Y0-AVA-521

Contents

PART ONE
POLICY PRACTICE: THE FOURTH DIMENSION OF SOCIAL WORK PRACTICE   1

Chapter One
The Importance of Social Policy Practice   3
Defining Social Policy 3
The Purpose of Policy 8
Defining Policy Practice 8
Policy Practice: Skills and Tasks 9
The Individual Versus the Environment 10
Expanding the Boundaries of Social Work Practice 12
Forces That Politicized the Human Services 13
Social Work and the Environment 16
The Conservative Backlash
   of the Reagan and Bush Years 19
Why Social Workers Failed to Conceptualize
   Policy Practice in the 1960s and 1970s 20
Demystifying Policy Practice 21
Toward Policy Practice: The Evolution of Theory 22
Issues in Conceptualizing Policy Practice 24
Policy Advocacy 26
A Foundation for Policy Practice 27
Summary 27
Suggested Readings 28
Notes 29

Chapter Two
The Ethical Rationale for Policy Practice 35
How Ethical and Nonethical Issues Differ 35
Beneficence and Professional Practice 36
Policy-Sensitive and Policy-Related Practice 37
Moving Toward Policy Practice 40
Policy Practice as Social Justice 43
Fairness and Advocacy for Outgroups 46
The Merits of Government Intervention 48
Other Ethical Principles in Policy Practice 50
Case 2.1 Patients' Access to Their Charts: An Agency Issue 51
Ethical Dilemmas 55
Personal Versus Professional Policy Practice 59
Do Social Workers Practice Policy
    Differently than Others Do? 61
Is Self-Interested Activity Ethical? 63
Ethical Issues in Phases of Policy Practice 64
Summary 64
Suggested Readings 65
Notes 66

Chapter Three
A Policy-Practice Framework: Skills, Tasks, and Action 68
Prerequisites for Practice 70
Applications of Policy Tasks and Skills 75
Episodes and Sequences of Tasks 81
Analyzing Policy Practice 81
Describing Policy Practice: A Case Example 82
The Diversity of Policies 87
Securing Mandates for Policy Practice 89
Discomfort with Power 90
Power, Assertiveness, and Policy Leadership 91
Policy's Role in Environmental Frameworks 92
Policy Practice as a Unifying Theme 93
Summary 93
Suggested Readings 94
Notes 95

Chapter Four
**The Big Picture: Policy Practice
in Governmental and Agency Settings**   **97**
The Players in Legislative and Governmental Settings   97
The Mind-sets of Elected Officials   109
The Mind-sets of Nonelected Officials   112
Strategy in Legislative Settings   114
The Political Economy of Organizations   114
The Political Economy of Programs and Social-Work Units   118
Mapping Agencies' Policies   119
The Players in Organizational Settings   124
Community Groups That Shape Policies   127
Summary   128
Suggested Readings   129
Notes   129

PART TWO
PREPARATORY WORK: BUILDING AGENDAS, DEFINING PROBLEMS, AND WRITING PROPOSALS   133

Chapter Five
Building Agendas   **135**
Taking the First Step   136
Why Preparatory Work Is Needed   137
Outmoded Theories   139
The Agenda Funnel   141
Three Streams and the General Policy Agenda   142
The Problem Stream   142
The Solution Stream   146
The Political Stream   148
Windows of Opportunity and Policy Entrepreneurs   151
Can Direct-Service Staff Help Build Agendas?   154
Advocacy for Powerless Populations and Unpopular Issues   155
Developing Links with Advocacy Groups   156
Summary   157

Suggested Readings 157
Notes 157

Chapter Six
Defining Problems   160
Using Policy Analysis 160
Classifying Problems Analytically 162
Measuring the Prevalence of Problems 165
Locating Problems within Society 167
Distinguishing Important Problems from Trivial Ones 168
Analyzing the Causes of Social Problems 168
Developing Interventions 172
Conceptual Issues in Defining and Measuring Problems 172
Paradigms of Policy Analysis 173
Variations in Problems 177
Challenges for Policy Advocates 178
A Policy-Practice Case 179
Case 6.1 Expanding a Preventive
    Program in a Mental Health Agency 180
Linking Analytic Skills to Other Policy Skills 183
Summary 183
Suggested Readings 184
Notes 185

Chapter Seven
Recurring Policy Options   188
Recurring Policy Issues 188
An Overview of the Proposal 204
A Case from the Human Services 204
Case 7.1 Policies for a New Program 205
Linking Policy Skills 208
Summary 209
Suggested Readings 209
Notes 210

Chapter Eight
Selecting Options and Writing Proposals   213
Trade-Offs: Systematically Comparing Policy Options 213
Value Issues in Constructing Proposals 220

Writing Memos 222
Case 8.1 Memorandum to the Commissioner 223
Developing Broader Policy Proposals 227
Policy Analysis: Putting It All Together 230
A Case Example 231
*Case 8.2 A Grant Proposal: The AIDS
   Preventive Education Project* 232
Summary 235
Suggested Readings 236
Notes 236

Chapter Nine
Strategies of Policy Persuasion 238
Policy Persuasion 238
Persuading Specific Audiences 239
Persuading Strategies 242
Assembling a Strategy 250
Case 9.1 Why a Presentation Was Successful 253
Combative Persuasion 259
Case 9.2 Attacking the Legislator's Measure 259
Win-Win or Collaborative Techniques 263
Summary 264
Suggested Readings 264
Notes 265

PART THREE
POWER AND THE POLITICAL PROCESS 267

Chapter Ten
Power and Policy Enactment 269
In Defense of Politics 269
Analytic and Political Approaches to Policy Practice 270
A Case from the Human Services 271
Case 10.1 A Preventive Mental Health Program 272
The Nature of Power 276
Person-to-Person Power 278
Substantive Power 280

Using Indirect Power 281
Successful Power Users 286
The Power of Autonomy 286
Discretion, Compliance, and Whistle-Blowing 287
Exerting Political Pressure 291
Power Differentials 291
Ethical Issues 293
Summary 294
Suggested Readings 295
Notes 296

Chapter Eleven
The Interactional Dimensions of Power 299
A Case from the Human Services 299
Case 11.1 Low-Budget Lobbyists 299
Attaining Power Resources 304
Outgroup Members' Problems 311
Developing Assertiveness 312
Can Direct-Service Staff Use Power Resources? 314
Group-Process Skills 315
Addressing Dysfunctional Group Processes 324
Summary 325
Suggested Readings 326
Notes 327

Chapter Twelve
Developing Political Strategy 330
A Case from the Human Services 330
Establishing Some Objectives 331
Grounding Strategy in Current Realities 332
Building Scenarios to Construct Political Strategy 340
Fleshing Out Strategy Details 344
Developing Strategy: An Agency Illustration 348
Developing Strategy: A Legislative Illustration 349
Developing Strategy in Governmental Settings 350
Developing Strategy in Organizational Settings 359
Developing Strategy in Community Settings 364
Summary 365
Suggested Readings 366
Notes 367

PART FOUR
AFTER ENACTING POLICY — 371

Chapter Thirteen
Implementing Policy — 373
A Framework for Implementing Policy 373
The Adoption Assistance and Child Welfare Act of 1980 381
The Policy Innovation 381
The Political and Economic Context 384
Problems in the Early Stages of Implementation 386
Problems in the Later Stages of Implementation 388
Developing Remedies 389
Ethical Issues: Compliance and Whistle-Blowing 397
Policy Advocates' Role 398
Outcomes of the Adoption Assistance and Child Welfare Act 398
Summary 401
Suggested Readings 403
Notes 404

Chapter Fourteen
Assessing Policy — 407
The Fundamental Logic of Policy Assessment 407
Similarities Between Assessing and Analyzing Policy 408
Similarities Between Policy Assessment and Policy Debates 410
Tools for Countering Criticism 412
Qualitative Evaluations 416
Policy Advocates' Use of Data 417
Why All Social Workers Should Assess Policies 418
Summary 419
Suggested Readings 419
Notes 420

PART FIVE
EPILOGUE — 423

Epilogue
Perspectives for Policy Practice — 425
Developing a Vision 425
Seeking Opportunities for Policy Practice 426

Taking Sensible Risks 426
Balancing Flexibility with Planning 426
Developing Multiple Skills 427
Being Persistent 427
Tolerating Uncertainty 428
Becoming a Policy Advocate 428
Combining Pragmatism and Principles 429
Summary 429
Notes 430

Name Index 431
Subject Index 437

Preface

Near the turn of this century, Jane Addams and her colleagues envisioned a profession that would make social activism integral to its work. This bold vision challenged the members of the fledgling profession to expand their work beyond interpersonal transactions. Unlike professions like medicine, law, nursing, or psychology, social work has retained this vision, even through ensuing conservative periods and in the face of pressures to make counseling the exclusive focus of the profession.

This idealistic vision has endured; however, it has not been consistently reflected in the school curricula or in the professional work of social workers in ensuing decades. Although many factors have contributed to this situation, I believe that the vision of Addams is not outmoded; indeed, many features of contemporary society—persistent patterns of inequality, major social problems like AIDS and homelessness, and attacks (such as funding cutbacks) on prerogatives of the profession—make the vision as compelling as it was nearly a hundred years ago.

The settlement-house leaders provided a vision but did not provide a detailed methodology for implementing it. The social work profession needs a framework in order to provide strategies and skills for reforming policies. This framework must be simple enough for a wide variety of practitioners to understand, yet complex enough to avoid suggesting that social change can be reduced to a few steps. It must be relevant for a range of professionals, including direct-service staff. In addition, the framework must be readily applicable to agency, community, and legislative settings. Rather than being limited to a single skill or style, the framework should include analytic, political, interactional, and value-clarifying skills; these skills reflect the actual work of those who strive to change policies. Further, the framework should belly the widespread impression that policy practice can be understood only by specialists, but it should also lay the groundwork to allow some social workers to enter policy-specialized positions. Finally, to be true to Addams's vision, the framework must emphasize advocacy for the powerless and oppressed.

In the decades following the progressive era, the profession failed to develop this kind of framework; the reasons for this failure are discussed in Chapter One of this text. I hope readers will agree that the framework presented in this book, which is a sweeping revision of the first edition (entitled *Social Welfare Policy: From Theory to Practice* and published by Wadsworth in 1990), meets some of the criteria listed in the preceding paragraph. Unlike the first edition, which was organized around the four policy-practice skills, the chapters in this edition are focused on the six policy-practice tasks: setting agendas, defining problems, writing proposals, enacting policies, implementing policies, and assessing policies. I reorganized the book in this way to provide a more concrete, task-focused approach to policy practice.

I argue that policy practice is an interventive discipline that holds promise of advancing reforming activity in agency, community, and legislative settings. By using such terms as *policy practice, policy tasks, policy skills,* and *tactics,* I have tried to convert social policy into a "doing" discipline with analytic, political, interactional, and value-clarifying dimensions. By placing policy practice squarely within ecological or systems frameworks that guide social work practice, I have sought to make it integral to the professional role. Further, I suggest throughout the book that policy advocacy to help the powerless and oppressed should be an integral part of social workers' policy practice.

The book is organized into four parts. In Part One (Chapters One through Four), I provide a rationale for policy practice that rests on an analysis of the following: the politicization of human services, pressing social problems in contemporary society, the interests of the profession, ecological frameworks, and the moral obligations of social justice and fairness. I discuss the policy-practice framework and ground it (and discussions in succeeding chapters) in a case study of policy practice. To provide orienting perspectives, I examine "the field of play" in a new Chapter Four that discusses policy-making procedures, key players, and the context of policymaking in agency, community, and legislative settings.

The remaining chapters focus on the six tasks of the policy-practice framework: agenda building, problem defining, and proposal writing are discussed in Part Two (Chapters Five through Nine); enacting policy is discussed in Part Three (Chapters Ten through Twelve); and implementing and assessing policy are discussed in Part Four (Chapters Thirteen and Fourteen). I conclude with an epilogue that explores strategies for making policy practice an integral part of the social work profession.

The aim of this book is to provide a methodology for carrying out, within contemporary society, the social reform that the settlement-house pioneers envisioned. When I list the perspectives that I hope graduates in social work will possess as a result of their social-policy curriculum, "willingness to assume leadership in improving agency, community, and legislative policies for disempowered groups" holds a prominent position. I hope this text contributes to that goal.

Acknowledgments

I first wrote about policy practice in 1984, in *The Theory and Practice of Social Welfare Policy* (Wadsworth). My efforts in revising and refining policy practice in the ensuing years, as well as my work on this text, has been made easier by the work and encouragement of colleagues across the country.

For words of encouragement about the viability of policy practice as an intervention method, I would like to thank Professors Chauncy Alexander, Ron Dear, George Haskett, Jacqueline Mondros, John Flynn, Scott Wilson, Will Richan, Barbara Friesen, Jack Rothman, Michael Fabricant, Aileen Hart, Steve Burghardt, Paul Kurzman, Marie Hoff, Charles Guzetta, Harry Wasserman, Howard Parad, Len Schneiderman, Rick Reamer, Jay Cohen, Terry Mizrahi, Mimi Abramovitz, Marie Weil, and Harold Lewis. In various master-teacher workshops that I have led under the aegis of the Council on Social Work Education, participants have been enthusiastic about using policy practice to revitalize the teaching of policy; I have benefited from their many suggestions. Professor Ram Cnaan and his colleagues provided useful insights at a workshop I led at the School of Social Work of the University of Pennsylvania, where I gave the Kenneth L. M. Pray Lecture as I was working on this manuscript. Norm Wyers and his colleagues at the School of Social Work at Portland State University have been leaders in teaching policy practice. They persuaded me to reconsider the role of social workers' personal beliefs in shaping policies and in focusing more specifically on line practitioners. I also benefited greatly from discussions with Nancy Amidei when she was a Milner lecturer at the University of Southern California—and from her ringing endorsement of policy activism as part of social work. Drawing on the suggestion of the late Griff Humphreys that I move my discussion of ethics nearer the start of this edition, I have devoted the second chapter of this book to social justice and equity. Professor Sheila Kamerman persuaded me to use the term *social policy* rather than *social welfare policy* to conform to international usage.

This manuscript was vastly improved by the insights of those who read full-length versions, including John D. Morrison, Aurora University; Elizabeth Thompson Ortiz, California State University, Long Beach; and Mary K. Rodwell, Virginia Commonwealth University.

I would like to thank Professor Ramon Salcido for commenting on Chapters Ten, Eleven, and Twelve; Professor Wilbur Finch for commenting on Chapters Four and Thirteen; and Adjunct Professor Anneka Davidson for comments on Chapter Five. Other colleagues have encouraged my line of inquiry, including Professors June Brown, Elsie Seck, Madeleine Stoner, and Sam Taylor, as well as Adjunct Professor Kathryn Wright. Professor Wilbur Finch has long been a supportive colleague; he has given me far more suggestions and encouragement than he has received in return. As the Dean of my school, Rino Patti created a working environment that enabled me to complete this revision.

In acknowledging those who have offered their assistance, support, and suggestions, I would like to add that any errors of omission or commission in this book rest on my shoulders alone.

I would like to thank Claire Verduin at Brooks/Cole for encouraging me to develop this new edition. Laurel Jackson skillfully moved the book through production, and Eve Kushner made many excellent editing suggestions.

Finally, I want to thank Betty Ann for her forbearance and support during the years I have labored on policy practice.

—Bruce S. Jansson

PART ONE
POLICY PRACTICE: THE FOURTH DIMENSION OF SOCIAL WORK PRACTICE

Chapter One argues that policy practice is as important as the other three interventive disciplines: direct-service, community, and administrative practice.

We see how policy practice has emerged over the last three decades in response to other changes. Unlike periods in the United States when the welfare state was virtually nonexistent (before the New Deal) or relatively simple (from the 1930s through the 1950s), social workers encounter policy issues virtually everywhere in the 1990s. They need to be conversant with social policies *and* be able to seek changes in them, both to help clients and to advance the interests of the profession.

Chapter Two discusses moral imperatives to engage in policy practice. Using the moral principles of beneficence, social justice, and fairness, we argue that ethical professionals should supplement their one-on-one counseling by changing policy in agencies, communities, and legislatures.

Chapter Three provides a framework for policy practice with a political and economic context, six policy-practice tasks, and four policy-practice skills. We argue that the concept of power needs to receive more attention in social work theory and curriculum.

Chapter Four contains an overview of legislative, governmental, social-agency, and community arenas. Policy practitioners need to understand the institutions and settings where they engage in their work. We discuss legislative procedures, governmental institutions, the political economy of organizations, organizational structures, and community institutions.

Chapter One

The Importance of Social Policy Practice

At first glance, social policy seems to divert social workers from the counseling, administrative, and community work on which they focus. However, social policy should play a crucial role in social work. Social policy provides social workers with theory about the human services. In addition, it enables them to represent powerless populations and to assume leadership roles, both within the human services delivery system and within society. Far from being esoteric, social policy helps social workers actualize policy and advocacy in their professional careers. This book establishes a framework and gives social workers vital skills toward this end.

For social policy to be relevant to social workers, it must provide them with a framework for policy practice, no matter what their specialization. While social work should educate policy specialists in the same way as administrative and community specialists, the profession should also provide all social workers, including clinical and direct-service workers, with concepts so they can make policy practice an important part of their work. This book seeks to provide such concepts. Policy practice should play a role in social work equal to that of clinical, community, and administrative interventions. Indeed, policy practice distinguishes social work practice from other counseling disciplines, such as psychology, psychiatry, and marriage-and-family counseling.

We will attempt to answer three questions in this chapter. First, what are social policy and policy practice? Second, what factors have led to the recent emergence of policy practice? Third, what basic skills and tasks do those who engage in policy practice need?

DEFINING SOCIAL POLICY

Definitions of social policy abound. Some emphasize the kinds of services and resources that social policies provide.[1] A course in social policy with this approach might stress the myriad programs in the American welfare state. Other definitions emphasize social policy's traditional interest in distributing resources to destitute persons.[2] A course with this view could analyze the inequalities in American society, how existing social policies do or do not reduce them, and alternative ways to create equal conditions and opportunities.[3]

This book uses a simple, problem-solving definition of social policy; we define social policy as *a collective strategy to address social problems*. Our definition is similar to that of the late Richard Titmuss, an English social-policy theorist.[4]

Defining social policy as goal-driven problem solving has several advantages. It emphasizes that social policies aim to alleviate social problems such as hunger, poverty, and mental illness. Table 1.1 illustrates the broad range of problems that social policies address. Some problems cannot easily be classified: Is substance abuse a physical problem, a mental problem, or antisocial behavior? Strategies to address these social problems can involve legislation, administrative regulations, agency policies, budgets, court rulings, and other policies.

Our definition suggests, as well, that social policy often addresses problems in the human services delivery system. When a social policy is implemented, it frequently encounters formidable barriers, such as lack of coordination between different agencies, lack of funds, lack of adequate financial management, or poorly trained staff. To appreciate the scope of changing social policy, imagine enacting legislation that provided prenatal services so as to decrease premature births and birth defects. Imagine, as well, that the person who sponsored the legislation found several years later that it had had little impact on rates of premature births or birth defects in an inner-city, Latino area. Assume the legislator also discovered that neither bilingual nor outreach staff had been hired, that clinic hours were limited to daytime hours, and that programs were located at inconvenient sites for the Latina women, such as at a distant public hospital. A legislator might seek to change social policy by (1) amending original legislation, (2) having a government agency issue regulations, (3) changing the budget that funded the program, or (4) changing policy at specific program sites, such as placing more emphasis on hiring bilingual staff. A frustrated legislator might decide that implementation is as important as the enactment as the original legislation, since failed implementation can sabotage enacted policies. The following are problems in the human services system that are often the targets of policy reform.

- *Fragmentation:* barriers make it difficult for clients or consumers to obtain services from multiple programs
- *Discontinuity:* clients cannot obtain consistent, accessible services over a period of time
- *Lack of access:* barriers make services hard to use at specific sites
- *Discrimination:* service providers are hostile or indifferent to specific kinds of clients
- *"Creaming":* providers deliberately seek clients with less serious problems
- *Wastage:* different providers serve the same population for the same problem, or services are not provided efficiently

TABLE 1.1
A Classification System of Social Problems

Material resources deprivation	Mental or emotional deprivation	Cognitive deprivation	Interpersonal deprivation	Deprivation of opportunity	Deprivation of personal rights	Physical deprivation
Inadequate income, housing, food	Various forms of mental illness	Developmental disability	Marital conflict Loneliness Destructive child-parent relations	Lack of education Lack of access to services or medical care Lack of fulfilling work	Lack of civil rights and liberties Victim of discrimination	Illnesses Disability

- *Lack of outreach:* providers make little effort to seek persons who do not currently use services
- *Incompetent staff:* staff are asked to perform tasks for which they have little training
- *Lack of cultural sensitivity:* providers make little effort to match their services to the cultural perspectives of the clients they serve

Defining social policy as goal-driven makes us ask whether specific policies actually address a social problem or whether other policies might be more effective. The definition forces us to stop merely describing policy and instead to analyze existing policies critically.

Moreover, a goal-driven definition aligns social policy with other disciplines that emphasize action, such as direct-service and administrative practice. These interventive disciplines all use various strategies to address problems. A direct-service practitioner helps clients define their problems and redress them. Administrators use an array of strategies to identify and fix various operating problems within specific organizations. Similarly, social policy practitioners address problems such as poverty, mental illness, and substance abuse. However, these practitioners frame their work not as providing services to specific persons, but as devising principles to shape the services or distribute resources provided by direct-service and administrative staff. When policy practitioners find that programs do not effectively address social problems, they try to change policies to correct institutional flaws. The literature on policy implementation suggests that even when policies have been officially enacted, policy practitioners do not cease their work.[5]

This definition of social policy eliminates the problem of establishing rigid boundaries between social policy and other kinds of policies. Most commentators agree that public welfare, child welfare, medical, and job-training policies are social policies, but less certainty exists about income tax, environmental, economic, transportation, and other policies.[6] Our definition suggests that specific policies *become* social policies whenever they influence social problems. For example, income tax proposals that increase or decrease the resources available to poor persons *become* social policies when they affect poverty and unemployment. By the same token, tax policies that regulate how corporations depreciate their equipment are not social policies.

Our definition does not apply only to legislative policies, because many kinds of policy exist in organizations and communities. For instance, consider the social problems of the mentally ill who do not want to enter psychiatric hospitals. Policies may come down from the highest levels: state mental health officials, county mental health departments, various courts, and even federal authorities. Although these *high-level policies* influence their work, staff in county mental health units may implement them in strikingly different fashions. One county hospital may commit many more persons than another hospital, because they define what constitutes an imminent threat to themselves and to other persons differently. Social workers cannot ignore these *local and organizational policies* when examining rules about the mentally ill in a particular state.

We include *policy objectives* in our definition because they shape the actions and choices of officials, executives, and staff. When a state mental health agency decides "to drastically reduce the populations of mental institutions," its officials and staff commit to this objective and to programs consonant with it. Imagine how services might change if, instead, top officials wanted to increase long-term institutional services for a range of mental conditions. By the same token, we include *rules and regulations* in our definition because many social policies constrain the activities of officials, staff, and consumers. A rule that denies a program to persons beneath specific income standards determines who can use it.

Formal, or *written, policies* can certainly be considered social policy, whether issued by legislation, court rulings, administrative guidelines, or budget documents. It is less immediately clear whether *informal,* or *nonwritten, policies* qualify. The issue requires some examination. When written policy contains relatively vague and ill-defined terms, officials must often develop informal policies to "fill in the gaps." For example, some laws restrict involuntary commitment to persons who pose an imminent danger to themselves or others; staff who require a strict standard may resist committing someone who has not actually attempted suicide, whereas other staff may believe that merely threatening suicide falls within this definition. Though such standards have not been recorded in official policy, they are policies because they have the same effect as written policy. They are collectively defined rules that profoundly shape the actions of direct-service staff and their administrators.[7]

Our definition of social policy, then, emphasizes rules, procedures, programs, and budgets external to specific persons that bind them to specific courses of action. But what about personal orientations, such as our preferences about social arrangements or which services we feel our agency should provide specific clients? Are these views "policies" or merely personal beliefs? A debate has emerged among social theorists on this issue. Some people, such as Wyers and Schorr, argue that personal views should be included in a definition of policy since social workers' actions are the ultimate actualization of policy.[8] Policies would be only paper or abstract creations if people, such as social workers in agencies, did not translate them into action. Other people, including prominent philosophers and theorists such as Mackie, argue that individual preferences or actions do not constitute policies, since they are not collective and binding phenomena.[9]

I take a middle course in this debate. I view court decisions, legislation, budgets, rules, and regulations as policies because they are external to persons and binding in nature. I view informal policies as analogous to formal policies; while not written, they bind or direct the staff in specific agencies by setting norms. I agree with Wyers and Schorr that personal orientations and actions profoundly determine whether written or informal policies are actualized in specific settings. However, I also agree with Mackie that the term "policy" loses its meaning if it includes official policies, informal policies, *and* personal orientations and actions. Were we to invest the term "social policies" with *all* of these meanings, it would never be clear *which* ones we emphasized.

Without suggesting that any of them is more or less important than the others, we might distinguish between four terms: (1) official, written policies, (2) informal, unwritten policies, (3) personal orientations toward policy (such as an aversion to specific rules), and (4) personal policy actions, such as obeying a policy in a specific work setting. Bisno calls this last type "policy-in-action," whereas I have named it "actualized policy."[10]

All these policy-related terms are important to social policy.

THE PURPOSE OF POLICIES

The controversial nature of social policy stems from its collective nature. If no policies existed, anarchy would reign. Staff members, consumers, agency directors, and public officials would pursue whatever they thought valuable. Left to their own, some staff might commit most persons with mental problems, even minor ones, to institutions, while other staff might commit no one, even those with life-threatening conditions. Anarchy has its virtues, but such random and personal actions would lead to confusion and unfortunate consequences for many consumers.

Anarchy would also threaten the rights of vulnerable persons, such as racial minorities or poor persons.[11] By defining which services and benefits persons can receive and clearly stating rules about determining eligibility, policies establish entitlements that cannot be violated by staff who dislike certain kinds of persons. Official policies also make clear to citizens which resources or services they can legitimately seek from social agencies.

Policy provides a mechanism for the general public, their elected representatives, and the governing boards of organizations to articulate and enforce their policy preferences. In light of scarce resources, societies and organizations cannot undertake an unlimited number of projects and cannot serve all who need assistance. Policies help establish policy priorities.

While policies allow policymakers to express their preferences, they also create accountability and enforcement. Elected officials are ultimately accountable to their constituents, who base their votes on which policies the officials support and oppose.[12] In turn, the agencies, programs, and staff that implement legislative policies are ultimately accountable to elected officials; if they flout legislative policies by not implementing them, they risk losing their funds and may be subject to prosecution.

DEFINING POLICY PRACTICE

We define *policy practice* as *efforts to influence the development, enactment, implementation, or assessment of social policies.* Policy practitioners can use rational and analytic tools such as data gathering, research, identification of policy options, and the drafting of policy proposals. They can use specific actions or verbal exchanges to encourage the deliberation of problems, the development of proposals, and the enactment and implementation of policies. These actions or verbal exchanges include discussions, presentations, debates, arguments, using specific power resources to modify other people's opinions or actions, and using coalitions, task forces, committees, and meetings.

Specific points during the policymaking process require *value clarification* or *ethical reasoning*. Policymakers have to decide what objectives or goals they favor when analyzing problems and developing policy proposals. Do they want drastic reforms or merely modest changes in existing policies? Values arise as well when policymakers define their motivations and loyalties. Do they identify with and seek to help certain powerless groups, the agency that employs them, or their particular work unit? Do they seek personal advancement through policy changes? Policy practitioners need to determine what risks they would take in questioning existing policies, such as risking the loss of their jobs in extreme cases.

Policy practitioners must wrestle with ethical issues related to procedural matters. Under what circumstances are deceptive, dishonest, or manipulative behaviors ethical? When is it ethical to undermine the credibility of another person or faction? When seeking support for a policy, is it ever ethical to make exaggerated claims about it?

Ethical issues arise about the substantive content of policies. For example, ethical principles conflict about involuntarily committing homeless persons with mental problems. Should laws protect homeless people's well-being or maximize their autonomy and self-determination?

POLICY PRACTICE: SKILLS AND TASKS

Policy practitioners often use four basic skills. With *analytic skills* they can identify policy alternatives, compare their relative merits, and develop recommendations. *Political skills* help assess policies' feasibility, identify power resources, and develop and implement political strategy. *Interactional skills* help practitioners make contacts, develop networks, build personal relationships, identify "old-boy" networks, and facilitate coalitions and committees. They use *value-clarification skills* to consider the morality of certain policy proposals and strategies to obtain support for them.

Other types of social workers need such skills as well. Direct-service practitioners analyze their clients' problems, use political skills to engage in case advocacy, apply interactional skills when helping clients, and recognize moral issues such as preserving client confidentiality. Similarly, administrators use analytic skills to diagnose problems and select remedies, political skills to develop support for new agency programs, interactional skills to develop rapport with their staff and boards, and value-clarification skills to examine various program and strategy choices.

Practitioners use policy skills to perform six tasks: setting agendas, defining problems, making proposals, enacting policy, implementing policy, and assessing policy. When presenting problems to agency, community, and legislative decisionmakers, they engage in *agenda-setting tasks*. John Kingdon's research on forming federal agendas identifies conceptual and political tools that practitioners use to place issues high on the policymakers' agendas.[13] When practitioners analyze how to present policy, they perform *problem-defining tasks*. They also define social problems such as homelessness, in classifying homeless persons, gauging the problem's prevalence in various communities, and analyzing its causes.

Proposal-making tasks involve identifying policy options, comparing their merits, and combining them into a proposal. Proposals can be relatively simple, such as one to change an agency's intake policies, or complex, such as one to establish a major social program. Practitioners engage in *policy-enacting tasks* when they develop strategy to have a policy passed or approved. When complex political processes are involved, strategy may consume major amounts of time and resources and demand frequent revisions. On other occasions, strategy may consist of one presentation at a critical meeting or personal discussions with a few highly placed decisionmakers.

Policy-implementing and policy-assessing tasks overlap with the administration and evaluation of programs. *Policy-implementing tasks* involve identifying why a policy is not adequately implemented and developing corrective strategies. As the expansive literature on policy implementation suggests, policy practitioners must often change official policy during the implementing process to correct whatever is contributing to the poor implementation. In many cases, they find that official policies cannot be implemented because of insufficient resources. These policy tasks are supplemented by administrative ones, such as hiring competent staff.

Policy-assessing tasks require deciding how to evaluate a policy and what changes to make in the wake of negative evaluations. Analytic, political, interactional, and value-clarification skills are needed to accomplish each of these six tasks.

THE INDIVIDUAL VERSUS THE ENVIRONMENT

From its inception, social work theory has been split between focusing on individuals (and their needs and problems) and the environment (as reflected by social conditions like poverty and social policies). When the profession originated just after the turn of the twentieth century, this split appeared in the competing conceptions of leaders such as Mary Richmond and Jane Addams.[14] Richmond certainly wanted to consider environmental factors in diagnosing clients' problems and needs. In fact, she admonished social workers to make home visits and become familiar with their clients' living situations. However, these assessments primarily served to gauge clients' motivations and capacities, not as tools for "changing social conditions and policies." As Wenocur and Reisch document, Richmond did not want the profession to emphasize social reform, partly because she thought it should focus on developing a scientific process of doing casework.[15] The settlement-house wing of the profession, led by persons like Jane Addams, countered Richmond. Addams and others found Richmond's formulations excessively narrow; she failed, Addams argued, to consider that the profession should acknowledge environmental factors that systematically harm classes of persons, such as women and children. She felt that social work should center around social reform.

Addams and her allies formed the Chicago School of Civics and Philanthropy and eventually the School of Social Service Administration of the University of Chicago. However, Richmond teamed with the Russell Sage Foundation and others to establish training institutes, the New York School of Philanthropy, and eventually the Graduate School of Social Work at Columbia University. Those wedded to Richmond's vision outflanked Addams and her colleagues. Philanthropic and university elites, as well as social agencies that depended on donations from wealthy people, found Richmond's vision appealing. It seemed to marry science with service to individuals, while avoiding the controversy intrinsic to social-reform activity. The settlement house movement had weakened greatly by the 1920s as a force for social reform. The many social work schools that were established in the 1920s eschewed social reform, although they often adopted the direct-service formulations of theorists like Richmond.[16]

Clinical theory in social work from 1930 to 1960 was dominated by two broad schools: Freudian theory and ego psychology.[17] In Freudian theory, the split between the person and environment became even more pronounced than in Richmond's work. Those social workers who subscribed to Freudian theory were taught to focus on their clients' internal conflicts and needs, which had developed in their interactions with their families. Even the community factors that Richmond encouraged social workers to consider in making diagnoses virtually disappeared in Freudian formulations. Good psychoanalysts should, they argued, concentrate on people's inner conflicts and defenses while trying to help them achieve psychic equilibrium through extended counseling. In this quest for internal equilibrium, psychotherapists were oblivious to external realities, such as poverty, bad housing, lack of jobs, lack of health care, and the oppression of specific populations. They did not realize that their methodology, which emphasized extended counseling sessions and introspection, was irrelevant to the vast numbers of persons concerned about immediate survival in a hostile world. Nor did ego psychology grant a significant role to environmental factors. Its theorists emphasized the emotional components of human functioning, the effects of familial history upon current behavior, and the "strengthening of ego functioning" to solve personal and familial problems.

At the same time as Richmond's theories, Freudian theory, and ego psychology dominated social work curricula, the descendants of the settlement house movement had obtained significant curriculum space for social welfare policy.[18] (Administration and community organization played more marginal roles in most schools' curricula.) But social welfare policy courses hardly bridged the chasm between persons and their environments either. Most schools taught some combination of social welfare history and current social welfare programs rather than skills to change the environment that shaped clients' lives. The social welfare policy offerings might have bridged the gulf by teaching techniques of social activism. Few realized that social workers could use these to change the environment either for specific clients (in case advocacy) or for groups of clients (in class advocacy).[19]

To be certain, no easy methods exist to bridge the worlds of clients and environments and to work in both realms. Lacking bridges between the casework and social policy, social workers probably graduated from 1920 to 1960 understanding clinical skills and social welfare institutions, but not seeing how to combine the two by being both clinicians and social activists, whether by enacting legislation in society or by changing specific policies in their agencies and communities.

Of course, despite their lack of techniques and theories of social activism, many social workers did become prominent leaders in social reform between 1920 and 1960. In the New Deal, for example, social workers led New Deal agencies and served in the top ranks of the Roosevelt Administration. Through their writings and their own social activism, many academic social workers tried to make policies more humanistic. But these salutary developments were hardly fostered, because theorists on both the clinical and the policy sides failed to articulate frameworks for combining clinical and social-reform work. In this book, it is argued that policy practice provides a methodology that all social workers can use to incorporate social reform within their work.

EXPANDING THE BOUNDARIES OF SOCIAL WORK PRACTICE

Several important developments in the late 1950s and early 1960s suggested that social work could include both direct service and social activism on a larger scale. In a massive study of social work curriculum, the Council on Social Work Education formalized community organization and administration as forms of social work intervention.[20] This reconceptualization added two interventive disciplines to the accepted one—direct service. Moreover, some social work educators advanced a concept of "generalist" social work practice, arguing that every social worker should have exposure to, and include in their professional practice, community organization, administration, and direct service.[21]

While these developments were important, it is not clear in retrospect that they prepared students much more fully than the older curriculum for careers that included policy practice. Early formulations of community organization by theorists such as Ross hardly mentioned social-reform work. Instead, they focused on community development through communities' self-help projects and central fundraising agencies that were not involved in changing policy.[22] Social work administrators focused on the nuts and bolts of agency administration, such as techniques of supervision and personnel management.[23] Generalist educators added courses, such as community organization, to the curriculum of all social workers, but we have already noted that administration and community organization materials hardly mentioned social activism.

Moreover, by the early 1960s, social welfare policy faculty still had not modified their curriculum to teach techniques for changing policies. Instead, they continued to cover a mixture of social welfare history and current policies.[24]

FORCES THAT POLITICIZED THE HUMAN SERVICES

After the early 1960s, the human services system changed dramatically. It became clear that policy profoundly shaped all social work, including direct service and clinical work. Emerging research and theory also suggested that clients' lives were inextricable from environmental forces, those given minimal importance in Freudian theory and ego psychology. At the same time, political changes swept through society, such as the civil rights movement, making social activism a viable option for some social workers. Although these factors, singly and in tandem, did not induce social work theorists to conceptualize policy practice, they provided a rationale for its eventual emergence in the 1980s.

In the 1950s, many social agencies could be neatly divided into public and nonprofit ones. Nonprofit agencies received most of their funds from nonpublic fund appeals such as United Way or Red Feather, sectarian fundraising efforts such as Federated Jewish Appeal, private donors, and fees.[25] These nonprofit agencies established their own fee structures, selected clients and the client problems they wished to serve, and, in some cases, shunned populations. For instance, they might exclude impoverished persons from service or hint that they should seek assistance elsewhere. Some family counseling agencies chose, for example, to serve poor persons, saying they were insufficiently motivated to solve their personal problems or unable to participate in the kinds of talking therapies that the agencies emphasized.[26]

Even public sector agencies, such as mental institutions and welfare agencies, widely assumed that professionals could dictate the terms of service.[27] Social workers in public agencies commonly had great freedom to determine which clients received what services and for how long. For example, social workers, who often staffed the intake and eligibility services in public welfare agencies, gave intensive help to clients they believed it would benefit. Within large, public bureaucracies, social workers had great autonomy as they applied their knowledge of human behavior to counseling strategies.[28] The social workers in welfare units or mental hospital units often had master's degrees, giving them considerable prestige within these bureaucracies.

The esteem they held contributed to the emergence of the Social Security Amendments in 1962, which gave federal incentives to hire social workers to provide services to welfare recipients. The policy obtained bipartisan support in Congress.[29] In 1963, community mental health legislation passed. It was widely assumed that social workers would now work through community-based agencies to serve deinstitutionalized patients.[30]

However, even in the early 1960s, social workers were not completely autonomous, for their employing agencies often placed many restrictions on their practice. These agencies were themselves profoundly influenced by community and societal pressures. In his classical study of the YMCA, for example, Mayer Zald noted that the YMCA's mission, as well as its need for revenues, created its emphasis on recreational programs, services to middle-class consumers, and suburban rather than inner-city services.[31] Some child guidance agencies taught staff prevailing psychiatric models and selected certain kinds of clients while rejecting others. Some welfare agencies insisted that their social workers implement relatively punitive policies, such as home visits, to determine whether recipients were cheating or had live-in partners, who were prohibited in many states.[32] But the prevailing social work literature of the 1950s and the early 1960s portrayed social workers as relatively autonomous in their work.[33]

A series of events, however, shattered this idyllic world in both the public and nonpublic sectors. Social services became more complex after funding changes in the 1960s, 1970s, and 1980s. Traditional nonprofit counseling agencies and public mental institutions were now supplemented by publicly funded programs. These consisted of: community mental health centers, mental hospitals, aftercare programs, and specialized profit-oriented psychiatric services. The latter type of agency might have been a substance abuse center, a halfway house, a board-and-care home, or a center for developmentally disabled persons.[34] Such complex sponsorship and specialization of services meant that social workers were increasingly influenced by interorganizational relationships in their work; they had to ask which clients "belonged" to whom, which ones should be retained or referred elsewhere, and whether to develop collaborative services, such as joint programs. Mental health agencies sometimes integrated with larger human services agencies that placed counseling, training, and welfare services under one roof.[35]

Patterns of financing services grew increasingly complicated, in turn affecting patterns of intake, the length of services, and the kinds of services that could be given to consumers. Mental health service funding became shared by private insurance, public programs like Medicare and Medicaid, county and municipal authorities, the states, foundations, United Way, Jewish Federated Funders, and federal and state programs for specific populations, such as disabled persons, substance abusers, and juvenile offenders.[36] Each funder placed specific restrictions on mental health services by prescribing their duration, the kinds of persons who could receive services, mechanisms for evaluating services, staff training qualifications, and the content of the services. Agency administrators became accountable to a dizzying array of funders. Moreover, administrators had to consider how to increase revenues from paying clients to remain solvent.[37]

Staffing agencies became more complex as new professions and rules developed, often removing requirements that M.S.W.s receive job preference. Social work's existence was endangered in some agencies by these new rules. In many public and child welfare agencies in the late 1960s and 1970s, M.S.W.s were often supplanted by nonprofessionals, B.S.W.s, or other professional counselors.[38]

The courts placed additional restrictions on agencies, making rulings about client confidentiality, involuntary commitments to mental institutions, informed-consent procedures when using psychotropic medications or other treatments with possible harmful side effects, due-process requirements when removing children from their natural parents, and minimum standards of service for the residents of institutions. Rulings from the various courts were so numerous and pervasive that they constituted a "phantom" welfare state that supplemented the programs and policies of legislators and government agencies.[39]

Federal and local governments gave so much money to social services in the 1960s and 1970s that the nature of human services fundamentally changed and the role of private donors and federated fundraising diminished. Many nonprofit agencies received the bulk of their funds from public authorities, who saddled the agencies with rules and regulations about how to use their funds.[40]

Moreover, community groups, theorists, government authorities, and professional associations vied to shape these regulatory policies. Mental health services had become politicized in a manner that would have been unthinkable a decade earlier. Patients often battled the American Psychiatric Association over involuntary commitment procedures; while patients wanted more rights and obstacles to commitments, the APA wanted to give professionals more discretion.[41] Representatives of children, the elderly, and ethnic minorities demanded more or better services for their clients, charging that they were excluded from services or received inappropriate ones.[42]

Philosophical and conceptual disputes emerged, encouraging such politicization. If patient advocates suggested that professionals wrongly diagnosed their clients, professionals retorted that these classifications were needed to promote scientific treatment.[43] While some persons wondered whether mental illnesses stemmed from poverty, unemployment, and environmental factors, other theorists continued to emphasize familial and emotional causes. African Americans, Latinos, and Native Americans often contended that social workers unfairly stereotyped them. Even when they exhibited the same symptoms as other persons, they were more likely to be diagnosed with serious mental conditions.[44] Child welfare workers were sometimes accused of imposing their cultural preferences when they removed children from parents who used physical punishment.[45] Theorists debated the relative importance of genetics, physiological imbalances, stress, poverty, unemployment, marital conflict, disability, role models, and other factors in causing mental disorders. A remarkable array of treatment methods appeared, including psychodynamic, behavior modification, cognitive, transactional, gestalt, and existentialism.[46]

Professionals increasingly felt pressured by their agencies, which increased in size and power to cope with policy, funding, and political turbulence. Social agencies had to market their services to new clients, keep abreast of current legal and policy developments, and meet funders' accountability requirements.[47] Agencies often had to develop new services, discard ones that lost funds, and devise more efficient methods of delivering services. Amid such pressures, agencies sometimes had to regulate direct-service staff, who were asked to implement the rapidly changing services of their organizations.

Aware of these changes, organizational theorists increasingly argued that agencies' internal dynamics had to be understood in their political and economic context. If traditional organizational theorists had emphasized agencies' internal processes and structures, advocates of a political-economy perspective contended that external policy, funding, and political environments shaped agencies.[48]

Policies both internal and external to agencies influenced social work. Thus, efforts to change or shape these policies necessarily became a part of professional practice, if only for defensive reasons. In the late 1960s, social workers' unions grew dramatically, especially in the public sector and nonprofit agencies.[49] Some social workers, as well as the National Association of Social Workers (NASW), increasingly opposed organizational and public policies that they viewed as inimical to their clients' well-being or to their own rights. NASW sought to represent social workers fired for objecting to specific policies.

These organizational and funding changes made it clear that social work practitioners were not autonomous. The external policies of funders, courts, government agencies, and legislatures profoundly affected direct-service staff, supervisors, administrators, and community organizers. These policies shaped the terms and nature of social services as well as the staff's working conditions.

Social workers clearly needed strategies against these various policies, either to improve their working conditions or to make social programs better address the needs of clients and the general population.

SOCIAL WORK AND THE ENVIRONMENT

We have noted that considerable social work theory in the 1950s emphasized how familial and emotional factors caused social problems. Although information about family members, employment, housing arrangements, and medical factors often helped shape diagnostic assessments and treatment plans, these data usually received less attention than clients' internal conflicts. For example, in the early 1960s many persons believed that social services could redress the widespread poverty of female heads of household. The idea was to counsel these women and help resolve marital problems so their husbands did not desert them. This approach overlooked issues of social class, the absence of subsidized day care, labor markets and training programs that discriminated against women, and racial discrimination.[50]

By the mid-1960s, however, many theorists began to give the external world more credit for human behavior. Some theorists, such as Abraham Maslow, emphasized meeting basic survival needs before fulfilling higher-order creativity needs.[51] Robert White suggested that humans possess a drive for competence; when they experience a chain of perceived failures, sometimes because of discrimination, they often freeze, flee, or make ill-advised choices.[52]

Other researchers and theorists probed how peers and groups influence individuals. Social psychologists observed how powerfully group norms affect their members, sometimes leading them to act self-destructively. Sociologists and psychologists widely debated what shapes behavior.[53] Researchers examined how situational stressors, such as divorce and unemployment, affect human behavior.[54]

Researchers examined the effects of poverty, segregation, and poor housing on human behavior.[55] Theorists in the 1960s explored how oppressive socioeconomic conditions create social problems such as poor health, substance abuse, and truancy. These problems, in turn, perpetuate poverty.

Debates also raged about the relationship between culture and poverty. Did poverty create cultural dispositions, such as living for the present, not the future? Or did this notion stem from middle-class researchers' imaginations and faulty methodologies? Was present-orientedness to the extent that it existed deeply rooted, or would it quickly disappear once persons were removed from poverty and oppression? Such debates illustrated increasing awareness that among people's environment, class, culture, and problems were related, even if the nature of these relationships remained controversial.[56] By contrast, a 1960 bibliography of academic writings on poverty consisted of less than a single page of citations.[57]

There was increasing recognition of culture's effect upon social problems and people's response to existing services.[58] People began to realize that the "melting pot" they believed in did not, in fact, eliminate cultural diversity as immigrants assimilated into the nation's dominant culture.[59] Theorists discussed how social workers need to consider the African-American, Latino, and Asian-American cultures to provide effective services. These concepts were not limited to racial concerns; feminists researched how women view the world differently than men and how their perspectives shape their interactions with other people and institutions.[60] With the increasing recognition that cultural diversity has not disappeared, people examined how other cultures perceive social problems and social services. Moreover, people noted that low-income persons often resisted using social services, either because they found them irrelevant to their immediate needs, were fatalistic about improving their condition, or lacked transportation or time to use them.[61] Services need to be tailored to populations' specific needs. When programs provide only a single approach or remedy, they risk ignoring the diversity of human experience.

Systems of social support were implicated by many theorists in cause and sustain social problems.[62] Research suggested that persons who lacked familial, neighborhood, and workplace support were more susceptible to illness and mental problems.[63] Professionals increasingly referred clientele to support groups, such as for alcoholism or cancer, whose members sought to comfort one another, provide survival strategies, and help other members negotiate bureaucratic systems.

Some research implicated the social service delivery system itself in causing or exacerbating social problems. Costly transportation and medical services, for example, cause many consumers to delay seeking help until their problems have become serious. Services that are excessively fragmented impede effective and multifaceted interventions.[64]

By the 1970s and early 1980s, numerous theorists developed frameworks acknowledging that environmental, policy, delivery-system, cultural, community, familial, and personal factors shape human behavior. This placed human behavior and individuals' problems in a broad context that included societal, organizational, cultural, and familial factors. Carel Germain and Carol Meyer developed ecological frameworks that required practitioners to use information about environmental factors as they helped clients.[65]

As these various environmental influences received increasing prominence in service and human behavior literature, the work of direct-service practitioners necessarily became more complex. A skillful social service professional had to ask whether an adolescent's truancy, for example, derived from substance abuse, dyslexia, a perceived absence of economic opportunities, negative familial role models, culture, peer pressure, physical ailments, conflicts with school faculty, conflicts with parents, or some combination of these. Social workers could use counseling, advocacy, referrals to specialized reading clinics, peer support groups, family therapy, or some combination of these interventions. Moreover, after examining the effects of diverse environmental factors, social workers sometimes conclude that they should provide clients with assertiveness, survival, job-seeking, and legal skills so that they can cope with ongoing adversities and discrimination. This strategy, which has been called *empowerment*, extends to communities, whose members can learn political and organizing skills to obtain policy concessions from governments, funders, insurance companies, and others.[66]

As environmental factors received more prominence, some theorists emphasized that social work practitioners should take on advocacy roles. If people's problems reflect oppression by landlords, welfare and other agencies, abusive spouses, and poor schools, perhaps social workers should represent individuals and classes of persons, such as low-income tenants or welfare recipients.[67] Advocacy can take two forms. *Case advocacy* seeks more equitable services for individuals within existing laws, regulations, and entitlements. *Class advocacy* tries to change defective laws and regulations and to develop new entitlements.[68] Class advocacy, in particular, plays an important part in policy practice.

By the 1970s, then, social workers possessed a more diverse set of skills than did their counterparts of the 1950s. The frameworks that became prominent in textbooks on human behavior and direct practice explicitly linked individuals' problems to a range of community, institutional, and societal factors. If theorists of the 1950s often assumed that white and middle-class behavior extended to all persons, many theorists in the two decades following the 1950s recognized that social class, gender, and ethnicity shaped people's problems, their perceptions of these problems, and their responses to social workers' interventions.

THE CONSERVATIVE BACKLASH OF THE REAGAN AND BUSH YEARS

It seemed briefly, in the John Kennedy administration (1961–1963) and the first two years of the Lyndon Johnson administration (1964–1965) that social-reform momentum, stalled since the New Deal of the 1930s, would reemerge. With relatively liberal policymakers and a sympathetic Supreme Court, it seemed that social workers could count on the enactment of progressive legislation. But a succession of developments, extending over nearly thirty years, made it clear that progress would not be automatic. The Vietnam War usurped scarce resources from 1965 through the early 1970s and divided the Democratic constituency into pro-war and anti-war segments, thus disrupting reform momentum in the Johnson administration.[69] While social spending increased dramatically in the early and middle 1970s, the nation's politics became polarized between anti-reform and reform groups. Using coded words like "the silent majority" and "the majority of law-abiding citizens," Presidents Richard Nixon (1969–1974) and Gerald Ford (1974–1976) sought to divide white Americans from persons of color by fostering resentment of social programs and social reforms. They tried to identify Democrats with "tax and spend" policies, busing, abortion, and social programs to help racial minorities.[70] Despite the brief interlude of the somewhat conservative Jimmy Carter (1977–1980), these Republican leaders were remarkably successful in pitting the nation against social reform, thus laying the groundwork for the conservative presidencies of Ronald Reagan (1981–1988) and George Bush (1989–1992).

This nearly thirty-year period of relatively conservative policies eradicated any assumption social workers might have had that progressive policies would emanate from the nation's capital or courts. It also became clear that social workers needed to assume proactive roles in local, state, or national policy circles. The National Association of Social Workers formed PACE (its Political Action Committee) to assist progressive candidates in 1975. Many social workers volunteered in various political campaigns as well as in advocacy groups that proliferated in the 1970s and 1980s to help children, the disabled, racial minorities, stigmatized groups such as gays and lesbians, women, the elderly, and other groups. Furthermore, as we discuss subsequently, theorists began to conceptualize an action or intervention arm of social policy.

While Bill Clinton's election to the presidency in 1992 seemed to break decisively with the conservative hold on the nation's politics, only 43% of Americans voted for him. Clinton was saddled, moreover, with the huge federal deficit, which has made it difficult for him to increase spending on the programs cut during the Reagan and Bush years. Nor were large parts of the Clinton constituency, such as "Reagan Democrats" and suburban voters, inclined to support reformist policies. So liberals and advocacy groups across the nation realized that activism would be needed in the coming years if reforms were to be enacted. A number of social-policy theorists realize that social workers need interventive skills to proactively shape policies.

WHY SOCIAL WORKERS FAILED TO CONCEPTUALIZE POLICY PRACTICE IN THE 1960S AND 1970S

We have discussed three developments in the decades after the 1950s that should have motivated social workers to engage in policy-reforming work: (1) the increasing importance of funders and policies as social services became politicized, (2) the increasing importance of a framework that implicated environmental factors, and (3) the conservatism of the 1970s and 1980s, which suggested the need for political activism. But the profession lacked theories or interventions to help its members develop this work and had only begun to articulate a "policy of practice" by the late 1980s. Several reasons account for this failure to develop policy practice. First, the study by the Council of Social Work Education in 1959 defined social welfare policy as supporting direct-service, community, and administrative interventions, not providing interventive skills to social workers.[71] Until well into the 1980s, the discipline did not provide practice skills, at least in the sense of other interventive skills in social work. Many policy theorists came to emphasize "policy analysis," which borrowed promising techniques from economics and public affairs, but required only analytic skills, not the political, interactional, and value-clarifying skills also needed by policy advocates.

Second, community organization came to be viewed in the activist 1960s as the intervention that would embrace social reform, thus, social policy faculty were relieved of this role. While theorists in community organization sometimes discussed policy reform, they were mostly absorbed in other topics, such as mobilizing and developing communities. When the Great Society collapsed and with it community organization, and conservative regimes ensued, room opened in social work for activism. Policy theorists, still focusing on providing theoretical, philosophical, and historical materials, failed to fill this opening.

Third, the environment versus individual debate persisted in the profession even after the introduction of environmental systems and ecological frameworks in the 1970s and early 1980s. These frameworks function in several ways. As Mary Richmond advocated decades earlier, emphasizing the environment encourages social workers to gather information about clients' living conditions. In this way, social workers need not try to change environmental conditions themselves, but can use conditions as aids to clinical work. I suspect that many social workers viewed frameworks in this light, which explains why the frameworks did not necessarily stimulate policy reform. Moreover, these frameworks were often eclipsed during the 1970s and 1980s by a never-ending stream of therapies that absorbed the attention of social work educators and students. These therapies gave scant importance to environmental, much less policy-changing, work.[72] Cognitive, behaviorist, transactional, existential, and gestalt approaches to clinical work may have enriched clinicians' work, but hardly emphasized social reform. The therapies may even have supplanted the frameworks in some schools and in the minds of some practitioners.

Policy practice has also been stunted by relatively scant attention to agency policies as a context for practice. A full-fledged theory of policy practice needs to include skills for changing *agency* policies, as well as community and legislative ones, because agency policies often shape social work. As Wasserman suggested in 1974, the employing agency is rarely discussed in practice methodologies, which assume that social workers can ignore the constraints of agencies' rules, policies, norms, customs, revenue needs, and external regulations from funding sources.[73]

DEMYSTIFYING POLICY PRACTICE

Social work practitioners and even some educators have resisted defining and developing a policy practice because of various myths they hold. The *great-person myth* maintains that only major policies are worth working on, such as Medicare, Medicaid, and welfare reform. In fact, direct service depends on many policies that extend from major ones, such as legislation establishing social programs and policies in community and agency settings. The great-person myth allows most of us to abdicate our policy responsibilities in our daily work because it limits policymaking to high-level officials or to those reformers who champion ambitious pieces of legislation.

The *specialization or expert myth* suggests that policymaking rightfully belongs to policy specialists with advanced analytic skills. Economists, program evaluators, and policy analysts have assumed increasingly prominent roles in policy discourse, but their expanded role does not mean other people cannot also partake in policy. Even well-conceived policy proposals deriving from sophisticated policy analysis have difficulty being passed and implemented. Reforms cannot usually be enacted without external pressures on legislators and officials. Because social workers actually implement policies and see social problems firsthand, they should help shape policies by sensitizing policymakers to shortcomings in existing policies.

The *myth of powerlessness* suggests that professionals and ordinary citizens cannot contribute to policymaking because they lack the power resources of interest groups and politicians. It is true that policymaking is often fraught with power imbalances. Many studies suggest, however, policy innovations stem not from single crusaders but from people acting in tandem through coalitions or professional associations.[74] Direct-service professionals can sometimes develop and use power resources within their agencies and communities.[75]

By suggesting that all policy is public policy, the *legislative-policy myth* neglects many other kinds of policy, including agency and community policies that influence the implementation of legislative policy. In the case of a community mental health center that receives most of its funds from state and federal sources, the agency establishes many policies when legislation does not provide details of implementation.[76] Indeed, "zones of discretion" enable agencies to define many details of their programs within certain parameters that high-level policy establishes. Even nonpublic agencies that receive most of their funds from public sources have considerable latitude in developing policies, including the ability to decide which public funds to seek.[77]

In demystifying policy, we do not want to suggest that anyone can be successful on most occasions. Even experienced policy practitioners do not often succeed in having initiatives enacted. If we become preoccupied with the problems and difficulties of practicing policy, however, we risk a sort of policy fatalism.

TOWARD POLICY PRACTICE: THE EVOLUTION OF THEORY

I cannot speak for other theorists who have developed policy-practice materials in recent years, but, after discussing the evolution of policy materials in recent decades, I will discuss why I began working on new approaches to policy when I coined the term *policy practice* in 1984.

Developing Analytic Skills

In 1956, Eviline Burns analyzed strategies to help destitute, unemployed, and elderly persons.[78] Although her book contained historical materials, she analyzed alternative approaches to these economic and social problems and compared the advantages of each. Burns suggested that many policy alternatives exist, each with advantages and disadvantages, and that choosing one requires comparing their strengths. For example, she contrasted ways to finance and structure welfare and Social Security programs. Neil Gilbert and Harry Specht, who portray themselves as disciples of Burns, continued this tradition by examining various "dimensions of choice," including policy alternatives to service-delivery, financing, and allocation issues.[79] Like Burns, they compared various policy options, such as alternative ways to determine who is eligible for a program. By identifying and comparing policy options, Burns and her successors moved beyond the chronicling and describing of policy toward a process of selection and choice.

Alfred Kahn suggested that policy analysts follow a series of conceptual steps when developing policy proposals; they should analyze the presenting social problem, develop policy alternatives, and devise policy proposals. He argued that policymakers should be rational and scientific in their approach.[80] Outside of social work, in fields such as economics and public affairs, theorists developed a host of analytic, research, and economic tools for analyzing problems and selecting policies.[81] Critics wondered, however, if policymaking can be as "rational" as these theorists implied. Many policy analysts hardly mentioned politics, old boy networks, and other realities that shape the selection of policies in specific settings.[82]

Using Values to Make Policy

In 1976, in a widely used text, David Gil contended that policymakers needed to use values to choose between policy alternatives. As a socialist, he strongly valued equality and redistribution to address social and economic needs.[83] Richard Cloward and Frances Piven provided radical analyses of the regulating functions of some social welfare policies. They contended that corporate and conservative interests often favored punitive programs, such as Aid to Families with Dependent Children (AFDC), that forced recipients into low-paying jobs by providing low benefits and deterring recipients from seeking welfare benefits.[84]

These radical perspectives provided a useful antidote to the analytic theorists, who often implied that values were irrelevant when selecting policies. Moreover, they suggested that policymaking is not entirely rational or scientific and that it may be entirely irrational when political pressures often dictate choices. But these theorists drew criticism as well. Could policymakers maintain radical perspectives when interest groups pressure them and when they need political skills to make compromises?[85]

Politics, Implementation, and Policymaking

During the 1970s and 1980s, theorists began to analyze the relationship between politics and policymaking. A growing number of writers emphasized political skills, including Maryann Mahaffey, Andrew Doblestein, Diane DiNitto, Thomas Dye, and Karen Haynes.[86] Ron Dear and Rino Patti collected empirical data to study why some pieces of social legislation are enacted while others fail.[87] Mahaffey's edited volume discussed testifying, lobbying, and coalition-building skills needed by policy advocates.[88]

In 1974, political scientists Jeffrey Pressman and Aaron Wildavsky contended that theorists were wrong in saying that policymaking ceases once policies are enacted. They argued that organizational, political, and economic realities sabotage many policies after enactment.[89] In the decade after Pressman and Wildavsky's book, theorists explored the successful implementation of specific policies.[90] Examining how high-level policies became operating programs, Kamerman and Kahn studied systems of social delivery in several cities.[91]

Theorists who examined political and implementation realities usefully expanded the boundaries of policy beyond the relatively narrow scope established by policy analysts. Their work implied that policy analysis must be coupled with knowledge of political and organizational realities.

Developing a Range of Policy Skills

Social welfare policy had traditionally fallen into social reform, historical, orienting, and descriptive materials. Even the analytic, political, and implementation literature that supplemented policy literature in the 1970s and 1980s usually failed to discuss how people might actually try to shape policies.

In the 1970s Willard Richan had emphasized that social workers, like lawyers, should be trained to develop and debate positions.[92] By the early 1980s, some theorists began to envision a practice component to social welfare policy. In a work published in 1981, John Tropman contended that practitioners need a range of policy competencies, such as persuasive skills, political skills, and skills in using committee and group processes to develop policies.[93]

Policy theorists had traditionally emphasized policymaking in legislative or government settings, but Tropman, Dean Pierce, and John Flynn suggested that executives and line staff need policy skills within social agencies.[94] Indeed, Herman Resnick and Rino Patti suggested that staff could help develop innovations within agencies.[95]

In a work published in 1984, I suggested that the discipline ought to define a multiskilled interventive component, which I called "policy practice," and contended that social workers could practice policy in agency, community, and legislative settings.[96] I suggested that policy practitioners need many skills, including analytic, political, interactional, and value-clarification skills. Drawing on political and policy science theory, I suggested that policy practitioners undertake tasks, such as developing, enacting, implementing, and assessing policies.[97] I amplified my discussion of policy-practice skills in 1990 with the first edition of this book.[98] Norman Wyers examined models of policy practice in 1992 and Figueira-McDonough advocated policy practice from a social-justice perspective in 1993.[99]

I evolved a policy-practice framework because it became increasingly obvious to me that social work educators failed to provide students with concrete skills and strategies for changing policies, even though the field claimed allegiance to the settlement house wing of the profession with its mission for social reform. While historical, analytic, and value-focused materials of social policy curriculum have merit, they have failed to provide a framework for social activism in times of festering social problems.

ISSUES IN CONCEPTUALIZING POLICY PRACTICE

Where does policy practice fit within the existing discipline of social work? Is it a new intervention or part of an existing intervention such as community organization or administration? Can generalist, direct-service workers engage in it, or must someone be a specialist, such as a lobbyist, aide to a legislator, or planner?

Is Policy Practice a New Intervention?

As we have discussed, the Council on Social Work Education decided in 1959 that three interventions constituted social work: direct-service, community, and administrative practice.[100] None of these disciplines focuses on changing policy, but it is partly relevant to each of them. Direct-service practice discusses the work of staff who implement policies. Community organization discusses mobilizing skills, such as forming coalitions. Theories about "political social work" that have recently emerged in social work literature come closer to policy practice, but focus only on its legislative aspects. Administrative social work discusses implementation issues. Human behavior theories discuss the causes of social problems.

I would argue that policy practice combines all the skills required to reinstill a social-reform mission in the social-work profession. Policy practice focuses exclusively on changing social policies. Theorists who evolve a framework for policy practice must uniquely draw concepts from the social sciences, organizational theory, evaluative research, communication theory, political science, and economics.

Expert or Generalist?

Some readers may conclude that policy practice is limited to experts or specialists. Of course, just as with administration and community organization, social work should prepare some of its graduates to be specialists unless it wants other disciplines to monopolize policy positions having to do with human services. (Professionals from economics, public health, public administration, and public affairs have supplanted the social-work policy roles in many governmental bodies.)[101] Specialists bring additional competencies to policy reform, such as advanced uses of research, but they cannot be effective without the skills we discuss in this book.

But all social workers, including direct-service, community organization, and administration practitioners, can and should participate in policy-changing work. This book seeks to identify the basic skills needed by *any* policy practitioner in *any* location, including agency and legislative sites. Generalists practice policy sporadically, fitting it in among all their other work. A social worker may try to change an agency's intake procedures or develop a new agency program. Another might participate in a community-wide coalition to improve services for AIDS-infected or homeless people. Direct-service practitioners, supervisors, administrators, and community workers practice policy *whenever* they try to improve policies, whether in their agencies, communities, or legislatures. At times, they may engage in little or no policy practice, only to become absorbed with it at another time. They sometimes practice policy on the spur of the moment when, for example, they initiate a point in a discussion with a colleague. They may develop a long association with a project to change existing policies.

Many social workers shape policies when they implement higher-level policies. They decide whether to implement, ignore, or modify specific policies.[102] Moreover, since social workers possess considerable autonomy, they must often make policy themselves. For example, until the recent federal legislation defined certain rights for the elderly, nursing home staffs had great latitude.

They could place their clients in restraints, in wheelchairs, under sedation, or in rooms separate from their spouses.

Self-Interest or Altruism?

Many of us think of policy practice as serving altruistic purposes, such as addressing social problems, but social workers can also engage in policy practice to advance the self-interest of the profession, or even a subset of the profession, such as "clinical social work." Indeed, Humphreys wonders if social policy would seem more relevant to clinical social workers if courses focused on the funding of services, the purchase of service arrangements, insurance coverage of mental health benefits, managed care, licensing, laws restricting sexual relations between therapists and clients, professional liability, and fee schedules.[103]

The distinction between self-interest and altruism in policy practice is often difficult to determine in the real world. Social workers who fight social problems often secure jobs when programs to remedy the problem are created. In many cases, then, we engage in policy practice both for altruistic reasons and out of professional self-interest.

I see no problem in directing policy practice toward self-interested goals, such as licensure and reimbursement by insurance companies. But we surely ought not limit policy practice to issues that bring a return to the profession; to fall prey to this approach would mean rejecting principles such as social justice and fairness.

POLICY ADVOCACY

I use the term *policy advocacy* in this book to refer to a special kind of policy practice that focuses on interventions to help powerless populations. These populations include African Americans, gays and lesbians, Latinos, Native Americans, poor people, and people with stigmatizing conditions such as AIDS, disabilities, and mental illness. Advocates may work on issues that draw widespread opposition in the general population, such as making sterilized needles available to drug addicts, distributing condoms to high school students, or ending capital punishment. They may take on taboo issues in specific agencies, such as extending services to marginalized populations when the agency staff largely opposes this. Advocates may seek to advance social justice by decreasing inequalities, such as that in the services of inner-city and suburban school districts.

Policy advocates use the same skills as if they had taken more popular positions. But they need personal characteristics, such as persistence and perspective, to decrease the likelihood of burning out when success does not come easily. They need to be able to form supportive coalitions and frame their arguments so as to gain support from potential opponents. Advocates encounter particular barriers and need special policy-practice skills, as we will discuss later.

Social workers are particularly suited to policy advocacy because of their traditions and the kinds of clients they often help. The settlement wing directed the social work profession to help relatively oppressed populations. While social workers work with a cross-section of society, they work with powerless populations more frequently than lawyers, doctors, and psychologists. Their professional organizations, such as NASW, are more clearly reformist than these other professions. This book seeks to discuss policy skills that policy practitioners in general and policy advocates in particular need.

A Foundation for Policy Practice

No one will emerge from reading this book with fully-developed skills to practice policy in agency, community, and legislative settings anymore than someone would finish a book on clinical, community, or administrative practice possessing practice-based skills. This book provides concepts, a framework, and many policy-practice cases to ground readers in theory and practice. With this foundation, a social worker can integrate a full-fledged policy practice into his or her professional career, whatever its focus or specialization.

Because policy-changing work is multifaceted, we have not tried to reduce it to a set of simple rules or steps. However, we have developed a framework that many policy practitioners have found helpful, including direct-service workers, supervisors, administrators, and advocates. By dividing policy-changing work into six tasks, this book seeks to show social workers ways to reform policy. This book discusses an array of policy-practice concepts, including ethical reasoning, windows of opportunity, trade-offs, policy options, policy persuasion, power resources, networking, assertiveness, political strategy, whistle-blowing, policy criteria, and coalitions. These concepts are integral to the work of reforming policy.

This book is also intended to help readers view policy practice as an intervention used in specific settings. In succeeding chapters, you will find many case examples that describe situations in which social workers have used policy-practice skills in specific agency, community, and legislative settings. As with direct-service administration and community work, professionals using policy practice must adapt their work to the traditions and realities of specific settings. Were these workers to use the same tactics in every setting and for every issue, they would limit their effectiveness in changing policies.

Summary

Social workers and their clients confront social policies at every turn of the road, whether agency, legislative, or administrative policies. Few of these policies are trivial. They determine who gets services, the content of services, whether personal rights such as confidentiality are protected, the distribution of resources in American society, the extent of preventive services for potential, personal problems, and the kind of staff who help clients in specific settings. Policies also shape the prerogatives of the social work profession, such as whether and how its members are licensed, which positions they can attain, and whether and how their services are reimbursed by government agencies.

Social workers need to be acquainted with existing policies because they have to help clients navigate the network of programs and services. But they also need skills to change existing policies or propose new policies. They cannot fully help their clients or protect the prerogatives of their profession without these skills.

For various reasons, the profession has only belatedly developed an interventive branch that focuses on changing policy. This book seeks to provide a framework and skills to make policy practice supplement direct-service, administration, and community-work competencies in social work practice.

Most social workers will not engage in policy practice full-time, but all social workers can add some policy practice to their other professional activities. We shall discuss in the next chapter why we think policy practice is a professional and ethical obligation.

Suggested Readings

DEFINITIONS OF POLICY AND SOCIAL WELFARE POLICY
Brian Hogwood and Lewis Gunn, *Policy Analysis for the Real World* (London: Oxford University Press, 1984), pp. 12-31.
Martin Rein, *Social Policy: Issues of Choice and Change* (New York: Random House, 1970), pp. 5-8.
Richard Titmuss, *Commitment to Welfare* (New York: Pantheon, 1968), p. 156.

MATERIALS THAT LINK POLICY TO DIRECT-SERVICE PRACTICE
Chauncy Alexander, "Professional Social Workers and Political Responsibility," in Maryann Mahaffey and John Hanks, eds., *Practical Politics: Social Work and Political Response* (Washington, DC: National Association of Social Workers, 1982), pp. 22-25.
Robert Goodin, *Reasons for Welfare: The Political Theory of the Welfare State* (Princeton, NJ: Princeton University Press, 1988), pp. 123-228.
Seymour Halleck, *Politics of Therapy* (New York: Science House, 1971), pp. 11-38.
Yeheskel Hasenfeld, "Power in Social Work Practice," *Social Service Review* 61 (September 1987).
Michael Sosin and Sharon Caulum, "Advocacy: A Conceptualization for Social Work Practice," *Social Work* 28 (January-February 1983): 12-17.
Alvin Schorr, "Practice as Policy," *Social Service Review* 59 (June 1985): 178-196.
Harold Weissman and Andrea Savage, *Agency-Based Social Work: Neglected Aspects of Clinical Practice* (Philadelphia: Temple University Press, 1983).

Overviews of Policy Deliberations
James Anderson, *Public Policy-Making* (New York: Praeger, 1975).
Bruce Jansson, *Theory and Practice of Social Welfare Policy: Analysis, Processes, and Current Issues* (Belmont, CA: Wadsworth, 1984), pp. 49–55.

Policy Practice
Bruce Jansson, *Theory and Practice of Social Welfare Policy: Analysis, Processes, and Current Issues* (Belmont, CA: Wadsworth, 1984), pp. 24–28, 53–60.
John Tropman, "Policy Analysis," in *Encyclopedia of Social Work*, vol. 2 (Washington, DC: National Association of Social Workers, 1987), pp. 268–283.
Norman Wyers, "Policy Practice in Social Work: Models and Issues," *Journal of Social Work Education* 27 (Fall 1991): 241–250.

Policy Practice in Specific Settings
Ron Dear and Rino Patti, "Legislative Advocacy," in *Encyclopedia of Social Work*, 18th ed., vol. 2 (Washington, DC: National Association of Social Workers, 1987).
Karen Haynes and James Mikelson, *Affecting Change: Social Workers in the Political Arena* (New York: Longman, 1992).
Maryann Mahaffey and John Hanks, eds., *Practical Politics: Social Work and Political Response* (Silver Spring, MD: National Association of Social Workers, 1982).
Herman Resnick and Rino Patti, *Change from Within: Humanizing Social Welfare Organizations* (Philadelphia: Temple University Press, 1980).
Ramon Salcido and Essie Seck, "Political Participation among Social Work Chapters," *Social Work* 37 (November 1992): pp. 563–564.

Notes

1. Martin Rein, *Social Policy: Issues of Choice and Change* (New York: Random House, 1970), p. 5.
2. Ibid., p. 5.
3. Ibid., p. 5.
4. Richard Titmuss, *Commitment to Welfare* (New York: Pantheon, 1968), p. 156.
5. Jeffrey Pressman and Aaron Wildavsky, *Implementation* (Berkeley and Los Angeles: University of California Press, 1974).
6. Rein, *Social Policy,* pp. 6–9.
7. Josephina Figueira-McDonough, "Policy Practice: The Neglected Side of Social Work Intervention," *Social Work,* 38 (March 1993): 179–188.
8. Alvin Schorr, "Professional Practice as Policy," *Social Service Review,* 51 (June 1985): 178–196; and Norman Wyers, "Policy Practice in Social Work: Models and Issues," *Journal of Social Work Education,* 27 (June 1985): 178–196.
9. When discussing moral rules, Mackie argues that "privately imagined rules or principles of action are worthless . . . we need expectations and claims (to have) moral rules." J. L. Mackie, *Ethics: Inventing Right and Wrong* (London: Penguin Books, 1977), pp. 146–148.
10. Conversation with Wilbur Finch, who attributed this phrase to Herb Bisno.
11. Robert Goodin, *Reasons for Welfare: The Political Theory of the Welfare State* (Princeton, NJ: Princeton University Press, 1988), pp. 123–228.
12. See Lewis Froman, "Interparty Constituency Differences and Congressional Voting Behavior," *American Political Science Review* 57 (March 1963): 57–61.

13. John Kingdon, *Agendas, Alternatives, and Public Policies* (Boston: Little, Brown, 1984).
14. Stanley Wenocur and Michael Reisch, *From Charity to Enterprise: The Development of American Social Work in a Market Economy* (Urbana: University of Illinois Press, 1989), pp. 47–78.
15. Ibid.
16. Ibid., pp. 115–135.
17. Harry Wasserman, "Social Work Treatment: An Essay Review," *Smith College Studies in Social Work* 45 (February 1975): 193.
18. Bruce Jansson, "Social Welfare Policy," in Rick Reamer, *Foundations of Social Work Knowledge* (New York: Columbia University Press, forthcoming).
19. Irving Weissman, *Social Welfare Policy and Services in Social Work Education*, vol. XII (New York: Council on Social Work Education, 1959).
20. See Werner Boehm, *Objectives of Social Work Curriculum of the Future*, vol. I (New York: Council on Social Work Education, 1959).
21. See, for example, Gordon Hearn, "Progress toward a Holistic Conception of Social Work," in Gordon Hearn, ed., *"The General Systems Approach: Contributions toward a Holistic Conception of Social Work* (New York: Council on Social Work Education, 1969), pp. 63–70; and Ann Hartman, "The Generic Stance and the Family Agency," *Social Casework* 55 (April 1974): 199–208.
22. Murray Ross, *Community Organizing* (New York: Harper & Row, 1955).
23. Yeheskel Hasenfeld, *Human Service Organizations* (Englewood Cliffs, NJ: Prentice-Hall, 1983), pp. 12–43.
24. Weissman, *Social Welfare Policy and Services*.
25. Elmer Tropman and John Tropman, *Encyclopedia of Social Work*, vol. 2, pp. 827–828.
26. Richard Cloward and Irwin Epstein, "Private Agencies, Disengagement from the Poor: The Case of Family Adjustment Agencies." In George Brager and Francis Purcell, eds., *Community Action Against Poverty* (New Haven, CT: College and University Press, 1967), pp. 40–63.
27. Robert Taylor discussed the tendency to deny that the agency context influences social workers or that they, in turn, influence clients. "The Social Control Function of Casework," *Social Casework* 39 (January 1958): 17–21.
28. Wenocur and Reisch discuss the "private agency ideal in the public sector" in *From Charity to Enterprise*, p. 260.
29. Gilbert Steiner, *Social Insecurity: The Politics of Welfare* (Chicago: Rand McNally, 1966), pp. 176–204.
30. U.S. Joint Commission on Mental Illness and Public Health, *Action for Mental Health* (New York: Science Editions, 1961), pp. 150–151.
31. Mayer Zald, *Organizational Change: The Political Economy of the YMCA* (Chicago: University of Chicago Press, 1970). Also see Robert Scott, "The Selection of Clients by Social Welfare Agencies: The Case of the Blind," in Yeheskel Hasenfeld and Richard English, eds., *Human Service Organizations* (Ann Arbor: University of Michigan Press, 1974), pp. 485–499.
32. Joel Handler, *Reforming the Poor: Welfare, Policy, Federalism, and Morality* (New York: Basic Books, 1972), pp. 25–46.
33. Taylor, "The Social Control Function of Casework."
34. Ted Watkins, "Services to Individuals," in James Callicutt and Pedro Lecca, eds., *Social Work and Mental Health* (New York: Free Press, 1983), pp. 45–68.

35. Laurence Lynn, *The State and Human Services: Organizational Change in a Political Context* (Cambridge, MA: MIT Press, 1980).
36. U.S. President's Commission on Mental Health, *Report to the President*, vol. 2 (Washington, DC: Government Printing Office, 1978), pp. 497–537.
37. Stephen Webster and Mary Wylie, "Strategic Planning in a Competitive Environment," *Administration in Mental Health* 15 (Fall 1988): 25–44.
38. David Hardcastle, "The Profession: Professional Organizations, Licensing, and Private Practice," in Neil Gilbert and Harry Specht, eds., *Handbook of the Social Services* (Englewood Cliffs, NJ: Prentice-Hall, 1981), p. 675.
39. Donald Brieland and John Lemmon, *Social Work and the Law* (St. Paul, MN: West, 1985), and Lester Schroeder, *The Legal Environment of Social Work* (Englewood Cliffs, NJ: Prentice-Hall, 1982).
40. Lester Salamon and Alan Abramson, *The Nonprofit Sector and the New Federal Budget* (Washington, DC: Urban Institute Press, 1986).
41. U.S. President's Commission on Mental Health, *Report to the President*, vol. 4 (Washington, DC: Government Printing Office, 1978), pp. 1362–1516.
42. Brenda McGowan, "Advocacy," *Encyclopedia of Social Work*, vol. 1, pp. 89–95.
43. Thomas Szasz attacks labels in *Insanity: The Idea and Its Consequences* (New York: Wiley, 1987). Robert Spitzer, Janet Williams, and Andrew Skodol defend diagnostic categories in "DSM-III: The Major Achievements and an Overview," *American Journal of Psychiatry* 137 (February 1980): 151–154.
44. Victor Adebimpe, "Overview: White Norms and Psychiatric Diagnoses of Black Patients," *American Journal of Psychiatry* 138 (March 1981): 279–285.
45. Andrew Billingsley and Jeanne Giovannoni, *Children of the Storm* (New York: Harcourt Brace Jovanovich, 1972), pp. 218–239.
46. David Mechanic, *Mental Health and Social Policy*, 3rd ed. (Englewood Cliffs, NJ: Prentice-Hall, 1989), pp. 37–40.
47. Noel Mazade, "Mental Health in Transition," *Administration in Mental Health* 14 (Spring-Summer 1987): 232–240.
48. Yeheskel Hansenfeld, "Power in Social Work Practice," *Social Service Review* 61 (September 1987): 475–476.
49. Dennis Chamot, "Professional Employees Turn to Unions," *Harvard Business Review* 54 (May 1976): 119–127.
50. Gilbert Steiner, *State of Welfare* (Washington, DC: Brookings Institution, 1971), pp. 35–40.
51. Abraham Maslow, *The Farther Reaches of Human Nature* (New York: Viking Press, 1971).
52. Robert White, *Ego and Reality in Psychoanalytic Theory* (New York: International Universities Press, 1963).
53. See, for example, Peter Berger, *Invitation to Sociology: A Humanistic Perspective* (Garden City, NY: Anchor Books, 1963), pp. 93–121.
54. Thomas Keefe, "The Stresses of Unemployment," *Social Work* 29 (May-June 1984): 264–268.
55. For discussion of 1960s theorists who studied social class's effect on human behavior, see William Wilson, "Cycles of Deprivation and the Underclass Debate," *Social Service Review* 59 (December 1985): 544–551.
56. See Barbara Solomon, "Is It Sex, Race, or Class?" *Social Work* 21 (November 1976): 420–421.

57. Henry Aaron, *Politics and the Professors* (Washington, DC: Brookings Institution, 1981), p. 17.
58. Wynetta Devore and Elfriede Schlesinger, *Ethnic-Sensitive Social Work Practice* (St. Louis: C.V. Mosby, 1981).
59. Nathan Glazer and Daniel Moynihan, *Beyond the Melting Pot* (Cambridge, MA: MIT Press, 1963), pp. 288–291.
60. Nancy Russo, "Women in the Mental Health Delivery System: Implications for Research and Public Policy," in Lenore Walker, ed., *Women and Mental Health Policy* (Beverly Hills, CA: Sage, 1984).
61. The classic discussion is found in August Hollingshead and Shirley Redlich, *Social Class and Mental Illness* (New York: Wiley, 1958), pp. 253–303.
62. Gerald Caplan, *Support System and Community Mental Health* (New York: Behavioral Publications, 1974).
63. Benjamin Gottlieb, *Social Support Strategies: Guidelines for Mental Health Practice* (Beverly Hills, CA: Sage, 1983), pp. 31–64.
64. Neil Gilbert, "Assessing Service-Delivery Methods: Some Unsettled Questions," *Welfare in Review* 10 (May 1972): 25–33.
65. Carel Germain and Alex Gitterman, *The Life Model of Social Work Practice* (New York: Columbia University Press, 1980); and Carol Meyer, *Social Work Practice: A Response to the Urban Crisis* (New York: Free Press, 1970).
66. Solomon, *Black Empowerment* (New York: Columbia University Press, 1976); and Hasenfeld, "Power in Social Work Practice."
67. McGowan, "Advocacy," pp. 90–91.
68. Ibid., p. 91. Also Michael Sosin and Sharon Caulum, "Advocacy: A Conceptualization for Social Work Practice," *Social Work* 28 (January-February 1983): 12–17.
69. Bruce Jansson, *The Reluctant Welfare State* (Pacific Grove, CA: Brooks/Cole, 1993), pp. 225–228.
70. Thomas Edsall, *Chain Reaction: The Impact of Race Rights and Taxes on American Politics* (New York: Norton, 1991), pp. 74–98.
71. See Werner Boehm, *Objectives of the Social Work Curriculum*, vol. I (New York: Council on Social Work Education, 1959).
72. Harry Specht, "Social Work and the Popular Psychotherapies," *Social Service Review* 64 (September 1990): 345–347.
73. Wasserman, "Social Work Treatment: An Essay Review," pp. 187–189.
74. See Robert Dahl, *Pluralist Democracy in the United States* (Chicago: Rand McNally, 1967).
75. Rino Patti and Herman Resnick, "Changing the Agency from Within," *Social Work* 17 (July 1972): 48–77. Also see Chauncey Alexander, "Professional Social Workers and Political Responsibility," in Mahaffey and Hanks, eds., *Practical Politics: Social Work and Political Response* (Silver Spring, MD: National Association of Social Workers, 1982), pp. 26–27.
76. Franklin Chu and Sharland Trotter discuss variations between community mental health centers' policies in *The Madness Establishment* (New York: Grossman, 1974).
77. Bruce Jansson, "Public Monitoring of Contracts with Nonprofit Organizations: Organizational Mission in Two Sectors," *Journal of Sociology and Social Welfare* 6 (May 1979): 362–374.
78. Eviline Burns, *Social Security and Public Policy* (New York: McGraw-Hill, 1956).

79. Neil Gilbert and Harry Specht, *Dimensions of Social Welfare Policy* (Englewood Cliffs, NJ: Prentice-Hall, 1974).
80. Alfred Kahn, *Theory and Practice of Social Planning* (New York: Russell Sage Foundation, 1969).
81. Yeheskel Dror, *Venture in Policy Sciences* (New York: Elsevier North Holland, 1971), and Edward Quade, *Analysis for Public Decisions*, 2nd ed. (New York: Elsevier North Holland, 1982).
82. See Edward Banfield, "The Public Interest," in Neil Gilbert and Harry Specht, eds., *Planning for Social Welfare* (Englewood Cliffs, NJ: Prentice-Hall, 1977), pp. 44–49.
83. David Gil, *Unravelling Social Policy* (Cambridge, MA: Schenkman, 1976).
84. Richard Cloward and Frances Piven, *Regulating the Poor: The Functions of Public Welfare* (New York: Pantheon, 1971).
85. Ron Dear and Rino Patti discuss the need for compromises in political arenas in "Legislative Advocacy," in *Encyclopedia of Social Work*, vol. 2, p. 37.
86. Maryann Mahaffey and John Hanks, eds., *Practical Politics: Social Work and Political Response* (Silver Spring, MD: National Association of Social Workers, 1982); Diane DiNitto and Thomas Dye, *Social Welfare: Politics and Public Policy* (Englewood Cliffs, NJ: Prentice-Hall; 1983); Andrew Doblestein, *Politics, Economics, and Public Welfare* (Englewood Cliffs, NJ: Prentice-Hall, 1980); Karen Haynes and James Mikelson, *Affecting Change: Social Workers in the Political Arena* (New York: Longman, 1986).
87. Ron Dear and Rino Patti, "Legislative Advocacy: Seven Effective Tactics," *Social Work* 26 (July 1981): 289–297.
88. Mahaffey and Hanks, *Practical Politics*.
89. Jeffrey Pressman and Aaron Wildavsky, *Implementation* (Berkeley: University of California Press, 1974).
90. For example, see Erwin Hargrove, *The Missing Link* (Washington, DC: Urban Institute, 1981); Eugene Bardach, *The Implementation Game* (Cambridge, MA: MIT Press, 1977); and Walter Williams, *The Implementation Perspective* (Berkeley and Los Angeles: University of California Press, 1980).
91. Sheila Kamerman and Alfred Kahn, *Social Services in the United States* (Philadelphia: Temple University Press, 1976).
92. Willard Richan, "A Common Language for Social Work," *Social Work* 17 (November 1972): 14–22.
93. John Tropman et al., *New Strategic Perspectives on Social Policy* (New York: Pergamon, 1981), pp. 181–247.
94. John Flynn, *Social Agency Policy: Analysis and Presentation for Community Practice* (Chicago: Nelson-Hall, 1985); Dean Pierce, *Policy for the Social Work Practitioner* (New York: Longman, 1984); John Tropman, *Policy Management in the Human Services* (New York: Columbia University Press, 1984).
95. Herman Resnick and Rino Patti, eds., *Change from Within: Humanizing Social Welfare Organizations* (Philadelphia: Temple University Press, 1980).
96. Bruce Jansson, *Theory and Practice of Social Welfare Policy: Analysis, Processes, and Current Issues* (Belmont, CA: Wadsworth, 1984), pp. 24–28.
97. Ibid., pp. 24–28.
98. Bruce Jansson, *Social Welfare Policy: From Theory to Practice* (Belmont, CA: Wadsworth, 1990).
99. Wyers, "Policy Practice in Social Work," and Figueira-McDonough, "Policy Practice: The Neglected Side of Social Work Intervention."

100. Boehm, *Objectives of the Social Work Curriculum of the Future.*
101. Conversation with David Austin.
102. Schorr, "Professional Practice as Policy."
103. Nancy Humphreys, "Integrating Policy and Practice: The Contribution of Clinical Social Work," *Smith College Studies in Social Work* 63 (March 1993): 177–186.

Chapter Two

The Ethical Rationale for Policy Practice

Some readers may remain unconvinced that policy practice should be an integral part of social work practice. After all, they might ask, do attorneys, physicians, nurses, or teachers, make policy-changing an integral part of their professional work?

In this chapter we shall argue that practice ought to be integral to the work of all professionals, but that social workers bear a particular obligation to engage in it. We shall discuss, moreover, the intent of policy practice. We will ask, for example, whether we can gear policy practice toward advocacy, or helping relatively oppressed groups, rather than toward upholding the status quo. After examining the moral imperative for policy practice in social work, we will study ethical dilemmas, meaning difficult choices that social workers must make. They have to choose between competing values, as well as between specific values and practical considerations such as political feasibility. Finally, we shall ask whether certain kinds of policy practice are compatible with the professional role, including engaging in electoral politics and advancing one's self-interest.

HOW ETHICAL AND NONETHICAL ISSUES DIFFER

Lest we imply that ethical issues confront policy practitioners at every turn, it is useful to define "ethical issues." Issues are ethical or moral *when they cannot be resolved without considerable recourse to personal values that define some "right" or "good" objective or criterion.*[1] When persons say "don't lie," "allow terminally ill persons to decide when they wish to forgo extraordinary medical measures," or "redistribute resources to poor people," they imply that certain actions or policies represent better values than other actions or policies. In their eyes, not lying is better than lying, allowing terminally ill persons to control their medical fate is better than making their medical decisions for them, and equalizing economic resources is better than allowing marked inequality to exist. An *ethical dilemma* exists when policy practitioners encounter at least two choices that each represent important values.

Ethical reasoning both simplifies and complicates policy practitioners' choices. It simplifies choices by declaring certain options unacceptable, at least in most situations. For example, few persons become habitual liars even if they lie on a few occasions. Similarly, most of us do not routinely betray confidences, support discriminatory policies, or defy the policies we are supposed to implement. Ethics establish certain boundaries for our choices in many situations.[2]

Because we take those kinds of limits for granted, we often fail to recognize their importance. Imagine a world in which people routinely lied to you, resorted to devious Machiavellian strategies, or developed discriminatory policies. With no ethical boundaries, life would become an unpredictable, tumultuous, and dangerous enterprise where powerful persons could routinely oppress whomever they disliked. Widely accepted ethical rules, such as honesty and fairness, establish boundaries that preclude specific options.

BENEFICENCE AND PROFESSIONAL PRACTICE

In this chapter, we develop an ethical rationale for policy practice in two stages. First, we discuss why, in their direct-service interactions with clients, social workers should include policy-sensitive and policy-related activities. (These terms are defined later in this chapter.) Second, we discuss why social workers should engage in policy practice—that is, in efforts to change policies.

Professionals of all kinds are bound by codes of ethics to place clients' needs first. We describe this moral imperative to help clients as "beneficence" because it is widely used in moral philosophy.[3] Professionals act unethically when they knowingly harm clients, whether by providing them with unnecessary or inferior services, lying to them, having sexual relations with them, or betraying confidences. Social workers share with other professionals a moral obligation to advance the well-being of their individual clients and refrain from harming them.

However, clients' well-being extends beyond the scope of the professionals they consult. A woman who cannot afford an adequate diet, for example, is unlikely to obtain physical well-being no matter how skillfully a physician treats her. The doctor who takes no interest in referring this patient to the Food Stamps Program, to a social worker, or to someone else who can link the woman with this program is not advancing the patient's beneficence. Similarly, a lawyer is morally derelict if she helps a woman obtain a divorce, but has no interest in her economic fate after the divorce is consummated. (So many women become mired in poverty when they must raise children singlehandedly that terms such as "the feminization of poverty" have evolved.) As was true of the physician, this lawyer should expand her professional work beyond merely performing a technical transaction.

Indeed, we can say that both the physician and the lawyer have two moral obligations: to make their professional recommendations with a sensitivity toward their clients' economic, social, and policy realities, and to engage in brokerage, liaison, and advocacy work for specific clients to improve these economic and policy realities.[4] The first moral obligation illustrates *policy-sensitive practice*, where professionals are aware that the client or patient often confronts (or will confront) negative and policy-related consequences that must be considered even when giving technical advice. Examples of professional work that is *not* policy-sensitive abound, as illustrated by physicians who prescribe diets or medications that clients cannot afford, lawyers who obtain divorces for clients with no thought to the economic realities they are likely to confront, and teachers or school administrators who are unaware of environmental factors (such as poor diet) that influence children's ability to learn. These professionals are morally obligated to shape even "technical advice" to help clients cope with realities in the external world. Perhaps physicians need to schedule time to discuss patients' situational realities rather than saying only "take this tablet three times daily for three weeks." Lawyers need to speak with clients about the needs they will have during and after specific legal actions. Teachers need to include parents in their teaching strategies. We call this policy-sensitive practice because it requires professionals to take into account clients' economic and social realities, many of which derive from societal policies.

Professionals also need to use brokerage, liaison, and advocacy services for specific clients. We call these policy-related services because they involve skills, such as mediation and conflict-management, that resemble skills used in policy practice. *Brokerage* means that the aforementioned physicians, attorneys, and teachers should negotiate services for specific clients with other institutions and persons. A physician could help parents of an asthmatic child decide how they will sacrifice some of their other needs to meet her exacting dietary and medicinal needs. A teacher may broker an agreement with a welfare office to obtain resources for a dyslexic child. They need *liaison* strategies to connect clients to other, related services. When a battered woman comes to a lawyer for divorce services, he may need to help her obtain access to a shelter. A physician should help low-income, pregnant women obtain free food from the Women, Infants, and Children (WIC) program. These professionals ought to "go to bat" for their clients by engaging in case-based *advocacy* when they are unfairly denied services from programs.[5]

We know, of course, that physicians, attorneys, and teachers often provide neither policy-sensitive nor policy-related services. This may be true because they are unaware of realities that affect their clients, have been trained to provide only technical and narrow services, or lack resources to expand their work. They may not want to take the time to discuss these external factors. With this attitude, they risk ignoring the beneficence of their clients because they fail to address their needs. Since we judge the morality of persons by omissions as well as commissions, we can rightly contend that professionals who do not engage in policy-sensitive and policy-related activities are morally deficient, even when they plead lack of time or knowledge.

POLICY-SENSITIVE AND POLICY-RELATED PRACTICE

Some readers may ask how our discussion of physicians, lawyers, and teachers applies to social workers. We have deliberately begun with other professions to emphasize three things. First, all professionals are morally obligated to advance clients' beneficence. Second, they cannot do so without policy-sensitive and policy-related practice. Third, we can make moral judgments about all professionals' work on the basis of acts of commission (such as lying to a client) and omission (such as not using policy-sensitive and policy-related practice). We are not holding social work to a different standard or moral code than other professions.

We argue, however, that social workers are even more morally deficient than other professionals if they do not engage in policy-sensitive and policy-related practice, because they occupy a unique position in the human services system. A physician who specializes in removing appendixes ought to be concerned about her patients after they leave the hospital, but her role in the human services is relatively focused and specialized. She is primarily concerned with surgical procedures, is trained to perform them, and is reimbursed by insurance carriers to treat appendixes, exclusively. Notwithstanding our moral objections to such narrow work, we often do not expect surgeons to go beyond their specific duties.

But beneficence takes on a broader meaning for social workers than for other professionals because of the unusual nature of social work. Many of their clients are trying to negotiate relationships, not just with individuals, but with institutions. Social workers in child welfare agencies, hospitals, mental health clinics, homeless shelters, AIDS treatment programs, schools, or family courts do not merely address specialized needs, such as appendicitis. They often deal with clients with emotional trauma, interpersonal and institutional relations, and a need for a professional to negotiate both the trauma and these relations. Consider a patient who has been disabled by a car accident and who, after a year of intensive rehabilitation, is about to be released from a hospital. This patient will need assistance in renewing his family life, rekindling marital relations, obtaining disability benefits, seeking vocational assistance, and surmounting prejudice against disabled persons as he reenters the job market. The ethical social worker has to engage in brokering, liaison, and case-advocacy to help this patient, rather than limiting herself to narrow clinical services.[6]

Beneficence requires social workers to help clients resolve emotional trauma, such as the disabled person's uneasiness about his loss of physical abilities. He might feel inferior because he has internalized cultural images of disabled persons that emphasize their helplessness or inadequacies. Policies, services, and programs greatly influence clients' well-being. This disabled person, for example, would likely feel threatened by inadequate disability benefits, denial of those benefits by punitive bureaucrats, lack of governmental enforcement of disabled people's rights, and inadequate homemaker aides during his recovery.

Our discussion suggests that beneficence cannot easily be conceived in narrow terms; no matter how skilled professionals are, they cannot help improve their clients' well-being without addressing clients' dysfunctional relations with their environment. Nor can social workers improve clients' well-being if they are continually exposed to oppressive relationships in their families, communities, or jobs. Clients must grapple with any cultural images that demean them by examining how oppressive ideology affects their personal activities and self-esteem. In all of these cases, helpers have to supplement traditional, direct-service interventions, which focus on intrapsychic matters, with other remedies. They might teach survival skills or assertiveness; help persons deal with discrimination; or use brokering, liaison, or advocacy interventions.

Ethical social workers also realize that they have limited time in which to help clients. Therefore, they need to teach clients skills to help themselves confront barriers, find resources, and manage their own cases. The social worker seeks to equip persons with the ability to take charge of their personal destinies in the future.[7] The term *empowerment* is commonly used to describe these survival skills.

While a physician can use knowledge of physiology to declare an infection to be a pathology, social workers need to wrestle with the proper definition of "pathology" when they work with specific clients. Assume, for example, that a member of an oppressed minority appears "paranoid," or seems excessively suspicious of other persons. Is this true paranoia or a reflection of actual encounters with other persons and institutions that have been oppressive? Assume that someone does not seem to know how to make and execute plans. Could this apparent pathology stem from living in an oppressive environment where "planning" is relatively futile because people lack the resources or the benign environment to make positive outcomes likely? Does beating one's children reflect pathology or the child-rearing practices of a specific group in the population? In each of these cases, social workers have to consider environmental and cultural realities even before making diagnoses, unlike the physician who can diagnose an infected appendix without recourse to these realities. With oppressed people, such as battered women, the social worker needs to educate clients about cultural forces, such as sexism, which they may have internalized. (Many women return to oppressive spouses, not just for economic reasons, but because they believe they somehow "caused" abusive treatment.)[8]

Social workers have to engage in policy-sensitive and policy-related practice if they wish to advance the beneficence of their clients. They risk ignoring the beneficence of their clients if they fail to place their work in a broader context and fail to provide services beyond merely discussing emotional matters.

When social workers perform policy-sensitive activities, they should recognize the following:

- Some problems or pathologies reflect situational and environmental pressures rather than deep-seated characteristics.
- Some apparent problems or pathologies are functional adaptions to oppressive realities.
- Survival skills are often as important to people (particularly persons who have been excluded from mainstream institutions) as intrapsychic interventions.

- Some persons need help overcoming feelings of inferiority that stem from exposure to oppressive ideology and institutions.
- Some people need help in becoming more assertive.
- Empowerment, or learning skills to counter oppressive realities, is often as important as purely intrapsychic interventions.

When social workers perform policy-related activities, they should realize the following:

- Often, they will need to negotiate service arrangements between clients and family members or institutions such as schools, welfare departments, child welfare departments, and clinics (brokerage).
- Often, they will need to connect persons to other persons, networks, or institutions (liaison).
- Often, they must be personal advocates for clients or empower clients to become their own advocates (case advocacy).

Moving Toward Policy Practice

We have argued, thus far, that all professionals need to broaden their work to include policy-sensitive and policy-related practice in their interactions with clients. We have also argued that the unique role of social workers in child welfare, hospital, clinic, school, industrial, and other settings suggests they in particular need to be attentive to environmental realities. We have made three, related assertions: (1) the beneficence of clients is intimately linked to their relationships with institutions, oppressive relationships, and oppressive ideologies, (2) social workers have to address or be aware of these relationships if they want to improve the well-being of many of their clients, and (3) social workers' failure to acknowledge key elements of clients' personal predicaments can be criticized on moral grounds as not contributing to clients' beneficence.

Having linked the beneficence of clients to policy-sensitive and policy-related interventions, we can now ask whether ethical social workers must also try to change defective policies and oppressive ideologies at some point in their careers. While we have discussed policy-sensitive and policy-related practice in direct-service practice to this point, we now move beyond direct-service practice to focus on changing policies in agency, legislative, and government settings. Possible activities include developing and working in coalitions, using power, developing tactics, lobbying, engaging in political campaigns, using persuading techniques, conducting policy-related research, drafting proposals, and reforming operating programs. (Recall that policy-sensitive and policy-related practice allow us to enrich and broaden our work with specific clients, but do not emphasize interventions to change policies in agencies or legislatures.) We make the moral case that policy practice that seeks to advance ethical principles should fall under the domain of all social workers, no matter their role in the human services system.

To discuss whether a moral imperative exists, let us examine other professions, such as medicine, law, and teaching, before returning to social work. Assume that physicians know that people's health depends on their access to primary health care on a regular basis and that millions of Americans currently lack access because they have no health insurance. Given the importance of access to health, we could clearly raise moral questions about physicians as a group and as individuals were they not to invest extraordinary effort in changing existing laws. They could be similarly indicted if their profession did not lead the effort to educate others about AIDS and to distribute condoms. In similar fashion, attorneys could be morally criticized if they failed to support expansion of government programs that provide legal aid for poor people. Teachers can be lambasted on moral grounds if they fail to fight overcrowding in inner-city schools. As Kozol's work suggests, many inner-city teachers must contend with staggering teaching loads in facilities that are far inferior to those in suburban districts.[9]

We know that physicians, attorneys, and teachers have often overlooked these policy defects. Moreover, the American Medical Association has often seemed more concerned about maintaining the fees and autonomy of physicians than supporting reforms in the American medical system.[10]

But social work would be in moral jeopardy equal to that of other professions were its members not to try to change policies. Even more than most other occupations, social workers serve stigmatized populations. Due to their relative lack of power and societal discrimination, these groups most need assistance from government laws, regulations, and programs. However, their powerlessness makes them vulnerable to the whims of the broader electorate, government budget crunches, cuts in regulatory agencies' staff, and the backlash in the general public's attitude toward social programs. Were social workers not to serve as advocates for these populations, they would risk the moral charge of not caring about them. No matter how skillful, policy-sensitive and policy-related, direct-service assistance cannot compensate for inadequacies in the broader society.

Even more than many other professionals, moreover, social workers serve as salaried employees in organizations. Their ability to advance their clients' well-being depends largely on organizational matters, such as employee morale, organizational policies, staff's ability to collaborate with one another and with other organizations, and adequate resources. We know many instances when meritorious policies came to naught because they were poorly implemented. While executives possess disproportionate influence, many lower-level staff can participate in the deliberations and politics of organizations to enhance their ability to deliver quality services that advance the beneficence of clients. Were staff wholly disinterested in organizational matters, they would risk the moral accusation (as would social workers who never try to change societal policies) that they do not care about the well-being of their clients.

Our discussion suggests that, far from constituting a distraction from ongoing, social-work practice, social policy is integral to it. An ethical social worker needs skills, concepts, and sensitivities drawn from social welfare policy to be a complete (and ethical) social worker. By emphasizing that environmental factors influence individuals' lives, especially members of specific populations (such as women, racial minorities, the disabled, gays and lesbians, and the elderly), policy powerfully broadens traditional interventions with clients. If social policy enriches direct-service practice, it also takes its place alongside direct-service, administrative, and community work. Policy practice requires skills and competencies just as any social work practice does. Every social worker seeking to advance their clients beneficence should practice policy practice some time in their careers, if only to improve agency, community, and legislative policies.

Social workers might initiate social-reform projects or work through chapters of the National Association of Social Workers or other professional organizations. Or their policy practice could sometimes take the form of helping existing advocacy and community groups. Indeed, "empowerment," or helping individuals assert their needs, extends to helping oppressed groups assert their rights collectively, whether through community-based organizations or advocacy groups that focus on the needs of specific, oppressed populations.[11] Social workers can volunteer their services to these advocacy groups, serve as consultants to them, help them find resources, and conduct research for them.

Policy practice can fully realize the environmental approach to social work practice. Policy practice aims to help populations by working on policies that affect them as groups rather than as individuals or families. If we change an agency's intake policy, develop a new program in an agency, or modify an existing law, we change the terms of service for many people, even if we initially engaged in our policy-changing work to help a single person or family. Without policy practice, social work practice gives only lip service to environmental frameworks. Clients' lives are powerfully shaped by societal factors that only policy practice can change, whether in agency, community, state, or national arenas. Without policy practice, the social work profession becomes, in effect, an apologist for existing institutions rather than a force for social reform.

Ethical social workers need to operate on several fronts during their careers. They must provide policy-sensitive direct-service practice, policy-related direct-service practice, *and* policy practice. They cannot engage in these disparate activities at all points in their careers; indeed, they are likely to engage in only episodes of policy practice. But these episodes ought to be a prized part of social work practice. They may only take the form of modifying agency policies, where the social worker urges the agency to meet important social needs, or modifying existing policies to make programs more responsive to their clients' needs. Even these relatively modest projects require that social workers possess skills and concepts not covered in direct-service literature and courses. We believe social-policy curriculum should fill the gap by devoting considerable time to them.

POLICY PRACTICE AS SOCIAL JUSTICE

We have justified policy practice to this point in terms of clients' beneficence. For example, we discussed helping disabled persons obtain benefits, services, access to job training and jobs, transportation, homemaker aides, and other forms of assistance that derive from high-level policies. In this perspective, we engage in policy practice to enhance the well-being of disabled persons by getting them more benefits, services, and rights.

But we can also justify policy practice from the vantage point of social justice, where policy practice seeks to reduce inequalities in society. Were we to engage in policy practice for this reason, we would pursue it because we find inequalities in society morally objectionable, whether they exist between social classes or between mainstream society and a specific population, such as disabled persons. But should we be concerned about inequality in society? Let us discuss varieties of inequality, some reasons inequalities violate ethical standards, and how policy practitioners use policy practice to decrease inequality.

Varieties of Inequality

If we were to analyze *current statuses* of American citizens in an array of dimensions, such as housing, income, neighborhood amenities, and health status, we would find vast disparities between them. Social class provides a shorthand method of summarizing many of these disparities, because persons in the upper classes (or quintiles) tend to possess more income (and therefore better housing, better neighborhood amenities, and better health) than those in the lower classes (or quintiles). We can also analyze disparities in current status between specific populations and the mainstream population. If we define "white adult males" to be the mainstream population, for example, we can compare their average income with that of a specific population, such as women, Latinos, African Americans, or children.[12]

We could also analyze disparities among citizens not by current income and related indicators but by access to opportunities, such as education, health services, assets (houses, for example), networks (for example, acquaintances with clout), and rights (for example, freedom from discrimination in jobs or promotions). Opportunity is, to some extent, the flip side of current status, since having opportunities allows us to obtain or improve current statuses, such as income.[13] When feminists complain that women are often excluded from old-boy networks, for example, they realize that promotions and jobs (current statuses) often depend upon contacts that give persons an inside track; excluded from these networks, women often lose jobs and promotions to males. Indeed, current statuses and access to opportunities are reciprocal; as someone's income increases, for example, they can afford expensive housing, which tends to be near better schools and jobs, which give them access to opportunities, which, in turn, allow their income to increase.

When Inequalities Violate Ethical Standards

Inequalities of status and opportunity are inevitable in any society. Short of fiat by someone with complete control over the economy who wanted equality, certain persons, classes, and populations develop greater "current statuses" and "access to opportunities" than others. Such inequalities exist even in noncapitalist societies, as illustrated by differences in wealth and status within Native American tribes or between noblemen and serfs in feudal society. But inequalities emerge in particularly striking fashion in capitalistic societies where those who control corporations or work in highly paid occupations such as law and medicine secure income, assets, and access to opportunities that are vastly discrepant from other people. Moreover, patterns of inheritance perpetuate these differences, as well as discrepancies in access to opportunities. The descendants of wealthy persons not only inherit wealth, but obtain access to opportunities by virtue of contacts, schooling, and other advantages.[14]

We confront formidable intellectual challenges when we ask "What degrees and kinds of inequalities are morally objectionable?" We have to be clear, for example, whether we discuss inequalities in statuses or access to opportunities. We need to discuss issues of *threshold;* at what threshold or amount is inequality morally objectionable? We also have to decide *why* inequality is objectionable, if at all. To the extent that we dislike inequalities, we must decide what kinds of policies should be used to reduce inequalities.

Nor do we have the ethical field to ourselves, because many philosophers have wrestled with issues of equality. It is beyond the scope of this book to summarize and analyze their different conclusions and arguments, but we will briefly analyze some tenets of the leading contemporary philosopher John Rawls to introduce us to the topic. In his seminal work, *A Theory of Justice,* Rawls argues that we can best construct our moral vision of a good society by trying to imagine its internal arrangements from behind a "veil of ignorance." With this veil on, we are unaware of our personal current status (such as income) or our personal access to opportunities.[15] Rawls says that if we are aware of our current status and are, for example, relatively well off, we would likely want a society that perpetuated our economic well-being, even if others did not share in it. Therefore, we should retreat behind a veil of ignorance where our personal income and opportunities are not known to us. When conceptualizing the ideal society in this manner, we would likely conclude that society should allow only those inequalities that would preserve or further the common good of society. We would reach this conclusion because we would not want to take the chance that we would be "stuck" in the lower reaches of society. Remember that when operating behind the veil of ignorance, we do not know in advance where we would be placed in society. We realize that we would probably end up in the lower reaches of a relatively inegalitarian society, because most people are in the lower reaches in these kinds of societies, in contrast to egalitarian societies where people have similar statuses and opportunities. Of course, we could take the chance, much like a lottery, that we would end up in the higher reaches of an inegalitarian society, but the odds would not be in our favor. The rational person would, Rawls concludes, opt for an egalitarian society. We would accept some inequalities. Occupations that require particular skill and training, such as brain surgery, would have relatively high salaries, so that the most skilled and dedicated persons would be attracted to them.

We can place Rawls's argument in simpler form by asking the reader, "If you had the choice at the start of your existence, before you had developed a liking for any specific society, if you did not know what position in society you would obtain, would you choose to live in the United States (with its relatively inegalitarian arrangements) or in more egalitarian societies such as Sweden, where discrepancies between affluent and less affluent classes are less marked, particularly when relatively equal access to health care and education are factored into the equation?" (Remember when answering the question that you possess no affiliation to any specific society, including its language and customs.) Rawls asserts that you would likely select Sweden because, on balance, you would not want to risk that you might "end up in" the American lower classes, which include many persons in blighted inner-city neighborhoods who have no health care.

Rawls's argument can be restated as the Golden Rule, which says "Do unto others as you would have them do unto you." If you are not willing to experience the inequalities of the inner city, for example, you should not support policies that perpetuate such inequalities. This argument suggests that failure to engage in *any* social reform, whether as a private citizen or as part of one's professional role, is tantamount to violation of the Golden Rule, or its equivalent in secular philosophy or other religions. If you (or I) do not want to live in inner-city areas without adequate health care and other amenities, we have a moral duty to try to improve the lot of inner-city residents, and other persons who experience inequality.

We can also support efforts to reduce inequalities with economic arguments. Extreme inequalities produce undesirable economic effects for the nation.[16] At a time when Americans compete with foreign nations, for example, they can ill afford vast reservoirs of relatively uneducated, unhealthy, and nonproductive citizens in the inner cities. But Americans have failed to invest in people, jobs, and infrastructure, which has, in fact, decreased the productivity of inner-city residents. By having to support a relatively unproductive group of citizens, Americans place themselves at a competitive disadvantage with other nations that possess more educated, healthier, and more contented citizens.

Similarly, vast disparities in statuses and opportunities probably produce undesirable social consequences. Persons in the lower reaches of relatively inegalitarian societies often despair about their chances to improve their lot. Such alienation often induces them to improve their lot through crime and drug-dealing, which harm their neighborhoods and the broader society. If they despair at working through the political system, they may also participate in violent, collective uprisings at enormous cost to themselves, their neighborhoods, and the nation, as the domestic disturbances of the 1960s and the 1992 Los Angeles uprising suggest.[17]

We can also advocate reducing inequality in the name of the common good. In recent decades, it has been fashionable to argue that self-interested and individualistic behavior constitutes the highest or best activity. Society benefits, conservatives have often said, when persons work hard, take risks, and build businesses to improve their incomes. Carried to an extreme, however, self-serving behavior ignores the social and economic realities that may *harm* the nation's collective good.[18] Many conservatives blithely assume that inequality is an unmixed blessing that girds all of us, including desperately poor people, to work hard to emulate people such as Bill Gates. But we have already argued that inequality over certain thresholds probably leaves many people at the bottom of the economic heap in a state of alienation, fear, and outrage. This combination is unlikely to produce positive outcomes! If we take "the collective good" as our starting point, we at least ask questions about those kinds and thresholds of inequality that are counterproductive from the vantage point of the broader society. And as our discussion of poverty's ill effects in inner-city areas suggests, it is unlikely that extreme inequality helps the nation during an era of international competition. (Conservatives might counter that efforts to improve the inner cities would require higher taxes and thus harm the nation's economy, but this assertion is refuted by the high economic growth rates of many other nations that have higher taxes than the United States.)[19]

Fairness and Advocacy for Outgroups

I find Rawls's approach to moral reasoning to have considerable merit because his arguments force us to ponder ideal, or preferred, social and economic arrangements. But some readers may find Rawls's arguments relatively abstract. They have company in many philosophers who note that it is almost impossible to operate behind a veil of ignorance since, try as we might, we cannot easily shed assumptions and knowledge that we currently possess.[20] Moreover, some persons may find Rawls's recommendations utopian. It is difficult to imagine converting a highly inegalitarian society such as the United States into one that even remotely approaches the Rawlsian ideal.

Why not proceed to social justice more directly by discussing specific groups who are clearly "unequal" from the dominant population? Why not seek to improve their lot on grounds that it is unfair for such groups to be unequal?

Indeed, we can advance a relatively simple, ethical goal undergirded by the notion of fairness, which most of us favor. The doctrine of fairness suggests that, if there must be some or even considerable inequality in society, why not seek a society where problems such as poverty are distributed randomly, rather than disproportionately located in specific populations such as African Americans and women? With this perspective, we do not seek to eradicate all or most inequality. That is probably an impossible task in a world where special and entrenched interests abound. Instead, we would reduce the inequality of specific groups in hopes that social problems and inequalities would be distributed more randomly. (We might hope, of course, that our assisting specific groups will ultimately reduce the general inequality in American society, even if that is not our immediate focus.)

Fairness is a simple concept that is related to but is somewhat different from equality. When we focus on fairness, we primarily want people to have the same chance of obtaining positive things (such as income) and negative things (such as lesser income or poverty). If society is unwilling to support equality, why not at least develop social arrangements that give individuals equal chances at both prized things and at inequalities that we are unwilling to eradicate? Of course, our seeking fairness does not mean we cannot also work for general equality so that no one experiences problems such as poverty.

Considerable evidence suggests that neither prized things nor inequalities are randomly distributed in the population. American society has a variety of "outgroups," or subgroups with a disproportionate share of social malaise.[21] These groups include: *racial outgroups* (for example, African Americans, Latinos, and Native Americans), whose physiological differences have often led to discrimination; *sociological outgroups* (such as women, the elderly, and disabled persons), whom employers often expect to occupy relatively low positions or to leave the work force; *dependent outgroups* (for instance, children), who need other people's assistance, but are often denied supportive programs because they lack political clout; *deviant outgroups* (which include welfare recipients, the mentally ill, gays, lesbians, and persons with criminal records), who suffer discrimination on grounds that they violate societal norms; and *model outgroups* (such as Asian Americans, white ethnic Americans, and Jewish Americans), who find it difficult to obtain supportive policies because society largely believes that they have no social problems. These outgroups experience different inequalities at different degrees, but each experiences inequalities compared to the mainstream population. Then, too, there are subgroups within outgroups that experience discrimination, such as Cambodian members of the Asian-American outgroup. The gay male population is, for example, relatively affluent compared to racial outgroups, but its members experience many forms of job-related, housing, and social discrimination, not to mention inadequate health-care services when they develop problems such as AIDS. The elderly population has made striking economic gains in recent decades, but many of them are devastated by the paucity of government-funded health services for persons who are frail or experience chronic conditions. As a group, children experience high rates of poverty, abusive behavior, the absence of quality child care, and poor educational services. We have already discussed the many problems of racial outgroups, who also encounter widespread racism from the general public and from police departments. While women have made important economic gains, they largely remain in gender-segregated jobs, experience high rates of poverty as single heads of households, are subject to high rates of abusive behavior, and often lack access to health care because they hold service jobs that do not provide health insurance.

Professionals, and social workers in particular, should work to ameliorate such inequalities, both by getting these outgroups better and more services in specific agencies and by seeking changes in local, state, and federal policies.

While we can use the principles of beneficence and social justice to support such efforts, we can also draw on the doctrine of fairness when we try to decrease their disproportionate inequality.

Take the case of expanding the Head Start Program to serve all low-income African-American children. We support the program because it enhances fairness by giving African-American children the educational, health, and child development services many white families have long taken for granted. Such families send their children to nursery schools, have easy access to doctors, and purchase computers and other educational aides for their children. While expanding Head Start hardly reduces societal inequality on a grand scale, as implied by Rawls's framework, it reduces some inequalities of African-American children when they are compared with, say, many white children.

It is relatively simple for social workers to try to help members of these outgroups through policy practice. Advocacy groups have developed in local, state, and national jurisdictions to assist these various outgroups. (We discuss in Chapter Eleven how to find directories of such groups in your local region.) Whether as a volunteer, member, staff person, or board member of one of these groups, social workers can participate in policy action by linking themselves to an advocacy group. Other avenues exist, such as local and state chapters of the National Association of Social Workers. Social workers can initiate their own projects, singly or in tandem.

The doctrine of fairness, as well as social justice, sometimes leads to painful predicaments, as with affirmative action. To decrease a specific outgroup's inequalities, sometimes we must take away opportunities from a privileged group, such as white males. Say that we have a limited number of positions in an organization, and we want to increase the number of women who hold those positions. We believe they are underrepresented because of past discrimination. We can only increase the number of female employees, at least in the short term, by reducing the number of male employees. Does favoring female applicants (which our doctrine of fairness supports) deny fairness to male applicants? The answer depends partly on our time frame and our ultimate objectives. The doctrine of fairness dictates a random distribution of problems such as unemployment or lower-paying jobs. Thus, positive discrimination for female applicants is justifiable because it makes men and women more equal (hence, it is fairer) with respect to jobs and higher positions, even if only within a particular organization. Were we to consider hiring women only when female applicants were better qualified than males, it would take decades to achieve parity. Affirmative "discrimination" *for* women was developed to move the clock ahead. In this perspective, it is hard to find an ethical alternative to affirmative action because any other policy would fail to redress historic patterns of inequality.[22]

THE MERITS OF GOVERNMENT INTERVENTION

If social justice and fairness provide moral imperatives for policy practice, they also suggest that we need to steer clear of the conservative philosophy that dominated national discourse during the Reagan and Bush presidencies.[23] Left to its own, unregulated devices, capitalism leads to considerable economic and social inequalities. In conservative economic theory, everyone has an equal or considerable chance of obtaining economic success by dint of hard labor. If this were true, the deciding variable in predicting economic success would be "character."

Comparing the affluent and nonaffluent classes suggests, however, that systematic structural factors make certain kinds of persons poor, even those who subscribe to the work ethic. Single women with children, African Americans, Latinos, persons with disabilities, and those in unskilled jobs are far more likely to be impoverished, for example, than white males. A range of environmental, social, and economic factors clearly work against these persons who, despite their personal character, will probably experience poverty and other social problems. In addition, once they encounter social problems, they are unlikely to have many resources to help them cope with economic uncertainty.

We can identify myriad structural impediments to economic equality. Denied access to northern industry until late in the nation's history, for example, African Americans and Latinos had to seek an economic foothold in a system dominated by white people. In many cases, these white citizens had moved to industrial cities more than fifty years before.[24] Discrimination in employment and childrearing responsibilities with no child support payments rendered many female heads of household impoverished. Inherited wealth helps perpetuate the status of certain social classes, who obtain assets and resources merely by the good fortune of birth. Ensconced in suburban sites, many affluent citizens find their economic superiority buttressed by schools, low crime rate, and other social amenities unknown to populations in inner cities or some rural areas.[25]

Problems also stem from the lack of regulation over economic processes. Left to their own devices, people may increase their income by fixing prices, advertising deceptively, and engaging in other unfair practices. Were we to adopt an economic and political philosophy that supported unregulated capitalism and a small, passive government, we would in effect accept inequalities as inevitable. While we may not know precisely what kind of regulation will work, we can nonetheless search for solutions rather than merely allowing rampant economic inequalities to flourish unmitigated.

Some of us gravitate to political ideologies, such as socialism or liberalism, which support government involvement in social and economic matters. These ideologies form a sharp contrast with the conservative ideology of Ronald Reagan and George Bush. Under these presidents, social and economic inequalities greatly increased because they reduced taxes on the rich, cut public-sector spending that would have had redistributive effects, and failed to offset economic devastation as American industry relocated abroad. Indeed, the American industry's displacement to other nations partly reflects how vested, economic interests use governmental power to advance their own purposes. Some corporations obtained provisions in the tax code, for example, to subsidize their relocation to other countries, where they could obtain low-cost labor and avoid American environmental regulations.

In contrast, liberal theorists espouse an activist government that would establish fair economic rules, use taxes to redistribute resources, support social programs that help poorer persons, and make opportunities, such as education, accessible. Although liberal policies are often timid, liberal philosophy at least gives the government some tools to offset inequalities inherent in capitalism.[26] Socialists extend this liberal logic to the capitalist order itself, urging government to operate significant portions of the economic order. As attractive as their philosophy may be, the United States has proven particularly nonreceptive to socialist ideology. In contrast, European nations have elected many socialist or even communist leaders.[27]

Although political ideologies provide general orientations toward government, they do not provide certain answers to specific issues. Liberal and socialist ideology nonetheless have merit in providing frameworks that allow collective remedies for social problems. These remedies may be imperfect, but at least they try to redress some inequalities rather than assuming that laissez-faire approaches are a panacea.

OTHER ETHICAL PRINCIPLES IN POLICY PRACTICE

We have emphasized the ethical principles of beneficence, social justice, and fairness as rationales for policy practice. We have argued that these principles require ethical social workers to engage in policy practice. But what about other ethical principles, such as honesty, self-determination (or autonomy), confidentiality, and preservation of life, namely the other ethical principles discussed widely in religious and philosophical literature?[28] When ethicists discuss various principles, they commonly refer to the following:

- Autonomy, or the right to make critical decisions about one's own destiny
- Freedom, or the right to hold and express personal opinions and take personal actions
- Preservation of life, or the right to continued existence
- Honesty, or the right to correct and accurate information
- Confidentiality, or the right to privacy
- Equality, or individuals' right to receive the same services, resources, or opportunities as other people
- Due process, or the right to procedural safeguards when accused of crimes or when benefits or rights are withdrawn
- Societal or collective rights, or society's right to maintain and improve itself by safeguarding the public health and safety.

Many philosophers have declared that right-living persons should adhere to these principles, as well as to the principles of beneficence and social justice that we have already discussed. It is beyond the scope of this chapter to discuss how philosophers have derived these principles. That subject would take us into branches of philosophy known as deontology, utilitarianism, and intuitionism. However, it is important to note that some philosophers, such as utilitarians, do not start with principles; they prefer to deduce ethics from the consequences of specific actions or choices.[29]

These principles often arise, of course, in professionals' interpersonal work, whether they are physicians, attorneys, teachers, or social workers. Professionals are urged by their codes of ethics to share information with their clients and not deceive them (honesty); to let their clients make the important decisions that arise during their interaction with professionals (self-determination); to preserve clients' privacy by not divulging information about them to other people (confidentiality); and to act to advance their well-being (beneficence).[30]

These ethical principles apply, as well, to policy practice, because we want ethical policies and procedures. Assume, for example, that people in your workplace routinely divulged client information to external sources and that you believed this violated one of the principles, such as confidentiality. It would be appropriate for you to change the defective policies to make them conform to these ethical principles. Indeed, we provide an example of such policy practice in Case 2.1, where a social worker tries to make records more accessible to clients in the name of self-determination.

CASE 2.1
PATIENTS' ACCESS TO THEIR CHARTS: AN AGENCY ISSUE

As a staff member in a mental health agency, I believe that patients should have access to written case records. Without knowledge about their diagnosis and problems, how can they fully participate in making a treatment plan? Far from causing them to become upset, reading and discussing case materials is likely to promote thoughtful contract making between social worker and consumer. But I now work in an agency where few patients see their records. This case illustrates ethical reasoning in the policymaking process. I examined prevailing policies and identified a policy issue that, I believe, merits further attention in this agency.

The Agency
The agency (henceforth called "Center B") is located on the grounds of a state hospital and was itself once a ward in that hospital. A year ago, Center B negotiated a contract with the county of Los Angeles under the terms of the Short-Doyle Act. This new contract meant that Center B was now to be separated from the hospital but would still remain partially under its control. Center B was also to maintain its location on the grounds of the state hospital.

Center B's formal mandate comes from both the county and the state. For example, the state and county share the funding and the responsibility to approve the agency's policies and constitution. Although the mandate is passed down and approved by two sources, the state actually has more direct control over Center B. For example, although no longer part of the state hospital, Center B must abide by the hospital's administrative manual and policies.

Center B is a community mental health and day-treatment facility where patients receive psychiatric treatment only during daytime hours, returning to their own homes in the evening. Center B provides a variety of services: group therapy, individual counseling, occupational therapy, recreational therapy, psychotropic medications, and vocational rehabilitation. Individuals with some mental disorder or life crisis who are able to function on at least a minimal level use these services.

Specifically, Center B's patients are individuals who have been hospitalized and do not need full-time care but are not quite ready to adjust to life outside a hospital setting, as well as persons who will always need some kind of supportive and therapeutic influence. Such patients would otherwise be hospitalized but can function with partial services.

Most of the patients are in the lower-income bracket and many must depend on some kind of government assistance, whether supplemental Social Security income, general assistance, or AFDC. Most patients have had very little formal education and are between twenty-five and forty-five years of age.

Charts are maintained for each person served by the agency and contain information regarding personal history, a psychiatric evaluation conducted at the initial intake interview, any correspondence that relates to the person, and daily notations charting progress at the center.

The staff is run on an "equalized interdisciplinary" principle. That is, each staff member functions as both a group and individual therapist. All staff members perform basically the same functions in their involvement and treatment of patients.

The staff consists of three social workers, two nurses, four psychiatric technicians, one marriage counselor, one psychologist, and one psychiatrist who functions as the agency's executive director. The entire staff meets formally once a week for an hour and a half. The director has an agenda and each staff member adds to the agenda before the meeting. The agenda is kept on the secretary's desk, where each staff member has access to it. At Center B all patients receive psychotropic medications and must walk through Center B's main office to collect their medications. When passing through the main office, each patient comes into visual contact with the medical charts, which are located in a three-sided cabinet. Each chart has a patient's name printed in bold letters and is held in a slot that enables easy visual access to the name.

A few months ago, several staff members at Center B became quite concerned about some patients' loitering in the main office and asking to see their charts. This problem was put on the director's agenda and brought up at a Thursday staff meeting. After much discussion, the entire staff agreed on a proposal to keep patients out of the main office as much as possible. Technicians and nurses were to hand patients their medication, and patients would then be instructed to leave the office area immediately. Patients were to remain in the office area only if they had some financial business with the billing clerk. Furthermore, patients who wanted to see their charts were to be referred to their personal staff therapist, who would decide whether to show it to them.

My research was directed toward interviewing a staff member from each of the disciplines represented at the agency to obtain an overall picture of staff attitudes regarding this issue. Of the six staff members I interviewed, all had at one time during the year been asked by a patient to see his or her chart.

All therapists felt that patients had the right to see their charts, yet they also felt that granting them this right depended on patients' ability to accept, understand, and fully interpret the material they read. Controversy centered on the issue of patients' rights versus therapists' discretion.

One of the most frequently used reasons for not allowing patients to see their charts was that it might jeopardize the patient-therapist relationship. Each therapist I interviewed was very much concerned that the patient might become angry, hostile, or intimidated by the therapist's written remarks and that the therapist would have to start building the relationship all over again or that the patient might not even be willing to continue.

The design of Center B ensures that all patients come into contact with a number of different therapists each day, although they may also have an individual therapist. Patients are considered almost a "community project," meaning that each therapist at the agency can feel free to talk to or help any patient. Because of this unique design, many members of the staff make comments in each patient's chart. Thus, therapists feared that patients might not trust any of them if the patients knew that the therapists shared information with one another. Many therapists also feared not feeling free to chart as they wished.

During my interview with the director, he suggested that patients might file slander suits against either an individual or the entire agency if they felt that a comment was malicious or harmful toward them. Although he felt that this situation was unlikely to occur, his comment suggested yet another rationale for opposing policy change. Some staff also feared a sort of domino effect; as one patient obtained access, others would also seek it.

It was also important to consider staff attitudes toward mentally ill patients. Four out of the six staff members I interviewed felt that patients' requests for their charts were probably a symptom of their illnesses. Several staff members explained that requests to see a chart might be a sign of paranoia, feelings of insecurity, or distrust toward the therapist or staff. Patients were also considered ill-equipped to read, accept, and understand chart material.

Three of the therapists stated that, when confronted by a patient, they would flatly say it was agency policy not to show patients their charts.

In fact, patients have exerted little pressure to increase their access to records. I think it is important to analyze this situation in an historical context. To begin with, the majority of Center B's patients have been discharged from the state hospital but still need some kind of therapeutic influence and support. At the hospital, patients were expected to follow hospital rules and schedules and were not allowed to disrupt hospital procedures. There was little room for individual freedom.

This approach actually reinforces the concept of mental illness. Lay people and professionals see patients as sick, out of control, and dependent. Therefore, hospital personnel put patients coming from the hospital in a passive role and see them as dependent on staff for help and treatment. Patients do not create demands to be met by the staff; rather, the staff sets the rules that the patients must follow. Essentially, patients receive an agency service over which they have no control.

Staff members as a whole were unwilling to let patients read their charts. As a result, staff used a number of tactics to end the issue once a patient raised it. The most widely used tactic was to tell patients that agency policy did not allow them to see their charts. Another tactic was to actually sit down with patients and explain why they could not see their charts. A third way to deal with the issue was to allow patients to read only specific excerpts from their chart. Some therapists, for example, would not let patients read the diagnosis, the correspondence, or the notations of other therapists, but would allow patients to read their own notations. Still another method was to explain to patients that the therapist wanted to think about letting patients see their chart. In this way, the therapist would put the issue off for an indefinite period of time, even though the issue eventually required a solution.

None of the therapists I interviewed had, at any time during their employment at Center B, allowed patients to see their entire chart, nor had any of the other therapists, as far as they knew.

An interesting aspect of the issue was the legal ambiguity of patients' rights to their charts. According to the agency's administrative manual (which is also the state hospital's manual), Center B staff did not have to provide access because the section discussing confidentiality of information does not discuss the issue. The manual presents a comprehensive list of persons other than the patient who may or may not have access to the chart, but mentions nothing about patient rights. The administrative manual adapts its policies from the Welfare and Institutions Code, which also noticeably omits any mention of patients' rights to see their charts.

During my research of the issue, I found a lack of information about the issue not only in the hospital's and Center B's procedures but also in the Welfare and Institutions Code. I did manage to find one source published by the American Medical Association that made some attempt to explicitly state a patient's rights. This source maintained: "In the absence of any statutory or court precedent that gives the patient the right of personal access to the medical record, hospital policy must be followed."

Because neither state statute nor hospital administrative policy makes any provisions, the issue of patients' rights to see their charts is open to agency interpretation. Historical precedent set down by the state hospital has been to restrict patients from seeing their charts. Within this framework,

Center B's director did indeed initiate an innovative policy when he allowed staff members to decide individually whether to provide access. However, they have chosen to adhere to traditional practice.

My personal experience with allowing consumers access to records suggests that they benefit from it. They are more likely to become collaborative participants in making decisions during their treatment. Further, I believe that these consumers have certain rights that cannot be arbitrarily ignored. At this point, some sense exists that prevailing policy is defective. But, if I pursue this issue, I will need to think carefully about how to proceed because there is relatively little interest in policy change and even considerable sentiment that patients should not obtain access.

SOURCE: This case is adapted from one developed by Michele H. Wilson, M.S.W. Names and locations have been altered.

ETHICAL DILEMMAS

We have discussed to this point ethical principles that many moral philosophers consider to have merit, such as beneficence, social justice, fairness, autonomy, and confidentiality. What happens, however, when these ethical principles *conflict* with one another so that we cannot easily determine what choice to make? What happens when an ethical principle conflicts with pragmatic considerations, such as political cost or administrative feasibility?

We use the term *ethical dilemma* to describe these common situations because in these circumstances, we find ourselves drawn in different directions. Our preceding discussion emphasized choosing "all-good" and "all-bad" options; when deciding whether to lie, for example, ethics helps us select the all-good option (do not lie) and reject the all-bad option (lie). In many situations, however, choices are far more complicated than this. People may encounter two partly good options.[31] When competing options both reflect positive values, ethics illuminate the dilemma.

We face many dilemmas, of course, but they only become ethical dilemmas when the choices reflect important values and when the resolution is not immediately apparent. I do not experience an ethical dilemma when I have to decide, for example, whether to take a coffee break now or in twenty minutes. Nor do ethical dilemmas exist when matters can be resolved purely by recourse to factual information, as when we compare the cost of two policies and make a final choice based entirely on economic considerations.

Of course, people sometimes do not realize when they have encountered an ethical dilemma. Physicians who routinely prolong the lives of terminally ill patients without consulting them may falsely believe that only one course of action (the prolongation of life) has merit. Indeed, as we note later, policy practitioners sometimes need to convince other people that they do in fact confront an ethical dilemma in a specific situation.[32]

Value-laden words such as *duty* and *responsibility* often reflect that ethical issues and dilemmas exist. Someone might say to the aforementioned physicians, for example, that they have a *duty* to consult terminally ill patients before prolonging their lives. One might tell someone who considers lying to another person that he has a *responsibility* to tell the truth in this situation. By contrast, it is unlikely that someone will say I have a duty to take a coffee break at a specific time or a responsibility to choose what movie to see on Friday. We will now explore three kinds of ethical dilemmas.

When Ethical Principles Conflict

Beyond looking for key words, like *duty*, how do we know when we confront an ethical dilemma? As we have noted, we need not ponder whether to lie, for example, because not lying is clearly the superior value and brings preferable consequences. If we routinely lie, we not only repudiate honesty (a value) but also jeopardize our reputations (a consequence). But people sometimes must consider lying when both lying and telling the truth would actualize important values and consequences.[33] Health-care providers often encounter ethical dilemmas, for example, when deciding whether to disclose to patients their true medical conditions, particularly with life-threatening conditions such as cancer. On one hand, full disclosure is appealing because it advances honesty and self-determination; patients often need facts about their medical condition to participate in medical decisions. Patients who do not know that they are terminally ill are unlikely to make intelligent decisions about further surgeries. On the other hand, not disclosing patients' true condition is appealing when patients request that health-care providers not tell them if they are terminally ill or have a potentially fatal disease such as cancer. Moreover, patients could experience serious emotional problems if providers truthfully told them the extent of their illness.

Health-care providers must decide not only whether to tell the complete truth or lie (for example, telling people they have a good prognosis when in fact they are terminal), but also whether to take various intermediate positions. Perhaps a provider should in some cases be noncommittal, except when patients specifically pressure them for additional facts. This course of action is a form of lying, but is not as blatant as providing false information.[34]

In this example, both courses of action exist and are associated with important values and consequences, creating an ethical dilemma. If people do not consider such an ethical dilemma carefully, they might choose the action that realizes both an inferior value and consequence.

However, events often conspire to hide ethical dilemmas from people; indeed, we need ethical reasoning not only to facilitate choices but also to recognize ethical dilemmas in the first place. In the case of lying in medical settings, health-care providers' increasing tendency to disclose information is relatively recent. Many health-care providers have not told patients about terminal illnesses for the following reasons. Medical staff wanted to avoid the trauma involved in telling patients such painful news. They also believed that divulging such a prognosis would cause the patient irreparable mental distress.

Finally, medical staff assumed that patients would not want to know the true extent of their illnesses when they were terminal. Each of these reasons blinded medical staff to the ethical dilemmas involved by making it appear that only one legitimate course of action existed, namely not disclosing information. We have already argued that disclosing important and even troubling, information to patients furthers the principles of honesty and self-determination and promotes positive consequences, such as allowing terminally ill individuals to make preparations for death. Indeed, in a shift from recent medical practice, many American ethicists currently contend that physicians *should* tell patients the true facts of their medical condition.

When ethical principles conflict, we have several possible courses. We can prioritize one of the principles, as when physicians tell patients their true medical conditions (the principle of honesty), which risks violating a patient's wish not to know about having a condition such as cancer (the principle of self-determination). Conversely, physicians could give precedence to self-determination by asking patients if they want full disclosure of medical information and giving it to them only if they do desire it. (In such cases, the physicians could obtain patients' sanction to give them only partial information.)

We can seek compromises when ethical principles conflict, as in one resolution to the ethical dilemma of euthanasia. Some persons want health providers to help them terminate their lives, whether by withholding food and water (passive euthanasia) or by administering a lethal drug (active euthanasia). (Requests may come from people who are unhappy with the quality of their lives for various reasons, including chronic, painful conditions and terminal conditions such as cancer.) Health providers encounter an ethical dilemma in these cases because patients' self-determination (their desire for assistance in dying) is pitted against the principle of not killing. Of course, we could give precedence to one of the principles by always acceding to the request for life-terminating assistance (which would favor self-determination) or by never acceding (which would favor not killing). In a middle course, we could place many conditions on euthanasia, thus limiting the taking of life to a relatively narrow range of persons. We could decide, for example, to limit it to persons who have received terminal diagnoses from two physicians. We could insist that single requests for euthanasia be denied. This would prevent patients from making ill-advised choices based upon situational factors such as temporary depression. Of course, those who want euthanasia available unconditionally and those who oppose euthanasia in all circumstances would oppose this resolution of the euthanasia dilemma.

When Ethics Conflict with Pragmatism

Consider the following argument: "The health-care system has runaway costs that are bankrupting the nation. We should take life-sustaining equipment away from all persons who have been comatose for more than one year, even if their relatives object and even if we know the patient would not have wanted to have 'the plug pulled.'" Should pragmatic realities, such as cost, be admitted into our ethical decisionmaking? Should we ration health-care services in order to save resources?[35]

We could argue, of course, that ethical choices should be untrammeled by such mundane considerations as cost. In this perspective, citizens' wishes should take precedence, no matter the economic consequences. Carried to an extreme, this view suggests that Americans should be able to obtain any medical procedure that they desire that does not harm them, such as cosmetic surgery.

But persons who believe in considering pragmatic matters say that, without rationing, the American health-care system will damage the American economy. Health costs now consume, for example, about 15% of the gross national product, make American corporations less competitive with those in other nations, and constitute a large share of the nation's budget deficit. They argue that we should sometimes consider costs even when this conflict with patients' wishes or their beneficence.

Indeed, some ethicists known as utilitarians or consequentialists often feature cost considerations prominently in their calculations. They frequently argue, for example, that we need to determine what medical procedures are cost-effective. We ought to measure a procedure's rate of success against the money expended on it. If surgery for a certain condition helps only one patient in a thousand recover, for example, they might argue that it should be canceled. Those medical resources could be expended instead on procedures that yield sizeable benefits, such as medical checkups for pregnant women.

I think pragmatic realities need to be considered sometimes, but they should never be chosen without also weighing various ethical principles. We should take pause in such cases, engage in ethical reasoning, and hope to find a resolution that makes sense for us even if we feel that it is imperfect.[36]

Cases with Competing Principles and Pragmatic Considerations

In other cases, ethical dilemmas involve competing principles *and* pragmatic considerations. At first glance, waiting lists for agency services appear to be above reproach because they advance the principle of fairness (first come, first served) and they make deciding whom to help relatively simple by making the choice into an administrative task (a pragmatic consideration).

A policy of first come, first served is fair because applicants are treated alike. However, most agencies must often breach this fairness by giving people with particularly serious problems immediate access to services. (This breaching of the normal policy advances the ethical principle of beneficence, or the redressing of suffering.) If many exceptions are made, however, the principle of fairness is undermined. Moreover, as the number and kind of exceptions increase, intake staff are given more power to make decisions. They might use this power to give special treatment to those who appeal to them or who are clever at "playing the system."

The first come, first served policy raises another, more subtle value issue—namely, its effects on different kinds of consumers. Assume that an analysis revealed that affluent persons were less likely than low-income persons to drop off an agency's waiting list and hence received more of the agency's services. The first come, first served policy might thereby decrease services to low-income clientele, which could impede the agency's efforts to serve a broad spectrum of the population. Should the agency in this example make exceptions to the waiting list on the basis of social class? As more and more exceptions are made, the intake staff's administrative burden increases, because the procedure is no longer automatic.

This example suggests that ethical issues lurk even behind relatively mundane policy issues. As in the case of divulging information to terminally ill patients, this example illustrates how people often do not recognize the ethical components of policies. When people are accustomed to certain kinds of policies, as in the case of waiting lists, they may be oblivious to their ethical implications. They might identify one value, such as fairness, while they ignore other issues, such as equality. Alternatively, they may give precedence to pragmatic considerations, such as cost and administrative feasibility, rather than also perceiving the need to weigh specific, ethical principles.

Rationale for Ethical Reasoning

Ethical reasoning provides a means or methodology for resolving dilemmas, but it does not necessarily lead to a consensus about specific issues. Ethical reasoning helps us recognize when we *do* encounter ethical dilemmas and encourages us to "take pause," or reflect before committing to specific choices or actions. The ultimate purpose of ethical reasoning is not, in our view, to obtain a single or objective truth. With some kinds of decisions, we have little need to take pause, such as trivial ones or decisions readily made with some factual information. If we must choose between two policies, concerned only that they be administratively feasible and if only one policy fits this description, we can quickly and confidently choose. Similarly, we can make minor decisions about our personal schedules without further ado.

When issues reflect important values and consequences, they should not be resolved impulsively. We should feel tugged in different directions, as if each alternative is serious and cannot be easily dismissed.[37] Were we to hurriedly resolve such issues, we might later decide that we had compromised important values and overlooked important consequences.

PERSONAL VERSUS PROFESSIONAL POLICY PRACTICE

Several years ago, a noted social work professor advocated that professional social workers should recruit clients to participate in electoral politics and urge them to support progressive candidates.[38] His suggestion was controversial; some faculty supported his suggestion on grounds that progressive candidates support programs that ultimately help clients, but other faculty believed he wrongly mixed personal political interests with professional work.[39] These latter faculty wondered, moreover, if clients would believe they had to follow his suggestions; because social workers act as authority figures, clients might even think they are required to take these political actions as a condition for receiving service.

This incident raises a broader question: which elements of policy practice should we pursue in our professional work and which in our private lives? When is it appropriate to engage in some forms of policy practice, such as helping political candidates, while working in agencies?

We could distinguish *electoral politics* from *politics.* A social worker does not participate in electoral politics when she testifies before legislative committees, helps draft legislation, or passes research findings to legislators, even if she limits her contacts to politicians of a particular ideology or party. She clearly seeks to advance the needs of her clients or other needy persons by such activity. When partaking in these activities, she engages in politics. Nor do social workers who organize or participate in coalitions or social movements to pressure politicians to enact progressive legislation engage in electoral politics. In contrast, a social worker who campaigns, raises funds for a politician, or registers voters probably engages in electoral politics. Were she to organize clients to engage in these activities for specific politicians, she would probably be participating in electoral politics, which could violate her agency's nonprofit status (if it is nongovernmental) or the terms of her employment in a civil-service (governmental) position.

The distinction between electoral politics and politics becomes murky, however, when the social worker helps a coalition develop lists of "acceptable" candidates during a forthcoming election or if she works with the Political Action Committee (PACE) of the National Association of Social Workers on behalf of specific clients. If she helps these coalitions or PACE as a private citizen in her nonworking hours, she would have no problem. However, if she devotes agency time to these projects, she may have gone too far.

If we declare electoral politics off-bounds for social workers during their regular work, they can and should engage in electoral politics as private citizens. That way, they can seek to advance ethical principles such as beneficence and social justice without jeopardizing their jobs. If we say electoral politics fall within our roles as private citizens, we can and should engage in nonelectoral political projects, including advocacy for our clients to legislative bodies. Nor do restrictions on participating in electoral politics in any way limit our duty to try to change agency policies when they violate ethical principles.

Indeed, our discussion wipes away an old-fashioned inhibition about policy practice that existed in some of the older professional literature. On the contrary, we suggest that ethical social workers should engage in many kinds of policy practice within their agencies, communities, and regions, not to mention with Congress and federal agencies.

CHAPTER TWO The Ethical Rationale for Policy Practice **61**

DO SOCIAL WORKERS PRACTICE POLICY DIFFERENTLY THAN OTHERS DO?

In concluding this chapter, it is worth asking whether social workers will engage in policy practice differently than other people. This question needs to be resolved empirically by obtaining solid evidence that compares the actions, behaviors, and arguments of different people in similar situations. Such comparisons could ascertain whether the members of different professions practice policy in a different or similar manner. At least three possibilities exist: social workers may practice policy in virtually identical fashion as other people, they may use entirely different approaches, or they may practice policy somewhat differently than other people (an intermediary position). Let us discuss these three possibilities.

We reject the possibility that social workers will practice policy altogether differently because people who try to change policies confront certain realities and contingencies no matter what their discipline. If social workers want to change policies, they will encounter power realities, for example, and they will have to use power resources in their work or suffer a string of defeats. Since none of us like to experience repeated failures in any endeavor, we try to adapt our actions, behaviors, and arguments to decrease their likelihood. We can guess, then, that over time, even social work practitioners who are initially ill-equipped to engage in policy practice will modify their work so that it resembles the policy practice of other people.

We surmise, however, that social workers are likely to practice policies differently from members of other professions because social workers possess somewhat different values. Values shape the goals and tactics of policy practice as our discussion has suggested. People who favor social justice, for example, are likely to develop a different kind of policy proposal than someone who focuses on cost-cutting, as comparisons of liberal and conservative legislators in Congress suggest. Social workers are more likely to advance issues that pertain to the social needs of oppressed minorities. They are more likely to try to correct administrative processes that promote inequitable treatment of stigmatized people.

If social workers have somewhat different values than other people, their policy practice may have some commonalities and some differences with the policy practice of other people. We see a suggestion that social workers possess different values in the comments of Maurice Bischeff, who runs simulations games in different professional schools of the University of Southern California. He compared the tactics of business school students with those of social work students when they played a simulation game known as *End of the Line*. This game asks participants to assume the role of elderly people who have limited resources, such as money and food, symbolized by paper clips. While various services are created to augment the supply of paper clips, competition and attrition lead some people to ''die'' when they lose their stock of paper clips. Students in the business school usually created a win-lose situation that led to a few winners and many losers. Social workers, by contrast, often invited destitute players to join supportive groups that shared their dwindling supplies of paper clips. The social workers defined the game in win-win terms that emphasized cooperative rather than competitive strategies.

While this anecdote does not provide definitive evidence, it suggests that social workers are somewhat more likely to identify with the underdogs, the downtrodden, and the oppressed. These groups include racial minorities, poor people, and stigmatized groups such as gay and lesbian persons and mental patients.

This tendency to empathize with the downtrodden does not mean that social workers possess radical or socialist ideologies, although a radical faction exists within the profession. As critics of the profession often suggest, its leaders have often been willing to accommodate the interests of relatively conservative funders and agency board members rather than engaging in vigorous advocacy for their clients.[40] Nor do we wish to contend that an interest in the downtrodden is always altruistic; social workers' jobs in agencies that serve oppressed groups depend, after all, upon their continued funding.

But these cautionary comments ought not detract from the likelihood that social workers place *relatively* more emphasis upon social justice than do the members of business, legal, public administration, and medical professions. They choose, after all, a profession that emphasizes work with stigmatized and oppressed groups.

Nor does most social workers' preoccupation with clinical work imply that the profession does not value social justice, as some critics of the profession have implied. Jerome Wakefield suggests that people who aspire to clinical work often possess a social-justice ethic; they want to build self-respect and self-esteem in people from families and environments that have made it difficult for them to cope with crises in life.[41] People with mental difficulties are like a disadvantaged group in a familial and sociological sense, if not an economic sense, because they often reach adulthood with profound relationship and problem-solving deficits. They may develop mental problems due to stress from environmental causes, such as unemployment and lack of support systems. People with severe or chronic mental problems are often subject to the kinds of job, housing, and social discrimination that we commonly associate with racial minorities and with other stigmatized groups. When their mental disabilities are severe enough to impede their ability to obtain and keep employment, they may become trapped in poverty. By devoting much of their time to helping people with familial and environmental deficits, clinical social workers practice distributive justice even though they emphasize clinical rather than policy interventions. They invest their professional energy in helping people who are members of a disadvantaged group and provide them with skills to help them to improve their lot, not to mention providing advocacy, brokering, and liaison assistance. While their work does not appear as obviously redistributive as that of civil rights activists, it focuses upon the needs of disadvantaged people who are subject to discrimination and poverty.

We should not overstate the extent to which clinical social workers emphasize social justice in their work. Many of them practice psychotherapy with affluent clients. However, social justice continues to receive considerable attention in social work texts.

Even when they do not favor redistributing goods and services to disadvantaged populations, social workers often adhere to beneficence. Increases in the funding of mental health programs, for example, do not need to be justified by recourse to social justice, but merely on grounds that mentally distressed people benefit from counseling.

To the extent that social workers place more emphasis than others on social justice and beneficence, we would expect their policy practice to reflect these values. When using analytic skills, they should consider social justice and equity more than those who emphasize cost or feasibility. Social workers should be more inclined to support reforms for disadvantaged populations than others. They should be more inclined to define problems in redistributive terms, focusing on how certain people are more deprived than other people.

Social workers should realize, of course, that they cannot rely exclusively upon their values in policy practice, because they need to use political, interactional, and analytic skills as well. They will often have to compromise when others value different criteria, such as cost considerations.

IS SELF-INTERESTED ACTIVITY ETHICAL?

We often engage in self-interested activity, such as trying to increase our salaries, seek promotions, or increase our power resources. Similarly, professions often try to enhance their own interests, even at the expense of other professions. When social workers seek licensing laws, which now exist in all the states, they want (among other things) access to reimbursements from insurance companies and Medicare. When they try to make certain positions "classified" (that is, reserved for people with social work degrees) in public agencies, such as in child welfare agencies, they seek to exclude other persons from those positions.

It is tempting to declare self-interested activity unethical because it reflects "baser" or lesser motives than ethical principles such as social justice. To gauge the ethical merits of self-interested activity, we have to ask why the person seeks resources or power and how they plan to use their gains. When Bill Clinton ran for president, for example, he clearly sought to advance his own interests by increasing his power. However, his policy goals may have had ethical merit, such as his desire to enact national health insurance, reduce defense spending costs, and pass legislation to help children. When employees seek promotions, we must also ask, "What do they intend to do with their power and do these intentions have ethical merit?" When the social work profession seeks licensing to help its members obtain jobs or when it reserves some child-welfare jobs for its own members by making them classified, we must ask whether these policies will enable more clients to obtain quality services. (Of course, people may disagree about the intentions of people who seek to advance their self-interest, whether through presidential bids, efforts to seek promotions, or professional licensing.)

As Salcido and Seck argue, however, those who act *only* out of self-interest are morally derelict.[42] We sometimes need to risk our self-interest in order, for example, to help powerless populations. Legendary activists, such as Martin Luther King, Jr., risked their lives and ultimately lost them in order to advance social justice and fairness. Professions should take positions on unpopular issues even if it gets them bad publicity, such as fighting for the economic and social needs of AFDC women, prisoners on death row, and persons with AIDS. Disturbingly, Salcido and Seck found evidence that some chapters of the National Association of Social Workers engaged only in licensing issues rather than broader issues.[43]

ETHICAL ISSUES IN PHASES OF POLICY PRACTICE

We have focused our discussion in this chapter on ethical imperatives that undergird social workers' participation in policy practice. But social workers encounter ethical issues at many points *during* policy practice. For example, they have to decide whether to use hardball tactics, to water down a proposal, or to engage in "whistle-blowing" when they disagree with agency policies.

Rather than trying to discuss these kinds of ethical issues here, we reserve them for other chapters on various facets of policy practice. We discuss ethical issues in building agendas in Chapter Five, defining problems in Chapter Six, writing proposals in Chapters Seven and Eight, enacting policy in Chapters Ten through Twelve, implementing policy in Chapter Thirteen, and assessing policy in Chapter Fourteen.

SUMMARY

We have argued that beneficence and social justice justify social workers' practicing policy in their agencies, communities, and legislatures. We defined policy-sensitive and policy-related direct-service practice and concluded that ethical social workers should link their direct-service work more to the external world.

Building on our discussion of policy-sensitive and policy-related practice, we argued that policy practice should also be part of social work. We drew heavily on the ethical principles of beneficence, social justice, and fairness to support this contention. But we suggested, as well, that policy practice can advance other ethical principles, such as honesty, confidentiality, and self-determination, by seeking rules, laws, and procedures that advance these principles. We saw this in Case 2.1.

We defined and discussed ethical dilemmas; that is, when competing policy options are each associated with important values or consequences. A central purpose of ethics, we decided, is to allow us to recognize these ethical dilemmas and to take pause before making choices.

Our discussion in this chapter suggests that policy practitioners need to understand the following about ethical reasoning:

- Its essential nature
- How beneficence, social justice and fairness suggest that professionals should expand their practice to include policy-related and policy-sensitive practice
- How beneficence, social justice, and fairness suggest that social workers should expand their practice to include policy practice
- How other principles, such as honesty, confidentiality, and autonomy, provide additional reasons for engaging in policy practice
- The nature of ethical dilemmas: for instance, when alternatives represent conflicting ethical principles and would cause different, important consequences
- The distinction between "personal" and professional policy practice
- How self-interested policy practice can be ethical but must be supplemented with policy advocacy

While we must often refrain from engaging in electoral politics in our professional work, we concluded that this limitation does not exclude a broad range of policy practice in our professional work. We concluded that the traditional argument, which emphasizes an incompatibility between policy practice and professional work, is outmoded and ethically flawed.

In the succeeding chapter, we will develop a framework of policy practice that sets the stage for discussing policy-practice skills and tasks.

Suggested Readings

UNDERSTANDING MORAL REASONING: UTILITARIAN APPROACHES
Jeremy Bentham, *An Introduction to the Principles of Morals and Legislation* (London: Athlone Press, 1970).

UNDERSTANDING MORAL REASONING: DEONTOLOGICAL APPROACHES
Robert Veatch, *A Theory of Medical Ethics* (New York: Basic Books, 1981).

UNDERSTANDING MORAL REASONING: INTUITIONIST APPROACHES
J. L. Mackie, *Ethics: Inventing Right and Wrong* (London: Penguin Books, 1977).

EXPLORING ETHICAL ISSUES THAT CONFRONT SOCIAL WORKERS
Frank Loewenberg and Ralph Dolgoff, *Ethical Decisions for Social Work Practice*, 3rd ed. (Itasca, IL: F.E. Peacock, 1988).
Frederic Reamer, *Ethical Dilemmas in Social Service*, 2nd ed. (New York: Columbia University Press, 1990).
Margaret Rhodes, *Ethical Dilemmas in Social Work Practice* (Boston: Routledge and Kegan Paul, 1986).

Exploring Ethical Issues about the Nature of "The Good Society"
John Baker, *Arguing for Equality* (London: Verso, 1987).
Robert Goodin, *Reasons for Welfare: The Political Theory of the Welfare State* (Princeton, NJ: Princeton University Press, 1988), pp. 227–359.
John Rawls, *A Theory of Justice* (Cambridge, MA: Harvard University Press, 1971).
Frederic Reamer, *The Philosophical Foundations of Social Work* (New York: Columbia University Press, 1993).

Notes

1. Frederic Reamer, *Ethical Dilemmas in Social Service* (New York: Columbia University Press, 1982), p. 3.
2. See J. L. Mackie, *Ethics: Inventing Right and Wrong* (London: Penguin Books, 1977), pp. 107–115.
3. Robert Veatch, *A Theory of Medical Ethics* (New York: Basic Books, 1981).
4. For example, physicians are often implored to address barriers that patients encounter when seeking medical care; see Elizabeth Rosenthal, "Despite an Infusion of Public Funds, Women Find Barriers to Prenatal Care," *New York Times* (January 6, 1993), p. 6.
5. Ibid.
6. See Julie Kosterlitz, "Enablement, the Disability Movement after 1990 Victory," *National Journal* (August 31, 1991), pp. 2092–2096.
7. Barbara Solomon, *Black Empowerment* (New York: Columbia University Press, 1976).
8. See Nancy Humphreys, "Integrating Policy and Practice," *Smith College Studies in Social Work* 63 (March 1993): 182–184.
9. Jonathan Kozol, *Savage Inequities* (New York: Crown, 1991).
10. The indifference of many physicians to obstacles that poor people encounter when seeking medical services is discussed by Paul Starr, *The Social Transformation of American Medicine* (New York: Basic Books, 1982).
11. For discussion of ways policy practitioners can help advocacy and community groups, see Kim Bobo, Jackie Kendall, and Steve Max, *Organizing for Social Change: A Manual for Activists in the 1990s* (Washington, DC: Seven Locks Press, 1991).
12. Lester Thurow, *The Zero-Sum Society* (New York: Basic Books, 1980), pp. 155–190.
13. John Rawls, *A Theory of Justice* (Cambridge, MA: Harvard University Press, 1971), pp. 83–90, 96–100.
14. Ibid.
15. Ibid.
16. Robert Reich, *Work of Nations: Preparing Ourselves for Twenty-First Century Capitalism* (New York: Knopf, 1991), pp. 171–261.
17. Ibid.
18. Robert Bellah et al., *Habits of the Heart* (Berkeley and Los Angeles: University of California Press, 1985), pp. 275–296.
19. Thurow, *The Zero-Sum Society*, pp. 155–190.
20. Mackie, *Ethics*, pp. 95–96.
21. I developed the term *outgroups* in my book *Theory and Practice of Social Welfare Policy* (Belmont, CA: Wadsworth, 1984), pp. 12–18.
22. A defense of affirmative action is provided by John Baker, *Arguing for Equality* (London: Verso, 1987), pp. 44–51.
23. For an example of conservative philosophy, see George Gilder, *Wealth and Poverty* (New York: Basic Books, 1981).

24. For a discussion of problems African Americans confronted when they moved North, see Nicholas Lemann, *The Promised Land: The Great Black Migration and How It Changed America* (New York: Knopf, 1991).
25. Reich, *Work of Nations*, pp. 282–300.
26. A liberal argument for regulation of capitalism is made by John Kenneth Galbraith, *Economics and the Public Purpose* (Boston: Houghton Mifflin, 1973), pp. 151–222.
27. Bruce Jansson, *The Reluctant Welfare State* (Pacific Grove, CA: Brooks/Cole, 1993), pp. 321–324.
28. Veatch, *Medical Ethics*.
29. Mackie, *Ethics*, pp. 125–168.
30. Various authors discuss first-order ethical principles that are applicable to social work. See Frank Loewenberg and Ralph Dolgoff, *Ethical Decisions for Social Work Practice* (Itasca, IL: F.E. Peacock, 1988); Frederic Reamer, *Ethical Dilemmas in Social Service*, 2nd ed. (New York: Columbia University Press, 1990); Frederic Reamer, *The Philosophical Foundations of Social Work* (New York: Columbia University Press, 1993); and Margaret Rhodes, *Ethical Dilemmas in Social Work Practice* (Boston: Routledge & Kegan Paul, 1986).
31. See Douglas Yates, "Hard Choices: Justifying Bureaucratic Decisions," in Joel Fleishman, Lance Liebman, and Mark Moore, eds., *Public Duties: The Moral Obligations of Government Officials* (Cambridge, MA: Harvard University Press, 1981), p. 38.
32. Reamer, *Ethical Dilemmas in Social Services*, p. 3.
33. Robert Veatch, *A Theory of Medical Ethics* (New York: Basic Books, 1981), pp. 79–107.
34. Mackie, *Ethics*, pp. 160–168.
35. Julie Kosterlitz, "Rationing Health Care," *National Journal* (June 30, 1990): pp. 1590–1595.
36. I discuss the need to balance consequentialism with first-order principles in *Social Welfare Policy: From Theory to Practice* (Belmont, CA: Wadsworth, 1990), pp. 265–269.
37. Yates, "Hard Choices," pp. 32–37.
38. Frances Piven and Richard Cloward, "New Prospects for Voter Registration," *Social Policy*, 18 (Winter 1988): 2–15.
39. Conversation with Maurice Hamovitch.
40. See Michael Reisch and Stanley Wenocur, "The Future of Community Organization in Social Work: Social Activism and the Politics of Profession Building," *Social Service Review* 60 (March 1986): 70–93.
41. Jerome Wakefield, "Psychotherapy, Distributive Justice, and Social Work: Part 1, Distributive Justice as a Conceptual Framework for Social Work," *Social Service Review* 62 (June 1988): 187–210. See also "Part 2, Psychotherapy and the Pursuit of Justice," *Social Service Review* 62 (September 1988): 353–384.
42. See Ramon Salcido and Essie Seck, "Political Participation among Social Work Chapters," *Social Work* 37 (November 1992): 563–564 for a critique of NASW chapters that focus their political activities only on issues of licensure and reimbursement.
43. Ibid.

Chapter Three
A Policy-Practice Framework: Skills, Tasks, and Action

Policy practice does not occur in a vacuum. The context provides both constraints and opportunities. Economic, organizational, political, and interpersonal factors, as well as existing policies, create the backdrop for a specific episode of policy practice. Historical factors play a role too; an issue that has generated considerable conflict before is likely to stir up differences of opinion again.

To obtain a dynamic, rather than a static, conception of policy practice, we need to view the skills, tasks, and objectives of specific policy practitioners in tandem. Relatively few theorists have developed dynamic models of policy practice. Texts often say policymaking involves a single skill, such as analysis. Alternatively, they describe policymaking as a series of steps or guiding questions, which minimizes the uncertainties and evolving nature of policy practice, not to mention its political and interpersonal components. Case studies and practical experience suggest that policymakers, no less than other practitioners, need to select interventions and conceptual tools to help them meet their goal.[1]

We define policymaking in social policy as deliberations in agency, community, and legislative settings in which participants advance their policy preferences. Cultural, political, legal, and economic factors, and historical precedents shape the deliberations profoundly. They sometimes provide *constraints* by limiting the policy options that participants can or do consider. If policy practitioners are aware of widespread opposition to a policy option, for example, they often discard or modify it to make it more acceptable. In other cases, contextual factors provide *opportunities*, such as when constituencies, research, precedents, legal rulings, and resources support specific policies (see Figure 3.1).

Of course, the policy context does not remain constant during policy deliberations; indeed, policy practitioners often want to make the context more conducive to their policies. As policy practitioners change people's opinions, for example, they modify the political components of the context, just as they influence interpersonal components when they become acquainted with other persons.

Policy deliberations describe the interactions of those who participate in policymaking (see the central portion of Figure 3.1). *Policy initiators* try to change

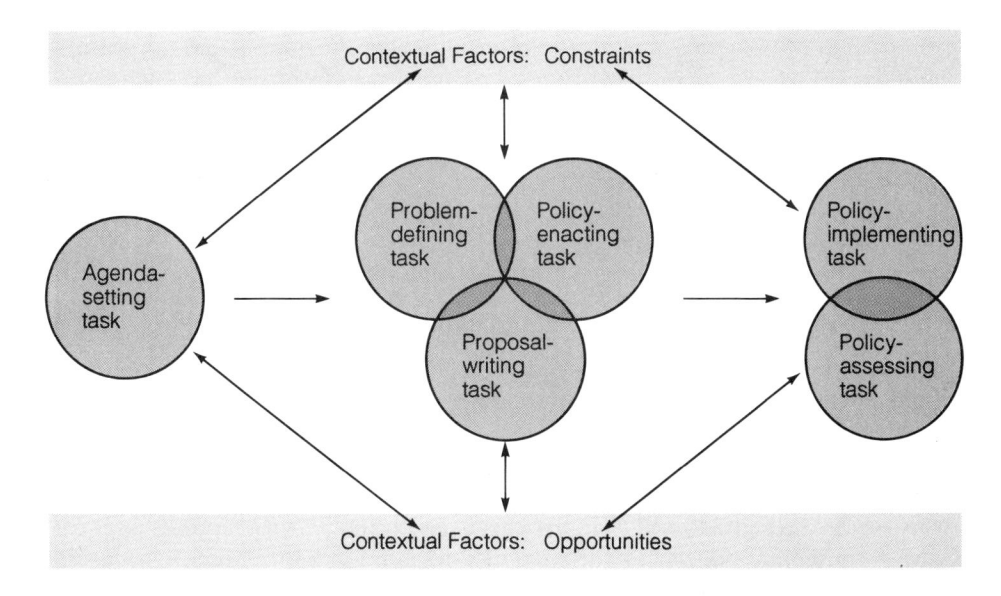

FIGURE 3.1
Tasks during policy deliberations

policy, whether by overturning an existing policy, recommending modifications of existing policy, or proposing new policies. Policy initiators may enter deliberations at many points; they may seek, for example, to put an issue on decisionmakers' agendas, participate in processing the issue, promote the enactment of a proposal, or help implement or assess an existing policy.

It would greatly simplify matters if we could assume that policy initiators work in isolation, as some theorists who provide step-by-step analytic frameworks suggest. But policy initiators usually do not have the field to themselves because other persons participate in policy deliberations. Some may join the ranks of policy initiators. Others are *bystanders* who take no part in policy deliberations. Still others are *policy responders* who seek to modify or change the policy proposals of the initiators. Finally, the *opposers* decide to block or modify proposals. These groups rarely remain fixed; people change groups as policy deliberations proceed. Indeed, initiators often want to expand their ranks by attracting people from other groups. However, opposers are often equally determined to convert persons to their positions. Nor do all groups emerge in policy deliberations; thus, an opposing group may not form when a consensus develops behind a proposal.

Issues spark different levels of conflict during policy deliberations. Some issues excite a great deal of disagreement, while others are resolved with minimal conflict. Participants' actions and rhetoric reflect the level of conflict. With high conflict, people use emotion-laden language, make vigorous efforts to outmaneuver other participants, rely on extraordinary tactics such as filibusters, publicize the issue by appealing to the mass media, and try to enlist others to support their positions. Polarization between factions and groups often occurs, such as conflict between political parties or conservatives and liberals in legislative settings, between different factions within specific neighborhoods in community settings, and between management and line staff in organizational settings. The absence of such actions and alignments usually suggests relatively low conflict or consensual deliberations.

Policy deliberations often last a long time. A piece of legislation, for example, goes through subcommittees, committees, and floor debates before it is forwarded to elected officials, such as the president or governor, for approval or veto. Proposals in agencies often proceed through sequences of deliberation, such as meetings, committees, and officials. Other issues, however, are resolved rapidly, such as decisions made in agency staff meetings to modify internal policies.

At some point, proposals are either enacted, whether in their original or amended form, or rejected. When analyzing these outcomes, we often ask, "Who won and who lost?" In many cases, amendments to proposals suggest that the practitioners realized their policy wishes. In some cases, we decide that apparent victors actually lost because their proposals are so diluted as to be meaningless, as Peter Bachrach and Morton Baratz note when they discuss "decisionless decisions."[2] (An example of a decisionless decision would be deciding to enact a new program when no resources are available.) Ultimately, we ask which segments of the population benefited or were harmed by the proposal's outcome, a question that forces us to evaluate policies. If a new social program distributes resources exclusively to affluent persons, for example, we might declare poor persons to have lost.

Once a policy has been enacted, policy deliberations focus on its implementation and assessment (see Figure 3.1). Considerable conflict can erupt during policy implementation as people and interest groups try to influence the priorities and directions of operating social programs. Unions, professional organizations, civil servants, and legislators, as well as heads of government, shape implementation.

Policy practitioners frequently assess programs established after policy enactment to see if they fulfill certain objectives. For example, researchers have assessed the Food Stamps Program to see if it has decreased malnutrition among specific segments of the population, evaluated the Head Start Program to decide if it enhances children's cognitive development, and analyzed the Adoption Assistance and Child Welfare Act to see if it has shortened children's stays in the foster care system.

PREREQUISITES FOR PRACTICE

To understand policy practice, we must analyze recurring tasks that policy practitioners undertake. We also need to discuss the skills they use to accomplish these tasks.

Policy Tasks

The *agenda-building task* describes when policy practitioners urge decision-makers to place policy issues on their agendas. When policy practitioners succeed in this endeavor, they shape the course of deliberations. Powerful presidents shape Congress's agendas, for example, whereas weaker ones lack this critical ability. Policy practitioners in social agencies are sometimes able to project specific issues to the forefront of policy deliberations by making timely presentations, discussing them with other staff, or sensitizing highly placed officials.

The *problem-defining task* describes when policy practitioners analyze the definitions, causes, nature, and prevalence of specific problems. For example, policymakers sometimes draw theory and research from the social sciences, economics, and medicine to inform their policy choices.

The *proposal-writing task* describes when policy practitioners develop solutions to specific problems. This work often requires them to examine various policy options, identify and weigh criteria, and select those policies that obtain relatively high scores or evaluations. Proposals can be relatively ambitious ones, such as a piece of legislation, or can suggest modest and incremental changes in existing policies.

The *policy-enacting task* occurs when policy practitioners try to have policies approved. Policy practitioners use various power resources to help enact their policies.

Policy practitioners continue to work even after policy enactment when they undertake *policy-implementing tasks.* If policy practitioners wish enacted policies to be realized in the real world, they must identify and address barriers to their implementation. Because this work requires knowledge of administrative and organizational theory, implementation requires policy practitioners to develop competencies that extend beyond the traditional boundaries of social policy.

Policy practitioners must evaluate programs when they undertake the *policy-assessing task.* Policy practitioners often try to construct meritorious policies when writing proposals. But it is difficult to predict how effective policies will be before they are implemented. When assessing implemented policies, practitioners often obtain data about the implemented policy's performance. Assessing policies can present daunting methodological and interpretative problems, but information helps revise policies or various details of their implementation to enhance their effectiveness.

When we discuss these policy tasks as separate entities, we risk suggesting that they are easily distinguishable. In fact, persons often engage in several of the tasks at the same time. For example, legislators undertake the policy-enacting task when they modify the proposals they are writing to enhance their prospects of enactment. They couple the problem-defining task with the proposal-writing task when they make a proposal address the basic causes of a social problem or the needs of a specific group.

Moreover, policy practitioners rarely accomplish the various tasks in a sequential and predictable fashion. Legislators may draft a proposal before devoting much time to defining the presenting problem. They may revise the proposal in response to a social scientist's comments at a legislative committee hearing. In this case, they begin with the proposal-writing task, revert to the problem-defining task, and return to proposal writing. Similarly, a legislator may attempt to rally support for a vague and ill-defined proposal (the policy-enacting task), only to return to problem-defining and proposal-writing tasks at a later time. Of course, this seemingly chaotic approach to policymaking departs from the sequential process that some policy analysts describe. However, events in the real world rarely correspond to any orderly approach.

To underscore the fluid nature of policymaking, we use overlapping circles in the center of Figure 3.1 to characterize relationships between the various roles.

The Context

A framework that describes the context and phases of policymaking, such as Figure 3.1, is useful because it provides an overview of factors that affect policy deliberations. Indeed, it encourages us to ask important questions about how policymaking works in specific situations and in general. We can ask, for example, whether political and economic forces determine the outcome of policy deliberations. In some cases, powerful interests possess such clout that they can singlehandedly shape the course of specific deliberations. The National Rifle Association, for example, has so many resources that it has repeatedly stymied efforts to control the possession of guns, including handguns and rapid-fire assault weapons. Interest groups with large constituencies and many economic resources have developed extraordinary power through mass mailing, marketing, campaign underwriting, and vote-counting technology. This has been true for corporate groups such as the American Association of Automobile Dealers or groups with mass membership, such as the American Association of Retired Persons.[3] With other issues, however, powerful external interests do not exist or are locked in opposition to one another. For instance, legislators have proposed cutting Medicare costs by placing ceilings on physicians' fees. The American Medical Association, which opposes this policy, contends with pressures from conservatives, some employers, and some unions that favor the policy.[4] Even these few examples suggest political and economic pressures vary in policymaking arenas. It provides policymakers with considerable latitude in some situations and imposes remarkable constraints on them in others.

Moreover, the context shifts over time, in response to both external events and policy deliberations themselves. Proposals to enact major federal day-care programs, for example, would have faced certain defeat in the 1960s, because few people believed women should work. By 1988, however, a determined group of children's advocates almost had a major day-care program enacted, and finally succeeded in 1990. As society changed in fundamental economic and social ways, the political and economic context of policymaking could also change. With the example of day-care, the numbers of employed women grew remarkably over time. Short-term changes in contextual factors can also occur. As people debate issues, they change the context by altering the opinions of specific groups, drawing into the debate groups who had been on the sidelines, or outmaneuvering potential opponents. Those who promoted child development legislation in Congress, for example, were able to exclude conservative politicians and interest groups from many of the policy deliberations. This created a far more favorable context for the legislation than exists for many social reforms. But this context became much bleaker when conservative politicians finally began to pressure the incumbent president to oppose the child development legislation. Such volatility is not uncommon in the political context because policymakers sometimes influence the context to make it more favorable to their proposals.

Our policy framework also poses interesting questions about the relationships between the phases of policy deliberations. The initial way an issue is defined in deliberations (during the agenda-building and problem-defining tasks) often shapes people's perceptions and choices during the ensuing deliberations. In 1987, for example, many politicians were concerned about the large enrollment in the AFDC program. To them, welfare reform meant reducing the enrollment. Framing the issue in this way led them to emphasize policy solutions that would reduce enrollment, such as requiring recipients to accept employment when it is available and providing training programs. Had the welfare reform issue been defined differently at the outset, policymakers might have emphasized other issues. Assume, for example, that legislators had focused on the "relative poverty of unskilled and single women with one or more children in their households." Had the issue been defined in these economic terms, legislators might have focused on raising women's income by increasing the minimum wage, increasing tax incentives to their employers, decreasing Social Security payroll deductions of low-paid workers, and increasing the AFDC benefits for those women who remained on the rolls.[5] The final welfare reform package that President Reagan signed into law in 1988 emphasized none of these solutions.

Similarly, activities in other phases of policymaking also influence the outcome. Writing proposals and implementing policy are closely related. When policymakers establish lofty goals but their proposals allocate relatively few resources, for example, they decrease the likelihood that their proposals will be implemented.[6]

Policy Skills

When undertaking these various tasks, policy practitioners need at least four basic skills. They need *analytic skills* to evaluate social problems and develop policy proposals, analyze the severity of specific problems, identify barriers to policy implementation, and develop strategies for assessing programs. They need *political skills* to gain and use power and to develop and implement political strategy. They need *interactional skills* to participate in task groups, such as committees and coalitions, and persuade other people to support specific policies. They need *value-clarifying skills* to identify and rank relevant principles when engaging in policy practice. Many theorists have discussed skills necessary for direct-service work, just as administrative and community theorists have discussed practice skills extensively within their domains. Policy theorists need to follow suit within their own discipline so that social workers have skills and strategies that will be effective in specific situations.

The policy-practice discipline has been hindered, however, by theorists' preoccupation with specific rules, norms, or techniques that social workers should use to develop "correct" positions. The analytic literature in social work and other disciplines says that social workers should use data and research to develop rational policies. The literature concerning values or ethics advocates identifying values, such as redistribution, that should guide policy development. Both types of policy literature assume that decisionmakers will accept policies that are technically correct (analytic theorists) or normatively correct (value-based theorists).

Policymaking is more complex and challenging than many rationalists and value-oriented theorists have recognized. While analytic and value considerations often should and do assume a major role in policy deliberations, they are often superseded by political and interactional factors. It is not enough merely to take positions; social workers have to enter the fray, develop game plans, and implement strategy. They must use competencies that extend beyond framing positions. Social workers need to adapt their practice to the realities they confront. If decisionmakers are not amenable to technical presentations, for example, practitioners need to use political or advocacy styles. Alternatively, they could supplement their analytic and value-clarifying work with political advocacy, such as using skilled presentations and group process.

Analytic and normative literature also underplays policymaking's pluralistic aspects. Policymakers often encounter a variety of viewpoints and engage in win-lose conflict where they seek to defeat their opponents. On other occasions, divergent interests are willing to compromise their different positions into a single position. In either case, policy is fashioned in the give-and-take of interactions, which are hardly discussed in the writings of many analytic and value-oriented theorists.

Policy practice will flourish only when we identify those actions, behaviors, and strategies that allow us to change policies in specific settings. Terms such as skills, tasks, context, and style, which receive considerable attention in direct-service, administrative, and community-work practice literature, need to appear in policy literature if the discipline is to become relevant to the everyday activities of professional social workers.

Policy practice seems more complicated when we say it involves four skills, not one. But we cannot simplify it when policy practice in agency and legislative settings rarely involves a single skill.

While many theorists emphasize one or another of these skills, effective policy practitioners need all of them when undertaking any of the policy-practice tasks. Although we associate certain skills and tasks (for example, analytic skills help in defining problems and writing proposals and political skills help in enacting policy), all of the skills assist the policymaking process. Value-clarifying skills are often needed to help policy practitioners resolve value-laden issues.

APPLICATIONS OF POLICY TASKS AND SKILLS

The skills and tasks intertwine during policy practice. Practitioners encounter analytic, political, interactional, and value-clarification challenges when they undertake the various policy tasks. We will briefly preview uses of policy-practice tasks and skills.

Building Agendas

People in agency and legislative settings can address an infinite number of issues. Thus, thousands of bills are drafted each year in legislatures across the nation. Most problems are consigned to outbaskets, so relatively few receive serious attention and reach legislative committees or agencys' boards or committees. Policy practitioners encounter analytic, political, interactional, and value-based challenges when they try to promote specific issues in agency and legislative settings.[7] Their analytic challenge is to provide technical information to convince decisionmakers that their problem deserves serious attention. They can argue that a problem, such as alcoholism, has sufficiently serious effects upon society that it demands attention. Policy practitioners often use trend data to suggest that a problem is becoming more serious with time, a tactic that suggests that inaction will increase the problem. Policy practitioners often use their analytic skills to create the impression that a crisis exists. When data point to a problem's severity and trend data track the problem over time, decisionmakers are likely to believe that it demands immediate attention.[8]

Policy practitioners use political skills to associate issues with political threats and opportunities in the minds of decisionmakers. People sense a political threat when they fear that actions will cause political losses. In 1989, the National Organization for Women (NOW) tried to convince both political parties that they should *not* enact state legislation to restrict access to abortion. NOW threatened to develop a new political party devoted to women's needs. By using this tactic, feminists hoped to convince establishment politicians that they risked massive defections of female voters from their parties if they restricted access to abortion. Decisionmakers see taking certain positions or actions as opportunities to attract new supporters. For example, African-American leaders have sometimes contended that Republicans could wrest some African Americans from the Democratic Party if Republican leaders would take certain civil rights and economic positions. Indeed, policy practitioners often magnify the political stakes that decisionmakers attach to certain threats and opportunities.

Policy practitioners have many ways of conveying the political importance of issues to decisionmakers. They can ask political leaders to attest to the issue's significance. They can point to analogous situations to demonstrate potential political threats or opportunities. A policy practitioner might tell a decisionmaker, for example, that someone else obtained considerable political advantage by championing a similar issue, or experienced important political losses by avoiding it. Once they have convinced a specific decisionmaker to commit to an issue, they can try to convince others that they will miss the boat if they fail to jump on board in the early stages.

Effective policy practitioners skillfully select propitious moments to inject issues into political deliberations. John Kingdon suggests that "windows of opportunity" exist when background factors are particularly favorable.[9] Perhaps a particularly scandalous condition has just been publicized, such as the neglect of someone with Alzheimer's disease. Perhaps a recently elected city mayor, whose mother suffers from Alzheimer's disease, supports funding a new initiative. Perhaps a new research report documents the dearth of services to families of Alzheimer's patients.

Policy practitioners use interactional skills to promote specific issues. They often hope to make decisionmakers conscious of specific issues by obtaining a privileged position for them in policy deliberation. Perhaps a committee leader agrees to address a specific issue at a forthcoming meeting. Perhaps an agency executive consents to form a task force to examine a problem. Perhaps the aide to an influential legislator agrees to discuss an issue with a powerful member of a legislative committee so that a bill receives preferential treatment in the committee's deliberations.

To secure a privileged position for issues, then, policy practitioners need to use persuasive, coalition-building, and credibility-enhancing strategies. In personal discussions, they need to convince others either that an issue is relevant to their beliefs, that important political threats or opportunities exist, or that credible people take interest in their issue.

Policy practitioners confront value issues when they seek a preferred position for issues in policy deliberations. To increase the prominence of an issue, policy practitioners sometimes inflate figures, exaggerate a problem's negative impacts on the broader society, or magnify political threats or opportunities. These tactics pose ethical issues that practitioners need to consider. In other cases, policy practitioners may display undue caution by avoiding relatively unpopular but important issues. In such cases, they need to decide whether their political caution leads them to ignore important policy issues that significantly affect oppressed groups.

Defining Problems

People often analyze social problems, asking about their causes and developing typologies. When coupled with empirical research, these analytic tools help us define the problems we may encounter.

Policy practitioners encounter the political challenge of framing specific issues so as to attract the attention of decisionmakers.[10] While technical or analytic people are accustomed to complex discussions of issues, many decisionmakers want relatively understandable and short presentations of problems. Policy practitioners need to develop words, titles, and explanations that are both comprehensible and palatable to decisionmakers. For example, in 1987 and 1988, advocates of AFDC reforms emphasized "family support" rather than "welfare reform" to make their measure more acceptable to conservative politicians. Proponents of reform argued that the measure would strengthen welfare families by helping the mothers to become more competitive in labor markets. Because welfare programs are often blamed for enticing people to avoid work, the legislation's supporters contended that it would prevent welfare by training and educating mothers, as well as providing day-care for their children. To undermine the notion that social reforms necessarily increase Washington bureaucracy, the legislation's supporters emphasized how it would fund innovative state programs and local government units. In framing the problem and their proposal, the practitioners selected symbols of children, families, prevention, and local innovation. These would be attractive to a broad spectrum of politicians, including many who would usually oppose projects to help AFDC women.[11]

Policy practitioners also need interactional skills to define problems. Often, they must link their problem-defining work to the culture or mission of a specific organization or setting. For example, in the discussion of techniques for enhancing personal credibility (see Chapter Eleven), we note how people often select problems or issues that are likely to be perceived as relevant to the mission or objectives of organizations. For example, a hospital social worker who wants to expand the hospital's services to older persons might base a proposal on the needs of this population.

Interactional skills help develop and tap into specific networks when social workers build agendas and define problems. Policy practitioners often want to garner support even before they develop proposals, so they need to be conversant with the decisionmakers and staff who form the leader corps in specific settings. A division of labor exists in many settings with respect to defining issues; certain people have expertise with specific issues but have negligible roles with respect to others. This division of labor is most obvious in legislative settings where the chairs and members of committees become known for expertise in specific issues. Less formally, a similar division of labor exists in some agencies. Policy practitioners need interactional skills to convince the officials with expertise on a specific issue to lead specific reforms.

When a coalition is formed to promote action on an issue, policy practitioners need to decide which terms, definitions, and paradigms members will use when discussing the issue with decisionmakers. When promoting child welfare and welfare reform issues in 1987 and 1988, various advocacy groups developed common themes that they emphasized in their testimony to Congressional committees. Proponents of welfare reform legislation rarely called it "welfare reform," but instead said "family support," "prevention," "employment and training," and "children." These common themes did not accidentally appear, but emerged after numerous meetings of the coalition that promoted the legislation.[13]

Policy practitioners use value-clarification skills to address a number of issues. To what extent should they define problems to accommodate decision-makers' or specific organizations' objectives? Some critics of the welfare reform legislation enacted in 1988 concluded that reformers had "sold out" to conservatives and had neglected important economic needs of welfare recipients in favor of relatively paltry training programs.[14]

Writing Proposals

People need analytic skills when they construct proposals. Policy practitioners must calculate trade-offs in order to select a policy from an array of competing ones. They identify and weigh criteria, score or rank competing options, and select the one with the highest score.

Were writing proposals entirely an analytic or technical matter, decision-makers would hire experts, give them specific instructions, and use the finished product in policy deliberations. Since political realities usually intrude, however, policy practitioners need political skills to develop proposals. Many policies are shaped through extended deliberations when various amendments are made. As Ron Dear and Rino Patti note, legislation often hinges upon its advocates' willingness to accept amendments; they may alter policies, such as a program's title, administrative details, the services it offers, its eligibility standards, the type of agencies that can deliver the services, and standards about which staff provide the services.[15] Moreover, amendments may increase or decrease a program's size.

Policy practitioners use political and value-clarification skills to decide when to accept or oppose amendments. People who favor the proposal offer friendly amendments, or relatively technical changes, to improve the proposal's political prospects. Practitioners' task is more difficult when hostile amendments suggest scuttling or fundamentally altering the proposal. Someone may wish to slash the proposal so profoundly that it no longer remains viable. Opponents may try to delete or modify certain standards, such as ones that govern staff qualifications. When faced with hostile amendments, the proponents of a proposal must weigh the political advantages of accepting the amendments against the substantive costs they impose. Of course, such calculations are often complex; opposing a hostile amendment may feel principled, but someone may regret opposing an amendment if that eventually defeats the proposal.

Policy practitioners often use political and value-clarification skills to decide whether to leave certain issues relatively vague in a proposal. Believing that vagueness reduces controversy and conflict, they do not precisely define the content of a proposal. Vagueness poses threats of its own, however. When proposals are vague, their implementors have considerable latitude in filling in the gaps after the policies have been enacted. If policy practitioners believe implementors are likely to possess different perspectives than their own, they will want to dot all the i's and cross all the t's to limit the implementors' discretion.

Practitioners need interactional skills at many points in developing proposals. Committees sometimes assume a central position in fashioning proposals, whether in legislative or agency settings. Personal discussions with a proposal's friends and foes orchestrate a succession of friendly amendments and soften or avert hostile amendments. Coalitions often assume a prominent role in proposal writing. For example, they may mobilize opposition to hostile amendments or oppose efforts to make a proposal excessively vague, at least with the matters they deem particularly important.

Value-clarification skills help preserve the integrity of proposals in the face of efforts to amend them. People have to decide at what point amendments violate their policies so extensively that they cannot accept them.

Enacting Policy

Practitioners employ analytic skills when developing a political strategy to enact policy. They analyze the context, identify the power resources available to them, and evolve a coherent political strategy. Policy practitioners often compare competing political strategies before they select one.

Policy practitioners use their political skills to implement this strategy. People with power must use their resources skillfully enough that other people modify their positions and accede to their wishes. When they exercise their power through intermediaries, they must convince other people to intercede for them in specific situations.

Interactional skills help practitioners during the political process. They use various tactics to develop and maintain their credibility with decisionmakers, including respected leaders and opinion-setters in their coalitions. They need access to people with inside information about strategies opponents are likely to use. They use their persuasive skills to convert people to their side and to keep opponents on the defensive. Policy practitioners need group skills, such as the ability to work in committees as leaders or staff, to develop and sustain coalitions, to diagnose why specific groups are not working, and to intervene to help task forces accomplish their work.

Policy practitioners confront some ethical issues during the political process. They must decide when tactics, such as dishonesty, are ill-advised or when they are necessary to defeat a well-organized opposition that resorts to its own hardball politics. It is difficult to establish inflexible ethical rules because realities, such as opponents' tactics often influence our judgment. Moreover, tactics often involve options that are not "all-bad," such as blatant lying, but "partly-bad," such as withholding sensitive information from opponents.

Implementing Policy

Policy practitioners use analytic skills to decide what kinds of organizational arrangements will aid in the implementation of specific policies. A practitioner might decide, for example, that bilingual staff and decentralized offices are needed to help Spanish-speaking people obtain preventive health services.

To attain organizational arrangements that are conducive to implementation, policy practitioners often must use political skills. Perhaps specific groups or individuals who wish to defend their "turf" decide to undermine the implementation of a program or to preserve outmoded procedures; perhaps legislators who promised to support a program decide to allot insufficient resources to it after it is enacted.

Implementing a social program requires developing collaborative relations between the program staff so that they work together. Moreover, many social programs cannot be implemented properly unless staff in other agencies and programs provide referrals, consultation, and resources. To develop collaboration, policy practitioners must often use interactional skills, such as mediating disputes and developing interagency agreements.

During implementation, many issues arise that require policy practitioners to clarify values. For example, because resources for social programs are scarce, staff members must decide which clients receive priority. When they are actual implementors of a policy, whether in direct-service or administrative roles, policy practitioners must decide whether and when to object to the failure of other staff to implement specific aspects of a program.

Assessing Policy

Policy practitioners often participate in assessing operating programs to ascertain whether they meet specific objectives or criteria, such as effectiveness or efficiency. When using analytic skills, practitioners use the burgeoning techniques of program evaluation to develop research to examine the outcomes of specific programs. They must decide, for example, what kinds of data they need, how to collect them, and how to interpret findings.

When assessing programs, policy practitioners often encounter political conflict. Perhaps people disagree about the selection of criteria to be used; for example, some people might want to know whether a program has actually improved its users' well-being, others might be interested in its efficiency. Or perhaps people disagree about how data should be interpreted.

To conduct an evaluation, policy practitioners must obtain the collaboration of many people. If high-level executives must grant permission to evaluate a program, for example, staff must share with researchers their insights about the program and about methods of obtaining data. Policy practitioners need interactional skills to fashion this collaboration.

Values intrude at many points during the assessment of programs. For example, criteria must be selected to decide whether a program has been "successful," but their selection is shaped by values. Take the case of a program to help homeless, mentally-ill persons; people could judge the success of the program by its effectiveness in "removing homeless people from the streets," "improving their sense of self-esteem," or "reducing welfare costs of the county." The interpretations of research data are also shaped by values. One person might decide, for example, that the findings of a study suggest that a program should be terminated. Another person might conclude that data suggest enough "success" to merit continuation of the program.

EPISODES AND SEQUENCES OF TASKS

The framework for policymaking that was established at the outset of this chapter (see Figure 3.1) divides policymaking into the six tasks previously defined. This framework suggests that we can describe policy practice during specific episodes—that is, relatively brief periods when practitioners perform one of the tasks. Or we can examine how policy practitioners perform a sequence of tasks, or an extended set of actions, verbal exchanges, and strategies through which the practitioner accomplishes several of the tasks. Indeed, we can envision a continuum extending from very brief episodes of policy practice, such as making a specific presentation, to an extended sequence that involves writing a policy proposal, seeking its enactment, and shaping its implementation.

Why do we want to focus on certain episodes or extended sequences of specific people's policy practice? If social policy includes a practice component, we have to describe and evaluate actual instances of policy practice. Direct-service and administrative practitioners and theorists describe and evaluate the work of their respective practices by dividing it into specific episodes or sequences. One can examine, for example, how a direct-service practitioner established a contract (a specific episode) with a client or managed an extended sequence of actions, verbal exchanges, and strategies from intake through the case's termination. Were we to evaluate this work, we could focus on the specific episode by asking whether the practitioner effectively established the contract. Or we could evaluate the extended sequence of work by asking whether the various phases of the case, such as making a contract, treating the client, and terminating the case, were effective.

ANALYZING POLICY PRACTICE

Our discussion of the six policy tasks and four policy skills helps us describe the work of specific policy practitioners. We must first decide which portion we wish to describe and evaluate. As the following list shows, we can describe and evaluate someone's policy practice in ascending levels of generality: (1) using specific skills when working on specific tasks, (2) using various skills when working on specific tasks, and (3) accomplishing sequences of related tasks.

At the simplest level, we examine the use of a specific skill when a practitioner engages in a single policy task. We can evaluate the use of analytic skills (a single skill) in developing a policy proposal (a single task) by asking whether the practitioner became familiar with important social science research, consulted someone with technical expertise, and researched possible funding sources. Alternatively, we could evaluate the use of political skills by asking whether the practitioner examined the proposal's political feasibility and consulted with people potentially instrumental in securing support for it.

At a more general level, we could inquire about the practitioner's effectiveness in accomplishing a specific policy task, such as writing a policy proposal. We could describe the combination of skills used in developing the proposal, whether some overall strategy existed at specific times, and whether the strategy changed as events unfolded. If this policy practitioner failed to supplement analytic skills with political ones in a politically charged situation, we might fault this omission.

At an even more general level, we can examine the work of a policy practitioner who engages in several related tasks. We can ask how a policy practitioner not only constructed a specific proposal (one task), but also sought its enactment and implementation (two additional tasks). We might conclude, for example, that the practitioner exhibited technical expertise in writing the proposal but lacked the political skills to obtain its approval from decisionmakers.

DESCRIBING POLICY PRACTICE: A CASE EXAMPLE

When we examine a policy practitioner's work, we often look for specific kinds of activities and strategies. We examine the type of tasks, strategy, and interactions the practitioner attempted. We must describe these activities and strategies before we can evaluate them.

The Context

A case from Edward Banfield's classic book, *Political Influence*, illustrates the policy-practice framework presented in Figure 3.1.[16] The staff of the Welfare Council of Chicago, directed by a social worker, felt that Cook County Hospital needed a new branch on the south side of Chicago, where a large, low-income, African-American community resided. The massive Cook County Hospital was located on Chicago's west side, and many residents could reach it only via a long ride on public transportation. Some south side African Americans obtained medical assistance from local nonprofit hospitals, such as Michael Reese Hospital or the Billings Hospital of the University of Chicago, but most had to travel a considerable distance to Cook County Hospital. Moreover, some African-American leaders were angry that some south side nonprofit hospitals "dumped" African-American patients, meaning they told low-income African-American residents to obtain medical assistance at the county hospital.

At the time of this case, the Democratic political machine and its leader, Mayor Richard J. Daley, dominated Chicago politics. Daley tightly organized the city of Chicago, which was overwhelmingly Democratic, providing tens of thousands of city service positions in return for Chicagoans' support. Chicago was ringed by white and largely Republican suburbs, which provided a constituency for some Republicans on the Cook County Board of Supervisors. (The county included both the city of Chicago and these white suburbs.) Democrats nonetheless firmly controlled the county board of supervisors under the leadership of Dan Ryan, himself a close political ally of Daley's.

Constructing a branch hospital on the south side, which the Welfare Council strongly favored, would not be easy. They would need county funds because public hospitals fell under the county's jurisdiction. Moreover, they would need medical staff willing to work at the branch hospital. They would need to make difficult decisions about which services it would provide. Should it, for example, provide only outpatient services, or should it provide surgical and diagnostic services as well?

These logistic, financial, and planning challenges dimmed when compared to the political problem of securing support for the branch hospital. Karl Meyer, the longtime director of Cook County Hospital, adamantly opposed building a branch hospital. Would it not be cost-effective, he asked, to expand the existing county hospital, rather than investing funds in a new facility? He also contended that it would be difficult to obtain interns, residents, and top-notch physicians at a nonteaching hospital (the county hospital was a teaching hospital). Some people believed Meyer also feared that a branch hospital would dilute his power at the county hospital, which provided many jobs for Democratic party supporters.

Moreover, Meyer was a close friend of the powerful Dan Ryan. Thus, he had an important possible ally in the forthcoming battle over the branch hospital. It was not certain, however, where Ryan stood on the issue. By contrast, the Welfare Council was poorly connected to the power structure of city or county politics. Its large board consisted of businesspeople and professionals. These people often sat on the boards of hundreds of Chicago social agencies, which the Welfare Council funded. They tended to be highly educated and affluent people who did not participate in the machine politics of the Daley administration.

Despite the seeming importance of the issue to south side African-American communities, no widespread support of the issue had developed. Traditional spokespersons and interests on the south side included a powerful newspaper, an African-American congressman affiliated with the Democratic machine, and some civil rights groups, such as the Urban League.

The Policy Tasks

Were we to analyze the policy practice of the Welfare Council leaders, we would describe how they addressed each of the specific policy tasks. (Because this is a complex and extended case, they addressed several tasks rather than merely one.) In building an agenda, the Welfare Council had to decide how to elevate interest in the issue. (The county board of supervisors was preoccupied with countless other issues and the county hospital system was under the board's jurisdiction.) Their primary strategy was technical; they asked their research and planning department, headed by Alexander Ropchan, to examine the feasibility of constructing a branch hospital.

In defining the problem, the Welfare Council established a rationale for constructing the branch hospital. Because the need for an additional facility seemed to be widely recognized, they focused on demonstrating that it would be feasible to build and staff the facility. Thus, they obtained evidence that interns, residents, and physicians could be found to staff it. Moreover, they developed data that suggested it would be less expensive to build and staff the facility than some critics suggested.

The Welfare Council undertook a proposal-writing task when it estimated cost and staffing and described the kinds of services it would provide. They hoped, for example, that it would not be merely an outpatient hospital but would also provide family practice, surgical, and speciality services. By contrast, some people suggested that it be merely a "feeder hospital" to the county facility, offering relatively few outpatient services.

They assumed a policy-enacting task when they sought funds from the county board of supervisors to build this full-service facility. When the county board eventually approved a bond issue to fund a major expansion of Cook County Hospital, the Welfare Council threatened to defeat the bond issue. This tactic enabled them to have the board make some concessions to them. They dropped the bond issue and plans for expanding Cook County Hospital and earmarked some funds to eventually purchase a site for a south side hospital.

Had the branch hospital been constructed, the Welfare Council might have assumed the policy-implementing and policy-assessing tasks. They would have participated in some issues regarding the policy's implementation. For instance, they would have tried to secure adequate annual funding from the county board, enhancing the hospital's outreach services to the surrounding community, and increasing its role in preventive programs, such as fighting lead poisoning among children who eat lead-based paint in tenement houses. They could have helped assess the policy by examining whether the branch hospital successfully prevented or treated specific kinds of illnesses, met certain cost or efficiency objectives, or fulfilled any other objective that they had established.

To understand the actions (or inactions) of the Welfare Council, we need to place their staff's policy practice in the context of political, technical, value-clarification, and interactional factors. Indeed, we could not evaluate their work without taking into account the Democratic machine, Dan Ryan's power, Karl Meyer's strong preferences, and the south side's lack of strong support for a branch hospital.

Using Skills to Accomplish Policy Tasks

To describe the Welfare Council's work in this case, we need not only to enumerate the policy tasks they undertook, but also to describe if and how they used analytic, political, interactional, and value-clarification skills.

To illustrate the use of various skills, let us examine the Welfare Council's work in defining problems, writing proposals, and enacting policy. When defining the problem of medical service on Chicago's south side, the council focused on the inaccessibility of medical services to African-American citizens. Moreover, the Council emphasized traditional outpatient and surgical services. Because they framed the issue in this manner, it was almost a foregone conclusion that they would advocate constructing a full-service public hospital on the south side. Indeed, they devoted much of their analytic work to proving that it was feasible to build and operate a large public hospital on the south side. They used their political and interactional skills to try to convince people, such as Dan Ryan and Karl Meyer, that they had framed the issue correctly. They issued a technical report and sent people to inform Ryan and Meyer of their conclusions.

Were we to evaluate their skills in defining the problem, then, we would conclude that they used analytic skills to document the dearth of hospital facilities for African Americans on the south side and political and interactional skills to disseminate their position to powerful decisionmakers.

They also used their analytic skills to develop a proposal for the south side hospital. Essentially, their proposal sought funds to build a smaller version of the existing county hospital on the south side. They used interactional and political skills to inform high-level officials of their recommendations and to demand that they obtain the funds so that construction could begin as soon as possible.

Convinced of the rectitude of their position and assuming that other people would soon concur, they saw no need to compromise or change their proposal to make it more acceptable. Indeed, the council leaders maintained a relatively intransigent position during most of the policy deliberations. When Ryan sought Council participation in a task force he established to study the issue, they maintained a relatively righteous posture. At one point they read their position to the task force members with the clear implication that they would not accede to amendments. They devoted their interactional and political skills to enunciating their proposal in relatively strident terms during the policy-enacting task.

When it became clear that other officials did not concur and, indeed, sought to enlarge the existing county hospital rather than building a south side hospital, the Welfare Council quickly shifted strategy. It sought to mobilize widespread opposition to Ryan's plan; he intended to seek voter approval to fund an expansion of the Cook County west side hospital. Throughout policy deliberations, the Council made clear that it did not want to amend or change its proposal.

When undertaking the policy-enacting task, the Welfare Council used its analytic skills to decipher political alignment on the issue. They apparently concluded that highly placed officials, such as Ryan and Meyer, were unlikely to favor a south side hospital. But they seem to have assumed that public opinion, particularly on the south side, would rally to their position and ultimately pressure the county to construct the facility. Indeed, this optimism increased their intransigence with Ryan and the task force he established to examine the issue. They used their interactional skills during the policy-enacting task to give Ryan and others the message that they would not negotiate.

When Ryan's task force recommended that the county vote on funding an expansion of the west side facility instead of a new south side branch, the Council decided that it was all up to public opinion. They assumed a negative or blocking role at this juncture as they sought to convince the county to withdraw its proposal. They organized a coalition of Chicago social agencies affiliated with the Welfare Council. They also allied with officials of Michael Reese Hospital, a nonprofit, south side hospital that wanted a public south side hospital to ease the burden of nonpaying patients on their facilities. The Council succeeded in obtaining some coverage in a major local paper, which criticized the plan to expand the county hospital. Members of the coalition packed a public meeting on the issue and voiced their displeasure at the county's plans.

The Council was chagrined to discover that their campaign to defeat the proposal did not attract broad support among south side African Americans. They had assumed that the major African-American newspaper, African-American politicians, and African-American community groups would rally to their side, since, after all, they sought to secure a major new medical facility in their district. They were so optimistic that they would receive widespread support that they had not extensively consulted African-American leaders or citizens. In fact, some African-American leaders, who were primarily concerned about discrimination against African-American patients by some south side nonprofit hospitals, feared that constructing the public hospital might encourage even more dumping of African-American, indigent patients. Other African-American politicians were beholden to the Democratic machine—and Ryan was a powerful member of that machine.

The Welfare Council eventually succeeded in forcing Ryan to change his position, since he doubted that the plan would be approved if public opinion was divided on the issue. He agreed to give much less money to fund a relatively small, outpatient clinic on the south side as well as a modest expansion of Cook County Hospital. It appeared in retrospect that neither side had prevailed: Ryan and Meyer failed to secure massive expansion of Cook County Hospital, and the Council failed to secure a large south side public hospital.

Were we to characterize their use of skills when enacting the proposal, we might conclude that the Welfare Council oscillated between a relatively optimistic posture early in the case (when they assumed most people would ultimately accept their position that a south side facility was needed) and a relatively negative posture in the latter portion of the case (when they assumed that Ryan would prevail without a determined and publicized campaign to block his plan).

We have not yet evaluated the Welfare Council's policy practice when defining the problem, writing the proposal, and trying to enact policy. Was the council too dependent upon their analytic skills during the problem-defining and proposal-writing tasks rather than using political skills as well? Did they make erroneous judgments about political realities? Could they have made skillful advances to Ryan earlier in the case and acceded to some compromises that would have led to the construction of a south side facility *and* an expansion of Cook County Hospital?

The way officials from the Welfare Council engaged in policy deliberations was influenced by various personal, organizational, and situational factors. As officials in a charitable organization that stood outside Chicago's political system, the leaders of the Welfare Council did not know how to play the rough-and-tumble political game of Cook County. The Welfare Council board members came from the relatively affluent and well-educated corps of business and professional leaders of Chicago and were disinclined to "play ball" with the political leaders of Chicago and Cook County. Accustomed to providing technical reports on a variety of social problems in Chicago from their detached position, it was not surprising that the Welfare Council resorted to a similar tactic in this situation.

While we can explain why the Welfare Council was not more inventive in its strategy, we can nonetheless criticize it. Various kinds of policy-practice errors exist, such as relying excessively on a single skill or failing to assess contextual realities.

THE DIVERSITY OF POLICIES

As the previous discussion of the post-1950s evolution of human services suggests (see Chapter One), social workers confront policy issues at virtually every turn in the road. The services they provide are dictated by policies from different sources. Policies come from legislatures, government agencies, courts, funders such as United Way, contracts and grants that governmental authorities use to purchase services from agencies, professional associations such as the National Association of Social Workers, licensing and accrediting bodies, boards of directors of agencies, and administrative staff. We argued in Chapter One, as well, that some policies emanate from the informal culture and agreements of the staff who implement policies.

We do not suggest that these policies are restrictive because they often provide implementing staff with considerable discretion. However, in many ways, these policies do shape the lives and work of citizens, clients, and implementing staff.

These policies vary in their effects and importance. Trivial policies have little importance, such as some of the detailed policies in agencies and programs. Other policies, however, have considerable impact on citizens and professionals; reformers should give these policies attention when they believe them to be dysfunctional.

Policies also vary in their malleability. Some policies are relatively simple to change because of their source, nature, and context. Policy practitioners find it easy to modify a relatively simple administrative agency policy that is enveloped in a nonconflictual context, as compared to a legislative policy that requires hundreds of legislators to concur and is highly controversial in nature.

Practitioners need not focus on a single kind of policy in their work; they can try to change simple or complex policies, agency or legislative policies, controversial or noncontroversial policies. Our focus in this book, indeed, is relatively generic because we are trying to provide concepts that apply to any policies.

It would be possible, of course, to study policy practice in a more specialized way, such as focusing on specific settings, such as agencies or legislatures. We could also focus on a specific style of policymaking, such as the analytic style. Alternatively, we could gear our discussion of policy to a specific sector, such as child welfare policy, rather than using a range of policy examples.

However, a broader treatment of policy practice has many advantages. Were we to concentrate on a single kind of policy, such as agency-based or legislative, we would imply that that kind should take preeminence in policy practice over other kinds of policies. This would also imply that social workers should have no connections with social movements or broad community coalitions. Were we to concentrate on policies that are relatively easy to change, such as some agency-based ones, we would imply that social workers ought not try to change more complex and controversial policies, such as legislative policies. Were we to concentrate on a single style of policymaking, such as an analytic style, we would imply that this style is effective in all or most situations.

A generic approach to policy practice underscores the need for policy practitioners to be flexible. Policy practice occurs in many kinds of settings and takes many forms. It varies with the nature of the issue and the context. It is better, we feel, to understand concepts, skills, tasks, and frameworks that apply to a range of policy-practice situations than limit ourselves to a single style or situation.

The need for versatility in policy practice stems from the diversity of policy practice that social workers can undertake. Policy practice can occur inside and outside agencies, such as with line staff, supervisors, executives, community organizers who work with community groups and social movements, and lobbyists. Policy practice can occur in formally sanctioned or official projects, such as when executives establish task forces to examine policy issues. It can be informal in nature, as when a direct-service worker decides to pursue an issue without the approval of higher officials. Policy practice can occur in planned fashion when someone develops a game plan, or it can occur in improvisational fashion, as when someone attends a meeting and decides on the spot to make a specific statement. Policy practitioners can assume affirming, blocking, or bystander roles. Practice can involve an extended sequence of actions, as when someone successively undertakes all six policy tasks, or it can consist of only one or two episodes, as when someone confines his work on an issue to several meetings. Policy practitioners may emphasize certain skills in specific situations, such as analytic skills, or they may use several skills in tandem. Policy practitioners might be leaders or initiators with respect to a specific issue or they could be followers.

A generic approach to policy practice, then, sensitizes us to the variety of policy-practice situations and actions that exist. It does not limit policy practice to specific styles, settings, or issues. It invites us to become participants in many ways and at different points in our professional work.

This generic approach offers no quick fixes or panaceas, however. Some issues are difficult to address and some policies are relatively intractable in nature. Policymaking does not occur on a level playing field; some people bring to the game more power resources, can invest more time, and have more skill than others. Policy practitioners take some risks when they engage in practice.

These cautionary notes should not, however, obscure the challenges and rewards associated with policy practice. Trying to change policies allows professionals to expand their boundaries and obtain the satisfaction that accompanies successful projects.

SECURING MANDATES FOR POLICY PRACTICE

Policy practice is in the job descriptions of lobbyists, politician's aides, and planners. How do other persons get mandates, or permission, to engage in it? Direct-service workers, supervisors, and administrators are not hired, after all, to engage in policy practice. Let us distinguish between policy practice that is part of one's job and that which is separate from employment.

Policy Practice as Part of Professional Work

While working in agencies, people can try to expand their professional role to include some policy practice. Someone might serve as their agency's liaison, for example, to a community-based organization, a community task force, or a governmental commission. A social worker might extend their work on an agency committee to explore an issue, or design a proposal, or implement a program. On hearing that another agency, coalition, or community group has initiated a policy change, a social worker could ask to be an agency liaison to it. In all these examples, social workers can seek official approval from their agencies to do policy-practice work as part of their paid employment.

Policy practice can be a part of one's work even when it is not a negotiated part of the job. When a social worker tries to change agency policies by forming an informal coalition, she engages in policy practice without seeking her employer's sanction for it. A social worker who tries to persuade another agency to address an unmet need in the community does not necessarily need formal approval from his employer.

Policy Practice Outside of Employment

Policy practice does not need to be restricted to one's official employment. People can engage in policy practice outside of working hours. They can work through a professional organization such as the National Association of Social Workers, a community-based coalition, or an advocacy group. Social workers can engage in policy practice independent of both the profession and an agency. When social workers participate in political campaigns, for example, they usually do so as private citizens.

DISCOMFORT WITH POWER

Many social workers do not participate in policy practice because they are disinclined to develop and use power.[17] Relatively powerless people sometimes enter a vicious circle; they are aware that they are relatively powerless and avoid participating in policy practice, which makes them even more powerless. Social workers often work in programs that receive relatively little support from broader society or from bureaucracies, whom social workers often must fight to save programs.

Moreover, most social workers are women. Rosabeth Kanter suggests that women are frequently excluded from inner circles of power, which may erode their confidence to participate in policy practice.[18] This male-dominated society has also accorded women background and supportive roles. When women and persons of color use power as white males might, they are often perceived as "aggressive," which prompts animosity toward them.

While developing and using power is only one of the four policy skills we have discussed in preceding chapters, it is essential to performing policy tasks. To give an issue prominence when building an agenda, for example, people must use power resources, such as expertise and authority, exercise procedural power to place it on committees' agendas, encourage highly placed officials to assume leadership, and draw on substantive power to make the problem seem important to decisionmakers. When defining problems, social workers manipulate symbols and paradigms to make a problem appear important to decisionmakers. When constructing proposals, policy practitioners must accede to political realities, because a proposal that decisionmakers find unacceptable will not be successful. Practitioners must wield substantive power when making proposals so as to accept amendments vital to securing support for their proposal. Policy practitioners must use process power when building agendas, defining problems, and writing proposals, because they have to decide whom to include in policy deliberations and when to escalate or decrease conflict.

In addition to using power skillfully and assertively, effective policy practitioners must devote considerable time to developing power resources. They need to enhance their credibility by making useful contributions to policy discourse. They require access to networks of people with information and power within specific settings.

If using power is helpful in building agendas, defining problems, and writing proposals, it is crucial in the policy-enacting task. Here, policy practitioners must draw on all their power resources to help enact their proposals or to block the proposals that they dislike. Power is also integral to implementing and assessing policy. It is often as difficult to secure reforms during implementation as to enact policies. Matters of turf, prestige, organizational hierarchies, and tradition cause many people to resist basic implementation changes. Assessment is also quite political. Selecting criteria, interpreting findings, and even deciding whether to undertake an evaluation are strongly influenced by the values and interests of those who implement programs.

Since developing and using power resources are integral to policymaking, social workers severely jeopardize their ability to be policy practitioners if they are uncomfortable with power. Moreover, social workers need leadership skills so that they can initiate and assume important policymaking roles.[19]

POWER, ASSERTIVENESS, AND POLICY LEADERSHIP

Social workers need to legitimize their power so that it seems like a resource in professional work, as do empathy, timing, and contracting in direct-service work. Social workers must realize that developing and using power are already endemic to social work. Yeheskel Hasenfeld suggests the following:

1. Clinical social workers often use power.
2. They interpret their clients' problems in ways that conform to the mission of their agencies. They establish certain expectations about clients' roles during the helping process.
3. They use sanctions and penalties for clients whose responses to services fall outside specific norms or expectations.
4. They enforce (or choose not to enforce) agency procedures governing eligibility, referrals, and termination.
5. They proffer comments and suggestions that steer clients toward certain actions or decisions.
6. They take sides in family or other conflicts, sometimes in subtle ways.[20]

Indeed, were power *not* used in clinical transactions, clients would probably be disappointed. They expect their helpers, who presumably have considerable expertise, to guide them, offer informed suggestions, and establish realistic expectations. As agency employees, moreover, most social workers are instructed to enforce policies, procedures, and protocols. Certain ethical limits should be placed on the use of power; however, power is integral to the clinical roles of social workers and is not, as some imply, an unprofessional, unethical, or unnatural adjunct to professional work. Similarly, administrators and community organizers use power resources at countless times, though the literature of these disciplines is less likely to deny this usage.

We need to demystify power and declare it a professional resource vital not only to clinical work, but to policy practice, as well. Power needs to be practiced, observed, and modeled, as with other professional skills. Simulations, role-plays, videotapes, and films, not to mention incorporating the concept into fieldwork, will all help make the subject relevant to social workers.

Assertiveness also needs greater attention in the profession because it provides concepts particularly germane to people who occupy low-status or low-power positions or who are continually reminded of their powerlessness. As the helpers of relatively stigmatized populations and as employees in chronically underfunded programs, social workers need to grapple with the psychology of power. They must address difficult issues: When is it futile to change specific policies or conditions? When can coalitions augment specific individuals' power? How does one overcome a vicious circle of helplessness that sometimes afflicts people with relatively little power?

We define "policy leadership" to mean taking the initiative in examining and remedying important problems.[21] People who initiate policy deliberations expose themselves to some risk, but they can also receive recognition and experience the psychological rewards of assuming a constructive, problem-solving role.

We need to perceive leadership not as a burden, but, similar to power, as an integral part of the professional role. If social workers fail to exert policy leadership, they allow other people with possibly less commitment to clients' well-being and oppressed minorities' needs to shape the human services delivery system.

Power, assertiveness, and leadership are related and mutually reinforcing concepts. The desire and ability to engage effectively in policy practice reflect ample amounts of these qualities in the practitioner. They serve as both means and ends. If using power allows people to be assertive and assume leadership roles, for example, their assertiveness and leadership contribute to their stock of power and their ability to make others heed their suggestions.

POLICY'S ROLE IN ENVIRONMENTAL FRAMEWORKS

Policy practice has always been implied in environmental frameworks, which continue to receive prominence in social work literature that discusses direct service and human behavior. Perhaps because the writers of this literature tend to come from the direct-service segments of the profession, they usually fail to devote sufficient attention to policy practice. The logic of environmental frameworks is clear; social workers who wish to help their clients have a professional duty to try to reform those factors that cause their clients problems.

Similarly, social policy theorists have neglected to link their discipline more explicitly to environmental frameworks. Indeed, the terms are rarely present in policy literature, perhaps because its theorists tend to view direct-service practice as different from and unrelated to policy issues.[22] Policy theorists ought not avoid the environmental framework, however, because it links policy to the activities of most social workers.

POLICY PRACTICE AS A UNIFYING THEME

As Phillip Popple suggests, it is romantic to aspire to a profession that is wholly unified when its members work in such different settings and undertake such different tasks. Indeed, he calls social work a "federated profession" that consists of various groups with different specializations and perspectives.[23]

At the same time, however, some unifying themes serve psychological and political functions. If the profession lacks *any* cohesion, it will fail to develop united positions and political clout on issues that affect our profession, such as licensing and funding. Moreover, social workers will lack the strong professional organizations that can influence decisionmakers.[24]

Perhaps policy practice can serve as one unifying theme, something that all social workers do, no matter what their specialization. It will allow social workers, singly and in tandem, to shape the world to be more congruent with their values. It will allow social workers to change those policies that profoundly affect the well-being of oppressed populations. Furthermore, it will allow social workers to infuse their professional work with the broader vision of the profession's founders, such as when Jane Addams tried to persuade decisionmakers to enact humane policies.

SUMMARY

Social policy has traditionally emphasized historical, philosophical, and descriptive content, but policy practice is gaining prominence in professional literature. Policy practice refers to the skills and strategies of those who seek to modify policies to make social welfare institutions more responsive to clients' needs.

Policy practitioners need to develop broader perspectives on the policymaking process, such as we have presented in this chapter. Policy practitioners ought to understand policy's role in professional work; understand a policy-practice framework; understand the political and economic context; be familiar with analytic, political, interactional, and value-clarifying skills; be familiar with building agendas, defining problems, writing proposals, and enacting policies, implementing policies, and assessing policies; and recognize the pivotal role of power in policymaking. Our policy-practice framework includes six tasks, which practitioners can accomplish using four skills. Each of these skills helps the practitioner be effective. They often work best in combination, even though much professional literature emphasizes only a single skill. Social workers function in a context that provides opportunities for changing policy, as well as constraining factors.

We can use this framework to analyze the work of specific policy practitioners, whether in agency, community, or legislative settings. We can analyze, for example, whether and how a policy practitioner used the various skills to accomplish a specific policy task or to undertake a sequence of tasks.

Social workers confront policy issues in countless places. Policies derive from their colleagues, their agencies, courts, funders, governmental sources, their professional ethics, and from many other places.

In addition to the four skills, social workers need to be able to develop and use power, because they can change relatively few policies without using power. Social workers need to legitimize power as a professional resource; indeed, we need to practice, observe, and model it as with other professional skills. Moreover, policy leadership needs to become an important part of social work.

Suggested Readings

VALUE-CLARIFYING SKILLS
Robert Moroney, "Policy Analysis Within a Value Theoretical Framework," in Haskins and Gallagher, eds., *Models for Analysis of Social Policy*, pp. 78–102.
Martin Rein, "Value-Critical Policy Analysis," in Daniel Callahan and Bruce Jennings, eds., *Ethics, the Social Sciences, and Policy Analysis* (New York: Plenum, 1983), pp. 83–111.

ANALYTIC SKILLS
Brian Hogwood and Lewis Gunn, *Policy Analysis for the Real World* (London: Oxford University Press, 1984).
Robert Mayer and Ernest Greenwood, *The Design of Social Policy Research* (Englewood Cliffs, NJ: Prentice-Hall, 1980).
Carl Patton and David Sawicki, *Basic Methods of Policy Analysis and Planning* (Englewood Cliffs, NJ: Prentice-Hall, 1986).

POLITICAL SKILLS
Eugene Bardach, *The Skill Factor in Politics* (Berkeley and Los Angeles: University of California Press, 1972).
Charles Lindblom, *The Policy Making Process* (Englewood Cliffs, NJ: Prentice-Hall, 1968).

CONSENSUS-BUILDING STYLES
Hedrick Smith, *The Power Game: How Washington Works* (New York: Ballantine Books, 1988).

BUILDING AGENDAS
John Kingdon, *Agendas, Alternatives, and Public Policies* (Boston: Little, Brown, 1984).
Smith, *The Power Game*, pp. 331–444.

DEFINING PROBLEMS
Allison Graham, *Essence of Decision* (Boston: Little, Brown, 1971).
Arnold Green, *Social Problems: Arena of Conflict* (New York: McGraw-Hill, 1975).
Hogwood and Gunn, *Policy Analysis for the Real World*, pp. 67–87, 108–127.
Patton and Sawicki, *Basic Methods of Policy Analysis and Planning*, pp. 103–138.

ENACTING POLICY

Charles Jones, *The United States Congress: People, Place, and Policy* (Homewood, IL: Dorsey Press, 1982).
Eric Redman, *The Dance of Legislation* (New York: Simon and Schuster, 1973).
Randall Ripley, *Congress: Process and Policy*, 3rd ed. (New York: Norton, 1983).

IMPLEMENTING POLICY

Yeheskel Hasenfeld, "Implementation of Social Policy Revisited," *Administration and Society* 22 (February 1991): 451–479.
Robert Montjoy and Laurence O'Toole, "Toward a Theory of Policy Implementation: An Organizational Perspective," *Public Administration Review* 39 (September-October 1979): 465–477.

ASSESSING POLICY

Richard Nathan, *Social Science in Government: Uses and Misuses* (New York: Basic Books, 1988).
Patton and Sawicki, *Basic Methods of Policy Analysis and Planning*, pp. 300–328.

Notes

1. Read any extended case study of policymaking as it actually occurs in agency, legislative, and community arenas. See the mixture of political, analytic, and interactional skills that Eric Redman uses when he seeks passage of legislation in the *Dance of Legislation* (New York: Simon and Schuster, 1973). Also read the cases in Edward Banfield, *Political Influence* (New York: Free Press, 1961). Many biographies of policymakers discuss the skills they use; see Doris Kearns, *Lyndon Johnson and the American Dream* (New York: Harper & Row, 1976).
2. Peter Bachrach and Morton Baratz, *Power and Poverty* (New York: Oxford University Press, 1970), pp. 17–38.
3. See Hedrick Smith, *The Power Game: How Washington Works* (New York: Ballantine Books, 1988), pp. 215–269.
4. Joseph Califano, *America's Health Care Revolution: Who Lives? Who Dies?* (New York: Random House, 1986).
5. For criticism of the 1988 welfare reform legislation, see Ann Nichols-Casebolt and Jesse McClure, "Social Work Support for Welfare Reform: The Latest Surrender in the War on Poverty," *Social Work* 34 (January 1989): 77–80.
6. Robert Montjoy and Laurence O'Toole, "Toward a Theory of Policy Implementation: An Organizational Perspective," *Public Administration Review* 39 (September-October 1979): 465–477.
7. For a discussion of building agendas, see Robert Eyestone, *From Social Issues to Public Policy* (New York: Wiley, 1978), and John Kingdon, *Agendas, Alternatives, and Public Policies* (Boston: Little, Brown, 1984).
8. Kingdon, *Agendas, Alternatives, and Public Policies*, pp. 95–105.
9. Ibid., pp. 182–184.
10. Smith, *The Power Game*, pp. 331–387.
11. The use of these symbols is obvious in testimony on the 1988 welfare reform legislation. See Congress, Senate, Committee on Finance, Subcommittee on Social Security and Family Policy, *Hearings on Welfare: Reform or Replacement?* 100th Cong., 1st sess., January 23, February 2 and 20, March 2, 1987.

12. Bruce Jansson and June Simmons, "The Ecology of Social Work Departments: Empirical Findings and Strategy Implications," *Social Work in Health Care* 11 (Winter 1985): 1–16.
13. Groups that participated in the coalition testified before Congress. See, for example, *Hearings on Welfare*.
14. Nichols-Casebolt and McClure, "Social Work Support for Welfare Reform."
15. Ron Dear and Rino Patti, "Legislative Advocacy," in *Encyclopedia of Social Work*, 18th ed., vol. 2 (Silver Spring, MD: National Association of Social Workers, 1987), p. 371.
16. Banfield, *Political Influence*, pp. 15–56.
17. See Eleanor Brilliant, "Social Work Leadership: A Missing Ingredient," *Social Work* (September-October 1986): 327–328.
18. Rosabeth Kanter, *Men and Women of the Corporation* (New York: Basic Books, 1977).
19. Brilliant, "Social Work Leadership."
20. Yeheskel Hasenfeld, "Power in Social Work Practice," *Social Service Review* 61 (September 1987): 475–476.
21. See Aileen Hart's dicussion of leadership in "Training Social Administrators for Leadership in Coming Decades," *Administration in Social Work* 12 (1988): 1–11. See also Brilliant, "Social Work Leadership," p. 326.
22. For an exception, see Carel Germain's contribution to Samuel Taylor and Robert Roberts, *Theory and Practice of Community Work* (New York: Columbia University Press, 1985), pp. 30–58.
23. Phillip Popple, "The Social Work Profession: A Reconceptualization," *Social Service Review* 59 (December 1985): 560–577.
24. See Nancy Humphreys, "Saving Social Services: Leading the Fight Against Cutbacks," *NASW News* 26 (February 1981): 2.

Chapter Four

The Big Picture: Policy Practice in Governmental and Agency Settings

We provide an overview of governmental, agency, and community settings in this chapter. To be effective, policy practitioners must understand how decisions are made in each of these arenas, how broader forces influence decision-making, what rules or procedures are commonly used, who the key players are, and what the mind-sets of key officials are.

Unfortunately, policy practitioners cannot work in isolation from myriad forces, factors, and institutions. They must contend with other persons and groups, often with divergent perspectives and proposals.

This chapter provides a roadmap to legislatures, communities, and agencies. The map does not tell us what route to take or how fast to drive, but orients us to the landscape so that we can better find our direction once the trip has started.

THE PLAYERS IN LEGISLATIVE AND GOVERNMENTAL SETTINGS

Anyone who conducts policy practice in the governmental sector must know who the key players are and what motivates them. Let us discuss elected officials (politicians), bureaucrats (unelected officials), and lobbyists and the interest groups with which they are affiliated (see Figure 4.1).

Elected Officials: Heads of Government

We can distinguish between three kinds of elected public officials: heads of government (such as a mayor, governor, or president), legislators (such as city councilpersons, members of county boards of supervisors, state legislators, and federal legislators), and officials elected to public, specialized entities, such as school boards.

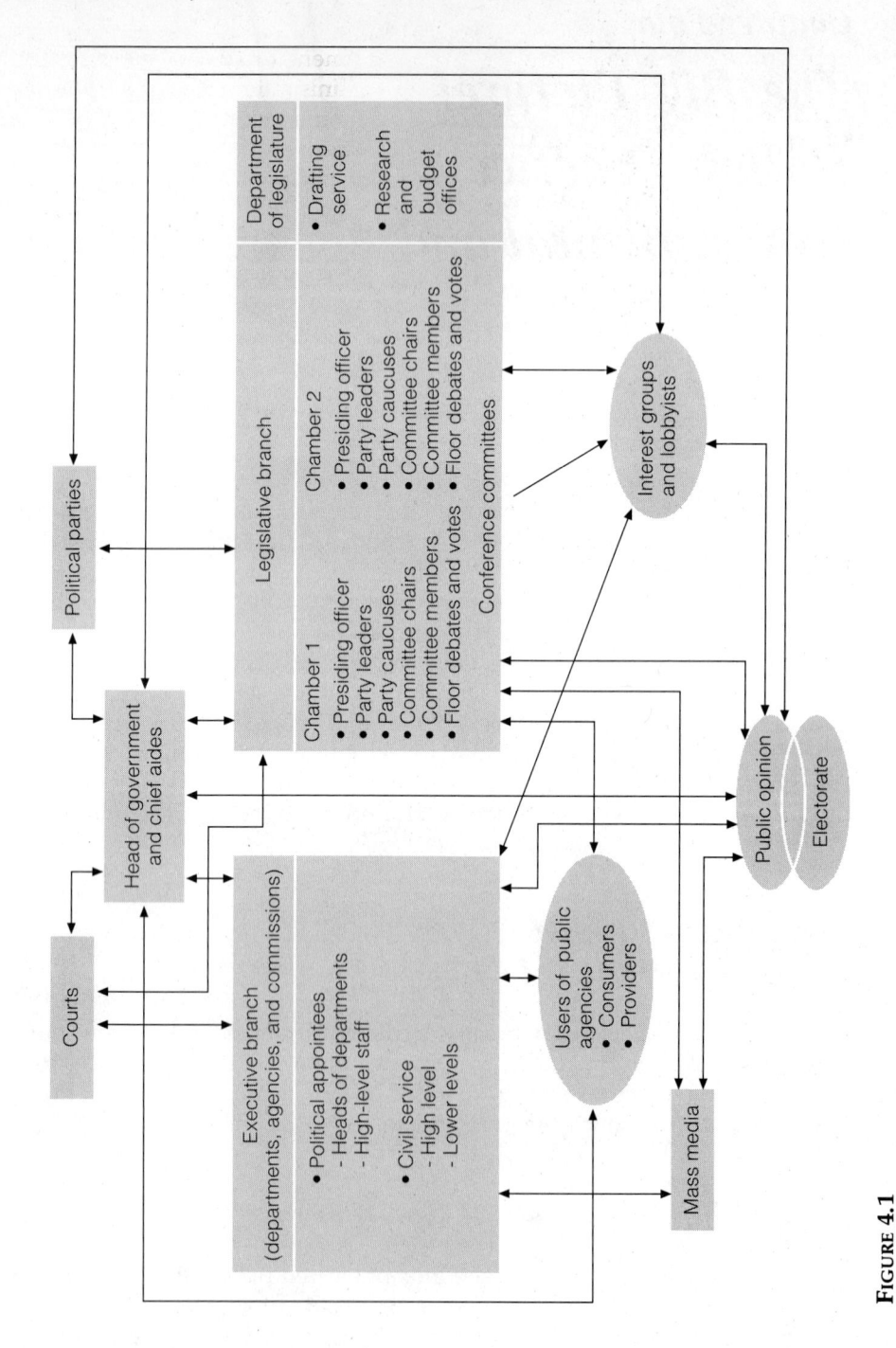

FIGURE 4.1
A schematic view of government and key players

Heads of government. The head of government (or chief executive) is the elected official charged with developing an administration. Thus, we name an administration after its leader, as in "the Clinton administration."

While some local governments have nonpartisan elections, heads of government are often the titular heads of their political party in their specific jurisdictions.[1] Once he was inaugurated, for example, Bill Clinton effectively became the national head of the Democratic Party, just as many mayors and governors head their political parties in their jurisdictions.

Heads of government usually have some guiding principles that shape their approach to the central issues they confront. As the differences between Ronald Reagan and Franklin Roosevelt show, we can often characterize a head of government as relatively liberal or conservative. Of course, ideology does not always predict how a politician will vote on specific issues, but it fosters a general approach to understanding how a politician approaches specific issues.

Heads of government and other elected officials want to establish a positive, popular record for their administrations that appeals to members of their own party as well as to other groups whom they hope will enlarge their political base.

Their central position in government and their constitutional powers make heads of government pivotal to the unfolding of policy during their regimes. First, presidents are in charge of the executive branch of government, which refers to the myriad agencies that implement federal governmental policies. These agencies are usually called "departments," such as the Department of Health and Human Services (DHHS) in the federal government (or the Department of Welfare in a state government). Heads of government appoint the high-level officials, such as the Secretary of DHHS, in these departments or agencies.

Second, heads of government usually initiate a budget, even though legislators ultimately make many of the final budgetary choices. This initiating role represents an important power because it allows chief executives to influence priorities within the executive branch.[2]

Third, chief executives usually develop a legislative agenda to which they often refer in general terms in speeches, such as the president's State of the Union speech. They have vast resources to help them fashion their legislative agenda. For instance, they have personal aides in their own office (such as the White House), in the executive branch (their political appointees), and in the legislature (political allies who occupy powerful positions in legislative committees or in the party).[3] Because heads of government have a central position in government and a high profile, their legislative proposals, which members of their own party or political allies introduce into the legislature, often obtain an advantage over that individual legislators' proposals. Even with such power, many heads of government's legislative proposals are defeated, particularly when the opposing party holds a majority in the legislature.

Fourth, chief executives often use their central position in government as a "bully pulpit." Capitalizing on the extensive coverage the mass media usually accord them, heads of government often try to gain support for legislative measures, rally opposition against legislators who may block their policies, or educate the public about specific issues.[4]

Finally, heads of government can veto legislation that the legislature has approved, an important power since legislatures often cannot muster the votes (such as the two-thirds of each chamber in the federal government) to override the veto. Some governors have line-item vetoes over budgets that legislatures have approved that allow them to unilaterally change budget figures.

Elected Officials: Legislators

Legislatures have responsibilities and powers that often rival those of heads of government under the division of powers in federal, state, and local jurisdictions. Foremost, legislatures can develop, approve, and reject legislation. They use this power to respond to legislation proposed by heads of government and to introduce their own legislation.

Legislatures possess extraordinary powers over budgets. When they write legislation, for example, they often authorize the maximum amount of funds for particular programs in a specific year. Heads of government cannot exceed these sums when they develop their budgets. In a separate process, they decide how much money to appropriate in a specific year and how to divide it among various programs. They usually begin with the budget proposed by the head of government but often make major changes in it.[5]

While not charged with actually implementing enacted legislation or writing the administrative regulations that shape it, legislatures engage in administrative oversight. Many of their standing committees hold hearings where they ask high-level executive branch officials to discuss the operations of specific programs. Legislators also receive feedback about operating programs from constituents. When legislators believe they have found defects or problems in operating programs, they have several remedies. First, they can amend the legislation that established the program. Second, they can convince executive branch officials to correct problems in programs by modifying their administration. Assume, for example, that legislators found that an existing program did not serve people with disabilities, even though they were intended to be part of the program when legislators originally enacted it. They might convince the program director to devote considerable resources on outreach to physically challenged persons. Third, they can use their hearings to put political pressure on heads of government and their appointees to correct certain problems. As when heads of government use the bully pulpit, legislators often use public hearings to expose issues, educate the public, and hear feedback on proposed legislation. Indeed, as Hedrick Smith notes when discussing Congress, many legislators like to use the mass media to publicize specific issues. They often do this in defiance of or without consulting senior legislators or party officials whose power has diminished in the decades since Watergate.[6]

Legislatures seem formidably complex, but, in fact, they are all structured in relatively similar fashion. A diagram of the Wisconsin state legislature represents the essential structure of most legislatures (see Figure 4.2). Legislatures are usually divided into two houses, such as the House of Representatives and the Senate at the federal level or the Senate and the Assembly at the state level. The two houses must usually both assent to legislation or a budget before it can become operative. As illustrated by Congress, many legislatures convene annually, but legislatures in some states convene only semiannually. Moreover, the length of legislatures' sessions varies widely; Congress meets almost nonstop each year, but other legislatures convene only for several months.

The members of each house or chamber of a legislature, whether in local, state, or federal jurisdictions, are elected by districts whose precise shape changes through time. Districts are reapportioned as population shifts and as courts decide that existing district lines are unfair to specific groups, such as Latinos or African Americans. To understand specific legislators, then, we must analyze the characteristics of their constituents, whose preferences influence their positions on myriad issues. We might ask: Is the district relatively affluent or poor? Does it have a mix of ethnic and racial groups, or is it dominated by a single group? Is it urban, suburban, or rural? Is it dominated by a single party or evenly divided between two parties?[7] We can also ask whether specific legislators occupy relatively "safe" seats or whether they will face closely contested elections.

To understand how specific chambers of legislatures operate, one must first ask, "Which party controls a majority of its members?" The majority party appoints chairs of key committees and has a majority in each committee of that chamber. Moreover, members of the majority party in each house elect the presiding officers for that chamber, such as the president of the Senate and the speaker of the House. These high-level leaders have considerable power in determining when specific measures are debated on the floor, in mobilizing support for or against measures, and in making important parliamentary decisions at critical junctures. Presiding officers often have authority to establish committees, assign members to committees, and appoint chairs of committees. They often have the power to decide where to route specific bills for deliberations. This power is critical because presiding officers can often kill a bill by insisting that it go through specific committees that are known to be hostile to it.[8]

A second tier of powerful leaders exists in each chamber. The floor leaders, who are also elected by caucuses, include the majority leader and the majority whip. Working in tandem with the presiding officer, these party leaders shepherd legislation through floor deliberations and decide which measures their party will support or oppose.[9]

A third tier of leaders consists of the chairs of the important committees of a chamber. These leaders are members of the majority party and have considerable power over the fate of legislation in their committees.[10]

Senate

- Staff
- Majority Caucus
- Minority Caucus
- Staff
- Chief Clerk
- Sargeant-at-Arms

Standing Committees

Administrative Rules, Review of
Aging, Business and Financial Institutions, and Transportation
Agriculture and Natural Resources
Audit
Education and State Institutions
Energy
Finance
Human Services
Insurance and Utilities
Judiciary and Consumer Affairs
Labor, Government, Veterans' Affairs, and Tourism
Senate Organization
State and Local Affairs and Taxation

Joint Legislative Bodies

Joint Committees
Administrative Rules, Review of
Audit
Debt Management
Employment Relations Survey
Finance
Legislative Council
Legislative Organization
Legislative State-Supported Programs Study and Advisory
Retirement Research
Retirement Systems
Tax Exemptions Survey
Commissions
Building
Interstate Cooperation
Uniform State Laws

Assembly

- Majority Caucus
- Minority Caucus
- Staff
- Staff
- Chief Clerk
- Sargeant-at-Arms

Standing Committees

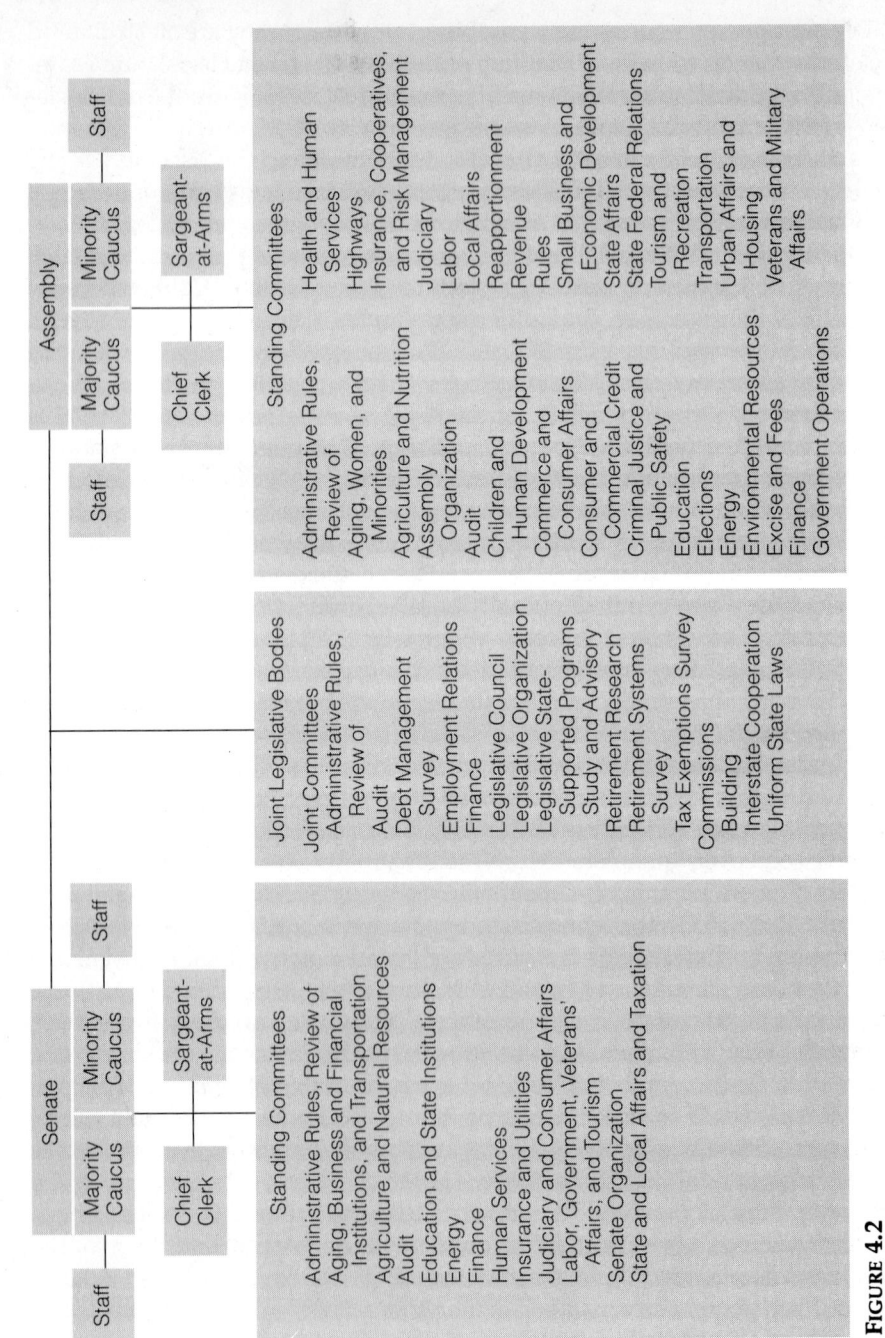

Administrative Rules, Review of
Aging, Women, and Minorities
Agriculture and Nutrition
Assembly Organization
Audit
Children and Human Development
Commerce and Consumer Affairs
Consumer and Commercial Credit
Criminal Justice and Public Safety
Education
Elections
Energy
Environmental Resources
Excise and Fees
Finance
Government Operations
Health and Human Services
Highways
Insurance, Cooperatives, and Risk Management
Judiciary
Labor
Local Affairs
Reapportionment
Revenue
Rules
Small Business and Economic Development
State Affairs
State Federal Relations
Tourism and Recreation
Transportation
Urban Affairs and Housing
Veterans and Military Affairs

FIGURE 4.2
The structure of the Wisconsin state legislature

Though at a disadvantage, a minority party often has considerable power in a specific chamber. It has its own leader, such as the House minority leader, who can mobilize support or opposition to pieces of legislation. The minority party is allocated seats on all committees of a chamber in proportion to its share of the chamber's total membership. Its members sometimes obtain a majority vote in committees by teaming with members of the majority party. Thus, in the era of Presidents Reagan and Bush, Republicans could defeat legislation that the Democrats strongly favored by joining with Southern Democrats, even though the Democratic Party had a majority in the House of Representatives throughout the period and controlled the Senate from November 1986 onward.

Because of their size and the myriad issues they consider, legislatures are divided into specialized committees. In the federal House of Representatives, for example, the Ways and Means Committee processes Social Security, Medicare, and tax legislation and the Committee on Labor and Public Welfare processes social programs such as Head Start. (See Figure 4.2, which lists the committees in each chamber of a state's legislature, and Table 4.1, which lists the committees in each chamber of the U.S. Congress.)

As we have discussed, the presiding officers of each chamber often have considerable discretion about where they refer measures. Many pieces of legislation go to multiple committees when they pose issues that cut across committee

TABLE 4.1
Standing Committees of the U.S. Congress

Senate	House
Agriculture, Nutrition, and Forestry	Agriculture
Appropriations	Appropriations
Armed Services	Armed Services
Banking, Housing, and Urban Affairs	Banking, Housing, and Urban Affairs
Budget	Budget
Commerce, Science, Transportation	District of Columbia
Energy and Natural Resources	Education and Labor
Environment and Public Works	Energy and Commerce
Finance	Foreign Affairs
Foreign Relations	Government Operations
Government Affairs	House Administration
Judiciary	Intelligence
Labor and Human Resources	Interior and Insular Affairs
Rules and Administration	Judiciary
Small Business	Merchant Marine and Fisheries
Veteran Affairs	Narcotics Abuse and Control
	Post Office and Civil Service
	Public Works and Transportation
	Rules
	Science and Technology
	Small Business
	Standards of Official Conduct
	Veteran Affairs
	Ways and Means

divisions. In Congress, for example, the House Ways and Means Committee and the House Committee on Energy and Commerce both consider health legislation.

Each legislative committee has its own internal structure. Its chairperson may be elected by the committee's members or appointed by the chamber's presiding officer. Committee chairs are usually powerful figures because, much like presiding officers of the overall chamber, they can kill legislation by not placing it on the committee's agenda, by referring it to a hostile subcommittee, or by merely raising strong objections to it when the committee discusses it.[11]

Each legislative committee has subcommittees *within* the broader committee that specialize in certain issues, such as a subcommittee on education. Subcommittee chairs also have considerable power over issues that fall within their domain.

Legislation that presiding officers refer to a committee falls into two categories. Some of it is consigned, more or less at once, to the legislative junk heap, because the committee does not consider it seriously, much less the full chamber. The subcommittees and committees take other legislation seriously and "mark it up" in committee deliberations, meaning that it is amended in various ways.

Most legislation, then, evolves in the course of deliberations that take weeks, months, or even years. Marked up in the committees of specific chambers, legislation can also be amended on the floor of the chamber when the whole chamber decides whether to amend, accept, or defeat a bill.

Figure 4.3 depicts the usual trajectory of legislative proposals, though many variations are possible. A bill usually starts in one chamber, progresses from committees to a floor debate and vote, and is then referred to the other chamber, where it follows a similar course. After the second chamber enacts their own version, representatives from each chamber seek a common version, which usually requires both chambers to make concessions. If the conference committee creates a joint version, each chamber must then ratify it before it goes to the president (or governor), who can then sign or veto it. Congress can override a veto if each chamber musters a two-thirds vote. Otherwise, the legislation dies.

Some legislative deliberations are relatively straightforward; relatively few amendments are offered and legislators move quickly to a decision. Other legislative deliberations, particularly over controversial issues, are marked by various parliamentary maneuvers, such as opponents' efforts to derail the legislation. In unusual cases, opponents will even filibuster a bill by talking nonstop to prevent a concluding vote.[12]

Officials elected to special bodies. Officials elected to political bodies, such as school boards, wield considerable power within their areas. Other political bodies, such as county boards of supervisors or city councils, have a markedly different structure from state or federal legislatures. They consist of a single chamber and they often have "nonpartisan elections," where candidates have no party affiliations on the ballot. Many differences exist between cities; while some have elected mayors, others elect their mayors on a rotating basis from the city council. It is beyond the scope of this discussion to elaborate on the

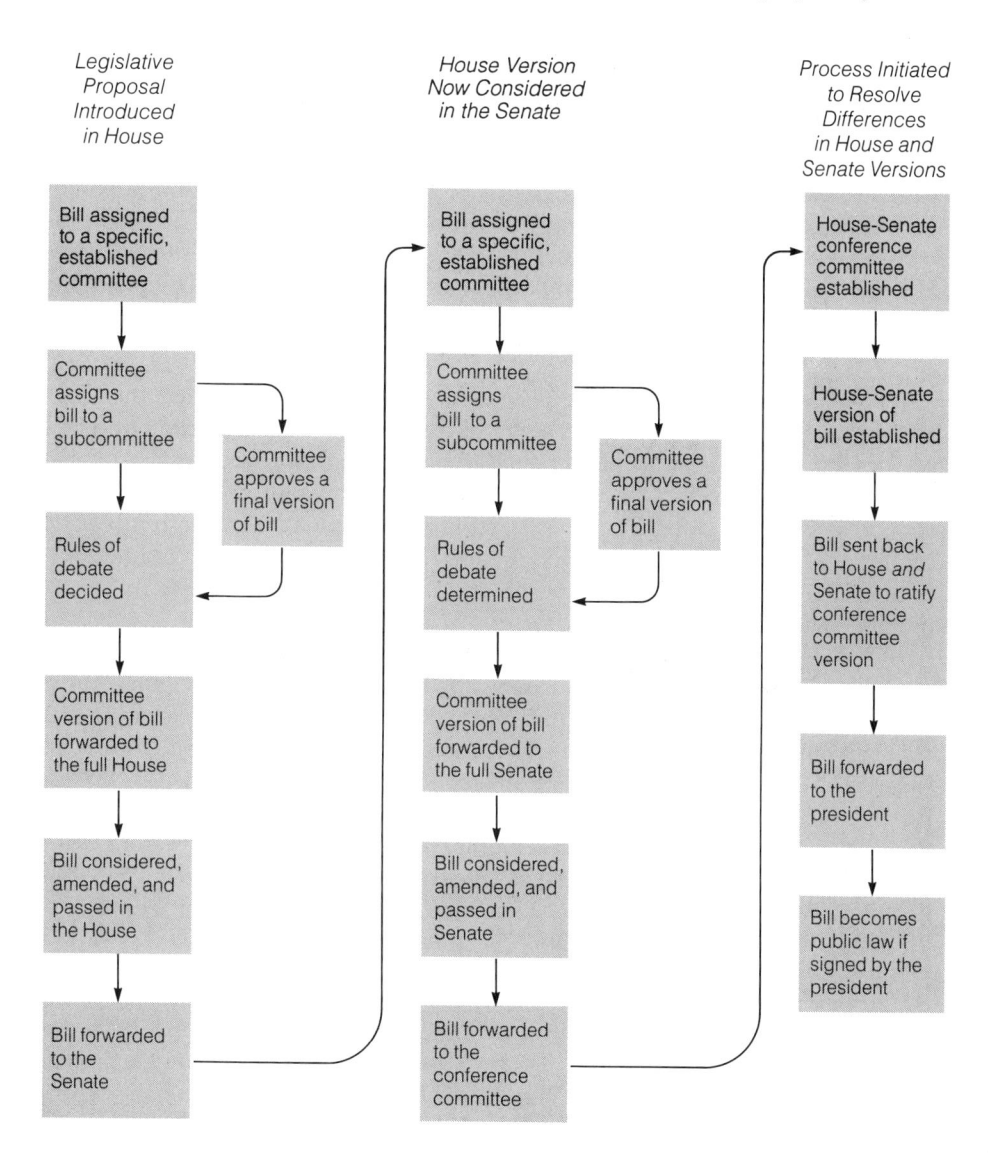

FIGURE 4.3
Route that a typical bill follows in the U.S. Congress

nuances of these different bodies, but policy practitioners need to be versed in them to participate in local politics.[13]

Bureaucrats (Unelected Officials)

Legislators are far outnumbered by public officials who work in government agencies in city, county, state, and federal jurisdictions. These public officials are either political appointees or civil servants.

Political appointees. Political appointees are high-level persons appointed to top jobs by heads of government, such as mayors, governors, or presidents. They serve at the pleasure of the heads of government. They do not have long-term job security because their mentor may dismiss them if they fall into disfavor, are considered to be a liability, or a new head of government comes into office. (This new leader usually dismisses the prior staff and appoints his own nominees.) Political appointees become spokespersons and representatives of their mentors, as when they discuss their administration's policy positions at press conferences. They will likely possess the same ideology as their mentor.[14]

Civil servants. Unlike political appointees, civil servants receive their jobs through competitive exams. Civil servants exist in a hierarchy marked by levels or "grades," with those in higher grades possessing more power than those in lower grades, though many exceptions exist to this generalization. (A civil servant is typically appointed to a specific level or grade and is promoted to higher grades based on annual job reviews by superiors.) Unlike political appointees, civil servants usually possess job security, though they can be terminated with funding cutbacks.[15]

Civil servants are the engines of government bureaucracies; they administer programs, draft regulations, collect data, and disburse funds to programs. Many civil servants outlast particular administrations; indeed, some people argue that civil servants are the permanent government, with powers that equal or even exceed those of some political appointees.

Even though they receive their positions from competitive exams rather than political appointments, some civil servants have close ties with legislators. They may have worked in the legislature as aides and they may have developed relationships with other aides or with the staff of legislative committees.[16]

Lobbyists and Interest Groups

Lobbyists are professional advocates who represent interest groups or causes. Hired by corporations, trade associations, professional organizations, or groups representing specific populations or issues, they voice their perspectives to legislators and officials in the executive branch of government.[17]

We can distinguish between relatively powerful lobbyists, who represent interest groups with considerable money and clout, and "shoestring lobbyists," who represent groups with relatively little money and clout. Lobbyists' power depends on several factors. Truly powerful lobbyists have funds not only to make campaign contributions to the legislators they wish to woo, but also to entertain legislators by hosting special events, taking them out to meals, paying them to address special meetings or conferences, and even by funding special trips for them. Powerful lobbyists often have considerable technical resources because their affluent interest groups can hire researchers and consultants to provide legislators with proposals and technical reports. Powerful interest groups, such as the American Medical Association in various states and in Washington, do not hire merely a single lobbyist; they often possess a team of lobbyists that has the resources to speak with most people in a specific legislature during a given period. They increase their clout further by forming coalitions with other lobbyists and interest groups with similar concerns. The American Medical Association, for example, can team with other medical interest groups and even some corporations to support or oppose specific pieces of legislation.[18]

By contrast, shoestring lobbyists serve smaller and poorer groups. Often acting solo, they lack the resources to make even minimal contact with many legislators, make large donations to campaign coffers, or entertain legislators. Their relative poverty should not imply, of course, that they are powerless; they can shape public policy on certain issues by carefully using their resources, establishing coalitions with like-minded interest groups and lobbyists, and mobilizing their constituencies to pressure public officials (for example, writing letters) on important occasions.

Lobbyists' character also shapes their effectiveness. While the general public widely views them as slippery and devious, lobbyists need reputations as "straight shooters" to be successful with legislators. Lobbyists who are caught telling lies, such as claiming someone supports a measure when they do not or giving deliberately misleading information, soon lose their credibility. Lobbyists must be persistent and not let specific defeats deter them. They need to like endless networking with legislators, civil servants, and interested citizens to form relationships that will help them achieve their goals.

Lobbyists' power hinges, of course, on the groups they represent. When we examine external pressures on legislators, then, we need to consider the power of specific interest groups. They obtain their power partly by hiring skilled lobbyists, but also by offering carrots (rewards and incentives) and sticks (implied or actual threats). The incentives include campaign contributions from Political Action Committees to specific politicians, supplying volunteers to help with campaigns, and technical assistance on issues. The threats include withdrawal of these carrots, endorsing opponents in primaries and general elections, and providing funds and volunteers to opponents.[19]

Some interest groups that begin with relatively scant resources possess considerable power and can augment their power by building reputations for the quality of technical information they give legislators. The Children's Defense Fund and the Center for Budget and Policy Priorities in Washington have, for example, attained key roles on an array of issues even though they lack the resources of the American Medical Association. By securing foundation funds, with which they built a core of sophisticated researchers and evolved a national constituency of members, these groups developed credibility for their research and their principled positions. "Think tanks" have also emerged that represent a range of perspectives. They issue periodic reports that carry considerable clout in Washington, DC, as well as in state capitals.[20]

Connections between Interest Groups, Legislators, and Bureaucrats

Important relationships exist between lobbyists, legislators, and bureaucrats. Many lobbyists, for example, are former legislators, civil servants, or political appointees. Many civil servants are former aides to legislators, with whom they maintain important relationships, such as passing them "inside information."[21]

While commentators sometimes exaggerate their power, "iron triangles" link civil servants, legislators, and lobbyists (or interest groups) when the legislature considers specific issues. For instance, if legislation about child abuse goes through a state legislature, several people who know each other and have worked together in the past, could become active, including: lobbyists associated with several children's advocacy groups; an association of the directors of public child welfare agencies around the state; professional associations, such as the state chapter of the National Association of Social Workers; a key civil servant in the state's welfare department; and the aide to a legislator with a long-standing interest in child abuse. Sharing similar points of view and past patterns of collaboration, these people might develop a policy by cooperating and bargaining, and then pool their resources to seek its enactment. They might even act in defiance of the incumbent governor if they think he or she will not support the measure.

We do not want to imply that such relationships exist with all issues or that the power of these collaborative relationships precludes important roles for other participants. But those who try to change policy in legislative settings need to be aware that these relationships exist and that they can be "tapped into" for technical advice or to enhance support for a specific measure.

Public Opinion

Politicians, bureaucrats, and lobbyists work in an environment marked by an uncertainty that derives from the electoral process. They realize that voters can end individual politicians' careers and can bring down specific administrations.[22] Bureaucrats are vulnerable to public opinion because scandals or unpopular decisions can ruin political appointees' careers.[23] Legislators often try to implement programs in ways that will please their constituents, as illustrated by politicians who oppose placing mental health facilities and prisons in their districts.

However, measuring public opinion is an uncertain art. Politicians often read polls, but they realize that even accurate polls cannot predict future changes in public opinion. Politicians often gauge public opinion from constituents' mail and from talking to constituents in their legislative offices and in their home districts.[24]

THE MIND-SETS OF ELECTED OFFICIALS

Those who engage in policy practice in governmental settings need to understand the mind-sets of heads of government, legislators, political appointees, and civil servants. Success in changing policy hinges on persuading these people to help and support them. They can only understand their mind-sets by examining the context that shapes their choices.

The Environment of Public Servants: Elected Officials

Imagine that you have just spent two years planning, fundraising, and campaigning to obtain your job. You narrowly defeated a determined foe who has already pledged that she will prevail, in the next election, which is several years away. In response to this threat, you will likely have reelection on your mind throughout your tenure. You will look at most issues with an eye to their effects on your reelection. You will spend hours wondering about the general public's preferences. To deduce their views, you study the following:

- Public opinion polls
- Recent outcomes of other elections in comparable districts
- The mail you receive
- The views of subgroups within your constituency, particularly those that you believe will support you in the next election
- The preferences of state or national organizations—for example, professional associations or groups, such as the American Association of Retired Persons—that might contribute funds to your next campaign.

Moreover, you would nervously eye the statements and positions of potential opponents in the next election. In some cases, you might support an issue to "steal the thunder" of your likely opponents, while in other cases you might openly support issues that they oppose in order to publicize your differences from them. In districts divided between liberals and conservatives, relatively liberal candidates often support liberal issues to solidify their support among liberals. They realize that, without committed support from this constituency, they could lose to conservative opponents.[25]

This nonstop campaigning would make you sensitive to the political ramifications of certain choices. Some issues, such as increasing funds for city parks, would cause you little or no concern. However, issues more controversial to important segments of your constituency could make you hesitate before committing yourself.

If elected officials often have their "ears to the ground," they also are extraordinarily busy. Assume that you are a member of several major committees and subcommittees. Each handles a large number of issues on which you need to brief yourself before and during policy deliberations. As you hurriedly read technical reports and briefing papers, you simultaneously try to raise funds for your reelection bid in several years. You make weekly trips back to your district to meet with citizens. You convene regularly with lobbyists from various interest groups. Citizens also come to your offices each day to speak to you. While a "caseworker" (this title is used even though these persons are not usually social workers) helps you process many constituent requests, you also devote some of your energies to specific constituent requests, such as that of an older woman who wants help coping with her husband's Alzheimer's disease.[26]

You would also be concerned about your relationships with your legislative and party colleagues. While you are, at times, a relatively independent entrepreneur who wants to make a name for yourself, you are also part of larger systems that, much as an organization controls an employee, place some limits on your actions, such as making you decide in certain situations to go along with policies and procedures you dislike. As you want to increase your status within these systems, you must play by their rules. As a member of legislative committees and subcommittees, you know that the chairperson holds great power and can often determine which issues receive a serious airing in the committee and what amendments are enacted. You belong to a political party, as well, which meets regularly, agrees collectively to support or oppose certain measures, and parcels out rewards and penalties, such as committee assignments and campaign funds. If you were a complete renegade, you could suffer reprisals from high officials in your legislative committees and your party.

Shortcuts: Aides, Lobbyists, and Priorities

With such a full agenda, you would need to develop shortcuts. You would have to rely heavily on aides to manage the bulk of your interactions with constituents, lobbyists, and others.[27] Nor would you be afraid to delegate much of your work to these trusted aides, because without them, you could not function. You would create a division of labor by hiring specialists in legislative matters and in handling constituent demands (such as the woman who wants help with her husband's Alzheimer's disease), as well as in fundraising and public relations. In other cases, you would rely heavily on lobbyists to do technical work for you, do reconnaisance with other legislators, help you draft legislative proposals, and help you write amendments to existing legislation.[28]

Early on, you decide that you have to develop priorities by taking some pieces of legislation seriously, while only giving lip service to others. Suppose a constituent wants you to "sponsor" a piece of legislation (by sponsoring it, you place your name at its head with those of other legislators), but you decide the legislation is not a priority for you. You agree to sponsor it as a symbolic gesture to keep your constituent's goodwill. You know you will not invest energy in promoting it. You decide, instead, to expend your "political capital" (your power resources) liberally on issues that could bring you large political dividends when you come up for reelection or that appeal to you for other reasons.

The Calculus of Choice

Any policy practitioner soon discovers that several factors shape legislators' choices. Indeed, precisely because so many factors intrude, policy practitioners should refrain from discounting legislators whose voting records make them appear unpromising. We can divide determinants of choice into eight categories. We have already discussed *electoral* considerations that lead politicians to support or oppose measures based on the preferences of voters, interest groups, and campaign donors.

However, electoral calculations are not always easy to make, since politicians often have poor information and must predict how the public will respond to an issue in future elections. Politicians often gauge what positions *existing and potential opponents* will take on issues. Then, the politicians can upstage their rivals, take important issues from them, or assert the opposite positions when they believe this will help in future elections.

Personal values and life experiences also shape politicians' positions; thus, many politicians who have had cancer show strong support for medical research.

Politicians sometimes support measures because they want to *obtain credit* for initiating a measure by "going public" before rival politicians take action. For this reason, politicians in the House of Representatives often vie with senators to develop legislative initiatives and Democrats often try to develop a measure before Republicans take the initiative.

Some politicians support measures in areas where they hope to become known as *personal experts*. Thus, in the late 1980s, Senator Dodd (a Democrat) and Senator Hatch (a Republican) sought reputations as experts on day-care legislation by vigorously and publicly engaging in the politics of the Act for Better Child Care.

While often focusing on the needs of specific interest groups, politicians sometimes attend to *the public interest*, particularly when they believe voters will hold them accountable for decisions that hurt the public interest.[29] Indeed, politicians sometimes support budget cuts and tax hikes even in defiance of powerful special interests.

Politicians often base choices on their estimations of a measure's *political feasibility*. They do not want to invest effort in measures that have little or no chance of passage. In some cases, of course, politicians support measures that they believe will not be enacted. They do this to publicize their positions to important parts of their constituencies.

Policy advocates must also remember that many issues have surfaced before in legislative settings. Similar to the rest of us, legislators are often creatures of habit; *habit or tradition* shapes their positions on some issues. Of course, people often change their minds as they receive new information or as political realities shift.

Politicians not only have to decide how to vote, but whether to invest considerable energy in specific issues. When they want to avoid offending someone but are not really committed to a measure, they may only give symbolic support for it. In other cases, when they personally favor an issue but fear some negative consequences, they support a measure, but try to keep their support low-profile. Sometimes, they openly campaign for an issue. At other times, they act as bystanders and may even absent themselves from the final voting in order to avoid offending either the supporters or opponents of specific legislation. In still other cases, they may openly oppose legislation.

Advocates for an issue are aware, of course, that their measures will most likely succeed if they have the support of particularly powerful politicians, such as committee leaders, the presiding officer of a chamber, and party leaders. These high-level leaders have extraordinary power not merely in expediting measures through the legislative process, but in attracting support for them from other, less powerful legislators. Practitioners' chances also increase as they obtain sponsors from both parties and from relatively liberal and relatively conservative politicians. (Of course, sometimes such breadth of sponsorship is not possible.)

Our discussion of the mind-sets of elected officials suggests that policy practitioners need to exercise caution in making premature judgments about legislators' choices. Many factors can impel them to support or oppose a measure and to invest any energy into it. Take the example of food stamps. Advocates for this legislation were tempted to write off some conservatives who usually opposed social reforms. However, they soon found that many conservatives became its ardent supporters, whether because they were beholden to agricultural interests (which believed the Food Stamps Program would enhance markets for farm products) or because they were genuinely troubled by the specter of malnutrition. Moreover, some Republicans did not want Democrats to get sole credit for enacting and expanding the Food Stamps Program, which they believed would be a politically popular program. Liberal advocates for enacting and expanding the Food Stamps Program, who would have faced an uphill political battle, found these conservative allies indispensable on numerous occasions.[30]

THE MIND-SETS OF NONELECTED OFFICIALS

Policy practitioners frequently seek assistance from nonelected officials, whether political appointees, civil servants, or lobbyists.

Political Appointees

One must always remember, when dealing with political appointees, that they received their appointments from high-level political allies, such as a head of government. They will not usually support, at least openly, legislation that these mentors would not approve. One can expect, therefore, that political appointees will seek permission from higher authorities before they commit themselves publicly to a measure.

In the real world, however, high-level political appointees, such as the Secretary of Health and Human Services, often make choices in a relatively ambiguous context. They may like a measure (or an amended version of it), but fail to get an unequivocal opinion about it from higher authorities, who cannot decide whether to support or oppose it and want the measure to evolve in the legislative process before they make definitive choices. In this situation, a high-level appointee might have some aides work on the issue and might even give technical assistance to advocates of the measure. In other cases, political appointees receive word from their mentors, such as a governor or president, that certain features of a measure are unacceptable to them and will cause them to veto it, while other features are acceptable. In these cases, a governor or president attempts to influence a measure by threatening to veto it if the final version contains certain provisions. In yet other cases, high-level appointees engage in a dangerous game of defiance; they quietly give background support to a proposal's advocates, even when they know that the head of government opposes the measure.[31]

Heads of government decide to support or oppose specific measures in a similar fashion to legislators. However, they are probably more attuned to a measure's *budgetary implications* than many legislators, because governors, mayors, and presidents initiate budgets.

The political appointees in government agencies are likely to be interested in facets of a measure that will be important during its implementation. They will, after all, implement it if it is enacted, so they attend to details such as: what agency will be asked to implement a measure, what resources will the measure need, what relationships will exist between different levels of government, and what rules (such as eligibility procedures) will be left vague or defined? As with heads of government, political appointees will also be interested in a measure's budgetary implications, because part of its funds may come from the department or agency.

Civil Servants

As nonelected officials who do not depend on politicians for their job tenure, civil servants often have a different perspective than politicians or political appointees. They commonly view themselves as professioanls with specific expertise. They are not under the same compulsion, moreover, to "act political," because they are not appointed by politicians. Nor can they commit their bureaucracies to a specific measure, because that prerogative is reserved for political appointees who head agencies.[32]

At the same time, however, civil servants work in a political environment. They have to be sensitive to the desires of the high-level political appointees who administer their departments, because they work under them and find their job promotions and job assignments influenced by these executives. As lower-level staff in the elaborate chain of command of governmental agencies, they often receive directives from high officials and may receive reprimands if they do not heed them.

Policy advocates who approach lower-level civil servants about proposed legislation, then, should not expect them to endorse it, because departmental or agency approval can only come from the director. However, lower-level civil servants can provide indispensable technical information, such as reports, studies, and data germane to writing a proposal.[33]

The degree of cooperation that a policy advocate receives from civil servants varies widely. Some civil servants are extraordinarily helpful to those who ask for technical assistance, while others are relatively cloistered and appear irritated by external requests. Their cooperativeness is often related to their personal disposition, their values (whether they like the proposed project), and their perceptions of the advocate (whether they trust him or her). Advocates must often be persistent when seeking help from civil servants, but also aware that they are besieged by numerous tasks.[34]

We should remember, too, that as with political appointees, civil servants sometimes give low-profile assistance to causes that they like, even without high-level departmental or agency approval. Advocacy groups sometimes find that they have reliable contacts in government agencies who give them inside information that enhances their work.

STRATEGY IN LEGISLATIVE SETTINGS

We have provided an overview of legislative and governmental settings. With knowledge of the procedures of these settings and the mind-sets of legislators and officials who inhabit them, policy advocates have to devise strategy for having legislation enacted. They need to know how to obtain assistance in developing strategy, find sponsors for their legislation, testify before committees, and use phone and letter strategies to pressure politicians. Moreover, practitioners often try to create favorable conditions for their policies in legislatures. Someone might, for example, participate in a politician's campaign, attend political clubs or parties, and contribute resources and time to a political action committee (such as PACE, the Political Action Committee of the National Association of Social Workers). We devote Chapter Twelve to methods of developing and implementing political strategy.

THE POLITICAL ECONOMY OF ORGANIZATIONS

Just as policy practitioners need to understand the structure and operations of legislatures, they must also be familiar with organizational processes. It is useful to analyze organizations' political economy as a prelude to examining their policies. To survive, organizations require ongoing, regular resources to meet their payrolls, not to mention their other overhead costs. Except in the case of a few lucky organizations that are massively endowed by private donors, the officials of organizations must frequently interact with institutions, accrediting bodies, and clients to maintain a steady flow of resources. When organizations stop receiving support from external sources or find these sources severely constricted, they go out of existence; downsize; merge with other agencies; or renegotiate their relations with the external world by changing their mission, their fundraising strategies, or their marketing strategies.[35]

Social agencies, which have always been shaped by their political and economic context, have been subjected to a particularly harsh set of realities in the 1980s and 1990s. Traditional sources of public funds have become constricted during the budget cuts and tax revolts of the 1970s, 1980s, and 1990s, when many citizens sought to reduce property taxes or objected to budget levels of local, state, and federal governments. Agencies that receive funds from federated fundraising campaigns, such as United Way and Jewish Appeals, have often found their allocations diminished. The resources of federated campaigns have been depleted by competition from other fundraising groups, national economic difficulties that have decreased corporations' contributions, and by scandals (in the case of the national United Way, whose chief executive was accused of misuse of funds).

The restricted flow of resources from governmental agencies and federal campaigns has meant that larger numbers of agencies have competed for the scarce resources of foundations, corporations, and private donors. As agency resources have been placed under pressure, many agencies have also found it difficult to maintain paying consumers. (The clients of many agencies have become poorer and beset by serious mental, economic, and other problems in an era of increasing inequality in the United States.)[36]

Even public agencies, which would seem at first glance to have relatively secure funding from governmental sources, have experienced a turbulent political and economic environment. We have mentioned the funding cuts and funding uncertainties of the last two decades in the public sector. Some public agencies have even had to seek some paying clients. These agencies have chosen, as well, to contract with nongovernmental agencies to provide some of their services, thus reducing the numbers of their own staff, as illustrated by public agencies that have contracted a considerable portion of mental health and child welfare programs with the private sector.[37] Many persons have advocated turning considerable numbers of federal welfare programs over to nongovernmental groups, whether not-for-profit or for-profit organizations, with the government providing consumers with funds (such as vouchers) that enable them to select between competing organizations.

Social agencies have also found themselves vulnerable to the policy preferences of governmental funders during a relatively conservative era. Fabricant and Burghardt argue that these preferences have taken away considerable discretion and autonomy from professionals in the public and not-for-profit sectors because public funders emphasize goals such as efficiency by insisting that service providers limit their encounters with clients; impose on agencies simplistic evaluative criteria that emphasize brief services, such as expecting that child welfare staff can "reunify" abused and neglected children with their natural families after just a few encounters; require agencies to devote large amounts of time to documenting their activities; and deemphasize hiring professionals, such as MSWs, in favor of noncredentialed (less expensive) staff.[38] We should note that "policy infringement" on professionals' work is not limited to social workers, because health professionals, such as physicians, also find themselves to have less autonomy, to be subject to many regulations, and to be evaluated by criteria such as efficiency.

When discussing the political and economic context of agencies, we cannot ignore, as well, changes that have occurred in the broader population during the 1970s, 1980s, and 1990s. Many social agencies find their clientele to have more difficult, serious, and complex problems. In those two decades, inequality has increased, conditions such as homelessness and AIDS have become rampant, substance abuse and crime have escalated in inner-city areas, and more affluent populations have "privatized" in suburban enclaves far removed from older social agencies. These growing problems have stretched agency resources and forced staff to focus their work on persons with relatively serious problems. Because the incidence of threats and violence against agency staff has increased—whether because clients have more serious problems or because staff members of agencies lack the time needed to provide intensive services—many public agencies have instituted security measures, such as guards and barriers.[39]

It is impossible to understand the policies of many public, nonprofit, and for-profit agencies without placing them in their political and economic context and acknowledging the harsh realities that agencies have encountered in the 1970s, 1980s, and 1990s.

The revenues of agencies come from a variety of sources. To survive, agencies need resources from fees, foundations, donors, and governmental sources. They also need clients.[40] Clients come directly to agencies from word of mouth, advertising, and outreach programs. Alternatively, referral sources steer them toward agencies, such as when agencies suggest clients use another agency's services, or when courts or probation departments require people to obtain specific services. Interorganization exchanges often shape the flow of clients to an agency, such as when the staff of two organizations agree to enter reciprocal relationships. These officials in the organizations may negotiate agreements whereby each agency focuses only on certain kinds of clients, while referring other clients to the second organization. Agencies may also develop joint programs that may be funded by collaboration in writing a grant proposal or seeking a contract.

Demographic, cultural, social, and technological factors also affect agencies profoundly, as when the population shifts, public opinion changes, and perceptions of social problems, such as family violence, evolve. These changes can influence the extent to which people use their services, the social problems they have, and the agencies they believe are relevant to their problems. While we usually think that agencies, once established, are permanent, many agencies cease to exist when their environments change. Many agencies used to provide places of residence for teenage, pregnant women, where they stayed before giving their newborns to adoption agencies. With legalized and safe abortions in some jurisdictions and with many young women choosing to keep their children, these agencies often went out of existence or markedly changed their mission.

Various pieces of legislation impose procedural requirements on social agencies. Legislation, such as the Americans with Disabilities Act of 1990, requires agencies to accommodate people with chronic physical and mental problems. Various state legislation requires agencies to: report certain social problems, such as child abuse; inform patients or clients about the risks of certain procedures; adhere to severe procedural limits when taking children from their natural parents; and work within restrictions when involuntarily committing people to mental institutions. Federal legislation places restrictions on the use of restraints in nursing homes. Court rulings, such as those forbidding discrimination against members of specific ethnic or racial groups, influence the procedures of many social agencies.

As we discussed earlier in this chapter, legislation that establishes and funds social programs often dictates the kinds of policies that agencies must follow when they implement them. Some program details left vague in the original legislation are defined later when the high-level government agency charged with implementing the program adds amendments or administrative regulations.

Some nongovernmental bodies issue regulations that agencies must meet in order to be accredited. They inspect the agencies regularly to ensure that they meet these regulations. Because unaccredited agencies may have difficulty hiring staff or recruiting clients, such regulations can powerfully shape their choices.

Nor should we forget community pressures on social agencies. Community groups, organized groups of clients, or individual clients may request or demand policy changes. Citizens can place pressure on agencies, particularly public agencies, by complaining to government officials about specific services or policies they disliked. Pressure can sometimes emanate from the mass media, such as "horror stories" about services clients received or did not receive.

Competition within the broader community places pressure on organizations, as well. Agencies seek security in relatively stable streams of clients and resources. When competition erodes traditional streams, agencies have to alter their programs or face retrenchment or termination. For example, by the 1970s, many YMCAs and YWCAs increasingly depended on fee-based recreation and exercise programs to middle-class people, but found their resources imperiled by the rise of profit-oriented exercise centers.[41] Many Y's faced retrenchment when they were unable to develop alternative programs.

To secure resources in the harsh era of the last two decades, organizations have had to negotiate and manage relations with their political and economic environments. They must: build relationships with existing and potential funders; develop services that appeal to sufficient numbers of consumers to provide revenues; satisfy external funders that their services meet specific, evaluative criteria; develop public relations campaigns to attract funders and consumers to the agency; and modify their services as competitors encroach on their traditional sources of clients. Funders and clientele shape organizations' policies, as do agencies' adjustments to their turbulent environment.

We do not mean to suggest that political and economic factors *determine* organizations' actions. Not-for-profit agencies have latitude in deciding, for example, which public contracts or grants to seek. Governmental policies that "descend" on public and nonpublic agencies are often vague or ill-defined on many points, so the staff in these agencies have considerable discretion in shaping many details of their services. While noncompliance with governmental policies poses legal and ethical issues, agencies sometimes disobey specific policies or bend the rules.

Our description of the harsh atmosphere for organizations in the 1970s, 1980s, and 1990s, such as funding restrictions, should not suggest that agencies cannot maintain humane, caring services. Even when such restrictions stretch staff resources to the limit, many agencies deliver effective services. Skilled leadership allows many agencies to keep up staff morale even in difficult circumstances.

As they manage and plan relations with their environment, agencies must attend, as well, to their internal operations: they have to build and maintain a staff, design programs, mediate internal disputes and conflicts, develop decisionmaking processes, produce budgets, attend to logistical tasks, and maintain their facilities. Indeed, agencies may be unable to obtain a steady flow of resources if their agency lacks a reputation for delivering quality services. In the case of not-for-profit agencies, for example, foundations often ask community leaders about a specific agency's reputation in the community. This reputation depends on people's perceptions of the services and staff when they interact with or hear about an agency.[42]

Executives of agencies, then, must juggle many tasks if they want their agencies to flourish. They must devote attention to their agency's relations with its environment, while trying developing internal processes that enable the agency to maintain quality services. Of course, executives can often delegate many tasks, such as using fund developers and planners for external relations and program directors for internal matters.

THE POLITICAL ECONOMY OF PROGRAMS AND SOCIAL-WORK UNITS

We have discussed organizations' political economy, but many social workers work in units of large organizations dominated by other professions, such as social-service units in hospitals, public welfare departments, corporations, and schools. Moreover, many social workers are employees of specialized units within a broader, social-service organization, such as adoption units within child welfare departments, programs for homeless persons within mental health clinics, and a program to help single mothers within a family counseling agency.[43]

Our discussion of organizations' political economy applies in double measure to these units or programs within larger organizations. They depend on their "host organizations" (the organizations that support them) for resources and for permission to perform specific roles or functions. In turn, political and economic factors that impinge on the host organization itself influence the programs' ability to command resources and mandates from their host organization.

To illustrate our discussion, take the case of a social-work department in a hospital. Such departments need to hire sufficient staff to help patients in many parts of the hospital, including the emergency room, oncology, and outpatient departments. They also need permissions from various units of the hospital, as well as the top management of the hospital, to assign personnel to these places. To obtain these resources and permissions, the social-work units must be exceedingly adroit at managing their relationships with officials and staff in the broader hospital; indeed, the "broader hospital" becomes a key part of the social-work unit's political economy. (We discuss in more detail political strategies these units can use to obtain resources in Chapter Eleven.) In turn, hospitals' propensity to allocate resources to their social-work departments hinges on factors in *their* political and economic environments, such as hospital accreditation standards and the extent to which Medicare and private insurances do or do not fund social-work services.[44]

Some program units within larger agencies derive funds from both the host organization and special, external funders. A project for homeless persons in a mental health clinic might, for example, receive funds from a governmental agency or a foundation and funds or supplies from the host organization. The directors and staff of such a program would need to be attentive to both sets of funders to ensure their own existence. If their external funding ended or decreased, they might try to convince the aency to increase its funding of the program.

MAPPING AGENCIES' POLICIES

Our discussion of agencies' political and economic context leads us to discuss the nature, varieties, and content of agencies' social policies. To better understand the nature of agency policies, try to imagine a social agency without policies. In such an agency, staff would "do their own thing" with little or no guidance from agency rules, regulations, protocols, or priorities. Such agencies would lack written mission statements or manuals that defined procedures. It would be difficult for them to describe their activities to outsiders, such as clients and funders, because, lacking clear priorities, they would lack direction. Clients would find it difficult to use agencies with no policies. How would they know if they qualified for service if no policies defined services—which services they could obtain and for how long? Nor would they easily understand their rights, since policies tell people if they are entitled to certain services and to certain protections or safeguards while receiving them.[45]

Policies govern the relationships of staff to each other within agencies, as well, so staff in agencies lacking policies could find themselves in a chaotic and unpredictable environment. Most agencies have personnel policies that establish staff's duties and rights, including rules for terminating staff and protection for staff from arbitrary treatment. Nor would such agencies have clear priorities as established by agency budgets, which are themselves a kind of policy.

Although policies do not shape many details of agencies' internal organization or regulate their internal dynamics, such as relations between staff, they typically provide an agency with central direction, priorities, and guidance for its operating programs. They also provide some protections for staff and clients by prescribing some of their rights.

To illustrate the variety of policies that agencies have, we will construct a hypothetical map of agency policies (see Figure 4.4). It is a complex diagram because agencies possess a range of policies that cannot be easily summarized. Some policies exist external to agencies but they "internalize" them, as when agencies accept policies when they take funding from governmental agencies. These policies establish specific rules for funded programs such as intake procedures, staffing requirements, content of services, reporting mechanisms, and a general statement about the program's purposes. When agencies have a number of programs funded by external sources (which is not uncommon now that not-for-profit agencies receive the majority of their funds from the government and foundations), an agency possesses multiple sets, or clusters, of these externally established policies. Some details of funded programs are left relatively vague, so the agency's staff must develop their own policies. (Of course, agency staff may ignore or even violate some of the policies that funders establish, though they incur not only ethical problems in doing this, but also the danger that their omissions or violations will be detected during audits and monitoring.) Court rulings often shape agency policies, as well, such as the Tarasoff decision, which required social workers to inform family members or others when a client tells the worker of his or her intention to inflict bodily injury on them. Social workers who decide not to inform these other persons of the threat risk being sued.[46] The policy preferences of external bodies, such as health insurance companies, that reimburse agencies (or their clientele) for specific kinds of services also affect agency policies.

Other agency policies are centrally established, even though external economic and social forces may influence their content. For example, most not-for-profit agencies have a "mission statement" that defines its priorities and direction.[47] One agency defines its mission as:

> A Career and Job Resource Center created to serve a broad spectrum of women by helping them recognize and attain their employment and earnings potential in the work world through providing job and career resources in a supportive environment.

As you can see from this example, mission statements are relatively vague, but they nonetheless establish the organization's general philosophy. In this example, the mission statement affirms certain activities—such as providing job and career resources—while not including other activities, such as counseling services or mental health services. In addition to a mission statement, staff often have certain objectives, goals, or priorities in common. When a staff member says, "What makes us unique is that we like preventive services," or "We like

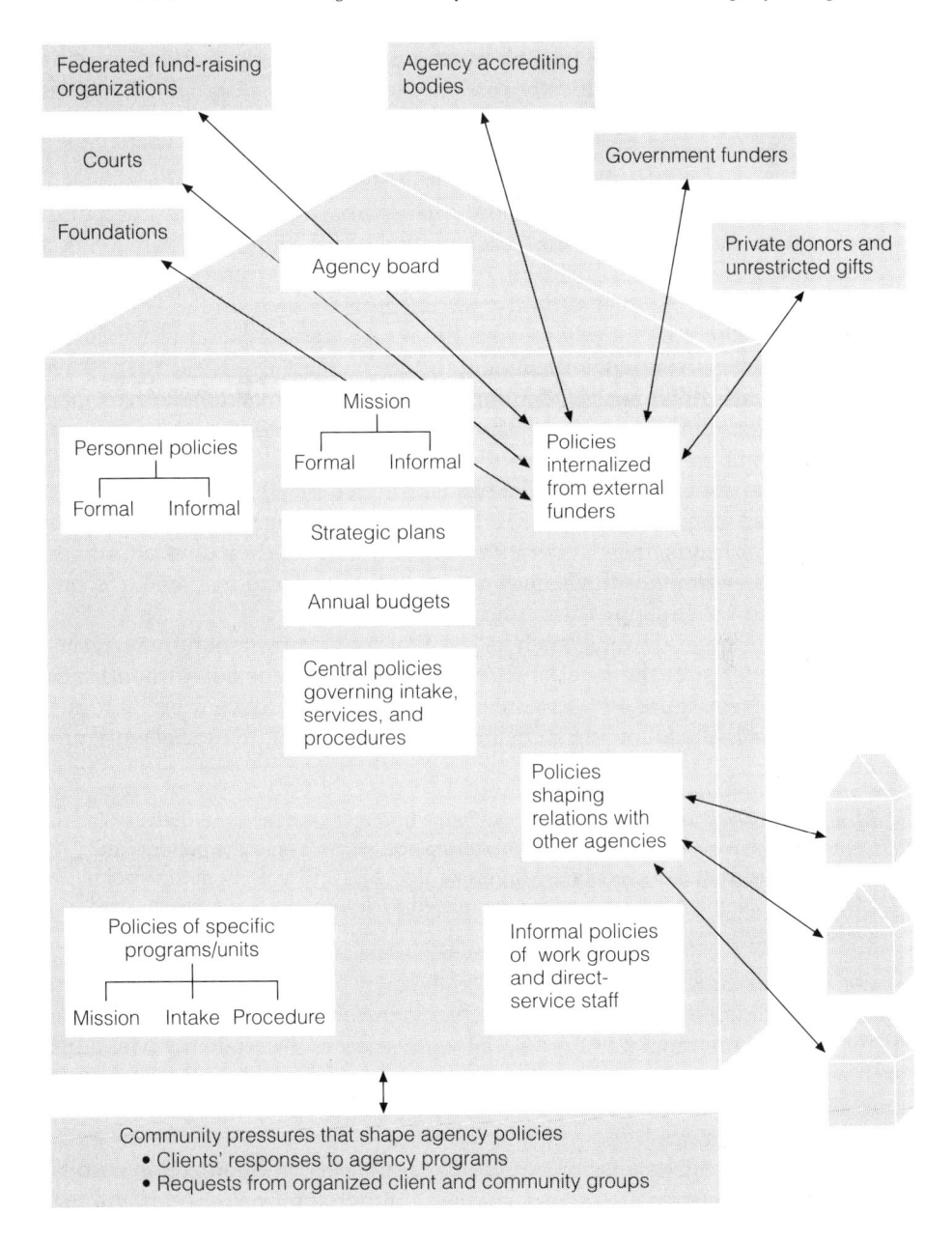

FIGURE 4.4
Map of agency policies

to use outreach," she suggests an overall approach to services that, she thinks, distinguishes her agency from other agencies.

Agencies' annual budgets serve as policy statements, at least in part, because they shape agencies' priorities by distributing resources to various programs or cutting funds for a program while increasing them for another. To understand fully an agency's policies, then, one must examine its budget and determine where its priorities lie. Specifically, one should look at its resource allocations to programs, both in the present and as those allocations have changed over the last several years.[48]

For those services that the agency funds by itself, the agency must establish its own internal policies, such as about intake procedures and the content of services. Take the case of a not-for-profit mental health clinic, for example, that receives fifty percent of its operating funds from external funders (who shape policies for those programs) and fifty percent from its own funds. The agency would decide internally how to govern the intake, services, and other details of those programs funded with its own money. Most agencies, then, have clusters of policies that shape programs funded by their own resources, particularly not-for-profit agencies that fund a significant portion of their own, internal programs.

Many nonprofit agencies receive funds from federated fundraising efforts, such as United Way or the Jewish Federated Fundraising. As a condition for giving agencies funds, these federations impose some of their own policies on the agency. They monitor the agency on a regular basis and may make recommendations to them about their internal priorities.[49]

In complex organizations, such as hospitals or government bureaucracies, many policies exist at the level of the unit, the bureau (or department), and the program (see Figure 4.5). Organizational units often have their own mission statements. The following is the mission statement of one social work unit in a hospital:

> It is the mission of the Social Service Department to enhance the delivery of comprehensive health services by providing social services to the patients and their families of the University of Minnesota Hospitals and to assist in the resolution of social and emotional problems related to illness, medical services, and rehabilitation.[50]

These units or programs usually have their own budgets, which staff of the hosts organization review and approve. A social-work department in a hospital might decide, for example, to fund social-work services in certain hospital units, such as the emergency room, while not in another unit, such as the neurology unit. These organizational units develop a number of policies to shape the direction of their programs.

Alongside budgets, missions, and official policies of organizations, units, or departments, many policies are fashioned through informal systems and networks. While not documented, informal systems shape staff's actions and choices at many points in their work and deliberations. Informal belief systems may vary with official, written policy, but they may also fill gaps when official policy is ambiguous.[51]

To illustrate the importance of informal policy in even the higher reaches of an agency, we will return to the discussion of an organization's mission. A written mission conveys a sense of unity usually absent in organizations, since different staff often possess divergent and subjective notions of an organization's

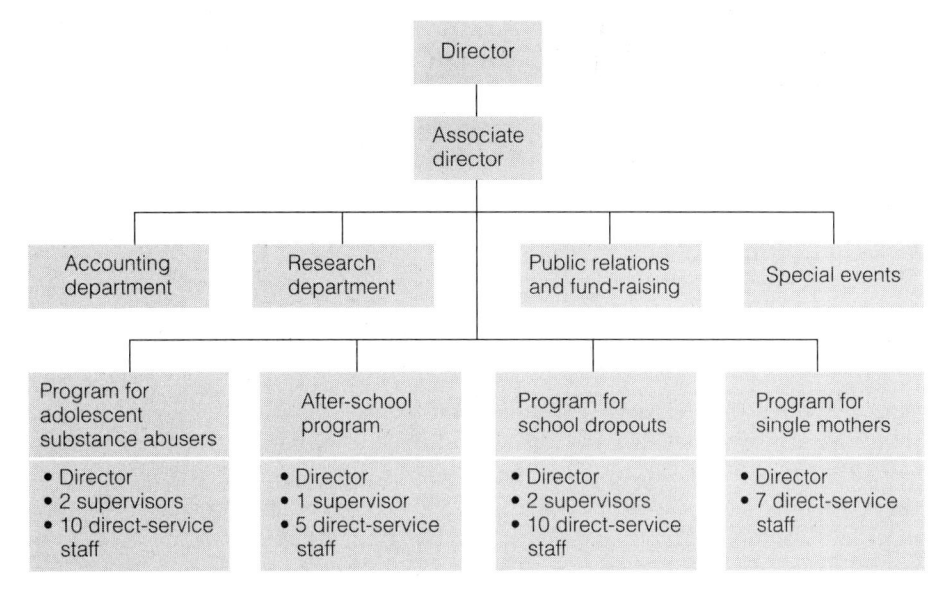

```
                          Director
                             |
                      Associate
                       director
                             |
   ┌─────────────┬───────────┴──────────┬──────────────┐
Accounting    Research          Public relations    Special events
department   department         and fund-raising
                             |
   ┌─────────────┬───────────┴──────────┬──────────────┐
Program for    After-school      Program for        Program for
adolescent     program           school dropouts    single mothers
substance abusers
• Director     • Director        • Director         • Director
• 2 supervisors • 1 supervisor   • 2 supervisors    • 7 direct-service
• 10 direct-service • 5 direct-service • 10 direct-service  staff
  staff          staff             staff
```

FIGURE 4.5
Sample organizational chart

mission. While the official mission might stress, for example, that it emphasizes services to families with single heads of household, some staff may want it to place more emphasis on serving intact families. People may disagree about the extent to which the organization should accept or seek governmental funds or the way intake policies should be structured. At times, divergent notions of the mission may erupt into conflict, such as when the organization selects a new director or during deliberations over the agency's budget.[52] In other cases, however, staff may sublimate their differences or even be unaware of some of them.

These differences about the agency's mission parallel subjective orientations toward organizational policies and can cause staff to hold divergent concepts. When confronting virtually identical client problems, for example, two staff members may proceed in different ways. One staff member might, for example, provide services based on traditional psychotherapy, while another emphasizes survival skills, advocacy, and empowerment.

Personal policy preferences, as well as binding, informal policies that many staff share, are neither good nor bad, but must be judged by the specific outcomes they cause for the clients and the agency. If we decide that a particular worker's personal policy preferences or informal policies of a group of staff prejudice them against certain kinds of clients, such as gays, we will want to modify these preferences or policies. But personal policy preferences and informal policies can sometimes lead to positive outcomes, such as advocacy and outreach, constructive efforts to help clients, and extraordinary efforts to assist clients above and beyond the call of duty.[53] Personal policy preferences and informal policies can sometimes help place legitimate limits on official policies, as illustrated by elderly patients under pressure from hospital and Medicare administrators to leave the hospital as soon as possible after medical treatment. Disoriented by surgery and medications, such older persons often resist early discharge and find ready allies in social workers who help delay their discharge for one or more days. While operating in apparent violation of higher-level policy, these social workers can often justify their actions as necessary for the well-being of their clients.

THE PLAYERS IN ORGANIZATIONAL SETTINGS

Anyone who seeks to change organizational policies encounters hierarchies and divisions of labor. These are the formal and structural characteristics of organizations that Max Weber emphasized in his classic writings.[54] *Hierarchy* describes the chain of command that vests in high-level executives such powers as creating high-level policies, hiring staff, and making budgets. The *division of labor*, or *specialization*, divides staff into units that focus on specific tasks, such as protective services, adoptions, and foster care in a child welfare office. While many organizational theorists have sought ways to soften hierarchy and specialization within organizations, they remain enduring, important features.

Some readers may not like these structural characteristics, associating them with control, rigidity, and fragmentation. However, we should remember that they also serve positive purposes. As productive collectives, organizations need powerful officials who focus on functions such as developing overarching policies, a mission, budgets, and planning. The complexities of tasks in the modern welfare state often do require specialization, both in the specific people's jobs and in the work of specific units or departments within larger organizations.

Figure 4.5 provides useful clues about hierarchy and division of labor in a particular organization. It identifies units in the organization's division of labor, including units that provide specific kinds of services to clients and units that perform work for the larger organization, such as research and accounting. It reflects the distribution of power within an organization, because people toward the top of the hierarchy possess certain formal powers. The chart mirrors people's affiliations within an organization because people associated with specific units often have loyalties to them and perspectives related to their tasks.

Were we to stop with the organizational chart, however, we would have an incomplete and distorted conception of the organization. Policy practitioners often want to know how power is distributed in organizations with respect to certain issues. While the organizational chart offers clues, for example, it may overstate or understate the power of specific individuals.[55] The director of a relatively small unit in an organization, for example, may have considerable power with respect to certain issues, but less power with others.

To obtain a more complete understanding of organizational power, as well as other dynamics and processes, we need to supplement the organizational chart with knowledge of interactions between the staff of an organization. We can conceptualize organizations as transparent overlays, placed on top of one another, that depict (1) the formal organizational chart, which displays the official hierarchy and division of labor; (2) the resources allocated to specific units, programs, or functions within the organization; (3) employees and internal programs that generate revenue, clientele, and prestige for an organization; and (4) informal relationships and patterns of consultation between members of the organization.[56] Of course, such overlays do not exist in the real world, but they provide a useful means of conceptualizing power and relationships within organizations. Together, these overlays provide useful, important information that allows us to build a fuller understanding of the dynamics of a specific agency.

Overlay 1: The Organizational Chart

Organizational charts tell us a considerable amount about the "players" in a specific organization. As we have discussed, people in high levels of the hierarchy, whether in specific units of the organization or in the broader organization, usually have powers and prerogatives that enable them to shape decisions. They can help make budgets; participate in hiring, firing, promoting, and supervising lower-level staff; obtain access to information about personnel, programs, and budgets of the agency; and have access to information about resources and institutions in the agency's external environment.

We can sometimes infer people's perspectives from their positions in organizations (see Figure 4.5). Top executives are often concerned about the budget implications of specific choices, whereas lower-level professional staff often emphasize implications for clients and staff workloads. As intermediaries between management and direct-service staff, supervisors often share the perspectives of both higher-level and lower-level participants in the organization. Those who direct or work in a specific program often view policy choices and agency budgets from the perspective of that program.

The board of directors of nongovernmental agencies make many important policy decisions. Boards establish an agency's high-level policies, such as its mission; hire its executive director; oversee the development of personnel policies; examine its budget; and serve as the general overseers. Some nongovernmental agencies and public agencies have advisory boards, as well, which offer suggestions to the top staff of the agency.[57] (The top executives of public agencies are ultimately responsible to those elected officials who appoint them, as we discussed in the first portion of this chapter.)

Were we to rely on organizational charts exclusively, however, we would likely have a distorted picture of the organization. Some people in the higher ranks of organizations defer to persons who are horizontal to them or even below them in the formal chart. Organizational charts do not tell us which units or programs in a specific organization have considerable resources or which ones top executives favor. In addition, organizational charts imply that high-level persons make most policy choices, but they do not tell us who has power with respect to specific issues. Many political scientists have observed that the distribution of power in community settings often varies with the issue; persons who are exceedingly powerful with respect to certain issues may have little or no power with other issues.[58]

Overlay 2: Budget Priorities

We have noted that budgets are important policy documents because they establish organizations' priorities. People who oversee program units with considerable resources, for example, often have more power than those who oversee units with relatively few resources. Examining budget trends in organizations can prove useful; if a specific unit has been losing staff positions while another has been gaining them, we can deduce that the power of each unit has changed. However, when taken by themselves, budgets can give us misleading impressions. Some persons who direct units with relatively small budgetary resources may have extraordinary power, for example, that derives from their close personal ties with other persons in the organization.

Overlay 3: Boundary Spanners and Mission Enhancers

Some persons are "boundary spanners" who possess links with institutions, officials, and agencies that could bring substantial resources to an agency. They may have links to funders, such as an agency program director; knowledge of funding sources or grant-writing skills; connections to elected officials (or their aides) who have power over funds that go to an agency; a seat on important committees in the host organization or in the community; or connections with key sources of referrals to an agency. Such people, who enhance agencies' resources and clientele, often derive power from these roles.[59]

"Mission enhancers" promote goals that highly-placed persons in organizations favor. If the top officials in a hospital want to increase the number of older clients, they are likely to view with favor those units or officials within their hospital whom they believe can advance this goal. Conversely, we can hypothesize that units or staff whose activities are peripheral to the organization's central objectives are likely to possess less power.

Overlay 4: Informal Relationships among Organizational Members

The connections between persons in organizations are partly predicted by the organizational chart, but proximity in the organization's hierarchy does not tell us about patterns of friendship and trust, enmity, or social distance. Nor does it tell us about human contacts that span different units of an organization or that cut across levels of the hierarchy. Policy practitioners need to know about these relationships to understand processes and choices in organizations.

Nor does the formal organizational chart tell us which persons band together to enhance their power within an organization. "Groupings" take many forms. Some are ongoing informal clusters of persons who share knowledge and support one another. Other groupings are constructed during specific controversies or crises, such as to oppose the termination of a program. Some groupings are relatively large; others consist of several staff.

COMMUNITY GROUPS THAT SHAPE POLICIES

It is not possible to study most social problems without taking community factors into account. People develop social problems, afer all, within their communities, and factors such as poor housing, social class, isolation, loneliness, and community violence, contribute to their development. Such factors powerfully influence the manner in which persons use specific social agencies, as illustrated by the way agencies develop reputations in different communities or among different populations within a community. An agency may be widely used by the members of one social class or ethnic group, for example, but not by others.

Many kinds of communities exist. They may be so heterogeneous that they cannot easily be described or they may be dominated by specific groups, such as "yuppies." Most neighborhoods within communities can be described by social-class or economic variables, as well as by ethnicity, racial, and age characteristics.[60]

As sociologists have long noted, communities have vertical and horizontal dimensions. When we discuss their vertical dimensions, we analyze economic, political, and social institutions that "descend" on communities from the outside, such as supermarket chains, corporations, state or federal policies, the mass media, or social movements that have local chapters or supporters. When we discuss their horizontal dimensions, we examine local civic associations (groups to advance a neighborhood's well-being), advocacy groups (local groups that form to promote specific causes), social agencies, neighborhood groups, and churches. Moreover, "social movements," meaning broad movements to foster social change, such as the civil rights movement of the 1960s and the Rainbow Coalition in the 1980s, sometimes develop local offshoots or chapters.[61]

These horizontal and vertical institutions become part of the political economy of communities and their social agencies. As we have noted, for example, many changes in YMCAs and YWCAs cannot be understood without considering their community contexts. When national corporations developed "fitness programs," such as Nautilus, fee-paying and recreational programs of the Y's became imperiled, because many middle-class persons joined private clubs. As communities changed their economic and racial characteristics and as many white residents moved to the suburbs, many Y's found they had to markedly change their mission or risk bankruptcy.

Policy practitioners interact with communities in several ways when undertaking the various policy-practice tasks. To place issues on agendas in local and state jurisdictions, they often need expressions of community interest, such as letters from community residents and officials. When defining problems, they must examine community factors that exacerbate or cause specific, social problems or that influence how persons use services. When constructing a proposal to develop outreach programs and halfway houses, they need to consider the perspectives of citizens and groups in the community. In trying to enact policy, practitioners often seek support from community groups for specific reforms. When implementing specific policies, practitioners should consider community factors, such as perceptions of the program, that could hinder implementation.

In seeking specific reforms, policy practitioners affiliate with, consult, or enlist the support of community-based groups. These groups can include civic associations, advocacy groups, local chapters of national groups, such as NOW or the NAACP, or local offshoots of social movements. Policy practitioners sometimes form coalitions representing social agencies and community groups when they want to oppose a specific measure, such as a cut in welfare benefits, or when they advocate for new programs, such as programs to help abused children.[62]

SUMMARY

Policy practitioners undertake their work in a context that provides constraints and opportunities. They must be familiar with the people, institutions, and procedures of legislative, agency, and community settings. Practitioners should understand the following:

- The "cast of players" in governmental settings
- The mind-sets of public officials
- The legislative process at a basic level
- Social agencies in their political and economic context
- The kinds of policies that social agencies have
- The "players" in organizational settings
- The community-based organizations that influence policies in agencies, local government, and legislatures

Policy advocates in legislative settings have to understand the cast of players who make policies in government, whether heads of government, political appointees, civil servants, legislators, aides to legislators, or lobbyists. They should understand the characteristic decisionmaking procedures used during the policy process.

Policy advocates have to understand the political and economic context of organizations in order to develop, enact, and implement policies. We have examined four "overlays" that allow us to understand organizations, including the organizational chart, budget priorities, persons who perform important boundary-spanning and mission-achieving roles, and informal relations between organizational participants.

Policy practitioners often must consider community factors when they devise and implement social policies. They often affiliate themselves with, consult, or seek the support of community groups, social movements, and advocacy groups during the policymaking process.

Suggested Readings

LEGISLATURES
R. Douglas Arnold, *The Logic of Congressional Action* (New Haven, CT: Yale University Press, 1990).
Hedrick Smith, *The Power Game: How Washington Works* (New York: Ballantine Books, 1988), pp. 119–160, 270–326.
J. Weatherford McIver, *Tribes on the Hill* (New York: Rawson, Wade, 1981).

GOVERNMENT BUREAUCRACIES
Laurence Lynn, *Managing Public Policy* (Boston: Little, Brown, 1987).

INTEREST GROUPS AND LOBBYISTS
Hedrick Smith, *The Power Game: How Washington Works* (New York: Ballantine Books, 1988), pp. 215–269.
Marilyn Bagwell, *A Political Handbook for Health Professionals* (Boston: Little, Brown, 1985).

POLICIES OF SOCIAL AGENCIES
Burton Gummer, *The Politics of Social Administration: Managing Organizational Politics in Social Agencies* (Englewood Cliffs, NJ: Prentice-Hall, 1990).

THE POLITICAL ECONOMY OF SERVICES
Michael Fabricant and Steve Burghardt, *The Welfare State Crisis and the Transformation of Social Service Work* (Armonk, NY: Sharpe, 1992).
Yeheskel Hasenfeld, *Human Service Organizations* (Englewood Cliffs, NJ: Prentice-Hall, 1983).

Notes

1. See James McGregor Burns, *The Power to Lead* (New York: Simon & Schuster, 1984).
2. For discussion of budget roles of the president, see Aaron Wildavsky, *The New Politics of the Budgetary Process* (Glenview, IL: Scott, Foresman, 1988), pp. 166–186.
3. Abraham Holtzman, *Legislative Liaison: Executive Leadership in the Congress* (Chicago: Rand McNally, 1970).
4. Hedrick Smith, *The Power Game: How Washington Works* (New York: Ballantine Books, 1988), pp. 388–428.
5. Wildavsky, *The New Politics of the Budgetary Process*, pp. 165–212.
6. Smith, *The Power Game*, pp. 41–57.
7. Smith, *The Power Game*, pp. 145–150. For a classic discussion of different orientations of conservative and liberal constituencies toward social legislation, see Lewis Froman, "Interparty Constituency Differences and Congressional Voting Behavior," *American Political Science Review* 57 (March 1963): 57–61.

8. Marilyn Bagwell, *A Political Handbook for Health Professionals* (Boston: Little, Brown, 1985), pp. 63–64.
9. Ibid., pp. 64–66. See also Richard Cheney and Lynne Cheney, *Kings of the Hill* (New York: Continuum, 1983).
10. Bagwell, *Political Handbook*, pp. 67–68.
11. Judith Meredith, *Lobbying on a Shoestring* (Dover, MA: Auburn House, 1989), pp. 65–78.
12. Lewis Froman, *The Congressional Process: Strategies, Rules, and Procedures* (Boston: Little, Brown, 1967).
13. Glenn Abney and Thomas Lauth, *The Politics of State and City Administration* (Albany: State University of New York Press, 1986), pp. 130–212.
14. Laurence Lynn, *Managing Public Policy* (Boston: Little, Brown, 1987).
15. Smith, *The Power Game*, pp. 270–326.
16. For a discussion of links between legislatures and civil servants, see J. McIver Weatherford, *Tribes on the Hill* (New York: Rawson Wade, 1981), pp. 87–111.
17. Interactions between lobbyists and legislators are discussed throughout Jeffrey Birnbaum and Alan Murray, *Showdown at Gucci Gulch* (New York: Vintage Books, 1987).
18. See Case 11.1 in this book for a detailed discussion of tactics used by lobbyists.
19. The role of funds from special interests and affluent Americans in campaigns and politics is discussed by Thomas Edsall, *The New Politics of Inequality* (New York: Norton, 1984).
20. See, for example, James Smith, *Brookings at Seventy-Five* (Washington, DC: Brookings Institution, 1991).
21. Weatherford, *Tribes on the Hill*, pp. 87–111.
22. See R. Douglas Brown, *The Logic of Congressional Action* (New Haven, CT: Yale University Press, 1990), pp. 1–87.
23. Lynn, *Managing the Public's Business*, pp. 68–73.
24. Brown, *The Logic of Congressional Action*, pp. 60–87.
25. Ibid.
26. Smith, *The Power Game*, pp. 119–159.
27. Ibid., pp. 119–159; and Willard Richan, *Lobbying for Social Change* (New York: Haworth Press, 1991), pp. 53–54.
28. Smith, *The Power Game*, pp. 270–284.
29. Brown, *The Logic of Congressional Action*, pp. 141–144.
30. For a discussion of the need *not* to "write off" conservatives when developing coalitions, see Nancy Amidei, "How to Be an Advocate in Bad Times," *Public Welfare* 40 (Summer 1982): 41.
31. As an example of the ambiguous signals that high-level political appointees often receive from heads of government, see the roles of Elliot Richardson and Edward Zigler in my case study titled "An Extended Policy-Practice Case: Child Development and Daycare" in *Social Welfare Policy: From Theory to Practice* (Belmont, CA: Wadsworth, 1990), pp. 350–377.
32. Richan, *Lobbying for Social Change*, pp. 60–62.
33. See Ron Dear and Rino Patti, "Legislative Advocacy: Seven Effective Tactics," in Maryann Mahaffey and John Hanks, eds., *Practical Politics: Social Work and Political Responsibility* (Silver Spring, MD: National Association of Social Workers, 1982), pp. 107–108.
34. An example of a civil servant's resistance to a policy advocate is provided by William Bell and Budd Bell, "Monitoring the Bureaucracy: An Extension of Legislative Lobbying," in Mahaffey and Hanks, *Practical Politics*, pp. 128–130.

35. Yeheskel Hasenfeld, *Human Service Organizations* (Englewood Cliffs, NJ: Prentice-Hall, 1983), pp. 43–49.
36. Economic pressures on human service organizations in the last two decades are discussed by Stepen Webster and Mary Wylie, "Strategic Planning in a Competitive Environment," *Administration in Mental Health* 15 (Fall 1988): 25–44.
37. Sheila Kamerman and Alfred Kahn, eds., *Privatization and the Welfare State* (Princeton, NJ: Princeton University Press, 1989).
38. See Michael Fabricant and Steve Burghardt, *The Welfare State Crisis and the Transformation of Social Service Work* (Armonk, NY: Sharpe, 1992).
39. Ibid., pp. 5–28.
40. Hasenfeld, *Human Service Organizations*, pp. 50–83.
41. Mayer Zald, *Organizational Change: The Political Economy of the YMCA* (Chicago: University of Chicago Press, 1970).
42. Jean Potuchek, "The Context of Social Service Funding: The Funding Relationship," *Social Service Review* 60 (September 1986): 421–436.
43. Bruce Jansson and June Simmons, "The Survival of Social Work Departments," *Social Work* 31 (September 1986): 339–344.
44. Bruce Jansson and June Simmons, "The Ecology of Social Work Departments," *Social Work in Health Care* 11 (Winter 1985): 1–16; and Bruce Jansson and June Simmons, "Building Department or Unit Power within Human Service Organizations," *Administration in Social Work* 8 (Fall 1984): 41–56.
45. Robert Goodin, *Reasons for Welfare* (Princeton, NJ: Princeton University Press, 1988), pp. 190–193.
46. See *Tarasoff v. Regents of the University of California*, 1976. 17 Cal. 4d 425.
47. Hasenfeld, *Human Service Organizations*, pp. 84–109.
48. For a discussion of the politics of money in organizations, see Burton Gummer, *The Politics of Social Adminstration: Managing Organizational Politics in Social Agencies* (Englewood Cliffs, NJ: Prentice-Hall, 1990), pp. 46–67.
49. For a critical view of federated fundraising, see Stanley Wenocur, "A Pluralistic Planning Model for United Way Organizations," *Social Service Review* 50 (December 1976): 586–600. See also Eleanor Brilliant, *The United Way: Dilemmas of Organized Charity* (New York: Columbia University Press, 1990).
50. Murray Gruber, ed., *Management Systems in the Human Services* (Philadelphia: Temple University Press, 1981), pp. 87–96.
51. A case study of the divergence between high-level, official policy and the actual, operative policies in agencies is provided by Franklin Chu and Sharland Trotter, *The Madness Establishment* (New York: Grossman, 1974).
52. Gummer, *The Politics of Social Administration*, pp. 10–11, 19–20, 162–163.
53. Goodin, *Reasons for Welfare*, pp. 190–193.
54. Hans Gerth and C. Wright Mills, ed., *From Max Weber: Essays in Sociology* (New York: Oxford University Press, 1946).
55. Gummer, *The Politics of Social Administration*, pp. 11–13.
56. Existing organizational theory, which presents a variety of factors that shape outcomes and behavior, is suggestive of the concept of overlays. Different authors emphasize different structural, political, and economic factors, as well as the informal culture of organizations. While placing organizational behavior in a political-economic framework, for example, Hasenfeld discusses these various factors in *Human Service Organizations*.
57. See, for example, Sheldon Gelman, "The Board of Directors and Agency Accountability," *Social Casework* 64 (February 1983): 83–91.

58. Robert Dahl, *Pluralist Democracy in the United States* (Chicago: Rand McNally, 1967).
59. Hasenfeld, *Human Service Organizations*, p. 8.
60. For a discussion of neighborhoods, see James Cunningham, "Are Neighborhoods Real? A Review Essay," *Urban Resources* 1 (Winter 1984): 19–22.
61. Roland Warren, *New Perspectives on the American Community* (Homewood, IL: Dorsey Press, 1977), pp. 260–365.
62. Milan Dluhy, *Building Coalitions in the Human Services* (Newbury Park, CA: Sage, 1990).

PART TWO
PREPARATORY WORK: BUILDING AGENDAS, DEFINING PROBLEMS, AND WRITING PROPOSALS

In policy practice, practitioners must shape proposals so that they can lead to actual changes in existing policies. They have to put specific issues onto decisionmakers' agendas, as we discuss in Chapter Five. They must define those problems that gave rise to their policy practice in the first instance, such as social or institutional problems. We discuss this in Chapter Six. Finally, they should use their ideas about the presenting problem to develop and present proposals, as we discuss in Chapters Seven, Eight, and Nine.

Chapter Five
Building Agendas

To use an analogy from baseball, experienced policy practitioners realize that their first challenge is to "get to first base." In policy practice, that means putting a policy issue onto decisionmakers' agendas in agency, community, or legislative settings. Before an issue can advance into the later phases of policy practice, decisionmakers must decide that the issue is sufficiently important to merit serious consideration. It is often difficult for a policy issue to reach first base because it must compete with myriad other issues for the scarce time and resources of staff, executives, boards of directors, governmental officials, legislators, mayors, boards of supervisors, and presidents. Policy practitioners often have to use a combination of political, interactional, and analytic skills to place their issues on decisionmakers' agendas.

How do we know when an issue *is* "on the agenda?"[1] In legislative settings, this has happened when legislation has been introduced into the legislative process, referred to a committee, and attracted the serious attention of some legislators (preferably ones with clout). In agency settings, an issue is on the agenda when it has become part of the agency's deliberations. Perhaps the executive director forms a task force or committee to study it. Maybe the staff or the agency's board plans to discuss the issue in a meeting. A group in the agency may decide to rally support for a policy change.

Of course, issues or proposals on legislatures' or agencies' agendas do not necessarily meet positive outcomes; many factors, such as opposition, can stymie them. Nor does placement on the agenda tell us precisely what kind of proposal or solution will finally emerge, because proposals are finalized in the give-and-take of deliberations. But placement on the agenda does tell us that a proposal is well-positioned to receive serious attention and that it has received an initial impetus, unlike many issues that do not even achieve this status.

In this chapter you will learn some policy-practice skills that help place proposals on agendas.

TAKING THE FIRST STEP

Assume that you work in an agency that provides job referrals and career assistance to women. You are perturbed that the agency provides little service to a specific client group, such as single, teenage mothers. While some services are available for these mothers, none of them, you decide, focus on their employment needs. While your distant challenge is to develop a proposal to help this population and perhaps secure funding for it, your immediate challenge is to convince other people, preferably decisionmakers at the agency, that the problem merits their serious attention. At this very moment, then, you are engaged in building an agenda. In this preliminary phase, you must place the issue on the agenda so that someone will examine the issue in more detail themselves or delegate it to someone else for further exploration. That "someone else" may be an executive, a staff committee, or a committee of the agency's board.

Agenda-building is a critical phase of the policy development process. Were we not to discuss it, someone might believe they could easily initiate policy reforms *without any preliminary work,* such as discussing the presenting issue, analyzing its feasibility, convincing other persons it merits attention, giving thought to who might get the ball rolling, and deciding when it is propitious to introduce the issue to others.

Agenda-building resembles the way a family decides where to take a vacation. Everyone has his or her own preferences, so they discuss and sell their idea to the other family members. If someone decides that no one else wants to go to Hawaii because it is too expensive, the family might choose a less expensive alternative in hopes that their second choice might be successful. Agenda-building is a kind of skirmishing, intelligence gathering, and strategy to convince others that a certain course merits consideration.

Persons who try to change policy in legislative settings encounter similar challenges. It is relatively simple to have a friendly legislator sponsor and formally submit a proposal into the legislative process, even though the legislator has no intention of putting effort into the project. The citizen who secured such endorsements and had her proposal introduced into a legislature would appear successful, but professional politicians would realize that at best a symbolic victory had been won. They realize that if a policy initiative lacks preparatory work and planning, it is unlikely that a legislative committee will discuss it, give it a public hearing, or vote on it—or that the legislative chamber will vote on it.

Most of us want not symbolic victories, but real commitments to our policies so that they stand some chance of success during the give-and-take of the political process. Skillful policy practitioners who are building an agenda try to create favorable conditions, interest, and support for a policy reform at the outset. Before we can discuss the specific actions of agenda-building, we need to gain a conceptual understanding of agenda-building processes.

Why Preparatory Work Is Needed

It is easy to see why most proposals fall by the wayside when we consider some simple realities that confront agency executives and legislators. Executives must manage organizations, raise funds, hire staff, adjudicate conflicts, and plan. These tasks often occupy most of their working hours. Executives also confront myriad policy issues, such as deciding what kinds of clients to serve, establishing which social problems fall within the purview of their services, naming overarching objectives or goals, developing policies and procedures within specific grant proposals, deciding whether to be advocates for their clients in the broader community or in a legislature, figuring out what kind of staff to hire, and developing policies and procedures to guide the staff. Some of these policies concern internal, procedural matters, while others concern the goals or mission of the organization in its political and funding context.

In light of these many issues, executives must ignore or defer many even when they seem important to a staff member, a board member, or a client. Were they to try to examine each of them in considerable detail, they would be exhausted by the monumental effort involved and frustrated because they would not be able to examine each issue in depth.

Executives also ignore or defer certain issues because they would embroil the agency in conflict. Some issues, even seemingly mundane ones such as changing an agency's intake procedures, can impassion people who want the issue left alone. Perhaps they like existing policy because it furthers their own interests, as when they receive a steady flow of certain kinds of clients to their units. They may like existing policy for ideological reasons; for instance, they might believe the agency should focus on the kind of clients it now predominantly serves. Perhaps they fear that some rival staff member has plotted the change in intake policy to obtain some advantage over them or even to cause them harm. In this political context, then, it is understandable that executives leave most issues alone. Often, they will act only when they are convinced that an issue merits attention in spite of possible political conflict and the time and effort the issue might take.

Nor are executives likely to invest time in an issue if they believe that other issues are more worth their time and effort. Executives give preference to certain issues for several reasons. To increase agency resources amid funding cuts, they may select issues that will obtain greater funds for their agencies. They may feel pressured by certain persons to focus on an issue. Or they may be more interested in certain kinds of issues than in others. Executives, then, must *ration* or limit the number of issues they consider.[2] They must also rank the issues to which they want to give attention in some order or *queue.*

Policy practitioners who want to bring their issues to the attention of executives and other agency personnel must *upset* or change this status quo. They develop strategy to convince executives that their issues merit attention.

Similar to executives, legislators ration issues and establish queues. Thousands of pieces of legislation are introduced into state legislatures and Congress, whether the legislators themselves, lobbyists, citizens, or professional associations conceived them. Were legislators to debate even a large fraction of them, they would work themselves to exhaustion and not give careful attention to any of them. When many people with different perspectives and constituencies are involved, it takes time and effort to consider even simple pieces of legislation. In each chamber of Congress, for example, subcommittees need to consider the policies, forward them to the full, legislative committee for further debate and votes, forward them to the full chamber for floor debates and votes, send them to a conference committee composed of members of both chambers if each chamber enacts different versions, and then forward the legislation to the president for his signature. Moreover, many legislators must spend endless hours during these long deliberations with lobbyists and citizens. It is no wonder, then, that leaders of the legislature decide not to devote time to most measures, thus reserving their scarce time for those pieces of legislation on which they want to concentrate.

Moreover, legislators often avoid those issues that appear to have little or no political payoff for them in terms of reelection. Politicians *deselect* those issues that appear unhelpful in obtaining or retaining constituents' support. A particular issue may seem too controversial or may antagonize an important faction or interest group, even if it pleases other people. Perhaps, after assessing that a policy does not stand a chance, they decide not to invest their energy in it.[3]

Unlike agency executives, who often want to avoid contentious issues that could disrupt their agencies, politicians are often attracted to issues associated with conflict if such issues can gain them support among constituents. Take the case of relatively liberal politicians. They may deliberately support an issue to anger conservatives if that will enable them to prove their ideological leanings to liberal supporters. They may opportunistically select issues that will give them media exposure so that they can have an advantage over opponents in upcoming election battles.[4]

Building an agenda does not ensure, of course, that a policy will ultimately be enacted. Agenda-building focuses merely on the preliminary portion of policymaking, when persons decide whether an issue deserves serious attention and may move it to a prominent position on deliberative agendas. Executives might decide to establish a task force or committee to examine the issue in more detail. They may instruct a staff member to research the issue, or they may look into it themselves. In legislative settings, the chairperson of a legislative committee may send a proposal to a subcommittee for initial examination or could place the issue on the full committee's agenda. By making these early, tentative commitments, the chairperson signals that a particular issue will not be consigned, at least for now, to the legislative scrapheap.

This decision to give attention or prominence to an issue in the early phase of policymaking does not guarantee success at subsequent points. An issue may attract great interest at the outset only to fizzle at a later point. It may become polarized between competing factions, only to lose in a climactic vote many months later. A policy proposal may be enacted but be so diluted or modified that its original proponents emerge dissatisfied. A policy may be enacted that does not adequately address or resolve the presenting issue. Then again, a proposal may be enacted only to be poorly implemented or not funded.

Even with these risks, skillful policy practitioners devote considerable attention to building agendas. They realize that they have virtually no chance of long-term success if they cannot garner significant interest in their favored issues in the early part of policymaking.

Outmoded Theories

Following John Kingdon's lead in his classic work, *Agendas, Alternatives, and Public Policies,* we use *agenda-building* to mean processes that lead to the selection of some issues and the rejection of other issues. We extend his analysis to agency settings, as well.[5] Before Kingdon began his work, many theorists had wondered how issues made it onto decisionmakers' agendas. Some of them assumed, for example, that agenda-building was a relatively rational process where decisionmakers chose specific policy issues through empirical research. Armed with the agency's latest service statistics, an administrator might develop a new program to reach a population underrepresented in the agency's services. After reading in a census report that the number of Asian immigrants in his jurisdiction had increased, a legislator develops policy to address one of their needs.

While acknowledging that some policy issues land on agendas by such rational means, Kingdon argues that purely rational explanations of agenda-building do not reflect how the agenda-building process *usually* works.[6] Administrators and legislators do not often consult technical information; rather, they respond to the entreaties of other people. They may place politics ahead of other considerations when choosing an issue to promote. Even when technical studies do exist, their recommendations are often ignored, as many of them gather dust on library shelves or in file cabinets. Moreover, decisionmakers often leap to solutions even before or without extended research or data gathering. Explanations of agenda-building that rely solely on rational considerations are insufficient, Kingdon argues, though we shall note subsequently that gathering research, data, and technical information can help policy practitioners build agendas.

Other theorists conjectured that *incrementalism* explains how issues get decisionmakers' attention. Incrementalists argue that executives and legislators prefer relatively small departures from existing policies because small changes are less likely to excite broad opposition or conflict. An agency with a program to help Latino males overcome substance abuse might expand the program to include Latina women rather than supporting a policy that proposed an entirely new program or a sweeping overhaul of existing services. Aware of this propensity, agency staff would suggest only minor modifications of existing policies. Incrementalists extend the same logic to legislators by arguing that they, too, prefer small departures from existing policies. Their arguments seem reinforced by the proliferation of minor changes to existing programs, such as expanding Head Start to include disabled children, the Social Security Act to include widows and the disabled, and civil rights legislation to include disabled persons, elderly persons, and women. Kingdon rightly argues, however, that decisionmakers, both in agency and legislative settings, often do support *major* changes in existing policy.[7] Agencies sometimes launch new programs that diverge markedly from their existing programs. For instance, President Bill Clinton decided in his first year of office to overhaul the nation's health care system. This is hardly incrementalism, even if his proposals fall short of those advanced by liberals.

Much like rationalists, then, incrementalists do not provide a comprehensive framework that allows us to understand agenda-building. Their frameworks do not teach policy practitioners a range of skills to help them secure a position for issues on decisionmakers' agendas.

Other theorists contend that policies rise to prominence on agendas primarily because of the pressure of interest groups. Few would doubt that interest groups have enormous influence over legislators and, in some cases, cause them to place some issues high on their agendas. But interest-group pressures do not tell us why, among the myriad ideas that thousands of interest groups champion, only certain issues are propelled onto agendas.[8] Moreover, some policy issues make it onto agendas without extensive pressure from outside interests. When Richard Nixon introduced his Family Assistance Plan to the surprise of both political parties, for example, he acted in the absence of widespread support for welfare reform.[9]

Another theorist developed the "garbage can theory" of agenda-building. Emphasizing organizations, he noted that many ideas bubble forth in settings where there are problems (such as social problems, service-delivery problems, administrative problems) and solutions (for instance, service-delivery, program, or administrative innovations).[10] These problems or solutions may surface at staff meetings. Perhaps they were discussed at a retreat of the executives and the board. Maybe a committee identified problems or potential solutions in its deliberations. The executive director, alone or in deliberations with other high-level staff, could have identified some problems or issues. Even when agency members consider an issue fleetingly, problems and solutions often retain a place in their memories. But issues remain in a state of limbo, in a figurative garbage can, until they are placed on the agendas of decisionmakers. Similarly, we can say that myriad problems and solutions exist in the "garbage cans" of legislatures or their environs. These problems and solutions derive from such sources as lobbyists, reform-minded legislators, think tanks, professional associations, and citizens.

The garbage can theory suggests a more fluid and dynamic process than the rationalist or incrementalist theories, but it does not discuss in sufficient detail how certain issues are "activated," or placed on policy agendas. At this point, Kingdon comes to our assistance by identifying three streams and introducing the notions of coupling, policy windows, and policy entrepreneurs. We shall now explore these ideas.

The Agenda Funnel

We have discussed policy agendas in general terms. We can now distinguish between *general agendas, decision agendas,* and actual votes or decisions, and we can illustrate these phases of the agenda-building process by using a funnel (see Figure 5.1). General agendas represent problems or solutions that have been discussed, usually fleetingly, in a given setting, even though high-level staff members have made no decision to give them detailed, serious consideration.[11] General agendas are illustrated at the top of the funnel in Figure 5.1. These problems and solutions may be selected for the decision agenda, as shown in the middle of the funnel.[12] An agency executive might decide, for example, seriously to consider improving services to Latino clients, choosing this issue from an array of problems in the agency's general agenda. The issue will then be forwarded to a deliberative body for serious consideration, and discussed during deliberative processes in one or more committees or forums. (At the

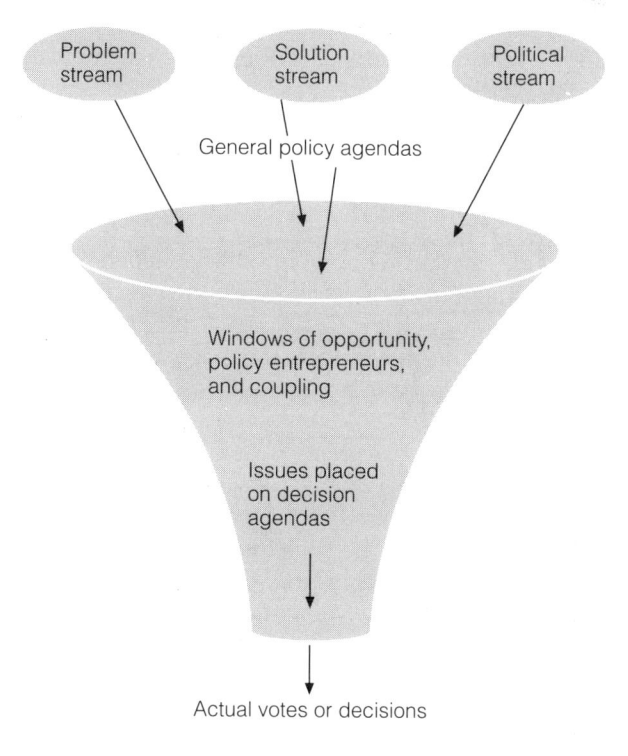

Figure 5.1
The agenda funnel

bottom of Figure 5.1, see "decision agendas," which often culminate in votes or decisions.)

It is admittedly somewhat difficult to tell where an issue exists in the funnel. Is it on the general agenda or the decision agenda? To answer this, ask the following questions. Has the issue been "floated" with little or no discussion? If so, it is on the general agenda. Has the issue been forwarded to a committee, task force, or other deliberative entity for further discussion? If so, it is on the choice or decision agenda. Has the deliberative entity disposed of the issue with a vote or decision? If so, it has left the agenda funnel. Of course, a specific issue may appear to be heading down the funnel, only to be sidetracked or delayed by an opponent or by competing issues. We cannot predict the ultimate fate of an issue even when it has reached the decision agenda, as many defeated pieces of legislation or rejected proposals in agency settings suggest.

THREE STREAMS AND THE GENERAL POLICY AGENDA

Kingdon suggests that three kinds of "streams" exist, largely separate from one another, in agency and legislative settings, namely, problem, solution, and political streams.[13] Events and persons in these three streams eventually help issues or proposals reach policy agendas.

THE PROBLEM STREAM

Problems often provide the starting point for policy deliberations, because policy practitioners often engage in their work when they worry about a condition in the world.[14] It is not enough for policy practitioners to personally express concern about a problem, however; they must convince others that the problem merits placement on the general and decision agendas of a legislature or agency.

To see that a problem stream exists in many agencies, one need merely examine developments in the agency during, say, the last ten years. Take the example of the aforementioned small social agency that provides job placement and career counseling services. The social worker who directs these services also founded the agency. In the beginning, the agency had a relatively narrow set of services, consisting mostly of posting job openings from area firms on a bulletin board and holding career planning seminars for women. In the ten years since its founding, staff, the executive director, and members of the board identified problems that the agency could address. They initially discussed some of these ideas in a meeting or in personal conversations, but over time, many ideas led to new programs, funded grant proposals, and cooperative projects with other agencies. In those ten years, the agency added special job placement and career planning services for Latinas, single teenage mothers, and displaced homemakers; a job placement program for unemployed women funded by the federal Job Training Partnership Act; and job fairs for high school women in a local school district. Each of these programs stemmed from a problem that someone placed on the agency's general problem stream in conversations or meetings. Of course, many other problems on the general problem stream did not progress to the lower end of the agenda-building funnel. The agency staff decided not to pursue one suggestion to provide a support group for unemployed women with a mental-health orientation because they believed it fell outside their mission, which emphasizes job referral, job search, and career development services.

Why Certain Problems Reach Agendas

The problem stream in a legislative setting consists of the problems that citizens, legislative, and government officials have floated in recent years. State legislators, for example, may have heard about lead paint poisoning in inner-city areas, lack of access to health care by the poor, lack of bilingual teachers, rivalry between state agencies that fund programs for homeless people, toxic waste dumps, lack of day-care programs for moderate-income persons, and a growing budget deficit.

What are some of the characteristics of problems that reach general policy and decision agendas in agency and legislative settings? By contrast, what kinds of problems tend not to receive serious consideration?[15] As Kingdon suggests, those who want decisionmakers to take their problem seriously have to convince them that it is a *problem* and not merely a *condition*. A problem poses a threat or danger to someone—for example, a group in the population.[16] Someone might argue that an agency will suffer dire consequences, such as a loss of funding, unless a specific problem is solved. They might say that if an agency does not reform its services, some group of persons, such as Latinos, will suffer. In the first year of President Clinton's administration, many persons argued that runaway health-care costs would bankrupt the nation if they were not reduced. Moreover, economists and corporate leaders warned that the high costs of health-care fringe benefits placed American corporations at a competitive disadvantage with other nations.[17]

But how does someone convince other persons that certain conditions are problems? They can use data to argue that a condition is serious in its absolute numbers, that some subset of the population is afflicted far more than other portions of the population, or that the problem is steadily becoming worse.[18] Absolute numbers, such as the percentage of women with inadequate or no childcare, can shock decisionmakers into believing that a condition is a problem. Someone with data indicating that Latinas lack adequate childcare in far greater numbers than white women could use this data to persuade legislators to fund day-cares for Spanish-speaking children. Data showing that a problem is worsening can convince legislators that a problem will reach crisis proportions without governmental intervention. Kingdon calls such statistical data "indicators."[19]

Advocates for corrective action often use words such as "crisis" to describe a condition. This word is overused, so the advocate needs some evidence or rationale for its use. Take the example of the dramatic spread of tuberculosis in the United States in the 1990s. Tuberculosis has hit AIDS patients and immigrants hardest. In addition, drug-resistant strains of the disease have spread because many persons fail to take prescribed medications for a sufficiently long period. Public health officials make a persuasive case that without strong corrective action, tuberculosis could become a national epidemic.

Sometimes an event—such as a catastrophic riot or fire, the death of a celebrity from AIDS or some other dramatic cause, or a publicized case of child abuse—can indicate that corrective action is needed. Kingdon calls such occurrences "focusing events."[20]

Advocates need to demonstrate, as well, that a problem is not hopeless and can be ameliorated. Advocates have often found it difficult to secure support for inner cities, the "underclass," or even homeless persons, because many legislators see these problems as unsolvable in contrast to simpler ones. Faced with this perception, advocates sometimes select subpopulations that do not seem to present chronic problems, such as "homeless children and youth" or particular sections of an inner-city community. This choice carries with it some ethical dilemmas, because it directs attention away from other persons who also need help. They may argue that a specific remedy or program has particular promise by drawing on research or successful pilot projects.

Advocates can appeal to values by arguing that society (or a legislature) has a duty to address an issue. Someone might say, for example, "How can one of the richest countries in the world fail to take care of its homeless persons, when they are scarcely found on the streets of European societies?" (Recall our discussion of ethical principles of beneficence, social justice, and fairness in Chapter Two.)

Because politicians often consider how taking corrective action will affect their careers, advocates often try to state problems in relatively broad terms. They may stress the absence of child-care for working women, the spread of Alzheimer's disease among all social classes and races, or inadequate sex education in schools. By presenting problems in general terms, advocates increase the likelihood all politicians will see the problem as important to their constituencies. However, advocates who use this tactic also risk making politicians fear that extraordinary resources will be needed to address the problem.[21]

Nomenclature is important when describing problems. Hence, the contemporary tendency to refer to "investment" in human needs rather than "spending." No practical difference exists between the two terms, because both mean using public resources. However, "investment" appeals to many politicians, including relatively conservative ones, because it implies that society receives a "return" on its investment. In contrast, "welfare" is interpreted as "throwing money at problems."[22]

Nomenclature can also appeal to socially acceptable symbols. With the Family Support Act of 1986, Congressional advocates, such as Senator Moynihan, called their reforms "family support" rather than "welfare reforms." They hoped that such words would attract more support from Congressional conservatives.[23]

As Kingdon notes, legislators' perceptions of the budget influence whether they act on specific problems.[24] Assume, for example, that an agency has had to lay off some staff; in such a financially strained environment, advocates for new programs would likely have trouble securing support. Indeed, the huge federal deficits of the 1980s and 1990s have retarded social reforms, because Congress increasingly demands that requests for new spending be accompanied by proposals to cut funding elsewhere. When faced with harsh fiscal realities, advocates try to show that a specific policy, such as increasing Head Start funding, will avert subsequent costly problems, such as welfare and crime. They may propose a pilot program in hopes of expanding it later.

Advocates encounter a double-edged sword when they use the word "prevention" to seek support for a problem. Prevention is, on the one hand, a culturally acceptable symbol since everyone prefers to prevent a problem than to fix it afterward. However, decisionmakers often perceive "preventive programs" negatively. They may wonder if a specific problem, such as teenage pregnancy or drug usage, *can* be prevented. They may not want to divert scarce resources to persons currently lacking a problem, because they want to help already afflicted persons. Those promoting preventive programs, then, need to find evidence that they will successfully avert problems.[25]

Advocates should be prepared for others' objections to their ideas. When a practitioner proposes a policy to help homeless persons, for example, an opponent might say that homelessness is unsolvable, that no known solution exists, and that programs to address it bring few political returns because homeless people rarely vote.[26] Moreover, some people may argue that the size of the homelessness issue has been vastly overstated and mismeasured with flawed research methodology. Similarly, someone who tries to place a problem on an agency's general or decision agenda may hear that "this issue does not fall within this agency's mission," "our agency lacks expertise or resources to address this issue," "we have no funds in our budget to address that problem," or "other issues should take priority." Advocates for a specific issue, then, must realize that they often do not have the policy field to themselves and must use arguments and data to counter opponents' tactics.

Tactics in the Problem Stream

Policy practitioners can use tactics to help place a problem on a general or choice agenda. They can use data to show that a crisis exists, nomenclature with broad appeal for legislators, evidence that a problem can be addressed and is not hopeless, discussion of budgetary implications, and in some cases arguments for prevention. They can discuss how not only a specific group, but society as a whole will benefit from our addressing a problem. They can emphasize to politicians that failure to address a problem could carry negative political repercussions for them.

The media can serve as an important educational tool in policy practice. Stories in the press, on radio, and on television about social problems can create powerful images in the minds of citizens and elected officials, who may decide to give them serious attention.[27] A social worker in an agency found, for example, that a reporter from a local paper became a frequent ally. When the social worker wanted the city to replace junkyards with low- and moderate-income housing, several stories in the newspaper about the blighted area prompted local politicians to take the neighborhood's problems seriously.

Policy practitioners can sometimes promote a specific problem by having citizens or clients become advocates. Practitioners commonly use this tactic in legislative settings, by asking people to write letters about a certain issue or visit legislators. It is more difficult to use this tactic in agency settings because agency executives do not like their staff to incite clients to demand new programs or better services. However, complaints from clients can have a powerful effect when they indicate that services are not relevant to their problems or that gaps exist in services.

THE SOLUTION STREAM

Rationalists often thought that solutions emerged only after a prolonged investigation of a problem, such as a decision to develop the Food Stamps Program after a long study of malnutrition. Kingdon observes, however, that solutions often exist on general agendas independent of specific problems.[28] Take a legislative setting, where solutions such as the following exist: health maintenance organizations, a value-added tax, multiservice centers in schools, foster grandparents, contracting out services, regional governments, and computer-assisted referral centers in neighborhoods. Similarly, agency settings often have solutions such as decentralizing services; collaborating with other agencies; developing a grant proposal to help single, teenage mothers; hiring a Spanish-speaking staff member; developing a strategic plan; or hiring someone from another, but related, discipline.

We can classify solutions into three broad groups. Some propose specific programs, such as interventions to help children, single mothers, or the elderly. Others aim to correct institutional problems, such as financing a program, changing an agency's fee structure, or enhancing the collaboration of different agencies when serving a specific client group. Still others propose methods of making decisions, such as setting up a task force, establishing a committee, or organizing an interagency planning committee.

Why Certain Solutions Reach Policy Agendas

As with the problem stream, only certain solutions make it to agency or legislative decision agendas. Those who examine solutions often test their fiscal, administrative, and political feasibility. Assume that a staff person in a job counseling agency for women advocated not only referring women to jobs, but actually training them. Some staff might be skeptical about the idea's feasibility. They might ask whether the agency, which had emphasized job referrals and job search, could develop training programs in fields such as computer literacy. Could it find facilities to house these services, foundations or government funders to fund them, and the needed staff? Could it place the graduates in actual jobs? Since this program represents a marked departure from current programs, it would likely encounter political opposition from some staff, as well as board members, who would question whether the proposal falls in the agency's mission. Some staff might fear, as well, that the proposal would detract from existing services.

Decisionmakers also judge a solution's likely effectiveness and technical merits. When people propose a solution to remedy rising American health-care costs, such as extensive use of health maintenance organizations, they often encounter skepticism that stems from the sheer number of failed solutions that have been tried in the past three decades to reduce American health-care costs. Advocates can counter such skepticism, of course, by citing evaluative research or by showing how a solution has been successfully used in model programs elsewhere.[29]

People may perceive specific solutions negatively because of prior deliberations. National health insurance provides a good example. When it was considered in the Nixon and Carter administrations, it became polarized between liberals and conservatives. Moreover, many powerful lobbyists, such as the American Medical Association, an association of health insurers, and the American Hospital Association, would deluge legislators with conflicting and often self-serving advice. It was not until the early 1990s, with the election of Senator Harrison Wofford on a plank to obtain national health insurance, that many politicians came to perceive national health insurance in a more positive light.[30]

Advocates of a specific solution must also show that no other solution exists that is preferable, on balance, to their solution. (We use the term "on balance" because most solutions have positive and negative attributes. We do not often seek a perfect solution, but one preferable to others when its positive and negative attributes are compared with competing solutions.) An array of reforms for the health system existed by the early 1990s, most addressing runaway costs. They included proposals to ration health care by limiting coverage of expensive procedures, such as bone marrow transplants. Other persons wanted to decrease malpractice suits against physicians on grounds that, practicing defensively, many physicians engaged in unnecessary surgeries. Still other persons wanted a "single payer" national health program, similar to the Canadian system, so that health insurance costs could be terminated. Advocates of these solutions sought to elevate their remedy from Congress's general agenda to its decision agenda. They hoped other legislators would believe that, on balance, their proposal was more efficient, politically feasible, and viable than competing proposals.

Policy practitioners often introduce solutions in private conversations with other persons, in meetings, or in the mass media. They want to see if they receive sufficiently favorable feedback to justify committing additional time, resources, and energy to the solution.[31]

Implications for Policy Practitioners

Our discussion suggests that policy practitioners must try to place a solution in a favorable light if they want it to make general or decision agendas. They must accomplish this task, moreover, in settings where specific solutions vie with one another for the scarce space on agendas. They should also recognize that they may encounter opposition from persons or groups who do not like their solution and who want to cast it in an unfavorable light.

THE POLITICAL STREAM

Background political developments powerfully shape the reception that specific problems and solutions receive when they are put forth in agency and legislative settings. It is useful to discuss the political streams in agencies and in legislatures separately, because they are quite different from one another.

Public and Nonpublic Agencies

Every agency, public or nonpublic, exists in a political and economic environment that shapes its high-level staff's decisions. Aware that their agencies require resources to survive, advocates of specific issues realize that they must consider funders' perspectives. Governmental or public agencies ultimately receive resources from appropriations of city councils, county boards of supervisors, state or federal legislatures, or some combination of these public authorities. These resources come to the agencies with directions about how they are to be used. Moreover, high-level government agencies develop administrative regulations to guide the implementation of publicly-funded programs. These regulations shape many service-delivery and eligibility procedures.

Not-for-profit agencies have more latitude than public agencies because some of their funds have fewer strings attached, such as funds from their own endowments, clients' payments, and private sources, such as foundations. Even these funds have some strings attached, however. For example, a particular donor may want her funds used in a specific manner, just as foundations usually do not write blank checks. Since at least half of the not-for-profits' budgets comes from public sources, however, part of their work is also strongly influenced by legislatures' dictates and government agencies' administrative regulations.[32]

Even more than not-for-profits, for-profit agencies receive most of their resources from nongovernmental sources, particularly from consumers' payments. While they also assume an important role in not-for-profit agencies, marketing considerations loom large in for-profit agencies, because they need to identify problems and seek solutions that will attract paying clients. Similar to not-for-profit agencies, many for-profit agencies also receive part of their funding from contracts from public authorities.

Executives in not-for-profit and for-profit agencies are influenced, not only by existing funders, but also by perceptions of potential funding sources. Staff in an agency that serves older persons, for example, may be attentive to up-and-coming issues, such as abuse of the elderly, new services for people with Alzheimer's, or projects to link housebound older people to social and medical services. Perceiving likely trends may lead agencies to aim for new resources linked to these emerging issues.

The goals of top agency executives provide a powerful context for agenda-setting because they often favor certain problems or solutions, while discriminating against other ones. Assume, for example, that hospital executives decide that the hospital should vastly increase its services to older persons. Someone who wanted to place services to help abused elderly people on the hospital's decision agenda would find their work far simpler than those who wanted to vastly increase services to children.[33]

Agencies' policies are influenced, as well, by court rulings, such as ones about the confidentiality of client records; commitment procedures; malpractice; and the hiring, firing, and promotion of staff. Court rulings have saturated the human services system in recent decades on myriad matters that are germane to the actions of staff in public, not-for-profit, and for-profit sectors.

Professional trends and developments also shape the activities of social agencies. While these trends and developments appear, at first, to affect direct-service activities rather than policies, they often have policy implications. As interest in multicultural diversity has increased dramatically in the 1980s and 1990s, for example, outreach, service to specific groups, and new patterns of staffing social agencies have developed.[34]

While "politics" customarily refers to electoral and legislative matters, it also refers to maneuvering in agencies between persons, factions, and organizational units, as well as between boards, executives, middle managers, and direct-service staff. Executives in agencies realize that they must listen to and frequently accommodate these various persons, groups, and interests to avoid excessive internal conflict in their agencies. These groups have policy interests and preferences and express them in deliberations within the agency, whether in formal meetings or informal exchanges. To be certain, some people in higher-level groups and groups such as top management, often possess more influence than direct-service staff. However, direct-service workers have unions on their side, and even when their power is not augmented by unions, they can sometimes have an important effect on policy choices within agencies.

Clients and external advocacy groups can also shape policy choices in organizations, though the extent of their influence varies in different agencies and by the specific issue at hand. For example, the National Welfare Rights

Organization pressured many public welfare agencies to process their clients less arbitrarily. The procedures have indeed improved, though court rulings also played a part in this development.[35]

Legislatures and the Public Sector

When we discuss the political stream in the public sector, we must analyze which factors predispose politicians toward specific problems and solutions. Politicians want to be reelected, so they are attentive to public opinion, whether gauged by polls, mail or personal conversations with constituents, or discussions with other legislators about the public's positions. Realizing its importance to most citizens, politicians are acutely aware of the mass media, such as editorials in newspapers and on television, documentaries on current issues, and coverage of daily news events.[36]

Interest groups, such as the American Association of Retired Persons, professional associations, civil rights groups, and unions besiege legislators, often with full-time lobbyists who are particularly knowledgeable about certain issues. Politicians are acutely aware of trends in recent elections that suggest what the electorate favors; if the electorate seem to be moving in a liberal direction, for example, politicians are more likely to favor social reform than if the electorate has recently voted in a relatively conservative fashion. Recent dramatic events, such as a budget crisis, a scandal, or a highly publicized fire in a tenement building, can shape public opinion and the news.

Legislatures have hierarchies of their own. Leaders in both of the major parties have considerable power in shaping party members' positions on many issues. A chain of command exists, as well, in legislatures' committees, where committee chairpersons and "ranking members" (those with the most years of service) possess more power than newer members. The predispositions of these powerful legislators shape, in turn, the problems and solutions that reach legislatures' policy agendas.

We must be careful, of course, in implying or stating that politicians' views are determined by any of these factors. Their views stem not simply from the pressures exerted on them, but also by their estimates of future trends. Politicians may take problems or solutions seriously, even without pressure from interest groups or citizens, if they believe the issue could become an important issue in the future.

Other officials shape policy deliberations in legislative settings, such as civil servants, think tanks, and lobbyists. Civil servants, particularly highly placed ones, outlast particular administrations. Thus, they accrue considerable technical knowledge and are often adept at gauging political trends, directing proposals to legislators, and helping legislators make their proposals more feasible. Think tanks have achieved considerable prominence in the past two decades in Washington, DC, as well as in many states; just as civil servants do, their staff often work with legislators to fashion proposals.[37]

Implications of Political Realities for Practitioners

Policy practitioners need to be aware of the political stream in both agency and legislative settings when they try to place items on general or decision agendas. On the one hand, political realities affect whether issues can or will be placed on policy agendas. In an agency whose funders and executives do not favor a specific problem or solution, for example, policy practitioners may find it impossible to place that problem or solution on the decision agenda, no matter how skillfully they present it in a favorable light. On the other hand, policy practitioners can try to influence the political stream by speaking with powerful people about specific problems and solutions, developing coalitions or groups that agree about certain policy matters, or participating in the campaigns of politicians who are sympathetic with progressive reforms in American society. At a more modest level, persons can sometimes educate others about political realities related to particular problems or solutions. When an agency staff member wants to make a political environment more favorable to a problem or solution, he or she can point to funding trends, court rulings, political trends or professional developments that support a specific change in agency policy. (The policy practitioner does not create these trends or developments, but merely sensitizes other persons to them in hopes of paving the way for a policy change.)

Windows of Opportunity and Policy Entrepreneurs

We have discussed general factors that influence whether specific issues or problems reach general or decision agendas. We now focus on how problems or solutions move from the general to the decision agendas.

Kingdon identifies two factors in this progression. First, a combination of propitious events must create a "window of opportunity" for a problem or a solution to advance from the general agenda to the decision agenda. Second, one or more "policy entrepreneurs" have to advocate the problem or solution during this window of opportunity.[38]

Windows of Opportunity: Precipitating Events

At key points in agency and legislative settings, specific events help a specific problem or solution move down the funnel we depicted earlier. Calling these key times "windows of opportunity," Kingdon suggests that they represent relatively brief moments when "the time is ripe" for specific initiatives. We will examine windows of opportunity first in legislative settings and then in agency settings.

Some events sensitize legislators to a specific problem or solution. Dramatic and publicized stories can make them suddenly aware, such as a homeless person's death from exposure, or a flagrant example of child abuse. A task force may issue a report that alerts people to a problem, such as when a 1993 task force described the amount of elder abuse in California. When the media covers such events extensively, people begin to feel that existing policies and programs are strikingly defective.

Pivotal events in the political stream can stir up support for a specific problem or solution. With Bill Clinton's victory in November 1992 after twelve years of Republican rule, many people became hopeful that issues that had lain dormant would now reach Congressional agendas. People variously hoped that national health-care reforms, parental-leave bills, expanded programs for children, job-training initiatives, pro-choice issues, deficit-reducing strategies, and a host of additional policies would receive attention. With renewed hope that their issues would now reach decision or choice agendas, people invested time and resources in publicizing and championing them.

Of course, Clinton inherited budget deficits. Even when pivotal, political developments occur, certain constraints exist. By limiting resources, the deficit dampened many social-reform ideas.

Regular, predictable windows of opportunity exist in legislative settings. Advocates can seek additional resources for problems or solutions during annual budget preparations. At this time, executives of various agencies submit budget requests and advocates can petition members of the legislature who are on budget or appropriations committees for additional resources.[39] When legislation is "reauthorized"—that is, renewed for another period of time—advocates can sometimes obtain changes in the legislation. Advocates often try to obtain policy changes when a new administration arrives. Other, unpredictable opportunities appear when random political events occur or when crises develop unexpectedly.

Pivotal events in social agencies create opportunities for changing policy, as well. A governor, mayor, or large foundation may announce new programs to deal with a problem related to an agency's mission. Dramatic events may sensitize an agency's executive director or board members to a problem that the agency does not currently address. An affluent person may bequeath unexpected funds to an agency, enabling it to start a new program. By contrast, fiscal crises sometimes force an agency to reconsider its priorities or search frantically for resources from new funding sources. Perhaps an accrediting agency is about to make a visit, causing the agency to make some changes so as to obtain a favorable report.

New tides in an agency's politics also creates opportunity. Shifts in agencies' personnel often create strategic opportunities, most dramatically when a new executive director arrives. While executives are not omnipotent, they occupy critical positions, similar to governors and presidents, that allow them to chart new directions for agencies. Advocates for specific problems or solutions can often find an attentive audience in the new director.[40] Changes in the boards of not-for profit agencies, such as the accession of a new president, can serve as the catalyst for reexamining agency priorities.

Policy Entrepreneurs

Policy entrepreneurs are those who capitalize on or create windows of opportunity. Their strategy involves (1) preparing for an opportunity by doing primary work on a proposal, (2) recognizing that a window of opportunity augurs well for a specific problem or solution, and (3) seizing the moment by seeking support for a measure.[41] In government settings, the policy entrepreneur is often an enterprising legislator with persistence, creativity, respectability, and good timing. At strategic moments, such legislators may intercede with powerful committee chairpersons, draft and introduce legislation before the window of opportunity closes, or use the mass media to dramatize and to build support for their legislative initiative.

They sometimes try to draw imaginative connections between the problem, solution, and political streams to increase the chances that their initiative will be successful.[42] Take the example of the Clinton administration's 1993 national-health reforms. As a policy entrepreneur, Clinton seized on health-care reform by linking the issue to other issues. He focused on the United States' growing inability to compete in world markets by arguing that corporations' health-care costs make their products noncompetitive with Japanese and European corporations who do not shoulder health-care costs. He argued that many American workers cannot be productive if they fail to receive quality health services. He proposed specific solutions to this lack of access to health care, including "managed competition" and "budget limits on American health care." Finally, he capitalized on the wave of support for health-care reform from corporations, uninsured persons, and AIDS patients' advocates.[43] As this example suggests, he linked the problem stream, the solution stream, *and* the political stream.

Coupling the three streams can occur in agency settings, as well. Perhaps someone in an agency has discussed "decentralizing services" (a solution) while someone else has noted the relative lack of services to the Latino population (a problem). A policy entrepreneur in the agency might suggest writing a grant proposal to develop outreach stations for the Latino population, a proposal that would couple the problem with the solution. We have noted how executive directors are in an ideal position to determine when an opportunity exists and to initiate proposals, but staff and board members can also generate ideas when events are favorable.

Policy entrepreneurs must be skillful bargainers and negotiators so that proposals are acceptable to a range of persons. Some advocates wanted Clinton to propose a nationalized health-care program like Canada's, where the government is the sole payer and private insurance companies hardly exist. However, Clinton feared he would face the wrath of the insurance companies that possess enormous power on Capitol Hill. Thus, he sought reforms that would include insurance companies but would restrict their actions, such as denying coverage to persons with preexisting health conditions. Although many liberals would have preferred that he support nationalized health care, Clinton refrained from this approach to garner the support of a broad-based coalition in Congress.[44]

As stated earlier, placement of an issue on a policy agenda does not guarantee its enactment. In late 1993, it was unclear whether Clinton would prevail. Moreover, successful placement does not mean that a proposal is above reproach. For example, many liberals questioned facets of Clinton's health-care proposal.

The Closing of Windows

Alas, windows of opportunity usually close, and often within a relatively brief period. Participants change, people think that a problem has been adequately addressed by some other measure, and new issues supplant older ones. The momentum of policy change can also be lost as persons haggle over the details of a suggested reform, as opposition to the reform emerges, or as budget exigencies prevent enactment of a specific reform.

CAN DIRECT-SERVICE STAFF HELP BUILD AGENDAS?

Our discussion suggests that policy practitioners within agency and legislative settings can strategize within the problem, solution, and political streams; identify windows of opportunity; and act as policy entrepreneurs.

Is agenda-building restricted to legislators and high-level agency staff, such as executive directors? To be certain, these persons are best situated to assume pivotal roles in building agendas, but direct-service staff can participate in agenda-building in both agency and legislative settings with the following activities.

Within the problem stream, staff can do the following:

- Discuss and publicize unmet needs in the human services system
- Obtain information to gauge the seriousness of specific problems
- Frame specific issues to make them appeal to executives or legislators
- Establish a coalition or action group to publicize a specific problem, such as elder abuse, whether in an agency or in the community
- Seek high-level support to establish a task force to study the issue

Within the solution stream, staff can do the following:

- Discuss or publicize a promising approach to a social problem
- Document how this approach or solution has been used successfully elsewhere
- Find information about the solution's feasibility, such as information about its cost and administrative requirements

- Establish an action group to obtain support for a specific solution, whether in an agency or in the community
- Seek high-level support to establish a task force to study the solution

Within the political stream, staff can do the following:

- Publicize specific problems or solutions in the mass media
- Work on or support the campaigns of candidates who advocate specific social reforms
- Lobby legislators or agency officials to sensitize them to specific problems or solutions

To identify windows of opportunity, staff can identify strategic points in agencies or legislatures when conditions would favor advancing specific initiatives. Finally, staff can work as policy entrepreneurs or in liaison with them by recognizing opportune moments for specific policy initiatives.

ADVOCACY FOR POWERLESS POPULATIONS AND UNPOPULAR ISSUES

Our discussion about agenda-building, to this point, has emphasized how agenda processes work and how a pragmatic policy practitioner can use these processes to reach policy goals. When we discuss how agenda processes actually work, however, we risk ignoring the important fact that they are often skewed against unpopular issues and powerless groups. Take the case of the Children's Defense Fund, established in 1973, which sought for almost 20 years to convince Congress to place day-care on its agenda, only to finally succeed in 1989. Advocates of massive programs for homeless persons have not yet succeeded, despite nearly a decade of lobbying and activism. Others unsuccessfully sought national health insurance since the 1930s, only to have a resurgence of hope in 1993. Those who want to change the American federal tax structure so as to truly reduce economic inequality have been relatively unsuccessful for decades.

Were we to promote only those issues that are likely to achieve prominence on agendas, we would ignore the need to support some issues even when we realize that short-term successes are unlikely. Recall our discussion in Chapter Two of ethical principles of social justice and fairness that often stimulate policy practitioners to seek social reform to address inequalities experienced by groups such as African Americans, Latinos, Native Americans, women, gays and lesbians, children, and persons with stigmatized conditions, even when short-term prospects are bleak.

Groups that plug away for unpopular issues and populations may be laying groundwork for subsequent policy changes. In the case of day-care and the Children's Defense Fund, advocates' diligent and sustained lobbying, as well as their assistance to grass-roots reform groups throughout the United

States, doubtless educated many politicians about the specific problems and needs of children. When pressure from feminist groups and corporations that hired large numbers of women finally placed day-care on Congress's decision agenda in the 1980s, the Children's Defense Fund spearheaded a coalition to seek specific legislation. Had they not promoted the issue in the preceding two decades, however, they may not have been successful in the 1980s. Or the legislation, which was hardly adequate in its funding and scope, might have been even more limited than the final version.

Militant groups, such as Act-Up, whose members engage in nonviolent protests and disrupt public functions to seek better care for people with AIDS, sometimes educate the public to desperate, unmet needs even if they do not use the tactics of persons inside the legislative process. Abolitionists in the 1850s, suffragettes in the early part of this century, and civil-rights advocates in the 1950s and 1960s used militant strategies to force neglected issues onto public officials' agendas. They persisted even in the face of criticism that their tactics were unethical or unwarranted. These kinds of groups sometimes "soften up" the electorate and decisionmakers so that they contemplate ideas they had not seriously considered before.[45]

DEVELOPING LINKS WITH ADVOCACY GROUPS

Policy practitioners who wish to build agendas in the broader community, but do not know how to get started, should consider connecting with an established advocacy group. (We discuss in Chapter Eleven how to locate and work with advocacy groups.) Effective advocacy groups try to shape public officials' agendas by pressuring them to consider solutions or problems, presenting research that underlines the importance of addressing specific, social needs, and publicizing stories in the mass media that dramatize certain issues. Would-be practitioners can join a local group, or a local chapter of a national group, meet the director of the advocacy group, subscribe to its newsletters and other materials, volunteer with its outreach and education projects, help its staff conduct research, and help the group lobby public officials. Those who want to be involved can work with local chapters, as well as the state chapter, of the National Association of Social Workers (NASW), whose leaders and lobbyists pressure legislators. Both advocacy groups and the NASW not only generate ideas for the general agenda, such as specific pieces of legislation, but place pressure on politicians to move these ideas toward choice or decision agendas. They often try to convince the chairpersons of pivotal legislative committees, for example, to hold hearings and seriously discuss proposals, rather than letting them slip into oblivion.

Policy practitioners can also campaign for those politicians who they believe would put certain issues on policy agendas. As we discuss in Chapter Eleven, for example, PACE (the political action arm of NASW) supports politicians who advocate certain policy reforms.

SUMMARY

Agenda-building processes develop and promote issues to help them reach agencies' and legislatures' policy deliberations. Building agendas is crucial, because problems and solutions that do not reach policy deliberations will not likely receive high-level and favorable attention. Practitioners need the following knowledge to build agendas:

- The importance of agenda-building processes to policy practice
- The three "streams" in agenda-building
- How social problems and solutions reach agendas
- How political processes shape agendas
- How windows of opportunity and policy entrepreneurs shape agendas
- How direct-service staff can build agendas
- The challenges policy advocates face in shaping agendas

Agenda-building requires each of the four policy skills that we identified in Chapter Three. Policy practitioners use political skills to analyze and engage in the political stream. They use analytic skills to develop and use data in the problem and solution streams. They use interactional skills to help problems and solutions reach policy deliberations in agency and legislative settings, persuade people to take specific problems and solutions seriously, participate in committees and task forces, and organize coalitions. They use value-clarifying skills to decide whether to invest energy in promoting an issue in the first place. We have noted that policy advocates often try to elevate issues that affect powerless or oppressed populations, even if they have a poorer prognosis than other issues.

As we have discussed, placing issues or proposals on decision agendas does not ensure their enactment or implementation. Agenda-building is merely a preliminary phase in promoting policy. We will explore subsequent phases in the succeeding chapters of this book.

Suggested Readings

Frank Baumgartner and Bryan Jones, *Agendas and Instability in American Politics* (Chicago: University of Chicago Press, 1993).
Robert Eyestone, *From Social Issues to Public Policy* (New York: Wiley, 1978).
Stephen Hilgartner and Charles Bosk, "The Rise and Fall of Social Problems," *American Journal of Sociology* 94: 53–78.
John Kingdon, *Agendas, Alternatives, and Public Policies* (Boston: Little, Brown, 1984).
Hedrick Smith, *The Power Game: How Washington Really Works* (New York: Ballantine Books, 1988), pp. 331–387.

Notes

1. Kingdon argues that an issue is on the agenda when "governmental officials, and people outside of government closely associated with those officials, are paying

serious attention" to it. See John Kingdon, *Agendas, Alternatives, and Public Policies* (Boston: Little, Brown, 1984), p. 3.
2. Robert Eyestone, *From Social Issues to Public Policy* (New York: Wiley, 1978), pp. 20–21; and Frank Baumgartner and Bryan Jones, *Agendas and Instability in American Politics* (Chicago: University of Chicago Press, 1993), pp. 250–251.
3. Ibid.
4. Hedrick Smith, *The Power Game: How Washington Works* (New York: Ballantine Books, 1988), pp. 331–444.
5. Kingdon, *Agendas, Alternatives, and Public Policies*.
6. Ibid., pp. 82–83.
7. Ibid., pp. 83–88.
8. Ibid.
9. Vincent Burke, *Nixon's Good Deed: Welfare Reform* (New York: Columbia University Press, 1974).
10. Michael Cohen, James March, and Johan Olsen, "A Garbage Can Model of Organizational Choice," *Administrative Science Quarterly* 17 (March 1972): 1–25.
11. We use the term *general agendas* here rather than Kingdon's term, *governmental agendas*, because we discuss agenda-setting process in both governmental and agency settings. Kingdon, *Agendas, Alternatives, and Public Policies*, p. 4.
12. Ibid., pp. 4, 150, 174–175.
13. Ibid., pp. 92–94.
14. Ibid., pp. 95–121.
15. Eyestone, *From Social Issues to Public Policy* (New York: Wiley, 1978), pp. 135–152.
16. Kingdon, *Agendas, Alternatives, and Public Policies*, p. 115.
17. Edwin Chen, "Clinton Aides Detail Health Plan," *New York Times* (January 9, 1993), p. 15.
18. Kingdon, *Agendas, Alternatives, and Public Policies*, pp. 95–108.
19. Ibid., pp. 95–99.
20. Ibid., pp. 103–105.
21. The work of advocates to place Alzheimer's disease on national policy agendas illustrates how advocates seek to dramatize the severity or pervasiveness of a social problem—even when precise data is lacking. See Julie Kosterlitz, "Anguish and Opportunity: Alzheimer's Disease," *National Journal* 23 (March 9, 1991): 2728–2732.
22. See Reich's use of the term *investment* rather than *spending* in Robert Reich, *The Work of Nations: Preparing Ourselves for 21st-Century Capitalism* (New York: Knopf, 1991), pp. 252–261.
23. Bruce Jansson, *The Reluctant Welfare State*, 2nd ed. (Pacific Grove, CA: Brooks/Cole, 1993), p. 293.
24. Kingdon, *Agendas, Alternatives, and Public Policies*, pp. 110–115.
25. The political problem of securing funds for prevention is illustrated by the AIDS epidemic; see Julie Kosterlitz, "AIDS Wars," *National Journal* 24 (July 25, 1992): 1727–1732.
26. As one example, conservatives were able to delay enactment of federal legislation to subsidize battered-women's shelters on the grounds that social workers had exaggerated the severity of the problem. See Liane Davis and Jan Hagan, "Services for Battered Women: The Public Policy Response," *Social Service Review* 62 (December 1988): 649–667; and *Congressional Quarterly Almanac* 35 (Washington, DC: Congressional Quarterly, 1979): 508–509.

27. For uses of the media to place issues on an agenda, see Smith, *The Power Game*, pp. 331–387; and Baumgartner and Jones, *Agendas and Instability in American Politics*, 103–125.
28. Kingdon, *Agendas, Alternatives, and Public Policies*, pp. 122–151.
29. Ibid., pp. 138–139.
30. Chen, "Clinton Aides Detail Health Plan," p. 15.
31. Smith discusses "trial balloons" in *The Power Game*, pp. 21–41.
32. Lester Salamon and Alan Abramson, *The Nonprofit Sector and the New Federal Budget* (Washington, DC: Urban Institute Press, 1986).
33. Richard Emerson, "Power-Dependence Relations," *American Sociological Review* 27 (February 1962): 31–40.
34. See, for example, Wynetta Devore and Elfrieda Schlesinger, *Ethnic-Sensitive Social Work* (St. Louis: C. V. Mosby, 1981); and Donna Ferullo, *Cultural Diversity in Social Work Practice: A Selective Bibliography* (Boston: Social Work Library at Boston College, 1991).
35. Guida West, *The National Welfare Rights Movement: The Social Protest of Poor Women* (New York: Praeger, 1981).
36. R. Douglas Brown, *The Logic of Congressional Action* (New Haven, CT: Yale University Press, 1990), pp. 119–146.
37. See, for example, James Smith, *Brookings at Seventy-Five* (Washington, DC: Brookings Institution, 1991).
38. Kingdon, *Agendas, Alternatives, and Public Policies*, pp. 174–193.
39. Ibid., pp. 110–115.
40. Ibid., pp. 160–162.
41. Ibid., pp. 188–193.
42. Ibid., pp. 181–188.
43. Robert Pear, "Clinton Health-Care Planners Are Facing Delicate Decisions," *New York Times* (March 23, 1993), pp. 1, 9.
44. Clinton decided not to use the single-payer, Canadian system not only because health-provider groups opposed it, but because the federal government would have been required to fund the entire package of benefits just as Clinton was trying to reduce the federal deficit. Ibid., pp. 1, 9.
45. Kingdon, *Agendas, Alternatives, and Public Policies*, pp. 134–138.

Chapter Six
Defining Problems

American society suffers from innumerable social problems, such as homelessness, family abuse, substance abuse, mental illness, and physical illness. These problems have defied resolution, despite legions of reformers' determined efforts. Moreover, numerous problems beset the human services system, which sometimes impede the implementation of social policies.

Policy practitioners must define, conceptualize, and measure social problems as part of their policy-changing work, or respond to the definitions, conceptualizations, and measurements that others have made. This problem-defining work has critical implications for the kinds of policies that are proposed and enacted in agency, community, and legislative arenas.

We provide several perspectives on social problems in this chapter, because, as complex phenomena, social problems can be viewed in different ways. We discuss tools used widely in analyzing social problems, including such quantitative research methods as needs assessment, census data, and correlational research. Other social scientists would also like to analyze social problems with qualitative techniques, such as intensive case studies that help explore the causes and nature of social problems.

A significant group of social scientists believe, however, that analytic approaches to social problems must be used with caution. They contend that our personal values and experiences and contemporary culture shape our perceptions and definitions of social problems to a great degree.

When defining problems, then, policy practitioners need to be familiar with analytic tools and qualitative research. They also need to consider how nonrational factors, such as culture and values, affect our definitions of social problems.

USING POLICY ANALYSIS

Considerable controversy exists about social problems. Can we scientifically define and measure them and determine their causes, or do nonrational factors, such as culture and politics, distort our perceptions so that we cannot be objective? This tension between analytic (or scientific) and nonrational perspectives resonates throughout this chapter, as we discuss both approaches. (We discuss in Chapters Ten through Twelve how political factors sometimes override rational considerations.)

We will begin our discussion with the "analytic approach." It is small wonder that many people want to improve the quality of policy choices, because policies intending to improve welfare, crime, substance abuse, public housing, urban development, and economic development have largely failed. Many factors conspire to make existing policies ineffective. Persons, groups, and institutions with power often select policies out of self-interest to increase their revenue, their prestige, and their power, and give them monopolies over specific services or tasks, sometimes with scant regard to citizens who need assistance. Tradition often shapes policies, even when existing policies are obviously outmoded and ineffective. Professional wisdom, which often fosters effective services, can sometimes lead practitioners to support dysfunctional policies, such as many surgeons' excessive reliance on radical mastectomies, hysterectomies, and heart bypass operations. Nor are policymakers immune to societal prejudices and misconceptions, as well as fads and presumed panaceas.

Why not, some theorists wonder, subject policy choices to careful deliberations to minimize the effects of power, tradition, fuzzy intentions, and intuition? Why not establish decisionmaking rules in advance so that only policy options that obtain positive evaluations are chosen? Why not make extensive use of research so that objective information guides policy choices?[1] As the definition of *analysis* in *Webster's New World Dictionary* suggests, the analytic approach emphasizes "breaking up of a whole into its parts to find out their nature."[2] Most analytic frameworks suggest a careful, step-by-step process of defining policy problems, collecting information, and reaching policy solutions after an extended and deliberative process.[3] In such frameworks, there are three steps. In Step 1, people analyze the problem at hand by asking the following questions:

- How do we define the problem so as to distinguish it from other, related problems?
- Can we establish a typology that defines subvarieties of the problem?
- How do we measure the problem's prevalence?
- How do we locate persons or institutions with the specific problem, or who might develop it?
- How do we assess the relative importance of the problem to society, to some group in the population, or to specific institutions?
- What causes the problem?

In Step 2, analysts compare possible remedies to the problem. They ask questions such as the following:

- What policy remedy will most effectively prevent or redress the problem?
- What array of policy options should be considered?
- What criteria and measures should be used to compare the options?
- Which policy option is preferable?

In Step 3, analysts disseminate technical data and policy recommendations to decisionmakers, hoping they will agree about the proposed remedy.

CLASSIFYING PROBLEMS ANALYTICALLY

Policy analysts try to bring rationality to our discussion of policy problems. They want to define problems with considerable precision, develop typologies to identify subvarieties, measure the prevalence of specific problems, assess the importance of problems to distinguish major ones from trivial ones, and examine the causes of problems.

Such an approach immediately raises issues of definitions and classifications. Analysts seek more specific terms to supplement broad ones, such as mental illness, alcoholism, and substance abuse, because such large problems usually embrace a variety of subproblems that differ significantly from one another.

To illustrate our discussion, we will examine Mark Moore's classification of heroin users (see Figure 6.1). First, he identifies heroin users at various *stages of development,* as seen by analyzing the model from the left (a susceptible but nonaddicted population) to the center (unsupervised users) to the right (users receiving services or in jail). Moreover, he analyzes patterns of movement between these stages (see the arrows in the model).

Moore distinguishes between unsupervised users in the left-center part of the model with descriptions such as "joy popper," "drug dabbler," "addict," "hustler," "drug-dependent," "conformist," "maturing-out user," and "burned-out user." To develop this typology, he used distinguishing characteristics to sort specific users into categories. Moore's distinguishing characteristics include: manifestations, phase of problem development, causation, and threshold.

Manifestations are outward behaviors that differentiate people. Some substance abusers, for example, do not appear mentally impaired or mentally disoriented, whereas addiction has damaged other people's mental functioning. Some substance abusers are frequently absent from work or perform their work erratically. Some are frequently involved in auto accidents or are arrested for driving-related infractions.

When classifying the *phase of problem development*, the analyst distinguishes between people at risk but without a problem, people in the early stages of a problem, people with serious problems, and people in the latter phases of a problem. In Moore's scheme, descriptions such as "susceptible population," "joy popper," "addict," "maturing-out user," and "burned-out user" suggest various phases in the development of drug use.

When examining a problem's *cause*, the analyst identifies patterns in its origin. In Moore's scheme, for example, "conformist" suggests that some persons take drugs because of susceptibility to peer pressure, whereas "drug-dependent" suggests that psychological or physiological factors contribute to usage.

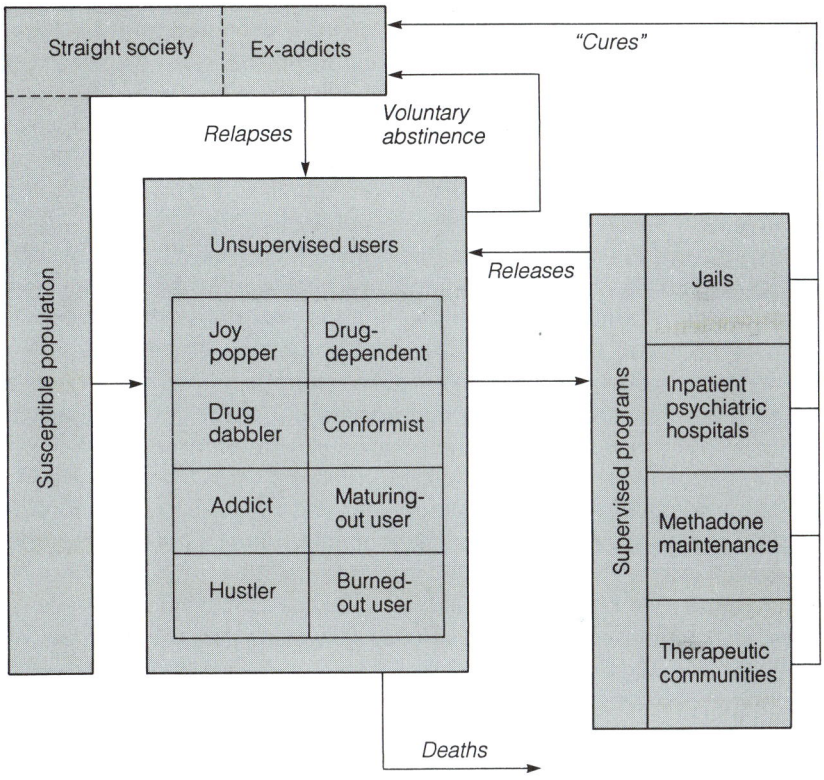

FIGURE 6.1
A dynamic model of heroin users
SOURCE: © 1976 by the Regents of the University of California. Reprinted from *Policy Analysis* (vol. 2, no. 3, p. 256) by permission.

Analysts must also wrestle with issues of *threshold* when defining problems. How much heroin is required, for example, to make one an "unsupervised user"? If people imbibe heroin several times a year at social events, can they still be classified as "joy poppers" or "drug dabblers"? In the case of alcoholism, at what threshold of consumption do we call people "social drinkers" or "alcoholics"? What level of anxiety or depression must be reached to call people "anxious" or "depressive"? Of course, these judgments are often influenced by cultural factors. Cocaine use, for example, was relatively widespread in all American social classes in the early part of the twentieth century. Thus, people had a far looser definition of addiction than do many contemporary Americans, who sometimes equate addiction even with occasional drug use.

What standard should be used in deciding the threshold? Using a *relative standard*, analysts compare the actions of one group with those of the rest of the population. If the national norm for drinking were two drinks a day, by a relative standard an alcoholic might be someone who consumed five or more drinks a day. Of course, a relative standard suggests a flexible or moving threshold; as the average usage of alcohol rises and falls in the population, for example, so does the threshold that defines alcoholism. Alternatively, we can use an *absolute standard* in which we base a threshold on expert opinion. Perhaps physicians contend that persons who imbibe more than two drinks a day or who use alcohol in the morning are alcoholic, because this behavior suggests compulsive patterns of use that can cause physical damage. Unlike relative standards, such absolute standards do not rise and fall with patterns of popular usage; if *everyone* in the United States consumed more than two drinks a day, for example, the entire population would be alcoholic.

By using concepts such as stages of development, manifestations, causation, thresholds, relative standards, and absolute standards, policy analysts develop *typologies*. Difficult as typologies such as Moore's are to develop, they increase our precision when discussing social problems. If we make no effort to develop classification schemes, we encounter serious problems. First, we cannot develop policies and programs that specifically address the idiosyncratic needs of certain groups.[4] Moore's scheme suggests, for example, that we should develop different programs for at-risk populations than for current addicts. Perhaps we also need different programs, depending on the reason for addiction, such as conformity or physiological or psychological needs. Second, if we have no classification system, it is difficult to evaluate how effective specific strategies are. As we couple classification systems with service strategies, we can evaluate whether certain kinds of counseling or other remedies are most effective with specific types of drug users. Third, a classification system allows us to establish priorities. If research suggests that certain people are most likely to become long-term users, for example, federal or state authorities might give priority to programs that target those people with prevention, counseling, or other services.

Classification helps us understand not only heroin use, but also other social problems, such as mental illness, poverty, child abuse, and marital discord. Many analysts and professionals have developed typologies of mental illness, for example, such as the *DSM-III* manual of the American Psychiatric Association.[5] When testifying before Congress in 1988 about welfare reform, some experts distinguished between impoverished persons, such as single, teenage mothers; recently divorced older women; and victims of structural unemployment, whose skills or work experience is rendered obsolete by changes in the global economy.[6] Because research suggested that single, teenage mothers were most likely to be on welfare rolls for ten or more years, the welfare reform legislation of 1988 required local authorities to give priority to this group in its training, counseling, and educational programs.

Analysts actually encounter formidable technical obstacles when trying to construct classification systems such as Moore's. Critics may ask, for example, whether his subtypes of heroin users are mutually exclusive; can "addicts" be neatly distinguished, for example, from "drug-dependent persons" and "conformists"? Classification systems sometimes create categories that lead policymakers and direct-service staff to stereotype people.[7] Thus, people who appear to belong to specific groups may be erroneously categorized or labeled. Some

African-American psychiatrists allege, for example, that mental health workers wrongly classify many African Americans as schizophrenic due to racism and a propensity to mistake some behaviors that derive from their social class or from African-American culture as pathology.[8]

Persons who construct classification systems often encounter a dilemma regarding the breadth of their categories. If relatively few categories are used, such as dividing the heroin population into preaddicts, addicts, and recovered addicts, it is difficult to develop specialized programs. If many categories are developed, the analyst risks making artificial distinctions between persons who, in fact, share many commonalities.[9] Moreover, categories can overlap.

It would make our work much simpler, of course, if we overlooked these conceptual problems. However, such oversimplification is one reason why we fail to remedy important social problems. We construct single solutions to the problems of welfare, homelessness, or substance abuse, rather than seeing the individual needs and dynamics behind these broad categories. When conservatives state, for example, that AFDC women are lazy and have children to obtain welfare payments, they fall prey to simplified, incorrect assumptions. Dependency in the AFDC population is caused by inadequate wages and jobs for single heads of households, inadequate child-care, job discrimination against women, and many other factors. Imperfect as it may be, Moore's scheme represents one attempt to examine many types of heroin users and suggests that heroin users need many kinds of services.

MEASURING THE PREVALENCE OF PROBLEMS

Assume that we have defined a social problem (such as homelessness) or a subvariety of it (such as homeless children). Policy practitioners often have to demonstrate that specific problems are sufficiently important to merit the attention of agency staff, funders, government officials, and legislators. Moreover, they have to discuss the nature and causes of specific problems so that people believe that interventions can effectively address them. Like the fabled blind man who gradually develops a composite concept of an elephant by examining different parts of the animal, practitioners can use a variety of technical approaches when measuring the prevalence of social problems.

Legislators, funders, and executives are more likely to invest scarce resources in programs that they believe address widespread problems. Rates, prevalence, and incidence are commonly used to measure the relative magnitude of social problems.[10] *Rates,* for example, measure the ratio of persons, such as white males between ages 18 and 25 who are arrested for drunk driving in a specific year, to a larger reference group, such as the total number of white males in this age bracket in the population that *year.* (Rates are expressed as percentages.) *Incidence* measures the ratio of *new* cases, such as comparing the number of new arrestees in 1990 among white males, aged 18 to 25, to a larger reference group, such as the total number of white males in the population that year in that age bracket. (Incidence is expressed as a percentage.) *Prevalence* measures the ratio of persons who *currently* experience a social problem to the total population. (Prevalence is expressed as a percentage.) Thus, a policy analyst might want to compare the number of persons currently under prosecution for drunk driving to the total number of drivers on a specific day. Each measure provides a somewhat different estimate of the problem's seriousness. These kinds of data are often available from city, county, state, or federal government agencies or from research literature in the social and health sciences.

When data are not available from government agencies or research literature, policy practitioners measure social problems in other ways. Jonathan Bradshaw contrasts measures of felt need, expressed need, expert need, and comparative need.[11] *Felt need* measures how much persons *believe* they experience a problem. An agency might interview a sample of working mothers with preschool children, for example, to assess the extent to which they believe they cannot afford day-care or whether they have so-called latchkey children. Of course, persons sometimes exaggerate their actual needs or, in the case of stigmatized conditions such as substance abuse, underreport them.

Expressed need measures the degree to which persons actually *seek* specific services. A policy practitioner might examine the length of waiting lists at drug-treatment centers, for example, or the number of calls that a hot line receives about substance abuse. Although clients' service-related behaviors are useful, they may not accurately reflect people's actual needs. Some persons do not seek existing services, for example, because they believe they cannot afford them, do not like agencies, are unaware of existing services, think they will receive ineffective services, fear they will be prosecuted, or fear they will be subjected to punitive services because of their stigmatized condition.

Policy practitioners sometimes use the *expert-need* approach by consulting experts, such as social scientists, social work practitioners, local executives, or government officials, to obtain their estimates of specific problems' severity. Experts can draw convincing evidence from current research, such as the extent of alcoholism among women. Of course, experts' biases or values can importantly influence their positions and credibility; someone who defines alcoholism as consuming many drinks each day will provide a lower estimate of the problem's seriousness than someone who uses a more stringent standard, such as defining alcoholism as consuming only several drinks a day.

A *comparative-need* approach measures unmet needs by comparing the distribution of services in different communities. Assume, for example, that certain neighborhoods possess relatively many drug-treatment programs, while others, with similar demographic characteristics, have relatively few. We can infer that more unmet need for drug-treatment services exists in the neighborhoods with fewer treatment programs. One should interpret comparative-need measures with caution because they rely on inference rather than measuring needs directly. For example, a neighborhood with relatively few drug-treatment programs might appear to have a shortage of services because it is compared with neighborhoods that have too many services.

Using several or all of these approaches helps us gauge the importance of specific social problems. If we were trying to promote drug-treatment programs in a specific neighborhood, for example, we might look into the length of existing programs' waiting lists (expressed need), ask high school students their perceptions of the seriousness of adolescent substance abuse (felt need), provide data that similar neighborhoods have more programs (comparative need), and obtain information from selected experts (expert need).

Measurements of social problems become more dramatic when they include trend data suggesting that a specific problem is becoming more serious. Such data can come from felt-need, expressed-need, comparative-need, or expert-need sources.[12] Someone could show that a community's substance-abuse problems have dramatically increased over the past decades by noting rising deaths from overdoses and longer waiting lists for drug-treatment programs.

LOCATING PROBLEMS WITHIN SOCIETY

It does us little good to determine that a problem is relatively widespread if we cannot locate and reach its victims or, in the case of preventive programs, its potential victims. We can use social science tools to locate people with a certain problem. Census data, gathered in a major national survey every ten years, do not collect data about problems, such as substance abuse or mental illness, instead stating demographic, economic, and housing data in aggregate terms for specific geographic regions.[13] Its data are nonetheless important to social workers, because social scientists have linked demographic or economic factors with social problems. Poor persons are more likely than affluent persons, for example, to experience specific medical problems, to be unemployed, to have poor housing, and to be pressured by drug dealers to use substances such as heroin. Members of certain ethnic groups are more likely than others to have some medical conditions, such as sickle-cell anemia and Tay-Sachs disease. By using economic, housing, demographic, and ethnic data, policy analysts can *infer* high rates of certain social problems in specific neighborhoods and areas within them.

Policy analysts need not confine themselves to census material. Local public health offices, various state agencies, municipal and county authorities, and some federal agencies, such as the National Institute of Mental Health, collect or compile various kinds of population-based data.[14]

Census and other public data can also shape marketing, outreach, and advertising strategies. An agency could publicize its services in certain neighborhoods with a high concentration of specific groups. For example, the agency could market its services to areas with working women (day-care), adolescents (substance abuse), or elderly persons (home health-care services).[15] Policy analysts can even inspect neighborhoods to decide where persons with specific kinds of problems reside. As a tenant organizer, for example, I discovered that I could easily locate substandard housing by observing the window frames in specific neighborhoods; flaking paint and the absence of putty often predicted the condition of the rental unit.

DISTINGUISHING IMPORTANT PROBLEMS FROM TRIVIAL ONES

Because finite resources exist for human services, policy analysts often have to decide which of them should receive priority. Data about a problem's prevalence are useful, but they can be misleading, because some widespread problems are relatively trivial. When an oral surgeon estimates that 25% of the population have defects in their teeth or jaws, a critic might respond that many of these "defects" are merely cosmetic and less important than social problems such as child abuse. Similarly, some experts have argued that marijuana use, while widespread, is relatively trivial compared to heroin, cocaine, or even cigarette use.[16]

How do we determine which problems deserve priority? Analysts often try to examine the impact of problems on their victims, their families and friends, and society. Considerable research suggests that alcoholism is quite serious, because it causes health problems, absenteeism, and loss of employment. These direct effects are supplemented by a tragic toll on families, including abusive behaviors and divorce. By providing a role model of excessive drinking to their children, alcoholic parents also increase the likelihood that their children will become alcoholics as adults. Numerous researchers have probed the economic effects of alcoholism on society, including the taxes lost when alcoholics are unable to work; the decreased productivity in corporations; the considerable medical costs that society pays to help alcoholics detoxify and to treat alcohol-related medical conditions, such as liver failure; and the economic and human costs of accidents caused by drunk drivers.[17]

After documenting a specific social problem's costs to victims, families, and society, policy analysts provide evidence that specific programs can reduce these costs. In some studies of the effectiveness of programs that treat alcoholism, for example, policy analysts contend that investing resources in preventive or ameliorative programs will save society some of alcoholism's current costs. Such programs will decrease destructive behaviors, such as absenteeism and drunk driving; decrease alcohol-related illnesses, such as hepatitis; decrease wife battering and child abuse; and increase the tax revenues that society receives as absenteeism and disability rates decrease.[18] Every dollar spent on a social program with a high benefit-cost ratio, such as alcohol-treatment centers, reduces the cost of specific social problems to society and increases society's tax revenues.

ANALYZING THE CAUSES OF SOCIAL PROBLEMS

When we have identified a social problem (or a subvariety of it), we often want to examine its causes. Why do people develop a problem such as heroin use or homelessness? Can we identify factors that caused the problem? Having discovered the cause, can we evolve primary, secondary, and tertiary preventive strategies for any of its potential or actual victims?

We should note at the outset that people develop many interventions or remedies in the health and human services without significantly understanding the causes of specific problems. Health-care providers or social-service providers may try a remedy only to find that it seems to be effective for unknown reasons. Research may disclose that those who follow certain practices do not (for unknown reasons) contract a specific disease or problem. For instance, research has found that taking aspirin every other day for many years makes people less likely to contract heart disease and colon cancer, although researchers do not know why this is true.

Be this as it may, policy analysts understandably want to use both quantitative and qualitative research to discern the causes of specific problems so that they can develop appropriate interventions. Two approaches are common. First, policy analysts compare persons with a social problem with persons who have none, and infer from their differences why certain persons develop the problem. Second, policy analysts can follow certain persons through time to try to find factors that lead them to develop a problem. It is far more difficult to conduct this second kind of research, because it extends over years, requires gathering data at many intervals, and depends on a significant number of subjects' agreeing to participate in the research over an extended period.

In either kind of research, policy analysts develop frameworks at the outset to guide their inquiry. Of course, they sometimes discover that their theoretical frameworks were partly or wholly erroneous and that they must examine other factors.

To understand how analysts approach their work, we will examine David Ellwood's recent work with poverty in the American family.[19] He did some conceptual work before he began his research. Ellwood decided to focus on families with children because he was particularly interested in the effects poverty has on children. He used the government's definition of poverty, which is computed by multiplying by 3 the funds needed to maintain a "minimally adequate diet." He divided families into three categories, because considerable literature and common sense suggested that their poverty could stem from somewhat different causes. Ellwood distinguishes between two-parent and single-parent families. Moreover, he examines inner-city families of *both* these types to find out whether they face particularly high poverty rates. This approach allowed him to identify distinctive patterns in each of the three groups. (We only discuss his findings about two-parent families.)

When studying two-parent families, Ellwood found that, not counting government benefits, 6% of the families with a full-time worker were poor; 61% of the families with partially employed or unemployed parents were poor; and 67% of families that lacked a fully employed wage earner *and* had at least one ill, disabled, or retired parent were poor. When calculating the percentage of poor two-parent families who fell into different categories, Ellwood found that 44% of the poor two-parent families had a full-time worker—a finding that suggested that low wages were a major cause of poverty in these families. Unemployment and partial employment were the second largest cause

Causes

- Low wages
- Unemployment and underemployment
- Disability of one or both parents
- Retirement of one or both parents

→ Family poverty ←

Possible Solutions

- Earned income tax credit and increases in minimum wage
- Access to health benefits
- Increases in benefits to retirees

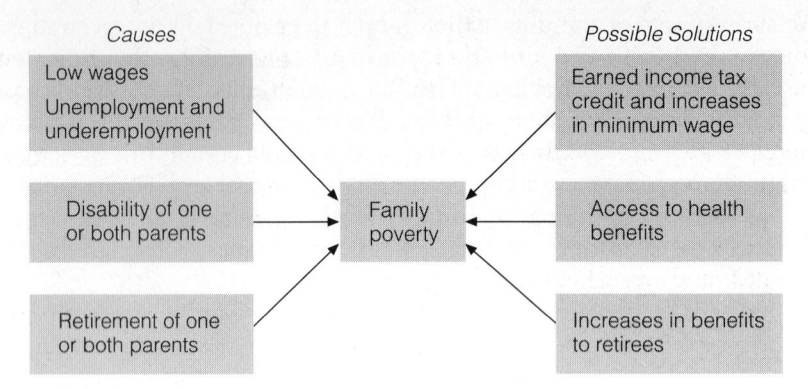

FIGURE 6.2
Poverty and remedies in two-parent families

of poverty in these families, because 35% of the poor two-parent families did not have a full-time employee. Disability and retirement were the third largest cause of poverty in these two-parent families, as 21% of them had a disabled or retired member.[20] (See Figure 6.2 for a schematic diagram that illustrates poverty in two-parent families.)

With this basic data, Ellwood supports remedies that address low wages, unemployment, and disability.[21] To rectify low wages, Ellwood wants to expand the earned income tax credit (which gives impoverished working persons a tax rebate sufficient to lift them above poverty) and to increase the minimum wage. He wants a "transitional assistance program," which couples training and wages, to help unemployed families obtain more secure jobs. He also wants a national health insurance program to give health benefits to families with disabled members. Moreover, Ellwood advocates increases in benefit programs, such as the Supplemental Security Income Program, for persons with disabilities.

After the initial analysis, researchers often do secondary analysis to locate the families with particular problems who need special assistance. The researchers might want to analyze the families with a disabled parent to ascertain which behaviors lead them into poverty. When low-wage families have a disabled parent, how does that disability influence the other parent's work? Does the parent without the disability have to spend so much time caretaking and transporting the other to medical services that he or she cannot find or maintain full-time employment? Will that parent's wages decrease because of frequent work interruptions?

In studying this kind of family, the analyst could obtain information directly from them and conduct a quantitative study. The analyst might discover, for example, that poverty increases with the extent and nature of the disability, but that the working parent is far more likely to earn relatively high wages when another relative, such as a grandparent, can help care for the disabled parent. The analyst might ask whether the well parent tends to work less when the family also has young children.

We have emphasized quantitative research to this point, but qualitative research is often needed, as well. Quantitative research is more efficient. A researcher can analyze quantitative data and obtain findings in a relatively brief period. However, we often want to be able to observe the social processes associated with problems, such as how the well parent copes with the spouse's disability. We want to track the problem's development over time. Often we do not even know what factors to examine in complex phenomena, such as the coping mechanisms of families with disabled parents. A policy analyst who used a qualitative approach might spend considerable time in the households of such families to observe their behaviors and to analyze how they coped with the disability. Such research might have as its initial, theoretical framework a diagram such as Figure 6.3, which suggests patterns of interaction between various factors. The qualitative researcher would refine the framework as new information appeared, possibly adding new variables.

Figure 6.3 suggests that poverty in these families increases as the extent of the disability increases, as the spouse of the disabled person lacks medical coverage, or as the family has more children. These guesses on the researcher's part would have to be tested by quantitative or qualitative research.

We can add depth to any causal scheme by going further back in time. We might ask, for example, why certain kinds of persons obtain such low-paying jobs that they cannot escape poverty. As we think about this, we would likely examine factors such as level of schooling, race, age, gender, job-search abilities, job training, parents' social-class, and the place of residence, such as inner-city, suburban, or rural areas. These factors, singly and in tandem, might shape people's occupational choices and employment opportunities.

Were we interested in preventive strategies, we would want to identify factors that predict which people will receive poverty-level wages and to develop preventive programs in response to these causal factors. Locating factors that will likely cause certain behavior or outcomes is difficult. Despite careful research, for example, social scientists still remain unable to predict who will be suicidal or violent with much accuracy. Considerable controversy surrounds studies that claim to identify the causes of such problems as drug addiction and alcoholism.

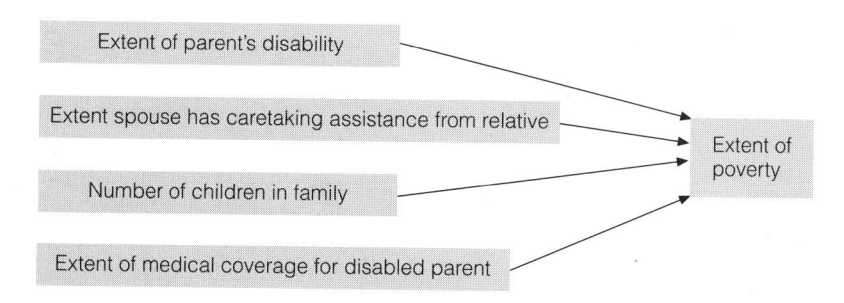

FIGURE 6.3
Poverty in two-parent families with a disabled parent

When we do develop preventive programs, policy analysts will only consider them truly effective after a program evaluation compares behaviors and outcomes of persons who do and do not receive the preventive services.

DEVELOPING INTERVENTIONS

Analytic frameworks, such as the ones in Figures 6.2 and 6.3, have promise in helping us to develop interventions, because they provide information about the causes of specific social problems. Policy analysts use a systematic, planned approach to addressing or preventing social problems. Ellwood uses his analysis to support several policies that could, in tandem, significantly reduce poverty in two-parent families. In families with a disabled parent, we would probably have to consider strategies beyond merely making the family eligible for medical benefits. The healthy spouse might need child-care, transportation, and in-home caretaking services to enable them to find and keep well-paying employment.

CONCEPTUAL ISSUES IN DEFINING AND MEASURING PROBLEMS

We will now "switch gears" in this chapter and discuss why a number of social scientists are less hopeful than policy analysts that we can define, measure, and conceptualize social problems with scientific rigor. We will explore some nonrational factors shape our perceptions of social problems.

As policy analysts wrestle with defining, measuring, and analyzing problems, they frequently confront the fact that problems are not "real" or "objective" entities, but constructs of the human mind.[22] Indeed, a number of social scientists contend that, despite quantitative methodology, culture, political interests, and traditions powerfully shape our definitions of social problems, the importance we attach to them, and the solutions that we seek for them.[23] Take the example of poverty. People have long argued about the definition of poverty. Does it only exist when persons suffer life-threatening conditions such as hunger? Is it best measured by an inability to purchase some "acceptable" amount of goods and services? If so, which level places someone at, below, or above poverty? Is it measured by comparing the economic condition of certain people, such as low-wage workers, with high-wage workers or "rich" persons?[24] Moreover, is poverty the inability to purchase certain amounts of services and goods, or must one also be involuntarily subjected to it? Indeed, must one also possess negative mind-sets, such as hopelessness and alienation? Such a stipulation would cast Mother Teresa outside the pale of poverty and would require us to examine not only people's financial resources, but also their routes into poverty and their attitudes about it. One could examine the length of economic deprivation; someone who is temporarily deprived of of resources after losing a job or after a bad day at the track might not be poor in contrast to those who experience poverty for extended periods.

Other conditions in the external world are subject to widely varying interpretations by experts and citizens. Some experts tell us that at least 40% of us suffer from "serious mental illness," whereas others place the number at 10%.[25] Estimates of the numbers of alcoholics, child abusers, and children who are neglected also vary wildly.[26] While these variations partly result from people's resistance to disclosing stigmatized conditions to researchers, they also underscore the role of judgments, values, and culture in defining social problems.[27] A mild bout of depression is, for some experts, "mental illness," but merely a normal response to a life event for other experts. Drinking several martinis after work each day represents alcoholism to some persons, but is merely social drinking to other analysts.

We have discussed social problems to this point, but our comments apply equally to problems in the social services. There is fraudulent use of services, bureaucratic waste, unresponsiveness of services to consumers, red tape, duplication of services, and discrimination. Extreme examples of these problems include: when an executive pockets agency funds, a consumer negotiates fifty forms to apply to a program, or agencies deny services to consumers based on their race or gender.

Values, culture, and traditions shape our perceptions of these conditions. Conservatives argue, for example, that most federal programs are unresponsive to consumers, inefficient, or tangled with red tape or fraud.[28] Although some fraud exists in many programs because it is impossible for intake staff to verify every piece of information that applicants submit, what amounts and kinds of fraud make it a serious problem? As in the case of poverty, definitions and thresholds determine the problem's severity. To some persons, any incorrect information by an applicant or any "bending of the rules" by intake workers constitutes fraud. Others impose a less stringent standard. Some persons are not concerned about fraud unless more than 10% of applicants receive benefits or services to which they are not entitled; others view it as a problem if it exceeds 5%.[29] Persons sometimes determine the seriousness by comparing different programs; liberal defenders of programs like AFDC and Medicaid note, for example, that lower rates of fraud exist in these programs than in the Internal Revenue Service.

As our examples of poverty and fraud suggest, policy problems are slippery concepts. We can disagree about their definitions, their seriousness, their causes, how they relate to other problems, their implications for society, and, not surprisingly, about strategy to address or prevent them.

Paradigms of Policy Analysis

Personal, psychological, economic, biological, environmental, and other perspectives powerfully shape or guide policy analysts' work. In *public health* or *ecological perspectives*, environmental factors such as occupational, economic, familial, peer, neighborhood, or advertising forces cause social problems.[30] Many environmental factors have been implicated as causes of alcoholism. Members of certain occupations, such as reporters who are subject to deadline and competitive pressures, have high rates of alcoholism. The liquor industry's targeting of youth has increased alcohol use among adolescents and college students. Peer pressure contributes to alcoholism among businesspeople, who often drink heavily during their frequent social and business interactions with colleagues and clients. Those with a public health perspective often advocate community, occupational, and societal interventions to stop alcoholism, such as placing limits on liquor advertising, reducing the stress in certain occupations, and developing preventive services for persons subject to high-level stress.

Persons with *radical perspectives* implicate economic and social inequalities, as well as the thwarted economic opportunities of certain populations, as causes of specific social problems.[31] Some radicals argue, for example, that the alienation and desperation of low-income persons contribute to relatively high rates of certain kinds of substance abuse in inner-city neighborhoods. The economic desperation of many persons in low-income communities stimulates some of them to become drug dealers within their communities. Radicals are likely to indict persons and interests who have an economic stake in perpetuating social problems, such as the mass media (which can glamorize the use of alcohol), the liquor industry, and international drug dealers. Because they implicate economic and political factors, radicals are often skeptical about the effectiveness of counseling remedies.

Analysts who use *medical* or *disease models* explore the physiological factors associated with substance abuse.[32] Considerable research suggests that genetic factors play a major role in addictions to alcohol, cocaine, heroin, and other drugs. Research suggests that various physiological factors sustain an addiction, so that some persons find it nearly impossible to overcome addictions. Such analysts often seek physiological remedies, such as medicines that can counter the addictive effects of a drug, substitute drugs such as methadone, detoxification, and early-warning systems for children who possess a genetic predisposition.

Biologists and medical researchers have begun to expand our knowledge of some social problems by examining the rates of specific problems, such as alcoholism, in twins who have been placed with different adoptive families at birth. Because children of alcoholics have a high tendency to be alcoholics, even when they are adopted by families where no substance abuse exists, the researchers surmise that genetic predisposition is an important causal factor. These kinds of studies have implicated genetic factors in a growing number of social problems, such as schizophrenia, depression, and alcoholism.[33] Moreover, some researchers believe that genetic factors may predispose some persons to multiple addictions; many alcoholics, for example, are simultaneously addicted to substances such as cocaine.[34]

Studies that implicate the genetic causes of specific diseases have been criticized, however, by many persons. While genes can predispose people to certain problems, for example, they are rarely the sole explanations, except with conditions such as Huntington's disease. Furthermore, scientists cannot isolate one problematic gene; if predispositions to social problems *are* genetic, patterns of multiple genes are to blame. It is often impossible to separate the effects of genes and environmental factors and stressors.

Persons who emphasize *intrapsychic factors* explore personal and familial causes of substance abuse. Perhaps, some contend, alcoholics drink to escape personal and familial dilemmas, to rebel against controlling parents, or, in the case of males, to escape dependence on their mothers. Analysts who emphasize intrapsychic factors often seek various kinds of counseling remedies.

In a departure from traditional counseling, some persons adhere to *behavioral frameworks.* Some social problems can be redressed in this perspective by providing rewards and disincentives to people with such problems as smoking. For example, behavioral counselors try to persuade smokers to participate in a regimen that provides them with rewards (such as increasing an amenity the smoker values) and disincentives (such as decreasing the valued amenity).

Some persons, such as those who believe that certain social behaviors are criminal, emphasize *deterrent strategies.* Many persons want to maintain criminal penalties for the use of many addictive substances, including marijuana, cocaine, and heroin, just as temperance crusaders sought to criminalize the use and sale of alcohol in prior eras. Some analysts believe that social problems can be redressed by raising the financial costs to those consumers who use them; why not, they ask, dramatically raise the cost of cigarettes and alcoholic beverages or make the users of addictive substances pay higher premiums for their health insurance?

Many political analysts are economists. Their perspectives and research have helped us understand the causes of specific problems, patterns of use of specific programs, and alternative policies.[35] Economic research provides useful information about employers' responses to employees' addictive behaviors, the impact of advertising alcohol on consumer behavior, the effects of fees in promoting or deterring people from drug-treatment programs, and the cost-benefit ratios of alternative policies that seek to redress alcoholism. Much economic research focuses on how financial motivations affect people's behavior. Economists can explore, for example, why some persons become drug pushers by examining the financial rewards associated with it. Or they ask what economic factors, such as fear of losing employment or the costs of treatment-related fees, shape people's decisions to seek or not seek help for their problem. Economists also examine how the financial motivations of institutions and corporations shape their actions and, at least in some cases, increase some social problems. Take the example of cigarette companies. The tobacco companies' financial motivations perpetuate cigarette smoking by generating extensive advertising. Indeed, political pressures from growers and corporations make it difficult to eliminate the federal government's massive subsidies to tobacco growers.

Economists also explore the effects of advertising on specific kinds of consumers' behavior. An economist might ask, for example, whether targeting wine cooler advertisement to teenagers actually affects their purchases of this product.

Economists also examine larger questions, such as the way government policies influence economic activity in the private sector. Economists explore the way taxes on products, such as cigarettes, influence cigarette purchases and the extent to which specific groups disproportionately pay such taxes, such as blue-collar families where rates of smoking are relatively high.

Economists also examine how specific government policies affect the nation's general employment and economic growth. Because unemployment and poverty are social problems in their own right, as well as problems that cause or exacerbate other problems, this kind of research is important to persons in social policy. Of course, as debates between schools of economic theory suggest, considerable controversy exists about the effects of specific economic policies on the general economy. *Supply-side economists* prefer tax policies that provide large-scale investors, such as corporations and affluent persons, with relatively abundant capital; *monetarists* emphasize maintaining a delicate balance of the money supply to avoid inflation and recession; and *Keynesian* or *demand-side economists* think consumers should have adequate purchasing power to keep consumer demand high to stimulate the production of goods and services. Many hybrid models of economic theories exist.[36]

Macro or societal economics, therefore, examines relationships between the supply of money, consumers' purchasing power, and the investment of capital. In addition, economists study how these factors produce specific economic effects, such as unemployment, inflation, and economic growth. Economists disagree because these relationships are so complex and because many additional factors, such as other nations' economic policies, intrude. To return to our example of substance abuse, for example, American internal policies about drug trafficking are often confounded by the policies of Latin American, Asian, and Middle Eastern nations.

Vigorous debates often break out between theorists, analysts, and researchers who adhere to the preceding approaches. Opponents of criminalizing drugs contend, for example, that it invites some persons, such as rebellious adolescents, to become addicts. Persons who implicate economic and environmental factors often contend that counseling represents an ineffective strategy. Radicals contend that, without remedying the inequalities in American society and the stress that poverty causes, many social problems will not be significantly alleviated. Contending groups often selectively cite research evidence to support specific remedies and to attack proposals of persons who use different paradigms.

These various frameworks and causal factors are not mutually exclusive; indeed, some experts argue convincingly that complementary strategies are often needed.[37] Moreover, the environmental frameworks that many social work theorists espouse suggest that social workers need to combine aspects of the various paradigms, such as environmental, social-psychological, and radical perspectives.

VARIATIONS IN PROBLEMS

When pointing to the problems in defining, measuring, and conceptualizing social problems, many persons stress, as well, differences between groups in the population. Alcoholism appears, for example, to have different causes and to take different forms among men and women.[38] Unlike men, whose alcoholism often stems from occupational stress and peer pressure, many women's alcoholism begins during points of family crisis, such as marital discord, divorce, or a child's death. Unlike men's drinking, which tends to occur in bars or with friends, many women sustain relatively secretive styles of drinking. These differences in both the causes and manifestations of alcoholism suggest that men and women may need different kinds of treatment, as well as different kinds of preventive services.

Moreover, cultural differences affect people's responses to services. Spanish-speaking families, for example, often defer to male heads of household before seeking assistance for specific problems. In contrast, in many white families, women often take the initiative in seeking services for specific problems. Social-service agencies that serve Latinos must try to include male heads of household in service transactions if they want to be successful.[39] Moreover, some ethnic groups require bilingual and bicultural staff who can interpret nuances of expression and probe for the meaning of verbal and nonverbal cues in ways not possible for staff from the dominant culture. Some persons respond favorably to one approach, such as a specific kind of counseling, whereas others respond to behavior modification or to membership in support groups such as Alcoholics Anonymous. Deterrent measures, such as increasing the cost of alcohol or cigarettes, appear to decrease some people's use, but they may be even more effective when supplemented with counseling programs and reductions in advertising.

The vast literature that has recently evolved on "culturally sensitive practice" and on "multidiversity" stresses the need to adapt programs to specific populations.[40] Our discussion suggests that this sensitivity has to occur on two, related levels. First, we need to examine how specific social problems occur differently in certain populations, as our discussion of alcoholism among males and females suggests. Second, we need to ask how we can adapt services to the culture and norms of specific ethnic and racial groups, as our discussion of Latinos suggests.

We should remember, as well, that the problems of oppressed populations are often caused or exacerbated by the hostile environments and the extreme poverty that many of their members encounter, particularly in inner-city communities. How can the rules of mental health, whether in diagnosing or treating conditions, not be modified, for example, when social workers help persons who live in areas that look like bombed-out cities, who are exposed to violence on a daily basis, who cannot obtain secure jobs that allow them to escape poverty, and who can obtain amenities such as health care only by waiting for days in clinics? Terms such as *paranoia, inability to make long-term plans,* and *flight,* which could be used to describe mental conditions or problem-solving deficits with middle-class citizens, must be used cautiously when discussing persons in these high-stress environments, where planning, trust, and permanent social arrangements are less feasible.

The term *empowerment* helps us reconceptualize some of the services that social workers provide to persons in high-stress environments, because they are besieged by economic stressors. (While empowerment is not limited to persons in high-stress environments, it may have particular relevance for them.) When seeking to empower persons, social workers often emphasize survival skills, such as helping persons cope with the fragmentation of services, understaffed services, and hostile bureaucrats. Rather than focusing on pathology, empowerment helps people develop personal plans to improve their lives. Indeed, some persons favor words such as *consumers of service* rather than *patient* or *client* to avoid labeling people. Some social workers advocate placing less reliance on mental health diagnostic categories, such as those in DSM-III, which label persons on the basis of deficits, rather than strengths.[41]

Social workers can use aspects of marketing theory and research to help match their services to clients' needs. Marketing theory, while often used to promote advertising, also focuses on research to discern specific groups by age, race, gender, ethnic group, or some combination of these factors. By using qualitative research techniques, such as small groups of consumers who discuss the services they desire, marketing researchers develop recommendations about where persons want to receive services, the nature of these services, and acceptable fees.[42] While it is beyond our discussion to examine marketing theory in detail, it allows policy analysts to ground their work in actual discussions and interactions with potential clients, rather than making assumptions about clients' needs.

CHALLENGES FOR POLICY ADVOCATES

We have noted that policy advocates who help oppressed populations encounter particular challenges in policy arenas because their issues frequently are unpopular. Certain kinds of issues and populations have a relatively privileged position within American culture, as can be seen by the success of organizations that specialize in them to secure a disproportionate share of resources. Fundraisers for hospitals, certain cultural undertakings, and educational organizations, such as private schools, have an enviable job in raising funds compared, for example, to shoe-string organizations that help stigmatized populations.[43]

Moreover, the broader population views the problems of stigmatized populations, such as homelessness or AIDS, through prejudiced lenses. Rather than viewing homelessness, for example, as stemming from an absence of halfway houses, decent social services, and affordable housing, many persons stress the personal failings of homeless persons as the major, even sole, cause of this condition.[44] Rather than viewing AIDS as an epidemic, similar to cholera in prior eras, many persons view those who have this disease through the lenses of homophobia, seeing it as stemming from an aberrant life-style choice.[45]

Problems of oppressed populations are, moreover, often viewed as relatively hopeless and unsolvable in nature, unlike those of more powerful populations. The "underclass" provides a good example; rather than mounting a national assault on the problems of inner-city residents, many Americans perceive their problems as too chronic and pervasive to be addressed. Moreover, they often believe inner-city residents have chosen to be unemployed, to take drugs, and to commit crimes, choices that make it impossible for the broader society to help them "until they really want to pull themselves up by their bootstraps."

When advocates use language that suggests that inequalities in American society, such as discrepancies in the incomes and opportunities of social classes, should be rectified, they are often dismissed as left-leaning radicals. In a society that lacks a strong radical tradition, the rhetoric of social equality is often dismissed.[46] But advocates of powerless populations and unpopular issues often realize that, without a fundamental redistribution of resources and opportunities, specific groups, such as inner-city African Americans, will remain on the periphery of American society. They will be unable even to imagine themselves significantly improving their lives relative to the broader population.

These common perceptions of the problems of oppressed populations underline the need for their advocates to educate people, whether through the mass media or personal discussions with highly placed officials. They must contest the definitions and conceptualizations of specific social problems, such as equating "welfare" with "bad character" rather than limited and low-paying jobs. They have to resist people's stereotypes by arguing that certain groups are, in fact, composed of persons with different needs and problems. For example, women may remain on AFDC rolls because they have disabled family members, lack job skills, or live in areas where virtually no jobs exist for relatively unskilled women.

A POLICY-PRACTICE CASE

A social worker aiming to develop a new program to address clients' unmet needs has to define specific social problems, collect data about their prevalence, propose specific interventions, and convince decisionmakers that new policies are needed to address the problem. In Case 6.1, a social worker tries to develop a preventive program in a mental health agency.

The social worker analyzes the problems that the LEAPS project, or the Learning Everything About Parenting Service, would address. She considers developing a research survey to ascertain what kinds of problems the project might address among families with young and adolescent children. Would it address several social problems, such as suicide and substance abuse, or focus on a specific one such as teen pregnancy? Which populations might LEAPS target? What kinds of outreach or publicity would make the program relevant to certain parents?

180   PART TWO   Preparatory Work: Building Agendas, Defining Problems, and Writing Proposals

As she ponders these questions, the social worker engages in policy analysis that focuses on defining, measuring, and conceptualizing specific social problems. Because social policy seeks to ameliorate social problems, this portion of policy practice is vital to social workers, who are well aware of unmet needs in the communities where they work.

Case 6.1
EXPANDING A PREVENTIVE PROGRAM IN A MENTAL HEALTH AGENCY

I work for a community mental health center (the Hobart CMHC) attached to a local hospital that provides it with some of its funds. The Hobart CMHC is currently in a state of fiscal crisis because the local hospital is experiencing marked budgetary deficits; indeed, there have been layoffs of clerical and administrative staff.

Thus, as a community mental health center, Hobart CMHC has become like Cinderella, a participant in a hospital family that views her as an unwanted stepchild. Like Cinderella, Hobart is considering looking to external sources for deliverance.

It would be too presumptuous of me to consider the program proposal I will set forth in this paper as Hobart's fairy godmother. However, perhaps it could be the glass slipper, an instrument for orienting Hobart to the concept of community mental health and a means for educating the local hospital about that concept. The family-child division of Hobart CMHC began a program called the Preschool and Infant Parenting Service (PIPS) several years ago. This program aimed to reach parents of young children (through five years) who had concerns about their children's development and behavior. A "warm line" free telephone service was established. Parents could call into the clinic and within twenty-four hours receive direct assistance from either staff clinical social workers, child development specialists, or volunteer paraprofessionals specifically trained for this program. Medical questions were not in the realm of service; rather, the objective was to provide suggestions, alternatives, information, referrals, and reassurance to callers. The name "warm line" described the response and the fact that this was not to be correlated with crisis or "hot line" kinds of programs. Calls averaged about forty-five minutes in length, and, generally, families who called received follow-up calls (callers could choose to remain anonymous, however).

Besides the warm line, the PIPS program offered a variety of brief services, usually about six weeks in length. Mothers and fathers with "normal" concerns about raising their children could speak with other parents in various group settings led by a staff member. The six-week groups cost twenty-five dollars per family. The PIPS program was an early (secondary) prevention program whose objective was to enlarge the population using Hobart CMHC while increasing "normal" families' comfort with using this kind of clinic. Every family participating is interviewed and evaluated separately and families with serious problems are referred to other programs at the local hospital.

PIPS was initially funded by a small federal grant, which has expired; it is now funded by the local hospital. It is a small operation that has never been evaluated for its impact and is currently in jeopardy of being eliminated. To provide more comprehensive mental health services and thereby increase community support and participation, I am seeking to expand the present PIPS program through increased publicity and staffing and by adding a similar service for families with young children and adolescents.

With tongue in cheek, I have already accomplished the first task of program development in devising an appropriate acronym. The new program is to be called LEAPS (Learning Everything About Parenting Service). Allowing myself to fantasize, I can envision a LEAPS program with a warm line and group technology serving families at all levels of the life cycle, including three-generational problems. (The area Hobart serves has a large senior citizen population, yet program development for that group has been minimal.)

The idea for a LEAPS program evolved from observing the warm line. Each time PIPS advertised its warm line service through the communications media, the warm line would receive calls from families with children over the age of five. Staff time and availability are limited, so these calls could not be adequately serviced. Professionally, I feel that expanding to a LEAPS program could lead to better services for a larger population.

Four sequential steps are needed before LEAPS can be implemented. One step is to document the LEAPS program comprehensively, including a definition of the LEAPS mission as it correlates with stated and implied goals for Hobart CMHC and its family-child unit. LEAPS would have to be described as capable of providing broader services to people needing emotional help and providing consultation and prevention objectives through innovative treatment in the family mental health field.

Documentation needs to include a description of program operation and the specific populations served. It should also anticipate statistics, such as estimates of the numbers who would use this service, operational costs, probable space needs, staffing needs and costs, and equipment needs and costs, including telephone and audiovisual materials. Some of these estimates could be based on studies of similar programs, including the PIPS project, suicide prevention, and other hot line services.

A preliminary market research survey could enhance the documenter's perception of the need for this program. It would also alert the public to the potential service and provide an avenue for community input in the planning stage. Market research is important because it puts the consumer in the position of contributing to decisionmaking.

The description of staff could strategically emphasize in-house control by appointing a staff member clinical administrator. To satisfy medical staff, a psychiatrist could be designated program consultant. This might also reinforce public legitimation of the project.

Because of the present dearth of funds, use of existing staff would be prudent. To mitigate conflicts with PIPS personnel, the PIPS staff should be LEAPS's core personnel. Hiring a community worker with additional communications and public relations expertise could be justified as saving staff time. I feel that infusion of new blood schooled in community work could be an important asset to the LEAPS program. Most of the present staff needs to be educated about consultation and community outreach, because few have participated in community projects.

Methods of record-keeping and evaluation also need to be improved. One important statistic that PIPS is not gathering is the number of referrals it makes to the family-child unit or other programs at Hobart CMHC. There has been much speculation that PIPS is a viable feeder for Hobart CMHC, and information to that effect would point to another merit of the program. Built-in methods of evaluation and research also seem to be needed as justification for continued funding.

A second step is to obtain approval from people within the agency structure. My first targets would be key personnel. The woman who originated the PIPS program is married to Dr. Jones, an influential physician. As Hobart CMHC chief and as the local hospital's envoy to powerful people, he is a pivotal contact. My observation of a parenting project now in existence at Hobart CMHC bears witness for seeking support from Dr. Jones for any new proposal. The parenting project, a longitudinal study of children and their families, was funded and staffed independently and was approved by officials at the local hospital without seeking aid from Dr. Jones, the Hobart CMHC chief. Consequently, the project staff faces obstacles, such as lack of space, and is subject to the criticism of Dr. Jones's chief, who publicly questions the validity of the study.

A third step involves community support for the project. Several influential persons on PIPS's advisory council want a project that serves a larger section of the population. External support may also come from the county child welfare agency, which is understaffed but working to develop a preventive strategy.

A crucial fourth step is to obtain funding from external sources. Informal contacts with officials from several local foundations suggest the possibility of funding for a larger program, especially if part of the funds can be assumed by Hobart CMHC and the county child welfare department. Hobart CMHC has several ongoing private fundraising groups; perhaps one of these groups could be persuaded to raise funds for a new program. Present financial difficulties preclude asking for a portion of existing funds. This program might need to be presented as a one-year "demonstration" project when initially approaching funding sources.

SOURCE: This case is adapted from one by Andrea Karzen, M.S.W. Names and locations have been altered.

Linking Analytic Skills to Other Policy Skills

As was demonstrated in Case 6.1, analytic skills must often be supplemented by political, interactional, and value-clarification skills if policy practitioners wish to promote new programs effectively. Analytic skills allow us to marshal technical evidence to show that a specific social problem is important. Thus, the social worker in Case 6.1 contemplates using a survey to ascertain what problems families with young children and adolescents might wish the LEAPS program to address.

As the case suggests, however, the social worker encountered some political obstacles. She notes, for example, that the current staff might view her proposed LEAPS program with some animosity, as might the originator of the PIPS program, which already had a warm line. PIP's staff might fear that LEAPS would compete with it for scarce funds or that the new program might diminish some of their prestige. Thus, the social worker contemplates securing support from Dr. Jones, an influential physician whose wife initiated PIPS.

She also realizes that she needs interactional skills. If a task force is established to develop the proposal, the social worker can assist its deliberations by using a variety of group skills. Moreover, she will need to have numerous personal discussions with persons such as Dr. Jones to persuade them that a new program is needed.

Value-clarification skills will help decide, among other things, whether the new program will address important enough social needs to merit spending scarce agency funds. Might other social needs be more important? Are preventive programs as necessary as curative programs? She will need value-clarification skills to decide which political tactics to employ. Is it ethical, for example, to use contacts with highly placed officials to take funds from the PIPS program and allocate them to the LEAPS program?

Even this brief discussion of Case 6.1 suggests that the analytic skills (such as qualitative and quantitative research) emphasized in this chapter must be coupled with the policy skills discussed in succeeding chapters.

Summary

Policy practitioners need considerable sophistication in thinking about social problems, which are complex phenomenon. Indeed, they need to be familiar with a variety of perspectives about social problems and different tools for analyzing them. Practitioners must understand the following:

- Cultural and political factors that shape perceptions of social problems
- Analytic approaches to classifying problems, measuring their prevalence, finding their location, determining their severity, and analyzing their causes
- Qualitative approaches to analyzing social problems

- How social problems vary in different populations
- How to contest definitions, measurements, and perceptions of social problems that stigmatize or stereotype oppressed populations

Concepts in this chapter, such as analyzing the causes of social problems and their prevalence, classifying social problems, and observing how they vary, figure prominently in the work of policy analysts, who hope to develop disciplined and scientific approaches to social problems. Skillful policy practitioners use these concepts both to develop policy proposals and to secure support for them from legislators, executives, and other decisionmakers. They also draw on supportive research and theories from the social sciences, biology, and economics.

We ought not minimize, however, the controversy that often surrounds attempts to define, measure, or conceptualize specific social problems. Ideology often influences what kinds of data and perspectives policy practitioners favor. Competing camps of experts often take divergent positions about the causes and nature of specific problems.

Policy analysts must be careful not to assume that the causes of problems, as well as consumers' responses to specific services, can be generalized across society. Different causes of problems, such as alcoholism, exist in different populations, such as between men and women. Members of different ethnic and racial groups respond in different fashion to specific services. An emphasis on empowerment is particularly useful with persons who live in oppressive environments, such as many African-American and Latino residents of inner cities. Marketing theory and research can be used to match social services to specific populations' needs.

Policy advocates encounter political challenges when trying to promote services for oppressed populations, but their determined efforts have often succeeded in shaping discourse about effective interventions.

Suggested Readings

DEVELOPING TYPOLOGIES
David Ellwood, *Poor Support: Poverty in the American Family* (New York: Basic Books, 1988).

POLICY AGENDAS
John Kingdon, *Agendas, Alternatives, and Public Policies* (Boston: Little, Brown, 1984).
Louis Koenig, *An Introduction to Public Policy* (Englewood Cliffs, NJ: Prentice-Hall, 1986), Chapter 4.
Julie Kosterlitz, "Not Just Kid Stuff," *National Journal* 20 (November 19, 1988): 2934–2939.

CONTROVERSIES IN DEFINING AND CONCEPTUALIZING SOCIAL PROBLEMS
Herbert Fingarette, "Alcoholism: The Mythical Disease," *Public Interest* 91 (Spring 1988): 3–22.
John Kaplan, "Taking Drugs Seriously," *Public Interest* 92 (Summer 1988): 32–50.
Ethan Nadelman, "The Case for Legalization," *Public Interest* 92 (Summer 1988): 3–31.

William Wilson, "Cycles of Deprivation and the Underclass Debate," *Social Service Review* 59 (December 1985): 541–559.
Steven Wineman, *The Politics of Human Services: A Radical Alternative to the Welfare State* (Boston: South End Press, 1984).

How Culture and Values Influence Definitions of Social Problems
Joel Best, ed., *Images of Issues* (New York: Aldine DeGruyter, 1989).
Arnold Green, *Social Problems: Arena of Conflict* (New York: McGraw-Hill, 1975).
Egon Guba, *The Paradigm Dialogue*. (Newbury Park, CA: Sage, 1990).
Barbara Solomon, *Black Empowerment* (New York: Columbia University Press, 1976), pp. 299–313.
Malcolm Spector and John Kitsuse, *Constructing Social Problems* (Menlo Park, CA: Cummings, 1977).

Technical Approaches to Analyzing and Measuring Social Problems
Jonathan Bradshaw, "The Concept of Social Need," in Neil Gilbert and Harry Specht, eds., *Planning for Social Welfare* (Englewood Cliffs, NJ: Prentice-Hall, 1977), pp. 290–297.
U.S. National Institute of Mental Health, *A Working Manual of Simple Evaluation Techniques for Community Mental Health Centers* (Washington, DC: Government Printing Office, 1976), pp. 99–146.

Notes

1. See Alfred Kahn, *Theory and Practice of Social Planning* (New York: Russell Sage, 1969); Robert Mayer and Ernest Greenwood, *The Design of Social Policy Research* (Englewood Cliffs, NJ: Prentice-Hall, 1980); Yeheskel Dror, *Venture in Policy Sciences* (New York: Elsevier North Holland, 1971); and Edward Quade, *Analysis for Public Decisions*, 2nd ed. (New York: Elsevier North Holland, 1982).
2. Webster's *New World Dictionary* (New York: Simon and Schuster, 1982), p. 16.
3. Mayer and Greenwood, *The Design of Social Policy Research*, pp. 67–76.
4. See J. K. Wing, *Reasoning About Mental Illness* (London: Oxford University Press, 1978), chapter 2.
5. Robert Spitzer, Janet Williams, and Andrew Skodol, "DSM-III: The Major Achievements and an Overview," *American Journal of Psychiatry* 137 (February 1980): 151–154.
6. See testimony of David Ellwood in Senate, *Hearings*, Subcommittee on Social Security and Family Policy of Committee on Finance (March 2, 1987), pp. 105–111.
7. See Thomas Szasz, *Insanity: The Idea and Its Consequences* (New York: Wiley, 1987).
8. Victor Adebimpe, "Overview: White Norms and Psychiatric Diagnoses of Black Patients," *American Journal of Psychiatry* 138 (March 1981): 279–285.
9. See David Mechanic, *Mental Health and Social Policy*, 3rd ed. (Englewood Cliffs, NJ: Prentice-Hall, 1989), pp. 16–44.
10. Martin Bloom, *Primary Prevention: The Possible Science* (Englewood Cliffs, NJ: Prentice-Hall, 1981), pp. 173–174.
11. Jonathan Bradshaw, "The Concept of Social Need," *New Society* 30 (March 1972): 640–643.

12. John Kingdon, *Agendas, Alternatives, and Public Policies* (Boston: Little, Brown, 1984), pp. 95-99.
13. See National Institute of Mental Health, *A Working Manual of Simple Evaluation Techniques for Community Mental Health Centers* (Washington, DC: Government Printing Office, 1976), pp. 99-146.
14. Ibid., pp. 99-146.
15. Phillip Kotler, *Principles of Marketing*, 4th ed. (Englewood Cliffs, NJ: Prentice-Hall, 1989), pp. 42-46.
16. Steven Mirin, et al., "Casual versus Heavy Use of Marijuana, A Redefinition of the Marijuana Problem," *American Journal of Psychiatry* 127 (March 1971): 1134-1140.
17. Department of Health and Human Services, Public Health Service, *Alcohol and Health: Report to U.S. Congress on Alcohol and Health* (Washington, DC: Government Printing Office, 1987), pp. 1-27.
18. Shelley Wood, "Alcoholism," *California Journal* 5 (June 1974): 199-201.
19. David Ellwood, *Poor Support: Poverty in the American Family* (New York: Basic Books, 1988).
20. Ibid., pp. 81-127.
21. Ibid., pp. 81-127.
22. Arnold Green, *Social Problems: Arena of Conflict* (New York: McGraw-Hill, 1975), pp. 67-115.
23. See Joel Best, ed., *Images of Issues* (New York: Aldine DeGruyter, 1989); Earl Rubington and Martin Weinberg, *The Study of Social Problems*, 4th ed. (New York: Oxford University Press, 1989); and Malcolm Spector and John Kitsuse, *Constructing Social Problems* (Menlo Park, CA: Cummings, 1977).
24. Victor Fuchs, "Redefining Poverty," *Public Interest* 8 (Summer 1967): 88-96.
25. Jeanne Giovannoni discusses problems in measuring rates of mental illness among children in, "Children," *Encyclopedia of Social Work*, 18th ed., vol. 1 (Silver Spring, MD: National Association of Social Workers, 1987), p. 251.
26. See Jon Conte, "Child Sexual Abuse," *Encyclopedia of Social Work*, vol. 1, pp. 255-256.
27. Green, *Social Problems*, pp. 67-115.
28. Martin Anderson, *Welfare* (Stanford, CA: Hoover Institution Press, 1978), pp. 160-161.
29. Frank Thompson, *Health Policy and the Bureaucracy: Politics and Implementation* (Cambridge, MA: MIT Press, 1981), pp. 134-147, 176-178.
30. *Alcohol and Health*, pp. 97-119.
31. Steven Wineman, *The Politics of Human Services: A Radical Alternative to the Welfare State* (Boston: South End Press, 1984).
32. For a critique of the medical model in substance abuse, see Dorothy Nelkin, *Methadone Maintenance: A Technological Fix* (New York: Braziller, 1973).
33. See, for example, Robin Murray and James Stabenau, "Genetic Factors in Alcoholism Predisposition," in E. Mansell Pattison and Edward Kaufman, eds., *Encyclopedic Handbook of Alcoholism* (New York: Gardner Press, 1982), pp. 418-420.
34. Mirin, "Casual versus Heavy Use of Marijuana," p. 1137.
35. For an overview of research in economics, see Joseph Stiglitz, *Economics of the Public Sector*, 2nd ed. (New York: Norton, 1988).
36. Green, *Social Problems*, pp. 67-115.
37. William Miller and Hester Reid, "Matching Problem Drinkers with Optimal Treatments," in William Miller and Nick Heather, eds., *Treating Addictive Behaviors: Processes of Change* (New York: Plenum Press, 1986), pp. 175-204.
38. Vasanti Burtle, ed., *Women Who Drink: Experience and Psychotherapy* (Springfield, IL: Charles C Thomas, 1979).

39. Vicente Abad, "Mental Health Delivery Systems for Hispanics in the United States: Issues and Dilemmas," in Moises Gaviria and Jose Arana, eds., *Health and Behavior: Research Agenda for Hispanics* (Chicago: Simon Bolivar Hispanic American Psychiatric Research and Training Program, 1987).
40. See, for example, Wynetta Devore and Elfrieda Schlesinger, *Ethnic-Sensitive Social Work* (St. Louis: C. V. Mosby, 1981); and Donna Ferullo, *Cultural Diversity in Social Work Practice* (Boston: Social Work Library at Boston College, 1991).
41. Barbara Solomon, *Black Empowerment* (New York: Columbia University Press, 1976).
42. Phillip Kotler, *Principles of Marketing*, 4th ed. (Englewood Cliffs, NJ: Prentice-Hall, 1989).
43. Jean Potuchek, "The Context of Social Service Funding: The Funding Relationship," *Social Service Review* 60 (September 1986): 421–436.
44. Joel Blau, *The Visible Poor: Homelessness in the United States* (New York: Oxford University Press, 1992).
45. Randy Shilts, *And the Band Played On: Politics, People, and the AIDS Epidemic* (New York: St. Martin's Press, 1987).
46. Bruce Jansson, *The Reluctant Welfare State* (Pacific Grove, CA: Brooks/Cole, 1993), pp. 321–324.

Chapter Seven
Recurring Policy Options

In Chapter Six we discussed some methods of defining, measuring, and conceptualizing social problems. Our focus shifts in this and the next two chapters to the proposal-constructing task, in which social workers develop proposals that address these kinds of problems. We will discuss how to use analytic, political, value-clarifying, and interactional skills to develop and defend proposals.

We focus in this chapter on a series of policy options that practitioners often encounter in the human services, such as eligibility, allocation, financing, and staffing options. To illustrate our topic, we discuss a case where a social worker develops a proposal for a national system of battered women's shelters. In addition, an agency-based case is presented at the end of this chapter.

At a more modest level, social workers often scrutinize specific policies within the human services system, such as the intake system, protocols for certain kinds of clients, outreach services, and the mix of preventive and curative services. In each case, they often identify and compare policy options before proposing specific changes to existing policy. In this chapter, we examine several policy options that often recur in the human services delivery system.

RECURRING POLICY ISSUES

When devising social policies, practitioners confront a number of issues. These include the following:

1. Establishing a mission
2. Designing the structure of service
3. Planning the resource path
4. Defining services
5. Rationing scarce resources

6. Addressing community factors
7. Overseeing policy implementation

To resolve each of these issues, policy practitioners have to make informed choices between policy alternatives. These choices can sometimes be difficult, particularly when considering a variety of criteria, such as efficiency, effectiveness, equity, and feasibility.

To illustrate our discussion, we will take the perspective of a hypothetical policy practitioner in Washington, DC, who wants to develop a federally funded program for the victims of spousal abuse.[1] She works for a shelter in Baltimore, but is connected with a coalition of service providers, feminists, victims of spousal abuse, and professionals who want the federal government to take a more active role in addressing this problem. (Their group is called the Stop Wife-Battering Coalition.) The policy practitioner knows that several local programs have been initiated for this purpose, mostly by underfunded nonprofit agencies that have sought assistance from foundations, private benefactors, and public sources, such as the Department of Housing and Urban Development. Despite their founders' determined efforts, these centers have proved woefully inadequate in helping the rising numbers of women who seek relief from spousal abuse. The coalition tentatively calls their proposed program the Federal Shelter program.

Establishing a Mission

While developing this program, the policy practitioner must develop some objectives for the Federal Shelter program. We have noted that policies usually contain explicit or implicit objectives that provide programs with an overarching direction. The preambles of legislation often provide this rationale.

When discussing the shelters with legislators' aides, she finds no consensus on the federal government's mission in responding to spousal abuse. Some legislators are uninterested in the issue, believing that advocates grossly exaggerate its importance and magnitude; indeed, one aide contends it is a "figment of the imagination of do-gooder social workers, who want to create more jobs for themselves." Other legislators favor a "get-tough" strategy that would provide federal funds and policy requirements to local governmental units to find, prosecute, and imprison offenders. However, they demur from direct federal assistance to shelters, which they think local jurisdictions should fund. Still other legislators want to provide federal assistance to a national network of shelters that offer shelter to battered women and their children.

While believing that better law enforcement is also needed, our policy practitioner, as well as other participants in the Stop Wife-Battering Coalition, decides to emphasize federal assistance to shelters; she thinks abused women need the immediate protection that shelters afford. (She realizes that many women lack the resources to find alternative sources of safe shelter.) The coalition also wants the shelter program to offer a service component to help women cope with their predicament and link them to legal, welfare, job-placement, and other services.

Their objectives, then, emphasize federal funding to establish shelters and serve the women who seek protection there. This mission has important consequences for the policies they will develop; had they adopted a mission that emphasized prosecuting spouse abusers, their proposal would have taken an entirely different form.

Designing the Structure of Service

Having established a general direction, this social worker and her allies encounter some practice issues: Who should ultimately oversee the new program? What kinds of agencies should receive funds for the program?

Affixing ultimate responsibility. Programs and agencies are typically classified in policy sectors, such as mental health, health, child welfare, public welfare, and gerontology.

Assigning specific programs to a sector is often arbitrary and sometimes contentious. In the case of the Head Start Program, the federal Office of Education and the federal Office of Economic Opportunity (OEO) vied for it at its inception. In truth, it could have been placed in either of them because it possessed educational components as well as the parent and community participation that OEO emphasized.[2] It was placed in OEO because its key founders feared that placing it in the Office of Education would render it a mere educational program that lacked advocacy, parent-participation, and child-development dimensions.

To return to our example, the policy practitioner has to decide who should receive ultimate responsibility for the program. Were the Federal Shelter program assigned to the National Institute of Mental Health, for example, its major focus could become providing counseling services (with less emphasis on providing shelter services). If it were assigned to the Department of Housing and Urban Development, social services might be eliminated. Of course, the policy practitioner could try to make it an independent agency that reported directly to the president, possibly linking it to other programs that assist victims of violence.

She needs to decide not only which governmental department should receive ultimate jurisdiction, but also to develop policies about implementation. Should state officials (perhaps from a state agency) or federal authorities oversee the program and choose which agencies receive federal funds? Who should collect statistics about how shelters use the funds so as to keep legislators informed? Who should attend to program problems, such as if shelters misuse funds or fail to comply with local building codes? Who should determine shelters' eligibility policies within a specific state? Should these policies be contained within the federal legislation, be defined by federal officials after the legislation has been enacted, or be left to the discretion of state officials?

In the 1960s, legislators often made federal officials responsible for many funding and operational decisions. Indeed, in many federally funded programs in the War on Poverty, local agencies applied directly to federal authorities for funds, and federal officials inspected and audited local projects. In subsequent decades, authority has increasingly been vested in state, regional, or county officials, who ultimately report some details of local programs, such as program statistics, to federal funders. (In the Reagan administration, even this reporting was minimized because he wanted to divest federal roles in favor of state and local ones.)

The policy practitioner must weigh the advantages of using the various levels of government.[3] If she believes that many local units would be particularly unreceptive to the needs of battered women, she could vest responsibility with the federal government. However, it is difficult for federal officials to superintend the operational details of thousands of shelters. Alternatively, she could choose a middle course by directing the federal funds to state authorities, while requiring them to follow specific standards and report specific information to federal authorities.

Kinds of agencies receiving funds. The policy practitioner has to decide which kinds of agencies can receive federal funds. Should nonprofit, public, profit-oriented agencies, or some combination of these receive funds?[4] Not-for-profit agencies have boards of directors, but their members are not allowed to have a financial stake in the agency, nor do the boards have shareholders or other investors who receive dividends. (Agency surpluses must be reinvested in the agency, whose staff receive fixed salaries.) Not-for-profit agencies are exempt from state and federal taxes, and contributors can usually deduct donations from their income, provided the agencies have a tax-exempt status with the Internal Revenue Service and with state authorities who oversee nonprofit agencies. Profit-oriented agencies are owned by private investors, whether private owners or stockholders, who expect a financial return on their investment. (Owners may assume a major role in overseeing their agencies or may cede management to outside managers who work under their general direction.) Public agencies are usually funded exclusively by public authorities and clients' payments. In actual practice, complex hybrids exist. Many not-for-profit agencies and some profit-oriented agencies receive contracts from public authorities. In these agencies, federal, state, or local authorities may partially reimburse clients' bills. Some nonprofits even have profit-oriented subsidiaries.

The policy practitioner has to compare these kinds of agencies when deciding whether to give them funds. Because public agencies lack a profit motive, they have no economic incentive to deceive or shortchange consumers. Indeed, theorists, such as the late social welfare theorist Richard Titmuss, contend that public agencies reinforce altruism by strengthening the notion that society should both fund and implement social programs.[5] Many critics have assailed public agencies, however. They are often bedeviled by red tape and by civil service and unionized employees who cannot be easily removed when they are ineffective. Although ultimately accountable to elected officials, many public agencies do not make extensive use of community resources, such as volunteers and support groups. Because public agencies have often emphasized services to poor persons, they are often shunned by working and middle-class citizens, who may also believe them to be excessively bureaucratic in their operations.[6]

Not-for-profit agencies are perceived as more innovative than public agencies because fewer regulations constrain their programs.[7] Because they tend to be smaller than public agencies and have boards composed of residents, some of them are probably more responsive to the needs of specific communities. Some critics nonetheless question whether not-for-profit agencies are actually more innovative than public agencies and note that their boards are often dominated by community elites, with scant participation by ordinary citizens.[8] Some of them engage so aggressively in marketing and fundraising that they are indistinguishable from profit-oriented agencies.

Profit-oriented agencies also have their defenders and detractors. Many who advocate privatizing the human services—that is, giving profit-oriented organizations expanded roles in delivering services—contend that private markets enhance the efficiency of human services while gearing services toward consumers' needs. They suggest that agencies that are inefficient or unresponsive to consumers should lose their clientele to competitors.[9] Many critics vigorously challenge this optimistic portrayal of for-profit agencies. They point out how profit-oriented nursing homes and day-care centers sometimes attract consumers with deceptive advertising, cut the quality of their services to increase their profits, and refrain from serving persons who cannot pay their fees.[10]

Planning the Resource Path

The policy practitioner realizes that fiscal resources are the lifeblood of the human services system and that many shelters desperately need funds to survive. She must choose a funding source for social programs, determine how much money to give specific programs, and select a funding channel.

Sources of funds for social programs. Policy analysts must choose from a variety of funding options.[11] The extensive *general revenues* of local, county, state, and federal governments fund many programs. Since the 1930s, the federal government has emerged as the major funder of social welfare programs, because it can raise more taxes than state or local governments. The federal income tax produces most federal revenues, far more than limited state income taxes or state (or local) property, sales, excise, and license taxes.

General revenues provide a useful source of funds for social programs, because they are generally unrestricted. However, many groups seek general-revenue funds, including thousands of existing social programs and the Defense Department. Moreover, in the wake of taxpayer revolts, in which many voters supported measures to cut tax rates—as happened in both federal and state governments in the 1980s—access to general revenues became even more problematic.

Payroll taxes fund Social Security and Medicare programs. These taxes take a certain percentage of employees' or employers' payrolls, or both. While payroll taxes are a predictable and stable source of revenues, it is virtually impossible to develop new payroll taxes, because Social Security and Medicare already preempt considerable shares of people's payrolls.

Consumer payments fund a significant share of the nation's social programs. Agencies or private practitioners, such as counselors and physicians, may impose these fees. Consumer payments deter the unnecessary use of social and medical services and sometimes (in the case of sliding fees) require relatively affluent persons to shoulder part of programs' operating costs. However, they often deter poor persons from seeking needed services.

Special taxes, such as on marriage licenses, auto licenses, and alcoholic beverages, are often earmarked for specific programs. For example, many states use special taxes on marriage licenses to fund battered women's shelters. As with payroll taxes, special programs provide a stable source of revenues for specific programs, but political interests, such as liquor companies, often oppose them, fearing the taxes will raise the costs of their products and erode their markets.

Private philanthropy, including federated community fundraising drives (such as United Way and appeals for Jewish and Catholic agencies), corporations, foundations, and individual donors, remains a major funding source for social programs, even though it has been eclipsed by government.[12] Private philanthropy provides funds that are often less restricted than government monies, because they are not usually earmarked for specific programs. As with the general government revenues, however, many people apply for scarce philanthropic funds. Established agencies or ones with popular causes, such as hospitals, attract a disproportionate share of these funds.

Determining levels of funds. Euphoric after the enactment of legislation, reformers often discover that the program receives inadequate funding. The funding of public programs usually follows a two-step procedure.[13] First, legislatures *authorize* funds by stipulating how much money (an upper limit) a specific program can receive in a given year. Second, the legislature *appropriates*— that is, actually commits—a specific amount of money to the program for a specific year. However, programs often receive far fewer funds than were authorized for them, because there are too many demands on the available funds during the annual appropriations process. Intensely political from start to finish, the appropriations process leads to winners (programs that receive their authorized levels) and losers (programs that receive far less than their authorized levels).

Legislatures sometimes provide *open-ended funding* for some programs, where they agree to fund whatever costs those programs incur in a specific year. The Medicare and Social Security programs illustrate such open-ended funding.

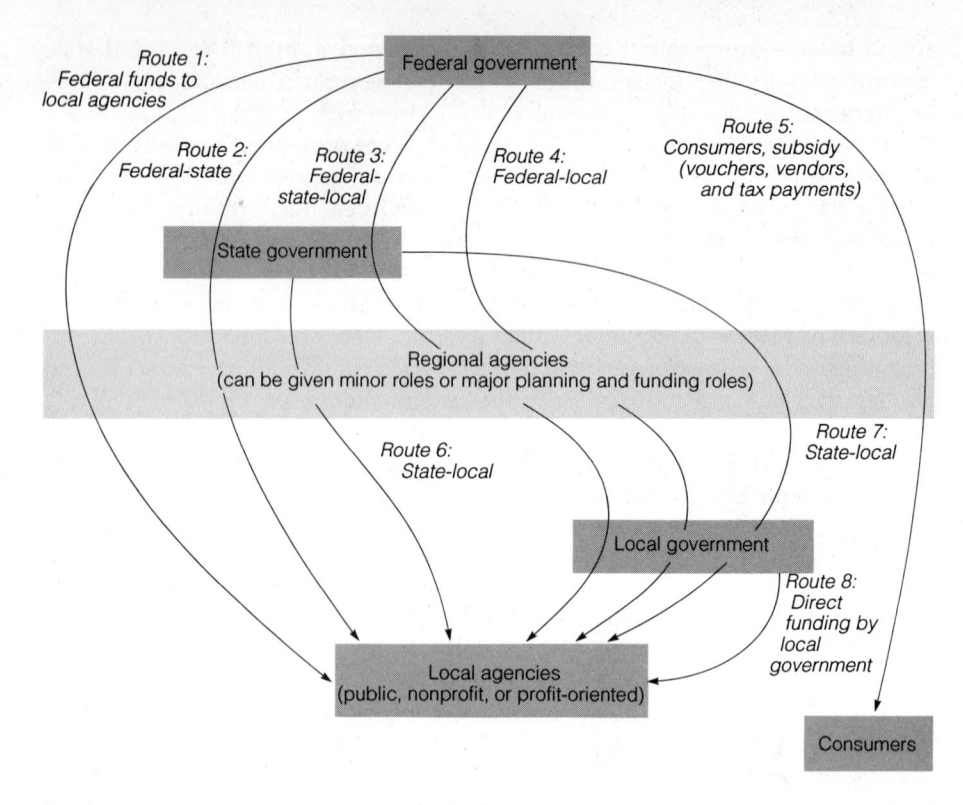

FIGURE 7.1
Possible funding channels

Funding channels. Once funds exist for a social program and some combination of public, nonprofit, and profit-oriented agencies have been chosen to receive the money, funding channels need to be devised to distribute these resources. We can visualize the funds as flowing from various levels of government to agencies or consumers through channels (see Figure 7.1).

Federal funders often provide money directly to the agencies, as in Route 1. Funding may take the form of project grants, where the federal government gives a shelter funds to provide services to battered women. The government could regulate the nature of services or could give local agencies relative latitude. Alternatively, the government can ask local agencies to bid for *contracts* that specify services the government wishes to provide.[14] If a project grant provides funds to assist battered women, a contract details specifically what the government seeks to purchase, such as "5,000 days of residential services, for battered women in Fargo, North Dakota."

Alternatively, some persons argue that federal funders should provide resources directly to consumers (Route 5). For example, some persons favor the use of *vouchers*—that is, funds consumers can use to purchase specific services, such as day-care. Government can place parameters on the kinds of commodities that can be purchased and can require providers to meet certain licensing standards. Government funds can also make *vendor payments* to reimburse providers for services they provide to specific clients.[15] For example, the Medicaid program reimburses hospitals and physicians for the medical services they provide to low-income patients.

In the federal-state channel (Route 2), the federal government distributes funds to the states, which then distribute the funds to specific agencies. Advocates of state government support this policy because it gives states enhanced roles in the human services system. Indeed, advocates of *block grants*, which are relatively unrestricted funds that the federal government gives states or local units of government, argue that they give recipients the flexibility to use the funds as they wish and adapt their programs to local needs.[16] Opponents of block grants often contend that they provide local jurisdictions with carte blanche use of federal funds for trivial or misdirected programs or allow them to underserve specific groups. These opponents favor federal funding of specific programs that require the recipient to use the money for specific purposes and adhere to numerous federal regulations. (These programs, such as the Head Start Program, are often called *categorical programs.*) In the Reagan administration a number of large block-grant programs were established, including one for maternal and child health and for social services. While the federal government placed some restrictions on how the states used these funds, there were fewer constraints than in the 57 categorical programs that they replaced. Alternatively, the federal government can fund local governments directly (Route 4), a favored tactic among some mayors and county supervisors who chafe at the extraordinary power of the federal government. In this case, local governments would fund battered women's shelters within their jurisdictions.

Similarly, states use myriad channels when they distribute their funds to local programs. They can distribute the funds directly to agencies (Route 6) or use local governments to distribute funds to agencies (Route 7).

Each funding channel has its critics and defenders. Those who favor the use of vouchers contend that it promotes healthy competition among agencies for clientele and decreases the need for government bureaucracy. Critics, however, point to many defects in market schemes. Although armed with vouchers, many low-income consumers cannot find quality providers because relatively few of them have agencies or practices in low-income areas.[17] Persons who want to maximize the federal government's role want to have it directly fund agencies or consumers, whereas persons who want to increase the states' role, such as many conservative politicians, want federal authorities to give states unrestricted block grants.

Indirect financing. We have focused on how federal and state governments can finance social welfare programs directly. Social welfare services can also be financed indirectly through the tax system.[18] Consumers are sometimes given *tax deductions* that allow them to deduct specific social welfare and housing expenditures, such as health expenditures or interest payments on their mortgages, from their pretax income, thus lowering their taxable income. *Tax credits* allow taxpayers to subtract payments to specific programs from their federal taxes; thus, many working women fund part of their day-care expenditures by subtracting a child-care credit from the taxes they would otherwise pay. *Tax exemptions* allow the taxpayer not to have to pay taxes on specific income. For instance, people can subtract from their taxable income an allowance for each dependent they have, thus lowering their taxable income.

In these indirect methods of financing social welfare, then, citizens receive money, not by direct government appropriations, but through tax concessions. The advantage of using the tax system is that it does not require appropriations and thus avoids political uncertainties. However, tax concessions often benefit wealthy persons disproportionately. For instance, the tax deductions for mortgage interest payments on expensive homes vastly exceed deductions for modest homes. (Tenants generally receive no assistance from the tax codes.) Although the government gives persons with tax-subsidized benefits a free hand in choosing their services, it does not usually regulate or monitor them. For example, persons who receive day-care credits can use services that do not meet basic standards.[19]

Some funding choices. With the preceding discussion as background, the policy practitioner has to state in her legislative proposal how much funding to request, to what extent states should match federal funds, whether states should receive funds with relatively few restrictions, and whether taxes on marriage licenses could be used in some states to fund shelters.

When examining funding channels, she has to review her predilections about the various levels of government. If she decides to emphasize the states' role in superintending the program, she could propose that federal authorities direct funds to states, which would then fund the shelters. If, by contrast, she wants to emphasize the role of the federal government, she may have federal authorities directly fund local agencies, or she may develop a categorical program providing funds to states that follow specific guidelines in using the funds.

She decides to ask for an authorization level of $450 million in the first year, with authorizations to rise to $600 million within three years. Although she wants more funds than this for the program, she realizes that conservatives, as well as some moderates and liberals, will object to a larger program during a period of federal budgetary deficits. She selects Route 2 from the funding channels—that is, for federal funds to give funds to states, who then fund local shelters. She would have preferred direct federal funding of shelters, but she doubts that this policy is politically feasible.

Defining Services

As she develops an initial outline of the Federal Shelter program, the policy practitioner must provide direction for the shelters' services, decide what mix of preventive and curative services to provide, and determine how to ration scarce resources.

Establishing an orienting framework. We can return now to our discussion of conceptual frameworks in Chapter Six, where we contrasted public health, intrapsychic, deterrent, and other paradigms frequently used in social policy. The policy practitioner has to articulate an orienting framework on which to base her services strategy.

The policy practitioner realizes that women who have been subjected to abusive behavior often experience multiple problems, such as legal, psychological, familial, medical, and economic issues. Many of them contend with divorce and police protection, suffer from anxiety and depression, have children traumatized by family violence and disruption, have serious physical problems from the violence, and face a loss of income after separating from their spouses. These considerations prompt the policy practitioner to favor multifaceted services integrated with residential services. As she struggles to define the services, she decides she wants some combination of advocacy, crisis intervention, and referral services that are integrated through a case-management system.

She is certain, however, that some shelters will not provide *any* social services, because they lack funds or are preoccupied with residential services. Thus, she decides to specify in the legislation those services that shelters receiving federal subsidies will need, including crisis intervention, referral services, and case-management services, to attend to battered women's multiple needs.

Of course, she realizes that formal requirements often do not shape the *style* of services. She does not want the shelters to become merely places of residence for battered women; indeed, she wants to link the shelters to their surrounding communities and feminist organizations. Moreover, she wants them to be advocates, not only for individuals, but also for battered women in general. She wants the shelters to support policies to increase prosecutions of spousal abusers and to include battered women in existing state programs that provide financial reimbursement to the victims of violent crimes. How can she promote these intangible attributes in her legislative proposal? Besides case management and other services, she decides to require advocacy for battered women, the use of volunteers, and, as we will discuss later, battered women's participation on shelters' governing or advisory boards. Even with these stipulations, she realizes that many shelters might seem to offer only a residence, not a multiservice center, because it is far simpler to define facilities' formal attributes than to shape their informal qualities, such as sensitivity, advocacy, or responsiveness to community needs.

Staff and licensing issues. The policy practitioner realizes that implementing these plans requires hiring competent staff. She also knows, however, that considerable competition among social service professionals might develop if she favors certain kinds of professionals, such as social workers, in her legislation.

Before we can understand her predicament, we need to discuss the way professions, including social work, develop their power and credibility. Professions develop out of both altruism and self-interest.[20] Members of specific professions want to protect consumers from incompetent persons (altruism), but they also want to reserve their title and access to certain jobs and private practices to persons who meet certain requirements (self-interest). Both altruism and self-interest encourage monopolies where professionals exclude "outsiders" who have not received specific training. Professions must establish minimal educational and training requirements, both to be certain that their members possess certain competencies and to distinguish these members from the general public and from other professions. (If no minimum requirements exist, *anyone* can use the title of the profession and pose as a member of the profession. This would undermine the profession's credibility because consumers and employers are likely to believe that the title means nothing.) To protect their members, then, professions specify minimum training and education provisions and develop methods for monitoring them. In the case of social work graduate schools, whose graduates use the degree M.S.W., cannot receive national accreditation from the Council on Social Work Education (CSWE) unless they follow minimal classroom and fieldwork requirements.[21] Similarly, persons who claim they have the B.S.W. degree must complete specified undergraduate education and fieldwork requirements that CSWE specifies. Programs not accredited by CSWE can graduate students, but their graduates could have trouble finding jobs, and their programs would have difficulty recruiting faculty.

However, professional organizations are rarely content, again for reasons of altruism and self-interest, to rely exclusively on accreditation to enhance their status. They also want government to use its *licensing powers* to reserve for its members certain titles, tasks, and positions.[22] *Licensing of titles* means that by state law, people can use titles such as "licensed clinical social worker," "physician," or "attorney-at-law" only when they have met certain training requirements, including graduating from accredited programs and engaging in postgraduate training. For example, in some states, requirements for the title Licensed Clinical Social Worker (LCSW) include working for a specified number of hours under a licensed clinical social worker's supervision.

Licensing of tasks or *functions* requires people to complete certain training before performing specified tasks, such as surgery or prescribing drugs in the case of physicians. This kind of licensing represents an even more potent form of protection for a profession because, unlike the licensing of titles that merely regulate the terms persons use to describe themselves, it reserves certain tasks to members of a profession.[23] Imagine the power that licensed clinical social workers would suddenly gain if *all* counseling were reserved to them just as surgery is reserved to physicians!

Professions often try to keep certain positions in government agencies to themselves by having them *classified*. When government authorities require certain credentials for a civil service position, such as stipulating that only social workers with master's degrees can fill supervisory positions in some child welfare agencies, they prevent members of other professions from competing for that position. It is small wonder that professional social workers have been perturbed by declassification, which removes the requirement that one must have a master's degree, or even a bachelor's degree in social work, for many positions in child welfare agencies, welfare programs, or other programs.[24] Licensing and classification issues are often controversial, because rival professions vie to reserve certain positions for themselves or to prevent other professions from monopolizing them.[25]

Our policy practitioner must decide whether to require the shelters that receive federal funds to hire certain kinds of professionals. The legislation could stipulate, for example, that each shelter's director of social services must have an M.S.W. degree and that only members of specific professions with a supervised practicum in clinical work can provide certain case-management and counseling services. Such requirements might enhance the quality of the shelters' social services and make their services billable to insurance. But the policy practitioner realizes that such staffing requirements would have some disadvantages. They will substantially increase the cost of maintaining the shelters, because shelters will have to pay the relatively higher salaries that professionals command. Professionals excluded from directing the shelters, such as marriage and family counselors and psychologists, could oppose the legislation. Some people might even argue that "professionalizing the shelters" will detract from their use of volunteer and community support because many feminists seek to enhance contributions of nonpaid women to programs that help women. The policy practitioner decides to require the shelter directors to possess an M.S.W. degree and the direct-service staff to have had a supervised practicum, but not to specify their professional affiliation.

Preventive versus curative services. Supporters argue that preventive programs can lead to significant savings by decreasing the costs of welfare, mental health, health, and other existing programs. Such programs provide either primary prevention (preventing problems before they arise) or secondary prevention (detecting and addressing social problems soon after they arise).[26] However, only a fraction of social welfare funds is spent on programs that provide consumer education or early detection efforts (secondary prevention) or on projects that address causes of problems, such as how substance abuse and poverty lead to spousal abuse in populations at high risk for family violence (primary prevention).

When contemplating whether to provide a major preventive component, the policy practitioner confronts difficult dilemmas. The number of women on shelters' waiting lists makes it difficult to justify spending large sums on prevention. It is difficult to know how to prevent abusive behavior in light of the complexity of the problem and the absence of definitive research. Abusive behaviors probably stem from some combination of exposure to abuse as a child; marital discord; substance abuse; cultural factors; sexism; situational stressors; such as unemployment and poverty; the ownership of guns by many Americans; a national culture that promotes violence; and possibly a genetic predisposition toward violence in some persons.[27] While large-scale reforms and national reforms could redress some of these causes, the policy practitioner could not easily address them in her legislative proposal. If primary prevention is difficult to accomplish, she nonetheless wonders whether her legislation could engage in secondary prevention with early detection of abusive behaviors. As members of her coalition brainstorm the issue, they decide that properly advertised local hot lines can encourage women to seek early assistance. Thus, she includes in the bill a section qualifying shelters to apply for funds to set up a hot line.

Rationing scarce resources. The term *rationing* sounds like something reserved for economies of wartime, Third World, or Eastern Bloc nations. Many consumers who use social programs need assistance, but every social agency and social program must engage in some form of rationing.[28] Our policy practitioner must grapple with this issue as she plans the legislation, because the resources that Congress might authorize will not be sufficient to address the large demand for services by battered women, who have formed long waiting lists for existing shelters. Moreover, if the Federal Shelter program were enacted and advertised, it is likely that many women who do not currently use services would seek them.

Formal or direct methods of rationing. One of the most common methods of restricting access is to give free services only to those who fall beneath a minimum level, such as the official poverty line; this method is called means-testing. Using income measures poses some problems, however.[29] An income limitation would prevent some women from entering shelters unless a sliding-fee scale allowed persons above the minimum level to pay fees adjusted to their income. An income limitation requires shelter staff to perform the time-consuming task of checking applicants' financial records. Financial tangles increase when abused women have left their spouses, placing their finances in a state of chaos. Can shelter staff accurately identify actual available income, as opposed to total family income, in these circumstances? Income-based eligibility, however, has some advantages. It allows social agencies to focus scarce resources on those persons who are least able to purchase services.

In addition to, or instead of, basing eligibility on income, the policy practitioner can use diagnostic criteria, such as the level of danger to women, the frequency or severity of the abuse, or the extent of applicants' personal trauma. As with mental health institutions, which often limit access (or at least involuntary commitments) to persons who are a danger to themselves or to others, the policy practitioner can limit use of shelters to women who have actually been abused rather than only receiving verbal threats. Diagnostic criteria have the advantage of limiting the programs to persons who appear to have the most serious problems. This is not an unimportant consideration when dealing with battered women whose lives are sometimes in danger. However, these criteria place applicants at the mercy of intake staff, who may misread the situation's seriousness or who may allow their own preferences to shape their judgments.[30] Indeed, intake staff's biases may make them more sympathetic to certain persons, such as members of their own racial or ethnic group or women with certain kinds of problems.

When analyzing her options, the policy practitioner may choose to use a number of eligibility criteria in tandem. She can, for example, limit free service to persons earning less than a certain amount *and* require shelter staff to give priority to women in danger of serious injury. She cannot resolve rationing issues without considering certain values or her original mission. If she wants a national network of federally subsidized shelters that provide a resource to most battered women, she may seek eligibility policies that are relatively nonexclusionary. Carried to its fullest, she can even declare shelters to be an *entitlement* with open-ended funding, much like Medicare or Social Security, receiving automatic funding for whatever services shelters provide to abused women during a given year.

We should note that buck passing is common with respect to eligibility. In order not to make difficult and sometimes controversial choices, federal or state legislators often yield eligibility decisions to states or agencies. Such ceding of eligibility standards in programs such as AFDC has some merit, because standards of living and demand for services vary in different parts of the nation. Critics contend, however, that more conservative and poorer states restrict eligibility excessively when given this power.[31]

Indirect methods of restricting access. Social agencies and programs devise policies that indirectly influence clients' access. One method of rationing is to place upper limits on the intensity or duration of services. To allow more persons to receive assistance, a program administrator can decide, for example, to limit residence in a shelter to a certain number of months. When placing limits on services, policy practitioners must balance effectiveness with equity. If the intensity, duration, or amount of services or benefits is markedly reduced, more consumers receive program benefits (equity is increased), but services may be distributed so thinly that persons receive ineffective or inadequate assistance.[32] Policy practitioners must make difficult choices when considering the relative intensity or amount of program benefits.

Another common method of rationing resources in social agencies and programs is to adopt a first-come, first-served policy in which consumers receive services in order of application. This approach appears at first glance to be equitable because no favoritism is possible. However, this policy has its own liabilities. Some people who have serious problems may need preferential access. Certain kinds of clients may be likely to drop off waiting lists.

Some critics argue that social agencies should reserve resources for underserved populations, much as affirmative action or quotas reserve employment slots for women and racial minorities. They should also, according to this argument, develop outreach services to these populations and examine service-utilization patterns to reach consumers who prematurely terminate.

Some social agencies ration services by *discouraging* specific populations from utilizing them. Overt discrimination is probably less serious than subtler forms.[33] Low-income populations, who want tangible assistance with economic and social problems, will probably not use some service approaches, such as extended "talking therapies." Similarly, a lack of bilingual and ethnic minority staff can deter ethnic minority consumers from using services. Agency personnel might not fully realize that their forms of service or their staffing patterns powerfully influence who does or does not use the program.

Agencies ration services indirectly in many other ways, including the placement of facilities, the use of specific program titles, and the selective use of outreach. When facilities are placed in low-income areas, they promote their use by poor persons, just as facilities in many suburban areas favor affluent populations. The importance of titles becomes obvious when one examines the differences between a "free clinic" and a "women's free clinic": the latter clearly would encourage female users and discourage male users. Patterns of outreach and advertising also influence access; if staff advertise their program to relatively affluent populations, for example, they bias access toward these persons and away from other populations.

Charging fees is another way to restrict access. As fees increase, low-income consumers are less likely to seek services or more likely to terminate at the earliest possible point. Some policies, such as restricting services to regular hours, impose a hidden but substantial burden on working persons and poor persons who must in effect pay a fee by taking time from their employment.

Our policy practitioner reluctantly decides that she has to ration the services financed by the Federal Shelter program, because of the enormity of unmet needs. She decides to restrict access to three months of residence in shelters unless the woman remains in imminent danger of physical abuse. She requires the shelters to disseminate information about their services to a broad range of community groups. She establishes a sliding-fee schedule for applicants, but allows it to be waived when family finances are disrupted by dislocation.

Addressing Community Factors

We noted earlier that the policy practitioner wants the shelters embedded in the community fabric to endow them with sensitivity, friendliness, and informality. Of course, no legislative strategy can ensure that staff possess these qualities, particularly when staff do not value them or when high-level officials do not monitor services. She decides she can indirectly promote these qualities through policies regulating the centers' governance and use of community-support systems, as well as requiring shelters to engage in advocacy for abused women.

She realizes that many shelters probably will not prioritize advocacy, the use of community support systems, or user-friendly services because the shelters may be overwhelmed by the sheer numbers of women who seek their services. Moreover, some staff would not give these objectives priority, because they do not value them as much as, say, providing residential or clinical services to battered women. The policy practitioner inserts provisions in the legislation to encourage shelters to spread word of their services to local self-help groups; local professionals who have extensive contact with women (such as stylists); female community leaders; and agencies that link women to schools, job placement, medical services, free clinics, and other agencies. She also requires the shelters to provide advocacy services, such as seeking greater protection by local police departments for women who have been abused.

Because shelters' staff and boards define priorities and objectives, the policy practitioner requires boards to select 51% of their membership from currently or previously battered women, female leaders in the community, and local professionals who work in self-help and other agencies. She hopes that this requirement will encourage shelters to implement these provisions, because these kinds of board members should be more sympathetic to her objectives than the businesspeople and professionals who usually dominate agencies' boards. To give the boards even greater powers, the policy practitioner also requires the boards to review programs and budgets in the hope that they will promote the full range of services included in the legislation, including advocacy, community-support systems, and outreach.[34]

Policy practitioners sometimes favor creating regional organizations to fund local agencies and shape policy choices.[35] Thus, Area Agencies for the Aging (AAAs) and regional boards sometimes assume these roles for various programs funded by states' block grants. These regional entities, some persons argue, are able to coordinate agencies' services in a relatively broad geographic area, identify underserved jurisdictions, and monitor the agencies' services in their areas. The policy practitioner could advocate creating regional boards and giving them substantial roles in funding and overseeing local shelters. She ultimately decides not to include regional entities in her legislation, because some members of the coalition fear that many conservatives, who tend to dislike "additional levels of bureaucracy," would oppose the legislation if they were added.

Overseeing Policy Implementation

While the boards and staff of local agencies play a major role in shaping the content and direction of services, officials in local, regional, state, and federal bureaucracies often monitor, assess, and regulate high-level, implemented policies. We call these functions *policy oversight. Monitoring* examines the extent to which local agencies actually implement official policies; *assessment* evaluates how much implemented policies help the recipients; and *regulations* provide steps, procedures, and reporting mechanisms for implementing agencies to use.[36]

We have already noted that the policy practitioner fears that if local agencies are unsupervised, they will neglect some important policies. She realizes, however, that it is unlikely that federal officials will be able to oversee every shelter under the Federal Shelter program. She decides to support a division of labor. Federal officials would provide administrative regulations, but whichever state agency distributes federal funds to shelters would receive a percentage of those funds (say 3%) for monitoring local programs. Moreover, each state would have to establish a Licensing Advisory Board composed of state fire, social-service, and health officials to develop minimum standards that each shelter must meet.

AN OVERVIEW OF THE PROPOSAL

We have seen our practitioner face a number of policy options and make some tentative choices. Here is an overview of her decisions. She established a mission by proposing a nationwide system of shelters for battered women. These shelters would provide a range of social services to these women. She designed the structure of service by placing the Federal Shelter program in the Department of Health and Human Services, using only nonprofit agencies, and setting some standards at the federal level, but requiring each state to appoint a lead agency to administer the funds to local agencies. She planned the infusion and circulation of resources by establishing an authorization level of $450 million, which would rise to $600 million within three years, and by using Route 2 (see Figure 7.1). She defined services by using an ecological paradigm, requiring services to include referral, crisis, case-management, advocacy, legal, and outreach services; proposing a regional hot line in designated regional areas; and requiring the shelter directors to possess an M.S.W. degree and direct-service staff to have had a supervised practicum. She rationed scarce resources by establishing a sliding fee, which can be waived when family finances are disrupted by dislocation; limiting residence to three-months, which can be waived when the resident remains in imminent danger of physical abuse; and by giving admittance priority to women in imminent danger of physical abuse. The proposal addresses community factors by requiring outreach to underserved segments of the population, links with community-support systems, advocacy, and 51% of the board to consist of currently or previously battered women, staff in agencies or support groups for this population, or community leaders. Finally, she arranged for the overseeing of policy implementation by earmarking 3% of funds to pay lead state agencies to monitor the shelter programs.

As we will note in the next chapter, it is relatively simple to list available policy options and to make preliminary choices, as our practitioner has done. But she and other members of her coalition have not yet encountered the hardships of the political process or persons who are not favorably disposed to her proposal. At that point, she will need to make some agonizing choices.

A CASE FROM THE HUMAN SERVICES

When social workers develop or restructure human services programs, they must identify several policy options and choose between them. In Case 7.1, for example, a social worker proposes an innovative community emergency service (CES) program for families that need immediate assistance.

CASE 7.1
POLICIES FOR A NEW PROGRAM

I was one of several coordinators assigned to develop an innovative program to provide community emergency services (CES) to families in a large metropolitan area. (The word *we* refers to the coordinators.)

We modeled this service system on a program in Nashville, Tennessee. Nashville had one large institution that housed the majority of children waiting to be placed. Public welfare staff members became aware of a lack of any real preventive system or alternatives to placement and developed a program model that incorporated six components (described later in this case) that could help a family in crisis.

Federal authorities recently chose an unincorporated area as a possible site for CES. Many people in the community recognized that this community had a problem delivering services to certain kinds of families. An initial exploration suggested that the community would be receptive to the program; thus, an administrator in the public welfare agency assigned us to the CES program to work with the community on devising policies.

Our initial focus as staff coordinators was to assess the community's needs, identify the problem areas, diagnose causes, and formulate solutions. The next step was to develop a constituency and devise strategies to effect necessary action. The regional administrator of the public welfare agency was helpful in providing two resources at this point. First, we received a list of various agencies and personnel in the community involved in providing services to families. The list identified key persons who could give information on the community's problems and on existing programs. We used this list and expanded it by contacting people informally to sound out problems that the community experienced. Second, we were given access to records of emergency family situations that the public welfare agency handled during the past two years. These records covered both day and evening situations and revealed that major defects existed in the community that the CES program could address.

During the day, the public welfare office and various community agencies handled families' emergencies. But the services sometimes overlapped and were not very well coordinated. The most severe problems, however, arose during the evening when no viable services for families existed. The sheriff picked up children from families in crisis and placed them in foster homes or in Duncan Hall (a county detention facility), because no emergency foster homes were available in the community.

These children, many of whom spoke only Spanish, were traumatized by being placed outside their homes in a strange community where no one could communicate with them. Often, when a parent was hospitalized on an emergency basis, the children went to Duncan Hall because no foster homes in the community were available at night for such families. Adolescents who were having family problems came into the court system because they were found on the streets at night. Some children came into placement because adequate housing was not available for the entire family. Finally, records revealed that service programs among various agencies in the community were not coordinated. In some instances, we found that various agencies were providing the same services to some families and none to others or were competing with one another for clients. Some families did not meet agencies' intake criteria and were denied services in a crisis.

The CES program developed six components:

1. Twenty-four–hour emergency intake
2. Emergency homemaker caretakers, who provide live-in parenting services when parents are temporarily disabled
3. Emergency foster-family homes
4. Emergency shelter for adolescents
5. Emergency shelter for families
6. Outreach and follow-up

Our next step was to develop a constituency and devise strategies to effect action. We accomplished this task in several ways. First, we met with various persons and agencies in the community about the problem they had identified and about what could be done from the community perspective. Next, we attended meetings of established groups in the community to learn more about community leaders and agencies, including the Interagency Coordinating Council, a group of ninety agencies that meet on a monthly basis and share resources and new program information. At these meetings, we began to network with agencies.

However, we began to face political problems. People in the community had strong feelings about the public welfare agency, some of which were negative. They asked whether the coordinators were really going to implement the services. In one instance, an agency executive in a small, private, community-based agency accused our agency of always talking but never producing results. We restated our commitment to the program and asked for community participation in the planning committees in order to make it both a public welfare and community system. Community people responded to our enthusiasm.

After a month and a half of reconnaissance work in the community, a large general meeting was held at a neighborhood center to bring together various community and agency personnel. The general meeting accomplished its goals by imparting information, garnering support, gaining legitimacy for the program, and making contacts in the community.

Six planning committees formed to focus on the six components. People received sheets at the general meeting to sign up for whichever component was most closely related to their interests or agency services. We facilitated weekly meetings. In December, two months later, another general meeting was held to inform people of the various committees' accomplishments with the hope of setting a time for the program's implementation.

After the first general CES meeting, we set up a meeting with the public welfare agency's administration to discuss what resources they would offer. It soon became obvious that, for a number of reasons, the key division chief did not fully support or understand the new CES project, which he described as an extension of an already existing twenty-four–hour hot line program in the public welfare agency. We were not part of the ongoing administrative staff and had not developed links within the department and therefore lacked credibility with this executive. Further, the executive had his superior's orders to explore the program, not approve it. (We were asking him to approve the plan to implement CES.) We realized we had made a tactical error and resolved to develop intradepartmental support for the CES program.

We spoke at meetings within the agency, informed line-staff supervisors and middle-management staff about CES, and asked for suggestions. We informally contacted staff in various offices of the public welfare agency to discuss the program and get support. These strategies were so successful that, when we requested a budget for CES, we were told that approval was likely by early January and that CES would begin on a trial basis by March. Resources that other community agencies offered helped keep projected costs relatively low.

It was the planning committee, however, that really influenced the public agency to sponsor the program. The twenty-four–hour intake committee found a twenty-four–hour phone line that CES could use. They set up intake guidelines for families coming into the program and they established written agreements with agencies about what services they would provide and who each agency's contact person would be after regular hours. Further, the public welfare agency agreed to assign six children's services workers to make home calls for the CES program at night.

Each of the committees submitted plans that recommended various resources. The emergency shelter committee was instrumental in gaining the county board of supervisors' support. Further, a powerful supervisor helped facilitate CES's working relationships with other county agencies by putting the coordinators in touch with key persons in the county medical center, mental health center, and the probation department.

By the first week in January, the public welfare agency had assigned eight homemakers to the program, two of whom were immediately available. Emergency bilingual and bicultural foster homes were developed in the Latino area for the CES program. Existing adolescent group homes in the community agreed to set aside beds for the CES program. The emergency shelter for families committee, in working with the Latina center, had found an old church building that they were preparing for use in one month. On the outreach component, various private and public agencies made written commitments to supply services once the program became operational.

In planning the project, the public welfare agency and the various community agencies divided up responsibility for providing services. As the project moved closer to implementation, the promise of services attained legitimacy for the program with community agencies, which maintained or developed closer ties with CES. We built links both external and internal because we knew that the program could not function without such connections (to the Public Department of Social Services). Service responsibilities among agencies were clearly defined, and community agencies gained prestige through association with the project.

SOURCE: This case is adapted from one developed by Mary Hayes, M.S.W. Names and locations have been altered.

LINKING POLICY SKILLS

From studying Case 7.1, we realize that practitioners must combine analytic skills in identifying, comparing, and selecting policy options with other policy-practice skills to be effective. Recall that the social worker wants to initiate a community emergency services program for families that need immediate assistance (such as when wife battering, child abuse, child neglect, severe marital conflict, illness, homelessness, and other conditions exist). Although the social worker is confident that she has developed an analytically sound proposal that includes six components, she has to convince public authorities and decision-makers that the proposal should be funded, a real political challenge in an era of scarce public resources. To meet this challenge, she employs political and interactional skills; by attending many community meetings and having personal discussions with highly placed officials (interactional skills) she *also* constructs a constituency for the proposal (political skills). Indeed, the social worker finds that she needs interactional and political skills to develop support for CES within the department where it would be housed. She uses value-clarification skills as she decides whether and how to put community pressure on her employers and as she contemplates acceding to department officials' attempts to diminish the proposed program's size.

As our example of the legislation to fund shelters for battered women suggests, policy practitioners must be acutely aware of political realities *as* they construct proposals. The women who drafted the legislation decided at several, critical junctures to incorporate provisions that our practitioner might have changed, had she not believed that she must heed political realities. She chose, for example, to include rather limited fiscal authorizations of $450 million in the first year. She also chose to use the states to administer the funds (Route 2), rather than giving federal authorities a more expansive role. In making these concessions to conservative and moderate politicians, she had to wrestle with the ethical dilemma, "Is half a loaf better than none?" (Recall our Chapter Two discussion of ethical dilemmas, which exist when ethical principles, such as social justice, are pitted against pragmatic factors, such as political realities.)

SUMMARY

We have discussed in this chapter policy options that practitioners often encounter when constructing social welfare proposals. They need substantive knowledge of these options. They need to understand the policy issues and options that recur in the American welfare state, including financing staffing, eligibility, and allocation choices. Furthermore, they should understand how many proposals contain combinations or clusters of policy options. Finally, practitioners need to know how to use political, value-clarifying, analytic, and interactional skills in tandem when developing policy proposals.

Policy practitioners need additional skills when developing proposals. When making policy choices, for example, policy practitioners must often grapple with the dilemma that each policy option has merits and weaknesses. Policy practitioners must frequently examine trade-offs to determine, on balance, which options appear preferable. They need to be able to fashion brief position-taking memos and construct longer proposals, such as grant proposals. They also need to be able to defend policy proposals by developing presentations, whether written or oral. We turn to these additional skills in the next two chapters.

Suggested Readings

FEDERAL, STATE, AND LOCAL RELATIONSHIPS

Paul Gorman, "Block Grants: Theoretical and Practical Issues in Federal/State/Local Revenue Sharing," *New England Journal of Human Services* 4 (Spring 1984): 19–23.
Richard Nathan and Fred Doolittle, "Federal Grants: Giving and Taking Away," *Political Science Quarterly* 100 (Spring 1985): 53–74.

PROFIT-ORIENTED, NOT-FOR-PROFIT, AND PUBLIC AGENCY RELATIONSHIPS

Harry Carroll, Ralph Conant, and Thomas Easton, eds., *Private Means—Public Ends: Private Business and Social Service Delivery* (New York: Praeger, 1987).
Harold Demone and Margaret Gibelman, eds., *Services for Sale* (New Brunswick, NJ: Rutgers University Press, 1989).
Alfred Kahn, "Public Social Services: The Next Phase," *Public Welfare* 30 (Winter 1972): 15–25.
Sheila Kamerman and Alfred Kahn, *Privatization and the American Welfare State* (Princeton, NJ: Princeton University Press, 1984).
Lester Salamon and Alan Abramson, *The Nonprofit Sector and the New Federal Budget* (Washington, DC: Urban Institute Press, 1986).
Stan Smith and Deborah Stone, "The Unexpected Consequences of Privatization," in Michael Brown, ed., *Remaking the Welfare State* (Philadelphia: Temple University Press, 1988), pp. 232–252.

Organizational Issues in the American Welfare State
Michael Murphy, "Organizational Approaches for Human Services Programs," in Wayne Anderson et al., eds., *Managing Human Services* (Washington, DC: International City Management Association, 1977), pp. 193–229.

Fiscal Issues
Harold Demone and Margaret Gibelman, *Services for Sale* (New Brunswick, NJ: Rutgers University Press, 1989), pp. 101–102.
Herman Leonard, *Checks Unbalanced: The Quiet Side of Public Spending* (New York: Basic Books, 1986).
Paul Terrel, "Financing Social Welfare Services," in Neil Gilbert and Harry Specht, eds., *Handbook of the Social Services* (Englewood Cliffs, NJ: Prentice-Hall, 1981), pp. 380–410.

Professional and Staffing Issues
Bruce Fretz and David Mills, *Licensing and Certification of Psychologists and Counselors* (San Francisco: Jossey-Bass, 1980), pp. 9–29.
David Hardcastle, "The Profession: Professional Organizations, Licensing, and Private Practice," in Gilbert and Specht, *Handbook of the Social Services*, pp. 666–688.

Allocation Issues
Richard Frank, "Rationing of Mental Health Services: Simple Observations on the Current Approach and Future Prospects," *Administration in Mental Health* 13 (Fall 1985): 22–29.
Neil Gilbert and Harry Specht, *Dimensions of Social Welfare Policy,* 2nd ed. (Englewood Cliffs, NJ: Prentice-Hall, 1986), pp. 66–91.
Richard Titmuss, "Laissez-Faire and Stigma," in Brian Abel-Smith and Kay Titmuss, eds., *Social Policy: An Introduction* (London: Allen and Unwin, 1974), pp. 33–46.

Prevention
Martin Bloom, *Primary Prevention: The Possible Science* (Englewood Cliffs, NJ: Prentice-Hall, 1981).
Neil Gilbert, "Policy Issues in Primary Prevention," *Social Work* 27 (May 1982): 293–297.

Staff Discretion
Robert Goodin, *Reasons for Welfare: The Political Theory of the Welfare State* (Princeton, NJ: Princeton University Press, 1988), pp. 184–228.

Notes

1. For an overview of one effort to secure federal legislation to fund shelters for abused women, see the *Congressional Quarterly Almanac* 35 (Washington, DC: Congressional Quarterly Service, 1979), pp. 508–509. Also see Liane Davis and Jan Hagen, "Services for Battered Women: The Public Policy Response," *Social Service Review* 62 (December 1988): 649–667.
2. Bruce Jansson, "The History and Politics of Selected Children's Programs and Related Legislation," (Ph.D. diss., University of Chicago, 1975), pp. 66–67, 76–77.
3. See Paul Gorman, "Block Grants: Theoretical and Practical Issues in Federal/State/Local Revenue Sharing," *New England Journal of Human Services* 4 (Spring 1984): 19–23; Robert Fulton and Ray Scott, "What Happened to the Federal/State Partnerships?" *New*

England Journal of Human Services 4 (Fall 1984): 38-39; and Allen Imersheim, "The Influence of Reagan's New Federalism on Human Services in Florida," *New England Journal of Human Services* 5 (Spring 1985): 17-24.

4. Some overview literature on auspices includes Ralph Kramer, *Voluntary Agencies in the Welfare State* (Berkeley and Los Angeles: University of California Press, 1981); Bruce Jansson, "Public Monitoring of Contracts with Nonprofit Organizations: Organizational Mission in Two Sectors," *Journal of Sociology and Social Welfare* 6 (May 1979): 362-374.
5. Richard Titmuss defends public agencies in, *The Gift Relationship* (New York: Pantheon, 1971). Alfred Kahn also makes such a defense in, "Public Social Services: The Next Phase," *Public Welfare* 30 (Winter 1972): 15-25.
6. For an overview of some criticisms of public agencies, see Ralph Kramer, "From Voluntarism to Vendorism: An Organizational Perspective on Contracting," in Harold Demone and Margaret Gibelman, eds., *Services for Sale* (New Brunswick, NJ: Rutgers University Press, 1989), pp. 101-102.
7. For a critical overview of the emergence and roles of nonprofit agencies in the federally funded welfare state, see Eleanor Brilliant, "Private or Public: A Model of Ambiguities," *Social Service Review* 47 (September 1973): 384-396.
8. For criticisms of voluntary agencies, see Kramer, "From Voluntarism to Vendorism," pp. 102-103.
9. For a defense of profit-oriented agencies, see Emanuel Savas, *Privatizing the Public Sector: How to Shrink Government* (Chatham, NJ: Chatham House Publishers, 1982).
10. For criticism of profit-oriented agencies, see Harold Demone and Margaret Gibelman, "Privatizing the Acute Care General Hospital," in Harry Carroll, Ralph Conant, and Thomas Easton, eds., *Private Means—Public Ends: Private Business and Social Service Delivery* (New York: Praeger, 1987), pp. 50-75.
11. For an overview of funding options, see Paul Terrel, "Financing Social Welfare Services," in Neil Gilbert and Harry Specht, eds., *Handbook of the Social Services* (Englewood Cliffs, NJ: Prentice-Hall, 1981), pp. 392-394.
12. Ibid., pp. 398-399.
13. Classic accounts of the authorizations and appropriations processes are found in Richard Fenno, *Power of the Purse* (Boston: Little, Brown, 1966) and Aaron Wildavsky, *Politics of the Budgetary Process* (Boston: Little, Brown, 1964).
14. See Demone and Gibelman, *Services for Sale*.
15. John Coons and Stephen Sugarman defend voucher and vendor payments in, *Education by Choice: The Case for Family Control* (Berkeley and Los Angeles: University of California Press, 1978). Frederick Thayer criticizes them in, "Privatization: Carnage, Chaos, and Corruption," in Carroll, Conant, and Easton, *Private Means—Public Ends*, pp. 146-170.
16. Various points of view on block grants appear in Richard Nathan and Fred Doolittle, "Federal Grants: Giving and Taking Away," *Political Science Quarterly* 100 (Spring 1985): 53-74, and Richard Williamson, "The 1982 New Federalism Negotiations," *Publius* 13 (Spring 1983): 11-33.
17. Thayer, "Privatization."
18. See Herman Leonard, *Checks Unbalanced: The Quiet Side of Public Spending* (New York: Basic Books, 1986).
19. Ibid., pp. 251-265, for criticism of the use of the tax system.
20. Bruce Fretz and David Mills, *Licensing and Certification of Psychologists and Counselors* (San Francisco: Jossey-Bass, 1980).

21. David Hardcastle, "The Profession: Professional Organizations, Licensing, and Private Practice," in Neil Gilbert and Harry Specht, eds., *Handbook of the Social Services* (Englewood Cliffs, NJ: Prentice-Hall, 1981), p. 677.
22. Ibid., pp. 679–683.
23. Ibid., pp. 666–687.
24. Robert Teare, *Classification Validation Processes for Social Services Positions* (Silver Spring, MD: National Association of Social Workers, 1984).
25. S. K. Khinduka, "Social Work and the Human Services," *Encyclopedia of Social Work*, 18th ed., vol. 2 (Silver Spring, MD: National Association of Social Workers, 1987), p. 691.
26. Martin Bloom defends preventive services in, *Primary Prevention: The Possible Science* (Englewood Cliffs, NJ: Prentice-Hall, 1981).
27. Neil Gilbert makes cautionary comments on prevention in, "Policy Issues in Primary Prevention," *Social Work* 27 (May 1982): 293–297.
28. For a discussion of rationing, see Richard Frank, "Rationing of Mental Health Services: Simple Observations on the Current Approach and Future Prospects," *Administration in Mental Health* 13 (Fall 1985): 22–29.
29. A general discussion of means tests appears in Neil Gilbert and Harry Specht, *Dimensions of Social Welfare Policy* 2nd ed. (Englewood Cliffs, NJ: Prentice-Hall, 1986), pp. 82–84.
30. For a discussion of staff discretion, see Robert Goodin, *Reasons for Welfare: The Political Theory of the Welfare State* (Princeton, NJ: Princeton University Press, 1988), pp. 184–228.
31. For differences in AFDC when states establish their own eligibility standards, see Joseph Heffernan, "New Directions in Welfare Reform Debate: The Problems of Federalism," *Journal of Sociology and Social Welfare* 15 (December 1988): 3–27.
32. See Noel Tichy, *Organization Design for Primary Health Care* (New York: Praeger, 1977), p. 100.
33. For subtle forms of discrimination and rationing, see Sharon Sepulveda-Hassell, *An Assessment of the Mental Health Treatment Process: Eliminating Service Barriers to Mexican Americans* (San Antonio, TX: Intercultural Development Research Association, 1980), and David Ramirez, *A Review of Literature on Underutilization of Mental Health Services by Mexican Americans: Implications for Future Research and Service Delivery* (San Antonio, TX: Intercultural Development Research Association, 1980).
34. A similar tactic was used in the Head Start program; see Jansson, "History and Politics of Selected Children's Programs," p. 131.
35. For discussion of regional agencies, see Eli Ginzburg, ed., *Regionalization and Health Policy* (Washington, DC: Government Printing Office, 1977).
36. For a discussion of monitoring, see Bruce Jansson, "The Political Economy of Monitoring: A Contingency Perspective," in Demone and Gibelman, *Services for Sale*, pp. 343–359, and Kenneth Wedel and Nancy Chess, "Monitoring Strategies in Purchase of Service Contracting," in Demone and Gibelman, *Services for Sale*, pp. 360–370.

Chapter Eight

Selecting Options and Writing Proposals

Although it is important to know about recurring policy options, such as those discussed in the last chapter, it is equally important to *use* those options to write policy proposals. Policy proposals can take many forms. Some are relatively brief, while others are lengthy; some are highly detailed, while others are relatively vague; some contain objectives and goals, while others emphasize methods of implementing policies.

Shaping a proposal is a critical juncture in policy practice, because it requires policy practitioners to translate their preferences into a tangible and presentable form. While practitioners often change or modify proposals in the course of deliberations, they provide a starting point for discussion.

In this chapter, we will discuss analytic skills used to select policy options and construct proposals, while noting that political realities often influence policy practitioners' choices. Having constructed proposals, policy practitioners must defend them in memos, presentations, debates, and negotiations. This requires interactional skills, which we cover in the next chapter.

TRADE-OFFS: SYSTEMATICALLY COMPARING POLICY OPTIONS

To make systematic comparisons of policy options, policy practitioners often proceed deliberately; they identify options, select and weigh criteria, and rank options and develop a decisionmaking matrix.[1] To explore further this analytic style of reasoning, we have selected a simple example, which should illustrate and demystify it. In our example, officials of an overcrowded school district weigh alternative policies before selecting a course of action. (We discuss analytic and qualitative approaches.)

Identifying Options

Policy analysts rarely feel comfortable with a single policy option; they want to compare and contrast alternative policies before making a final selection.

Someone seeking to end malnutrition in certain segments of the population, for example, might examine the merits of distributing food directly to certain persons, changing the Food Stamps Program, and changing existing welfare programs to give low-income persons more funds to purchase food. These three policy options might in turn be contrasted with how expanding income tax credits to poor persons would affect food consumption. By identifying these four options, the policy analyst hopes to avoid prematurely committing to a specific policy.

Policy analysts sometimes examine, not alternative policies, but yes-and-no options. Take the case of a state-funded social program that has never been formally evaluated. Deciding that they can no longer take its effectiveness for granted, state officials decide to subject it to a rigorous evaluation that will determine whether the program provides sufficient benefits to merit its continuation. In this case, the options are "continue the program" or "terminate the program," a choice that many policy analysts hope would be made on the issue's merits, rather than because a political faction has the power to obtain its preferences.

Selecting and Weighing Criteria

In order to select an optimal policy, practitioners must first identify criteria to use as a basis of comparison. In simple cases, a single criterion suffices; given three policy options, for example, and the single criterion of cost, the cheapest policy option would be selected. In most cases, however, analysts identify several criteria. For example, they often consider costs, administrative feasibility, and effectiveness in addressing consumers' needs. After selecting more than one criterion, policy analysts need to weigh their relative importance.

To illustrate the selection and use of multiple criteria, take the example of a school district with overcrowded schools. The district must decide whether to build more schools (Option 1) or keep the facilities in year-round use (Option 2). The second option would be possible if each student and teacher received three six-week breaks staggered during the academic year, rather than the traditional eighteen-week summer vacation. By staggering the breaks, the school would be filled during each month of the year. In a public meeting about this issue, a variety of criteria emerge. One school official believes that cost is the most important criterion because, he argues, the district is strapped for funds. A leader of the teachers' union contends that teachers' morale will be devastated if teachers have to take three six-week vacations during the year, rather than the traditional eighteen-week summer vacation; she insists that teacher morale be an important criterion. Some working women with several children in schools wonder if their day-care problems will be exacerbated by the year-round option. They say it will be difficult to find day-care programs for six-week blocks at scattered points during the year. These parents insist that day-care considerations be included as an important criterion.

Even this brief example suggests the sheer number of criteria that policy analysts can consider. When multiple criteria exist, someone has to decide which of them are important, which are relatively trivial, and which should not be considered at all. As this example illustrates, value and political considerations strongly influence both the selecting and weighing of criteria. If the teachers' union has considerable power, for example, it is likely to persuade the school board to seriously consider the impact of a year-round schedule on morale of teachers. By contrast, unrepresented or powerless groups who might be harmed in important ways by a scheduling change may find their concerns relegated to a secondary status in policy deliberations. Assume, for example, that many low-income students need to have summer jobs and that they are unlikely to find jobs for three six-week vacations scattered throughout the year. Unless someone taken seriously by school board members articulated this problem, this economic issue might not be considered at all.

Varieties of Criteria

As was discussed in Chapter Two, *value-based criteria* are reflected by such terms as *equality, equity, social justice,* and various freedoms, such as the right to free speech, the right to privacy, the right to receive accurate and honest information, and the right to self-determination.[2] (Moral philosophers, religious leaders, the due process clause of the Fourteenth Amendment to the Constitution, and the Bill of Rights discuss these value-based criteria.)

Consumer-outcome criteria define specific policies' effectiveness in redressing social problems. In the social services, for example, people often scrutinize how various policy options will affect clients' well-being. To return to our example of the schools, one could ask whether students learn more effectively with a three-month summer vacation or with three six-week vacations scattered throughout the year. Of course, effective learning constitutes only one measure of student well-being; others, such as their social, economic, and developmental well-being, could be considered as well.

Terms such as *efficiency* and *cost* reflect *economic criteria*. School board officials want to know the relative costs of constructing new school buildings and mandatory year-round attendance, because they have scarce resources. However, it is sometimes relatively complicated to compute the costs of various policy options. The old adage "penny-wise and pound-foolish" illustrates that options that save funds in the short run sometimes cost more in the long run. In this case, a decision not to build more schools would bring short-term savings, but the board might encounter long-term costs if it built new schools in fifteen years when the costs of land and construction have risen dramatically. These long-term costs might offset the short-term savings of delaying construction. Costs can also be difficult to assess when policy choices bring hidden costs. Were the school board to decide not to construct new buildings, teachers might demand higher salaries as compensation for the inconvenience of teaching on a year-round schedule.

Feasibility criteria pertain to the political and administrative practicality of specific policy options. An option might seem quite attractive, but be rejected because it could not be implemented or was not politically tractable. For example, some persons believe we should decriminalize certain drugs, such as cocaine, by selling them at relatively cheap prices in state-regulated stores. However, many practical details could confound the administration of the new policy. If cocaine were legalized, what about countless substances such as PCP ("angel dust") and others not even yet invented? If cocaine were legalized, the state-regulated stores might offer a wide assortment of mood-altering substances. Who would pay for growing or manufacturing the currently illegal drugs? Should poor persons be allowed to use their food stamps to purchase them? Could federal authorities easily override state laws that declare mood-altering substances to be illegal? Would authorities have to limit the amount of drugs someone could purchase, or could persons obtain unlimited quantities? Could drugs in such an open market be kept from adolescents or schoolchildren, or would older friends, siblings, or even some parents supply them? Some politicians would likely assail this policy for threatening to corrode our youth's morals by making drugs too accessible.

Externalities criteria assess how a policy option affects institutions or persons who initially appear unrelated to a policy. If drugs were decriminalized, including hallucinatory ones, policy analysts would have to ask whether driving accidents would markedly increase. This externality could not be dismissed as trivial because as many as 35,000 Americans die each year from the effects of driving while under the influence of alcohol, a decriminalized and accessible drug. However, some positive externalities might offset these negative ones. The reduced price of drugs and the increased availability in state-regulated stores would drive criminal elements, gangs, and foreign profiteers from drug dealing and would make it unnecessary for addicts to steal to support their habits.

Terms such as *cost effectiveness* reflect how we can combine several criteria into single measures.[3] In cost-effectiveness studies, analysts want to know which policy will most benefit consumers at the lowest cost. One policy option may yield considerable benefit to consumers, but at a prohibitive cost; another option may yield few benefits, but at a low cost; and a third option may provide considerable benefits at a relatively modest cost. A policy analyst who wants a cost-effective policy would probably select the third option because it balances cost and effectiveness.

Creating a Decisionmaking Matrix

To help select policies, policy analysts often construct a decisionmaking matrix that graphically portrays the options and criteria.[4] In our case of the school board, they want to display the two policy options (year-round attendance versus construction of new buildings) and four criteria (cost, teacher morale, parental daycare considerations, and students' educational achievements). As can be seen in Table 8.1, a decisionmaking matrix organizes the options and criteria into a table.

CHAPTER EIGHT Selecting Options and Writing Proposals 217

TABLE 8.1
A Decisionmaking Matrix

	Criteria			
Policy options	Cost	Teacher morale	Parents' day-care needs	Student learning
Schedule year-round attendance with staggered vacations				
Initiate a major construction program				

TABLE 8.2
Policy Options Ranked by Criteria

	Criteria				
Policy options	Cost (.50)	Teacher morale (.15)	Parents' day-care needs (.10)	Student learning (.25)	Total
Schedule year-round attendance with staggered attendance	⑧ 4	④ .6	③ .3	⑩ 2.5	7.4
Initiate a major construction program	③ 1.5	⑦ 1.05	⑧ .8	⑩ 2.5	5.85

The school board members must rank the two options' relative merits by assigning scores in the cells of the decisionmaking matrix. They will then select the policy option with the best score. To score the options, the school board must first rank the relative importance of the four criteria across the top of the matrix. As with any rating system, some rules must be established.[5] While there are several scoring mechanisms, they decide to rank each criterion from .001 to .999, based on its importance to them. Moreover, they decide that the criteria's four scores must add up to 1.0 to force them to decide the criteria's comparative value. The board decides to rank cost as .50, teacher morale as .15, parents' day-care needs as .10, and student learning as .25. By ranking the criteria in this manner, the board has decided that cost counts the most, parents' day-care needs and teacher morale count the least, and that students' educational needs receive middle-range importance. They place these rankings directly beneath each criterion in parentheses at the top of Table 8.2.

The board must next assign the two policy options scores with respect to each of the four criteria. They can use some combinations of research data, expert opinions, and their best guesses. Again, they need some ranking system. They decide to rank the options from 1 (poor) to 10 (outstanding) and place these rankings in circles next to each policy option (see Table 8.2). The board rates the full-year option as 8 with respect to cost, because it will be less costly than a major construction program, and the new-construction option as 3, because of the high cost of construction. By contrast, the board gives the new-construction program a higher ranking (7) than the year-round option (4) with respect to teacher morale, because most teachers prefer summer vacations to staggered vacations. Similarly, the board ranks the new-construction program relatively high with respect to day-care needs (8), because working parents have persuaded them that it would be difficult to arrange day-care if vacations are staggered; the year-round option receives a ranking of only 3 on this criterion. Both policy options receive the same score of 10 with respect to student learning, because the board does not feel that either option will jeopardize their education.

The board must now calculate scores that combine its ranking of the options for each criterion (the circled scores) and the relative importance of each criterion (the numbers in parentheses).[6] The board decides to multiply the circled score in each cell by the number in parentheses at the head of each column. This will produce a final score in each cell. (The summary scores are underlined in Table 8.2.) The year-round option thus obtains a score of 4 with respect to cost (.50 x 8 = 4), while the major construction program obtains only 1.5 in that category (.50 x 3 = 1.5). The year-round option obtains the same score as the construction program with respect to student learning and lower scores in teacher morale and day-care needs.

Which option should be selected? When the board adds the underlined scores in the various cells next to each option, it finds that the year-round option achieves a somewhat higher score (4 + .6 + .3 + 2.5 = 7.4) than does the construction option (1.5 + 1.05 + .8 + 2.5 = 5.85). The biggest difference between the two options occurred with respect to cost, partly because the board gave such importance to this criterion in its deliberations.

The term *trade-offs* refers to assessing the comparative advantages of policy options. In the case of the school board, we can visualize the two competing options as weighing down the ends of an old-fashioned balance scale; the analyst seeks to discover which option has the most *weight*—that is, has the greatest net score on criteria that the policy analyst has identified and ranked.[7] Thus, the board selected the first policy option, even though the second option is superior with respect to teachers' morale and parents' day-care needs.

When reviewing this example of a decisionmaking matrix, it is important to dwell not on the details of the scoring rules that the school board adopted, but rather on its *style* of analytic reasoning. Other numeric rules could easily have been used to rank the criteria and the various options and to compute summary scores. When using an analytic style of reasoning, the policy analyst breaks the selection process into a series of sequential steps that eventually lead to an overall score for specific options.

Using policy matrices, such as Table 8.2, does not necessarily eliminate conflict, because persons can disagree about the criteria selected, their relative importance, and specific options' scores for those criteria. Recall that the board had ranked new construction as superior to year-round schooling with respect to day-care services because the board believed that working parents would have difficulty finding child care during the staggered vacations that would occur with year-round schooling. Had they taken part in the deliberations, for example, some parents might have vigorously contested the board's assertion that new construction was superior to year-round schooling with respect to daycare, because the board could incorporate into the new buildings some childcare facilities. Teachers might have objected to the assertion that year-round schools are more harmful to teacher morale than schools with traditional summer vacations. Considerable guesswork and intuition often enter the rankings, even if some policy analysts believe that they are approaching the decision scientifically.

When policy analysis occurs before a policy is enacted, as in the case of the school district, analysts must predict the outcomes, costs, and consequences of policies; in many cases, these kinds of estimates turn out to be inaccurate. The school board could discover, to their chagrin, that they grossly underestimated the costs of a policy option or its effectiveness in redressing a social problem.

Even when data exist, they can often be disputed. Perhaps researchers found another school district that had already adopted a year-round schedule and concluded that its teachers had, on balance, liked it. A skeptic might ask if this research was flawed; perhaps researchers surveyed an inadequate sample of teachers or used inadequate data-gathering instruments, or perhaps the teachers in the other district possessed different preferences than those in the school board's district.

Qualitative Rankings

Had the board not been quantitatively inclined, it could have *qualitatively* ranked the two policy options. Some critics of quantitative techniques would readily support this tactic on grounds that existing data does not allow accurate quantitative rankings. (We have noted even in this simple example that it is difficult to make scientific estimates of "teacher morale" or "student learning" and how weighting the different criteria profoundly reflects the values and interests of those persons who make these rankings.) However, persons making qualitative rankings (such as "high," "medium," and "low") would still have to develop options and criteria and weigh the criteria in order to judge the relative merits of the two policy options.

Table 8.3 portrays some trade-offs that social workers in agencies often encounter. Indeed, the practitioner in Chapter Seven who developed legislation to help battered women would have encountered each of the trade-offs in Table 8.3 when designing shelter programs at the local level.

TABLE 8.3
Trade-offs for Policy Options

Policy options	Advantages	Disadvantages
Intensive rather than extensive services	Provides in-depth services with greater impact	Denies services to large numbers of consumers
Development of community-based rather than institutional services	Decreases stigma of service; helps integrate consumers into mainstream	Is difficult to orchestrate several community services and involve transient populations
Using generic rather than specialized services or staff	Focuses on client as a whole person	Staff members lack specialized expertise relevant to consumers' specific needs
Providing preventive rather than curative services	Allows early detection and treatment of social problems and educates consumers to forestall development of problems	May neglect the needs of people who already have a serious problem
Universal rather than selective eligibility	Allows staff to serve all applicants; makes imposing means tests unnecessary	Makes it difficult to target scarce resources to those with particularly serious problems
Decentralized rather than centralized services	Makes outreach to consumers possible; improves access to services and use of community networks	Is more expensive to operate than centralized facilities
Using multiprofessional teams rather than single professions	Allows many professions to contribute to service	Makes interprofessional conflict possible

VALUE ISSUES IN CONSTRUCTING PROPOSALS

We have emphasized analytic and interactional skills in this chapter, but policy practitioners also use value-clarifying skills. Values come into play at numerous points in the analytic process; people must decide how to define social problems, which policy options are even worth considering, and how to weigh criteria. Moreover, they must meld options into an embracing proposal that reflects important values, while also considering realities that may force them to make concessions.[8]

Many paradigms help examine social problems, such as intrapsychic, ecological, and radical ones, as we discussed in Chapter Six. Definitions of problems shape the solutions people propose. Those who define AIDS as only a physiological problem, for example, are likely to concentrate exclusively on providing medical services, while those who use an ecological framework are more likely to help AIDS patients cope with discrimination, economic destitution, and mental trauma.[9] Selecting paradigms bears ethical implications. Defining AIDS in narrowly medical terms risks violating the principle of beneficence, because this paradigm overlooks ameliorative programs, such as ones that prevent discrimination against AIDS sufferers in medical clinics, residential arenas, and workplaces.[10]

Some practitioners deliberately omit certain policy options from deliberations to ensure that they will not be included in the final proposals. Perhaps they dislike options that call for fundamental reforms of existing policies, that could harm their personal interests or that force them to alter traditional modes of providing services.[11] Practitioners can omit disliked policy options from deliberations in several ways. Individuals who support them can be excluded from deliberations. Such individuals could be scapegoated by calling them "troublemakers" or other pejorative names. (Scapegoating silences critics effectively by exposing them to peer pressure that impugns their ideas and reputations.)

Selecting program options also has ethical implications. If practitioners refuse to consider options that challenge existing (and defective) institutions, they risk violating beneficence and social justice. At the same time, inattention to practical political realities can also be attacked on ethical grounds, because it may prevent legislation from passing. Policy practitioners who enact modest programs, even ones that fail to achieve reformers' full objectives, sometimes obtain services that might otherwise not exist.

Criteria can skew the evaluations of policy options so that certain options are selected or rejected. If cost is the only criterion, for example, policy options that are somewhat more costly than other options will be rejected, even when they have considerable merit. A policy option that would be highly effective in addressing clients' needs may be prematurely rejected solely because it is more expensive than another.

Many critics of contemporary policy analysis have faulted the tendency to select only criteria that lend themselves to quantitative measurements. In this process, value-based criteria, such as reducing inequality, fairness, and restoring public trust in social services are sometimes excluded.[12] To be certain, some value-based criteria are difficult to define and controversial, as was discussed in Chapter Two. Promoting equality, for example, raises many questions. Do we want to redress inequalities in access to specific services, or to make certain people's life conditions (such as housing) equal to those of others?[13] *Whose* inequalities do we wish to decrease? Should we put highest priority on helping women, racial minorities, or groups with stigmatized problems, such as mental health issues or poverty, or some combination of these (or other) characteristics? *How much* equality is feasible or desirable? Individuals who wish to reduce certain inequalities for specific groups are likely to stimulate spirited opposition from those who contend that this would jeopardize the rights or needs of *other* people. Critics of affirmative action maintain, for example, that preferential treatment of racial minorities and women brings "reverse discrimination" against white males.

The difficulties of defining certain criteria, such as equality, ought not deter us from using them, however. If no one uses them, important values such as equality and social justice will be excluded from policy deliberations.[14] Indeed, as was argued in Chapter Two, social workers, whose founders often sought to help disadvantaged people, should envision their policy practice as including advocacy for unpopular causes and unpopular criteria.[15]

While policy practitioners should include several criteria in their analysis of policy options, they should realize that such inclusiveness often makes selecting options more difficult. As we add criteria, we increase the chances that the criteria will conflict, as the example of involuntary commitment procedures for mental patients shows. If a department of mental health only uses the criteria of minimizing short-run costs and maximizing the self-determination of people with severe mental conditions, for example, it might emphasize strict limits on psychiatric evaluation teams' (PET teams) freedom in committing persons to mental institutions. This policy would also restrict commitments to hospitals, thus limiting the mental health department's costs. If the department *also* adds the criteria of enhancing the general public's safety and decreasing the likelihood that persons with severe mental conditions will harm themselves, its process of policy selection becomes more difficult. Not only must it consider more options, but the criteria now conflict. The department staff members are likely to feel pulled in different ways; if they restrict the intake staff's ability to use involuntary commitments, they risk jeopardizing the safety of some clients, as well as that of the general public. Conversely, if they allow staff to commit patients whenever staff believe a patient needs intensive care, they risk violating the self-determination of those patients who oppose commitment.

It is tempting to simplify complex issues such as commitment procedures to expedite solutions, but that risks ignoring important issues. When different principles are involved that suggest conflicting policy options, practitioners ought not avoid such dilemmas. In the case of commitment procedures, we should value patients' self-determination and well-being *and* the well-being of the general public. As was already noted, we should often feel pulled in different directions when we develop policy proposals—a conflict we can only partially resolve by seeking compromises.

When resources are scarce, policy practitioners often wonder which issues or problems should be given priority. For example, a mental health agency that decides to focus on attracting relatively affluent clients to obtain fees could fail to seek funds to help homeless or other impoverished clients. The principles of beneficence and social justice suggest that social agencies have an ethical duty to direct their scarce resources, as well as their fund-raising and political energies, to helping particularly needy populations.[16]

WRITING MEMOS

Another way to compare and choose options is to write a memo. Case 8.1 is a good example of a memo that delineates a number of options, examines their advantages and disadvantages, ranks them qualitatively, and reaches a conclusion at the end.

A social worker actually prepared this memo in the early 1980s for the Commissioner of the Department of Mental Health (DMH) where she examines policy options with respect to her state's services for mentally ill persons. The author compares (1) deinstitutionalization, (2) liquidating existing state schools, and (3) implementing a purchase-of-service (POS) system of community care, where public authorities reimburse nongovernmental agencies for providing specific community-based services. At the end of the memo, she chooses deinstitutionalization coupled with retaining smaller hospitals.

Of course, as with any policy conclusion, someone can take issue with her analysis and conclusions, whether by questioning her criteria, by questioning her rankings of the options, or by proposing options not even presented in her memo. The importance of this memo for our purposes lies not in its specific conclusions on a policy issue at a particular point in Massachusetts history, but *in its style of reasoning* about options, criteria, trade-offs, and conclusions. All social workers could develop similar analyses of issues and problems, even ones that arise in the agencies where they work.

CASE 8.1
MEMORANDUM TO THE COMMISSIONER

I. Policy Issue

In the context of the next five-year plans, what should be the role of state hospitals for the mentally ill? Specifically, should DMH care for its remaining institutionalized clients completely within existing institutions, completely within the community by purchase of services (POS), or somewhere in between? How can the department shape its personnel policy accordingly?

Recommendations: The goal for mentally ill clients should be liquidating existing state hospitals, leaving one small institution in each of the seven regions to serve violent patients. The proposed facilities would be operated by private auspices under state contract. Community-care services should be completely POS. DMH's personnel policy should be, implicitly, one of attrition, where civil servants in DMH are trained and transferred to other state positions and to community service settings under public auspices in settings like municipal hospitals. Explicitly, DMH should work closely with unions to arrange for three options: early retirement, training and transfer to other state positions, and training and transfer to community-service settings under public auspices to preserve vesting but not civil service protections. These places might include municipal hospitals, state university–sponsored settings, and so forth.

II. Summary and Analysis of Issues

The impetus for deinstitutionalization stems from a belief, buttressed by research findings, that large institutions inhibit and discourage mentally ill individuals' potential to function independently. Prevalent in the past twenty years, this belief underlies passage of the Community Mental Health Centers Act of 1963. Legal developments, especially several Supreme Court decisions, have hastened deinstitutionalization by prohibiting involuntary commitment without provision of treatment. Social programs, such as Medicaid, Medicare, Title XX, and SSI, have provided heretofore absent funding for community services. These developments have taken 370,000 people out of public mental hospitals from 1955 to 1975. In Massachusetts, 7000 people have left state hospitals between 1971 and 1978.

Current situation: These deinstitutionalized clients have frequently been placed in nursing homes that lack the resources and the inclination to meet the needs of mentally ill residents. Many other individuals reside in substandard boarding houses, do not receive rehabilitation or treatment services, frequently decompensate, and are readmitted to state hospitals. Still other individuals are simply lost to follow-up treatment.

This situation stems from gaps in community services for a deinstitutionalized population, the availability of services not tailored to the needs of the mentally ill individual but offering a protective environment, and pressure to deinstitutionalize quickly due to mounting costs and a desire to avoid legal suits. This urgency precludes planning to fill service gaps and foster receptive community attitudes.

What should the optimal community care system look like? What is needed? The literature abounds with descriptions of successful and unsuccessful community-care programs for deinstitutionalized, mentally ill people. The same essential program elements emerge again and again as keys to success or failure. They are: targeting chronic patients, which is a priority; links to other resources—for example, vocational rehabilitation; community provision of the full range of functions associated with institutional care; individually tailored treatment; culturally relevant programs tailored to local communities; specially trained staff attuned to the survival problems of mentally ill clients living in noninstitutional settings; public or private beds; and internal evaluation of these resources.

The problem at hand is how to move states such as Massachusetts from having half-filled institutions and underserved, deinstitutionalized clients to a fully community-based model that incorporates these eight program elements.

III. Available Options

Option 1: Discontinue deinstitutionalization. Devote scarce resources to upgrading institutions.

- *Pro:* This option appeals to those who doubt mentally ill individuals' potential for growth and who, due to concern or contempt, want them off community streets. It is administratively simpler, leaving the state in complete control. However, it is likely to be more costly than using community services, because community-based programs have federal funding sources, such as SSI and Medicaid.

• *Con:* Research offers strong support that large institutions reduce individualization, thereby discouraging ego development necessary for independent functioning. Current concern for civil liberties will not tolerate this option, particularly with regard to the mentally ill.

Option 2: Develop a complete community-care system, incorporating the eight program elements. Fund the services with POS.

• *Pro:* Critics of POS say that providers dominate the state, which loses control and is dominated by providers. However, this has largely been due to a lack of state planning, an abundance of personnel trained in direct-service, rather than management, and a state inferiority complex. These deficiencies can be altered. State legislatures must be persuaded to keep providing funds to support institutional care and new funds to develop community services. Once community settings are in place, institutional expenditures can be converted to community expenditures, and new funds can be discontinued. This interim support of two systems is vital to planning efforts. Administrative personnel can be retrained and direct-service personnel phased out. Liquidating property assets and converting direct-service expenditures into POS monies provide the state with buying power it need not be afraid to exercise. Community mental health centers and other financially distressed community-service settings will welcome state funding.

• *Con:* As exemplified by community mental health centers, community programs reject the mentally ill as "unrewarding." Community residents reject the mentally ill out of fear, disgust, and concerns about property devaluation. Although some programs may welcome state funding, delayed payment creates prohibitive cash-flow problems.

Option 3: Develop a community-care system incorporating the eight key elements using POS, but maintain small, regionally located, state institutions to treat violent, mentally ill individuals. The proposed facilities would be privately managed and staffed. Develop a limited number of direct-service community programs under other public auspices, such as municipal hospitals and state university–sponsored settings. Staff them with transferred institutional personnel.

• *Pro:* This option is particularly suited to the mentally ill. Violent patients frequently cannot be treated safely in community-hospital settings. Small, secure institutions in each region will provide more humane, cost-effective care than will large institutions preserved for this purpose. The rationale for private administration, as for POS versus direct services, rests on the assumption that personnel currently serving in state institutions would recreate negative institutional practices that suppress client development in the proposed small institutions. As institutional personnel are moved into community settings, they can be purged of their institutional ways; literature describes how this has been done successfully. Most of the best personnel have now left the state systems. Private community programs are fiercely resisting incorporating the remaining state personnel, even the professionals. However, because unions are strong and influence state legislators, and out of a sense of fairness, employee concerns about jobs and retirement benefits must be considered. Three options may meet state personnel's needs, while preserving the state's policy of attrition: early retirement benefits, training and transfer to other state positions, and training and transfer to community settings under other public auspices.

• *Con:* Any residual institutional role is dangerous, because it will be overutilized. The incentives needed to attract private management and professional staff for the proposed facilities would outweigh any cost-effectiveness the facilities would provide.

IV. Recommendation

Recommendation: Choose Option 3.

Rationale: The mentally ill have few, if any, advocates (families are often nonexistent for one reason or another), and suffer from a fluctuating disease requiring several treatment methods. As a result, inpatient beds must be available, and some of these beds must be in a secure setting to protect others from violent patients and suicidal patients from themselves.

V. Implementation Factors

How can legislators be persuaded to keep supporting both an institutional system and develop community-based services? They must be impressed with the horrors of a poorly planned deinstitutionalization process. Plenty of examples exist, probably even locally. Use them to gain crucial planning time.

How can unions be persuaded to comply with an implicit attrition policy that will no doubt be perfectly explicit to them? The state administration must convince local legislators—that is, those whose areas are most affected by deinstitutionalization—that institutions are inhumane, anachronistic relics that must be abolished (the state can point out that Senator Backman has been vocal in this regard), but that the state wishes to be fair to employees caught in the middle.

DMH management should be sure to broaden the base when dealing with unions. They should meet not only with union leaders but also with rank and file and respected professionals. DMH should be sensitive to employee anxieties and committed to retraining and relocation efforts. New York State has been successful in this area and offers a good model.

What about the future? Should the state aim to dismantle all direct-care services permanently? No. Once the current system has been dismantled and POS has been in operation for a while, DMH should evaluate the cost-effectiveness of direct-care services versus POS, especially for outpatient services.

SOURCE: This case is a modified version of one by Dr. Marcia Mabee.

DEVELOPING BROADER POLICY PROPOSALS

A high-level official in the Kennedy and Johnson administrations once said that those who take a stab at drafting a proposal often obtain considerable power precisely because their initial version establishes certain ideas and options that often are retained in subsequent versions. When first configuring a proposal, a policy practitioner should not become excessively absorbed with details; the original version should contain essential points and an overarching rationale. In the case of legislation, an initial version might contain a title, a brief preamble containing the purpose of the legislation, a discussion of policy options that describe the content and structure of the program, and some practical administrative and budgeting details. Often, supplementary appendix materials contain some fiscal and implementation details, such as an estimate of the proposal's likely costs.

Establishing a Rationale

Proposals will not succeed unless decisionmakers believe in a compelling reason to consider and enact them. Proposals perceived as trivial are usually discarded amid decisionmakers' crowded schedules. Either as part of a proposal or in a brief, attached statement, policy practitioners must establish a convincing rationale.[17] When proposals attempt to redress existing policies' deficiencies, such as unmet consumer needs, gaps in existing services, or ineffectiveness, the rationale might emphasize how the new program would better meet an important social need. When proposing new service approaches, practitioners often specify the innovative nature of their proposal.[18]

Perhaps it addresses clients' needs by transferring techniques currently used with other populations. (Someone in a mental health clinic could propose the use of biofeedback technology in stress-reduction programs, though it has traditionally been used in medical settings.) An innovative technique may be to provide outreach services to a population that currently does not use social services. A proposal may identify a new way to link different services, such as schools, hospitals, and mental health clinics, in a specific region to address adolescents' substance abuse. A proposed program may use new kinds of staff.

Some innovative policies hinge on the research and conceptual work we discussed in Chapter Six. Someone may propose outreach services for a population particularly at risk of developing specific problems, such as children whose parents are severe substance abusers. A program might draw on research showing that persons who lack support from family and community are most likely to develop specific problems; in such cases, practitioners might try to link such persons to support systems.

Research on cultural and ethnic factors might suggest using new approaches with subgroups, such as helping Spanish-speaking women address substance-abuse problems or teaching inner-city youth safe sex practices.

Drawing on Research Findings

We can now return to our discussion of social problems in Chapter Six. Because most policy proposals purport to address specific problems, they should not only refer to these problems, but also demonstrate that the proposed program will remedy the problem. Take the case of the school board. The proposed year-round option makes little sense if it is not linked to the problem of school overcrowding. Is this a truly serious problem? Do trend data suggest that it is becoming more serious? Do demographic data about birth rates and population mobility suggest that it will worsen in a particular area? Take the issue of battered women from Chapter Seven. A proposal to secure federal subsidies for shelters would obtain more support if its framers analyzed the incidence and causes of wife battering. Were the program to provide *preventive* services to decrease spousal abuse, its framers would have to link their proposed remedies to prevailing research about the causes of the problem.

Constructing Proposals

Practitioners rarely select only one option. Many proposals contain clusters of options that, when taken together, describe a new social program, an innovation, or a change in existing policy. As we noted in Chapter Seven, for example, a practitioner who proposed federal funding battered women's shelters would have to define several policy options to remedy the seven policy issues we described.

When constructing proposals, one must identify the goals, as well as the administrative and decisionmaking mechanisms.[19] Take the example of an agency's grant proposal for a new program that the agency wants a foundation to fund. The foundation will want to know what goals give direction to the activities within the project and what priorities provide the project with some internal focus. It would want to know who will ultimately administer the project. Moreover, the foundation would seek a logical link between the proposal's rationale and the policies, procedures, and budgets it outlines. If the agency wanted to establish outreach services to a neglected and foreign-speaking population, for example, but made no mention of hiring bilingual staff, the foundation might wonder if the goals could be achieved.

Proposals must also be coordinated with existing institutions, laws, and programs. New programs do not exist in a vacuum, but must coexist with existing policies. When writing proposals, practitioners should ask whether coordinating mechanisms are needed, whether existing agencies and programs are likely to cooperate with new ones, and whether certain proposal goals will be frustrated by any policies of existing programs. Will those who must approve the proposal fear that it intrudes on similar, existing services and programs?

Implementation and Evaluation

Proposal writers often try to convince readers that their proposal is not only conceptually sound and important, but also that it will actually achieve the major objectives it identifies.[20] Many readers of proposals are cynical because they have seen so many impressive proposals fail during implementation.

Most policy proposals discuss the details about implementation. A proposal to begin a demonstration program in an agency, for example, may include timetables or schedules, methods of evaluating the program, budgetary details about supplies, salaries, and facilities and ways to publicize the program.

Practitioners can try to convince readers of their proposals' effectiveness by developing plausible scenarios in which these implementation strategies play a prominent part. They can develop time lines to show what the project will look like three, six, nine, and twelve months after its enactment in terms of cost, as well as services rendered, staff hired, and other program details. They can provide flowcharts to show how clients will move through a new program from intake to the completion of services. They can illustrate referral patterns from external sources to the program and from the program to outside agencies.[21]

Scenarios can help practitioners identify possible errors at the outset. It is common, for example, to believe that a project can achieve greater results than its staff and resources can deliver. Funders are adept at spotting this weakness. A proposal framer may underestimate the time it takes to put a project into operation, to publicize it, or to make links with other agencies whose programs intersect with it.

Of course, implementing programs causes unexpected problems and obstacles to emerge. Proposal writers should explain how they plan to detect errors during implementation, such as by advisory groups' evaluations, monitoring, outside reviews, and overseeing. Indeed, many foundations and government funders require that proposals contain a plan for evaluating new programs after they have been implemented.[22] Proposal writers may actually include a formal plan for evaluation or may leave the details to be resolved later.

Garnering Support for the Proposal

Policy practitioners have to decide where to route their proposals. In the case of legislative policies, they consult advocates and legislative aides, as well as government officials, to obtain advice about politicians and committees interested in certain issues. Within relatively small agencies, proposals reach the executive director's desk and the director often participates in developing them. In larger bureaucracies, proposals can take several routes. An initial sponsor must guide it to people who can promote it before it ascends to higher authorities.

When proposals will be submitted to external funders, policy practitioners should draw on the extensive grant-writing literature that lists government, foundation, and corporate sources of funding, which is beyond the scope of this text. Suffice it to say that many funding alternatives exist for most proposals. Practitioners will need to do some research to find appropriate sources. Once they have identified potential sources, such as particular foundations or government agencies, policy practitioners should tailor their proposal to address the issues, information, and requirements that particular funders desire.

Decisionmakers often want evidence of a proposal's widespread support.[23] Policy practitioners need to find legislators who will sponsor their proposal. Drafters of legislation often try to assemble a broad list of sponsors that includes persons from both parties, all geographical regions, and different perspectives and ideologies. Public testimony before legislative committees by a range of people, including well-known figures, also reflects support. When submitting nonlegislative proposals to funding sources, proposal writers often attach letters of endorsement from executives in other agencies, experts, and community leaders to attest to the proposal's importance and the proposal writer's ability to implement it.

Revising the Proposal

Proposals rarely emerge full-blown from first drafts, but are gradually revised. In the legislative process, amendments to bills are written in successive committee deliberations. Indeed, legislative committees often publish copies of amended bills that show precisely how they altered a prior version; lines are drawn through excised words and new provisions are italicized. Grant proposals to foundations, government authorities, and other funding bodies, are also revised gradually from start to finish. In some cases, for example, the framer will write a one-page version and circulate it to other persons, including a staff member in a foundation or government agency. A later version, which may be four or five pages by now, will be circulated for comments again as a prelude to a more lengthy final version.

Translating complex ideas into fluent prose requires considerable skill. Excessive jargon, longwindedness, complex sentences, and poor syntax diminish interest in a proposal.[24] Many decisionmakers, such as legislators, who lack technical understanding are disinclined to read dense, lengthy materials. Policy practitioners can sometimes err, of course, in the opposite direction; if their proposal is too brief and fails to address important issues, their work may be discarded as superficial. Proposal writers must use analytic, political, and value-clarification skills in tandem, as they present their ideas. Perhaps political considerations dictate leaving certain topics out, using certain words rather than others, and developing a proposal title that appeals to certain persons.

POLICY ANALYSIS: PUTTING IT ALL TOGETHER

In Chapter Seven, we discussed how to combine various policy options to form a coherent legislative proposal. We now focus on a broader array of proposals, including grant proposals to foundations or government authorities. We can conceptualize proposal writing as combining the concepts we discussed in the last three chapters (see Figure 8.1). This combining creates four overlapping

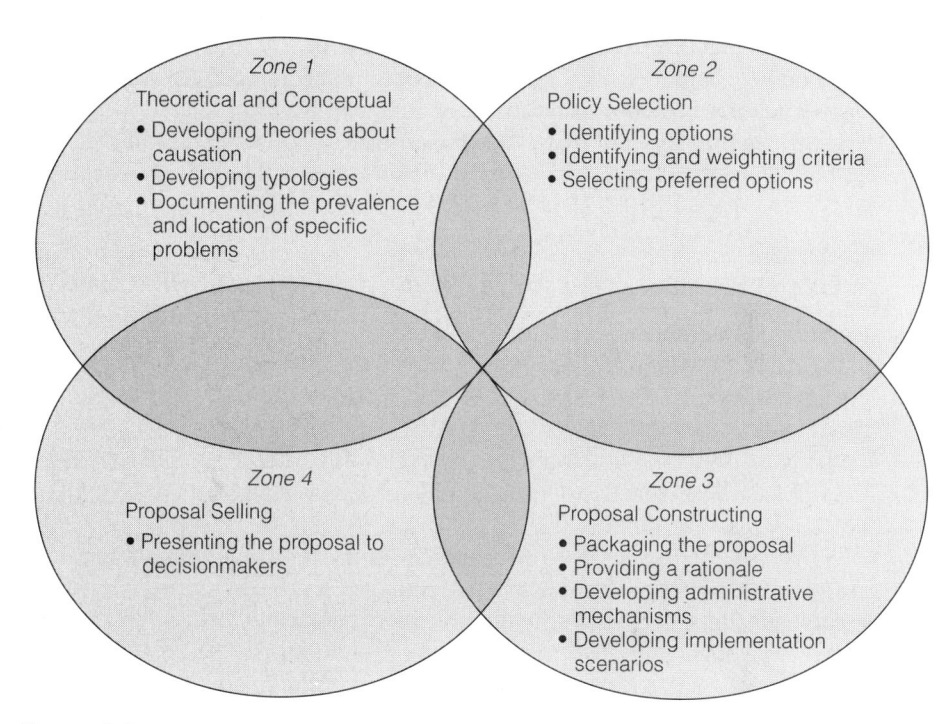

FIGURE 8.1
Four zones in policy analysis

```
Zone 1
Theoretical and Conceptual
• Developing theories about causation
• Developing typologies
• Documenting the prevalence and location of specific problems

Zone 2
Policy Selection
• Identifying options
• Identifying and weighting criteria
• Selecting preferred options

Zone 4
Proposal Selling
• Presenting the proposal to decisionmakers

Zone 3
Proposal Constructing
• Packaging the proposal
• Providing a rationale
• Developing administrative mechanisms
• Developing implementation scenarios
```

zones. Zone 1 emphasizes the theoretical and conceptual tasks that we discussed in Chapter Six. By drawing on relevant research in the social sciences, for example, the policy practitioner hopes to ground a policy proposal in existing knowledge of specific social problems, interventions, and populations. In Zone 2, the policy practitioner identifies several policies, as we discussed in this and the last chapter, and then compares and contrasts policy options before selecting some for the final proposal. Zone 3 reflects the process we have just discussed, in which practitioners construct a proposal. They provide a rationale, identify goals, select administrative mechanisms, develop a budget, and create implementation scenarios, sometimes only after extensive consultation and revision. Finally, as is discussed in more detail in the next chapter, policy practitioners must present their proposals persuasively to decisionmakers, funders, and legislators, as we see in Zone 4.

A CASE EXAMPLE

Case 8.2 presents a proposal written by a social worker. It requests $54,043 to provide preventive services for persons at high risk of HIV infection. Note how it contains the first three zones; it discusses the presenting problem, or the risk of HIV infection, and proposes a remedy (Zone 1); it develops a strategy to achieve this goal (Zone 2); and it combines the problem, objectives, strategy, and methods of evaluation into a coherent document (Zone 3). We do not know how its writer tried to convince other persons that it warranted funding, but we can surmise that she had many discussions with officials within her agency, researched alternative funding sources, and submitted it to a promising source.

CASE 8.2
A GRANT PROPOSAL: THE AIDS PREVENTIVE EDUCATION PROJECT

Problem Statement
In the fall of 1989 the City Council of Pasadena heard a report from the City Health Officer on "The Status of AIDS in Pasadena." As a result, the City Council appointed the Pasadena AIDS Strategic Planning Task Force on January 1990. The task force was charged with developing a proactive plan to determine what Pasadena and public and private organizations could do to address the AIDS crisis.

The task force consisted of Pasadenans, including AIDS service providers, politicians, persons with HIV, doctors, school board members, religious leaders, and public health officials. They formulated the following mission statement: "No member of our community will be newly infected by HIV and those infected will get appropriate care."

To begin to assess AIDS-related needs in Pasadena, the task force developed a continuum of care model. It consisted of four major categories into which all educational and treatment services would fall. The continuum included preventive education, early intervention, symptomatic intervention, and extended care.

Recognizing that preventive education is the best "cure" we have for HIV, the task force focused much of their attention on it and dedicated nearly four times as many recommendations to it as to other sections of the continuum of care. Several recommendations focused on guidelines for HIV preventive education in relation to substance abuse, calling for educational materials and programs. The plan urged community groups and institutions to become involved in preventive education.

These recommendations gave rise to this proposal, which aims to train the staff of drug treatment facilities to teach its clients behaviors that will decrease their chances of becoming infected with HIV.

Agency Description
The mission of the All Saints AIDS Service Center (ASASC) is "to serve people whose lives are affected by HIV and AIDS by providing service, preventive education, and advocacy for an appropriate community and government response." It is a nondenominational, not-for-profit agency established in 1988 that has offered direct services to 750 persons with AIDS, as well as preventive outreach programs to thousands in the San Gabriel Valley Region of Los Angeles County, including Pasadena. Four hundred clients are currently registered with the center, and 60 new clients register for these services each month. More than 300 people attend one of the

center's 13 support groups, which are conducted in English and Spanish. The center's health education team provides outreach services to public agencies, local corporations, prisons, parole officers, Head Start programs, Planned Parenthoods, schools, colleges, and other health-care agencies. The staff has 25 members and 600 volunteers. The ASASC implements its education and prevention programs in its Education and Prevention section. The programs mentioned in this section are described in an attached appendix.

Proposed Program
Goals
The primary goal of the preventive education plan is to teach the staffs of six to eight Pasadena agencies facts about HIV/AIDS, information about the relationship between addiction and HIV, and training in behaviors that reduce the risk of acquiring the disease. It is hoped that, by focusing on the staffs of these agencies rather than on their clients, community preventive education will continue, even after this grant's 12-month period.
Objectives
To achieve these goals, the proposed project will meet these objectives:

1. ASASC will develop a training curriculum in collaboration with a representative from the Public Health Department. This curriculum will build upon ASASC's existing AIDS 101 curriculum to change the attitudes and behaviors that place the substance-abusing population at risk. This curriculum will be developed by the end of the first six weeks of the project.
2. ASASC will conduct four intensive sessions per agency for the staff of six to eight agencies. These sessions will occur between the third and ninth months of the twelve-month period.
3. Two months after the final education session, ASASC will conduct one follow-up session for each agency to address successes and challenges specific to that agency. ASASC will conduct two follow-up evaluative sessions during the tenth and twelfth months for all involved agencies.
4. ASASC will seek specific levels of demonstrated competence from the staff of drug-treatment centers at specific points in this project:

    - 80% of the trained drug-treatment staff will meet specific criteria during teach-back presentations at each agency's fourth intensive session.
    - 80% of the trained drug-treatment staff will exhibit a 90% rate of knowledge at the end of the project imparted to them between the first and the final sessions.
    - 50% of the trained drug-treatment staff will demonstrate that they have disseminated HIV/AIDS information by making formal presentations during the twelve months of the project.

Proposed Plan
ASASC will train staff of at least six to eight Pasadena agencies that treat users of drugs, including alcohol and intravenous drugs. The training will

include four intensive sessions with direct-service personnel the agency has chosen to participate in the training.

Training will consist of a pretest to gauge the level of knowledge with which participants enter the program; information addressing interconnections between low self-esteem, risky behavior, and substance abuse, and discussions of the possible origins of addictive and risky behavior; role playing about safe sex, in which drug-treatment staff deepen their understanding of the discomfort and difficulties in making behavior changes; basic information on HIV/AIDS, such as how infection occurs, how infection spreads, and the biology of AIDS; a list of community resources and discussion about how to access them; information about psychodynamic issues that emerge when substance abusers became aware that they have been at risk and want to be tested; and discussion of homophobia and how it shapes the views many persons have of HIV and AIDS.

Month-by-Month Time Line

The first two months of this twelve-month project will focus on set-up tasks, including: recruiting a health educator to implement the program, having the health educator and Public Health Department collaborate to build a curriculum for training drug-treatment center staff, contacting drug-treatment agencies who might participate in the project, and assembling reading material for the educational project.

In the next six months (months three through nine), the health educator will conduct training, sometimes in conjunction with other staff of ASASC's education and prevention section.

The final three months (months ten through twelve) will emphasize discussions among the trainees of the various drug-treatment centers. They will meet at ASASC offices to explore problems they have encountered in helping their substance-abuse clients modify their risky behaviors. These meetings provide ASASC with feedback about their training strategies. They will also help the trainees see ASASC as an ongoing resource.

Staffing and Evaluation

The health educator will be hired by and report to ASASC's coordinator of the education and prevention program. ASASC already has an Education Advisory Committee, including experts on immunology, psychology, child-abuse prevention, nursing, legal issues specific to HIV and AIDS, social work, and education. Members of this committee, in liaison with the Public Health Department and the health educator, will develop instruments and materials used to evaluate this project at various intervals. Methods of evaluating the "teach-backs," where trainees teach clients through role play, will also be developed.

Budget

Personnel costs

Coordinator of Education and Training	(1/5 FTE* @ $32,000)	$6,400
Health educator	(1 FTE @ $28,000)	28,000
Fringe benefits @ 18%		6,192
	Subtotal for personnel	$40,592

Travel

100 miles per month of local travel @ $.28/mile for 12 months	$336
Airfare to project meeting in Washington, D.C.	300
Conference costs	550
Subtotal for travel	$1,186

Direct costs

Educational materials	$1,750
Printing/copying	575
Postage	75
Advertising	75
Supplies	175
Software support	75
Equipment repairs	75
Books and publications	125
Refreshments	50
Subtotal for direct costs	$2,975

Indirect costs

Rent	$5,750
Telephone	1,150
Insurance	500
Janitorial	300
Audit	375
Copier maintenance	250
Miscellaneous	125
Administration	840
Subtotal for indirect costs	$9,290
Total cost of project	$54,043

*Full-time equivalent

SOURCE: This is part of a proposal prepared by Katrina Gould, M.S.W., in collaboration with staff at the All Saints AIDS Service Center.

SUMMARY

We have emphasized analytic skills in making choices while writing proposals. Policy practitioners need to examine the trade-offs of contending policy options. This means comparing policy options' relative merits by ranking them on criteria, which in turn have been ranked. Practitioners can use quantitative or qualitative approaches when making these rankings.

Having made difficult choices, policy practitioners must be able to fashion legislative, program, or grant proposals. Brief memos are an important kind of proposal in agency, legislative, and governmental settings. Policy practitioners sometimes write grant proposals when they seek funding from external sources.

In many cases, policy practitioners must be able to defend or attack policy proposals in written or verbal exchanges. Indeed, effective policy practitioners devote considerable time to such exchanges, which often determine whether they can obtain support for the proposal. In the next chapter, we discuss strategies of "policy persuasion."

Suggested Readings

Analytic Approaches to Policymaking
Brian Hogwood and Lewis Gunn, *Policy Analysis for the Real World* (London: Oxford University Press, 1984).
Carl Patton and David Sawicki, *Basic Methods of Policy Analysis and Planning* (Englewood Cliffs, NJ: Prentice-Hall, 1986).

Applications to Social Welfare
Kent Portney, *Approaching Public Policy Analysis: An Introduction to Policy and Program Research* (Englewood Cliffs, NJ: Prentice-Hall, 1986), pp. 111–112.

Critical Discussions of Policy Analysis
John Dryzek and Brian Ripley, "The Ambitions of Policy Science," *Policy Studies Review* 7 (Summer 1988): 705–719.
William Dunn, "Methods of the Second Type: Coping with the Wilderness of Conventional Policy Analysis," *Policy Studies Review* 7 (Summer 1988): 720–727.
Charles Wolf, "Ethics and Policy Analysis," in Joel Fleishman, Lance Liebman, and Mark Moore, eds., *Public Duties: The Moral Obligations of Government Officials* (Cambridge, MA: Harvard University Press, 1981), pp. 131–141.

Ethical Issues in Policy Analysis and Assessment
Peter Brown, "Assessing Officials," in Fleishman, Liebman, and Moore, *Public Duties*, pp. 289–303.
Ruth Hanft, "Use of Social Science Data for Policy Analysis and Policymaking," in Daniel Callahan and Bruce Jennings, eds., *Ethics, the Social Sciences, and Policy Analysis* (New York: Plenum Press, 1983), pp. 213–248.
Martin Rein, "Value-Critical Policy Analysis" in Callahan and Jennings, *Ethics, the Social Sciences, and Policy Analysis*, pp. 96–100.

Developing Broader Proposals
Mary Hall, *Getting Funded: A Complete Guide to Proposal Writing*, 3rd ed. (Portland, OR: Continuing Education Publications of Portland State University, 1988).
Armand Lauffer, *Grantsmanship and Fund Raising* (Beverly Hills, CA: Sage, 1983).
Craig Smith and Eric Skjei, *Getting Grants* (New York: Harper & Row, 1980).

Notes

1. The analytical process of identifying and selecting options is discussed by: Edward Quade, *Analysis for Public Decisions*, 2nd ed. (New York: Elsevier North Holland, 1982); Alfred Kahn, *Theory and Practice of Social Planning* (New York: Russell Sage Foundation, 1969); Yeheskel Dror, *Venture in Policy Sciences* (New York: Elsevier North Holland, 1971); Robert Mayer and Ernest Greenwood, *The Design of Social Policy Research* (Englewood Cliffs, NJ: Prentice-Hall, 1980); and Brian Hogwood and Lewis Gunn, *Policy Analysis for the Real World* (London: Oxford University Press, 1984).
2. Bruce Jansson, *Theory and Practice of Social Welfare Policy: Analysis, Process, and Current Issues* (Belmont, CA: Wadsworth, 1984), pp. 51–52.
3. See Tony Tripodi, Phillip Fellin, and Irwin Epstein, *Differential Social Program Evaluation* (Itasca, IL: F.E. Peacock, 1978), pp. 101–104.

4. See, for example, Robert Francoeur's "decision matrix technique" in *Biomedical Ethics: A Guide to Decision Making* (New York: Wiley, 1983), pp. 127–137.
5. Ibid., 127–137.
6. Ibid., pp. 127–137.
7. Noel Tichy portrays competing policy options on the ends of a balance throughout *Organization Design for Primary Health Care* (New York: Praeger, 1977).
8. Charles Wolf, "Ethics and Policy Analysis," in Joel Fleishman, Lance Liebman, and Mark Moore, eds., *Public Duties: The Moral Obligations of Government Officials* (Cambridge, MA: Harvard University Press, 1981), pp. 131–141. Also see Bruce Jansson, "Combining Advocacy and Technical Skills: The Interaction of Politics and Numbers," *Administration in Social Work* (1990).
9. Martin Rein, "Value-Critical Policy Analysis," in Daniel Callahan and Bruce Jennings, eds., *Ethics, the Social Sciences, and Policy Analysis* (New York: Plenum, 1983), pp. 96–100.
10. Katherine Briar and Scott Briar, "Clinical Social Work and Public Policies," in Maryann Mahaffey and John Hanks, eds., *Practical Politics: Social Work and Political Response* (Silver Spring, MD: National Association of Social Workers, 1982), pp. 45–54.
11. Wolf, "Ethics and Policy Analysis," pp. 131–141.
12. Ibid., pp. 133–137.
13. John Baker, *Arguing for Equality* (London: Verso Press, 1987), pp. 3–13.
14. Ibid. Also see Wolf, "Ethics and Policy Analysis," pp. 133–137.
15. Bruce Jansson, *The Reluctant Welfare State: A History of American Social Welfare Policies*, 1st ed. (Belmont, CA: Wadsworth, 1984), pp. 108–109.
16. Charles Levy, *Guide to Ethical Decisions and Actions for Social Service Administrators: A Handbook for Managerial Personnel* (New York: Haworth, 1982).
17. Craig Smith and Eric Skjei, *Getting Grants* (New York: Harper & Row, 1980), pp. 173–181.
18. Ibid., pp. 173–181.
19. Armand Lauffer, *Grantsmanship and Fund Raising* (Beverly Hills, CA: Sage, 1983), pp. 238–246.
20. Ibid., pp. 80–84.
21. Ibid., pp. 236–246.
22. Mary Hall, *Getting Funded: A Complete Guide to Proposal Writing*, 3rd ed. (Portland, OR: Continuous Education Publications of Portland State University, 1988), pp. 127–144.
23. Smith and Skjei, *Getting Grants*, p. 152.
24. Marya Holcombe, *Writing for Decision Makers* (Belmont, CA: Lifetime Learning Publications, 1981).

Chapter Nine
Strategies of Policy Persuasion

As we have discussed, policy practitioners must not only develop meritorious proposals; they also need to defend them with communication skills, whether in one-on-one discussions, presentations to larger audiences, or debates. Without "policy persuasion" skills, policy practitioners cannot attract sufficient support for their ideas to be effective.

We will distinguish between "friendly" and "adversarial" communications. In friendly communications, a policy practitioner tries to *decrease* opposition to a proposal with conflict-reducing techniques. For example, a presenter might stress commonalities he or she shares with the audience. In adversarial communications, a policy practitioner tries to best a person or group with opposing points of view, such as through debates. Alternatively, the policy practitioner could use negotiating skills to develop a compromise with a person who has different policy perspectives but is willing to bargain.

POLICY PERSUASION

A considerable part of policy practice involves using language to influence other people's attitudes, preferences, and actions.[1] We may try to influence people through interpersonal discussions, proposals, speeches to large audiences, memoranda, formal reports, debates or arguments, messages (such as editorials), or through the mass media. In each case, we initiate various communications to change others' perceptions.

It is difficult to understate the role persuasion plays in policy practice. In order to enact policies, practitioners must rally people's support. However, they often face significant challenges when other people are deeply opposed to their position, encounter pressure to oppose it, or are apathetic.

Persuaders need to develop strategy to overcome such obstacles. People highly skilled in the art of persuasion tailor their messages to specific audiences and situations to increase the likelihood of influencing them.

Persuasive encounters are transactional in nature. In other words, persuaders hope to change the beliefs or actions of their audience (which may be individuals, large groups, or the general public, in the case of mass-media communications). However, their endeavor requires activity on both sides. The presenter must send a message and the audience must decide whether to heed (and be changed by) the message or to ignore (and not be changed by) it.[2] No matter how loudly persuaders shout at someone or how articulately they make their case, their efforts come to naught unless the audience sees merit in the message and decides to heed its prescriptions.

The social context can often be important. One persuader might convince some people to accept certain beliefs or take certain actions if she has the luxury of interacting with them in relative isolation. However, she may find her work frustrated on a specific occasion by "external noise," such as peer pressure or competing messages from other senders, as well as inertia that stems from her audience's habits or beliefs.[3] For instance, political campaigners seldom have the luxury of extended personal discussion with voters. When faced with opposing candidates' messages, pressure from families and friends, and people's traditional political loyalties, politicians often fail to secure votes from people who might be sympathetic to their candidacy.[4]

Verbal and written messages are the vehicles of persuasion. Even in relatively brief messages, persuaders rely primarily on the message's content to convince others to change their beliefs or actions, but the manner in which verbal messages are delivered is also important. As we will discuss later, persuaders have many options when constructing messages.

Persuading Specific Audiences

Before persuaders can decide how to fashion a message, they have to establish objectives. Do they want major or minor changes in the audience's beliefs or actions? Are they content for the listeners to maintain their beliefs or habits, or do they want to change them markedly?

Determining Objectives

Objectives can be ranked on a continuum extending from ambitious to modest.[5] Persuaders with ambitious objectives hope to effect dramatic changes in their listeners. At the most ambitious level, persuaders hope both to markedly modify the audience's beliefs *and* to convince them to take specific actions, such as helping to change a policy, performing specific tasks, or pressuring decisionmakers to support a proposed policy. At a somewhat more modest level, a persuader may be content, at least in the short term, merely to modify others' beliefs, perhaps as a precursor to having them take action. (As we will discuss later, changes in people's beliefs do not necessarily cause them to change their actions.) Hoping to convince an agency executive to support a new policy eventually, a staff member might send him information about an unmet need in the community or a promising pilot project in another agency.

Efforts to maintain an audience's beliefs and actions fall between the ambitious and modest ends of the continuum. Assume, for the moment, that agency members fear that someone will soon question a favored program. The agency members want to head off this possibility by maintaining, or even strengthening, their director's support for the program. Assume, as well, that the executive has funded the program relatively generously. The agency members need to send messages that reinforce the program's importance, so that the director will not be unduly influenced by the impending attack.[6] While this endeavor sounds relatively modest in nature, it is more ambitious than merely educating others, because it aims to influence others' beliefs and actions.

We also need to distinguish between the short- and long-term objectives of persuasion. When planning a message on an occasion, a practitioner may have a relatively modest objective, such as sensitizing an audience to an issue. But he or she may anticipate relaying a series of messages to an audience that ultimately change their beliefs and rally their support around a new policy. Indeed, policy practitioners often hope to persuade people bit by bit. A campaign might consist of interpersonal discussions, a memorandum, and a formal presentation, each planned to educate an audience and to move them toward support of a policy.

It is more difficult to develop a series of presentations, of course, than to convince an audience in a single presentation to support a policy or to change their beliefs. Numerous discussions, memos, and presentations may be required. The policy practitioner not only must develop a series of presentations, but also must decide when to proceed beyond educating the audience to seeking their support for new policies and beliefs. The policy practitioner may proceed too cautiously or too rapidly from modest to ambitious objectives.

Diagnosing Audiences

Policy practitioners often try to "diagnose" audiences, even if they do not use the therapeutic classifications of direct-service practitioners. They often want to know the audience's beliefs, degree of motivation in an issue, fears and hopes, and the extent to which they are subject to situational or historical factors that might influence their response to a message.[7]

When examining audiences' beliefs, policy practitioners gauge the degree of opposition to their messages. Audiences are most hostile to a message when they oppose its value premises and its fundamental argument.[8] When liberal policy practitioners seek to expand the nation's welfare programs and address a conservative audience, they are likely to find the audience disagrees with their value premises that society is obliged to help impoverished people and that government should expand its social welfare roles and their assertion that unemployment and low-paying jobs, rather than the size of existing welfare grants, have caused welfare rolls to expand. Many conservatives believe that government is not obligated to help most poor people and that the current welfare system exacerbates welfare problems by encouraging dependency.

Audiences are less hostile when the value premises and logic of the message approximate their own beliefs or when they have flexible or undefined positions. When an audience has a fairly broad zone of tolerance, it is relatively open to other ideas, values, or perspectives. Practitioners who want to make major changes in the audience's beliefs encounter a difficult challenge when the zone of tolerance is relatively narrow.[9]

Audiences also differ in their levels of motivation or involvement in specific topics. All of us have been part of audiences that could not care less about a message. Perhaps we have been inundated with boring messages about the same subject or do not perceive its relevance to us.[10]

When an audience is hostile to a policy, persuaders have to try to figure out why. Indeed, theorists suggest that audiences are most receptive to messages relevant to their fears and hopes.[11] When a new program is proposed in an agency, for example, some staff may fear it will jeopardize their current responsibilities, will divert funds from favored projects, or will cause new burdens that they do not wish to shoulder, such as learning new skills or working longer hours. Skillful persuaders carefully allay these kinds of fears in their messages.

Similarly, practitioners often identify positive factors that could motivate some audience members to support a policy. A new program in the aforementioned agency, for example, might allow staff members to develop new skills, increase their job security by bringing in new revenues, and enhance the agency's prestige and that of its staff members. Moreover, many professionals respond favorably to policy initiatives that address important or unmet client needs.[12]

The social context may influence the audience's response to a particular measure. If a social agency is cutting costs, for example, its staff members are unlikely to support a costly new program. Audiences often respond to historical factors. Assume, for example, that a specific issue has been presented before to some members of the audience. Their recollections of these discussions, which they often transmit to those who were not present, can powerfully shape people's responses. If an issue was divisive, for example, it may generate extensive conflict when it is reintroduced. By contrast, policy issues associated with positive traditions often have a good chance of meeting a positive audience response.[13]

To this point, we have assumed that audiences are relatively homogeneous in their orientations toward a subject. In fact, audiences usually contain a range of perspectives; one faction may support a new policy, while another faction may be opposed. Practitioners must identify a mixed audience's factions.[14] They should decide how to address the subgroups' different needs in their messages. Perhaps a section of a message can appeal to one segment of the audience ("some of you fear that . . ."), while a second section can address another segment ("others of you believe that . . ."). Even with audiences that have divergent perspectives, practitioners can identify and appeal to common values, hopes, or aspirations; they can note, for example, that "despite our differences on this issue, we all agree that this agency needs to diversify its services."

Tailoring Objectives to the Audience

Persuaders often encounter the difficult dilemma of establishing objectives that are too modest or too ambitious. Persuaders may falsely believe that an audience is so hostile to their messages that they can only hope to achieve minor changes. This mistaken judgment predisposes them to be too timid. By contrast, persuaders establish unrealistic expectations because they falsely believe that their audiences are (or can soon be) similar to themselves. Those with liberal perspectives, for example, may unrealistically expect to make an extremely conservative audience accept a policy that stems from liberal premises, only to find that the message merely unites the audience in its preexisting opposition to "these knee-jerk liberals."

PERSUADING STRATEGIES

With objectives, audience, and situation in mind, policy practitioners must develop a persuading strategy. That requires selecting a medium, a sequence of presentations, a format, and a presentation style. After discussing these components, we will discuss tactics for specific audiences.

Selecting a Medium

Persuaders rely on symbols, such as words and visual aids, to influence audiences' ideas and actions, but they can present these symbols in many ways, such as through speech, documents, graphic aids, or some combination of these methods. Because these modes of communication are so familiar, we often do not consider their relative merits.

Public speaking allows presenters to interact with the audience. As they perceive fears and hopes that impede or facilitate a positive response, presenters can address them; indeed, they can elicit these perceptions and emotions during the course of their presentation. Oral communication allows persuaders to be flexible; if they are skilled at thinking on their feet, they can change their message midway through to respond to unforeseen developments. When persuaders want an audience to become emotionally involved in an issue, they often use arguments that culminate in a call to action, where members agree to support a cause actively.[15]

Written communications, such as memoranda, letters, and reports, allow precision, unlike spoken communication, where definitions and details are often relatively vague. When presenters want audiences to commit to a course of action, they can elicit relatively binding agreements with documents; a memo may ask people, for example, to check specific categories at the end of the memo, such as "agree or support," "disagree," or "undecided." Written communications help explain relatively technical subjects, such as implementation details for a specific policy or a summary of existing research, because it is difficult to convey technical subjects in brief addresses.[16]

Graphic communications, such as graphs and slides, simplify complex materials. Graphic materials often help capture the attention of a hostile or indifferent audience; someone who seeks support for vulnerable populations, for example, can use pictures or slides to promote sympathy or interest. If used to excess, however, graphic materials can lose an audience's attention.[17]

Using a Sequence of Presentations

When we envision presentations, we customarily think of one-shot episodes, where people try to influence an audience with a formal presentation. In this light, persuaders have only one chance to convince an audience to take a specific position on an issue. In fact, skilled persuaders rarely approach their work in this manner, because they realize that they will be more effective if they use a sequence of persuasive encounters. Even when a formal presentation culminates the sequence, it may be preceded by a variety of written, interpersonal, and other communications. A persuader might decide, for example, to use some informal, personal encounters to discover where people stand on issues and what they fear or dislike. A persuader may use these informal encounters to obtain information about the audience and to initiate the process of changing the audience's knowledge or beliefs.[18]

Selecting a Format

A format is the most critical part of a presentation. Most audiences fear a presentation that rambles or is inappropriate for the subject. Moreover, presenters need to believe they have mastered their topic in order to present it more confidently.

Every speech has a beginning, a middle, and an end. Your challenge is to command your audience's attention at the outset, impart important substantive information in the middle, and make the conclusion serve the presentation's essential purpose (such as persuading the audience to take action, set up a committee, or take a specific problem seriously).

When thinking about your presentation, it is useful to decide what you want the audience to achieve or do upon leaving the presentation. You might decide, for example, that you want the audience to set up a committee to study an issue, emerge believing that a condition *is* serious, or leave with new knowledge about an issue.[19] Once you have stated your essential objective, you can develop a format that specifies how you will achieve it.

Do not lock yourself into a single format prematurely. Try different versions of your speech. Think about novel points you can make at the outset or in the conclusion that might appeal to your audience. Brainstorm to develop alternative outlines.

Skilled persuaders usually develop a basic format for certain communications.[20] These formats are critical, because they establish an integrating logic for a presentation. There are seven kinds of presentations in Box 9.1.

BOX 9.1
Possible Formats

• To *discuss how a problem developed*, you can use a *time* structure, where you note the sequence of events that caused the problem. Such a speech might begin, "I want to discuss how the problem with our agency's intake developed by taking you through a sequence of events. . . ."

A. Intake procedures in 1985
B. Revisions of intake procedures in 1986
   1. Why revisions were made
   2. The nature of the revisions
C. Changes in the composition of our agency's clients between 1987 and 1991
D. Intake problems caused by these changes in clientele
E. Options we should consider in revising our intake procedures again
   1. Option 1
   2. Option 2
F. Call for a task force or committee to make recommendations

• To *explain a problem*, you can use a *topical* structure that discusses a problem's components. Such a speech might begin, "I want to discuss operating problems in our agency as a prelude to some policy recommendations. . . .")

A. We are experiencing a number of problems in our agency's program for school dropouts
B. Problem 1
C. Problem 2
D. Problem 3
E. Relationships among these three problems
F. Options we should consider to address these problems
   1. Option 1
   2. Option 2
   3. Option 3

• To *establish that a problem exists* and needs attention, you can use a *criticism* structure to describe the situation and criteria to suggest that it *is* a problem. For example, you might say, "Our intake procedures are faulty because clients with serious problems do not receive prompt attention and because the procedures are unfair. . . ."

A. An overview of our intake procedures
B. Why our intake procedures need to be overhauled
   1. Problems of fairness
   2. Problems encountered by clients who are denied immediate service

continued

BOX 9.1 continued

    3. Administrative problems
    4. Staffing problems
C. The need to collect more information about Problems 2 and 4
D. Call for a committee to collect the information and make some recommendations

• To show a *cause-effect relationship,* use an *association* structure. Say, "I want to discuss how the problem with our intake procedures stems from the rapid increase in our waiting list. . . ."

A. Discuss problems with intake policy
B. Discuss specific changes in nature of clientele using the agency during the past five years
C. Link the problems with the changes in clientele
D. Discuss possible implications for changing intake policy

• To gain *acceptance for a plan,* use an *argument* structure, where you present the elements of the problem and the central features of your corrective plan. Begin, "I want to discuss why our intake policies are faulty and then present a five-part plan to deal with the situation. . . ."

A. Discuss problems with intake policy
B. Provide a solution
C. Discuss how the solutions address specific criteria
    1. Administrative feasibility
    2. Fairness
    3. Cost

• To *criticize* someone else's statement of a problem or plan, use a *refutation* structure, where you state their central tenets and then present your arguments about why their statement was flawed. Say, "I want to discuss why the plan Susan Smith offered to correct our intake system is flawed. . . ."

A. Provide an overview of the intake problems
B. Describe the central elements of Smith's plan
C. Discuss how it fails to address certain criteria
    1. It is not administratively feasible
    2. It is not fair to certain kinds of clients
    3. It would be too costly
D. Discuss an alternative approach and how it better meets these criteria

• To *influence people to take action,* use a *directive* structure, where you state reasons why immediate, emergency action is needed. You might say, "This situation is urgent. We should send a delegation at once to see the head of the welfare agency."

continued

> *BOX 9.1 continued*
>
> A. Why this problem has taken on urgency
>   1. Effects on clients
>   2. Possible political ramifications
>   3. Implications for our funding
> B. Why a delay in addressing it would be calamitous
> C. Alternative courses of action
>   1. Write a letter
>   2. Contact head of welfare agency by telephone
>   3. Send a delegation
>   4. Other actions
> D. A call to action
>   1. Send a delegation
>   2. Have the delegation make the following arguments
>   3. Supplement the delegation with other actions
>   a. Call the mayor
>   b. Contact a member of the county Board of Supervisors

Our discussion suggests that policy presenters should tailor their outline to the subject they discuss. While outlines can take different forms, they need to develop a logical sequence of topics that structures the presentation both for the presenter and for the audience.

Fine-Tuning a Presentation

Once presenters have developed a medium, selected an audience, and developed an outline, they can fine-tune the presentation in numerous ways, and in the process revise the outline. Presenters often use specific techniques to make their presentation more interesting to the audience. They might add case examples, because most audiences appreciate arresting illustrations. They may elicit audience participation during part of the presentation by asking, "Which of these options do you prefer?" or "Can you think of an option I have not considered?" They could use a particular visual aid, such as passing out a chart or presenting it with an overhead projector.

The presentation's basic structure suggests an outline, as we illustrate with a speech to the staff of an agency about its flawed intake procedures. This speech uses a criticism structure.

   I. Initial statement—an overview of the presentation: I will discuss three reasons why I think intake policies are flawed.
  II. Why do I think they are flawed?

A. Certain clients with serious conditions have to wait long periods. (Discuss Client A as an illustrative example.)
B. Certain kinds of people disproportionately drop off the waiting list. (Discuss Client B as an illustrative example.)
C. Our waiting-list procedures make certain clients feel frustrated. (Discuss Client C as an illustrative example.)
III. Ask the audience to share any experiences they have had with the intake procedures.
IV. Recommendation: establish a committee to find alternative ways to structure our intake procedures.

Developing an Effective Presentation Style

Your effectiveness as a presenter hinges not just on the substantive content of your presentation, but also on your *delivery style*. This involves your relationship with the audience, your speech patterns, and your use of gestures.[21]

You have to feel comfortable with your basic outline before you begin your presentation. And you need to have mastered it by rehearsing so that you need only look at the bold headings from time to time as you make the presentation. Most audiences like presenters to make eye contact with them.

To offset the fear that you will ramble, you may tell the audience at the start the presentation's basic logic. You could say, "I will discuss the following points with you today. . . ." Select an interesting case example, visual image, or analogy to interest the audience in your topic at the outset. You need to make clear transitions as you move from topic to topic by making statements such as, "Having discussed why intake procedures are flawed, we can now move to possible remedies." You also need to "wrap things up" in a thoughtful conclusion that draws on the preceding sections of your presentation.

Avoid distracting habits, such as fumbling with papers, excessively rapid or slow speech patterns, or pacing back and forth. Some experts in presentations suggest that we all videotape ourselves prior to making presentations to discern unconscious, distracting patterns.

Our discussion suggests that presentations, as with many other topics in this book, rely partly on *interpersonal* actions and exchanges that must be practiced and observed. If making presentations is critical to policy practice work, we need to build skills as with other aspects of social work.

What do you do if you are frightened about making speeches? Most important, try not to run away from public speaking opportunities, difficult as they may seem. Some of us develop "fright instincts" when making speeches and can only break this pattern with practice. Many people find it useful to pause momentarily before speaking to gain equilibrium, to master the points they will use at the outset to put them in the flow of the presentation, and to master the presentation's outline. Other people find it helpful to videotape their presentation several times beforehand. This tactic allows them to correct a tendency to speak too quickly or too slowly.

Tactics for Specific Audiences

You can modify your outline as you consider the likely nature of your audience. We will discuss hostile, apathetic, and expert audiences. Policy practitioners sometimes encounter *hostile audiences* who possess values or beliefs that predispose them to oppose a specific message.

Various techniques can decrease hostility. You can identify common values, perspectives, and practical concerns that link the persuader to the audience.[22] These commonalities could include certain memberships, educational affiliations, or demographic traits. You can appeal to higher values that you share with the audience, such as by saying, "all of us share concern for the homeless people we see on the streets."[23] Some policy advocates seek conservatives' support for social programs by appealing, for example, to their patriotism; if Americans want the nation to remain competitive in international markets, these advocates could argue, they need to redress the high dropout rate in schools.[24]

You can establish your credibility with hostile audiences by citing authorities or experts whom the audiences are likely to respect and by discussing credentials or experiences of your own that make you credible to the audience. To seem reasonable, you can present "both sides" of complex issues and freely admit that alternative viewpoints are inevitable when addressing complex issues. Rather than alerting your audience to your conclusion at the outset, you can gradually "build a case" in hopes that by presenting evidence, you can gradually change their minds about a topic. You might reach your eventual proposal only after rejecting or refuting alternative positions.[25]

Humor often calms tense situations. Perhaps persuaders can make fun of themselves so that the audience perceives them as unceremonious and unpretentious.[26] If told with skill, anecdotes at the start of presentations can ease audiences into subjects that they find difficult or stressful. (Do not attempt humorous anecdotes at the start of presentations if you feel uncomfortable delivering them.)

Apathetic audiences present similar challenges to persuaders. It is important not to overwhelm apathetic audiences with complex arguments or data, which can intensify their apathy. Nor is it wise to tell the audience that they should care about the issue; this intrusive technique is likely to make them retreat even further into apathy. The skillful persuader needs to make the presentation interesting and lively, stress few themes or arguments, present a simple argument, and offer interesting and unusual evidence that the audience has not heard on prior occasions.[27]

Expert audiences are composed of persons who perceive themselves to be well-versed on the presentation topic. Presenters need to spend considerable time displaying an array of perspectives and evidence to such audiences and discussing the merits of alternative options, rather than moving quickly to a single option. Acknowledge that existing knowledge is imperfect and that choices are difficult. You should pay tribute to the audience's expertise by noting that they "have thought extensively about this subject." You might want to elicit opinions or suggestions from the "experts" in the audience.[28]

Other Tactical Choices

Additional options can help presenters modify their outlines.

Single-sided or two-sided arguments? Should persuaders present the strongest possible argument for a specific policy (a single-sided argument), or should they consider both sides of an issues (a two-sided argument)? One might contend that a new policy is needed, that it has some liabilities (such as its cost), but that it is desirable on balance after considering both positive and negative considerations. Conversely, they might emphasize the strengths of their proposal and hope that opponents do not find its weaknesses.

Some social psychologists suggest that two-sided arguments are particularly useful for critical or hostile audiences, because the persuader anticipates and defuses some criticisms and thereby appears reasonable and open-minded. If presenters excessively emphasize the weaknesses of their position, however, they risk providing ammunition to opponents.[29]

How much dissonance? All persuaders want to change their audiences' beliefs, actions, or a combination thereof. But they have to decide how much dissonance, or discrepancy between the audience's beliefs and the proposal, to introduce. If they ask for massive changes, they risk alienating their audiences. If they ask for minor changes, they risk undermining support for their policies.

When persuaders anticipate a hostile audience, they should probably refrain from suggesting massive changes from the outset. Several presentations should be scheduled, with the first one seeking to educate the audience, rather than securing commitments to major changes. When encountering sympathetic audiences, persuaders can state their case more dramatically and secure public commitment to major changes.[30]

Climax or anticlimax? Social psychologists have researched whether it is better to make the strongest points at the beginning of a presentation or at the end. Their findings are contradictory, but some show that audiences pay the most attention to the introductory and concluding portions of speeches. The weakest points should usually be inserted in the middle sections.[31]

Who should present? When a choice exists, persuaders need to ponder carefully who should take the lead in presenting information to specific audiences. With hostile or apathetic audiences, presenters should be relatively credible with them or possess styles of communication suited to overcoming hostility and apathy. It is sometimes useful for multiple presenters to take responsibility for different portions of a presentation.[32]

Adapting the setting. Skillful persuaders sometimes find or create settings where specific audiences will most likely heed their messages. Relatively intimate settings could be substituted for formal settings to increase the rapport between presenters and specific audiences. Seating arrangements can be devised to facilitate exchanges between the presenter and the audience. Graphic aids, such as slides, can help overcome an audience's apathy. In some cases, the audience can be broken into smaller groups that reconvene at a later point to share their solutions to specific problems.[33]

Honoring protocols and expectations. Audiences often have specific expectations about presentations. In the case of testimony to legislative committees, for example, legislators expect presentations to be relatively brief—that is, not to exceed 10 or 15 minutes.[34] (Detailed materials and the text of the presenter's comments are submitted separately.) Audiences may also have certain expectations regarding the formality, tenor, and style of a presentation. An audience of persons who consider themselves experts on a subject expect the presenter to offer alternative viewpoints, whereas an audience of activists often expect a "call to action." To understand these expectations, presenters need to speak with audience members in the weeks before their presentations or with people familiar with the audience.

ASSEMBLING A STRATEGY

We see that persuaders have several options when creating a persuading strategy. They must make choices about the audience, the social context, and their objectives. To explore a strategy's development, we will discuss the audiences that Rand Martin, a lobbyist for a gay group, might encounter as he seeks legislative reforms for AIDS victims. (We discuss Martin's lobbying more extensively in Chapter Eleven.) These hypothetical vignettes illustrate the reasoning that persuaders use as they develop strategy for specific audiences.

The Hostile Audience

Assume that Martin wants to convince some conservative Republicans—the people most likely to be critical of the gay community and to believe that AIDS victims "brought it on themselves"—to support a major legislative initiative. The legislation would expand the state's funding of home-health-care programs to serve AIDS patients. It would cover homemaker, visiting-nurse, and physical-therapy services. Not only Medicaid recipients but also persons considerably above the poverty line would receive these services. (Currently, counties fund most state home-health services and only for individuals who meet restrictive income standards.) Admittedly, the new program will be expensive, because many AIDS victims who are not eligible for existing county programs will need extended home-health services.

With this skeptical and hostile audience, Martin decides to make two presentations, the first to capture their interest and cut through their stereotypes and the second to obtain their suggestions for legislative strategy.

Even before the first presentation, he obtains the assistance of several sympathetic Republican legislators, who agree to moderate the sessions and expedite discussion. He wants his introduction to make some of the conservatives perceive the problem in human and personal rather than abstract and ideological terms. He decides to present several case histories of HIV-positive people who have encountered dilemmas when seeking home-based services. To decrease the audience's perception of the problem as belonging only to "gay radicals," he relates several cases of conservative Republicans who have contracted the disease. He also makes analogies to elderly and disabled persons to communicate that the AIDS population's home-health needs and problems are similar to those of other, more accepted populations. He concludes the first presentation with a question-and-answer session about the dimensions of the problem.

During the second presentation, he uses a rational format with a two-sided argument. After quickly summarizing some factual information from the first session regarding the problem's dimensions, he lists some alternative remedies: these include the cost-effectiveness of establishing different levels of eligibility for home-health services, the merits of working through local nonprofit agencies rather than through the counties' home-health programs, and the benefits of focusing the services on specific subgroups of AIDS patients. Some legislators wonder if the program should emphasize home-health services for AIDS victims who can still work, but who are least covered by the county home-health programs. After discussing the merits of these various options, he provides them with a legislative proposal that a bipartisan group has tentatively drafted but not yet introduced into the legislative process.

The Sympathetic Audience with Some Hostile Members

Assume that the legislative proposal is introduced into a legislative committee, most of whose members are sympathetic, but a minority of whose members are hostile. Martin, who hopes to intensify support for the proposal, encounters the dilemma of addressing "mixed audiences." Should he "write-off" the minority and direct his comments to the sympathetic members, or should he target his comments to the hostile minority, because he expects the majority to support the proposal?

Martin decides to focus his comments on the majority, but to include points in his presentation that can attract some swing votes from the minority. For the sympathetic majority, who do not need an extended argument but want a brief and dramatic message to energize them to support the proposal, he uses a relatively emotional format, rather than a rational one. Indeed, he focuses his presentation on a particularly poignant case. To appeal to the hostile minority, however, he selects a case that illustrates how providing a homemaker and other services can allow some people with AIDS to remain productive workers (and hence taxpayers) for a longer period than if these services were unavailable.

The Expert Audience

Assume that the lobbyist seeks support for the proposal from hospital administrators, whose professional association wields power within the state. Unlike most legislators, who possess scant knowledge of the intricacies of healthcare programs, hospital administrators are familiar with existing programs. With this audience, Martin decides to emphasize practical cost and administrative issues, such as how the proposal would be implemented, how the state would monitor it, and how it would affect the duration of AIDS patients' sojourn in hospitals.

To enhance his rapport with this audience, Martin cites evidence and arguments that he obtained from a hospital administrator and some hospital social workers who specialize in discharge planning. Because the proposal's funds would be funneled through nonprofit agencies, he discusses how these agencies would coordinate their services with hospitals.

Interpersonal Discussions

As this legislation progresses from initial proposal to drafted legislation to (hopefully) enacted legislation, the lobbyist will have countless interpersonal discussions with foes and friends of the legislation, officials in the state bureaucracies, local officials, and community activists. These interpersonal discussions would take many forms. Some of them would be to solicit information about people's positions, biases, and perspectives. In these contacts, Martin would maintain a fact-finding posture. Of course, his patience would be tested when individuals assume a hostile stance toward people with AIDS, such as when a legislator maintains that "the solution to the AIDS problem is to require all testing centers to turn over the names of HIV-positive persons to public health officials." As Lewis Dexter suggests, the lobbyist should remain "benevolently neutral" in some of these hostile discussions. While he need not disingenuously agree with these legislators, he does not need to attack them, either.[35] Indeed, he might indicate that "we share a desire to bring this epidemic under control, but what ideas do you have about how to help AIDS patients remain productive members of society in the interim?"

In some of these interpersonal discussions, Martin uses a directive communication format, where he seeks support for a proposal. He might wish an action-oriented group's leader to mobilize support for the legislation by obtaining letters and phone calls from key legislators' constituents. He might use a combination of flattery and emotional language—for instance, "We've turned to you many times in the past and you have never let us down. . . . How do you think we can place pressure on these five legislators who are 'swing votes?' "

Other interpersonal discussions might follow a rational format, such as ones with health experts. In these conversations, the lobbyist might seek assistance in defining the home-health needs of AIDS patients, the cost implications of specific provisions in the legislation, and administrative considerations.

We can often improve presentation skills by studying the work of successful presenters, such as when Governor Mario Cuomo nominated Bill Clinton for president in summer 1992. (See Case 9.1.)

CASE 9.1
WHY A PRESENTATION WAS SUCCESSFUL

In the presidential election of 1992, Governor Mario Cuomo of New York State made a pivotal speech at the Democratic Convention. He nominated the Democratic candidate for president, Bill Clinton. Cuomo's speech was widely viewed as a rousing success. As an exercise, try to analyze why this was true. Ascertain whether Cuomo has a coherent outline. Analyze whether and how he adapted his presentation to the kind of audience he confronted. Why did the audience respond favorably? What kind of presentation techniques did Cuomo avoid that might have been less successful with this audience?

I don't want to go overtime. They warned me I might wind up playing the accordion on the Arsenio Hall Show, so let's—

Tonight, tonight I will have the great privilege and honor of placing before you the name of the next President of the United States of America, Gov. Bill Clinton of Arkansas.

It seems to me that this is not a matter of our wanting Bill Clinton, it is much, much more than that. We need Bill Clinton because he is our only hope for change from this nation's current disastrous course.

Eight years ago, in San Francisco, some of us tried to convince America that while President Reagan was telling us we were all one "shining city on a hill," there was another city, where people were struggling, many of them living in pain. And we tried to tell America that unless we changed policies—unless we expanded opportunity—the deterioration of the other city would spread.

Well, we Democrats failed to reach enough Americans with that message, and now the nation has paid an awful price. We cannot afford to fail again.

Lives of Pain
The price is too high.

For the first time in their lives, millions of Americans who took for granted the basic right to make a living with one's own hands and mind and heart, have been denied the dignity of earning their own bread.

Today, a 50-year-old father lives nearly in terror at the prospect that if he is laid off now—as so many people around him have been—in addition to losing everything else, he'll lose his health insurance, too.

"What if I'm struck by cancer? My God, what about the mortgage? What about my son in college? And my daughter who's graduating high school? How will they get an education? And will they find a job even if they get an education?" How could it have happened? In a country where the executives of companies that fail, the presidents and chairmen of companies that make profits by trading solid American jobs for cheap labor overseas, can make $5 million, $10 million, $15 million a year?

How did it happen? How can our middle-class workers be in such terrible jeopardy?

A million children a year leaving school for the mean streets, a million a year surrounded by prostitutes and drug dealers, by violence and degradation of all kinds.

Some of them growing up familiar with the sound of gunfire before they've ever heard an orchestra; becoming young adults, only to be instructed by the powerful evidence of their surroundings, that there is little hope for them—even in America.

Nearly a whole generation surrendering in despair—to drugs, to having children while they're still children, to hopelessness. How did it happen, here, in the most powerful nation in the world?

It's a terrible tragedy. Not only for our children, but for all of America.

They are not my children, perhaps. Perhaps they are not your children, either. But Jesse is right: They are our children.

And we should love them. We should, we should love them. That's compassion.

But there's common sense at work here as well, because even if we were hard enough to choose not to love them, we would still need them to be sound and productive, because they are the nation's future.

Failed Economic Policy

It would be bad enough if we could believe that all of this unhappiness and failure is the result of a terrible but only a temporary recession.

But this, ladies and gentlemen, is more than a recession. Our economy has been weakened fundamentally by 12 years of conservative Republican supply-side policy, so called.

In fact, in fact supply-side was just another version of the failed Republican dogma of 65 years ago, then called "trickle down," which led to the Great Depression. And it has failed us again!

Think about supply-side. Supply-side operated from the naive Republican assumption that if we fed the wealthiest Americans with huge income tax cuts, they would eventually produce loaves and fishes for everyone. Instead, it made a small group of our wealthiest Americans wealthier than ever and left the rest of the country the crumbs from their tables. Unemployment, bankruptcy, economic stagnation.

Today, today, as we've heard so many times, a $400 billion annual deficit and a $4 trillion national debt hang like great albatrosses around our nation's neck, strangling our economy, menacing our future. Remember, we became a great nation by making things and selling them to others for their marks and their yens. But today, we buy from Japan and Germany and other nations the things we used to make and sell to them—automobiles and radios and televisions and clothing—giving them our dollars for their goods.

And then at the end of the year, because we spend so much more than we collect in these reduced taxes, we borrow back those dollars, paying billions more of our dollars in interest, increasing our debt—decreasing our ability to invest in our children, our schools—perpetuating a mad economic cycle that threatens to spin us totally out of control.

In no time at all, in no time at all, we have gone from the greatest seller nation, the greatest lender nation, the greatest creditor nation to, today, the world's largest buyer, the world's largest borrower and the world's largest debtor nation. That is Republican supply-side.

And that, ladies and gentlemen, that is the legacy of the Bush years. The slowest economic growth for any four-year Presidential term since Herbert Hoover. An economy crippled by debt and deficit. The fading of the American dream. Working-class families sliding back down toward poverty again, deprivation, inexplicable violence.

Desire for Change

And after 12 years, Americans are disillusioned, and they are angry, and they are fearful. And Americans showed that with the quick embrace they gave to the sudden appearance on television of a provocative, wealthy businessman who said he'd like to be President. Before he told anyone what he intended to do or how he would do it, he used one word and applause broke out all over America. The word was "change!"

Of course, the American people want change, of course we want something better than George Bush and the politics of decline, decay, and deception.

And beginning with this convention, we—you and I—must demonstrate to all the American people that change for the better is at hand, ready, able, eager to serve—in the person of—yes—Gov. Bill Clinton of Arkansas, and this time, this time we cannot afford to fail to deliver the message, not just to Democrats but to the whole nation. Because the ship of state is headed for the rocks.

The crew knows it. The passengers know it. Only the captain of the ship, President Bush, appears not to know it.

He seems to think—no, no, no, you see the president seems to think that the ship will be saved by imperceptible undercurrents, directed by the invisible hand of some cyclical economic god, that will gradually move the ship so that at the last moment it will miraculously glide past the rocks.

Well, prayer, prayer is always a good idea: but our prayers must be accompanied by good works. We need a captain who understands that, and who will seize the wheel—before it's too late. I am here tonight to offer America that new captain with a new course before it is too late and he is Gov. Bill Clinton of Arkansas.

Politics of Inclusion

Bill Clinton, Bill Clinton understands that a great political party must apply the best of its accumulated wisdom to the new configurations of a changing reality. He cherishes the ideals of justice and liberty and opportunity and fairness and compassion that Robert Kennedy died for. But he knows that these ideals require new implementations, new ways to provide incentive, to reward achievement, to encourage entrepreneurship, to develop jobs. Bill Clinton believes, as we all here do, in the first principle of our Democratic commitment: the politics of inclusion—the solemn obligation to create opportunity for all of our people, not just the fit and the fortunate.

For the aging factory worker in Pittsburgh and the schoolchild in Atlanta; for the family farmer in Des Moines and the eager immigrants, sweating to make their place alongside of us, here in New York City, and in San Francisco. For all the people; for the bright, young businesswoman in Chicago; all the people from wherever, no matter how recently, of whatever color, of whatever creed, of whatever sex, of whatever sexual orientation, all of them, equal members of the American family, and the neediest of them, the neediest of them deserving the most help from the rest of us. That is the fundamental Democratic predicate. Surrender that Democratic principle, and we might just as well tear the donkeys from our lapels, pin elephants on instead, and retreat to elegant estates behind ivy-covered walls, where, when they detect a callus on their palms, they conclude it's time to put down their polo mallet.

Bill Clinton believes that the closest thing to a panacea that we have is described by a simple, four letter word "work!" He has been living that truth all of his life.

So, Bill Clinton believes that what we most need now is to create jobs, by investing in the rebuilding of our cities; the shoring up of our agricultural strength; by investing to produce well-trained workers, new technologies, safe energy, entrepreneurship, laying the foundations for economic growth into the next century with free enterprise for the many, not free enterprise for the few, pulling people off welfare, off unemployment, giving people back their dignity and their confidence.

And unlike the other candidates—unlike the other candidates—and they all talk about jobs, Bill Clinton has a solid, intelligent workable plan to produce these jobs.

On Will and Wealth

But President Bush disagrees with Bill Clinton. President Bush says we cannot afford to do all that needs to be done. He says we have the will but not the wallet.

Bill Clinton knows that we have the wealth available, we have proven it over and over every time the dramatic catastrophe strikes.

Remember the savings and loans?

Governors and mayors had gone to Washington, and I was among them, to plead for help for education, for job training, for roads and bridges, for drug treatment. "Sorry, there is none," said the President. "We're broke. We have the will but not the wallet." And we put our heads down.

And then Americans discovered that wealthy bankers—educated in the most exquisite forms of conservative, Republican banking—through their incompetence and thievery, and the Government's neglect, had stolen or squandered everything in sight!

The world's greatest bank robbery and we heard no moralizing about values from our Republican leaders then, did we?

Instead of castigations, *mirabile dictu*—all of a sudden—the heavens opened, and out of the blue, billions of dollars appeared.

Not for children. Not for jobs. Not for drug treatment or for the ill or for health care. But hundreds of billions of dollars to bail out failed savings and loans. Billions for war. Billions for earthquakes if they strike, God forbid, and hurricanes and Bill Clinton asks, if we can do all of this for these spectacular catastrophes when they occur, why can we not find the wealth to respond to the quiet catastrophes that every day oppress the lives of thousands, that destroy our children with drugs—all the quiet catastrophes, the quiet catastrophes that kill thousands with terrible new diseases like AIDS, that deprive our people of the sureness of adequate health care, that stifle our future.

Bill Clinton asks the question, Bill Clinton has the answer. And America needs Bill Clinton, too, because he understands that we must deal with what could be—eventually—the most lethal problem of all: a degraded environment—one that kills life in our lakes with acid rain; allows cancer-causing rays to pierce a deteriorated ozone shield and threatens to convert the entire planet into a cosmic hothouse.

Bill Clinton made clear how well he understands that when he announced Senator Al Gore would be the next Vice President of the United States of America.

Attributes of Leadership
America—America needs Bill Clinton. America needs Bill Clinton for still another reason.

We need a leader who will stop the Republican attempt, through laws and through the courts, to tell us what God to believe in, and how to apply that God's judgment to our schoolrooms, our bedrooms, and our bodies.

Bill Clinton, Bill Clinton knows the course from here, past peril, to a new era of growth and progress for this nation that will enable us to share our power and our abundance with the whole world community.

He was born and raised, fortunately for us, with the personal attributes needed for leadership: God-given intelligence, vitality, and an extraordinary quality of character that allowed him to survive the buffeting and the trauma of a difficult youth. He was born poor in Hope, Ark. Now the accents, even the colors may have been a tint different but the feelings were the same that many of us experienced on the asphalt streets of some of the nation's great cities. The same pain, the same anguish, the same hope. He has lived through years of hard challenges since that difficult youth. And with each new challenge he has grown wiser and stronger as he demonstrated so well with his remarkable resiliency in the recent bruising Democratic primaries.

I will tell you this. In a world of fragile and thin-skinned politicians, he was an admirable aberration.

Bill Clinton has always been driven by the desire to lift himself above his own immediate concerns, to give himself to something larger than himself.

His entire life has been devoted to helping others through public service and for 11 years now, he has been the Governor of his beloved state, protecting Arkansas from a Federal Government that has been depriving the states and cities for over a decade, balancing 11 budgets in a row, doing the things that governors and presidents are supposed to do—enforcing the laws, providing education and opportunities for children and young adults, expanding health care, attracting new jobs, and reaching out to heal wounds caused by 300 years of unfairness and oppression.

He has done it so well that the nation's other governors, both Democratic and Republican, have repeatedly acknowledged him to be a national leader.

All this time, all this time, all this time Bill Clinton has worked to relieve other people's discomfort because he remembers his own struggle.

That's why we need Bill Clinton—because Bill Clinton still remembers, because he is equipped to break the awful gridlock in Washington and to deliver effective government finally—because he will remind that nation that we are too good to make war our most successful enterprise. That's why we need Bill Clinton. We need Bill Clinton because he does not believe that the way to win political support is to pit one group against another.

Bill Clinton does not believe in the cynical political arithmetic that says you can add by subtracting, you can multiply by dividing. He rejects that. Instead, instead he will work to make the whole nation stronger, by bringing people together, showing us our commonality, instructing us in cooperation, making us not a collection of competing special interests, but one great, special family—the family of America!

For all these reasons, we must make Bill Clinton the next President of the United States of America.

Visions of a Great Parade

Ladies and gentlemen, a year ago in this great city led by our great mayor—Mayor Dinkins—we had a great parade in New York City to celebrate the return of our armed forces from the Persian Gulf.

I'm sure you had one too.

But as joyous as those parades were, I'd like to march with you in a different kind of celebration, one, regrettably, that we cannot hold yet.

I'd like to march with you behind President Bill Clinton through cities and rural villages where all the people have safe streets, and affordable housing and health care when they need it.

I want to clap my hands and throw my fists in the air, cheering neighborhoods where children can be children, where they can grow up and get the chance to go to college, and one day own their own home.

I want to sing—proud songs, happy songs—arm in arm with workers who have a real stake in their company's success; who once again have the assurance that a lifetime of hard work will make life better for their children than it had been for them.

I want to march behind President Bill Clinton in a victory parade that sends up fireworks, celebrating the triumph of our technology centers and factories, outproducing and outselling our overseas competitors.

I want to march with you—I want to march with you—knowing that we are selecting justices to the Supreme Court who are really qualified to be there and justices—justices who understand the basic American right of each individual to make his or her own private moral and religious judgments.

I want to look around and feel the warmth, the pride, the profound gratitude of knowing that we are making America surer, stronger, and sweeter. I want to shout out our thanks because President Bill Clinton has helped us to make the greatest nation in the world better than it's ever been.

So step aside, Mr. Bush. You've had your parade!

It's time—it's time for change. It's time for someone smart enough to know; strong enough to do; sure enough to lead.

The Comeback Kid. A new voice for a new America.

Because I love New York, because I love America, I nominate for the office of the President of the United States, the man from Hope, Ark., Gov. Bill Clinton!

COMBATIVE PERSUASION

We have emphasized "friendly persuasion" thus far by presenting techniques with which persuaders can change an audience's beliefs and actions. Rather than confronting the audience, persuaders try to use written and verbal language that engages the audience in a cooperative and transactional enterprise. When such language is used skillfully, audiences are hardly aware that their perspectives have changed or that the persuader has spent considerable time developing a strategy.

When using *combative persuasion,* presenters use confrontive strategies to modify the opinions and actions of those who oppose their perspective.[36] Two kinds of combative situations exist. In the first type, persuaders have coercive, one-on-one confrontations to change an adversary's position. In a confrontational meeting, for example, the presenter—the leader of a social movement—might demand that an agency executive make the agency's services more responsive to a specific population's needs. In other cases, persuaders debate an adversary hoping to convince *observers* to accept their point of view over that of the adversary. In a staff meeting, for example, a woman might argue with another person to convince staff members to accept her position. We can illustrate the use of combative persuasion by discussing adversarial debates, coercive messages, and negotiations.

Adversarial Debates

Three parties exist in adversarial debates: the persuader, the adversary, and an audience of observers. Debates rarely follow a structured format, aside from when school debate teams meet, but argumentative situations often arise.[37] Perhaps someone presents a proposal in a staff meeting, which one or more persons criticize and then its initiator defends. Perhaps someone testifies against a proposal to a legislative committee to oppose mandatory HIV-testing for prostitutes. Perhaps someone argues with an individual in the presence of another person. Persuaders sometimes hope to change the minds of both their immediate adversary and the audience that hears their argument.

Rand Martin, the lobbyist for an AIDS advocacy group, attacked a conservative legislator's proposal to require all testing services, both public and private, to give state public health officials the names of all persons who test positive for HIV. To illustrate the array of arguments that debaters can use, in Case 9.2 we present twelve arguments Martin could use. Assume that Martin debates the legislator in a public forum, such as before a student audience.

CASE 9.2
ATTACKING THE LEGISLATOR'S MEASURE

Martin could do the following:

• Attack the *values* implicit or explicit in the proposal. A debater can contrast *any* value premise with an alternative value premise. While the legislator values control to protect the public's health, Martin favors protecting the privacy and freedom of people who test positive for HIV. Such privacy, he contends, conforms with traditions embedded in the Bill of Rights. Persons who are HIV-positive but may remain free of AIDS symptoms for many years particularly need privacy to protect them from discrimination.

- Attack the proposal's *feasibility*. Public health departments would ask HIV-positive individuals to list persons with whom they have had sexual relations. Department officials would then alert each of those partners to their possible infection with HIV. However, it is extremely time-consuming to develop these lists and contact the persons on them, particularly because health departments lack sufficient staff to implement this policy. "If public health officials lack the staff to adequately accomplish their existing functions, how can we expect them to assume these added functions?" Martin might ask.

- Attack the legislator's *motives* by saying, "He wants a witch-hunt, not humanistic services, for those who are HIV-positive."

- Attack some *unanticipated* or *adverse consequences* of the proposal. People who fear they carry the virus may avoid testing if the results are not confidential. Many people would likely forgo testing, fearing that their identities would be revealed to employers, landlords, and others.

- Attack the legislator's use of *specific analogies*. Assume that the legislator contends that public health departments have long required divulging the names of persons with syphilis and gonorrhea. The legislator says this information has led to successful efforts to alert sexual partners to their possible infection. To attack this analogy to other sexually transmitted diseases, Martin might note that syphilis and gonorrhea are currently epidemics *despite* these practices. Moreover, discrimination against people with these treatable diseases is not nearly as marked, he might argue, as with persons who are HIV-positive. Unlike syphilis and gonorrhea, the initial infection with HIV is often followed by a lengthy period—sometimes more than ten years—when the person has no serious symptoms, much less AIDS. "If we breech the confidentiality of persons with a disease of such duration," Martin might argue, "we risk extended damage to their careers and reputations that does not occur with treatable diseases, such as syphilis."

- Attack the legislator's *uses of data* and *analytic assumptions*. Assume, for the moment, that the legislator contended that the proposal had already been used in Colorado and that it had been successful. Martin could criticize specific quantitative studies that the legislator used to buttress this claim. Martin could attack the methods used to collect data, the applicability of the Colorado data to his state, and the way the legislator interpreted the data. (We discuss methods of criticizing quantitative studies in more detail in Chapter Thirteen.)

- Attack *implicit models of human motivation* in the legislator's rationale for the proposal. Requiring that testing centers report HIV-positive persons' names to the public health department implies that most HIV-positive persons will not *voluntarily* cooperate with public health officials.

This assumption suggests that most HIV-positive persons lack a strong sense of social responsibility. Martin might assert that many HIV-positive individuals are (or can become) concerned about former and current sexual partners *if* given access to high-quality counseling that does not infringe on their confidentiality. When they receive their test results, for example, they could be told about voluntary counseling and the need to inform current and prior sexual partners of the risks they encounter. Martin could reframe the issue, moving away from *forcing* HIV-positive persons to assume social responsibility to providing assistance to HIV-positive persons to help them channel their inherent altruism. The gay community's remarkable generosity toward people with AIDS and the proliferation of support networks they have established support this contention.

- Attack the legislator's conception of the *chain of events* that would follow the enactment of his proposal. The legislator assumes that: testing centers will provide names of HIV-positive people to the state's public health department; this department will contact HIV-positive people; HIV-positive people will agree to provide the names of previous sexual partners or persons with whom they shared needles when using drugs; public officials will contact these partners; and the partners will agree to be tested for HIV, will practice "safe sex," and, if they test positive, will provide public officials with names of their partners. Martin could contend that this chain of events would often be broken at one, two, or more points. We have noted that public health departments often lack the staff to make these contacts. When forced to divulge names, some HIV-positive persons might decline to be cooperative because of the violation of their privacy and the imposition of mandatory procedures. In the case of casual sexual encounters or needle sharing, HIV-positive persons might be unable to supply names. Because of the population's mobility, it would be difficult to locate some of the partners, even if authorities had their names.

- Expose *vagueness* in the legislator's proposal that might make it seem less attractive to other people. Perhaps his proposal fails to describe how the testing services, some of them private ones, will be linked to the state's public health department. Perhaps the proposal fails to discuss how the mandatory-reporting policy will be evaluated to assess its effectiveness in slowing the spread of HIV.

- Attack *unacceptable trade-offs* in the legislator's proposal. He might commend the legislator for wanting to stem the spread of HIV (a desirable objective) but argue that, noble as it may be, this objective should not cost tens of thousands of individuals their privacy (a valued objective) or cost the government exorbitant amounts. When making this kind of argument, the lobbyist in effect says that we need to stem the spread of HIV with methods that do not violate personal privacy and that are not so costly.

- Argue that the legislator's proposal will be *rendered ineffective* by unforeseen future events. Assume, for example, that impending technology allows individuals to test themselves for HIV in the privacy of their homes. This technology would render moot the mandatory-reporting law, because many people would bypass public or private testing centers. Alternatively, assume that legal rulings render the mandatory-reporting law unconstitutional or delay its implementation.

- Offer a *counterproposal.* Because tracking partners is expensive, Martin could argue that scarce public resources ought instead be invested in public education projects, such as efforts to promote safe sex by the use of condoms. Perhaps scarce resources should be invested in teaching addicts and prostitutes how not to become infected and how not to spread the disease to other people. The lobbyist might conclude that "the state will get a far better return on funds invested in an educational program than in a mandatory-reporting program."

Coercive Messages

Policy practitioners sometimes use coercive messages with decisionmakers whom they believe would otherwise oppose their positions.[38] People who use coercive messages usually assume—often correctly—that cooperative messages will not work, because political and ideological factors, discriminatory attitudes, and tradition make decisionmakers unwilling to accept their policy proposals. These lawmakers may feel that existing resources are already so committed to other programs that they cannot support a new program.

With this assumption in mind, people try to make their program seem important. They develop a message that contains several elements.[39] First, at the outset, practitioners make a formal demand, such as asking for a commitment to fund a specific program. The message may include threats, either explicit or veiled; persuaders may refer to taking further steps, such as litigation, protests, or sending delegations to even higher authorities, if decisionmakers do not comply with the request. Threats also contain incentives or rewards, such as promising *not* to use coercive measures if the request is granted. The practitioner can threaten to publicize the issue through the mass media, if the media have not already been apprised of the issue.

Practitioners often try to influence the social context when they use coercive messages. They may insist that the decisionmaker listen to a delegation, rather than to one or several persons. They may physically surround the decisionmaker with members of their group. In some cases, persuaders inform the mass media of the encounter before it has occurred in order to place even more pressure on decisionmakers.

Coercive messages can be effective in some situations, particularly when no other recourse exists and when decisionmakers feel vulnerable to adverse publicity or to the coercion. But coercive messages also carry certain dangers. If decisionmakers do not feel vulnerable to coercion, they are unlikely to comply with the requests and may in fact harden their positions and take retaliatory measures.[40] Assume, for example, that some staff in an agency used coercive messages with their executive director with respect to a specific issue; were the director not to sympathize with them and to believe they lacked the power resources that they claimed, she might fire, demote, or otherwise retaliate against the leaders of the delegation. Moreover, once coercive messages have been initiated by one side in a dispute, a vicious circle of escalating intransigency and reprisal often begins that makes it increasingly difficult for opposing sides to cooperate.[41] Both sides will begin to view the conflict as win-lose, rather than win-win, so that *any* concession to the other side becomes a personal defeat.

Negotiations

Negotiations take place when two or more opposing parties in a conflict meet to develop a final position.[42] Skillful negotiators want to emerge from the negotiations with their positions intact, but they often realize that they have to make some concessions.

Practitioners usually decide before the negotiations which positions are nonnegotiable, which are less important to them, and which concessions they might make at some point during the negotiations. They make these initial choices as they analyze their opponents' positions, motivations, and power resources. If they think their opponents are unlikely to make concessions, they may decide to be tough at the outset. They may also set a tough negotiating stance at the outset if they think their opponents will accede to concessions. Negotiations usually begin with each side presenting their initial positions. As the negotiations proceed, each side decides whether and when to grant concessions to the other side, either as a means of testing their intentions, as a sign of good faith, or as a quid pro quo for a concession the opponent has made. As the negotiations proceed, each side has to decide how tolerable a stalemate would be, whether the other side will match its concessions, and when to make concessions. If both sides believe it is necessary to resolve the conflict, concessions emerge in the course of deliberations. Each party, much like a poker player, gradually reveals where it is willing to make concessions. The two sides will probably use delays, veiled or open threats, and inducements to persuade the other side to make concessions.

As Burton Gummer notes, negotiations do not have to be as formal as our preceding discussion suggests. When persons engage in give-and-take discussions in any setting, such as committees or private conversations, negotiation often takes place.[43]

WIN-WIN OR COLLABORATIVE TECHNIQUES

We may have conveyed the misleading impression that policy practitioners mostly use combative, or win-lose, tactics. Indeed, emerging feminist literature suggests that administrators, as well as policy practitioners, should make greater use of collaborative techniques. We began this chapter by discussing "friendly persuasion," so it is fitting that we end it with an emphasis on collaborative strategies.

Most of us associate negotiations with hardball tactics. Some theorists advocate noncombative techniques, where each side seeks to understand the other side's views, list alternative remedies, and reach a consensus through collaborative decisionmaking. Conflict-reducing language aids a collaborative process, which can lead to a solution that meets both parties' needs. Eliciting ideas from the other side also helps throughout the negotiating process.[44]

Policy practitioners sometimes act as mediators in disputes between contending factions. Assume that two factions in an agency have opposing views on a policy issue and that they have been embroiled in conflict for a sustained period. Also assume that they *do* want to resolve the conflict, but that they do not know how to achieve this resolution. As the mediator to the dispute, you approach both parties and signal your willingness to help mediate the dispute. After talking with both sides to better understand their positions, you have the two sides agree to attend a meeting where you act as mediator. As the meeting unfolds, you encourage both sides to state their positions, you identify possible points of compromise, you encourage both sides to discuss these points during an interlude, and you help them develop a compromise when they reconvene. For mediation to be successful, each party to a conflict has to believe that the mediator does not manipulate the situation to the other side's advantage.[45] People can, of course, mediate in less formal ways, such as promoting a compromise in a staff meeting. Mediators must convince both parties that they are neutral arbitrators who will help each side develop a collaborative situation.

SUMMARY

Policy practitioners need skills to persuade others to support their positions. Whether presidents, government officials, agency executives, or line staff, policy practitioners need to be able to devise persuading strategies to accomplish their objectives with specific audiences. They should establish objectives and diagnose their audience as hostile, sympathetic, apathetic, or expert. They need to construct outlines for their presentations in light of their subject matter, objectives, and audience. They have to be able to make effective presentations by keeping eye contact, pacing their delivery, and stimulating audience participation.

Policy practitioners sometimes engage in "friendly communication," where they shape their presentations to elicit a favorable response from the audience. On other occasions, they engage in "combative communication," where they use directives, debating strategies, and hardball negotiating approaches. They may also act as mediators, using win-win modes of negotiation.

Suggested Readings

POLICY-PERSUADING STRATEGIES
Austin Freeley, *Argumentation and Debate*, 6th ed. (Belmont, CA: Wadsworth, 1986).
Willard Richan, "A Common Language for Social Work," *Social Work* 17 (November 1972): 14–22.
Herbert Simons, *Persuasion*, 2nd ed. (New York: Random House, 1986).

NONCOMBATIVE NEGOTIATIONS AND MEDIATION
Herb Bisno, *Managing Conflict* (Newbury Park, CA: Sage, 1988), pp. 98–147.
Jay Folberg and Alison Taylor, *Mediation* (San Francisco: Jossey-Bass, 1984).
Margaret Gibelman and Harold Demone, "Negotiating a Contract: Practical Considerations," in Harold Demone and Margaret Gibelman, eds., *Services for Sale* (New Brunswick, NJ: Rutgers University Press, 1989), pp. 131–148.

Notes

1. Willard Richan, "A Common Language for Social Work," *Social Work* 17 (November 1972): 14–22.
2. Herbert Simons, *Persuasion*, 2nd ed. (New York: Random House, 1986), pp. 18–21.
3. Donald Cegala, *Persuasive Communication: Theory and Practice*, 3rd ed. (Edina, MN: Bellwether, 1987), pp. 13–15.
4. Simons, *Persuasion*, pp. 227–251.
5. Cegala, *Persuasive Communication*, pp. 70–75, 97–98.
6. Simons, *Persuasion*, pp. 23–24, 141–142.
7. Karlyn Campbell, *The Rhetorical Act* (Belmont, CA: Wadsworth, 1982), pp. 69–118.
8. Ibid., pp. 101–116.
9. Simons, *Persuasion*, p. 25.
10. Campbell, *The Rhetorical Act*, pp. 69–118.
11. Cegala, *Persuasive Communication*, pp. 152–155.
12. Stan Paine, G. Thomas Bellamy, and Barbara Wilcox, *Human Services That Work* (Baltimore: Paul Brooks, 1984), pp. 42–44.
13. Morton Deutsch, *The Resolution of Conflict: Constructive and Destructive Processes* (New Haven, CT: Yale University Press, 1973), pp. 124–152.
14. Segmentation is discussed extensively in marketing literature; see Phillip Kotler, *Principles of Marketing*, 4th ed. (Englewood Cliffs, NJ: Prentice-Hall, 1989), pp. 42–46. Also see Simons, *Persuasion*, pp. 143–146.
15. George Brager and Stephen Holloway, *Changing Human Service Organizations* (New York: Free Press, 1978), pp. 199–203.
16. Ibid., pp. 199–203.
17. See Marya Holcombe and Judith Stein, *Presentations for Decision Makers* (New York: Van Nostrand Reinhold, 1983).
18. Ibid., pp. 16–25.
19. Ibid., pp. 11–13.
20. Gerald Phillips, *How to Support Your Cause and Win* (Columbia: University of South Carolina Press, 1984), p. 96.
21. Holcombe and Stein, *Presentations for Decision Makers*, pp. 132–145.
22. Simons, *Persuasion*, pp. 153–154.
23. Ibid., 124–129.
24. Robert Reid, *Work of Nations: Preparing Ourselves for the 21st Century* (New York: Knopf, 1991), pp. 154–168.
25. Simons, *Persuasion*, pp. 148–154.
26. Ibid., pp. 210, 213.
27. Ibid., pp. 153–154.
28. Ibid., p. 153.
29. Cegala, *Persuasive Communication*, p. 136.
30. Simons, *Persuasion*, p. 153.
31. Cegala, *Persuasive Communication*, p. 134.

32. George Brager, Harry Specht, and James Torczyner, *Community Organizing*, 2nd ed. (New York: Columbia University Press), pp. 342–343.
33. Paul Ephross and Thomas Vassil, *Groups that Work* (New York: Columbia University Press, 1988), p. 157.
34. George Sharwell, "How to Testify Before a Legislative Committee," in Maryann Mahaffey and John Hanks, eds., *Practical Politics: Social Work and Political Response* (Silver Spring, MD: National Association of Social Workers, 1982), pp. 85–98.
35. Lewis Dexter, "Role Relationships and Conception of Neutrality in Interviewing," *American Journal of Sociology* 62 (September 1956): 153–157.
36. Simons, *Persuasion*, pp. 253–254.
37. Ibid., pp. 190–192.
38. See Brager, Specht, and Torczyner, *Community Organizing*, pp. 355–357.
39. Simons, *Persuasion*, pp. 253–256.
40. Ibid., pp. 259–261.
41. Ibid., pp. 253–256.
42. See Margaret Gibelman and Harold Demone, "Negotiating a Contract: Practical Considerations," in Harold Demone and Margaret Gibelman, eds., *Services for Sale* (New Brunswick, NJ: Rutgers University Press, 1989), pp. 131–148. Also see Burton Gummer, *The Politics of Social Administration: Managing Organizational Politics in Social Agencies*. (Englewood Cliffs, NJ: Prentice-Hall, 1990), pp. 153–185; and Herb Bisno, *Managing Conflict* (Newbury Park, CA: Sage, 1988), pp. 99–147.
43. Gummer, *Politics of Social Administration*, pp. 160–162, 174–177.
44. Bisno, *Managing Conflict*, pp. 100–101, 121–123, 137–139.
45. See Jay Folberg and Alison Taylor, *Mediation* (San Francisco: Jossey-Bass, 1984).

PART THREE
POWER AND THE POLITICAL PROCESS

Policies are not fashioned in a vacuum, but are shaped by political realities in decisionmaking arenas, such as legislatures, the boards of agencies, or city councils. We discuss the nature and varieties of power in Chapter Ten because the concept of power lies at the heart of the political process.

Policy practitioners must often be skilled in, not just using power, but developing power resources in the first instance. We discuss the interactional dimensions of power in Chapter Eleven.

To have policies enacted, policy practitioners have to devise a strategy for using power resources. We discuss techniques for building strategy in Chapter Twelve.

Chapter Ten

Power and Policy Enactment

Practitioners often want to shape policy choices in legislative and agency settings. To do this, they need a conceptual understanding of power. They should explore what power and assertiveness are and how they are used. We devote this chapter to these kinds of conceptual issues as a prelude to discussing ways to develop personal power resources (Chapter Ten) and political strategy (Chapter Eleven).

IN DEFENSE OF POLITICS

People sometimes call those preoccupied with political realities opportunistic, power-hungry, or wedded to special interests. Some truth often exists in these assertions, but they obscure how important politics can be in policymaking. Before we discuss some of these functions, we will define the word *politics* more precisely. Some people equate it with government policymaking; indeed, one part of Webster's definition declares it "the politics and aims of a government [and] the conduct and contests of political parties."[1] Certainly, these government and party functions belong within a definition of politics, but what about "wheeling and dealing" in other settings, such as social agencies, professional associations, and communities? Webster comes to our aid by also including in his definition, "the political connections or beliefs of a person [and] the plotting or scheming of those seeking personal power, glory, position, or the like."[2] Webster's choice of *plotting* and *scheming* suggests a certain disdain for such activity, though he usefully notes that politics includes power-related struggles in *any* setting. We need a definition that does not cast aspersion on persons who develop and use power, because such leaders as Franklin Roosevelt, Lyndon Johnson, and Bill Clinton sometimes used power for noble ends.

At the risk of rewriting the dictionary, let us hazard our own definition. Politics represents "efforts by people in government and nongovernment settings to secure their policy wishes by developing and using power resources." When defined in this manner, politics becomes relevant not only to highly placed officials, but also to *anyone* who tries to influence policymaking.

It is difficult to imagine a world where politics does not exist, because political processes are endemic to social discourse. Were such a world to exist, people who lacked the formal authority to develop policy positions would have no recourse but to obey existing policies or to seek remedies through other means, such as force. In dictatorships, of course, politicians face these grim prospects. However, democratic regimes allow interests, factions, and individuals to occupy legitimate roles in policy deliberations, even if some people possess greater power than others.

The political process provides a way to address the many value-laden issues in policymaking that no analytic methodology can resolve. When people have conflicting values or reach opposite conclusions, they can resolve their differences through the political process. While some policy analysts claim to be purely objective or scientific in their approach, even a casual examination of their methodology reveals many value-laden choices, as we discussed in Chapter Eight when we noted how values powerfully shape the selection of criteria, options, results, and decisionmaking rules.[3]

ANALYTIC AND POLITICAL APPROACHES TO POLICY PRACTICE

Unlike policy analysts, who select options on technical grounds, people who use a political model usually do not want to waste their scarce resources and time on losing issues when they might invest them in winning ones.

Because of their preoccupation with power, people who ascribe to the political paradigm devote considerable time to calculating political feasibility; they examine patterns of support and opposition associated with specific issues, options, and proposals, not only before they begin, but also during the course of deliberations. By making these calculations, they hope to assess whether a proposal can be enacted and to develop political strategy to help them outmaneuver likely opponents.[4]

A political model differs markedly from the analytic approaches we discussed in the preceding four chapters. If the analyst wants to discover technically superior solutions to problems by using quantitative and qualitative techniques, the adherent of the political approach wants to understand existing political realities so as to select feasible options and develop effective political strategy. If the analyst assumes that "the truth will win out," the politician assumes that "might will prevail." If analysts devote most of their time to technical tasks, political practitioners devote considerable time gauging political realities, developing power, and implementing political strategy. (Of course, sophisticated policy practitioners can creatively *couple* analytic and political approaches in specific situations.) Box 10.1 presents the political approach to policy practice by asking questions typical of that orientation.

> **BOX 10.1**
> **A Political Model**
>
> *The Distribution of Power*
>
> - What persons, interests, and factions are likely to participate in certain policy deliberations?
> - What are their power resources?
> - What are their likely positions on a proposal?
> - How strongly do they hold these positions?
>
> *Political Stakes in an Issue*
>
> - What political benefits and risks will I encounter if I participate in certain policy deliberations?
> - Should I be a leader, a follower, or a bystander?
>
> *Political Feasibility*
>
> - What patterns of opposition and support will likely be associated with specific policy options?
> - Which of them, on balance, should I support?
>
> *Political Strategy*
>
> - What power resources do I (or my allies) currently possess that are relevant to these deliberations?
> - What power resources might I (or my allies) develop that will be relevant to these deliberations?
> - What strategies will we use as the deliberations proceed?
>
> *Revising Strategy*
>
> - How should I change my strategy in light of evolving political realities, including my opponents' likely moves?
> - As political realities evolve, how should my role change?

A CASE FROM THE HUMAN SERVICES

Case 10.1 illustrates the need for political skills in policy practice. In the case, a social work intern tries to develop an innovative program in a mental health agency. She notes that the agency, which considers itself an advocate for children's mental health needs, lacks a program to help children whose parents have been institutionalized for psychiatric problems. She hopes to obtain approval for an eight-week crisis model of services to these children, but soon realizes that she encounters numerous political barriers. Would private-practice psychiatrists and staff in area hospitals, who admit patients to mental hospitals, cooperate with the new program by making referrals to it? Would agency officials support a preventive program when they believe the agency should address the existing mental problems of children and adults? Would the executive director, who wishes to use existing resources to eliminate a waiting list, oppose the innovation because it would divert funds from this priority?

CASE 10.1
A Preventive Mental Health Program

It is curious that the Mountain View Child Guidance Clinic considers itself an advocate for children's mental health needs when it neglects children of the psychiatrically hospitalized parent. Such children are in crisis and experiencing extreme family disequilibrium at the time of the parent's hospitalization. They need immediate assistance in understanding and dealing constructively with feelings and thoughts associated with this experience. It is preferable that this intervention occur at or near the time of the crisis, when defenses are most fluid and before maladaptive patterns of functioning have solidified. To meet this need, I am trying to develop, in addition to the brief services offered by the clinic, a crisis group for children of psychiatrically hospitalized parents.

The coordination and cooperation necessary for such a program would be a landmark in the clinic's history. Its success would depend on the referrals of psychiatrists who assist patients admitted to local public and private psychiatric hospitals. If the clinic bypassed the physician's authority and accepted referrals directly from hospitals' social-service departments, it would alienate some physicians, who might imperil the program by boycotting it.

Announcements could be sent to the hospitals, their social-service departments, and specific physicians. The service must offer support to both the physician and the hospital.

The politics of this agency dictates that the new program not be called preventive, lest funders and policymakers not favor it. Because they believe that no room exists in the budget for prevention, this program will be called crisis intervention.

We could approach four local hospitals with announcements of the new clinic program. A follow-up phone call would add a personal touch and hopefully clinch the process. As a staff member, I would persuade physician-friends of its merit, while soliciting membership and support.

There are a number of barriers to change in this agency. The clinic focuses its energy on the quantity rather than the quality of services. Of primary importance to the executive director is avoiding a waiting list. To this end, he mobilizes all forces, and automatically shelves any program change that would deter this aim. Further, staff are usually inundated with work and have little time to create innovative services. Similarly, the agency values efficiency in programming and expenditures. Clinic executives believe that they cannot afford to risk any revenue by applying funds to areas other than those directly funded and approved. Another barrier to innovation is the agency staff's disinclination to participate in program development, which deprives the agency of new program ideas. Staff members seek what fulfillment is available through the clients themselves but leave the business of the clinic to the bureaucracy.

I am only a student intern in this agency, but I want to get this innovation off the ground before my field experience ends. Considering the nature of the agency, it is essential to introduce the change in an administratively sanctioned way through approved channels. Therefore, I initially broached the idea of the innovation to the director of outpatient services, Mr. Jones, who is my preceptor for short-term and intake cases. On first mentioning the plan, I was careful to make it appear an idea that I had developed in the course of discussions with him. I told him I saw the idea as consistent with comprehensive mental health care for children, an ideal he often espouses. Underscoring that the services would take only eight weeks, which he likes, and stressing its efficiency in terms of the waiting list, I ventured to actually propose a pilot plan. He groaned and suggested that I "write it up," with no explanation as to what that meant. Rather than irritate him further, I did not mention the project for several weeks. I then told my regular field instructor that I was discussing with Mr. Jones a new program for children of hospitalized patients and I received her approval to use this as a learning experience in program design.

Several weeks later, I found that Mr. Jones completely had forgotten my plan. But, in further discussion, he expressed strong interest and even brainstormed an initial strategy with me that would help the innovation gain gradual support in Mountain View Child Guidance. He argued that we should develop a two-phase strategy. In phase one, I would develop a pilot project. Because I am a student intern, it would not need formal clearance from high-level executives or the agency board. He would simply notify the executive that a student intern was establishing a pilot group for children of institutionalized parents. He urged a low profile during this initial period. After we initiated the project, he would develop a strategy for a formal proposal that would go to the executive director and hopefully eventually to the board. That would be phase two. If all went well, the agency would formally earmark funds for the program. He hoped that my experience with the pilot project would provide useful information for writing the formal proposal and orally presenting it to the executive and the board. He concluded our meeting by saying, "You know you will have to do the entire program in the pilot phase. All the screening and everything." He seemed tantalized by the idea of obtaining increased service with no additional expenditure of staff time.

To date, I have succeeded in involved Mr. Jones sufficiently in planning to encourage his sense of investment in the program. I have abided by the rules in recognizing his authority and decisionmaking powers and deemphasizing my own initiative. My short-term strategy, then, is to begin the program myself. But a number of obstacles could still interfere with program acceptance by key decisionmakers, even during the pilot phase.

One obstacle is the issue of community coordination. Currently, the clinic has superficial coordination with local mental health agencies, only exchanging cases sporadically. No clear plan exists for coordination of services. This program necessitates an intermediate type of coordination, a case-planning coordination organized into a whole-family approach. The current fragmentation in treatment of families with a disturbed member would be a danger in this program, because it would undermine the purpose of comprehensive care. What factors are involved in this coordination process?

First, there is the issue of goal conflict. On the surface, there appears to be little; both the psychiatric hospitals and the clinic serve and are concerned with families' mental health needs. But is that really the case? In fact, the hospitals view treatment of the parent-patient from a pathology model rather than a family systems perspective. In that case, they may choose to refer the child, not for group, but for individual treatment as an "impaired" family member. It will be important to impress on these staff members that the groups help the child in crisis, rather than providing long-term therapy. With regard to the power relationships between agencies, the major snare seems to be the physicians' autonomy. The administrators of local psychiatric hospitals may perceive the children's group as highlighting their own program deficiencies and choose to provide a similar service themselves.

At present, the agencies do not consider themselves interdependent. Instead, they coexist in separate realms of the psychiatric community and rarely communicate. More positively, though, they may cooperate with this project, not only because of the children's emotional needs, but also because child and adult agencies are complementary community services that do not usually compete for the same clientele.

To alleviate some of the tension between agencies and to facilitate the common goal of improved community mental health, I will plan individual visits to each hospital's social-services department. I may be invited to present this program to the monthly meeting of hospital psychiatrists, which will create a direct encounter with most of the staff physicians. In addition, I will invite representatives of each hospital to the clinic for an orientation and open house, which should improve relationships between clinic and hospital and emphasize the community nature of the project.

Within the clinic itself, a political process will follow the initiation of this program. When Mr. Jones seeks its official approval, he must submit it to the medical director for confirmation; he in turn takes it to the executive committee for approval, and they then present it to the board of directors for final approval. However, because Mr. Jones is the most powerful person in the agency, his approval should lead to its acceptance.

A complicating factor is the director of training, Ida Brown. To be candid, she does not particularly like Mr. Jones and often opposes any proposals he initiates. She may interfere in the decisionmaking process by pushing for a nondecision; that is, she may suggest that the plan be initiated only after lengthy study or pending location of special sources of external funding. Another problem may arise because many in the agency focus on the child of an institutionalized adult as a patient, which clashes with the program's preventive mission.

I also see several other groups developing in relation to the program. One consists of the senior administrator and the chief of program development (also the director of support services). These two men are allied in their unstated mission of increasing clinic prestige and influence in the community. They will probably support the program from their stated positions of commitment to enriching the quality of service available to the community. This would appear reasonable and underscore the senior administrator's interest in the efficient business operation of the clinic.

The executive director himself will probably support the program in deference to Mr. Jones, to whom he defers on all issues pertaining to the outpatient part of the agency. The outpatient service functions virtually independently from the day-treatment and other components of the agency.

The medical director is also a figurehead, whose medical degree is valued by the agency. He will most assuredly remain neutral lest he find himself in the middle of a political battle. He appears to have little power in the agency.

The board of directors also has little power in this agency. They are most concerned with what mural is painted on which wall and how chairs are grouped in the waiting room. Program development is not their expertise, and they usually abide agreeably with decisions made by the executive director.

In the future, I see this program as an integral part of the clinic's services, if it can survive pilot and approval stages. The children served during their first experience with a parent's hospitalization may choose to return to us if the parent is rehospitalized. Children who have experienced numerous parental hospitalizations will be able to compare previous episodes with the one eased by clinic services. We may then see self-referrals by children and families, reducing the need for physician referrals.

Mr. Jones wants me to assist him in writing the formal proposal after my pilot project has been in operation for five months. The project has made me realize that good clinical skills need to be supplemented by program design and political skills. How else can social workers develop and institutionalize innovative services?

SOURCE: This case is adapted from one developed by Stacy Stern, M.S.W. Names and locations have been altered.

As she ponders these kinds of questions, the social work intern examines her own power resources, such as her ties to her preceptor, Mr. Jones. She thinks about how she can best present the proposal to him to increase the likelihood that he will support it. She subsequently discusses with him a two-phase political strategy to obtain support for the proposal to lead (she hopes) to eventual approval of the project by the executive director and the board of the agency.

This case, which emphasizes possible political barriers to the acceptance of a new policy, is not unusual, because opposition to new policies often exists in agency, community, and legislative settings.[5] Had the intern been unable to think and act in political terms, she would most certainly have failed to obtain approval for this proposal. Had she not realized that she had power resources, such as ones that derived from her ties to her preceptor and even from her status as an intern, she might not even have realized she could initiate a new program.

THE NATURE OF POWER

If politics is both inevitable and, at least in some cases, beneficial, policy practitioners have to understand power and develop skills in using it. We can begin by discussing the elusive concept of power, which lies at the heart of politics. We will use Case 10.1 to illustrate power and how it is used.

When the social work intern wanted to develop an innovative program to help children, she realized at once that it could be an uphill battle, because various barriers to preventive programs existed in the agency. We will begin our discussion of power with a simple two-person situation, where X "sends" power and Y "receives" it. X wants Y to take an action that Y would not normally have taken. We can argue that X succeeds in exercising power by convincing Y to take an action that he would not otherwise have taken. The social work intern has influenced her preceptor, Mr. Jones, if he assents to a program that he would not otherwise have supported.[6] (The intern has not exercised power if Mr. Jones would have initiated the innovation anyway.)

How does X influence Y to take an action he might otherwise not have taken? If X uses physical coercion, Y has virtually no choice, as is illustrated by a criminal suspect who is forced to enter a police car at gunpoint. In some situations, of course, it is difficult to determine where voluntarism begins and coercion ends; people in desperate economic straits may believe they have little choice but to accede to specific requests if they fear they will lose jobs, pay increases, or promotions. Even in such cases, however, receivers have some choice; some people *do* leave jobs to follow the dictates of their conscience.[7] Were the intern to make Mr. Jones to support the innovation by holding a gun to his head, she would have forced him to make this decision. We agree with Peter Bachrach and Morton Baratz that force is not power, because forcing someone to do something gives them little or no choice.[8]

When power *is* used, it involves transactional rather than unilateral relationships and choices.[9] The receiver in a power transaction (Y) can choose whether to accede to the sender's (X's) suggestions. Y has many options. He

```
X                         Y
(sender)  ───────────▶  (receiver)
          ◀───────────
```

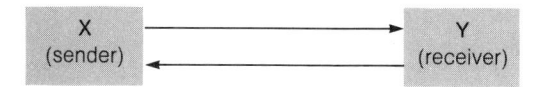

FIGURE 10.1
Direct power transactions

can refuse to follow X's suggestions altogether; he can say that he is undecided; he can agree but not really mean it; he can enthusiastically agree; or he can give an ambiguous response. The social work intern had to discuss the program innovation with Mr. Jones on two occasions before he formally committed to the project. He probably gave only his symbolic support on the first occasion (probably not wishing to discourage the intern), because he had completely forgotten the plan when the intern reintroduced the idea several weeks later. However, he seemed to support the idea "enthusiastically" on the second occasion, even to the point of initiating ideas about strategy. When we declare the exercise of power to be transactional then, we argue that it is not possible to understand it by examining only one of the partners in the relationship. Both X (and X's actions or verbal expressions) and Y (and Y's responses to X's entreaties) are integral to power transactions. We can portray power relationships graphically by placing arrows between X and Y (see Figure 10.1).

Power's transactional nature has important consequences for political strategy. Even in this simple two-person example, success in using power hinges on a number of considerations. X has to decide in the first instance that a particular issue warrants the expenditure of power. The intern's commitment to children's well-being, as well as to preventive mental health, led her to put effort toward securing the innovation. X (the intern) has to use the power resource skillfully enough for Y (Mr. Jones) to accede to her wishes. The intern "was careful to make it appear an idea that (she) had developed in the course of discussions with him" in order not to appear too intrusive or pushy. She couched the idea "as consistent with comprehensive mental health care for children," because he had often supported this goal.

Power often enters into transactions that involve more than two persons. As a person with little formal power, the intern realized that officials in the upper reaches of the organization would ultimately have to approve the plan. Feeling she lacked the ability to shape their actions directly, she had to work through Mr. Jones, hoping that he would ultimately convince them to support the innovation.[10] In this case, two sets of transactional relationships exist; the intern (X) tries to convince Mr. Jones (now Z) in hopes that he will persuade, say, the director of medical services (Y). See Figure 10.2, where the dashed line signifies the intern's exertion of power over the medical director by the use of Mr. Jones as an intermediary. (Intermediaries are commonly used in legislatures and agencies.) We will now discuss various power resources that people use in direct relations with other people.

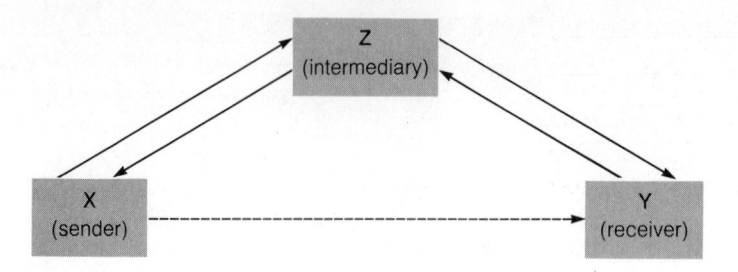

FIGURE 10.2
Indirect power transactions

PERSON-TO-PERSON POWER

Policy practitioners sometimes exert power in personal discussions with other individuals. We call this kind of power *person-to-person power*. In their classic article, John French and Bertram Craven discuss the uses of expertise, coercion, reward, charisma, and authority as power resources.[11] When using *expertise*, senders display their personal credentials and (presumed) knowledge to convince others that they should adopt certain positions. For such entreaties to be effective, of course, receivers have to believe that specific senders *are* experts. The student intern in Case 10.1 realized that high-level officials would be more likely to approve her innovation if she and Mr. Jones could say that it had been successfully implemented as a pilot project. This tactic would increase their credibility because they could argue, "We know how to implement this kind of innovation."

Policy practitioners threaten penalties when they use *coercive power*; someone might hint at loss of a job, promotion, or desirable position if another person does not accede to a specific policy. Politicians sometimes threaten to "punish" someone who fails to support a measure by opposing legislation *they* want, cutting programs or funds from their districts, and not granting them positions in key committees. Threats can backfire, as well, because they can alienate people who become angry when threatened.

When using *reward power*, policy practitioners promise inducements to other persons, such as promotions, pay increases, financial or other support in upcoming campaigns, and bribes. They may also promise a quid pro quo arrangement, where they will support someone's policy request on a future occasion if that person accedes to their specific request. Lyndon Johnson skillfully used reward power, not by providing rewards each time a legislator supported one of his policies (an approach that would have made politicians expect rewards on frequent occasions), but for an extended pattern of supportive votes.[12] As with coercive power, reward power can backfire if people feel that they are unfairly pressured to adopt positions and their ethical sensibilities are offended.

Charismatic power exists when people use personal qualities of leadership, moral authority, and persuasiveness to stimulate others to follow their wishes. (People who possess *authority* often exercise power by using power that stems from their position in an organization's hierarchy. Followers may also hope to receive rewards and avoid sanctions by following their superiors' suggestions.)

We have discussed person-to-person power in dyads, but it also exists when a sender gives presentations to larger groups. An executive might say to her staff, for example, "Support this policy or our agency will suffer severe financial repercussions" (coercive power); or a politician might say to a neighborhood group, "Have people vote for me if you want this neighborhood improvement" (reward power). Indeed, political campaigns are candidates' efforts to influence the general public's opinions through political advertisements and debates with opponents.

As we have noted, person-to-person power can also be exercised indirectly through third parties. One person may ask another to intervene with a third person, as when a politician asks an ally to persuade a fellow legislator to support specific legislation. Even mentioning a third party's *possible* intentions involves indirection. Someone may suggest, for example, that another person or institution, such as a funder, will harm an agency if it fails to adopt certain policies. A person might invoke someone else's expertise when seeking support for a specific policy, such as the research findings of a respected academician.

Exercising person-to-person power is most effective when the sender selects the kind of power that the receiver is likely to honor. Someone may respond to expertise, for example, but not to coercion. Effective users of power often have considerable knowledge of how the people they seek to influence are predisposed.

We have already noted the importance of selecting power resources carefully and applying them skillfully. Practitioners who use expertise as a power resource, for example, have to marshal persuasive evidence and make the receiver believe that the "expert" is an expert.[13] The social work intern in Case 10.1 tried to exert power subtly by not pushing Mr. Jones too hard when he seemed initially "irritated" by her innovation.

Power resources can be used singly or in tandem. Someone may use a combination of a "carrot" (reward power) and a "stick" (coercive power) to persuade someone to support a specific policy. One may try different power resources over time; if using rewards fails, someone may then try coercion or expertise.

People sometimes exercise power by asking others for advice on a difficult issue, even those they fear might oppose their views on the issue. Persons are often flattered to be consulted and are less likely to oppose a proposal when they have contributed some of its features. We sometimes call this method of increasing power "cooptation." Indeed, the student intern increased her power over Mr. Jones by appearing *not* to wield power. She solicited his advice and made every effort to make it seem as if the innovation had evolved in her discussions with him.

SUBSTANTIVE POWER

People often form opinions about a policy, not because they have been encouraged to support or oppose it, but because of how they view its substantive content. Policy practitioners exercise *substantive power* when they shape policies to elicit support from specific persons. Assume, for example, that two persons favor providing low-income housing subsidies in a government program, but one wants the subsidies to primarily go to people beneath poverty standards, while the other wants the subsidies to go, as well, to people with moderate incomes. The initiator of a housing-subsidy proposal might decide not to define the precise income levels within the legislation in hopes that *both* persons would vote for it. Indeed, *vagueness* is often an effective tactic when persons disagree about specific details of a proposal.[14] Vagueness, can, of course, be counterproductive in certain situations because an excessively vague proposal can arouse opposition in those who strongly favor including specific measures in it. Moreover, when key points of legislation are not defined, the implementors of the legislation have more leeway. If the members of one party believe that the other party will control the presidency (and thus, top appointive positions in implementing agencies), they might not want to leave key points ill-defined because they fear that their political foes will implement the legislation contrary to their wishes. For example, in 1988, some Democrats, fearing that Republicans would not insist on minimum child-to-staff ratios when implementing a national day-care proposal, tried to place specific ratios in the federal legislation.[15]

Policy practitioners exercise substantive power when they change a policy proposal to enhance specific decisionmakers' support for it. In the aforementioned day-care proposal, advocates inserted many provisions to allay conservatives' opposition, such as putting a modest ceiling on the program's costs and giving the states significant roles in shaping the programs within their boundaries. These changes can occur at the outset, when initially drafting legislation, during deliberations, or when the bill goes before Congress. Substantive power often involves compromises, where someone modifies a provision in exchange for another faction's changing another provision.

Policy practitioners encounter dilemmas when using substantive power. They may change a policy proposal to obtain a specific person's support, only to find that they have alienated someone else. When they make numerous concessions to obtain opponents' support, proposals can become so diluted as to be, in the words of Bachrach and Baratz, "decisionless decisions," or merely symbolic measures.[16]

For example, Senator Hubert Humphrey and Representative Augustus Hawkins initiated a legislative proposal in the 1970s requiring the federal government to create jobs whenever the national unemployment rate exceeded 3%. By the time the legislation was enacted, it included only a vague statement that the federal government would seek full employment. It did not require the government to take specific actions, such as developing public works when considerable unemployment existed.[17] To avoid excessive compromises, skillful policy practitioners often refrain from offering changes in a proposal until they are certain that compromises are needed for its passage.

A practitioner using substantive power may also couple a relatively unpopular proposal with more popular ones. In "Christmas-tree legislation" (so named because of the "gifts" many legislators place in it for certain persons or interest groups) in Congress, politicians place various unenacted proposals in a larger piece of legislation just before the session finishes at the end of December; politicians who oppose certain measures in this multifaceted legislation nonetheless vote for it because it contains some of their own measures.[18] A controversial proposal attached to a popular proposal may be swept to victory by support for the popular one. Foes of abortion discovered this when they attached a proposal prohibiting the use of Medicaid funds for abortions to appropriations bills for the Department of Health and Human Services.[19]

Proponents often shape a proposal so that it is nonthreatening to potential opponents. A proposed program may be deliberately designed and portrayed as a pilot project to defuse opposition to it.[20] Proponents may place a proposed program under a specific government unit's jurisdiction to make it more appealing to potential opponents. Proponents enhanced support for the Supplementary Security Income (SSI) program, which would provide income to destitute elderly and disabled persons, by proposing that it be placed under the jurisdiction of the Social Security Administration. That unit of government is more acceptable to conservatives than those that administer welfare programs, such as AFDC.[21] Proposals' titles are often selected to make them more acceptable to conservative politicians; thus, Senator Moynihan emphasized "family support payments" rather than "welfare payments" when discussing a welfare-reform initiative in 1988.[22]

Christopher Matthews contends that many successful politicians avoid discussing basic principles when considering legislation.[23] Realizing that mentioning fundamental principles can often alienate valuable allies with different perspectives from their own, they often focus on precise details of legislation. It is better, they reason, to win battles over the content of legislation than to have shouting matches about ultimate purposes. Of course, this substantive-power tactic can be used to excess; policy practitioners often need to enunciate basic principles to rally support for a measure and assert important values.

USING INDIRECT POWER

We have discussed the use of power, to this point, in direct transactional relationships. However, power can also be used in *indirect* ways by changing the environment in which power transactions occur rather than by influencing people in a straightforward way. Skilled policy practitioners often try to influence processes, decisionmaking bodies, and contexts to give their proposals a strategic advantage.

Decisionmaking Power

Policy is often fashioned by *decisionmaking* or *procedural power* in the course of deliberations. In legislatures, for example, numerous people, committees, and bodies must all assent to a policy before it can finally be enacted.[24] (Recall Figure 4.3, which depicted the normal course of legislation through both chambers of the Congress.)

There are many parliamentary techniques and strategies for increasing a proposal's chances of enactment (or for blocking someone else's proposal). Clever strategists often try to bypass persons, committees, and meetings that seem unfavorable to their proposal, while routing the proposal to more favorable settings. In some cases, practitioners try to persuade party officials to steer a proposal to the committee most favorably disposed to it. Practitioners sometimes "leapfrog" a meeting or procedure to help their proposal. They use person-to-person power with key decisionmakers, such as chairs of important committees, not only to obtain their support, but also to secure their assistance with logistic details. A committee chair can place a proposal in a preferred position on meeting agendas, insist that policies undergo further subcommittee deliberations, and abbreviate lengthy deliberations to help or prevent a specific measure's enactment. Clever strategists are well-versed in such tactics; they use them to outmaneuver legislative foes on the floor of Congress.[25]

Using specific procedural tactics can sometimes be counterproductive, however. Someone can be accused of unfairly stifling dissent by rushing a proposal through Congress, stacking the cards in favor of or against a proposal, or bypassing normal channels. Ethical objections can also be raised when persons exclude others from policy deliberations.

When initiating proposals, it is necessary to ask who the key decisionmakers are, whether they favor a proposal, and whether proponents can overcome opposition. In the early years of the Reagan administration, Republicans controlled the Senate committees because their party possessed a majority of Senate seats. White House staff members helped these Republican chairs mobilize party support for bills that Republicans favored. Disgruntled Democrats discovered that many of their legislative initiatives never made it beyond these committee gatekeepers, even when they had considerable support in the House, where Democrats chaired committees. When the Democrats regained control of the Senate in the 1986 elections, they also regained control of the Senate committee chairs, which they in turn used to scuttle many of the legislative proposals of the Reagan administration.[26]

Various decisionmaking procedures also exist in agencies. A staff member, committee, or executive may propose a new agency program. A staff committee may develop the proposal and bring it to the full staff for consideration. The executive may then take it to the board of directors, which may refer it to a board committee before taking a final vote. Or simpler procedures are sometimes used, as illustrated by a hospital social-services director who wants to develop social-work services on the neurology ward but also merely seeks the concurrence of the medical director of neurology. Only after the staff member has been on the service for some time may he even obtain formal approval from a higher hospital official, possibly when he needs additional funding from the hospital's budget.

In Case 10.1, the social work intern carefully considered procedural options as she developed strategy for her program innovation. With her preceptor, she planned a two-phase strategy. First, she would develop a pilot project as a student intern *without* securing high-level, formal clearance. Then, after initiating the pilot and proving it workable, they would develop a formal program proposal. The proposal would go to the executive director and several other persons, optimally culminating in the board's approval. Because of barriers to this innovation in the agency, such as tight budgets, the intern and the preceptor decided their innovation would be doomed if they *began* with a formal proposal to the executive director. Assume that the intern and preceptor were correct—that their proposal was ultimately accepted because they chose a procedural route that gave it a better shot than another might have. They have clearly exerted power in improving their proposal's chances. They exerted this power *not* through efforts to convince other people of its merits, but by shaping the decisionmaking process. Were we *not* to consider decisionmaking power in this case, we would not fully understand why the intern had been successful.

Process Power

Policies are shaped in the give-and-take of deliberations, which are characterized by their tenor, tempo, and scope of conflict. *Tenor* describes the level of conflict; *tempo* refers to the timing, pace, and duration; and *scope of conflict;* describes the numbers and kinds of persons who participate in them.

Policy practitioners use *process power* when they influence the tenor, tempo, or scope of conflict of these deliberations in order to help enact a specific proposal. Let's begin with the crude analogy of a schoolyard dispute to illustrate process power. The two parties to this conflict must not only develop their positions in the dispute but also must decide how to resolve their dispute. For example, each shapes the tenor of deliberations; will they use brute strength (a fight), have an amicable discussion, or take some middle course in which they shout at each other but do not fight? Each must decide, as well, what tempo of deliberations will help their cause. Do they seek a speedy settlement or protracted deliberations? They determine who should participate in the conflict; if they want a narrow scope of conflict, they exclude most other persons from their interaction, but they invite others to join the fray if they believe a broad scope of conflict will help their cause.[27]

A bully with physical superiority might decide to initiate a fight, whereas the proverbial "ninety-pound weakling" might want to expand the scope of conflict to include other, more powerful allies. Some protagonists believe that speedily resolving an issue will aid their cause by not allowing opponents to organize an attack. People may decide that their cause will benefit from relatively low conflict by using behind-the-scenes deliberations, where opponents are effectively screened out of the deliberations.[28] Note how the social work intern in Case 10.1 wanted to keep the innovation "low profile" during its pilot phase, in order *not* to make it the subject of controversy.

We can usefully contrast win-lose politics with win-win politics. In win-lose politics, each side in the contest believes that it loses each time the other side obtains a victory. With this mentality, both sides want to contest every point. In win-win politics, each side believes that it can obtain mutually beneficial concessions or victories. While parties to win-win politics do not want to concede all points, they are eager to compromise so that both sides can emerge better off than before deliberations. It would be a more pleasant world if people perceived win-win possibilities in more conflicts and people transformed conflicts into win-win situations. In many cases, however, this is not feasible. Parties may have conflicting values, may not trust opponents, and may believe they will suffer severe losses if they make concessions.

Individuals can sometimes influence the level of conflict. People who wish to intensify conflict, for example, use emotion-laden words, refer to fundamental values at stake, enlarge the scope of conflict by publicizing the issue or entreating friends to join the deliberation, or use unusual tactics, such as the filibuster in legislative settings.[29] These people can also clearly state that they do not want amicable resolution, such as by saying, "we plan to fight to the finish" or "we will accept no significant changes in our proposal." People who believe that conflict will be detrimental to their cause take actions or make statements that diminish conflict, such as emphasizing a proposal's technical features, identifying common interests among all parties to the conflict, and discouraging those who will raise the level of conflict from participating.

Policy practitioners influence the pace of deliberations by encouraging or discouraging amendments to a policy or by shortening or lengthening the time allocated to its discussion. The timing of a disputed proposal often favors a specific side. If someone introduces a proposal at an inopportune moment, its chances may be imperiled, no matter how skillful its defenders or how great its merits. Whether in agency or legislative settings, such background factors as budgetary deficits, a crowded agenda, or an unsympathetic executive can provide a harsh environment for a policy proposal. When a favorable context exists, a proposal defeated at a prior time may suddenly "sail through" the political process.[30]

Policy practitioners often have limited power to influence political interaction. Someone who wants to limit conflict, for example, may find her goal sabotaged by opponents who succeed in escalating conflict. Someone who wants to restrict the scope of conflict may be unable to stop someone else from publicizing it in the mass media, as the frequent leaks to the press in government settings suggests. Even skillful policy practitioners can miscalculate. Someone who introduces a proposal at a seemingly opportune moment may soon discover that background factors scuttle it. Moreover, policy processes often develop a momentum that defies attempts to change them; when conflict becomes heated, for example, it is often difficult for persons to diminish it, no matter what they do.[31] Tradition also frustrates policy practice, because issues that have previously generated high conflict, such as national health insurance, will stir up conflict if reintroduced.[32] The nature of an issue powerfully shapes the course of conflict; proposals for massive changes in the status quo will more likely polarize liberals and conservatives than will more modest proposals.[33]

Shaping Contexts

We have already noted that power transactions occur within a context and that people often change the scope of conflict by encouraging other persons to participate or avoid the fray. We need to give even greater prominence to the context, however, because pressures from external sources often shape political transactions within agencies and legislatures. Skillful policy practitioners often try to use these external pressures to their advantage.

Policy practitioners may try to stimulate persons external to decision arenas to support specific measures at strategic times. Advocates of the Brady Bill, which seeks to limit handgun purchases, encouraged supporters to pressure legislators. In addition, they planned for this pressure to come at specific points during the unfolding of congressional legislation, such as when key committees were making decisions and during important debates on the floor of each chamber. Hedrick Smith argues that television has revolutionized political tactics in Congress, particularly when coupled with the declining power of leaders of political parties and legislative committees, whose power was eclipsed by various procedural changes and by giving party members greater power to select them.[34] Viewing themselves as quasi-independent persons who seek a national constituency for themselves, many politicians develop videotapes on a regular basis, which they forward to media outlets in their constituencies. The mass media, then, becomes a vehicle through which politicians can develop personal reputations and increase public support for those issues that they believe will enhance their popularity.

In some cases, proponents of specific measures actively organize grass-roots coalitions to pressure legislators to support specific proposals. Realizing that the National Rifle Association possessed extraordinary power, advocates of gun control organized their own groups to exert pressure on legislators.

On other occasions, politicians decide *not* to publicize issues so as to decrease external pressure on legislators. They may fear that interest groups who hear about a specific measure will mobilize opposition to it. They may worry about adverse public opinion. At strategic points in deliberations, then, legislative committees go into executive sessions where they do not talk to the media or to lobbyists. They deliberately give certain measures "a low profile."

In an era of tight budgets, advocates of innovations in agencies must often find external referral and funding sources *before* finding support in their agencies. The social work intern in Case 10.1 realized that her innovation would be more successful if she could obtain the approval of local psychiatric hospitals. She needed a substantial flow of referrals, she decided, to show that the idea was viable and to provide revenues for the project. She realized that this would require her to convince social-service departments and individual psychologists and psychiatrists to refer children of institutionalized patients to the project.

Successful Power Users

Many case studies of successful politicians and social movement leaders suggest that personal characteristics increase some persons' ability to shape policy outcomes. Take *persistence*, for example. People such as Jane Addams and Martin Luther King, Jr., persevered over decades despite repeated failure in their quest for social justice. Even our student intern in Case 10.1, who might have been rebuffed by her preceptor's initial "irritation" about her proposed innovation, brought up the issue several weeks later, and secured a positive response. As we noted in Chapter Five when discussing agenda-building, some issues "float" in a latent state for years, only to resurface because someone was sufficiently persistent to reintroduce the measure.

Successful users of power are often able to avoid personalizing issues, even when they are subject to unfair attacks.[35] Those who focus on issues' substantive content, while avoiding attacks on the motivations or character of opponents, are often viewed in a more positive light than those who make personal attacks. As we point out in the next chapter, even though we often have to *respond* to attacks that unfairly characterize our intentions or motivations, it does not usually enhance our personal power to *initiate* such attacks.

Skillful policy practitioners must also establish that they are not willows that bend in every breeze. Personal credibility, which often lies at the heart of the effective use of power, can be eroded if someone seems excessively opportunistic. It is acceptable to demonstrate basic convictions, even in the face of opposition.

While they do not want to bend with every breeze, successful policy practitioners must also be skilled at fashioning compromises. A fine line sometimes exists between having convictions and having the ability to compromise. Compromises are frequently needed to obtain people's support in agency and legislative settings for specific proposals.[36]

The Power of Autonomy

We have argued thus far that the effective exercising of power often occurs when a person influences someone else's actions or opinions. In some cases, however, people possess power when they can free themselves from others' attempts to control their actions and opinions. This kind of negative or defensive power allows people to "call their own shots." This kind of power is significant when people are pressured to support policies that they find objectionable.[37]

Autonomy is important in the human services, because it allows direct-service staff to shape many of their personal choices, even in defiance of existing policies. Remember that social-work practice consists of transactions with clients, often in the privacy of offices, hospital wards, or somewhere in the community. We have also noted that social workers can possess policy preferences that shape their choices in their daily work. Indeed, their daily work is, at least in part, a manifestation of policy. A social worker who does not want to serve certain kinds of clients, for example, can often obtain this result by discouraging them or by referring them elsewhere, even when this practice contradicts higher-level policy. In effect, the social worker in this case makes her own policy and she can "get away with" this practice because she possesses considerable autonomy in her personal work.[38] Of course, the power of autonomy can be abused, such as when social workers do not support desirable policies. Moreover, social workers can incur penalties for themselves and their agencies when they sabotage certain policies.

DISCRETION, COMPLIANCE, AND WHISTLE-BLOWING

The interrelated issues of discretion, compliance, and whistle-blowing confront direct-service and other social-service staff throughout their careers. Considerable controversy sometimes exists in specific agencies about the general issue: how much discretion, or autonomy, should policymakers and administrators grant human services workers? In what circumstances, we ask, should social workers be able to disobey policies they believe are unethical? When should social workers be able to take their disagreements about internal agency matters to external parties, such as the mass media?

Defining Zones of Discretion

When analyzing policy implementation, we often think in broad terms, such as about agencies' budgets and leadership. In other words, we take a "top-down" perspective. Alternatively, we can take a "bottom-up" perspective by beginning with the line worker, who translates policy into action.

Some persons might think that high-level policies dictated virtually all the actions of direct-service staff. However, a considerable portion of direct-service staff's work occurs within "zones of discretion," where their judgments and choices shape their actions.[39]

Why do agencies cede so much discretion to their direct-service staff? Assume that you are a high-level policymaker and you are quite certain about the intake policies you want for a children's program. You write "definitive" standards in legislation, such as "only children from families with XYZ income shall obtain admittance to this program." This kind of policy is binding because it is clear-cut and allows no exceptions. Assume, however, that you want the program to help children who have "learning disorders" and who meet these income standards. Assume also that, despairing of defining "learning disorders" with precision, you do not attempt an exact definition. You cede to those who implement this policy considerable discretion in selecting children with "learning disorders." Moreover, you let professional workers judge when a child has sufficiently mastered learning skills to make them ineligible for continuing services. Professionals would need to determine when the child had stopped making "sufficient progress" or had reached some degree of learning competence to graduate from the services. Realizing that some people will need extended help, while others may overcome their problem in a brief period, you decide not to write a blanket rule that establishes a maximum period of service.

Our discussion suggests that professionals often are given so much discretion because their work often requires judgment calls that arise with complex social problems, human motivation, and clients' progress. High-level officials may decide that professionals need latitude to make exceptions to policies, thus allowing discretion in a program's official policies. Assume, for example, that legislators are aware that some psychotic patients need to be committed to institutions, even though they are not suicidal and have not physically threatened other persons. Rather than decreeing that only those who have threatened violence against themselves or others should be institutionalized, legislators might allow commitments based on people's "current threats of violence against themselves or other people *or* professional judgment, even though such discretion could sometimes lead to unnecessary commitments.

When discussing the autonomy of direct-service workers, we must note, as well, that the location and nature of their work makes it impossible to oversee all of its details. Direct-service workers conduct much of their work in private interactions with clients. Moreover, many human-services agencies do not conform to the bureaucratic models discussed by Max Weber; rather than having tight controls in centralized structures, many of them are "loosely coupled" organizations with several quasi-independent programs, units, and branches. In such organizations, it is difficult for top administrators to regulate the work of direct-service staff.[40]

It must be noted that ceding discretion to professionals bears some risks. What if this freedom leads some social workers to discriminate against certain persons in the name of "professional judgment," such as a professional who decides that people with specific learning disorders ought not be allowed into a program? The professional might be prejudiced against persons with certain kinds of learning disorders or have erroneous perceptions about their condition.[41]

Professionals sometimes take advantage of discretion to further their own material interests or their own sometimes narrow approach to service delivery. Franklin Chu and Sharland Trotter discovered that many mental health professionals failed to implement policies prescribed by federal legislation they were uninterested in working with psychotic or low-income persons.[42] Unethical as it may be, a few social workers have even siphoned clients from their public agencies to their private practices, in spite of widely held ethical norms that prohibit this practice.

There is a tension between maximizing professional discretion and making binding rules to prevent discrimination against clients and to protect the public interest. This tension sometimes leads social workers, chafing at restrictions, to disobey policy in the name of "professional judgment."

Our discussion of discretion and binding rules underscores, however, a critical issue surrounding policy implementation. When should discretion be expanded to enhance professional judgments and when should it be contracted to enforce high-level staff's priorities? This issue must be analyzed in the context of specific situations. We may decide in certain cases that policies grant too much discretion, allowing people to abrogate a policy's intent with personal judgments. In other cases, we may decide that policies excessively bind professionals, thus preventing them from exercising needed discretion.

Issues of Compliance

Social workers at the direct-service level encounter dilemmas when they do not want to implement specific policies. A social worker in a public welfare setting may dislike specific, punitive policies. A social worker in a child welfare office may object to pressures to "reunify" families when the natural families have not been adequately analyzed or helped. Social workers can adopt several strategies. First, they can keep their noncompliance secret even from their supervisors by bending or violating rules, ignoring rules, enforcing rules halfheartedly, or counseling clients about ways to circumvent specific policies. Second, they can comply with official policy, but use every available means to bend the rules by seeking exemptions for specific persons. As we have discussed, social workers who want to help an elderly person avoid early discharge from a hospital can claim, for example, that no nursing-home beds can be found. While technically complying with official policy, these social workers might only halfheartedly look for such beds or even lie about the beds' availability. (Such deception returns us to the first strategy discussed above.) Third, they might comply with official policy in every respect, even when believing it to be defective, and make no effort to change it. Fourth, they might comply with official policies, while trying to change them.

No easy answers exist for such dilemmas. The duty to obey official policy cannot be dismissed lightly; professionals' credibility would be severely jeopardized if they *routinely* flouted the rules. Yet some policies are unethical or harmful to clients, whether to all clients or just those with idiosyncratic needs. Beneficence requires us to consider disobeying policies that appear inimical to clients' needs or in violation of professional ethics. However, it is difficult for them to protest policies when high-level officials strongly promote them or when agency officials fear that higher authorities, such as legislators, will retaliate if they discover noncompliance with high-level policies.

By the same token, direct-service social workers sometimes want their fellow staff to comply with a specific policy. They may find that their colleagues do not implement policies that *do* possess ethical merit. (Social workers may not implement meritorious policies because they have narrow helping philosophies that deemphasize activities such as outreach, believe that they lack expertise or resources, feel burned out, or are prejudiced against certain kinds of clients.) In such cases, social workers should try to change their colleagues' behavior through educational techniques, technical assistance, or even by alerting higher management to the noncompliance. Changing peers' behavior can pose a formidable challenge, however, particularly when the agency atmosphere is not conducive to challenging norms.

Whistle-Blowing

Individual staff members often should try to work through normal channels. However, what if individuals find specific policies or other staff members' actions (such as corruption) so morally flawed that they cannot abide their continuation? Furthermore, what if they fear that open opposition to these policies will cause their dismissal or other penalties? An emerging literature suggests that staff members can ethically publicize flawed policies and actions by divulging information to persons outside the organization, such as the mass media, legislators, state authorities, regulators, or funders.[43] They can reveal this information to outsiders, either using their own names or speaking on condition of anonymity in order to prevent personal reprisals. They can also give the information to the National Association of Social Workers, who can protect their identity while making the information public. (However, whistle-blowers who make their names public are sometimes perceived as more credible than those who leak charges anonymously.)

Whistle-blowing is an attempt to reform implementation processes by calling external parties into the conflict. It is ethical if: the policies or actions are major violations of ethics or professional standards, not trivial ones; the whistle-blower has extremely good evidence that he or she cannot modify policies through conventional means; and the whistle-blower has excellent evidence that he or she will be subjected to serious penalties by raising questions about the policies or conduct. (Despite recent legislation in some states that protects whistle-blowers, as well as sanctions that the National Association of Social Workers can exact against employers who fire whistle-blowers, persons sometimes have justifiable reason to believe that they will be in jeopardy if they engage in whistle-blowing.) At the same time, whistle-blowing can be abused when persons raise trivial issues, such as minor indiscretions within an agency, or when they have not fully considered alternative means of changing policies.[44]

Our prior discussion of discretion suggests that social workers often encounter *not* objectionable high-level policies, but vague policies that require them to *develop* policies to fill the policy vacuum.

EXERTING EXTERNAL PRESSURE

To this point we have discussed power that policy practitioners use from *within* agency and legislative settings. In other cases, they try to influence policymakers from an external vantage point, whether from community groups, external agencies, coalitions, interest groups, or professional associations.

As we have discussed, legislators' positions on issues often result from pressure from lobbyists, interest groups, experts, officials within the government, and constituents. These people may exert pressure during personal interactions in legislators' offices, at social occasions, during legislative hearings, or by correspondence. In some cases, legislators bear the brunt of the pressure, while on other occasions lobbyists and constituents try to persuade legislators' aides.[45]

Practitioners often encourage these sources to convince legislators that they will suffer severe repercussions if they oppose a measure. But pressure must be carefully timed, focused, and planned so that it constructively contributes to support for a specific proposal.[46] Unfocused pressure can sometimes be counterproductive, as illustrated by letter-writing campaigns that use form letters (politicians like individualized expressions of support) or when coalition members give conflicting testimony at legislative hearings. Pressure is sometimes particularly effective when it is carefully timed to precede important votes. Supporters of a proposal often form coalitions of diverse groups and institutions to exert pressure on politicians. (We discuss coalitions in more detail in the next chapter.)

External pressure can be placed, not only on legislatures and government agencies, but also on social agencies. As Yeheskel Hasenfeld and other organizational theorists with a political-economy perspective note, organizational policies are shaped by many forces external to them.[47] Funders, courts, community groups, and community leaders shape organizations' internal policies in many ways and to varying degrees. Just as policy practitioners sometimes pressure legislators, they sometimes pressure social agencies to modify specific policies or to consider program innovations. For example, local chapters of the National Welfare Rights Organization frequently picketed or sent delegations to local welfare offices to challenge discriminatory practices in the 1960s.

POWER DIFFERENTIALS

Our discussion to this point may falsely suggest that all of us have an equal opportunity to wield power, that if we put our minds to the task, we can each be successful in having policy proposals enacted. This optimistic conclusion ignores harsh realities, such as power differentials that give some people a significant advantage in transactions.

Legislators and high-level government officials have *formal authority*. Their positions give them powers to approve or disapprove certain policy initiatives, to make proposals, and to obtain access to program, budget, and technical information. Their positions give them access to other highly placed people who yield information and assistance that are not available to others. They are often likely to command obedience from other people when they issue directives or make recommendations. Executives of agencies and government bureaucracies possess considerable authority that stems from their power over subordinates, the deference subordinates accord them, and their experience and knowledge. Technical experts with information about specific topics often possess extraordinary power in governmental and agency settings.

The leaders, staff members, and lobbyists for groups that have large constituencies, such as certain interest groups, professional associations, and social movements, may derive power, not only from their technical expertise, but also from their access to constituencies. These constituents can exert influence on decisionmakers who do not heed policy suggestions. In turn, leaders, staff members, and lobbyists have expertise and clout that make it simpler for them to cultivate personal relationships with decisionmakers, which further enhances their power. Some interest groups increase their power, as well, by making large contributions to the campaigns of politicians who support their positions. In a compelling account of how the mass media and large interest groups (such as the American Association of Retired Persons and political action committees) influence policies, Hedrick Smith contends that groups and lobbyists with well-organized, grass-roots constituencies, extraordinary resources, and access to the mass media increasingly wield power in legislative settings.[48]

Individuals who help shape and enact budgets, such as legislators on appropriations committees and officials who develop budgets in bureaucracies, often have extraordinary power, because "those who pay the piper dictate the tune." A professor of mine once lamented social workers' tendency to seek jobs in organizations' personnel sections, because the staff in the budget and fiscal departments usually have more power to shape the policies and programs of bureaucracies. Officials in the federal Office of Management and Budget (OMB) are key players in establishing the nation's domestic policy, because they shape the president's budgetary recommendations.

In some cases, authority figures can even command obedience when their suggestions are ethically flawed.[49] The impulse to obey authority figures sometimes stems from peer pressure, loyalty to the organization, lack of information about specific issues, or fear of sanctions.

Nor should we overlook the role of cultural symbols in giving certain persons and groups more power than others. Officials affiliated with socially acceptable topics, such as children, health, and education, are often more influential than people associated with socially stigmatized groups, such as mentally ill people, welfare recipients, or ex-offenders.[50]

Discrimination patterns in broader society influence power transactions. Rosabeth Kanter suggests that women are often excluded from decisionmaking in large organizations because of gender-based prejudice and because they lack access to old-boy networks.[51] Members of minority groups often encounter similar problems.

Although few people would disagree that power differentials exist, some theorists, such as C. Wright Mills, suggest that a power elite, such as leaders of well-financed interest groups, often exists. This elite monopolizes power and consigns other people and interests to marginal roles.[52] Indeed, tightly organized factions, interests, or even individuals often possess such power that they control policy deliberations. Were we to accept this thesis in every situation, however, we could easily succumb to resignation, fatalism, and cynicism. "Pluralist" theorists, such as Robert Dahl, suggest that many interests and people shape policy choices.[53] They point to multiple interest groups that shape policies in municipal, county, state, and federal jurisdictions to support their contention.

Who is right? Each side is correct in certain situations. In some situations, specific people and interests possess the power to dominate policymaking. Other policy choices are associated with a political process, where just about anybody can successfully join the fray. In yet other situations, certain people and interests may possess a preponderance of power in setting agendas and shaping choices, but determined and well-organized groups may be able to force them to make important concessions. As we discuss in the next chapter, policy practitioners need to be realistic in assessing the distribution of power in specific settings.

The case of the student intern illustrates how persons with little formal power can sometimes wield surprising might. By taking the initiative, working through an intermediary (Dr. Jones), developing an effective innovation, and securing support for the innovation from other psychiatric hospitals, the intern mapped a sophisticated strategy to secure a major policy change in her agency.

Ethical Issues

Some social workers believe that developing and using power is unprofessional. We argued in Chapter Three, however, that social workers use power frequently in their work, including their direct-service work, even when they are unaware of this. Whenever they "guide," "direct," or "suggest options to" clients, they use power. When they make recommendations to supervisors or external authorities, such as courts, they use substantive power. Indeed, we argued in Chapter Two that social workers can be unethical by *not* using power in certain situations, such as questioning defective policies or seeking policy changes in the external world. In such cases, we said, social workers (and other professionals, such as teachers, attorneys, and physicians) may not advance beneficence, social justice, and fairness.

Power can be used in unethical ways, as with dishonesty and manipulation, but we must take care not to make simple, ethical rules. When someone is blatantly dishonest to gain a strategic advantage, that person has used unethical conduct. An example might be giving false data or telling someone that they will not use a tactic or procedure that they subsequently use. But blatant lying can be distinguished from lesser forms of dishonesty, such as not divulging unsolicited information. Why would someone volunteer to an opponent that she will attack his position in a forthcoming meeting? Moreover, as we discussed in Chapter Two, we sometimes encounter ethical dilemmas when we use power, such as when honesty and social justice conflict. Assume, for example, that enacting a measure to help low-income persons hinged on your telling an opponent of that measure a falsehood. Faced with this ethical dilemma, you might tell the falsehood because of your allegiance to social justice. (Of course, we are seldom in such situations and would want to reflect and seek consultation before acting.)

Ethical issues surrounding manipulation also defy easy resolution. Assume that you want to win. You are convinced that you cannot win if you do not use a devious parliamentary maneuver that places your opponent at a disadvantage, have someone in authority threaten another person so that they will not oppose your measure, or suppress data that would make your position appear less tenable. All of these behaviors are manipulative in the sense that they seek to give your side an advantage at the expense of open discourse, normal deliberations, and free choices. Such tactics are usually unethical and even counterproductive, because they might cause others to distrust you and even oppose your positions. However, certain manipulative behaviors, much like some forms of dishonesty, can be justified in certain, limited situations. You might rightly decide that: ethical principles, such as social justice and beneficence, are at stake; your opponents are using hardball tactics, putting you at a decided disadvantage if you do not use them yourself; and you will lose if you fail to use some form of manipulation. Here, too, you would want to reflect, seek consultation, and use manipulative behaviors only if you believed them ethically warranted.

SUMMARY

We have discussed many power resources in this chapter, as well as the nature of power transactions. People often exercise power in transactional relations, using person-to-person power resources (such as expertise, reward, and coercion) to persuade others to take positions or actions. Practitioners often use substantive power to elicit support by altering provisions in proposals. Practitioners often exercise power indirectly, by using decisionmaking and process power to affect policy deliberations. Practitioners can elicit support from within decisionmaking arenas or from external vantagepoints, such as through advocacy groups.

Social workers often obtain power through having autonomy in their work. Because of the nature of their work and because policymakers and higher-level staff deliberately granted them discretion, many social workers have considerable power to make unsupervised decisions. Social workers often confront difficult dilemmas, however, when asked to comply with policies that they believe to be unethical or ineffective. In unusual cases, when they find that they cannot change unethical policies or practices by conventional means, they resort to whistle-blowing. To use power well, practitioners should understand the following:

- Some positive functions of politics in policy deliberations
- The transactional nature of power relationships
- Person-to-person and substantive power resources
- How to shape policy outcomes indirectly
- Personal characteristics that enhance political effectiveness
- Issues of autonomy, discretion, compliance, and whistle-blowing
- The importance of power differentials
- External and internal vantage points when making policy changes

We see that policy practitioners need to be adept in using power. They cannot use it, however, if they do not *possess* it or if they fail to use resources that they do have. We discuss in the next chapter how people develop power resources.

Suggested Readings

THE NATURE OF POWER
Peter Bachrach and Morton Baratz, *Power and Poverty* (New York: Oxford University Press, 1970).

VARIETIES OF POWER
John French and Bertram Craven, "The Bases of Social Power," in Dorwin Cartwright and Alvin Zander, eds., *Group Dynamics: Research and Theory* (New York: Harper & Row, 1968), pp. 259–269.
Lewis Froman, *The Congressional Process: Strategies, Rules, and Procedures* (Boston: Little, Brown, 1967).
Christopher Matthews, *Hardball: How Politics Is Played* (New York: Summit Books, 1988).
Hedrick Smith, *The Power Game: How Washington Works* (New York: Ballantine Books, 1988).

A DEFENSE OF POLITICS
Eric Schattschneider, *The Semisovereign People* (New York: Holt, Rinehart & Winston, 1960).

USING POWER FROM INTERNAL VANTAGE POINTS
Burton Gummer, *The Politics of Social Administration: Managing Organizational Politics in Social Agencies* (Englewood Cliffs, NJ: Prentice-Hall, 1990).
Bruce Jansson and June Simmons, "The Survival of Social Work Units in Host Organizations," *Social Work* 31 (September 1986): 339–344.
Herman Resnick, "Tasks in Changing the Organization from Within," in Herman Resnick and Rino Patti, eds., *Change from Within: Humanizing Social Welfare Organizations* (Philadelphia: Temple University Press, 1980), pp. 200–212.

Using Power from External Vantage Points
Karen Haynes and James Mikelson, *Affecting Change: Social Workers in the Political Arena* (New York: Longman, 1986).
Nancy Humphreys, "Competing for Revenue-Sharing Funds: A Coalition Approach," *Social Work* 24 (January 1979): 14–20.
William Whitaker, "Organizing Social Action Coalitions: WIC Comes to Wyoming," in Maryann Mahaffey and John Hanks, eds., *Practical Politics: Social Work and Political Response* (Silver Spring, MD: National Association of Social Workers, 1982), pp. 136–158.

Power Resources of Direct-Service Staff
Michael Lipsky, *Street-Level Bureaucrats: Dilemmas of the Individual and Public Service* (New York: Russell Sage Foundation, 1980).
David Mechanic, "Sources of Power of Lower Participants in Complex Organizations," *Administrative Science Quarterly* 7 (December 1962): 349–364.

The Problem of Assertiveness
Rosabeth Kanter, *Men and Women of the Corporation* (New York: Basic Books, 1977), pp. 158–197.
Linda MacNeilage and Kathleen Adams, *Assertiveness at Work* (Englewood Cliffs, NJ: Prentice-Hall, 1982).
Stanley Milgram, *Obedience to Authority* (New York: Harper & Row, 1975).

Ethical Issues in Politics
Chauncey Alexander, "Professional Social Workers and Political Responsibility," in Mahaffey and Hanks, *Practical Politics*, pp. 22–25.
George Brager, Harry Specht, and James Torczyner, *Community Organizing*, 2nd ed. (New York: Columbia University Press, 1987), pp. 316–339.
Joel Fleishman, "Self-Interest and Political Integrity," in Joel Fleishman, Lance Liebman, and Mark Moore, eds., *Public Duties: The Moral Obligations of Government Officials* (Cambridge, MA: Harvard University Press, 1981), pp. 52–92.

Notes

1. *Living Webster Encyclopedic Dictionary of the English Language* (Chicago: English Language Institute of America, 1977), p. 737.
2. Ibid., p. 737.
3. Martin Rein, "Value-Critical Policy Analysis," in Daniel Callahan and Bruce Jennings, eds., *Ethics, the Social Sciences, and Policy Analysis* (New York: Plenum, 1983), pp. 96–100.
4. William Coplin and Michael O'Leary, *Everyman's Prince* (North Scituate, MA: Duxbury, 1976).
5. Tom Burns, "Micro-Politics, Mechanisms of Institutional Change," *Administrative Science Quarterly* 6 (September 1961): 257–281.
6. Peter Bachrach and Morton Baratz, *Power and Poverty* (New York: Oxford University Press, 1970), pp. 17–38.
7. For discussion of dilemmas of those who receive power resources, see Stanley Milgram, *Obedience to Authority* (New York: Harper & Row, 1975).
8. Bachrach and Baratz, *Power and Poverty*, pp. 17–38.
9. Ibid., pp. 17–38.

10. Edward Banfield, *Political Influence* (New York: Free Press, 1961), pp. 307–314.
11. John French and Bertram Craven, "The Bases of Social Power," in Dorwin Cartwright and Alvin Zander, eds., *Group Dynamics: Research and Theory* (New York: Harper & Row, 1968), pp. 259–269.
12. Doris Kearns, *Lyndon Johnson and the American Dream* (New York: Harper & Row, 1976), pp. 190, 224–227.
13. See Christopher Matthews, *Hardball: How Politics Is Played* (New York: Summit Books, 1988), pp. 21–43.
14. Bruce Jansson, *Theory and Practice of Social Welfare Policy: Analysis, Processes, and Current Issues* (Belmont, CA: Wadsworth, 1984), p. 184.
15. Julie Rovner, "Daycare Package Clears First Hurdle in House," *Congressional Quarterly Weekly Report* 46 (July 2, 1988): 1833–1836.
16. See Bachrach and Baratz, *Power and Poverty*, pp. 17–38.
17. *Congressional Quarterly Almanac* 34 (Washington, DC: Congressional Quarterly Service, 1978), pp. 272–279.
18. Jansson, *Theory and Practice*, p. 184.
19. Joseph Califano, *Governing America* (New York: Simon and Schuster, 1971), p. 67.
20. Gerald Zaltman and Robert Duncan, *Strategies for Planned Change* (New York: Wiley-Interscience, 1977), p. 100.
21. Vincent Burke and Vee Burke, *Nixon's Good Deed: Welfare Reform* (New York: Columbia University Press, 1974), pp. 195–204.
22. Congress, Senate, Committee on Finance, *Hearings Before the Subcommittee on Social Security and Family Policy*, pp. 2–14 (January 23, 1987).
23. Matthews, *Hardball*, pp. 144–154.
24. Lewis Froman, *The Congressional Process: Strategies, Rules, and Procedures* (Boston: Little, Brown, 1967).
25. Eugene Bardach, *The Skill Factor in Politics* (Berkeley and Los Angeles: University of California Press, 1972), pp. 234–240.
26. Bruce Jansson, *Reluctant Welfare State: A History of American Social Welfare Policies*, 1st ed. (Belmont, CA: Wadsworth, 1988), pp. 212–214, 222.
27. Eric Schattschneider, *The Semisovereign People* (New York: Holt, Rinehart & Winston, 1980), pp. 20–46.
28. Jansson, *Reluctant Welfare State*, p. 217.
29. Morton Deutsch, *The Resolution of Conflict: Constructive and Destructive Processes* (New Haven, CT: Yale University Press, 1973), pp. 124–152.
30. John Kingdon, *Agendas, Alternatives, and Public Policies* (Boston: Little, Brown, 1984), pp. 1–22.
31. Deutsch, *The Resolution of Conflict*, pp. 124–152.
32. Ibid., p. 368.
33. See Theodore Lowi's discussion of the politics of redistributive measures in, "American Business, Public Policy, Case Studies, and Political Theory," *World Politics* 16 (July 1964): 677–715.
34. Hedrick Smith, *The Power Game: How Washington Works* (New York: Ballentine Books, 1988), pp. 388–444.
35. Matthews, *Hardball*, pp. 144–154.
36. Ron Dear and Rino Patti, "Legislative Advocacy," in *Encyclopedia of Social Workers*, vol. 2 (Silver Spring, MD: National Association of Social Workers, 1987), p. 37.
37. Michael Lipsky, *Street-Level Bureaucrats: Dilemmas of the Individual and Public Service* (New York: Russell Sage Foundation, 1980), pp. 13–16.
38. Ibid., pp. 90–98.

39. Ibid., pp. 16–18.
40. Kenneth Weick, "Educational Organizations as Loosely Coupled Systems," *Adminstrative Science Quarterly* 21 (March 1976): 1–9.
41. Robert Goodin, *Reasons for Welfare* (Princeton, NJ: Princeton University Press, 1988), pp. 184–228.
42. Franklin Chu and Sharland Trotter, *The Madness Establishment* (New York: Grossman, 1974).
43. Sissela Bok, "Blowing the Whistle," in Joel Fleishman, Lance Liebman, and Mark Moore, eds., *Public Duties: The Moral Obligations of Government Officials* (Cambridge, MA: Harvard University Press, 1981), pp. 200–215.
44. Ibid.
45. George Sharwell, "How to Testify Before a Legislative Committee," in Maryann Mahaffey and John Hanks, eds., *Practical Politics: Social Work and Political Response* (Silver Spring, MD: National Association of Social Workers, 1982), pp. 85–98.
46. Ibid., pp. 81–84.
47. Yeheskel Hasenfeld, *Human Service Organizations* (Englewood Cliffs, NJ: Prentice-Hall, 1983).
48. Smith, *The Power Game*.
49. Milgram, *Obedience to Authority*.
50. Richard Fenno, *The Power of the Purse* (Boston: Little, Brown, 1966), pp. 366–390.
51. Rosabeth Kanter, *Men and Women of the Corporation* (New York: Basic Books, 1977), pp. 129–163.
52. C. Wright Mills, *The Power Elite* (New York: Oxford University Press, 1956).
53. Robert Dahl, *Pluralist Democracy in the United States* (Chicago: Rand McNally, 1967).

Chapter Eleven

The Interactional Dimensions of Power

Our discussion of the transactional nature of power in the preceding chapter suggests that it is wielded in interpersonal relationships rather than by fiat. In this chapter, we will examine in more detail some interactional dimensions of power; how do people obtain it in the first instance, how do they decide when and whether to use it, and how do they use power in groups or coalitions? Moreover, what special obstacles do members of oppressed outgroups, such as women, gays, and racial minorities, confront as they seek to obtain and use power in specific settings, such as agencies?

A CASE FROM THE HUMAN SERVICES

To illustrate the interactional dimensions of power, we provide a case example of "low-budget lobbyists" who encounter particular challenges in obtaining power. They lack the resources and funds of lobbyists associated with well-heeled and powerful constituencies, such as the American Medical Association and the American Association of Retired Persons. As you will see in Case 11.1, Rand Martin (whose debate with a conservative legislator we discussed in Chapter Nine) and Sherry Skelly must develop power from scratch by using several strategies. They work in a legislative setting, but the challenge of developing power resources also exists for people in organizational settings and involves similar strategies.

CASE 11.1
LOW-BUDGET LOBBYISTS

The phone rang a dozen times before a harried Rand Martin could grab it. He disconnected the caller when he tried to put the line on hold so he could finish another call. Such is life when you are between secretaries and cursed with a cheap, quirky phone system.

He would probably receive little sympathy from Sherry Skelly, who lacks not only a secretary but, until recently, a desk, typewriter, and an office. Until she managed to scrape up the money, she had been using a donated hallway as her headquarters. She still makes do with a single phone line and an answering machine, however.

Martin and Skelly are lobbyists, Martin for the AIDS-oriented Lobby for Individual Freedom and Equality (LIFE), and Skelly for the California Children's Lobby. You can tell they are lobbyists because they work bills, meet with legislators and consultants, and testify at hearings. Their pictures are also in the Secretary of State's *Directory of Lobbyists*.

But if you look for other signs that signify "lobbyist" to most of the public, you will not find any. The organizations they represent never show up on the lists of heavy campaign contributors. They keep their fingers crossed when they send their cards to legislators on the floor, hoping to speak with them, for, unlike their heavyweight counterparts, Martin and Skelly are unable to command an audience. They do not have legions of staff to keep them posted on the dozens of bills they must track. If they hit the Sacramento hot spots at night, it is to relax and enjoy themselves; their budgets do not allow for the drinks or dinner that might further connections with lawmakers and legislative staff.

In short, what these two lack is money.

Of course, they are not alone. The Fair Political Practices Commission lists 762 registered lobbyists. Ranking lobbyists by affluence, there are only eleven big operators at the top. Those eleven receive in excess of $500,000 in client fees and spread around hundreds of thousands of dollars more in campaign contributions.

Much lower in rankings are the lobbyists for public interest groups— California Common Cause, Consumers Union, American Civil Liberties Union—along with lobbyists for state agencies, departments, and commissions. Although they have no money to grease the wheels of power, they usually have enough resources to track bills, produce position papers, and rally the public.

Scraping dead bottom are a subgroup of public interest entities, such as LIFE and California Children's Lobby, whose annual budgets detail how many stamps may be used and how many photocopies may be made in one month. Martin runs his operation on a budget of $80,000, including office rent, his salary and that of a secretary. Skelly makes it on $63,000.

Clearly neither of them is in it for the money. If it is true that money turns the wheels in the capital, then one would expect Martin's and Skelly's work to be mostly futile. So who are these penny-pinching lobbyists, how do they get by, and what can they possibly accomplish?

"A lobbyist is a be-all," says the twenty-seven-year-old Skelly. "I feel like I'm a mediator and a resource who can provide expertise on an issue. If you have no money, you end up working closely with consultants, and consultants are very detail-oriented."

Expertise, a flair for detail, credibility—these are the tools a low-budget lobbyist brings to work every day. Some of the weight such a lobbyist carries is personal, earned over years of consistently giving good advice and testimony; some of it comes from the organization he or she represents.

California Children's Lobby, for instance, is an umbrella group for child-care providers, child-care educators, and parent groups around the state. Skelly says the lobby has a twenty-year track record of grass-roots activism that makes it an effective advocate on children's issues.

"It's a very sophisticated network," she says. "With the phone tree we have, we can get forty calls into a member's office on a particular bill within an hour. These people know the [legislative] members in their areas; they write letters, make phone calls, and involve the parent groups. This committed network has been developing for the past ten or twenty years, and now it's primed and ready to go."

Skelly, who has been with California Children's Lobby for almost a year, says she is the only full-time lobbyist for children's issues in Sacramento. Although that has the drawback of spreading one person too thinly over hundreds of bills, it does mean that Skelly has become a focal point for children's issues and a natural funnel for information, studies, and trends.

But beyond the clout of her organization, Skelly works on developing her own ties and credibility. She knows about one-quarter of the members of both houses.

"When I meet a member, I don't just talk about my bills," she says. "Education bills, minimum wage—if I know a certain member is interested in something this year, then I talk about that. Then they know I'm interested in their concerns and views and not just pushing my agenda."

Just as important are her consultant contacts. "Consultants tap into [lobbyists] as a resource. You have to prepare good amendments for bills and make good suggestions well in advance of hearings if you are going to influence the outcome."

The 34-year-old Martin, who has been a lobbyist on health issues for three years, says he is always working on his recognition and credibility with both legislators and consultants. Unlike Skelly's organization, Martin's group is still learning to flex its political muscles.

While children's issues may be simmering on a front burner this year, Martin's issue has been boiling at high speed for a couple of years.

Martin was instrumental in forming the Lobby for Individual Freedom and Equality, an umbrella organization for 42 California organizations concerned about AIDS. He has been its sole lobbyist since it began.

The first full year of operation, he felt swamped, working out of his living room to track 65 bills. Confronted with 142 bills this year, last year is beginning to look calm in retrospect.

"The number of bills, so many legislators and staff to get to know, plus keeping a fledgling organization afloat—it's been difficult," Martin says.

The difficulties are not just in the part of the job that deals with bills. He has learned quickly that a discount lobbyist not only needs to keep an eye on developments in the capital but also needs to educate, guide, and cajole the groups he represents. One of his biggest tasks is forming his backers into a cohesive, effective voice.

"Gays and lesbians have always been very adept at turning people out on a single issue, but they've been unable to do it on a consistent basis," Martin says. "LIFE has been working to build that kind of network. LIFE illustrates a new political maturity that acknowledges the need for a group to have continuous visibility."

Networking and consensus-building are slow processes, however, and the AIDS epidemic is moving very quickly. "Building a network takes longer than gaining personal access to an individual legislator, but it's every bit as important," Martin says.

Important, yes; comfortable, no. Martin is often caught between a legislative agenda that threatens to move ahead without LIFE and purists on his board who believe compromise is synonymous with evil. "It puts us in a tough position, because we have liberal legislators who want to side with us telling us we have to give on some things," Martin says. "But then we have those who believe LIFE needs to maintain a pure image in the gay-lesbian community. And there's a need for those kinds of people: they create such a pure position, we look like moderates in comparison."

So Martin frequently finds himself in the role of an educator, not just to consultants and legislators, but to his own group members, who need to understand how the process works and what is probable, feasible, and impossible.

Skelly agrees with the vision of a lobbyist as an educator. She conducts seminars and attends the monthly meetings of a half-dozen child-oriented organizations. It's important for the folks back home to understand how Sacramento works and how they can affect what comes out of the capital.

"The Children's Lobby network can produce a teen parent and her partner, holding a baby, to give testimony at a hearing," Skelly says. "We can call on experts in the field and find out anything a legislator might want to know. These people are on the scene where state programs are actually working, so they are in a good position to know what's wrong and what needs to be done. They need to be able to convey that information to the legislature."

Skelly says that such personal testimony at hearings can have a "significance beyond dollars."

But dollars do count, no matter how optimistic or well-armed with statistics a lobbyist may be.

"A lobbyist without money just doesn't have the access," Martin says. "It's most visible when lobbyists are giving testimony. The committee members sit up and listen when it's someone with clout or money; they pay attention."

Martin says this matter-of-factly, with little bitterness in his voice. He regretfully accepts reality; lobbyists without the big bucks have to be more diligent in preparing arguments, supplying statistics, and proposing improvements—sometimes to no avail.

"You take a lot of frustration home. But then there have been people we've turned around on a particular issue," Martin says. "I think we've had a lot of impact on Dr. Filante [Assemblyman William Filante] and helped build his leadership on the AIDS issue among Republicans."

Skelly says her biggest victory came last year when she helped secure $500,000 in the 1987–88 state budget for California State University child care. The governor had already vetoed a $1.2 million expenditure, so getting the partial funding past his blue pencil was a plus. "These campus centers had been struggling along for twenty years without any state funding, and many of them were on the verge of closing," she says. "So this was the first time general-fund money was ever committed to campus child care, and I was very excited about it."

The upbeat Skelly cannot remember a defeat that left her depressed in the past, but even an optimistic nature will not block reality this year. California Children's Lobby's top priority is a statutory cost-of-living adjustment for child care. The governor has already vetoed similar legislation in the past. The governor also placed an equitable cost-of-living adjustment in his budget proposal this year, cutting the ground out from under Skelly's arguments by removing the need for immediate action. "I have to admit I'm beginning to anticipate a problem," she says.

Like all lobbyists, Martin has experienced both victories and defeats. His biggest victories have been killing two of GOP State Senator John Doolittle's ten-bill AIDS packages, and his worst defeat was the passage of a bill to test prostitutes for AIDS.

Victories that come by defeating bills are often fleeting. One of Doolittle's bills would have substantially relaxed AIDS test confidentiality laws, including turning results over to public health officials, and the other would have allowed widespread testing in psychiatric institutions. Those two are dead, but other measures this year are likely to accomplish at least some of Doolittle's goals.

The prostitute bill's passage was the type of fluke that leaves lobbyists with nightmares. The bill swept out of the Assembly, not as a well-reasoned policy decision, but on a Gang-of-Five tidal wave while Martin watched helplessly. "It happened so fast, and most of it was behind closed doors," Martin says, "so we really couldn't do much about it."

Had the Gang of Five, a group of dissident Democrats, not been trying to find common ground with Republicans so they could successfully challenge Speaker Willie Brown, the prostitute bill would have stayed buried or at least could have been modified to be less objectionable to LIFE, Martin says. But it is just one of several bills on which Martin expects defeat, leaving him feeling stressed and making his shoestring-budget operation all the more depressing.

"Burnout is common with public interest lobbyists," Martin says. "The ones you see around the building who have been here for 20 or 30 years work for industries, big-buck clients."

So if Martin received an offer from a big-time lobbying firm, would he switch?

"I couldn't leave LIFE dangling in midsession," says Martin, who is gay and deeply committed to the fight against AIDS. "But in the longer term, yes, I'd probably move on. You can have a deep personal commitment to an issue, but it only lasts until burnout hits."

Martin, whose father is a Washington, DC, lobbyist, is already well sidetracked from the theater career he had planned. He keeps his hand in acting and directing with a Davis community theater group, but his future is in the capital. "It's in my blood," he says simply. "The more I've been involved in government activities, the more I've been fascinated with what is going on in Sacramento."

The fascination is still there for Skelly, as well. "I really enjoy lobbying. It's exciting and stimulating."

Skelly didn't start out as a lobbyist. An active role in starting a child-care program at UC Santa Barbara put her in the limelight when the university's student association needed a lobbyist. Two years there and anther year with the Children's Lobby have satisfied her itch to do something professionally that focuses on children.

"I have a bottom-line commitment to education and children's issues. I might move on to something else in the future. But I'm pretty dedicated to children's issues and, right now, I couldn't imagine doing anything else."

SOURCE: Adapted from Kathy Beasley, *California Journal,* 1988.

ATTAINING POWER RESOURCES

When people use power resources in transactional relationships, their success depends on several factors. They must *believe* they possess certain power resources, such as expertise, even in order to try using them. They need to have knowledge, often "insider knowledge," about the agency or legislature that they wish to influence. They can only obtain this knowledge by knowing persons familiar with who has power, what tactics will most likely be effective, when to initiate a proposal, and what contacts are needed with insiders. They must actually *try* to use their power resources rather than merely storing or saving them. Someone who is excessively fearful, for example, may not ever try to use power resources. The people they attempt to influence must take their initiatives seriously or they will not yield to them in any way. If a lobbyist tries to persuade a legislator on the basis of expertise, the legislator should believe the lobbyist *is* an expert.

The effective use of power, then, depends on several factors that must be present simultaneously in transactional relationships. To understand power, then, we need to explore in more detail the sociology and the psychology of power, or how persons believe they possess power *and* gain the confidence to use it. We also need to examine what leads *other* people to heed rather than ignore a practitioner's requests.

People often develop power resources and the confidence to use them by interacting socially with others over an extended period. People who meet successively with colleagues over time, for example, are likely to sense their personal power, particularly if they have established a rapport with those colleagues. In contrast, persons who are relatively isolated from their colleagues may be less likely to believe they can initiate policy suggestions that will be taken seriously.

Similarly, we respond to other people's power initiatives based on our prior experiences with them. If we have had many interactions with them and have come to trust their judgment, for example, we are more likely to respond favorably to their suggestions than someone with whom we have had little or no contact.

Because power accrues through successful interactions over time, skillful policy practitioners try to *embed* themselves in the interactions of specific settings, both to develop confidence in their own power resources and to increase the chances that other people will respond favorably to them.

Building personal credibility, networking, and developing links with external movements, associations, and groups all help individuals develop power resources. We note at several points in this chapter how Rand Martin and Sherry Skelly, the two "low-budget lobbyists," use these strategies in a legislative setting to develop power resources. Staff members in agencies develop power with the same strategies.

Building Personal Credibility

Whether they are attorneys, physicians, or social workers, professionals require a certain level of personal credibility to be effective with their clients. Without this credibility, they would soon find their practices jeopardized, because clients would not seek or trust their services. Similarly, the personal credibility of people who seek to change policy influences the degree to which others listen to them. Credibility refers to personal characteristics that other people value in a practitioner and that influence their responsiveness to that practitioner.[1]

Several tactics can enhance individuals' personal characteristics and hence their credibility. Policy practitioners can emphasize that they are reasonable and pragmatic, are team players, abound with integrity and authoritativeness, have a positive track record, and are affiliated with successful institutions. People often use Machiavellian tactics, as well, to enhance personal credibility, although not without ethical and practical risks.

Appearing reasonable and pragmatic. As we noted in Chapter Ten, policy practitioners can sometimes increase their credibility with decisionmakers who have different values by *not* emphasizing a proposal's underlying principles and, instead, by focusing on substantive provisions.[2] Assume, for example, that a policy advocate wants to redistribute resources to poor people by substantially increasing the benefits of the Food Stamps Program. This advocate has a radical perspective. When dealing with the aide of a conservative legislator, such as Senator Robert Dole of Kansas, the policy practitioner might downplay his radical ideology in order to emphasize both the details of the reform and the objective of "increasing distressed farmers revenues." By downplaying his ideology, which is dissonant with the ideology of conservative politicians, the policy practitioner will seem more credible to the aide than would an openly radical person.[3]

This strategy can be carried to extremes if policy practitioners sacrifice their preferences excessively in their zeal to appear reasonable and pragmatic. Indeed, it can be counterproductive if other people perceive the policy practitioner as disingenuous.

Appearing as team players. Adherents of power-dependence theory suggest that others view us as credible when they depend on us.[4] To illustrate this theory, contrast two social-work units in two hospitals. The unit in Hospital 1 contents itself with providing crisis-intervention services to patients, whereas the unit in Hospital 2 fills several functions besides the traditional counseling ones. The staff members assume highly visible roles in discharging elderly patients, providing financial counseling for patients, providing social services to rape victims, serving as intermediaries between the hospital and the Department of Children's Services in suspected cases of child abuse and neglect, operating a substance-abuse clinic, and providing home-based services to frail, elderly persons. Top decisionmakers in Hospital 2 depend on the staff for several services. Indeed, they can hardly imagine how their hospital could function without this social-work department. By contrast, top decisionmakers in Hospital 1 hardly know that the social-work unit exists, much less that it is vital to the hospital. According to power-dependence theory, decisionmakers are more likely to heed suggestions of the director or other staff of the expansive social-work unit (Hospital 2) than of the other unit (Hospital 1).[5]

Power-dependence theory suggests, then, that practitioners can increase their stature by assuming multiple functions within their organizations to supplement their relatively narrow job descriptions. As the director of a social-work unit once said to me, "I might even consider washing windows!" These expansive functions serve several purposes; they make high-level administrators feel beholden to units and individuals who perform a variety of positive tasks for the agency, and they make these units and individuals appear to be team players who have the institution's broader interests in mind.

Policy practitioners can also enhance their credibility by taking the initiative to make specific changes within an organization. Assume, for example, that a social worker has a casual conversation with a hospital administrator about some problem. The administrator remarks on "the turnover of nursing and social-work staff in the pediatrics unit during the past five years, which has severely jeopardized the quality of services and staff morale." If the social worker seized the initiative by offering to survey the staff before discussing possible causes of the turnover, she makes the administrator dependent on her by performing some necessary work. Volunteering these services makes her appear to be a team player. If she continues to assume additional roles on this project, such as chairing a committee, she continues this proactive and positive role.

We can imagine that these assertive actions would enhance her credibility with respect to this issue.

People can also increase their image as team players by shaping policy proposals germane to an organization's mission.[6] A policy practitioner would enhance his credibility by developing and supporting policy proposals consonant with one or several of these objectives.

Of course, ethical concerns limit the use of this tactic because we should not make proposals consonant with morally objectionable values. If a hospital wished not to serve any poor patients who lacked insurance, even ones with emergency conditions, a social-work unit ought not seek funds for additional staff to help screen out such people.[7]

Increasing personal integrity. Some people may rightly wonder whether some of these tactics for increasing personal credibility might not imperil practitioners' integrity. If we must constantly appear reasonable and as team players, when can we speak out for specific causes or *not* be team players when we think "the team" needs fundamental reforms?

Policy practitioners may take heart that many effective legislators combined moderate approaches with principled and outspoken positions on certain issues. Hubert Humphrey, Phillip Hart, and Claude Pepper often championed social causes before they became popular or fashionable, with some risk to their political well-being. Yet these men were highly successful legislators, were overwhelmingly reelected on numerous occasions, and enjoyed immense popularity among their legislative peers. Perhaps one reason for their credibility was that many people perceived them as having integrity, as being able to draw the line when their most fundamental beliefs were challenged.[8] Humphrey became a determined advocate for civil rights legislation, as did Pepper in defending Social Security. Even people who disagree with others' values often admire that they will take risks to defend these values. In contrast, people who bend as willows do with every passing breeze do not command the same respect. Of course, even the aforementioned politicians had to determine when to invest their energies and when to take risks; on many issues, they were more willing to accommodate others.

Increasing authoritativeness. When we want to change a policy in an agency, community, or legislative setting, opposition often arises, as people say change is not warranted. Perhaps some faction or person merely wants to increase their own interests. The policy practitioner can often diminish such inertia by conveying a sense of authoritativeness about the subject, whether by citing important research, documenting similar changes in other settings, or quoting reputable experts.[9] The policy practitioner may find some evidence that supports a policy change. In the case of the high rate of staff turnover in the pediatrics service of a hospital, the social worker might conduct her survey of the situation by using a standardized instrument that measures staff morale. As individuals appear to be authoritative with a specific issue, they increase the likelihood that they will be perceived as authoritative on future occasions.

Developing a positive track record. One cannot develop credibility merely by using rhetoric; people have to observe firsthand, or hear secondhand, that someone is competent, trustworthy, or authoritative, or that their department performs indispensable services.

Secondhand reports can be quite helpful in establishing credibility. As people initiate useful policies and try to change existing policies, they obtain good reputations in the eyes of those whom they directly encounter and those who hear positive feedback about them.

Affiliating oneself with successful institutions. Credibility stems not only from individuals' actions and attributes, but also from their affiliations. To illustrate this point, assume that a hospital administrator receives requests for additional funding from the directors of two units within the hospital. The first request comes from a director whose unit has been marked by chronic and repeated turmoil and that the administrator does not perceive as providing quality services. The second request comes from the director of a unit widely viewed as outstanding; the hospital administrator has received many positive reports about its services and staff. Although both directors may possess similar personal characteristics, we can guess that the hospital administrator will be more likely to heed the second request.

The lesson for social workers who work in bureaucracies is simple. Personal credibility stems in part from being associated with well-regarded and effective units. Those units, in turn, derive their reputations from the quality of their work and of their staff.[10] Practitioners can enhance their credibility indirectly by improving the services of the unit that employs them.

Using Machiavellian tactics. Some individuals try to enhance their credibility by using negative tactics, such as harming others' reputations, buck-passing, sandbagging, and turf- or empire-building. Those who use Machiavellian tactics often assume that a win-lose situation exists, where their reputation will improve only if they impugn colleagues' characters. (In political campaigns, where candidates are pitted against one another and where only one person can be elected, win-lose situations often exist, but some persons extend this logic to all situations.) In the case of buck-passing, people blame others for specific failures in hopes of clearing their own names.[11] In sandbagging tactics, people seek to diminish others' successes by contending that other people, perhaps even themselves, were really responsible for these successes.[12] As any participant in bureaucratic politics can confirm, many people excel in turf- or empire-building where they accumulate power and responsibility by wresting them from others.[13] People malign colleagues to diminish their initiatives by suggesting that the proposals reflect ulterior and evil motivations, such as a desire for status or power.[14]

These negative tactics can be quite effective in some political campaigns or in helping some people, such as Richard Nixon, attain power. Some administrators also obtain power by using one or more of these tactics. But the credibility of those who use them can suffer, because others may perceive people who rely on negative tactics to be immoral.

Illustrations from Case 11.1. The case at the outset of this chapter illustrates how many interactional skills low-budget lobbyists need to develop power resources. Rand Martin tells us that his power depends on his being "reasonable and pragmatic" in dealing with legislators, though it is difficult to make concessions that he and his allies do not want to make. He discusses the need for personal integrity and authoritativeness by providing well-researched, accurate information to legislators. Both he and Sherry Skelly mention the need to develop a track record of timely and responsible contributions to legislators.

Networking

Networking refers to the nature, number, and range of supportive relationships that people possess.[15] These relationships are important to policy practitioners in several ways. Individuals with broad networks develop "early-information systems" where they learn about issues, problems, and trends relevant to their work as policy practitioners. Perhaps the priorities of top decisionmakers in an agency will decisively change in coming months in ways that will affect their units and the agency's services. Policy practitioners with broad networks can call on other individuals for advice as they develop policies and strategies. When seeking to remedy a specific problem in the agency, someone may ask a trusted colleague for input.

There are many kinds of networks. *Lateral networks* consist of relationships with colleagues, whereas *vertical* and *subordinate networks* consist, respectively, of persons who are superior to and beneath a person in an organization's hierarchy. People have relatively *heterogeneous networks* when they have supportive relationships with others in a range of positions both within and outside their work. A social worker in a hospital possesses a heterogeneous network, for example, when it includes members of different units or departments in the institution and different professions. Some relationships in networks are short-term, perhaps fashioned in response to a specific problem, while others are long-standing.

Many strategies help in expanding personal networks. They include enhancing one's visibility, seeking inclusion in decisionmaking bodies, cultivating mentors, obtaining access to informal groups, such as old-boy networks, and developing links with social movements.

Enhancing personal visibility. Some people develop networks by increasing their visibility in specific bureaucratic, community, and legislative settings. Indeed, one school of management, which is called "Management by Walking Around," exhorts managers to broaden their personal networks. Some individuals resort to visiting places where persons socialize to expand their circle of acquaintances.[16]

The nature of relationships during these personal contacts becomes important to the policy practitioner. Christopher Matthews tells the story of the young Lyndon Johnson, who lived in a boardinghouse in Washington, DC, when he first arrived as an aide to a legislator. To meet other aides who lived in the same boardinghouse, he brushed his teeth three or four times each morning and took several showers. In these encounters, he asked them about their jobs and their interests, a tactic that convinced each aide that he cared about him.[17]

Indeed, politicians often employ a tactic that others can use. Although exchanging information and socializing are important, both as ends and as methods of establishing relationships, they need to be supplemented by actively seeking advice, support, or suggestions from others. As Matthews notes, people usually like to be asked for advice because it makes them feel important and wanted.[18] Of course, too much can be made of a good thing, as when individuals make excessive requests.

Obtaining inclusion in decision-making bodies. Agencies often establish committees to examine specific problems, whether ongoing committees or time-limited ad hoc groups.

Membership on some of these task forces is sometimes limited to people who are placed on committees by top officials in an organization. However, individuals can seek membership by displaying interest in an issue. Individuals can also suggest that a committee be established to examine a problem. Committee deliberations offer an excellent opportunity to obtain an inside position on important issues, improve one's credibility, and extend one's network.

Seeking mentors and inclusion in old-boy networks. When researching why women have difficulty obtaining promotions in corporations, Rosabeth Kanter implicates their exclusion from mentoring relationships and old-boy networks.[19] Males, she observes, informally develop relationships with high-level male officials. These officials become mentors to these men, giving advice and information about the internal workings of the corporation, its politics, taboo subjects, informal factions, upcoming policy issues, and strategies for obtaining promotion. Mentors introduce these neophytes to acquaintances, including important officers of the corporation, both in formal decisionmaking arenas and in informal or social situations. On occasion, mentors "go to bat" for neophytes when they need high-level assistance.

Mentors introduce neophytes to informal cliques and relationships. As J. McIver Weatherford notes with respect to legislatures, old-boy networks span the legislative, bureaucratic, and lobbying spheres of government as people move between them in their employment.[20] In both state and federal capitals, for example, powerful legislators have an intricate network of acquaintances, many of them former aides, in lobbying and bureaucratic capacities. They tap into these rich networks at many points in their work; a legislator might contact acquaintances within government agencies when contemplating whether to introduce legislation, when seeking to help a constituent with a specific problem, and when searching for issues to use to enhance his or her reputation as an initiator of new legislation.

These old-boy networks contain a wide-ranging set of contacts that provide assistance, information, business connections, and job possibilities to their members. Many high-level decisions are made during the social encounters between the people in these networks; those outside the networks are not consulted about these decisions and lack the advantage of having advance notification of upcoming policy changes.[21]

The workings of the mentor system and the old-boy networks are manifestly unfair, at least from the perspective of those not included in them. Lacking allies within the networks, many women and racial minorities are excluded, as are "loners," or those disinclined to maintain a network of relationships.[22] Declarations about their evil nature, however, will not make them disappear, nor will the moral victories of those who avoid them erase the disadvantages this exclusion brings.

Both Rand Martin and Sherry Skelly make clear that low-budget lobbyists depend on having contacts within the state's legislature and governmental agencies. While lacking money to entertain legislators and their aides, they can nonetheless develop a range of connections. They need to focus on increasing their visibility in an arena filled with other lobbyists, who often possess greater resources.

Links with External Groups, Persons, or Movements

Some people develop links with groups that take interest in issues such as AIDS, reforms for children, disabled persons, and mentally ill persons. The members of such groups, which often possess minimal resources, are highly knowledgeable about specific issues and deeply committed to them. Other people become active in local chapters of professional organizations, such as the National Association of Social Workers. Others form relationships with specific politicians or civil servants.

These connections can increase the power of persons within their own organizations. Persons known to possess these contacts will likely be viewed as more credible than those who lack them. They can bring into their organizations ideas and information that come from these external contacts.[23] To help the external groups or movements, they can sometimes recruit other staff or even clients to help them, though they must be certain that their clients do not believe that they must participate in order to receive services.[24]

Sherry Skelly tells us in Case 11.1 that maintaining several external allies is critical to a low-budget lobbyist's success. She inherited and helped maintain a sophisticated network of children's advocates throughout the state. She uses the network to increase her expertise on myriad issues and to place pressure on legislators at pivotal points.

OUTGROUP MEMBERS' PROBLEMS

We have already alluded to Rosabeth Kanter's pioneering work on problems that female executives confront when seeking power in organizations. Her observations apply, as well, to persons of color, gays and lesbians, people with disabilities, and members of any groups that confront prejudice.[25]

Members of these groups must work even harder than others to obtain power in certain settings. They have to use the same techniques we have already discussed, such as networking, but they must be even more diligent and persistent. They should try to develop contacts with other members of their own group in their workplace, such as women who have obtained positions of power before them, to provide them with special assistance, support, and advice. When these contacts are lacking within an organization, they should seek help from mentors *outside* the organization—for example, in similar or related organizations.

Members of outgroups can also find allies among "mainstream persons" who could, for example, take the lead to diversify an agency's staff or include a broader range of staff in supervisorial and other positions.

The case about low-budget lobbyists illustrates how persons with marginal power resources can nonetheless gain significant power with careful strategy.

DEVELOPING ASSERTIVENESS

People sometimes fail to seize strategic opportunities to shape policies because they assume they cannot win. In some cases, as our discussion of power differentials suggests, the deck *is* stacked against them. In many other cases, however, individuals undermine their effectiveness by becoming fatalistic.

To use power effectively, people must first decide that they possess power resources, that they can use them successfully, and that they want to use them. The word *assertiveness* describes this proclivity to test the waters, rather than being excessively fatalistic.

Assertiveness is undermined, however, by two dispositions that chronically lead some people to underestimate their true power resources. First, some people have a victim mentality, which disposes them to believe that other people will conspire to defeat their preferences.[26] A director of a social-work department in a hospital might believe, for example, that nurses and physicians will systematically oppose *any* proposals of social workers. Second, some people are fatalistic about using power in a more general sense; they believe that only high-level persons or powerful interests wield power successfully. Such fatalism suggests that people outside these exalted categories cannot effectively participate in policy deliberations.

Both the victim mentality and fatalism create self-fulfilling prophecies. If people believe that others conspire against them and that only a restricted group can use power effectively, they will not exercise personal power resources. If others perceive them as disinclined to participate in policy deliberations, these other people are more likely to run roughshod over them, ignore their occasional suggestions, and exclude them from policy deliberations. These negative experiences further reinforce the victim mentality and fatalism in a vicious circle.[27]

Fatalistic practitioners ignore the diverse power resources that most of us can attain. Fatalists falsely assume that we each possess a fixed supply of power resources that will not increase, even as we enhance our credibility, expertise, connections, and other sources of power. Although some people *are* relatively powerless, they can change this situation by finding allies, establishing relationships, developing expertise, and obtaining information.

To understand this problem, recall our Chapter Ten discussion about the sender of power (X) and the receiver of power (Y) as illustrated in Figure 10.1. Assume that you are Y, that you work in an agency, and that your program director intimidates you. Through his demeanor toward you, his intimidating remarks, and even his veiled threats, your director seeks to dissuade you from making changes in the program. You encounter, then, a problem that both distresses and frightens you, especially in terms of your job security.

What can you do about this situation?[28] You can realistically assess both the risks and benefits likely to accrue from efforts to change defective policies. Persons who intimidate other people often derive power from a kind of mind trip that they inflict on their victims. Once the "victim" believes that her options are foreclosed and that she has no recourse but to follow the intimidator's suggestions, the intimidator has won. You should ask, "Is his power as extensive as he suggests, or can I use my own power resources without incurring unacceptable penalties, such as losing my job?" You can test the waters by asking other people how they perceive a specific policy to see if your perceptions have merit. You can discern whether other people also feel intimidated and whether your director's actions are exclusively directed toward you. You can try authentic, direct communication with your program director, focusing on substantive issues to see if he is more "bark than bite." It is sometimes problematic to accuse someone of seeking to intimidate you, since this can make the situation even worse. You can start, however, by stating your substantive positions about specific issues where you differ with him.

In situations where you are subject to intimidation, you should not expect easy answers. Perhaps the situation can be eased by direct, honest communication, but it may defy easy resolution. An assertive person will not passively accept the situation, but will try to diagnose it, identify possible strategies, and select one of them. An assertive person will often try several options sequentially in search of a remedy that works.

Here is an example of assertiveness. The director of a social work department in a hospital requested increased budgetary resources for her department, but was denied. She noticed, however, that unsuccessful entreaties educated top officials to social-work programs. Indeed, she surmised that some officials actually felt guilty about denying well-presented and justified requests. She decided not to be intimidated but to make further requests for funds for her department. She discovered that skillfully and frequently requesting funds caused increases in her unit's budget. Unlike departments with more timid executives, her department gained size and stature as she assertively sought resources for her department on several occasions, even in the wake of unsuccessful requests.[29]

Case 11.1 illustrates how policy advocates with relatively minimal resources must combat "burnout" and "fatalism" when working in the state's capital as low-budget lobbyists. They frequently observe lobbyists with munificent resources wining and dining legislators, offering them campaign contributions, and performing several technical tasks for them. Low-budget lobbyists cannot employ these strategies because they lack the needed resources. Were they to succumb to pessimism, they would leave their positions, but both of them have persevered and obtained notable successes in spite of minimal resources.

CAN DIRECT-SERVICE STAFF USE POWER RESOURCES?

Our discussion of outgroup members' special problems and of assertiveness leads naturally to the question, "Can people 'at the bottom of the heap,' such as direct-service staff members, use power resources, or does their subordinate position in organizational hierarchy consign them to a powerless position?" We must acknowledge that organizations vary considerably; if some executives elicit and even expect input from direct-service staff, other executives are relatively authoritarian and exercise considerable power resources.[30]

Direct-service staff can develop considerable person-to-person-power resources, such as expertise, that stem from their personal knowledge of an agency's problems. Many supervisors and executives value suggestions from direct-service staff about a range of agency matters and respond to well-conceived suggestions for changing existing services. Direct-service staff should realize that executives depend on them for their agencies' reputation, efficiency, revenues (when agencies charge for services), and public relations with clients and other agencies. By any reckoning, most agencies would cease to exist if they lacked reasonably competent front-line staff.

Direct-service staff also possess considerable power to reward and coerce. As they do their work well, they enhance their reputations and credibility. In turn, the superiors often recognize that direct-service staff members' attentiveness to the program and policy concerns further enhance the quality and productivity of their work. When unions exist, direct-service staff members can threaten in an implied or stated way to disrupt their work if certain demands are not granted; these demands primarily involve salary and work-load issues, but unions sometimes seek changes in policy. Even when unions do not exist, direct-service staff can vigorously protest some policies by making their case directly to high-level staff.

Direct-service staff often have access to certain agency decisionmaking processes, such as staff meetings, retreats, unit meetings, and meetings with supervisors. If they have developed their power through the strategies we discussed earlier in this chapter (such as enhancing credibility, networking, enhancing personal visibility, and developing relationships with external bodies), they are likely to increase their power in these agency deliberations. In some cases, moreover, they can seek membership on specific agency committees or even suggest that a committee be formed to examine a specific issue.

Direct-service staff can also wield power indirectly, as we discussed in the preceding chapter, by influencing a supervisor to initiate a suggestion. They can form coalitions within their agencies and pressure administrators to modify specific policies. However, staff members should be realistic about the realities of power within their organizations during such endeavors.

As we discussed in Chapter Ten, direct-service staff members often derive power from their autonomy.[31] Many regulations influence direct-service staff by governing the length and intensity of services, recommending procedures, and establishing priorities. However, regulations are difficult to enforce because direct-service staff members' work is relatively shielded from high-level scrutiny. Moreover, it is often possible to bend some rules without technically violating them. Carried to an extreme, autonomy can bring anarchy when staff members systematically disobey existing policy, but it nonetheless represents an important kind of power that they can use.

While we have discussed the use of power during decisionmaking, direct-service staff members can also shape outcomes by helping to build agendas, define problems, and construct proposals, as we discussed in Chapters Five through Nine. For example, direct-service staff can try to place certain issues on policy agendas, contribute to discussions where social problems are defined and analyzed, and—as we discussed in Chapters Seven, Eight, and Nine—they can help shape proposals.

Direct-service staff do not, of course, have the power resources that executives, funders, or legislators do, so they need to enhance their power resources imaginatively and selectively choose issues and situations where they can influence policy deliberations.

Group-Process Skills

Some discussions of power imply that individuals "take on" the establishment by themselves. In fact, policy practitioners often work with groups, such as committees, community task forces, coalitions, or legislatures. Policy advocates often work with local advocacy groups, such as a chapter of a national civil rights organization or a gay-lesbian advocacy group in a specific city. Professionals can work within local or state chapters of their national organization, such as the National Association of Social Workers.[32] There has been a veritable explosion of nongovernmental organizations at the national, state, county, and city levels that champion the needs of persons with special problems (such as blindness, breast cancer, and dyslexia) and outgroups (such as women, Latinos, and refugees). Some groups focus on a special population that has a particular social problem, such as helping women obtain employment in the building trades or seeking greater assistance for Latinos with AIDS.

All policy practitioners need to find out, *before* they become fully engaged in issues, what groups currently exist in the jurisdiction where they want to work. Several reference books provide an excellent starting point (see Box 11.1). Assume, for example, that someone wants to seek better services for older persons with Alzheimer's disease in Kansas City. By consulting these catalogues of associations, one could quickly find existing organizations in Kansas City, in other cities in Kansas, and in Washington, DC, that deal with (1) older persons and (2) Alzheimer's disease.

> **BOX 11.1**
> *Reference Works Listing Advocacy and Professional Groups*
>
> *Associations Yellowbook: Who's Who at the Leading U.S. Trade and Professional Associations* (New York: Monitor, 1993).
> *Directories in Print* (Detroit: Gale Research, 1989).
> *Encyclopedia of Associations, 1993* (Detroit: Gale Research, 1993).
> *National Trade and Professional Associations of the United States* (Washington, DC: Columbia Books, 1993).
> *Regional, State, and Local Organizations, Encyclopedia of Associations*, 7 vols. (Detroit: Gale Research, 1993).
> *State and Regional Associations of the United States* (Washington, DC: Columbia Books, 1989).
> *Washington Information Directory: Guide to Government Agencies, Associations, Congressional Committees, Congressional Staff, and Congressional Caucuses* (Washington, DC: Congressional Quarterly, 1993).

Moreover, someone could focus on a problem by starting a local organization or initiating a coalition that pooled the resources of several agencies and groups. A social worker could form a coalition of groups concerned with mental health, health, and older persons' needs to improve policies and services for Alzheimer's patients in a specific locality.

Working with Task Groups

Policy practitioners need skills in working with *task groups* within places of employment or the broader community. They can serve as members, staff, or leaders in these groups. Task groups "focus on producing or influencing something external to the group itself." In contrast to groups for treatment, therapy, and education, task groups do not emphasize members' personal growth or learning.[33]

A remarkable range of policy-related task groups exists.[34] Some groups concentrate on making and enacting policies, whether they are the boards of agencies, legislative committees, or legislatures themselves.[35] These groups often rely, however, on policy recommendations from "feeder groups," such as deliberative committees, subcommittees, task forces, study groups, or commissions. These various feeder groups develop recommendations and forward them to decisionmaking entities.[36] Some of these groups are ongoing entities, such as an agency's program committee or the Select Subcommittee on Children and Youth in Congress. Executives or political leaders establish other groups to study specific problems and make recommendations, only to terminate them after they have done so.

Other task groups specialize in implementing policies.[37] Assume, for example, that a county mental health and substance-abuse agency developed a new program for students in the school district. To oversee the new program, the agency could establish an ongoing overseeing committee, which might suggest policy changes if they believed the new program was not realizing its objectives. A multitude of ongoing coordinating committees exist, as well, to promote communication and policy development between various agencies.

Additional groups advocate the policy preferences of specific factions or interests. Unions have become a potent power source in the human services system by mobilizing vast numbers of employees in public and nonprofit agencies.[38] Community organizations, such as those modeled on the theories of Saul Alinsky, represent specific neighborhoods.[39] A remarkable array of groups serve as advocates for specific groups and institutions with varying amounts of power and resources. Social movements spawn many groups and an overarching purpose, usually to advance the needs or perspectives of a specific segment of the population. This was true of the civil rights and welfare rights movements of the 1960s and, more recently, the movement to help homeless people.[40] While often seeking national goals, social movements often have local affiliates, such as chapters of NOW or of a civil rights organization. As we discuss later, coalitions merge the resources and power of discrete groups.[41] Many committees exist in agencies to examine specific issues, committees that staff can and should join.

Why develop task groups? Task groups serve needs that could not easily be met if individuals tried to shape policy on their own. For example, people sometimes turn to task groups for cognitive reasons.[42] When confronting a serious problem, individuals often find it useful to pool their ideas to reach a joint solution. Of course, using groups to make decisions is not a panacea, because groups sometimes make flawed choices. People use task groups, as well, for political reasons.[43] People sometimes establish specific task groups to mobilize pressure for reform because such groups can be highly powerful if they obtain resources, effective leadership, and policy-practice skills. Highly placed officials often initiate task forces, such as committees, to "cover their bases" in order to avoid being accused of excluding various interests from their deliberations, or they may control the membership of a task force so it will approve only their preferred options. Some executives also try to increase political support for specific measures by developing blue-ribbon committees because such groups can bring legitimacy to specific policies, since their membership consists of influential persons. (In the case of appointed task forces, advocates often try to convince highly-placed officials to place one of their members on the group in hopes of influencing their deliberations.)

Policy practitioners' roles in task groups. Practitioners can be leaders, staff, or members in task groups. Indeed, the role they assume often influences the nature of their work. *Leaders* are comparable to an orchestra's conductor or a football team's quarterback. They facilitate the group's work by helping to develop a mission and acquire resources, such as funds and staff. They expedite the group's ongoing work by developing agendas and presiding at meetings. They help shape its structure and membership by developing subcommittees and a nominating process. They intervene at specific points to promote members' participation and decisionmaking. As facilitators, they avoid or diminish excessive internal conflict or dysfunctional processes, such as scapegoating specific members. Besides the president or chair of a group, there are other leaders, such as treasurers and secretaries, who perform important logistical tasks.[44]

Staff expedite and facilitate issues in the group. As expediters, they collect information, assemble materials, perform secretarial functions, and attend to logistical details to allow others to concentrate on developing ideas and taking specific actions. As facilitators, they attend group meetings and help group processes to allow the group to achieve its goals. They often work with group leaders between meetings to help them plan upcoming sessions and accomplish specific tasks.

The staff's role places certain limits, however, on their interventions within groups. Their role requires considerable circumvention and restraint, because they are background facilitators and expediters, rather than members or leaders. They may disagree with the group's decisions, but they often refrain from speaking out from their own perspectives, preferring to shape decisions more discreetly.[45]

Members of task groups provide ideas, perform specific tasks, give the group power by linking it to interests, lead subgroups within the task group, provide resources, and (in the case of some members) assume leadership in the group after a period of apprenticeship. While leadership is crucial, few task groups are successful without motivated and active members.[46]

What successful task groups need.   Many task groups are highly successful. They establish and realize their objectives in the course of deliberations and activities. Other groups flounder, split, procrastinate, or dwindle to nothingness, as many of us have experienced in our professional and personal lives.

Theorists and researchers have identified several factors that lead task groups to succeed and other groups to fail. These factors include the group's mission, leadership, developmental needs, procedures, structure, deliberative and interactional processes, staff and resources, and their context. Indeed, many theorists and researchers suggest that we need to examine the structure and processes of groups, as well as the actions of specific persons in them, to understand why some of them succeed while others fail.

Task Groups' Missions

Successful groups have to develop a mission that defines their objectives or goals. Although the mission often changes during deliberations and events, members should decide what they want to accomplish during the early stages of the group's existence. Several dangers exist. A group may establish unrealistic expectations, such as hoping to enact a major piece of legislation in a brief period. When it cannot accomplish its objectives, its members' morale and its leaders' reputation may suffer. It may fail to develop a consensus about its objectives, so that different factions and members have different expectations. In some cases, overt or manifest expectations may clash with hidden ones, as when leaders possess personal agendas that they do not share with members.

The mission also includes agreements about procedural matters, such as the frequency of meetings, the way leaders are selected, the group's size, and its relationship to external bodies. Without agreeing about these matters and about their major goals, groups can encounter controversies and misunderstandings.

Task Groups' Leadership

Successful groups have skillful leaders with an array of qualities that facilitate their work. Skilled leaders walk a tightrope between alternative vices: they should be directive and assertive, yet not dominate; they should encourage dissenting perspectives, yet not allow the group to become encumbered with excessive or destructive conflict; they should perform several tasks, yet encourage group members to perform other tasks; they should represent the group to the external world, yet not excessively seek personal credit; and they should emphasize the group's accomplishment, but not neglect the group members' social and emotional needs. Unskilled leaders may be domineering, passive, confrontational, dictatorial, or self-promoting.

Skilled leaders understand groups' developmental, structural, and process needs and develop strategies to address them. A leader might discern, for example, that "this group needs to engage in relatively unstructured brainstorming" at this point in its existence or that "we need to reach closure on this topic" at another point.

Leaders need certain value orientations. Effective leaders are committed, for example, to democratic values; they want to give group members a considerable role in shaping their decisions, although good leaders realize that discussion can be carried to excess. They do not want the group to engage in actions destructive to certain participants, such as scapegoating members with legitimate and dissenting perspectives.

Task Groups' Developmental Needs

Groups develop, or evolve, through time as they strengthen their missions, engage in deliberations, and accomplish tasks. In early phases, for example, they must agree about their mission, leadership, and procedures, and form realistic expectations. During middle phases, they need to update their mission, develop and implement procedures, experience successes that instill and maintain a sense of momentum, and develop a division of labor that allows and requires a range of people to participate in the group's activities. In later phases, some groups should terminate themselves when they no longer are needed, whereas others need to regenerate by revising their mission and seeking new members.

Some groups do not progress between these stages of development. Having not established their mission, some groups keep returning to the question, Why do we exist? Other groups fail to change their mission as events unfold. With their original mission accomplished or rendered obsolete, some groups continue to exist when they should be terminated.

Task Groups' Procedures

Some people falsely equate leadership and group effectiveness with minutes, agendas, and bylaws, which are procedures. Procedures, however, serve a useful purpose.[47] They allow thoughtful people to review the group's accomplishments and, in the case of agendas, to anticipate and plan forthcoming events. They provide a history of the group that can be periodically reviewed to ascertain how the group has evolved and to analyze what new tasks it might undertake. Bylaws provide mechanisms for selecting leaders, replenishing membership, dividing tasks among officers and subcommittees, and handling funds.

Task Groups' Structure

Task groups must organize themselves internally by establishing subcommittees or ad hoc groups to facilitate a division of labor. They have to decide how large they wish to be to accomplish their mission and, in the case of groups that pressure decisionmakers, to obtain political clout. They have to examine their relations with external bodies; do they wish to merge with other groups, participate in coalitions with other groups, or maintain an independent existence?

These kinds of structural issues pose significant challenges for some groups. A group that becomes excessively decentralized with numerous committees, for example, may lack direction, but a group that is too centralized might fail to delegate responsibilities to its members. A group could lose its identity if it merges with other groups or becomes excessively active in coalitions, but it may lack clout if it remains isolated from other groups.[48]

Task Groups' Deliberative and Interactional Processes

To be productive, groups need to develop modes of deliberation and interaction that allow their members to examine options, assess their strengths and weaknesses, make informed choices, and develop strategies to implement their choices. Positive modes of deliberation include an open atmosphere where members feel free to contribute ideas, dissent is permissible, persons believe their ideas will be taken seriously, and brainstorming precedes the selection of ideas.[49] Moreover, group members need to respect each other and the deliberative process sufficiently and honor decisions that the group makes.

The decisionmaking process can be stifled or abbreviated, however, if leadership and group processes do not favor dissent, brainstorming, and a democratic process. The social psychologist Irving Janis suggests that some groups succumb to "groupthink," where they move too rapidly to unanimous positions, scapegoat dissenters, and do not fully consider the strengths and weaknesses of their positions.[50] Intolerant leaders, membership that fails to represent a variety of perspectives, and truncated deliberations contribute to this phenomenon.

Janis, Robert Bales, and other researchers suggest that groups should progress through a series of stages when considering issues. They should brainstorm options in a risk-taking and tolerant atmosphere.[51] With care and considerable effort, they should gradually reduce these options so that a revised list emerges. Only after an extended process of considering the strengths and weaknesses of these options should the group develop its final position. This movement from large numbers of options to final choices can only occur if group members feel free to take risks and if the group tolerates internal dissent.

Task Groups' Staff and Resources

Groups that engage in relatively complex work need staff and resources to help them accomplish logistical tasks, provide them with technical assistance, and facilitate the work. Staff can come from institutions, such as agencies, or they can be volunteers. Resources can come from institutions, memberships, special events, private donors, or corporate or foundation donors.

Just as low-budget lobbyists can achieve some goals but are disadvantaged compared to lobbyists with access to staff and resources, groups that lack resources or staff operate at a marked disadvantage compared with other groups. Of course, resources and staff do not guarantee success, because staff need to possess various group-process skills to be effective.

Task Groups in Their Context

Groups exist in a context that can facilitate or impede their work. Groups have varying degrees of autonomy; while some of them are given considerable independence, others become political appendages of officials who establish them. These latter groups may be unable to establish sufficient autonomy to allow them to function at a high level. Effective groups need to obtain some independence if they wish to develop their own identities, while still maintaining linkages to officials in their environment.[52]

Forming Coalitions

Policy advocates frequently want to pool the resources of several groups into a single coalition that has a "common cause" to seek policy reforms. Coalitions are often temporary associations created to provide support for a specific issue, such as a piece of legislation. (We discuss ongoing associations, called "networks," subsequently.)

Why do policy practitioners seeking policy reforms for oppressed populations particularly need coalitions? As Case 11.1 suggests, groups representing relatively poor, powerless, or stigmatized segments of the population have an uphill battle, because powerful interests and public apathy or opposition often impede social reforms. Moreover, relatively powerful groups have coalitions of their own, such as coalitions of trade associations, agricultural interests, and tax-cutting groups. The U.S. Chamber of Commerce has state-level affiliates, as well as a powerful national organization, that lobby legislatures extensively and that often oppose social reforms. With respect to specific issues, such as abortion and gun control, coalitions present conservative positions to legislatures. When confronting these obstacles, reformers must increase their power through their own coalitions and networks.

Coalitions are different than many task groups, such as committees within specific organizations, because they bring the representatives of disparate organizations into a single group that seeks common action. The representatives agree to share the costs and labor of their shared endeavor in a sort of division of labor. When seeking to enact a piece of legislation, for example, one member of a coalition might handle mailings, another member might lobby, and another member might organize a constituency to telephone legislators at critical intervals.[53]

Coalitions can be successfully organized by attending to some of the issues and dynamics of task groups that we have just discussed. As Milan Dluhy suggests, for example, successful coalitions need to evolve leadership through a small, executive council that meets frequently and invests considerable energy in planning and overseeing the coalition. A single person can spearhead a coalition, but a coalition obtains power through the *combined* efforts of different organizations and persons. Thus, a coalition is enhanced when a number of persons invest in its success. Indeed, because many persons participate, coalitions can share credit for their work, thus decreasing the chances that members will resent the publicity that a single person or organization receives.[54]

The group that leads the coalition must, most importantly, define its goals and mission. Do they seek to enact a single piece of legislation, place ongoing pressure on legislators (or agencies), educate and sensitize people about a social problem or population, develop innovative programs, or some combination of these or other goals? They have to decide, as well, when to disband the coalition or whether to transform it into an ongoing association (see our ensuing discussion of networks).

Having developed a mission, the coalition's leadership needs to divide labor. The leading group should establish subcommittees to focus on tasks, such as research, lobbying, developing a phone bank, obtaining funds, and public relations (including creating a newsletter and reporting events to the mass media). The central leadership group could perform the coalition's real work, but using committees encourages a broader range of persons to participate. (The chairpersons of the committees often sit on the central leadership council.) With a division of labor established, the leadership council meets on regular occasions to monitor the committees' work and to develop a coordinated strategy for accomplishing its work.[55]

The leaders of coalitions have to decide what kind of membership to seek. It is easier to form coalitions of like-minded persons and groups, because less effort will be needed to fashion agreements on policy and strategy matters. If someone wants to obtain greater funding for child-welfare functions in a local jurisdiction, for example, that person could form a relatively homogeneous coalition of children's advocates, social work leaders, and children's institutions. Coalitions that represent a broader range of perspectives are more challenging to develop and maintain, because their leaders have to devote more time to developing a consensus on goals and strategy. Yet coalitions with relatively heterogeneous membership sometimes have more clout because they include members who can appeal to different kinds of legislators, agencies, and citizens. Assume, for example, that the local chamber of commerce joined the aforementioned coalition; its leaders might not share some assumptions with children's advocates, but they might be able to convince some moderate or conservative politicians to support funding increases for child-welfare services.

Establishing Networks

While coalitions are usually temporary alliances of groups for joint action that end when they have accomplished their purpose, policy practitioners also establish ongoing networks of persons and organizations. On a regular basis, these networks inform members about certain kinds of legislation, increase their members' political awareness, and foster the members' participation in the political process.[56] Indeed, Rand Martin's organization, the AIDS-oriented Lobby for Individual Freedom and Equality, is a network because it is an ongoing organization with a governing council.

Assume that persons interested in child-welfare reforms in a state wanted some mechanism for sharing information about legislation, hearing about program innovations in different counties, and keeping abreast of national legislation. Envisioning their network as an ongoing organization with agency affiliates and individual members, they might establish an executive council that would establish a division of labor, central offices, and a newsletter. This executive committee would schedule occasional meetings and workshops to supplement its newsletter. Like a coalition, it could mobilize the pooled efforts of its membership to support or oppose important pieces of legislation.[57]

ADDRESSING DYSFUNCTIONAL GROUP PROCESSES

We have discussed some attributes of effective task groups, coalitions, and networks. The effectiveness of these groups often hinges on policy practitioners' ability to intervene skillfully when problems arise.

The degree to which practitioners can intervene depends on the position they hold in the group. If staff usually stay in the background and facilitate, leaders and members can more assertively participate in the give-and-take of a group's deliberations. While leaders directly shape agendas and procedures, staff usually offer leaders behind-the-scenes suggestions about them. While leaders often summarize and clarify members' statements and positions and see if agreement exists, members are often more free than leaders to state their opinions in a forthright way.

Despite the constraints and opportunities that are provided by these different roles, all participants can diagnose or anticipate specific problems. When a task group or coalition loses momentum, for example, someone can ponder whether the problem lies with a failure to develop a coherent mission, inadequate leadership, flawed internal processes, inadequate procedures, flawed structures, an inadequate process of deliberations, or insufficient resources. We make diagnoses by observing the group's operations from the vantage point of our role in the group. We often form our judgments, as well, from discussions with other participants who may, for example, complain about a facet of the task force or coalition. We may also decide that something is wrong when we observe specific group outcomes, such as poor attendance and failure to achieve specific tasks.

Having diagnosed the problem, a participant in a task group needs to evolve a corrective strategy, often in tandem with other persons. Interventions include having behind-the-scenes discussions, developing ideas during group deliberations, assuming some leadership functions, using power, mediating, directly assuming specific tasks, using humor, and having discussions with persons and institutions external to the group.

Group members can make many kinds of comments during meetings to help develop ideas and proposals. They might say, "Don't we need to spend more time discussing this idea?", "Isn't it time to reach closure?", "Can we couple this idea with one that was made earlier?", and "Is there a different way to look at this problem?" They can suggest certain procedures to consider ideas, such as "Shouldn't we break up into smaller groups to seek solutions to this problem?"[58]

Even when they are not leaders, group participants can assume some leadership functions on specific occasions. Assume, for example, that a leader appears to move a group prematurely toward closure on a specific issue; a member or a staff member can say, "I would like to hear more about another option that was briefly raised a few minutes ago." Persons adept at the use of parliamentary tactics can sometimes use them to inject new perspectives and delay decisions. Members can directly contact leaders between meetings to add additional issues to agendas or to register their opinions on procedural, process, or structural matters. Of course, members and staff can risk alienating leaders or can erroneously usurp their functions if they do not use discretion.[59]

As in any collectivity, participants in groups have power resources. It might be nice if groups' deliberations and processes were purely reflective and scholarly in nature, but political realities often intrude. Disagreements often develop about specific issues or even the leadership, processes, or structure of groups. Participants often use their power resources to shape decisions, whether by invoking their expertise, asserting their authority, or suggesting parliamentary procedures that they think will give them an advantage over someone else.[60] Members sometimes try to influence other members' positions by interceding with them between meetings. Factions that adhere to specific positions often develop within groups.

People need to use power resources in groups with discretion and without overriding the normal, deliberative group processes. Excessive use of power resources by the group members can render them miniature legislative bodies whose members substitute threats, coercion, and parliamentary maneuvers for normal deliberative processes. At the same time, however, power resources sometimes need to be used to overcome stalemates, stop destructive activities such as scapegoating, bring acceptable decisions to "important players" in a group's environment, or make groups more responsive to the needs that they have neglected.

We discussed the use of mediation in Chapter Nine. All groups need persons willing to mediate at specific points in their deliberations, particularly when groups become polarized into competing factions.[61] Mediators can help group members identify their common values and the benefits of compromises. They can suggest specific structural or process strategies that diminish conflict, such as bringing in an outside facilitator with a neutral perspective. They can identify specific compromises that may allow conflicting sides to believe that their central concerns have been addressed.

We have noted that persuaders often use humor to defuse conflict. Effective group participants inject humor into their deliberations at key points to ease tension, place members at ease, and encourage persons not to take their positions (at least on some occasions) too seriously.[62] Humor can sometimes help in discussing specific group problems, as when a leader says, "At the rate we're proceeding, all the legislators we know will be dead before we come up with a bill."

Participants in groups or subcommittees can sometimes "take the bull by the horns" by volunteering to undertake difficult or conflict-producing tasks that other members shun. When a subcommittee completes a task or develops a position on a difficult issue, for example, it gives all group members a sense of accomplishment and momentum.

SUMMARY

We have discussed some interactional skills associated with power in policy practice. These include methods of developing power resources and skills in working with task groups, coalitions, and networks.

To enact policy, practitioners should understand the following:

- How policy practitioners develop power resources
- How members of specific outgroups encounter challenges when seeking and using power
- The psychology of power as illustrated by intimidation and assertiveness
- The dynamics of task groups, including committees and coalitions

Policymaking does not occur on a level playing field, because some persons and interests possess more power resources than others. Formal authority in bureaucratic and policymaking hierarchies, access to resources and powerful constituencies, and policymaking skills give some participants an advantage. Considerable theory and evidence nonetheless suggest that individuals and groups can often shape policy outcomes by using power resources, such as expertise, autonomy, indispensability, reward, and coercion to advance their policy preferences.

Persons can attain power and knowledge about specific systems, such as agencies or legislatures, by building their credibility, networking, enhancing their visibility in specific settings, and developing links with external groups and organizations.

People who have a victim mentality or believe that using power is unethical or unprofessional often impede their own ability to participate in policy deliberations. Such passivity makes them unlikely to influence the selection of policies. This failure often strengthens their fatalism and their sense of victimization. When subjected to intimidating behaviors by other persons, policy practitioners need to diagnose the situation and evolve corrective strategies, such as honest, authentic communication.

Policy practitioners also need skills in working with, developing, and using groups. They have to learn how to work with existing organizations, such as advocacy groups, when engaging in policy practice. Whether as staff, members or leaders, they need skills to work with community-based or agency-based task groups, such as committees, chapters of professional organizations, or local advocacy groups. They may need to work with coalitions or networks formed to pool several resources.

When in task groups or when acting by themselves, policy practitioners need skills in developing and implementing political strategy, where they develop an overarching plan to use power resources to achieve their policy goals. We devote the next chapter to methods of developing strategy.

Suggested Readings

BUILDING PERSONAL CREDIBILITY

Richard Emerson, "Power-Dependence Relations," *American Sociological Review* 27 (February 1962): 31–40.

Bruce Jansson and June Simmons, "Building Department or Unit Power Within Human Service Organizations: Empirical Findings and Theory Building," *Administration in Social Work* 8 (Fall 1984): 41–50.

Bruce Jansson and June Simmons, "The Ecology of Social Work Departments: Empirical Findings and Strategy Implications," *Social Work in Health Care* 11 (Winter 1985): 1–16.
Christopher Matthews, *Hardball: How Politics Is Played* (New York: Summit Books, 1988).

NETWORKING

Rosabeth Kanter, *Men and Women of the Corporation* (New York: Basic Books, 1977), pp. 129–163, 181–197.
Noel Tichy, *Strategic Change: Technology, Politics, and Culture* (New York: Wiley, 1983), pp. 69–94.
J. McIver Weatherford, *Tribes on the Hill* (New York: Rawson, Wade, 1981), pp. 87–111, 250–253.

WORKING WITH TASK GROUPS

Milan Dluhy, *Building Coalitions in the Human Services* (Newbury Park, CA: Sage, 1990).
Paul Ephross and Thomas Vassil, *Groups that Work* (New York: Columbia University Press, 1988).
Irving Janis, *Victims of Groupthink* (Boston: Houghton Mifflin, 1972).
John Tropman, Harold Johnson, and Elmer Tropman, *The Essentials of Committee Management* (Chicago: Nelson-Hall, 1979).

Notes

1. See Herbert Simons, *Persuasion*, 2nd ed. (New York: Random House, 1986), p. 130. Also see discussion of credibility by George Brager, Harry Specht, and James Torczyner, *Community Organizing*, 2nd ed. (New York: Columbia University Press, 1987), pp. 342–347.
2. Christopher Matthews, *Hardball: How Politics Is Played* (New York: Summit Books, 1988), pp. 144–352.
3. Rochelle Stanford, "Beleaguered Lobbyists for the Poor—Taking Allies Where They Can Find Them, *National Journal* 12 (September 20, 1980): 1556–1560.
4. Richard Emerson, "Power-Dependence Relations," American *Sociological Review* 27 (February 1962): 31–40, and D. J. Hickson et al., "A Strategic Contingencies Theory of Organizational Power," *Administrative Science Quarterly* 16 (June 1971): 216–229.
5. For research findings on power-dependence theory in hospital settings with social work departments, see Bruce Jansson and June Simmons, "Building Department or Unit Power Within Human Service Organizations: Empirical Findings and Theory Building," *Administration in Social Work* 8 (Fall 1984): 41–44, 49–50.
6. See Bruce Jansson and June Simmons, "The Ecology of Social Work Departments: Empirical Findings and Strategy Implications," *Social Work in Health Care* 11 (Winter 1985): 1–16.
7. Bruce Jansson and June Simmons, "The Survival of Social Work Units in Host Organizations," *Social Work* 31 (September 1986): 342.
8. Joel Fleishman, "Self-Interest and Political Integrity," in Joel Fleishman, Lance Leibman, and Mark Moore, eds., *Public Duties: The Moral Obligations of Government Officials* (Cambridge, MA: Harvard University Press, 1981), pp. 67–77.
9. Eugene Bardach, *The Skill Factor in Politics* (Berkeley and Los Angeles: University of California Press, 1972), pp. 204–206, 216–220.
10. Jansson and Simons, "Survival of Social Work Units," p. 341.
11. Matthews, *Hardball*, pp. 207–209.
12. Ibid., pp. 203–204.

13. J. McIver Weatherford, *Tribes on the Hill* (New York: Rawson, Wade, 1981), pp. 87–111.
14. Matthews, *Hardball*, pp. 194–211.
15. Noel Tichy, *Strategic Change: Technology, Politics, and Culture* (New York: Wiley, 1983), pp. 69–94.
16. Weatherford, *Tribes on the Hill*, pp. 20–24. Also see Tom Peters and Nancy Austin, "MBWA (Managing by Walking Around)," *California Management Review* 28 (Fall 1985): 9–34.
17. Matthews, *Hardball*, pp. 21–33.
18. Ibid., pp. 59–73.
19. Rosabeth Kanter, *Men and Women of the Corporation* (New York: Basic Books, 1977), pp. 181–184.
20. Weatherford, *Tribes on the Hill*, pp. 87–111.
21. Ibid., pp. 87–111.
22. Ibid., pp. 250–253.
23. See how a social movement led to legislative reform in Wyoming in William Whitaker, "Organizing Social Action Coalitions: WIC Comes to Wyoming," in Maryann Mahaffey and John Hanks, eds., *Practical Politics: Social Work and Political Response* (Silver Spring, MD: National Association of Social Workers, 1982), pp. 136–158.
24. See Frances Piven and Richard Cloward, "New Prospects for Voter Registration Reform," *Social Policy* 18 (Winter 1988): 2–15.
25. Kanter, *Men and Women of the Corporation*.
26. Ibid., pp. 158–160, 196–197.
27. Ibid., pp. 196–197.
28. Linda MacNeilage and Kathleen Adams discuss various strategies in *Assertiveness at Work* (Englewood Cliffs, NJ: Prentice-Hall, 1982).
29. Jansson and Simmons, "Survival of Social Work Units," pp. 339–340.
30. David Mechanic, "Sources of Power of Lower Participants in Complex Organizations," *Administrative Science Quarterly* 7 (December 1962): 349–364.
31. Michael Lipsky, *Street-Level Bureaucrats: Dilemmas of the Individual and Public Service* (New York: Russell Sage Foundation, 1980), pp. 13–18.
32. John Tropman, Harold Johnson, and Elmer Tropman, *The Essentials of Committee Management* (Chicago: Nelson-Hall, 1979), pp. ix–xiii.
33. Paul Ephross and Thomas Vassil, *Groups that Work* (New York: Columbia University Press, 1988), p. 1.
34. Tropman, Johnson, and Tropman, *Essentials of Committee Management*, pp. xiii–xiv.
35. Ibid., pp. 179–186.
36. Ephross and Vassil, *Groups that Work*, pp. 16–18, 22–24.
37. Tropman, Johnson, and Tropman, *Essentials of Committee Management*, pp. 196–203.
38. Dennis Chamot, "Professional Employees Turn to Unions," *Harvard Business Review* 54 (May 1976): 119–127.
39. Saul Alinsky, *Reveille for Radicals* (New York: Vintage Books, 1969).
40. Simons, *Persuasion*, pp. 253–261.
41. Samuel Bacharach and Edward Lawler, *Power and Politics in Organizations* (San Francisco: Jossey-Bass, 1980), pp. 48–69; and Brager, Specht, and Torczyner, *Community Organizing*, pp. 193–200.
42. Robert Bales and Fred Strodtbeck, "Phases in Group Problem Solving," in Dorwin Cartwright and Alvin Zander, eds., *Group Dynamics: Research and Theory* (New York: Harper & Row, 1968), pp. 380–398. Also see David Sink, "Success and Failure in Voluntary Community Networks," *New England Journal of Human Services* 7 (1987): 25–30.

43. See Bacharach and Lawler, *Power and Politics in Organizations*, pp. 48–69; Brager, Specht, and Torczyner, *Community Organizing*, pp. 193–200; and Bardach, *Skill Factor in Politics*, pp. 215–230.
44. Tropman, Johnson, and Tropman, *Essentials of Committee Management*, pp. 5–23. For a compilation of literature on leadership, see Ralph Stogdill, ed., *Handbook of Leadership: A Survey of Theory and Research* (New York: Free Press, 1974).
45. Tropman, Johnson, and Tropman, *Essentials of Committee Management*, pp. 38–48.
46. Ibid., pp. 24–37.
47. Ibid., pp. 63–139.
48. Ephross and Vassil, *Groups that Work*, pp. 84–87, 166–183.
49. Irving Janis, *Victims of Groupthink* (Boston: Houghton Mifflin, 1972).
50. Ibid.
51. Bales and Strodtbeck, "Phases in Group Problem Solving."
52. Ephross and Vassil, *Groups that Work*, pp. 84–87, 166–183.
53. Milan Dluhy, *Building Coalitions in the Human Services* (Newbury Park, CA: Sage, 1990), pp. 53–57.
54. Ibid., pp. 59–63.
55. Ibid., p. 62.
56. Ibid., p. 52.
57. Marilyn Bagwell and Sallee Clements, *A Political Handbook for Health Professionals* (Boston: Little, Brown, 1985), pp. 189–194.
58. Ephross and Vassil, *Groups that Work*, p. 164.
59. Tropman, Johnson, and Tropman, *Essentials of Committee Management*, p. 45.
60. There is surprisingly little discussion of positive and needed uses of power in committees and task groups. Power is usually viewed as destructive of group processes.
61. Jay Folberg and Alison Taylor, *Mediation* (San Francisco: Jossey-Bass, 1984).
62. Ephross and Vassil, *Groups that Work*, pp. 158–159.

Chapter Twelve
Developing Political Strategy

We have emphasized the nature and varieties of power, but we have not yet discussed how policy practitioners use their power resources to create political strategy in agency, community, or legislative settings. *Political strategy* is "a planned sequence of actions and verbal exchanges in a specific time frame to increase the likelihood that a proposal will be enacted."

A CASE FROM THE HUMAN SERVICES

Recall that Case 10.1 discussed a social work intern's efforts to obtain a preventive program in a mental health agency. (The program would provide eight-week crisis services to the children of parents who were institutionalized because of their mental problems.) Although it was important for her to identify her sources of power, such as her connections with a preceptor (Mr. Jones), she had to incorporate these kinds of power into a coherent political strategy.

Before she could develop a political strategy, however, she had to assess the political realities of the case. She quickly decided that many political barriers existed, such as many top officials' dislike of preventive programs, the agency's scarce resources, and patterns of competition among the agency, area hospitals, and psychiatrists. However, she also identified various individuals and forces that supported or could support her innovation, such as Mr. Jones and some officials, who wanted to develop innovative projects that would enhance the agency's prestige.

After considering these realities, she and Mr. Jones developed a two-phase strategy. They would begin with a low-key approach, where the intern would develop a pilot project without consulting or seeking approval from highly placed officials, and would proceed to a formal presentation to the executive director after the project had already demonstrated its success.

In this chapter, we will further explore forming such strategies in the context of political realities. Social workers need these kinds of political skills because, as Case 10.1 suggests, even relatively small and inexpensive proposals often encounter opposition from multiple sources. Ill-considered strategy often leads to failure; had this intern *immediately* sought approval from the executive director for the project, for example, she would probably have failed to obtain it. Although intelligent and skillfully implemented strategy does not guarantee success, it often increases the likelihood that policy practitioners will obtain their policy preferences.

ESTABLISHING SOME OBJECTIVES

To develop intelligent strategy, policy practitioners have to first answer the question, Why am I participating in the political process? They have to decide what side they are taking and the degree and kind of policy changes they seek.

Determining a Position

Strategists must first decide whether to do the following:

1. Initiate their own proposal (an affirmative position)
2. Change others' proposals (an amending position)
3. Oppose others' initiatives (an opposing position)
4. Assume no role (a bystander position)

These choices are important because they commit the strategist to certain obligations and risks. People who develop a proposal have to invest considerable time in research, discussion, meetings, and negotiations and may expose themselves to criticism along the way. Advantages accrue to those who initiate proposals, however. By seizing the initiative, they make it more likely that their ideas will figure prominently in ensuing policy deliberations.

In contrast to strategists who initiate proposals, some people decide to amend them. Assume, for example, that someone is generally in accord with another person's position but does not wish to invest time in developing a proposal. By amending the proposal during policy deliberations, this person can advance his or her preferences for specific changes.

People sometimes assume a blocking role to stop the enactment of an objectionable proposal. It is easier in some respects to block proposals than to develop them, because opposers need only pinpoint their flaws, which is simpler than developing them in the first instance. Blockers encounter risks of their own, however. They can be perceived as naysayers who lack constructive alternatives and may be accused of opposing changes because they benefit from existing policies.

Strategists sometimes adopt bystander roles; that is, they remain aloof from the deliberations over an issue. They may believe that they lack power to influence outcomes, want to save their scarce political resources for a future issue, believe that involvement in deliberations will require them to antagonize one or both sides in a controversy, or want to stay on the sidelines until they can assume a mediating role.

Strategists' roles often depend on their analysis of a proposal's prospects. If the prognosis for passage of a proposal is extremely bleak, for example, some practitioners are reluctant to develop proposals, just as they might not obstruct a proposal that had attracted widespread support. However, policy practitioners sometimes oppose objectionable policies or develop proposals in the face of overwhelming odds, whether because they believe fundamental principles are at stake or because they want to convince some segment of their constituency that they will champion their interests.

Selecting Policy Changes

Policy practitioners must decide whether to seek relatively major or incremental changes. This choice, can often be difficult to make. A policy practitioner may believe that a particular group or program needs major changes. Fundamental changes are often not politically feasible, however, and require relatively large investments of time and energy.[1] Political realities contribute to this choice; if a considerable number of people oppose a specific initiative, for example, policy practitioners may have to settle for relatively modest changes in existing policy. In some cases, policy practitioners aim only to educate people about a problem, because it is impossible to develop and enact policies if people do not first believe that a problem exists.

Selecting a Time Frame

Policy practitioners often ask, "Do we want specific changes to be enacted in the short term, such as during an upcoming meeting, the present year, or the present session of a legislature, or will we accept a longer time frame?"[2] People with a long-term perspective do not need to develop strategy that will bring instant results, although they encounter the formidable challenge of maintaining interest in an issue when tangible results are not forthcoming. Selecting a time frame depends both on the distribution of power and the practitioner's policy objectives; when the power distribution is unfavorable for a proposal, for example, it is difficult to enact it immediately, no matter how skillful its proponents.

GROUNDING STRATEGY IN CURRENT REALITIES

Political strategy must be firmly linked to existing realities, including power distribution, contextual factors, situational realities, impending developments, and the setting.

The Power Distribution

Kurt Lewin, the noted social psychologist, pioneered the concept of force-field analysis to assess the distribution of power in specific situations.[3] To obtain a rough estimate of the support for a proposal, Lewin suggests that we enumerate persons (by name) and indicate the strength of their support or opposition in numeric terms, say, from 1 (weak support or opposition) to 10 (strong support or opposition). We can graphically illustrate their names and their positions by placing the opponents on the underside of a line and the proponents on the topside (Figure 12.1). The line lengths correspond to the strength of their opposition to or support of the policy. We can discern the preponderance of sentiment in opposition to the policy in Figure 12.1 by comparing the number and length of lines beneath the horizontal line to the lines above it.

To gather a complete depiction of the strength of support of and opposition to a specific policy proposal, we would need to obtain considerable information. First, we must know someone's relative ability or power to shape policy on a specific issue, because people with such power could be particularly critical to our strategy development. A committee chair who considers an issue, for example, often has more power than someone who does not occupy this strategic position. Second, we need to estimate the relative salience or importance that specific individuals attach to an issue. Someone might have strong convictions about an issue and be well-positioned to affect policy, for example, but not become involved in the issue, whether because he believed it fell within someone else's purview or because he was more interested in other issues.

William Coplin and Michael O'Leary have developed a simple scoring system to assess the distribution of power and sentiment with respect to an issue.[4] Take the example of a family of four who must consider two issues: whether to have Grandma move into the house after a recent bout of illness

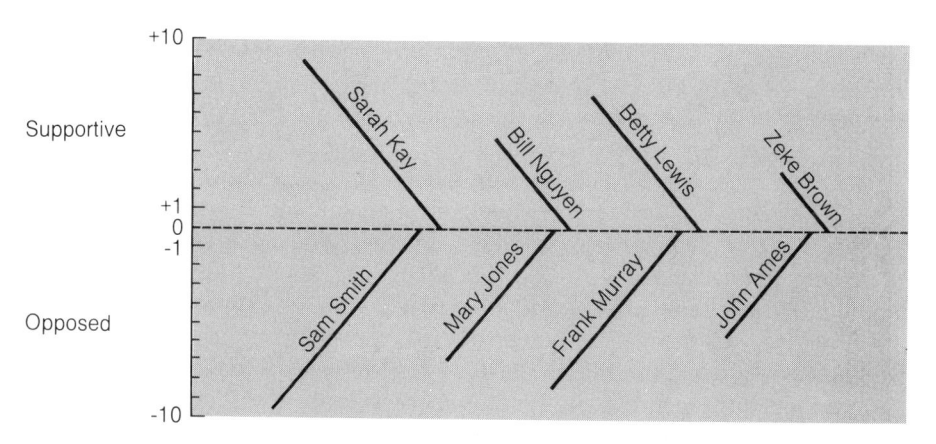

FIGURE 12.1
Support and opposition to a measure

and whether to allow the eighteen-year-old son to own his own car. The two parents (Mary and Frank) and the two children (Sam and Diane) have decided to reach these decisions democratically, but, as we noted in the preceding chapter, policymaking does not usually occur on a level playing field. Assume that we know the family well enough to construct the data in Table 12.1, which represents the positions, salience, and power of the family members. (The initials M, F, S, and D stand, respectively, for the mother [Mary], the father [Frank], the son [Sam], and the daughter [Diane].)

First, we give each person a score with respect to their formal positions on the issues (extending from −10, very negative, to +10, very favorable). Table 12.1 shows that Mary strongly favors allowing her mother to reside in their home (she receives a score of 10), whereas Frank opposes the move (he receives a score of −5). The children are mildly supportive and receive scores of 2 and 4. *All* family members support allowing Sam to have a car, respectively receiving scores of 4, 2, 10, and 8, although, predictably, the two children support this policy more strongly than either of their parents.

Second, we score each person with respect to the salience, or importance, that they give each issue on a scale from 1 (low salience) to 10 (high salience). Both parents attach considerable importance to each of the issues; hence, their scores of 8 on the issue of Grandma and 7 on the issue of Sam's car. The children attach much more importance to the issue of the car (they both score a 7 on Issue 2), while attaching less importance to Grandma's residence in their home (their scores are 3 and 4 on salience).

Third, we estimate people's relative power to influence choices on a scale from 1 (low power) to 4 (high power). The parents possess far more power than the children; thus, they score a 3 on each issue, while the children score a 1 or 2 on each issue.

To obtain an overall reading of the distribution of sentiment, salience, and position, we multiply each person's scores on each issue. Mary receives a score of 240 (10 × 8 × 3) on Issue 1 and 84 (4 × 7 × 3) on Issue 2, whereas Frank receives scores of −120 on the issue of Grandma (−5 × 8 × 3) and 42 (2 × 7 × 3) on the issue of Sam's car. The two children receive considerably higher (more favorable) scores of 140 and 56 on the issue of the car than on the issue of Grandma, where they receive scores of 6 and 16.

After finding people's total score on each issue, we simply add the participants' scores on each issue to obtain a total for issue 1 and 2. Because a higher score indicates a more favorable prognosis for a proposal, it appears that Sam is more likely to have a car (84 + 42 + 140 + 56 = 322) than is Grandma to obtain residence in the family home (240 + −120 + 6 + 16 = 142). Table 12.1 shows that a single *negative* score by a powerful participant (father or grandmother) can markedly decrease the likelihood that a specific issue will be enacted.

A numbers approach to force-field analysis may seem far-fetched, but the skeptical reader should realize that politicians in legislative bodies sometimes use this kind of analysis, crude and imperfect as it may be. They keep numeric tallies to determine the prognosis for specific pieces of legislation.[5] If a proposal

TABLE 12.1
Estimating the Distribution of Sentiment, Salience, and Power

	Issue 1: Grandmother				Issue 2: Car			
	M	F	S	D	M	F	S	D
Positions on the issues (−10 to +10)	10	−5	2	4	4	2	10	8
Salience (1 to 10)	8	8	3	4	7	7	7	7
Power to influence the outcome of this issue (1 to 4)	3	3	1	1	3	3	2	1
Totals for each participant (multiply the numbers down each colum)	240	−120	6	16	84	42	140	56
Grand total for each issue (add the totals for each person)		142				322		

receives an extremely low or unfavorable score, policy practitioners may decide the situation is hopeless, unless they develop strategy that enables them to change the positions, alter the salience, or modify the power of persons who support their position.

Moreover, identifying important participants, as well as their positions, salience, and power, helps policy practitioners develop strategy.[6] The data in Table 12.1 suggest several strategy options. Assume that Mary wants Grandma to move into her home. She could try to bring Frank at least to a neutral position, she could hope to reduce the salience he attached to the issue (perhaps by contending it would be a brief stay), or she could try to isolate him from the decisionmaking process, thus reducing his power to influence the outcome. She could seek to alter the children's positions, salience, and power, perhaps by promising them support for the car in return for their support on the grandmother issue! Table 12.1 does not include coalitional power, but Mary could increase her power by "ganging up on" Frank, which means forming a coalition with her children. She could also try to add new participants to the struggle.[7] Perhaps she could persuade Grandma to make an impassioned plea to Frank, or secure the family physician's support, if he says that residence in the family's home would be more beneficial to Grandma than entering a nursing home. To convince Frank that other people would share in entertaining and caring for Grandma, Mary could enlist support from other relatives, who might even offer to visit Grandma after her move to the family home.

We should note certain dangers in force-field analysis. If people wrongly estimate others' positions, they may falsely judge a position's prognosis. Misreading evidence may lead them to commit two kinds of errors: they may falsely refrain from pursuing a proposal that could be enacted, or they may promote a proposal that cannot be enacted.

These errors in calculating positions, salience, and power can be compounded by another kind of error. When we estimate at one time that a proposal is or is not politically feasible, we sometimes assume that the current distribution of sentiment, salience, and power will remain constant in the future. In fact, positions, salience, and power often change during the course of deliberations. Indeed, effective reformers are skillful at transforming bleak and seemingly hopeless situations into more positive ones by developing and implementing strategy. Indeed, our discussion of some of Mary's strategy options suggests how strategists can modify existing realities.

These cautionary notes about force-field analysis do not render it useless. If we make no effort to gauge the support and opposition to specific measures, we can often blindly commit ourselves to issues that are not politically feasible. Additionally, if we do not estimate the degree of difficulty in enacting a policy, we cannot estimate the time and political resources that we will require. It is better to go into battle, some would say, with our eyes open to the realities that we confront.

Identifying Contextual Realities

Although it is useful to tally the relative support of and opposition to a policy, we need to supplement these calculations with broader considerations of *why* certain persons take specific positions or how they are likely to act when an issue enters into policy deliberations. Analyzing prior traditions of deliberation, vested interests, and participants' underlying values provides a more complete understanding of people's positions and likely actions than does merely estimating their current positions.

Prior traditions. Many issues may have been considered on prior occasions. Decisionmakers, interest groups, and the general public respond to policies depending on their recollections or reports and accounts of the prior deliberations.[8] Deliberations are more likely to be conflictual, for example, when an issue has been associated with ideological polarization on prior occasions, as illustrated by controversy that arises whenever Congress considers national health insurance, gun control, or abortion. Indeed, many politicians avoid such issues, because they do not want to become embroiled in controversy that pits various constituents against one another or that commit them to an extended legislative battle with uncertain outcomes. In organizations, too, participants sometimes refrain from reintroducing issues or policies that have been associated with controversy on prior occasions.

Policy practitioners can sometimes erroneously conclude, however, that traditions associated with an issue will continue. After President Nixon's veto of legislation that would have funded a national day-care program (among other things), children's advocates found it difficult to persuade many legislators to reintroduce or support similar legislation. But a determined coalition nearly obtained the enactment of major day-care legislation in 1988 when a combination of factors, including pressure from corporations and from an expanded pool of female workers, created a more favorable environment. They finally prevailed in 1990 with the enactment of the Child Care and Development Block Grant. Indeed, skillful strategists try to offset the negative effects of traditions by emphasizing developments that have made a position more feasible than on a prior occasion. Supporters of the day-care proposal in 1988, for example, realized that many more women were in the workforce than in the early 1970s and that many corporations had become convinced that they needed subsidized day-care to attract and retain female employees.[9]

Vested interests. People often form positions on specific issues out of self-interest. In some cases, they fear that policies will harm their interests.[10] Politicians may worry, for example, that a certain policy will antagonize some of their constituents, enable the other party to expand its constituency, or allow an opposing politician to obtain an electoral advantage. An executive of a social agency or government bureaucracy may fear that a proposal will shift resources or program responsibilities to rival agencies, impose controls or regulations on their activities, or diminish their revenues. Alternatively, people support specific issues or policies because they believe that the policies will enhance their power, prestige, or resources.

It can be difficult to predict how people will calculate the impact of a policy on their interests. Specific politicians may not know how their constituents will respond to a proposal, may mistakenly assume that constituents will support or oppose them, or may not realize that some losses, such as antagonism from one interest group, will be offset by gains from other groups. Skillful strategists often try to identify a position's positive effects on the interests of those people whose support they hope to garner. For example, supporters of the day-care proposal in 1988 told many politicians that they risked losing a large share of the female vote if they opposed the proposal.[11]

Cohesion of likely opponents and proponents. Although we can sometimes calculate with considerable precision specific individuals' positions on an issue or policy, our analysis is incomplete if we fail to examine their relationships. Assume, for example, that we discover that support for and opposition to a proposed policy are evenly balanced. This discovery makes us predict a stalemate, because neither side will prevail. To our astonishment, the proponents subsequently win a one-sided victory because their close working relationships allow them to evolve strategy and to work together to implement it. Their opponents are not, by contrast, unified. Moreover, the nature of the leadership associated with specific issues is often vitally important. If leaders with knowledge, commitment, political expertise, and considerable power support a specific issue, it is more likely to be successful. Moreover, successful leaders are adept at assembling and maintaining supportive coalitions.

Situational Realities

Situational realities often shape the course of policy deliberations. In legislative settings, for example, specific policies are often influenced by upcoming elections, the balance of power between contending parties, rivalries among powerful legislators, rivalries among members of different legislative chambers, the budgetary situation, changes in leadership, the other proposals vying for attention, and the remaining time in a legislative session.[12]

These kinds of background factors all influence people's interest in specific issues and the extent of conflict associated with them. When national elections are imminent, for example, politicians of both parties begin to jockey for position; they want to take "out-front" positions that will appeal to major segments of their existing constituencies or draw some of their opponents' constituents to their side. For example, liberal Democrats from northern cities may support certain social programs and publicly oppose conservative initiatives, such as efforts to rescind regulations that promote affirmative action. Conservatives not only promote issues that will solidify support among their traditional constituencies, but also advance social measures that will attract some Democrats to their cause; thus, George Bush developed a tax-credit scheme to fund daycare for middle-class women in the summer of 1988 to counter a more liberal proposal from Michael Dukakis.[13] By the same token, however, impending elections may make members of both parties avoid issues offering no partisan advantage or fraught with significant political risks. For example, some liberal Democrats who normally support federal financing of abortions may avoid this divisive issue in the year preceding an election.

Personal and institutional rivalries often exacerbate conflict and efforts to initiate proposals. Legislative committees may jealously attempt to preserve their jurisdiction over certain issues; when their leaders hear rumors—for example, that another committee will soon develop a proposal—some of the members may hurriedly develop their own proposal to preempt the issue. This kind of rivalry can exist between committees within a legislative chamber or between rival committees in different chambers, as between leaders in the House Committee on Education and Labor and those in the Senate Committee on Labor and Public Welfare. In the early phases of so-called child-development legislation in 1971, for example, these two committees developed proposals amid considerable rivalry.[14]

Situational factors also influence the political process in organizations. Neither elections nor party rivalries exist in organizations, but the succession of leaders, internal institutional and personal rivalries, tensions between the boards and staff of agencies, budget realities, and changes in external funding can significantly influence the politics of specific proposals.[15] After a new executive takes over, for example, a relatively fluid political situation exists; the executive and individuals and factions within the organization develop positions on issues on the policy agenda and seek support for them. Indeed, theorists contend that many major changes in organizational policies occur in the aftermath of new leadership.[16]

Institutional and personal rivalries pervade most organizations as different factions and units vie for scarce resources, possess somewhat different views of where the organization should be heading, and seek recognition for their respective programs. As in legislative settings, these rivalries sometimes influence people's positions on specific proposals; thus, someone may oppose a rival's initiative simply because the rival proposed it or initiate a proposal to beat her to the punch. The structure of many organizations invites institutional rivalry, because they are divided into units that have overlapping jurisdictions and seek funds from the organization's limited budget.[17] Considerable competition often exists, for example, between nursing, psychology, and social-work units within hospitals as each seeks enlarged functions and budgets.

Predicting Future Developments

We have noted that calculating a policy's support can falsely imply that political interaction is static and can be analyzed only once. In fact, people change their positions on measures as supporters, opponents, and bystanders interact and as events unfold. Assume, for example, that a person who is relatively neutral about a policy proposal at Point 1 observes at Point 2 someone's nasty and unethical effort to steamroll her perspective. She may become so incensed by this power maneuver that she opposes the proposal. As this example illustrates, it is sometimes difficult to develop strategy, because people's positions on specific issues change during the give-and-take of the political process.

The political process also shapes people's strategies. Supporters of a measure may decide that they need only spirit a measure quietly through a legislative committee and onto the floor of Congress to secure its enactment. However, if they learn that opponents plan to attack the measure in emotional terms and publicize it in the mass media, they may quickly develop more militant strategies. Indeed, theorists have developed a body of knowledge called *game theory* that examines how people respond to opponents' tactical maneuvers.[18]

Because people change their positions during the political process, effective practitioners have to revise their strategy in response to anticipated and unexpected events.

Adapting Strategy to the Setting

Skillful policy strategists realize that they have to adapt their strategy to a specific setting. We discuss later in this chapter, for example, how agency politics differ from legislative politics. However, these are many types of agencies. If a win-win and team-building atmosphere characterizes some agencies, for example, other agencies have more conflictual relationships between staff or units. A legislative committee may have different norms and operating procedures than another committee. If the members of the House Committee on Labor and Education are used to relatively wide-open conflict between liberals and conservatives, for example, the members of the House and Senate appropriations committees have traditionally prided themselves on quiet, private deliberations, where they seek behind-the-scenes solutions to budgetary issues.[19] Policy practitioners must adapt their tactics to different settings' idiosyncrasies.

BUILDING SCENARIOS TO CONSTRUCT POLITICAL STRATEGY

Our discussion thus far has been oriented toward the *future* (setting objectives) and toward the *present* (examining current realities, such as the distribution of power and sentiment, germane to policy deliberations). Political strategy allows us to conceptually link the present with the future by identifying likely actions and verbal exchanges that will help practitioners obtain their policy preferences.

Developing Alternative Scenarios

Policy practitioners sort through a series of political options, much as a quarterback surveys possible plays to use in a tight situation. Indeed, creative strategists run through successive what-if scenarios in which they explore whether various actions or statements could help them obtain their policy preferences.[20]

To portray these what-if scenarios, imagine three possibilities. In Scenario 1, the policy practitioner asks, "What would happen if I (or my allies) made a *single* presentation to a decisionmaker, suggesting a course of action?" This presentation might involve a request that a problem be taken seriously enough to be placed on a committee's agenda, or suggest that a policy option be seriously considered. In some cases, this single presentation (a modest strategy) will suffice, particularly if the practitioner correctly assesses that a propitious and supportive environment exists.

When policy practitioners decide, however, that such a minimal strategy will probably be unsuccessful, they turn to other, more ambitious strategies. Practitioners sometimes develop at least two additional scenarios. In Scenario 2, the strategy is somewhat more ambitious; perhaps the single presentation is coupled with discussions with key decisionmakers in order to make them more sympathetic to a policy. Scenario 3 is even more ambitious and could involve developing a coalition, cultivating a constituency, coupling presentations with many personal discussions, allocating specific roles and tasks to a range of people, and mixing internal pressure with external pressure. As an example of ambitious strategy, in the early 1990s, a coalition of organizations, in which the National Organization for Women was a central participant, developed a legislative proposal for family leave, which would allow parents to obtain unpaid leave from work following the birth of a child, a parent's illness, or the death of a family member or close relative. Its members not only had personal liaisons with legislators and government officials, but also exerted extensive external pressures on congressional members through letter writing and articles in the mass media.

We will contrast the three preceding strategies with an improvised one. In some cases, policy practitioners decide *not* to develop a strategy, but to seize opportunities as they arise.[21] At an opportune moment, they may inject an idea into committee discussions, a staff meeting, or a conversation with an official in their organization. Improvisational strategies are sometimes useful because policy practitioners lack the time or do not know "the lay of the land" sufficiently to develop more refined strategies. However, unlike the three preceding strategies, improvisational strategies may not enable the policy practitioner to mobilize and use power resources systematically.

Policy practitioners need not invest major resources in this preliminary development of strategies, because they only delineate the *broad outlines* of strategy at this point. In effect, they ask, "Does this issue require a major investment of resources and time on my (and my allies') parts, or should we address this issue with a modest or improvisational strategy?"

Selecting a Strategy

Pragmatic considerations and stylistic preferences shape the selection of strategy. Policy practitioners obviously want to select a strategy that will help enact their policies, so they review strategy options in light of the realities we have discussed in this chapter. If their force-field analysis suggests that there is extraordinary opposition to their proposal, for example, they may select an ambitious, complex strategy that requires a significant investment of time and energy. Policy practitioners want a strategy sufficiently robust to offset the opposition that their proposal will likely encounter.

They must consider their own resources and time. Accordingly, they often seek a strategy that allows their measures to follow a "path of least resistance."[22] If a proposal can be enacted with a relatively simple strategy that requires few resources and little time, most policy practitioners will select it. Even when they fear a more ambitious one is needed, they may select a relatively modest strategy, because they lack time or place higher priority on another issue.

Practitioners' strategy choices are also influenced by their stylistic preferences. Individuals often have distinctive styles when participating in the political process, whether in legislative, community, or agency contexts. Consider the case of the 1992 presidential candidates.[23] Tom Harkin, the Democratic senator from Iowa, was an "old-fashioned populist" who championed social programs to help minorities and poor people at numerous points during his career. He was often less interested in having specific bills passed than in championing social and moral causes. Like Jesse Jackson, the candidate whose career began in the ministry and the civil rights movement, Harkin hoped to educate the public to the merits of an expansive welfare state. Paul Tsongas, the former senator from Massachusetts, was a centrist who focused on the economy in a low-key, academic manner, even giving long-winded lectures. He seemed *not* to want to incite conflict to the point of downplaying his liberal positions on various issues. As the quintessential "outsider," Jerry Brown, the former California governor, sought to distance himself from the political powers of the Democratic Party and identified himself with outgroups, such as the homeless and African Americans. Ross Perot also painted himself as an outsider to the extent that he developed an independent party; unlike the other politicians but like Tsongas, he preferred to focus on economic measures, complete with technical lectures on television. Bill Clinton was a curious combination of populist (as when he spoke like an outsider to Washington who wanted to reform national politics by bringing it closer to the common people) and insider (as when he freely sought and accepted funds and endorsements from various power figures).

These varied political styles suggest that each of us possesses distinctive approaches to politics. Some of us state our positions directly, whereas others discuss them in private deliberations. Some people like to precipitate conflict by advancing controversial positions, whereas others serve as mediators. Some people initiate and enact policies, whereas others prefer implementing roles.

Each of these styles has advantages and disadvantages. Mediators facilitate compromises, but are sometimes accused of failing to develop their own perspectives. Champions of ideological positions initiate bold changes, but sometimes lack compromise skills that are needed in the end. (Many persons perceived Harkin and Brown as ideologues.) Persons who only select "sure winners" or who avoid controversial issues are seen as lacking courage or leadership.

Policy practitioners' personal styles often extend to the political interaction that they favor. We will distinguish between high-conflict and polarized politics, high-conflict but consensual politics, low-conflict and technical politics, and moderate-conflict but compromise-oriented politics.[24] People who use a *high-conflict and polarized style,* such as those who introduce liberal versions of national health insurance legislation into Congress, deliberately choose controversial policy measures that they know will polarize others into supportive and opposing camps. Unafraid of conflict, such people do not hesitate to raise the stakes. Thus, a liberal who initiates a national health insurance plan would criticize the "self-serving tendencies" of the American Medical Association, the greed of health-care providers and insurance companies, and the inequalities of the current health-care system. This style of politics is useful in a number of situations. It can educate citizens and build reform-oriented constituencies, even when passage is unlikely. People can also use this style when they believe their side possesses a numeric majority in a deliberative body, such as Congress, or could obtain a majority if the proposal aroused the general public so much that they pressured their legislative representatives. When the Democrats obtained sweeping majorities of both congressional houses in the New Deal and the Great Society, Presidents Franklin Roosevelt and Lyndon Johnson, respectively, were able to obtain sweeping legislative reforms by using a conflictual style of politics.[25]

A *high-conflict and consensual style* occurs when policymakers want to obtain credit for a highly popular measure, such as increased funding for a program.

In such cases, both sides in a political conflict advance proposals that they claim will "do the most" for the program and contend that their opponent's proposal is insufficient. Because the measure is extremely popular, however, both sides seek an eventual solution in order not to be tagged as obstructionists; in the final analysis, they compromise with their opponents. In this style of politics, conflict is combined with a willingness to compromise, unlike the high-conflict and polarized style where both sides seek to defeat their opponents during a protracted period of conflict.

A *low-conflict and technical style* of politics is sometimes used when practitioners fear a measure will become enveloped in controversy if it is publicized or dramatized. Seeking to obtain passage, strategists portray an issue as "merely technical" or "small-scale." They shun publicity for the measure, provide a technical rationale for its passage, and make extensive use of parliamentary maneuvers, such as attaching the measure to another, more popular measure to usher it quietly and quickly through the legislative process.

Strategists seek a *moderate-conflict but compromise-oriented style* of politics when they want to foster a give-and-take process of deliberations.[26] The measure lacks widespread public support, cannot be presented as "merely technical," and is somewhat controversial. Its advocates want to encourage a process of deliberations that eventually produces a compromise that is acceptable to all parties. Unlike conflictual politics, however, and like the politics of technical issues, much of the compromising and amending process occurs in the proverbial "smoke-filled rooms" of committees and party caucuses.

Of course, strategists cannot always stimulate the style of politics that will lead to the enactment of their measure. Someone who favors the technical style may find that it becomes enveloped in polarized conflict. Conversely, someone who wants moderate conflict and a consensus may discover that the issue is widely dismissed as "merely technical" and generates only low conflict and an emphasis on the issue's technical aspects.

Although we have related these styles to legislative settings, they also exist in organizations. People in organizations sometimes stimulate polarized politics that divide their staff and officials into contending factions, although this occurs less frequently than in legislatures. On other occasions, people in organizations seek support for issues by portraying them as technical or minor. For example, someone may propose a temporary demonstration project to decrease opposition from those who would object to a major innovation.[27] Skillful strategists can use a variety of styles and adapt them to specific situations.

Revising the Strategy

The preceding discussion fails to capture the fluid nature of devising strategies. We have noted that it can be difficult to predict who is likely to support or oppose a specific policy. People cannot make strategy without anticipating how possible opponents will act. How cohesive and organized are they? For example, do they possess coalitions, leadership, and strategies, or are they merely scattered individuals? If they possess strategy, what is it likely to be, how are they likely to attack the substantive content of the proposal, which persons are they likely to try to convince, and what procedural powers might they use? Of course, strategists may have little or no idea about opponents' strategies, but they at least need to consider them.

To the extent that they can guess opponents' likely strategies, strategists need to decide whether and how to counter them. Assume that opponents assail a policy's costs. Proponents might show that it will reduce other costs, might alter the proposal to make it less costly, or might contend that the additional costs are offset by benefits to clients. Anticipating opponents' strategy enables proponents to more effectively counter it.

Interventions devised at Point 1 need to be revised later as policies evolve, as events unfold, as new configurations of support and opposition to a policy develop, and as opponents' strategies change. During revision, strategists encounter the same challenge that confronted them initially, which is how to capitalize on and strengthen the sources of support for their policy and how to offset or neutralize opposition.

During this process, the policy itself may change markedly. In congressional settings, for example, legislation is modified in the give-and-take of committee deliberations, in floor debates, and during negotiations between proponents of the bill and legislators and their aides.[28] At certain points, proponents concede to changing the legislation to decrease opposition to it, whereas in other cases, powerful people or factions impose changes on them.

Fleshing Out Strategy Details

Policy practitioners must identify which power resources will help them achieve their policy preferences in a specific situation. It is rarely sufficient to identify those power resources that, at a single and climactic moment, can help enact a policy. Instead, a sequence of power transactions, often extending over months or years, provides the groundwork that allows a proposal to be developed, obtain some initial clearances, and reach a culminating vote or process of ratification. A number of people may help devise and implement these power transactions. Strategy usually requires, then, the successive and repeated uses of power, often by many people in many situations.

Moreover, some overall style or approach is needed when devising strategy. Is a low-conflict or high-conflict approach to be used? Will strategists mobilize a relatively large group to pressure decisionmakers, or will they rely on behind-the-scenes discussions? Will they seek a sweeping reform or settle for a relatively modest one?

A detailed strategy identifies specific actions and verbal exchanges that one or more persons will make during a specific time frame to achieve those policy objectives. There are many types of strategies. Some are relatively ambitious and involve many people; others are relatively simple and involve one person's actions or verbal exchanges. Some strategies, such as ones to enact a major piece of legislation, cover an extended time frame, whereas others are devised for a single event, such as an important meeting. Effective strategy addresses certain issues that can be placed in six categories (Box 12.1).

Establishing a Time Frame and Policy Goals

Proposals are usually only enacted after a series of maneuvers, meetings, discussions, presentations, and other interactions. People who seek ratification of their proposals often set time frames in which they expect one or several episodes to ensue.[29] Someone may specify a time frame, for example, for obtaining an affirmative vote during an important meeting, establishing a supportive coalition, or having an item placed on a meeting agenda. By defining goals and time frames as events unfold, policy practitioners can lend focus and discipline to their work.

BOX 12.1
Six Issues Strategists Often Address

Establishing a Time Frame and Policy Goals
- What do proponents wish to achieve within a specific time frame?

Specifying a Proposal's Content
- What minimal features or content should the policy proposal contain?
- On what points can we negotiate or compromise?

Organizing a Proposal's Proponents
- Who will provide leadership? Who will perform what tasks?

Establishing the Style
- What decision route, or parliamentary approach, will be sought?
- What level and scope of conflict will proponents seek?

Selecting Power Resources
- What kinds of person-to-person, substantive, process, and agenda-setting power resources will be used?
- Who will use these power resources and in what situations?

Revising the Strategy
- How should the game plan be revised in light of opponents' strategies?
- What new events or background factors suggest a change in strategy?

Specifying a Proposal's Content

Practitioners ultimately aim to have their proposal enacted, but they must often ask, "Precisely what proposal?" They have to decide what points of a proposal are most important to them, thus resisting efforts to change or delete them. Policy practitioners encounter difficult dilemmas; if they are willing to compromise excessively, they risk "ending up with nothing," but if they are excessively rigid or dogmatic, they may be unable to have any proposal enacted.

Organizing a Proposal's Proponents

The proponents of specific measures often want to pool their ideas and power resources, but they cannot accomplish this if they are not organized. With relatively small and homogeneous groups, such as colleagues in a social-work agency, coordinating mechanisms are relatively simple to form and may build on the leadership and communication patterns that already exist.[30] Coordination is more difficult when many heterogeneous groups or interests are represented and where mistrust exists, as well as fundamental differences about the policy.

As we discussed in the last chapter with respect to task groups, coalitions, and networks, proponents need to address issues of coordination, leadership, the building of constituencies, the resolution of conflict, division of labor, and communication. Moreover, they must attend to these issues, not only at the outset, but also as events unfold. People may lose interest or become disenchanted with the cause, disagreements may develop about strategy, people may feel that others unduly seek credit for a proposal, or people may become restive after setbacks.

Even before establishing these coordinating mechanisms, a pool of proponents must be gathered. Strategists have to avoid fatalism and naiveté when searching for potential allies. Fatalists wrongly assume that specific persons will oppose a certain initiative; thus, liberals sometimes assume that moderates and conservatives will necessarily oppose social reforms without fully considering constituencies, values, and other factors that might impel them to support a proposal.[31] Naive strategists wrongly assume that an initiative will attract support from several persons and interests, even when evidence suggests that it will be controversial. Unaware of political realities, naive strategists fail to take action or engage in discussion to offset opposition.

When deciding whether certain people, groups, or interests will support a proposal, strategists examine *motivating* factors. Do their past positions on a similar issue suggest an orientation? Are they likely to believe that a proposal could protect or advance their interests, such as constituency support, resources, or prestige? Will an existing or potential ally command sufficient respect to sway others to support an issue? Will certain people perceive a proposal as supporting an organization's central mission? These motivating factors are difficult to assess, but they provide important clues. In many cases, of course, people have mixed motivations where their values may dispose them to support a policy, but their vested interests may suggest opposition.[32]

Establishing the Style

We noted in the preceding discussion that a practitioner needs an overarching style, or approach. Practitioners must decide what kind of political interaction and which procedural or parliamentary approaches will most help their proposal. Will behind-the-scenes and nonconflictual deliberations suffice, or is more conflictual and publicized interaction advisable? If a choice exists, which committee will treat a proposal favorably? Should the introduction of an initiative be delayed until background conditions are more propitious?

Others may contest these choices, of course, such as the measure's opponents, who want procedural or parliamentary approaches that will lead to defeat of the proposal or initiative.

Selecting Power Resources

To realize their strategy, a policy's proponents must use their power resources in certain situations. Their challenge is to decide *who* uses *which power resources* in *which situations*. If several people are involved in a project, they can divide responsibilities for talking with specific people, making presentations, doing research, developing lists of supporters, and other functions. For example, people who seek policy changes in an agency may decide that, "Joe will propose a place on an upcoming staff meeting agenda to discuss modifying the intake procedure, Mary will comment on inadequacies in the existing procedure at the staff meeting, Tom will make some comments that support Joe and Mary, and Elise will suggest forming a task force to devise a new policy." Moreover, this group might decide to approach certain people before the staff meeting to obtain support for the policy change. Similarly, a coalition of groups seeking a change in federal day-care policy might seek an important legislator's sponsorship and allocate lobbying tasks to various persons.

Revising the Strategy

Proponents who hold rigidly to a strategy often imperil their success. Perhaps they made miscalculations when they established their strategy, such as underestimating the strength of the opposition. Perhaps specific opponents devised a counterstrategy to circumvent them. Unanticipated events may have powerfully shaped deliberations. A measure's proponents must then modify their strategy and respond improvisationally to unanticipated events.

Developing Strategy: An Agency Illustration

How do strategists put together a strategy from all the elements that we have discussed? Much like chefs who visualize different combinations of ingredients before trying them, strategists brainstorm several strategies and then speculate how events might unfold if each were used. We will consider an agency example and then a legislative example to discuss the way strategists think about strategy.

Recall Case 10.1, where a student intern wants to establish an innovative program for children of institutionalized mental patients. Astonished that neither her clinic nor any psychiatric clinics in the area had developed group services for these children, she develops a political strategy to plan a course of action. Her force-field analysis suggests that Mr. Jones occupies a position of great power in the agency as the director of outpatient services. Her force-field analysis also suggests that there are many barriers to the innovation. The executive director of the agency will not, she surmises, support the innovation, because it would divert scarce resources from existing services and might even lengthen the waiting list, which he is dedicated to shortening. Certain persons, moreover, might oppose the innovation if it is immediately introduced, such as Ida Brown, the director of training, who "does not particularly like Mr. Jones and often opposes any proposals he initiates."

The intern concludes that once the innovation has been tested and proven effective as a pilot project, Mr. Jones can then successfully present it to the executive director, who "defers (to Mr. Jones) on all issues pertaining to the outpatient part of the agency." Indeed, she thinks that the innovation, which would draw referrals from other agencies and give her agency a visible role in the community, would gain the support of the senior administrator and the chief of program development. These two men "are allied in their unstated mission of increasing clinic prestige and influence in the community." She believes that the rubber-stamp board will approve the innovation once it has received support from highly-placed officials in the agency and survived the likely attack from Ida Brown.

Everything depends, she concludes, on receiving Mr. Jones's vigorous support, establishing the innovation on a pilot basis, obtaining referrals from area agencies so that the program is viable, and keeping the pilot project "low profile" until it has proven successful. In short, the intern and Mr. Jones emphasize the timing of presenting the innovation for formal ratification in the agency policies.

In making this strategy, the intern and Mr. Jones implicitly reject alternative strategies, such as seeking support for the program even before it has been pilot-tested. The student intern also decided not to take the innovation to persons other than Mr. Jones, partly because she "reported" to him in the chain of command and partly because she believed he had extraordinary power in policy matters dealing with outpatient services.

DEVELOPING STRATEGY: A LEGISLATIVE ILLUSTRATION

We see an example of alternative scenarios in the case study of a young legislative aide, Eric Redman, who wanted to develop a National Health Service Corps. His idea was that young physicians who worked for two years in rural and urban clinics that serve low-income citizens would receive salaries from federal funds.[33] He initially wanted to develop a relatively modest strategy, extending the existing public health program, which allows some physicians to substitute public health duties for serving in the armed forces, to include the doctors who serve low-income citizens. (At the time of the case study, physicians were required to serve in the armed forces.) To accomplish this goal, he and his allies would need to convince officials in the Public Health Service (PHS) to expand their existing program. Indeed, Redman was not certain that he even needed legislative approval for his modest proposal; perhaps the PHS could implement it by merely expanding their current practice. Physicians could continue to be exempted from military service, but now some of them would provide medical services to poor people, instead of providing traditional public health services.

At the other extreme, however, Redman could imagine developing and seeking enactment of a relatively ambitious piece of legislation. This proposal might allow a larger program than one merely tacked onto the existing public health program, but it would also present major political problems. Might some politicians believe that the National Health Service Corps would be a kind of national health insurance, which has traditionally evoked extraordinary political controversy and conflicts between liberals and conservatives? Moreover, even if the legislation were enacted, the relatively conservative, Republican president would probably veto the legislation due to pressure from his party. The American Medical Association would probably use its remarkable lobbying resources to defeat a bill that placed large numbers of physicians in public, salaried positions. (The PHS had escaped this controversy because its physicians were allowed only to "prevent" illnesses through inoculation and educational programs, rather than providing medical services to patients.)

As he compared the modest with the ambitious proposal, Redman did a force-field analysis. He concluded that he had to select the modest proposal if he hoped to be successful. He soon had to revise his strategy, however, when he discovered that the existing public health legislation forbade PHS physicians from actually treating ill patients. Moreover, he depended upon officials in the federal bureaucracy to cooperate in order to expand the PHS, and they refused to cooperate with him, either because they did not want to work with the legislative aide of a prominent Democratic senator or because some high-level officials did not favor the proposed program.

Redman enlisted the assistance of some legislative aides to draft legislation that described and authorized funds for a National Health Service Corps. Thus, he had to revise his first, relatively modest strategy in light of changing events and new information. He assembled a group of legislative sponsors, including prominent politicians from both political parties.

This example describes Redman's successful and evolving strategy to enact his policy proposal.[34] He consistently used a low-profile and nonconflictual political style to obtain broad bipartisan support for his measure and to avoid opposition from conservatives that would certainly have doomed his legislation. He developed a low-conflict style of politics by shunning publicity in the mass media, emphasizing the small size of the intended program, and skillfully using rivalries between various politicians in Congress to entice them to develop competing versions of the legislation. His low-profile strategy was successful, although he had to mobilize external pressures on specific legislators and on the president just before he signed the legislation. He skillfully built support for the legislation among rural legislators from both parties—who traditionally oppose social reforms—by emphasizing the relevance of the program to rural populations unable to obtain sufficient medical personnel.

DEVELOPING STRATEGY IN GOVERNMENTAL SETTINGS

Assume that you are concerned about a social problem that you believe requires a legislative policy reform, whether a revision of existing legislation or a new piece of legislation. You would need to spring into action, whether you worked by yourself on this issue or through an existing advocacy group. Your actions might include seeking up-front consultation; receiving technical assistance; obtaining sponsorship and official support; receiving parliamentary assistance; lobbying; forming supportive coalitions; testifying, using the mass media; orchestrating telephone, visiting, and letter-writing campaigns; and working in political parties and campaigns.

Seeking Up-Front Consultation

Recall that any advocate must work in a political environment where lobbyists, interest groups, legislators (and their aides), and political appointees or civil servants have already formed relationships. Moreover, most problems in the human services system are associated with a web of existing policies, including legislation, administrative regulations, and even court rulings. Unless someone is already versed in these realities, they have to collect considerable information just to understand the political and policy context. They need to seek consultation through a series of brief, focused contacts with several people.[35]

Advocates need to come into these informational discussions having identified some issue that concerns them. Since they want information at this point, rather than support for specific proposals, they should ask whether the respondent *also* believes the issue to be serious and worthy of a policy remedy, whether the issue has been broached on prior occasions (and by whom and with what outcomes), what kinds of policies are most germane to the problem (for example, high-level administrative regulations, legislation, policies of agencies or agency units, or court rulings), and what technical information exists that would illuminate the scope of the problem. The advocate can ask what key persons or groups would likely be interested in the problem and whether any of them have already addressed it by seeking changes in existing policies.

Advocates will need to adapt their discussions to the characteristics of the interviewee. With the staff of advocacy groups or with aides to legislators who have established records of social reform, they can use somewhat different language than with a "number crunching" civil servant or aide to a relatively conservative legislator.[36] When seeking information in these early stages, the advocate wants to appear "benevolently neutral" to many interviewees, someone diligently seeking good information in order to develop a responsible policy position. Of course, some interviewees will be more helpful to an advocate if they believe that they share similar perspectives.[37]

Policy advocates can also obtain technical information from library sources and federal agencies, as well as advocacy groups and officials in other jurisdictions. They may have heard that another state has enacted legislation to address a problem or that an advocacy group in another part of the nation has sought corrective policies. Computerized library searches, as well as computer networks that link advocates across the nation, will allow advocates to obtain information more rapidly during the coming decade.[38]

Receiving Technical Assistance

At some point, advocates need to develop a policy document or, in the words of Willard Richan, a "policy brief," that states the problem, places it in the context of existing policies, names a possible remedy, and discusses the feasibility of a policy change. The remedy could outline a piece of legislation, an administrative regulation, or a change in the policies and procedures of one or more agencies.[39] This initial policy brief has to be relatively succinct and clearly written, since it aims not to provide an exhaustive treatment of an issue, but to point to possible or likely remedies.

Of course, advocates do not necessarily have to write the policy brief if they find someone else to take the lead, such as the staff person in an existing advocacy group, an aide to a legislator, or a lobbyist. Indeed, in our specialized world, policy advocates should sometimes see themselves as catalysts who incite other persons (those with specialized knowledge and access to decision-makers) to act. On some occasions, however, they may have to take the initiative if others cannot.[40]

The policy brief serves several functions. First, it helps the advocate crystallize in a brief format, such as two to ten pages, a problem and a remedy. Second, it allows advocates to enlist help from others whose help is sought in revising the brief. Third, as we discuss subsequently, the final policy brief can help in obtaining sponsorship for the project.

In the case of legislation, advocates must translate their ideas into a "legislative bill." This is a legislative proposal printed in an official form that includes its title and number (such as H.R. 1 for a bill numbered "1" in the House of Representatives), a list of sponsors, a preamble, and specific provisions. Advocates will need the help of legislative aides, experts, or legislative drafting services that exist in most capitals to put their ideas into this format.[41]

When constructing a legislative proposal, advocates should consider the breadth of support they will need to get it enacted. They should not dilute or compromise their interests excessively, but the legislation has to appeal to a range of politicians and interest groups to be enacted. They may decide to leave specific details relatively vague to avoid controversy. They might seek a more modest measure than they had originally anticipated. Alternatively, they might broaden a measure so that larger numbers of persons will benefit from it, thus making it more appealing to politicians and interest groups.

Obtaining Sponsorship and Official Support

Policy advocates need sponsorship and support if their bills are to be enacted. They need to find legislators who will agree to place their names as "sponsors" (or introducers) at the top of the legislation. The proposal will more likely be enacted if it has numerous sponsors, including sponsors from both political parties, sponsors from highly placed persons in a legislative chamber, such as the presiding office, the majority whip, and chairpersons of those committees that will hear the legislation.[42] Of course, as we have already discussed, a legislator's agreement to sponsor a bill is not an agreement to invest considerable energy toward its enactment. Advocates often hope that their discussions with legislators or their aides will convince them to commit personal resources to it.

Advocates would also like formal support for the legislation from the head of government, such as a governor, president, or mayor, and from the director of the department or agency that will be charged with implementing it. Of course, their support cannot always be obtained, as many liberal advocates have discovered when they confront conservative administrations.[43]

Enactment of legislation, then, requires many contacts in the early phase of the policy process. Policy advocates often need to develop a team approach, where several persons work together to secure these early commitments from powerful persons.

Advocates have several choices when trying to develop a coalition to enact a piece of legislation. They can write the legislation and then approach interest groups, such as advocacy groups, to seek their support. They can form an ad hoc coalition composed of representatives from interest groups, even before legislation has been drafted, and have members of this coalition help shape the legislation. They could form an ad hoc coalition after they have drafted the legislation to work together to support the legislation. They can also approach a standing coalition, one that already promotes legislation for a specific population such as children, and seek its assistance in developing or supporting the proposal. No matter what the approach, the advocate wants commitments from persons and groups who will help mobilize support for the legislation later.

Receiving Parliamentary Assistance

Once advocates have introduced the legislation and obtained formal commitments from persons both inside and outside the legislature, advocates should move the bill expeditiously through the legislative process. They do not want it to be delayed or sidetracked. (In many legislatures, bills not enacted within a specific period, such as two years after its introduction, are terminated.)

As we discussed in Chapter Four (see Figure 4.3), legislation often begins in one chamber, proceeds through committees to the floor of the chamber, and is then sent to the relevant committees of the other chamber, where it progresses through a similar deliberative route. There are many exceptions to this pattern. Sometimes the two chambers process legislation simultaneously. Alternatively, legislation approved by one chamber may proceed directly to the floor of the second chamber if someone attaches it to other legislation already on that chamber's floor.

Advocates outside a legislature need the collaborative assistance of legislators and their aides to move their legislation through the process, whatever its precise route. They need to make contact with these collaborative aides at various points in the legislative process to be certain that the legislation is indeed proceeding. In some cases, they may need to mobilize pressure from groups and persons outside the legislature to convince a powerful person, such as a committee chair, to keep their bill moving through the legislative process.[44]

Lobbying

Advocates often have personal discussions with legislators or their aides to elicit support for their bills. Persons who lobby should not feel apologetic about their work because, as we discussed earlier, legislators and their aides *need* lobbyists to obtain information about many of the issues that they confront. Because they often deal with lobbyists, most legislators are expert at distinguishing credible, honest advocates from ones who do not know their subject, give one-sided or inaccurate information, or do not know how to present their message briefly.

Successful lobbyists realize that their effectiveness hinges on several factors. They must have a succinct and clear message that states what proposal they support, what problem it seeks to alleviate, its central provisions, and when they need the legislator's support, both in the short term (such as a vote in a legislative committee) and in the longer term (a vote on the floor of a chamber).[45] Advocates often give legislators brief fact sheets summarizing the major provisions of legislative proposals and the measures' rationale.

Effective lobbyists are appropriately assertive during their brief encounters with legislators. They want to present a bill clearly, affirmatively, and confidently. Yet they do not want to bully legislators. They also want to legitimate legislators' perspectives by listening attentively to their questions, criticisms, or objections, while giving their best, reasonable answers to these questions and points. When asked questions to which they do not have answers, they can say that they will provide the information later.[46]

Forming Supportive Coalitions

We discussed task forces and coalitions in Chapter Eleven, such as issues in forming them, keeping them functioning, and troubleshooting problems that arise in them. Supportive coalitions can persuade legislators that significant numbers of constituents care about a proposal and that many persons and groups will be intensely displeased if the legislation fails. As we have noted, advocates can form this supportive coalition before legislation is drafted or after introducing a proposal to mobilize pressure to secure the bill's enactment. Advocates can also work through an existing coalition, such as ones that focus on a specific population's needs or ones that support reformist legislation for several groups. Once advocates have formed or joined a coalition, various arrangements are possible. The coalition members can meet regularly to plot and implement strategy. They may decide, after an initial meeting, to allow someone to orchestrate their work. This orchestrating would involve telling the coalition at key points to undertake certain tasks, such as finding persons to testify at hearings, mobilizing letter-writing campaigns, or participating in a press conference.

Testifying

Legislative committees usually convene hearings, which indisputably enhance a proposal's visibility and helps convince reluctant legislators that it has significant support. Advocates and their allies need to be certain that they are scheduled to testify at congressional hearings on their proposal.

Legislative testimony follows a specific format. Persons are allowed to make brief statements, usually no longer than five minutes, which they supplement with written testimony that they submit to the committee. The committee members who attend the hearings usually ask testifiers questions, which they field by themselves or in a panel with several other testifiers.

In giving legislative testimony, proponents of legislation often focus on key points that show why existing policy is defective, how the proposed policy will improve on existing policy, and why the proposal is budgetarily and administratively feasible. They should make these central points succinctly, while asking legislators to refer to their written statement for fuller information on any of the points in the verbal testimony. In their testimony, they should refrain from "overreaching," or making exorbitant claims for their legislative proposal, and from digressing into ideological statements, because they want to appear reasonable and well-informed.[47]

They can expect some questions that criticize the legislation or some facet of it. It is important in this phase of testimony that testifiers stick to what they know or can reasonably infer from available information. If no information exists about a specific point or if it is difficult to predict what effects a program will have in the future, they should admit some uncertainty, but follow this admission with a positive statement such as, "Our best information suggests that . . ." or "We have good reason to believe that. . . ." They can indicate that they will send the legislator further information if they do not currently possess it. Testifiers do not need, after all, to prove that their policy proposal will lead to *perfect* outcomes, but merely that they will lead to *better* outcomes than existing policies. Of course, testifiers do not want to err in the opposite direction by being too modest about a policy that they propose; they should assert wherever possible a proposal's likely positive outcomes and refrain from discussing possible problems or negative outcomes unless a legislator asks about them.[48]

Testifiers should never personalize things by lashing out at a questioner because they want to convey an impression of reasonableness, professionalism, and credibility. Nor should they usually bring political ideology into their testimony, because this digression could embroil the reform in ideological polarization. As Christopher Matthews discusses in his book, *Hardball*, successful politicians often focus discussion on legislative provisions rather than on philosophical principles.[49]

Using the Mass Media

Advocates often use the mass media when trying to enact legislation in order to reach a broad audience that can place pressure on politicians to take action.[50]

Advocates have several options. They can call a press conference to make their case for a proposal, sometimes on the same day as critical events, such as legislative committee hearings. They can announce such press conferences by sending various news organizations a one-page summary of the issue and information about the persons who will testify. If the issue is perceived as important, dramatic, and relevant for large numbers of persons, significant numbers of the press will attend these events, though minor technical revisions of policy are not likely to attract wide attention from the media.

Advocates can also *target* the mass media in pivotal politicians' districts. Assume, for example, that the chair of a legislative committee has bottlenecked a proposal; an advocacy group in his district might call a press conference to pressure this chairperson into supporting the legislation.

Advocates can write guest editorials, which they send to the editorial offices of newspapers, radio stations, and television stations. It is more likely that such editorials will be published if well-known persons write them and if they convey a dramatic, well-written message that does not exceed about 800 words.

Orchestrating Telephone, Visiting, and Letter-Writing Campaigns

Advocates can develop campaigns to call or write the offices of legislators, whether particularly powerful ones or all the members of a committee or chamber.[51] They may use the membership lists of community or professional groups to develop a cadre of letter writers. They need to provide letter writers with suggested themes but should take care to avoid the "mimeographed letter syndrome" because legislators consider individualized letters more credible than standardized letters.

Advocates can mobilize persons to visit legislators on a certain day to advocate supporting a proposal. They may, for example, rent buses to flood the capital with petitioners.

Working in Political Parties and Campaigns

Policy advocates' success ultimately depends on securing support from legislators who are sympathetic to their cause. However, their work is vastly simplified if they can help elect progressive legislators or if they help progressive legislators retain seats that they currently hold. Policy advocates can engage in partisan politics in five ways: (1) they can become active members in their political party; (2) they can join a political club that promotes the kinds of candidates they favor; (3) they can help a PAC; (4) they can participate in specific candidates' campaigns; or (5) they can run for office themselves.[52]

Participating in a political party. Assume that a policy advocate believes that the Democratic Party, for all of its flaws, nonetheless represents the most promising vehicle for social reforms in the United States. As a registered voter, she is automatically a member of her party's precinct or ward caucus, which not only elects a precinct committeeperson, but also elects delegates to a county convention. In turn, the county convention elects delegates to the state convention, which then elects delegates to the national convention. As a participant in the party, the policy advocate should support persons who represent a reformist perspective on social issues in county, state, and national conventions. She also should help the party by participating in voter registration drives, as well as voter turnout drives on election days.[53]

Joining a political club. Political clubs exist in most jurisdictions that raise funds for social-reformist candidates. These clubs meet regularly, raise funds for their club, decide which candidates (or other issues on the ballot) to support, and give funds to candidates and issues they have endorsed.

Helping an existing organization's PAC. Because organizations might lose their tax-exempt status if they engage in partisan politics, many of them have created a spin-off organization, called a political action committee (PAC). (Some PACs also exist independently of other organizations.) For example, the National Association of Social Workers (NASW) formed PACE, its political action arm, in 1975. PACE solicits its funds from members of NASW, but it keeps these funds in separate accounts from NASW. PACE endorses both national candidates, as well as candidates in state elections.[54]

Endorsing candidates is an important function of PACs. They choose candidates by assessing their positions on specific issues, whether by analyzing their voting records, their responses to a questionnaire the PAC has sent them, or their positions in personal interviews with the candidate. Candidates who obtain endorsements often freely publicize them to obtain support from the members and friends of specific PACs.

PACs also participate directly in specific elections. They recruit volunteers for the campaigns of endorsed candidates, do research for them, and encourage their members to vote for the candidate. They also fund endorsed candidates. Powerful PACs, such as the PAC of the American Association of Retired Persons, raise millions of dollars and have a veritable army of volunteers that participates in the campaigns of endorsed candidates. PACE has injected social workers' perspectives and resources into many campaigns.

Participating in political campaigns. Many people believe campaigns are solo undertakings by specific candidates. In fact, campaigns are temporary organizations, whose success or failure often hinges on the collective activities of campaign staff, the candidate, volunteers, and cooperating groups, such as the political party, PACs, and benefactors.[55]

As organizations, most campaigns have many branches or units. In addition to the candidate, most of them have a manager and various directors who oversee tasks, such as registering voters, encouraging people to vote, recruiting volunteers, raising funds, and doing research. Larger campaigns also have specialized media and advertising personnel, as well as pollsters. Many campaigns, such as those in many state and federal races, possess considerable technical capabilities, such as computers to locate specific voters and target mailings to them. The campaign director is, of course, a pivotal figure in the campaign, because he or she coordinates the entire enterprise.

High-level strategy is often critical in a campaign. Each candidate examines the profile of those who are likely to vote, whether in a primary campaign (when the candidates within one party vie for the party's nomination) or a general election. They "segment" these likely voters into groups based on demographic characteristics (such as age, gender, race, and social class), life-style (such as yuppies, hippies, and gays), positions on specific issues (such as welfare, abortion, and gun control), general ideological orientations (whether relatively liberal or conservative), and geographic area. In sifting through profiles of voters, candidates gauge which voters fall into three groups: likely opponents, likely supporters, and "swing" voters (who are undecided). While it may sound wrong to declare some voters to be "hopeless," as in the first group, candidates must save their scarce resources for those persons who *can* be persuaded to vote for them. Candidates sometimes choose not to expend significant resources on the second group unless they believe that ignoring these almost-certain voters could decrease their turnout rate on election day or decrease the funding and other assistance they give the campaign. Many elections depend on how successfully candidates attract swing voters.[56]

As even this cursory discussion suggests, electoral political activity hinges not only on developing correct strategy, but also on candidates' ability to target swing voters with messages and campaign resources, such as volunteers and the candidate's personal attention. Candidates may need to revise their strategy as the campaign proceeds. In some cases, candidates even discover that their foes place spies in their campaigns to alert the opponent to the candidate's tactics. Candidates develop an overall strategy, then, at the outset of their campaigns, but they soon find that they have to revise it to offset the strategy that their opponents have devised to counter *their* strategy!

In the push-and-pull of the campaigns, candidates project *positive* messages to gain certain voters' support, such as specific positions or general images (for example, "caring for older citizens"), and *negative* messages that attack opposing candidates to make them appear less attractive to specific voters. In the case of state and federal elections, candidates use the mass media extensively to convey these themes, whether through advertisements or through the general coverage that the media give them. As many commentators have noted, American campaigns often emphasize negative messages, such as impugning an opponent's motives; "digging up dirt," such as scandals or corruption; attacking the opponent's personal life; or misrepresenting the opponent's positions. Of course, no one candidate has a monopoly on the airwaves; as candidates publicize positive and negative messages, opposing candidates often try to counter them.

Campaign managers and fundraising staff become pivotal in many campaigns. Campaign managers not only oversee the entire campaign and coordinate its staff, but also help the candidate form strategy. They must decide what positive and negative messages to convey and when to convey them. A campaign manager often decides, for example, to save some messages until the final weeks, while using other issues earlier. The fundraising staff members must find resources to allow candidates to implement their strategy. Media advertisements and mailings constitute a large share of most campaign costs and can play a critical role, particularly in the closing weeks. Funds are also needed to rent offices, pay some campaign staff, and finance the candidate's travel and living costs.

Even our brief discussion of campaigns suggests that policy advocates can play a number of roles in campaigns. They can serve as paid staff members or as volunteers by helping to raise funds, secure volunteers, oversee volunteers' work, supervise telephone campaigns, oversee mailings, walk the precincts to solicit support, register voters, encourage people to vote on Election Day, host events for the candidate, or help distribute yard signs. They can also do research, such as helping a candidate obtain information about issues and about voters in the district, or helping solicit endorsements from PACs and individuals. (To become involved in any of these activities, someone merely calls or visits the campaign office and volunteers to work.)

Running for office. Increasing numbers of social workers are running for political office themselves at all government levels. These candidacies sometimes flow from long-standing work in campaigns for other officials, work from which the social worker gains contacts and experience. In some cases, however, social workers have successfully launched campaigns with little experience in electoral politics. During the past decade, as women have become more numerous in elective bodies at all levels, the political prospects for female social workers have markedly improved.

DEVELOPING STRATEGY IN ORGANIZATIONAL SETTINGS

Policy practitioners often want to obtain changes in the agencies' policies, whether "from within" or as advocates working from an external vantage point, such as from an advocacy group or a community-based coalition.

Legislative versus Organizational Politics

There are obviously great differences between the politics of organizations and legislatures. While legislators are elected, organizations' staff and executives are appointed to their positions. While legislators are acutely aware of public opinion and constituents' views, organizations' staff and executives are more attuned to persons and organizations that give them funds, referrals, and program guidelines. Legislators are used to open, protracted, and public conflict between members of different parties and persons with different ideologies. Indeed, they use conflict over specific issues to prove to their constituents in elections that they represent their interests better than members of opposing parties. In contrast, organizations' staff members tend *not* to want ongoing, protracted conflict, partly because staff members have to work together on a daily basis to implement agency programs. (Some leaders of organizations often actively quell conflict, whether to preserve their own power and preferences, to emphasize win-win decisionmaking processes, or to enhance the implementation of agency programs.)

Other differences between agencies and legislatures also deserve discussion. While legislators concentrate on enacting official policies, such as legislation and annual budgets, agency staff members also consider how they will respond to policies that descend on them from external sources, such as legislatures, government agencies, insurance companies, and courts. Their responses include: deciding not to seek certain funds (thus avoiding specific policies), seeking externally-funded programs whose policies they enthusiastically support, and seeking externally-funded programs whose policies they partially accept.

Some readers may ask, "How can agencies accept funds from external sources, such as government agencies, *without* also accepting the policies that come with them?" As the experience of many externally funded programs suggests, many agencies do not adhere to the policies that accompany the funds they receive. To examine issues of compliance, we need to look at the actions of several agency staff members, from the top officials (what messages they convey to direct-service staff), the supervisors, and direct-service staff members (how their personal policy preferences, as well as informal policies, shape their implementation of policies from external funders).

Shaping informal policies is an important policy arena in social agencies. (Recall that in Chapter One we stated that the shared beliefs and norms of staff constitute one form of social policy and that these informal policies can predispose staff to ignore specific official policies.) When they believe that informal policies block implementation of other, desirable policies, staff members can modify informal policies by interventions with their colleagues. They can also work around their colleagues by seeking support from higher-level officials to change aspects of informal policies. In addition, they could shape informal policies by influencing hiring and promotion decisions; thus, they could bring people into the agency whose policy preferences concurred with their own.

Policy practitioners in agency settings often work indirectly to change agency services. They can try to influence who oversees specific programs, where services are provided, what budget allocations specific programs receive, and what kinds of funds the agency seeks from external funders. In each of these cases, a policy practitioner shapes the implementation of policies by influencing implementing and budget choices rather than by trying to change official agency policies.

While legislators realize that others measure their influence by how they shape the content of specific legislation, agency staff members have many options. They can try to shape official policy at the highest levels of the agency. They can concentrate on policies in specific agency units or programs, even deciding not to bring an issue to the attention of higher-level staff. (Recall that the student intern in Case 10.1 decided with her preceptor not to bring the innovation to high-level staff until it had been implemented as a pilot program.)

Our observations about differences between legislatures and organizations suggest that organizational politics often take a different form and concentrate on different issues than legislative politics. Conflict is not as open or protracted, though it can and does exist and it can occasionally become intense.

Burton Gummer notes that some organizations are more politicized than others. He speculates that organizations are most likely to be politicized when they have scarce resources for their goals or programs; when there is considerable internal conflict over the priority of different programs; when staff members have different service approaches or philosophies, such as different treatment methods; and when there is conflict between units, programs, or departments.[57] (He also notes that *most* organizations have some of these features, so practitioners will frequently encounter politics in them.)

People can work on many fronts when participating in their agency's politics. They can try to change official agency policy, informal policy, implementing and budget choices, policy at higher levels of an organization, or policy in specific units.

Force-Field Analysis in Organizations

Recall our discussion of organizations in Chapter Four, where we analyzed the political economy of organizations and the four "overlays": the organizational hierarchy and formal interrelationships, the budget, the roles of boundary spanners and mission promoters, and the informal relations between organizational members.

Analyzing an issue's political economy. Astute tacticians within organizations place their work in a larger political and economic framework. When doing force-field analysis, they ask whether a specific policy will attract a steady stream of clients and resources to the organization or deter them. They will note a policy's specific, *positive* implications for the well-being of the organization; by highlighting how it will enhance the agency's reputation, its flow of clients, support from funding sources, or support from accrediting agencies. Because executives often favor maintaining staff morale, reducing internal conflict, and providing quality services, tacticians can also emphasize these kinds of positive consequences. Recall how the student intern in Case 10.1 planned to argue that developing group services for children of institutionalized patients would increase referrals to her clinic and its prestige in the community.

The formal organization. Skillful tacticians view organizations' formal attributes, meaning its hierarchy and division of labor, as both constraints and opportunities. Indeed, tacticians should not reach premature conclusions about specific issues; even when matters look bleak, people may find that support exists for an issue if it is framed correctly and if process-tactics (such as timing and the use of intermediaries) are chosen well. When viewed as a constraint, hierarchy intimidates persons who believe that their superiors oppose a policy change. In organizations that lack a team-building atmosphere, some persons may understandably fear that their promotions, pay increases, or jobs are at stake when they support even relatively small changes that top officials do not embrace. Where intimidation or fear exists, support for specific proposals may be significantly reduced. When social-service organizations are unionized (many public and nongovernmental agencies have unions), lower-level staff may be more emboldened to support policy changes, though many union leaders restrict themselves to "bread and butter" issues, such as employees' wages and working conditions.

Yet hierarchy also provides opportunities to astute tacticians. They can defuse the formal organization's negative aspects by finding allies for a proposed change within the higher ranks of administration. In rarer instances, they can use top officials' opposition to a suggested change to rally lower-level staff against top officials, a tactic trade unions often use. This tactic must be used with caution, however, because it can merely entrench higher-level officials against a proposal and lead to recriminations. The student intern hoped to defuse opposition to her proposal by obtaining Mr. Jones's support, as other staff deferred to him on issues relating to outpatient services.

The division of labor is a constraint when it fragments organizations into competitive units, causing unit members to oppose policy reforms that may benefit other units. When this win-lose ethos prevails, a policy practitioner may find it difficult to establish broad-based support for a change in existing policies. Indeed, the student intern in Case 10.1 feared that the director of training, Ida Brown, would oppose the innovation because it had come from Mr. Jones, a person she viewed as a rival. Organizations' divisions into separate units can also provide policy practitioners with rich opportunities for coalitions if they can devise proposals that appeal to persons with different perspectives and interests. Someone might frame a proposal so that various units each have "part of the action." Perhaps a quid pro quo arrangement can be developed so that the staff members of one unit, who initiate a proposal, agree to a concession for another unit if the second unit supports their proposal.

To offset the constraints of hierarchy and the division of labor, reformers can try to create a win-win atmosphere by saying a policy will help a range of persons within the organization. This amicable strategy will only work, of course, if persons *can* be united behind a policy change.

The budget and policy change. Because organizations tend to have scarce resources, policy reformers in agencies must usually place budget implications "up-front" in their force-field analyses. An innovation's prognosis is usually far bleaker if it will cost the organization considerable funds from its own budget and if it has little long-term prospect of generating offsetting funds from fees or external funders. Since it is unclear whether the student intern's innovation would generate fees or resources from funders, she probably should have devoted more energy to examining its fiscal implications.

When examining a proposal's budgetary implications, policy practitioners need to consider fee-generating possibilities, whether external funders may be interested in funding it, whether start-up costs will be offset by revenues once the innovation is institutionalized, and whether an inexpensive "pilot phase" is possible.

Agency mission and boundary spanners. Policy changes that advance central, important goals of the agency—or at least ones that people in top management value—probably have a better chance than ones that are seen as irrelevant to them or as detracting energy and resources from them.[58] The student intern's innovation appealed to Mr. Jones precisely because he viewed it as furthering his commitments to community mental health and to outpatient services. When considering an issue's relationship to the agency's mission, policy practitioners should also refer to the agency's political economy. Perhaps a proposal is not congruent with an agency's current mission, but it may represent an innovation that high-level staff will favor in the long run because it addresses emerging community needs or issues that specific funders prioritize.

It is easy to forget that practitioners can obtain support for some proposals by emphasizing their relevance to clients' beneficence, or well-being. As we discussed in Chapter Two, the hallmark of professions is their expressed, ethical interest in helping clients. When conducting force-field analysis, then, a policy practitioner needs to ask who they can likely persuade, and with what kinds of evidence, that a specific proposal *will* advance clients' beneficence? Expert opinions, feedback from clients, evaluators' findings, and social scientists' work can buttress the case that a proposal will help clients. (The student intern could have buttressed her case for the program had she found evaluative or theoretical literature suggesting that her innovation would significantly help children.)

Recall our discussion in Chapter Four of boundary spanners, who derive power from their ability to lead an agency to sources of funds and referrals that enhance its survival. Strategists enhance support for a proposal when they show that it will bring new funds and referrals to their agency or will enhance its prestige in the wider community.

Informal relationships. A practitioner must gauge informal relationships between organizational participants when assessing a proposal's potential support in an organization. We sometimes conduct force-field analysis by examining agency employees' separate opinions, but this kind of analysis ignores important *relationships* between agency staff members. People often take cues from others that they know or respect, so "converting" a single, pivotal person can often bring many other persons' support. Policy practitioners need to be able to understand longstanding patterns of association and deference in their agencies when they try to predict a policy's prognosis.[59]

Using intermediaries, which we discussed in Chapter Ten, is particularly important in the politics of organizations, because of their formal characteristics (hierarchy and division of labor) and informal associations between persons. A policy practitioner who is a direct-service worker usually seeks higher-level intermediaries' support for a proposal, so that other employees will follow their superiors' leads. It is also useful to seek the support of intermediaries in other units of the organization, because some people only defer to superiors from their own units.

Strategy Options

To illustrate the large number of strategy options in organizations, we will list a number of choices that members of organizations possess, while realizing that many other options exist.

Option 1. A direct-service worker decides to implement (or not implement) a policy without consulting anyone. (We discussed issues of autonomy in Chapter Ten.)

Option 2. A social worker decides, much like the student intern in Case 10.1, to begin a pilot program with the support of her supervisor *before* seeking high-level policy clearance.

Option 3. A social worker decides to organize a broad-based coalition within an organization to seek a specific policy change. He decides to use a confrontive, polarizing style of politics, even though he realizes that the outcome is uncertain and that he risks alienating important, high-level officials.

Option 4. A social worker decides to develop a program innovation, but only after consulting extensively and striking deals with several people that result in extensive modifications of her original proposal.

Option 5. A social worker decides to change staff members' informal norms because she decides that they harm certain kinds of clients by giving them misdirected services. She persuades a high-level official to bring an external consultant to the agency to give technical training to its staff about new approaches to service delivery.

Option 6. A social worker promotes using a task force to seek a win-win, collaborative solution to a problem in an agency. She believes that a collaborative planning project will produce a better solution than a conflictual, polarizing approach.

Option 7. Convinced that a proposal will be accepted only if it has the executive director's support, a social worker uses her supervisor as an intermediary to seek the executive director's approval for the proposal.

Option 8. Despairing of any other approach, a social worker settles on "whistle-blowing," or taking an issue directly to the mass media in hopes that external pressure on the agency will make its officials remedy some of its staff members' unethical behaviors.

Option 9. A policy practitioner does not take an active role in developing a proposal, but waits until a strategic moment to place pressure on people so as to modify the proposal. She uses her negotiating and mediating skills to develop a compromise proposal.

DEVELOPING STRATEGY IN COMMUNITY SETTINGS

Social workers often try to change the policies of community institutions. They may want a school, for example, to help dropouts or provide condoms to students; a zoning board to approve a halfway house for mental patients in a specific neighborhood; or a city to fund an innovative program.

In each of these cases, social workers have several strategy choices. They can persuade highly placed officials to approve the policies in a manner that would discourage publicity and therefore conflict. These strategies would require the cooperation of high-level officials within the schools, the zoning board, or the city's human services department. Some community issues, however, such as distributing condoms to high school students, would likely attract opposition from many community residents, even if highly placed officials agreed with the policy. In volatile, public confrontations, practitioners need skills in mobilizing community groups, developing coalitions, and working with the mass media in an extended process of conflict.

With less contentious issues, a policy practitioner might wish to develop a win-win, collaborative process of solving problems. She might decide that people who lived near the site of a proposed halfway house would support its development if the proposal honored certain safeguards. She might convene a meeting of the community residents to develop safeguards, such as declaring that the residents of the halfway house could not leave it after 10:00 P.M.

Persons who advocate the needs of oppressed or powerless groups, such as children, often work with community-based advocacy groups. These groups use research, lobbying, and mobilizing tactics to persuade legislators and public officials to change existing policies. Advocates sometimes work for agencies, as well. Those who want to start an advocacy group need to plan "the architecture of the organization" carefully at its outset. They must decide issues such as whether the organization seeks to advocate, to educate, to provide services, or to emphasize some combination of these goals; what the organization's geographic basis is (whether it is based in a neighborhood, housing development, or political district, such as a city, county, or state); what the basis of membership is (individual members or a coalition of organizations?), and what its funding base is (funding from members or outside donors?).[60] Advocacy groups can be short-lived and focused on specific issues, such as obtaining increased funding for a program or having a reform enacted. The groups can also be long-lasting, such as ones that advocate a population's needs. In some cases, a strong public education or advocacy function can be implanted within a social-service agency, although the agency would have to think through implications for its tax-exempt status.

Any advocacy group must devote a considerable portion of its time to developing a membership base, because its "clout" with legislators and its ability to raise funds require a constituency. The group's leaders have to plan events that draw attention to its efforts, such as meetings with public officials, demonstrations, and press conferences. It has to develop a strategy for recruiting members, developing leaders, and raising funds.[61] In light of these logistical challenges, advocates often seek assistance from an existing group, rather than starting a new one, if one can be found that is willing to take the lead on an issue.

SUMMARY

Political strategy puts power resources to use and requires practitioners to plan a pattern of actions and verbal exchanges. To form strategy, policy practitioners need to understand the following:

- The importance and nature of political strategy
- Force-field analysis

- Elements of strategy
- How to develop strategy in agency, community, and legislative settings
- How to have legislation sponsored, drafted, and enacted
- How to testify before committees and organize pressure campaigns

Skillful strategists can sometimes make a seemingly hopeless situation more promising by carefully analyzing the distribution of power and sentiment, developing what-if scenarios, selecting a strategy, and revising strategy as circumstances change.

Devising strategy requires considerable guesswork because of the sheer number of imponderables. It is often difficult to gauge where individuals or interests stand with respect to a proposal or to predict how they will respond to arguments or presentations. A strategy that seems meritorious at one time may be rendered useless by opponents' unexpected tactical maneuvers.

Skillful policy practitioners view power and political strategy as indispensable tools for achieving their policy objectives. Practitioners need to adapt their strategy to the decisionmaking procedures of specific settings. We discussed strategy options in legislative, agency, and community settings in this chapter. Legislative strategists need specific parliamentary, negotiating, testifying, lobbying, and proposal-writing skills. As we discussed in Chapter Four, they need to understand legislative procedures and the mind-sets of elected officials.

Strategists in organizations encounter settings that are markedly different than legislatures. They need to be familiar with an institution's political economy, because proposals that increase an agency's resources and clients often fare the best. Strategists need skills in framing issues so that the proposals do not pose budgetary problems and are relevant to the organization's goals. They can often gain support for their proposals by working through intermediaries and taking people's informal relationships into account. As in legislative settings, tacticians in organizations have many tactical options.

When policy practitioners seek policy changes in community institutions, they must sometimes work with community groups, citizens, and highly placed officials. They can sometimes develop win-win, collaborative strategies, but other issues become enveloped in conflictual politics that require mobilizing support and building coalitions. When tackling an issue, practitioners can develop a community-based advocacy group or enlist the aid of an existing group.

Suggested Readings

GAUGING POLITICAL FEASIBILITY
George Brager and Stephen Holloway, *Changing Human Service Organizations* (New York: Free Press, 1978), pp. 57–92.
William Coplin and Michael O'Leary, *Everyman's Prince* (North Scituate, MA: Duxbury, 1976).

UNDERSTANDING AND PREDICTING CONFLICT
Morton Deutsch, *The Resolution of Conflict: Constructive and Destructive Processes* (New Haven, CT: Yale University Press, 1973), pp. 124–152.

DEVELOPING AND IMPLEMENTING POLITICAL STRATEGY
Eugene Bardach, *The Skill Factor in Politics* (Berkeley and Los Angeles: University of California Press, 1972), pp. 183–240.
Ron Dear and Rino Patti, "Legislative Advocacy: Seven Effective Tactics," *Social Work* 26 (July 1981): 289–297.

CASE STUDIES OF LEGISLATIVE POLITICS
Jeffrey Birnbaum and Alan Murray, *Showdown at Gucci Gulch* (New York: Random House, 1987).
Eric Redman, *The Dance of Legislation* (New York: Simon & Schuster, 1973).
Bruce Jansson, "An Extended Policy-Practice Case: Child Development and Daycare," in *Social Welfare Policy: From Theory to Practice* (Belmont, CA: Wadsworth, 1990), pp. 50–377.

POLICY PRACTICE IN LEGISLATIVE SETTINGS
Karen Haynes and James Mickelson, *Affecting Change: Social Workers in the Political Arena*, 2nd ed. (New York: Longman, 1991).
Willard Richan, *Lobbying for Social Change* (New York: Haworth Press, 1991).

POLITICS IN AGENCY SETTINGS
Brager and Holloway, *Changing Human Service Organizations*.
Burton Gummer, *The Politics of Social Administration: Managing Organizational Politics in Social Agencies* (Englewood Cliffs, NJ: Prentice-Hall, 1990).

POLITICS IN COMMUNITY SETTINGS
Kimberly Bobo, Jackie Kendall, and Steve Max, *Organizing for Social Change: A Manual for Activists in the 1990s* (Washington, DC: Seven Locks Press, 1991).
Steve Burghardt, *Organizing for Social Action* (Newbury Park, CA: Sage, 1982).
Si Kahn, *Organizing: A Guide for Grassroots Leaders* (Silver Spring, MD: National Association of Social Workers, 1991).

Notes

1. Ron Dear and Rino Patti discuss the need for compromises in policymaking in "Legislative Advocacy," *Encyclopedia of Social Work*, 18th ed., vol. 2 (Silver Spring, MD: National Association of Social Workers, 1987), p. 37.
2. George Brager and Stephen Holloway, *Changing Human Service Organizations* (New York: Free Press, 1978), pp. 107–128.
3. Kurt Lewin, *Field Theory in Social Science* (New York: Harper & Row, 1951).
4. William Coplin and Michael O'Leary, *Everyman's Prince* (North Scituate, MA: Duxbury, 1976), pp. 7–25.
5. Stephen Frantzich, *Computers in Congress* (Beverly Hills, CA: Sage, 1982), pp. 248–250.
6. Coplin and O'Leary, *Everyman's Prince*, pp. 20–25, 170–175.
7. Eric Schattschneider, *The Semisovereign People* (New York: Holt, Rinehart & Winston, 1960), pp. 1–19.
8. See the discussion of organizations' traditions, objectives, and ideology in Brager and Holloway, *Changing Human Service Organizations*, pp. 57–66.
9. See Julie Kosterlitz, "Not Just Kid Stuff," *National Journal* 20 (November 19, 1988): 2934–2939.
10. Brager and Holloway discuss the role of persons' tangible interests in shaping their positions in *Changing Human Service Organizations*, pp. 85–92.

11. Kosterlitz discusses feminist pressure in "Not Just Kid Stuff," pp. 2934-2939.
12. See John Kingdon, *Agendas, Alternatives, and Public Choices* (Boston: Little, Brown, 1984), pp. 152-170.
13. Warren Miller and Donald Stokes, "Constituency Influence in Congress," *American Political Science Review* 57 (March 1963): 45-56.
14. Bruce Jansson, "The History and Politics of Selected Children's Programs and Related Legislation," (Ph.D. diss., University of Chicago, 1975), pp. 248-274.
15. See Yeheskel Hasenfeld, *Human Service Organizations* (Englewood Cliffs, NJ: Prentice-Hall, 1983), pp. 43-49.
16. See Perry Smith, *Taking Charge* (Washington, DC: National Defense University Press, 1986), pp. 17-26.
17. Samuel Bacharach and Edward Lawler, *Power and Politics in Organizations* (San Francisco: Jossey-Bass, 1980).
18. Thomas Schelling, *The Strategy of Conflict* (Cambridge, MA: Harvard University Press, 1960).
19. Richard Fenno, *The Power of the Purse* (Boston: Little, Brown, 1966), pp. 193-195.
20. See Schelling, *Strategy of Conflict*.
21. Eugene Bardach, *The Skill Factor in Politics* (Berkeley and Los Angeles: University of California Press, 1972), pp. 188-189.
22. Brager and Holloway, *Changing Human Service Organizations*, pp. 140-141.
23. Characterizations of these candidates stem from journalistic commentaries in the *New York Times* and the *Los Angeles Times*.
24. Also see comparisons of consensus, collaborative, and contest styles of strategies in Rino Patti and Herman Resnick, "Changing the Agency from Within," *Social Work* 17 (July 1972): 48-57.
25. Both of them were able, as well, to appeal to conservatives. See Bruce Jansson, *Reluctant Welfare State: A History of American Social Welfare Policies*, 2nd ed. (Pacific Grove, CA: Brooks/Cole, 1993), pp. 183-184, 214-216.
26. See Theodore Lowi's model of "distributive" politics in "American Business, Public Policy, Case Studies, and Political Theory," *World Politics* 16 (July 1964): 677-715.
27. Brager and Holloway, *Changing Human Service Organizations*, pp. 194-195.
28. Bardach, *Skill Factor in Politics*, pp. 183-194.
29. Ibid., pp. 235-236.
30. Herman Resnick, "Tasks in Changing the Organization from Within," in Herman Resnick and Rino Patti, eds., *Change from Within: Humanizing Social Welfare Organizations* (Philadelphia: Temple University Press, 1980), pp. 210-212.
31. Nancy Amidei, "How to be an Advocate in Bad Times," *Public Welfare* 40 (Summer 1982): 41.
32. Carol Weiss, "Ideology, Interests, and Information: The Basis of Policy Positions," in Daniel Callahan and Bruce Jennings, eds., *Ethics, the Social Sciences, and Policy Analysis* (New York: Plenum, 1983), pp. 213-248.
33. Eric Redman, *The Dance of Legislation* (New York: Simon and Schuster, 1973).
34. Ibid.
35. Kimberly Bobo, Jackie Kendall, and Steve Max, *Organizing for Social Change: A Manual for Activists in the 1990s* (Washington, DC: Seven Locks Press, 1991), pp. 164-174.
36. Willard Richan, *Lobbying for Social Change* (New York: Haworth Press, 1991), pp. 50-71.
37. Lewis Dexter, "Role Relationships and Conception of Neutrality in Interviewing," *American Journal of Sociology* 62 (September 1956): 153-157.
38. Bobo, Kendall, and Max, *Organizing for Social Change*, pp. 199, 200.
39. Richard, *Lobbying for Social Change*, pp. 105-116.

40. Ibid., pp. 23–26.
41. Marilyn Bagwell and Sallee Clements, *A Political Handbook for Health Professionals* (Boston: Little, Brown, 1985), pp. 68–69.
42. Ron Dear and Rino Patti, "Legislative Advocacy: Seven Effective Tactics," *Social Work* 26 (July 1981): 289–297.
43. Ibid.
44. Bagwell and Clements, *Political Handbook for Health Professionals*, pp. 128–135.
45. Ibid., pp. 136–156.
46. Ibid., pp. 136–156.
47. Karen Haynes and James Mickelson, *Affecting Change: Social Workers in the Political Arena*, 2nd ed. (New York: Longman, 1986), pp. 76–78.
48. Ibid., pp. 76–78.
49. Christopher Matthews, *Hardball: How Politics Is Played* (New York: Summit Books, 1988), pp. 144–152.
50. Bagwell and Clements, *Political Handbook for Health Professionals*, pp. 216–234.
51. Ibid., pp. 189–194.
52. Haynes and Mickelson, *Affecting Change*, pp. 141–153.
53. Bagwell and Clements, *Political Handbook for Health Professionals*, pp. 162–184.
54. Haynes and Mickelson, *Affecting Change*, pp. 111–125.
55. Ibid., pp. 126–140.
56. Ibid., pp. 133–134.
57. Burton Gummer, *The Politics of Social Administration* (Englewood Cliffs, NJ: Prentice-Hall, 1990), pp. 25–26.
58. D. J. Hickson, et al. "A Strategic Contingencies Theory of Organizational Power," *Administrative Science Quarterly* 16 (June 1971): 216–229.
59. Rosabeth Kanter, *Men and Women of the Corporation* (New York: Basic Books, 1977), pp. 129–163.
60. Bobo, Kendall, and Max, *Organizing for Social Change*, pp. 20–33.
61. Steve Burghardt, *Organizing for Social Action* (Newbury Park, CA: Sage, 1982), pp. 37–48.

PART FOUR
AFTER ENACTING POLICY

Once policies have been approved, implementation and assessment take place. Many factors determine whether and how policies are implemented. We provide a framework for analyzing implementation in Chapter Thirteen and illustrate it by discussing the implementation of the Adoption Assistance and Child Welfare Act of 1980.

Evaluations of implemented policies have become increasingly important in the last two decades. We explore alternative methods of assessing policies in Chapter Fourteen and discuss the way politics intrudes even into this seemingly technical part of policymaking.

Chapter Thirteen
Implementing Policy

Policy implementation is no mere afterthought to policymaking; rather, implementation determines whether enacted policies are actualized. When someone says that a policy exists "only on paper," they suggest that the enacted policy has little effect on the implementors, such as the direct-service staff of a social agency. When people say that direct-service staff members "only halfheartedly" implement a policy, they suggest that staff members have only marginally honored the policy. Implementation is vital to policymaking, because it can lead official policies to be meaningless symbols, while allowing others to be actualized. If we content ourselves merely with enacting policies, then, we risk ignoring implementing processes that shape ultimate outcomes.

Implementation raises profound ethical questions for the staff of social agencies. We discussed in Chapter Ten, for example, that direct-service staff members sometimes decide not to heed, or to obey only partially, some high-level policies that they consider unethical. Indeed, we also discussed how, in unusual circumstances, staff members of social agencies might even engage in "whistleblowing," where they divulge information about unethical agency practices to outsiders, such as professional associations, regulators, or the mass media.

In this chapter, we provide a systems framework to the implementation process and an overview of how policy innovations are implemented in their political and economic context. We suggest alternative strategies for improving the implementation of specific policies.

A FRAMEWORK FOR IMPLEMENTING POLICY

We can conceptualize policy implementation as a systems diagram that includes (1) a policy innovation; (2) a political economy with profound implications for policy implementation; (3) implementing processes; (4) policy practitioners' efforts to reform the implementing processes; and (5) ultimate outcomes. These five components are depicted as interlocking rectangles. (See Figure 13.1.)

A systems framework is useful because it allows us to "track" a policy from its introduction to its final outcome, place the innovation in its political and economic context throughout its implementation, analyze processes of

Policy's Political Economy
- Extent that preexisting conditions support policy
  - Standard operating procedures
  - Mind-sets
  - Patterns of resource allocation
  - Preexisting relations between organizations
  - Orientation of staff toward the innovation
- Support
  - From funders
  - From public opinion
  - From organized interests
- Opposition
  - From funders
  - From public opinion
  - From organized interests

Implementing Processes
- Leadership
  - Top officials
  - Supervisors
- Interpretations of official policy
- Implementing milieu
  - Agency sites
- Staff's activities
- Patterns of interorganizational behavior
- Intended beneficiaries' responses to policy
  - Users
  - Nonusers

Efforts to Reform Implementing Processes
- Efforts to modify policy
- Efforts to reform implementation processes
  - By participants, such as leaders of direct-service staff
  - By external actors, such as pressure groups, legislators, or funders

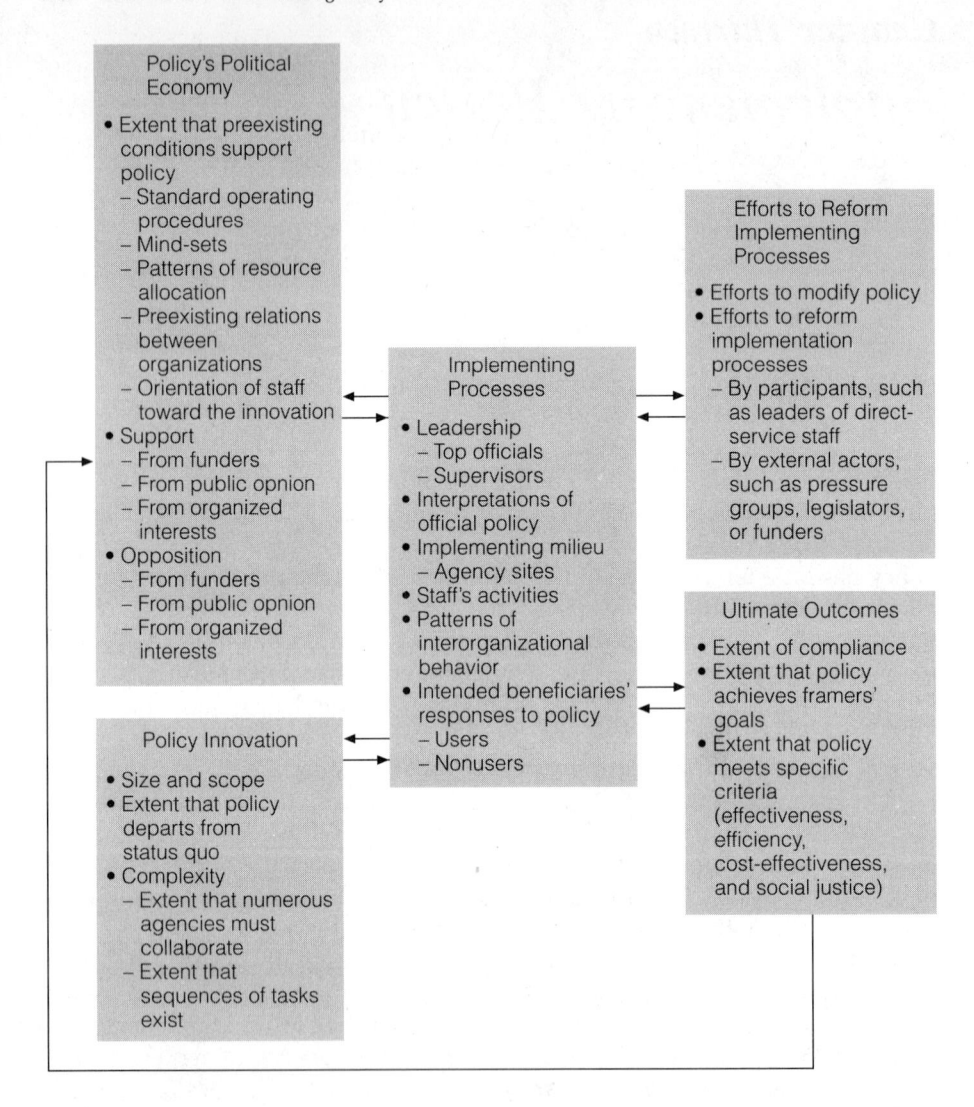

Ultimate Outcomes
- Extent of compliance
- Extent that policy achieves framers' goals
- Extent that policy meets specific criteria (effectiveness, efficiency, cost-effectiveness, and social justice)

Policy Innovation
- Size and scope
- Extent that policy departs from status quo
- Complexity
  - Extent that numerous agencies must collaborate
  - Extent that sequences of tasks exist

FIGURE 13.1
Systems framework for policy implementation

implementation, examine efforts to influence the implementing process, and analyze final outcomes. We can only understand how a policy innovation fares during implementation by analyzing its evolution in a specific context. We will now discuss the five elements of Figure 13.1.

Policy Innovations

Policy innovations are defined by the language of legislation and proposals and the understandings and interpretations that people possess at their inception.

Written policies are relatively easy to identify, although some vague terms may obscure their precise meaning. Ambiguous terms such as *increasing economic opportunity, full employment,* and *quality day-care* often appear in written policy.[1]

If we confined ourselves only to written policy, however, we would overlook the *policy intentions* of those decisionmakers who enacted the policy.[2] These policy intentions are often not reflected in the formal or written policies. For example, in 1965, the framers of Medicaid legislation wanted to increase poor people's access to physicians and hospitals that middle-class people used to allow them to escape class-based segregation in county and municipal hospitals. The program fulfilled many of the legislation's written policies, but most of its recipients continued to use public hospitals, so it failed to mainstream poor people into the larger medical system. Were we not to examine the persistence of such medical segregation, we would neglect a critically important failure of Medicaid.[3]

There are many kinds of policy innovations. Some of them are simple, such as a proposal to modify an agency's intake services in a minor way. Others are highly complex, such as national health insurance. Some policy innovations require many people and agencies to collaborate, while relatively few persons and one agency can implement others. Some policy innovations involve only a single task, such as changing intake procedures, while others require a sequence of tasks. To stimulate jobs in the inner cities, for example, we would need to lure industry into the cities, provide job training, improve the educational system, and enhance the infrastructure. Some policy innovations require vast amounts of resources, while other innovations need very few. Some policy innovations are mandated by higher authorities in a highly detailed way, while others are vaguely defined.[4]

Even this cursory discussion suggests that some policies are simpler to implement than others. A straightforward change in an agency's intake procedure that requires few resources and that the executive director has defined precisely can usually be implemented without much difficulty. Contrast this simple change with an ambitious, nationwide effort to make sweeping reforms in the child welfare system. We can hypothesize that innovations become more difficult to implement as they require major changes from the status quo, when they require many institutions to collaborate, and when a sequence of tasks must be accomplished.

Implementing policy innovations becomes more problematic, as well, when they contain *internal contradictions* and *flawed strategies*. Assume, for example, that a policy innovation seeks ambitious changes in existing programs, but allocates only minimal resources. This internal contradiction is illustrated by the ill-fated War on Poverty in the 1960s and by the Family Support Act of 1988. In each case, the policy innovations sought sweeping changes, such as the "elimination of poverty" in the United States or "the employment of large numbers of welfare recipients," but the resources allotted to these sweeping goals were miniscule.[5]

It is easy to overlook the actual substance of policy innovations when predicting their fate. A policy is likely to be unsuccessful if it proposes ill-conceived strategies.[6] Take the Family Support Act of 1988 as an example. The legislation proposed giving many women on welfare jobs when well-paying, blue-collar jobs were in sharp decline and women had minimal access to unionized jobs in the trades, such as plumbing and carpentry. Moreover, many studies revealed that most female welfare recipients had educational deficits; indeed, many of them had not even completed high school. The Family Support Act proposed "lifting" numerous welfare recipients into jobs without fundamentally addressing these economic and educational realities; instead, the legislation proposed modest training, educational, and day-care remedies. Nor did the legislation acknowledge that many women's net economic condition might deteriorate if they lost access to Medicaid, public housing, and food stamps, even after obtaining low-paying jobs. By requiring states to contribute a considerable share of the training and education costs, the legislation overlooked many states' budget deficits, which would likely restrict resources for these training and educational programs.

When we examine implementation, then, we should ask, "Do the actions of the people charged with implementing policies correspond to the formal policies, and do the enacted policies achieve the farmers' hopes or expectations?" In some cases, we can predict a policy's likely prognosis, even before it has been implemented, by examining its content and whether it contains internal contradictions and flawed strategies.

The Political Economy of Policies

Recall that in Chapter Four we discussed the political economy of organizations. In similar fashion, policy innovations have a political economy that includes the policies and budgets of the organizations that implement them.

These organizations have *standard operating procedures* that their staff members have evolved, such as techniques for reaching their clientele, organizing waiting lists, addressing clients' needs, and making referrals. These standard operating procedures may prove well-suited to a particular innovation, but they may also frustrate its implementation by being contrary to the procedures needed to implement a new policy.[7]

Organizational members have certain *mind-sets* that powerfully shape their perceptions of social problems and service strategies. While educators tend to focus on children's cognitive needs, for example, social workers are more inclined to emphasize their developmental and familial needs. These orientations can lead staff members to support or oppose the implementation of a new policy.

Organizations' *priorities* are reflected in their budgets and in their perceptions of problems. In the case of a policy to help dropouts, staff members in some schools may view students' attrition as outside their central priority of providing educational services to students who do attend classes, whereas staff members in other schools may believe assistance to dropouts should receive the highest priority.

Organizations' *patterns of resource allocation* may profoundly shape a new policy's fate. If an agency has had to make numerous budget cuts before initiating a costly policy, its officials and staff members may not support its implementation, but they might support it if it brought sizeable resources to the organization, such as from a funded grant.

Human services organizations may be interdependent, collaborative, competitive, autonomous, or opportunistic in their relations with other human services organizations.[8] A relatively self-contained program will not require collaboration between organizations, but agencies that are autonomous may be ill-suited to implement an innovation that requires clients to receive a variety of services. It is often difficult to develop collaborative relations between organizations if their prior relations have been competitive or if their staff members view one another with suspicion.

The importance of interagency relationships is illustrated by the Family Support Act of 1988. Many unemployed women on welfare need job training, remedial reading, child care, public transportation, career planning skills, job search skills, and help in caring for disabled members of their families. Administrators of programs to help these women must develop collaborative relations with public, not-for-profit, and profit-oriented agencies. Were staff in public employment agencies to decide that they did not want to work with welfare recipients, preferring instead to work with other kinds of clientele, they would undermine the effectiveness of the family support programs. Yet policies can sometimes create collaborative arrangements where they did not exist, particularly if the "lead agency" has resources to contract or purchase services from other agencies.

The prognosis for a policy innovation improves if implementors receive supportive pressure or assistance. We noted in Chapter Four that *patterns of external pressure* can influence organizations' staff members. Assume for example, that a school district designates a high school as the place where single mothers go to classes. If other children's parents strongly object to this decision, saying that they do not want their children exposed to so many young, single mothers, the school's principal and teachers might ask the school district to designate another school. This would hardly be a promising development for activists who hoped to develop supportive programs for single mothers. In other cases, external organizations, such as citizen groups or professional associations, may strongly support a new policy by providing volunteers, seeking greater funding for it, or helping with outreach.

When analyzing the success or failure of a policy's implementation, we often examine the sort of *leadership* that preexisted the policy's introduction. Leaders' values, commitments, and priorities often influence whether they lend their prestige, authority, time, and resources to a policy's implementation. When executives believe that a policy is unwise or intrusive, they are less likely to support its implementation.[9] They may also inject their perspectives into its implementation by not enforcing some of its goals or provisions. When executives like an innovation, by contrast, they may monitor its implementation, invest their own political capital to ensure its success, and ask staff members to "go the extra mile."

Thus, policy innovations are more likely to be implemented when an organization's standard operating procedures, key officials' and staff's mind-sets, organizational priorities, patterns of collaboration between organizations that must implement the innovation, and leadership strongly support them. Moreover, implementation is more likely when an innovation has wide support from the general public and organized interests. When the Head Start Program was created, the founders *created* a supportive context by forming wholly new agencies to implement it. They did so because they believed that educational institutions would be indifferent to the program's child-development, parent-participation, and advocacy components. They developed a national network of parent groups that lobbied public officials to increase funding for the program and to oppose efforts to place the program under the control of local schools.

When policies are introduced into a nonsupportive, polarized context, their prognosis is bleaker, as the discussion about programs to help welfare recipients find work suggests. Many Americans believe welfare recipients are "freeloaders." Because this ideology prevails, politicians often fail to secure ample resources to train and create jobs for welfare recipients. Nor have employment agencies, vocational training programs, child-care programs, and public transportation systems provided sufficient services to these work-training programs. Job-training programs enter an unsupportive economic environment in which relatively unskilled women have encountered discrimination in job markets and have often been limited to minimum-wage positions, even after extended training. With meager incomes from these jobs, they have often found it less profitable to work than to stay on welfare rolls, where they at least receive medical benefits, food stamps, and public housing benefits.

Implementing Processes

Once a policy is launched, its fate hinges on the beliefs and actions of various people and groups. If our discussion of a policy's political economy focused on preexisting orientations, we emphasize actual, unfolding beliefs and actions of decisionmakers, executives, staff, and clients when we discuss implementing processes (see the center rectangle of Figure 13.1). We want to know whether leaders charged with implementing a policy invest energy and political resources in doing so. We also want to know whether they believe the policy is important and whether it furthers their values, prestige, resources, or power. In addition, we want to know if specific leaders fear negative consequences, such as reprimands or loss of funding, if they do *not* vigorously implement a policy. In the case of multifaceted policies, we want to know which facets they support or oppose.

We want to know how decisionmakers and implementors interpret specific policies in light of the vagueness of many written policies. For example, when implementing legislation designed to help female welfare recipients find and retain work, do some administrators believe the policy requires them to force women into employment when they do not join job-training programs, or do the administrators emphasize recruiting volunteers? Do they believe the intent of the policy is for them to concentrate their job-training resources on those welfare recipients who have the best job prospects or to emphasize services to those with the bleakest prospects? (The original policy might be vague on these points.) In some cases, we may discover that, when reading the same policy, people interpret it in different ways. Or some might be ignorant about certain facets of a policy, even when the policy is precisely defined.

Policies are implemented in many sites, whose characteristics shape implementation processes. The division of labor and hierarchy was discussed in Chapter Four, where internal characteristics of agencies were described. Agencies' structural characteristics shape the implementation of specific policies in powerful ways. For example, they determine which persons and units within a bureaucracy are responsible for overseeing implementation of specific parts of a policy. They also determine how the work is to be divided among specific units. Later in this chapter, we will consider how staff turnover, morale, patterns of communication, and leadership styles affect implementation.

The fate of many policies hinges on the beliefs and actions of line staff. In Chapter Ten, we discussed how staff possess considerable discretion because of their autonomy. What is staff's understanding of a policy? How committed are they to its implementation? Do they have enough technical training to understand and implement it? Is the agency's informal culture supportive of the policy? If the staff are unionized, do union leaders support the policy, or do they attempt to hinder implementation, such as by opposing in-home visits on the grounds that they impose undue burdens on staff?

We have discussed the importance of interorganizational relationships to implementation. Implementors often can offer to other organizations inducements for cooperation, such as partnership that foster a division of labor in helping specific kinds of clients. Implementors can also hire case managers to help clients obtain resources from other agencies. However, these interorganizational links can be time-consuming to develop and maintain. Further, they can be difficult to develop when the staff of other agencies, already overburdened by existing commitments, believe they are being asked to shoulder additional burdens without such inducements as additional resources.

Usually ignored in the burgeoning literature on implementation, *the responses of a policy's beneficiaries* profoundly shape the course of implementation. For example, assume that high-level officials, wanting to "get homeless people off the streets," fund a project in which outreach workers attempt to persuade homeless people to enter shelters. Even if the workers implemented this policy diligently, their work would come to naught if large numbers of homeless people refused to enter shelters, either because they saw the outreach workers as unwelcome authority figures or because they believed the shelters were inferior to life on the streets. Indeed, marketing theory, which we discussed in Chapter Six, suggests that consumers will not respond favorably to programs that do not seem to offer benefits that offset the costs and risks they associate with them. For instance, they might perceive the time or effort involved in using services as a cost. They make these calculations, moreover, from the perspective of their culture, values, and previous experiences.

Reforming the Implementing Process

Our discussion to this point may falsely suggest that various forces *determine* a policy's fate once it has been initiated. In fact, implementation processes *evolve* in the months and years after an innovation has been enacted. The actions of various levels of staff and the responses of intended beneficiaries cause a policy's ultimate success or failure.

Implementation also depends on the evolving political and economic context. After the early stages of a policy's implementation, political, economic, demographic, cultural, and social factors may arise that impede or facilitate its implementation. Indeed, when a policy is enacted, its advocates cannot easily predict what developments may ensue, such as the election of governmental figures who oppose or support it and how many budgetary resources it will or will not receive.

By the same token, specific people can shape a policy's destiny by diagnosing why its implementation is flawed and developing interventive strategies. (See the upper right rectangle in Figure 13.1.) The prognosis for a policy innovation becomes more promising when several persons take a personal interest in its fate. Indeed, Eugene Bardach argues that innovations need a "fixer," or a powerful person willing to invest extraordinary time and political capital in following an implemented policy, identifying obstacles, and seeking remedies.[10] Later in this chapter, we discuss various tactics that advocates can use to reform the implementing process.

Ultimate Outcomes

On the right side of Figure 13.1, we place the "ultimate outcomes" of policy implementation. We want to know if official, high-level policies are implemented *as their framers intended* and whether the implementation processes advance the framers' specific goals, such as social justice, fairness, effectiveness, and cost-effectiveness.

It is often not easy to evaluate these outcomes objectively. We often rely on reports and statistics from those who actually implement a policy to ascertain whether it is implemented. However, agencies and providers often slant these data because they know their continued funding requires "compliance." Program evaluations that assess policies' implementation require considerable time and resources to complete, as well as the cooperation of agencies that implement the policy. (We discuss program and policy evaluation in more detail in this chapter and in Chapter Fourteen.)

Perceptions of program outcomes, whether based on empirical studies, secondhand reports, or informal observations, often become an important part of a policy's political economy (see Figure 13.1). When some legislators believe that implementing staff do not comply with existing policy, they may cut the funding of a program or try to modify the original legislation to make official policy more precise. For example, at many points in the last three decades, conservative politicians sought to "tighten" welfare programs because they believed agency staff did not enforce work-requirement provisions. The negative findings of a national evaluation of the Head Start Program led to presidential efforts to cut the program's size, whereas more recent research, which documented positive outcomes, fostered fuller funding of the program. Of course, people's preexisting orientations often shape which evidence they choose to emphasize or ignore when they consider a program's outcomes. These orientations also shape the interpretations people place on evaluations. When viewing a study that suggests a program achieves modest results, someone who initially opposed it might argue that "the glass is half empty," while someone who had supported it might declare that "the glass is half full."

THE ADOPTION ASSISTANCE AND CHILD WELFARE ACT OF 1980

Our discussion of Figure 13.1 suggests that policy implementation must be viewed as a multifaceted process that involves a policy innovation, a political and economic context, implementation processes, efforts to reform the implementing process, and policy outcomes. When we decide that a policy has or has not been implemented, we usually have to examine the various factors, singly and in tandem, that yield this outcome, rather than seeking a single cause. Our lead example will be the implementation of the Adoption Assistance and Child Welfare Act of 1980.

THE POLICY INNOVATION

The Adoption Assistance and Child Welfare Act of 1980 proposed a major overhauling of the child welfare system. Most children reside in their natural homes with one or more parents. When someone reports child abuse (typically physical abuse) or child neglect (when a child's nutritional, clothing, and other physical needs are not met), child-welfare staff investigate the home to see if the charges appear to have merit. They place the children in protective custody, often in a short-term detention center, pending an initial investigation. A dispositional hearing of the juvenile court ensues, with the court deciding whether to return the child to the natural home or place the child in foster care until later dispositional hearings. After those later hearings, the child can return to the natural home or stay in long-term foster (or institutional) care. They may eventually be placed in adoptive homes.

Before this legislation passed, many people were alarmed by the dramatic increase in the numbers of children placed in foster care due to their parents' alleged abusive behavior or neglect of basic needs. (The number of children in foster care had risen from 177,000 children in 1961 to more than 500,000 children in 1979.)[11]

The Adoption Assistance and Child Welfare Act of 1980 reflects the importance of both official, written policy and policy expectations to implementation. To understand its framers' policy expectations, we need to examine the child welfare system as it existed in 1980. Senators such as Alan Cranston and professional associations such as the Child Welfare League of America promoted the legislation, because they were worried that so many children, mostly minorities and teenagers, remained in foster homes or children's institutions for years after being removed from their natural homes.[12] Juvenile courts had taken the children from their natural homes not only because of neglect and physical abuse, but also because the children were "incorrigible"—their parents could not control or discipline them. (The courts took most of these children from the parents, though some parents voluntarily relinquished them.)

Framers of the legislation wanted permanent arrangements to replace the "state of limbo" that many children experienced as they moved between placements, whether in foster homes or in institutions. The framers realized that two sets of officials and staff members were the pillars of the child-welfare system. First, the child-welfare staff, conducted most of the counseling, screening, and placement services for the children, as well as for the foster home parents, the natural parents, and the adoptive parents. Second, the juvenile court judges made pivotal decisions about the children's dispositions.

The framers believed that impermanency plagued most children who were taken from their natural families for several reasons. Many child-welfare staff and juvenile court judges had become so accustomed to temporary arrangements for children that they did not assertively seek permanent arrangements. Despite legislation in some states that provided subsidies to adoptive parents to ease the financial burdens of assuming legal responsibility for a child, relatively few persons volunteered to adopt children, particularly adolescents, minorities, or children with serious physical or mental problems. In some cases, local staff members did not even try to rehabilitate the natural families to allow the children to return to them. This may have been true partly because the federal government funded the ongoing foster care costs for AFDC children, not rehabilitation costs.[13]

Critics of the child-welfare system saw other flaws, as well. They believed that subtle forms of racial prejudice and social-class bias influenced child-welfare workers to remove children from some homes. Did they not, critics asked, sometimes mistake authoritarian modes of child rearing, which are relatively common in lower-class families, for child abuse? Did they overlook that low-income parents sometimes neglect their children because they lack economic resources to provide them with basic amenities?

The framers hoped to make fundamental changes in the decisions made in the child-welfare system. They wanted tens of thousands of children to obtain permanent arrangements, either by returning to their rehabilitated natural families or by finding adoptive parents. The framers ingeniously combined incentives and requirements to accomplish these sweeping objectives. Because they knew that the existing child-welfare system was grievously underfunded (many social workers' caseloads exceeded eighty families), they wanted to provide additional funds to the child-welfare system. Moreover, they wanted to provide adoptive parents with subsidies to defray the cost of raising adopted children, because they knew that financial reasons deterred many parents, particularly poor ones, from adopting children. They feared that pumping more money into the system could be counterproductive if they did not require states to promote permanent arrangements for children, so they made states' receipt of the funds contingent on setting certain policies in motion, such as improved record-keeping systems and having courts periodically review cases.

The framers also established certain national standards. They required each state to have a tracking system so they could monitor each child's progress and so that no children became "lost" in the foster-care or institutional system. Moreover, they required each state to have external reviewing bodies (either the courts or administrative bodies) assess each child's progress. The framers charged the courts with initially determining that a child should be removed from its natural parents, so as to protect the natural parents' rights. They mandated a case review, as well, after the child had been in foster care for six months and again at twelve months to ensure that caseworkers had planned permanent arrangements. They also ordered a formal review at eighteen months to ensure that the permanency plan had been implemented, meaning the child had either been returned to the natural parents or adopted. To provide counseling and other services to natural parents, both before and after abusive and neglectful behavior, the legislation greatly increased the amount of federal money states would receive to fund child-welfare services. The framers hoped this money would increase efforts to reunify families, find adoptive parents, and develop permanent arrangements.

The legislation's framers used a three-pronged strategy, then, to reform the child-welfare system.[14] First, they provided subsidies to adoptive parents. Second, they required the states and courts to track children's progress in foster care and to review cases initially, as well as at six-, twelve-, and eighteen-month intervals. Third, they provided more funds for child-welfare services to encourage states to reunify families and make permanent arrangements.

The Adoption Assistance and Child Welfare Act was an ambitious and complex innovation that required many institutions to collaborate. It established a national mandate for fundamentally changing the child-welfare system by proposing that hundreds of thousands of children be placed in adoptive homes or reunified with their natural families. It proposed to change the actions of child-welfare workers, judges, potential adoptive families, child-welfare institutions, and natural parents. Moreover, the framers hoped that state legislatures would increase their funding of child-welfare services and that Congress would appropriate substantial sums to implement the policy in the years following its enactment.

Ambitious and complex innovations can be successfully implemented, of course, but their prognosis is uncertain when they are cast into problematic and unpredictable environments, where considerable funding problems, opposition, and institutional rivalries exist. We will now discuss the unfolding political and economic context of this policy innovation during the 1980s and early 1990s.

THE POLITICAL AND ECONOMIC CONTEXT

To understand why certain policies have been implemented and others have not, we need to examine implementation realities that preceded a policy innovation. Every policy is inserted into a context that can help or hinder its implementation. Moreover, we need to identify societal factors that impinged on the human delivery system before a policy's enactment.

For example, few professional, community, or client groups exerted pressure on politicians to increase funding for child-welfare services in the decades before 1980.[15] Many jurisdictions had already declassified child-welfare services, which means filling child-welfare positions with people who lacked master's degrees in social work or even bachelor's degrees in social work or the social sciences.[16] Local and state tax revolts, which began with Proposition 13 in California in 1978, bore ominous implications for funding of local child-welfare services.[17] Moreover, although many federal legislators did not sense it prior to Ronald Reagan's election in November 1980, considerable public sentiment had developed to cut federal social spending.[18] These political developments had severe repercussions for the implementation of the Adoption Assistance and Child Welfare Act, as we will discuss later. Another societal development with important implications was the sharp increase in reports of child abuse and neglect flooding child-welfare offices in the late 1970s. These calls, which may have stemmed more from public awareness of maltreatment of children than from actual increases in its incidence, severely limited workers' ability to devote much time to processing children already inside the foster-care system.[19] Finally, the rapidly rising number of women in the workforce, which began in the 1950s, continued in the 1970s and 1980s, exacerbating the problem of finding women or families willing to be foster parents or adopt children after the enactment of the Adoption Assistance and Child Welfare Act.[20]

Because we want to know whether various participants favored the innovation's underlying objectives and policies or whether they opposed them, we include both positive and negative factors in Box 13.1.

As this list shows, many factors form the context of a major innovation, such as the Adoption Assistance and Child Welfare Act. In this welter of positive and negative factors, it is often difficult to predict how a particular innovation will fare, on balance, once it has been enacted. Even a cursory examination of this list suggests that the context was uncertain in the early 1980s; if some evidence suggests that many persons and institutions would welcome sweeping reforms, other evidence indicates that numerous funding, institutional, and political factors could sabotage the reform.

The overriding question to ask with respect to any policy innovation is whether its provisions and resources will be sufficient to overcome resistance to reforms. Because the existing child-welfare system was swamped with excessive work loads and crises, many persons wondered whether the legislation would create permanent arrangements for hundreds of thousands of children, whose ranks included many hard-to-adopt adolescent, minority, and disabled youth.[21]

BOX 13.1
The Political and Economic Context of the Adoption Assistance and Child Welfare Act

POSITIVE FACTORS

- Because rapid increases in foster care became extraordinarily costly to local and state governments, they wanted to make the system more efficient.
- Many states had developed their own adoption-subsidy programs and seen some increases in adoptions as a result, even before the enactment of the Adoption Assistance and Child Welfare Act of 1980.
- Subjected to litigation and adverse publicity stemming from scandals, such as ill-advised placement decisions and poor foster care, many officials and staff in child-welfare departments wanted to reform their services.
- Finding it difficult to recruit foster care parents or adoptive parents, particularly for handicapped, ethnic, and adolescent children, many state and local officials were eager to cooperate with legislation to decrease the numbers of children in foster care and to promote adoptions.
- Many juvenile court justices wanted to assume a more active role in reviewing cases and promoting permanent arrangements.
- Attorneys had increasingly publicized and defended natural families' rights to due process in court proceedings. This development made juvenile courts and child-welfare staff less inclined to remove children quickly from their natural families.
- African-American and Latino communities had developed considerable interest in same-race adoptions, rather than transracial adoptions, thus enlarging the pool of adoptive parents in ethnic communities.

NEGATIVE FACTORS

- Top administrators of child welfare in state and county positions were so preoccupied with responding to child-abuse and child-neglect cases that they lacked time to give intensive services to children or natural families.
- Rigid hierarchies in social services precluded top officials' communication with low-level staff.
- In light of allegations that many children had been harmed when prematurely returned to their natural parents, many high-level administrators emphasized child removal, rather than efforts to improve the parenting skills of natural parents.
- Unions, which represent direct-service and clerical staff, emphasized pay, fringe benefits, and work loads, rather than service-related issues.

continued

BOX 13.1 continued

• Many legislators did not believe powerful constituents supported major improvements in child-welfare programs.

• State legislatures and county boards of supervisors did not fund child-welfare services sufficiently to allow caseloads to be reduced, due to local tax revolts and the absence of political or community constituencies concerned about child welfare.

• Institutions, which received funds for children who stayed with them, had economic incentives not to return children to their natural families or to place them with adoptive families.

• Because of declassification, where many local and state governments removed professional training requirements from specific jobs, many supervisors and direct-service staff in child-welfare departments lacked training in social work. Lacking treatment skills and concepts, they could not easily perform the complex tasks required by the new legislation.

• Many natural parents viewed the child-welfare staff and juvenile court as adversaries who primarily want to take their children from them. Because direct-service staff were so burdened with child-removal and investigation functions, they had scant interaction with natural parents. (Increasing numbers of natural parents obtained attorneys.)

• Many parents neglected their children because they lacked sufficient financial resources; thus, children were insufficiently fed and clothed. Moreover, poverty contributed to some abusive behavior by exacerbating intrafamilial tension. Yet no system existed within child-welfare agencies for providing job-training or employment-referral services for parents.

• Innovative services, such as residential centers where troubled families can reside while receiving counseling, did not exist in most localities.

PROBLEMS IN THE EARLY STAGES OF IMPLEMENTATION

Once enacted, the Adoption Assistance and Child Welfare Act was soon implemented in the various states. Each of them, as the act required, passed legislation mandating juvenile courts to hold disposition hearings at six-, twelve-, and eighteen-month intervals. The states also established procedures to "track" children who were removed from their natural homes.

Federal policies soon imperiled the implementation of the legislation. Seeking to devolve power to the states, Ronald Reagan tried to place the legislation within the Social Services Block Grant. This move would more or less have removed federal direction and leadership from child welfare by giving each state a carte blanche. Unlike the framers of the legislation, who wanted federal authorities to take an aggressive leadership and funding role, Reagan viewed the legislation as simply another categorical program to be phased into block grants. Moreover, Reagan sought to cut funds from the legislation and diminish federal surveillance of state programs. Children's advocates were able to keep the legislation out of the block grant and avert major funding cuts by federal authorities, but they could not obtain assertive monitoring of programs in an administration committed to diminishing the federal oversight of social programs.[22]

Children's advocates also encountered uphill battles in each of the states. To obtain federal funds, states had to maintain or increase their own, matching funds for child welfare in a period when many states experienced budget cuts. To cut the costs of their foster-care program, some states and counties tried to encourage child-welfare workers and juvenile courts to return children to their natural families, even when those families had not been provided intensive, social services. Nor did most states and counties move assertively to increase the numbers of child-welfare workers or supervisors with graduate degrees in social work.[23]

Still, encouraging signs existed. The numbers of children in foster care replacements plummeted from 500,000 children in 1977 to 251,000 children in 1983, even if some of these children were ill-advisedly returned to natural parents who continued to abuse or neglect them. The federal government spent almost $150 million for adoption subsidies for about 6,500 children in 1983. The legislation had begun to "shake up" the traditional institutions in child welfare, had decisively changed the mind-sets of many child-welfare workers, and had sensitized some officials to the need for more trained staff.

However, many child-welfare agencies continued to provide an unfavorable milieu for humanistic services to children, much less for implementing this policy innovation. Wanting to analyze the organizational milieu, Nora Gustavsson, a doctoral student, collected data from direct-service workers and foster care parents in a California child-welfare office in 1985.[24] While representing only a single county in one state, her data strongly suggested that "firing-line, direct-service staff" poorly understood the new high-level state and federal policies. She found that many child-welfare workers only minimally understood the state and federal legislation, that they often believed their supervisors had scant understanding of it, and that they received little or no in-service training to perform the tasks it required. Many of them reported that they rarely or never discussed the state's legislation. Most important, the child-welfare workers said that relatively few changes had occurred in their jobs since the federal and state legislation had mandated permanency planning; their caseloads remained the same, their time for client contact had not increased, and they had no greater "placement resources."[25]

Gustavsson also discovered an unintended consequence of the legislation—the number of foster parents who adopted children, became their guardians, or became their long-term foster care parents seemed to increase. Unable to reunify some children with their parents and recruit large numbers of adoptive parents in African-American and Latino communities, child-welfare workers increasingly viewed foster care parents as "permanent arrangements." However, this development had some adverse consequences, such as depleting the ranks of foster care parents as they filled these new roles and reducing the pressure on the child-welfare workers to find adoptive parents.[26]

PROBLEMS IN THE LATER STAGES OF IMPLEMENTATION

Other practical problems frustrated permanency planning. It had been widely assumed that many adoptive families, particularly from minority groups whose children were least likely to be adopted, would be lured by subsidies to become adoptive parents. (Some subsidy programs in various states had been successful in attracting adoptive parents.) However, the framers of the 1980 legislation miscalculated on several fronts. The incentives were probably insufficient to attract many parents to adopt children with difficult mental and physical problems. Free, long-term medical and counseling services existed only for conditions that existed at the time of adoption and only when children qualified for AFDC at the time of adoption.[27] Further, as members of minority groups became more affluent, many of them became less committed to helping poorer members of their groups, such as children in foster care.

Other practical problems frustrated implementation. It is difficult in the best of circumstances to determine whether a specific child should return home or be adopted; the insistence on an eighteen-month deadline for removing children from foster care, which works well in clear-cut situations, can be dysfunctional when social workers encounter families that require extended counseling to be able to provide adequate parenting.[28] Moreover, despite marginal increases in the federal funding of child-welfare services, the sustained and intensive provision of services to these families was often not feasible because of social workers' preoccupation with investigating new cases.[29]

Indeed, this preoccupation was prompted, in part, by a veritable explosion of reports of abused and neglected children, which increased by 147 percent between 1979 and 1989 for an astonishing total of 2.4 million reported cases in 1989 (child-welfare staff are required to investigate these cases). In addition, new kinds of cases had arisen; by 1993, more than 300,000 cocaine-addicted babies were born to drug-dependent mothers; each of these babies required time-consuming and intensive services to determine where they would be placed. The economic problems of the lowest quintile of the population worsened markedly during the Reagan and Bush administrations, adding to the numbers of children reported to be abused and neglected. Inundated by these kinds of problems, child-welfare staff were often unable to provide services to needy families. In fact, some critics feared that local staff often reunited children with their families without adequate investigations and with no follow-up services to see if abusive or neglectful behaviors still existed.[30]

Logistical problems also existed in the thousands of local child-welfare offices and juvenile courts across the nation. Permanency planning requires a team approach in which child-welfare workers, workers who locate adoptive families, judges, social work staff from juvenile courts, natural parents, foster parents, and supervisors work together to develop and implement plans. In some local offices, however, bureaucratic modes of operation emphasized top-down and specialized functions, precluding the formation of teams. Bureaucratic rivalries between juvenile courts and child-welfare departments sometimes impeded collaboration.[31] Most child-welfare departments did not possess close working relations with health, education, job-training, and mental health departments. Such links are vital if natural parents and children are to benefit from case-managed services that could address their problems.

The top-down mode of bureaucratic organization also interfered with direct-service staff members' understanding of the new permanency-planning policy. Often, they did not receive in-service or technical training to allow them to implement it. High rates of turnover, which were linked to excessive work loads, poor pay, and declassification, further frustrated implementation.[32]

Because of their optimistic assumptions, it is unlikely that most framers of the legislation realized that states and localities would resort extensively to questionable practices, such as returning many children to natural parents without adequate investigations or follow-up services, pressuring foster care parents to adopt children who had been placed with them, or placing severely disabled children with adoptive parents who were not fully informed of the extent of their physical or mental needs. Few adoptive families received follow-up services.[33] Each of these dubious practices was more likely to occur when the ambitious policy mandate to reform the child-welfare system was not coupled with massive increases in federal funding for child-welfare services.

DEVELOPING REMEDIES

It is interesting to speculate what the framers of the Adoption Assistance and Child Welfare Act could have included in their proposal had they guessed that federal and state authorities would not generously fund it or that the Reagan administration would not zealously monitor it.[34] They might have increased the federal funding of services even more. Had they realized how difficult it would be to find adoptive parents, they might have provided them even greater financial incentives or included broader health and counseling benefits. They might have questioned the advisability of rapidly moving hundreds of thousands of children from foster care back to their natural parents, had they realized that many children would be returned without receiving intensive services. A sort of revolving door developed, where children were taken from their natural parents and placed in foster care, reunited with their parents without adequate services or even diagnostic work, and then taken from their parents again after new reports of abuse or neglect. In this scenario, they could have increased the training and subsidies of foster care parents, and increased the status of foster care by defining it as a career that deserves a salary. Perhaps they could have established community group homes instead of focusing so heavily on permanency planning.

We could also make a radical critique of the Adoption Assistance and Child Welfare Act. While the legislation enhanced the record-keeping and adoptions of some children, it failed to address the poverty, unemployment, poor housing, substance abuse, and other causes of child neglect and child abuse.[35] Of course, policy options remedying these problems would have had drawbacks of their own, but the framers might have considered them more carefully had they anticipated the funding and program realities that their innovation would encounter.

Once the legislation was enacted, child-welfare advocates in various cities and counties were able to secure several victories that improved its implementation. In Los Angeles, for example, children's advocates pressured the County Board of Supervisors to increase the fiscal resources for child welfare markedly, hire an innovative and committed leader to head the Department of Children's Services, and embark on an ambitious program of professionalizing many direct-service and supervisory positions. (Many positions that had been declassified in the preceding decade were now defined as requiring an M.S.W.)

Policy practitioners can use at least six strategies to improve implementation: they can amend the original legislation, change the content of administrative regulations to shape implementation, mobilize pressure to increase a program's funding, enhance monitoring and high-level leadership, engage in community-based advocacy projects, and make the setting where the policy is ultimately delivered more amenable to the program.

Legislative Strategies

Legislation is not written in stone. In subsequent legislative sessions, policy advocates can convince legislators that they made some mistakes in their original version. Advocates often find it difficult to reopen the original legislation for amendments in the years immediately following its enactment, because having developed the legislation only through elaborate compromises, they are reluctant to reopen "Pandora's box." Moreover, some legislators may argue, "That problem can be addressed by changing the administrative regulations, not the legislation itself." If they can make a good case, however, that the legislation was fundamentally flawed, advocates can make incremental changes in the original legislation by finding legislators who will agree to sponsor these changes and developing action systems. The Adoption Assistance and Child Welfare Act was modified several years after its initial passage to allow adopted children to retain their eligibility to Medicaid. Advocates hoped that this amendment would encourage people to adopt disabled children or children with health problems.

Shaping Administrative Regulations

Once legislation is enacted, several implementation details must be resolved. The legislation usually names that agency or governmental department charged with implementing it, but it leaves unresolved many of the fine details of eligibility, personnel, treatment approaches, hours of service, evaluation mechanisms, reporting mechanisms, and issues surrounding the organization. To resolve these questions, the government agency must issue *administrative regulations,* which spell out these details and have the force of law once they have been finalized.

If government agencies were allowed to issue these administrative regulations by fiat and in secrecy, policy advocates would find themselves precluded from shaping them. While local variations exist, these agencies are required to follow a specific procedure that includes drafting a set of regulations; publishing the initial draft in a public document, such as the *Federal Register;* holding public hearings; allowing a period of time, often thirty or more days, for public comment on the proposed rules; and showing evidence that the public's comments were considered in revising the regulations. Policy advocates, then, can exert considerable pressure during this critical process by attending hearings, writing letters, and discussing critical issues with agency staff members who write the regulations.[36]

Mobilizing Pressure to Increase Funding

We have already noted that the funding for the Child Welfare and Adoption Assistance Act of 1980 did not meet the expectations of many persons who had supported the legislation. Recall that we discussed in Chapter Seven the distinction between authorizations, where legislative committees define the highest amounts that can be spent for specific programs, and appropriations, where legislative committees determine each year what will *actually* be spent on specific programs. Huge discrepancies often exist between authorizations and appropriations; if legislators authorize or allow relatively munificent funding for a program in the legislation that establishes it, they often budget far lower sums.

Policy advocates can try to increase appropriations for legislation in several ways. First, they can pressure the director of the agency charged with implementing a program to demand more money from the head of government, whose budget shapes the resources a program receives. Whether a mayor, governor, or the president has fashioned the budget, the head of government initially estimates his or her needs for a coming budget year by asking the heads of agencies to do the same. Because heads of government rarely increase the funds for a program beyond these initial estimates, a program's funding is particularly jeopardized when agency directors are too timid in seeking additional resources. Second, advocates can pressure the head of government to increase a specific item in the budget. Advocates can write top personnel in the state's budget office or the Office of Management and Budget in Washington, D.C. to argue that a program needs greater funding.

Finally, advocates can lobby the legislature when it creates a budget each year. Each legislative chamber has an Appropriations Committee, which it divides into subcommittees based on specific components of the budget, such as human services, education, and energy. Advocates can lobby the members of the subcommittee that deals with their issue, as well as legislators on the overall Appropriations Committee, which melds the subcommittees' recommendations into an overall budget. Of course, just like other pieces of legislation, budgets are ratified on the floors of each chamber, so advocates can try to find allies who will seek to increase a program's funds on the floor.[37]

Enhancing High-Level Leadership and Monitoring

Any policy innovation requires the continuing attention of high-level leaders, such as officials in governmental agencies, legislators, and directors of implementing agencies. In the welter of programs and issues that confront these leaders, they often fail to give attention to a specific policy innovation unless its advocates alert them to it. Moreover, advocates must sometimes pressure high-level leadership to institute a monitoring process, which would include periodic visits, collection of data, and surveillance of a policy's implementation. During budget shortages, monitoring is often sacrificed to other, immediate needs. This decision sometimes causes agencies to stop complying with key policy provisions. (Monitoring is not, of course, a panacea; a monitor might emphasize compliance with specific reporting requirements while barely examining whether agency staff were providing ethnic-sensitive services to members of specific ethnic groups.)[38]

Participating in Community-Based Advocacy Projects

Once the administrative regulations have been issued and the program is operating, policy advocates can often exert pressure on policymakers from external vantage points. Take the Adoption Assistance and Child Welfare Act, which advocated intensive services to natural families. That would enhance their parenting skills and ensure that they were ready to resume parenting after proven child abuse or neglect. Upon hearing that many children were reunited with such families without such services, local children's advocacy groups can and should pressure administrators, government officials, and legislators to develop corrective measures to remedy this omission.

Changing the Milieu

Policy practitioners often try to change the milieu where a policy innovation is delivered. We have already noted that in 1985, Nora Gustavsson found many barriers to the implementation of the Adoption Assistance and Child Welfare Act in a child-welfare agency in San Bernardino, California. Staff members received minimal education about the policy, bore excessive caseloads, lacked in-service training, and had inadequate supervision.

We can distinguish between changes within a milieu that are *directly* focused on a policy innovation and changes that *indirectly* shape its implementation. In the first case, a policy practitioner would seek funds, in-service training, education, collaborative relations with external agencies, the gathering of statistics, and supervision that focuses resources, attention, and staff skills on the policy innovation. Had public officials placed priority on permanency planning and services in the mid-1980s, for example, they would have sought far-reaching changes within child-welfare agencies to ensure their implementation, such as increasing in-service training to help staff provide ethnic-sensitive services.

However, if agency-wide problems, ones that go beyond a specific innovation, impede implementation of a policy, then changes that indirectly improve its implementation are needed. Assume, for example, that a child-welfare agency had problems with staff morale, staff turnover, and staff burnout before the Adoption Assistance and Child Welfare Act was enacted and that these problems persisted when this policy was implemented. It is possible that introducing a policy that asks staff members to commit time and energy to a new set of complex tasks can exacerbate preexisting agency problems. In the case of the Adoption Assistance and Child Welfare Act, workers were asked to develop permanency plans within tight deadlines, while retaining their large caseloads and not receiving much technical assistance. Skillful administrators needed to initiate reforms to maintain staff morale in these circumstances.

When using direct or indirect strategies, policy practitioners have to use analytic, political, interactional, and value-clarification skills.

Analytic skills: developing diagnoses. We will identify the factors that policy practitioners must consider when seeking to improve policy implementation in programs and agencies.

Leadership is critical to the implementation of policies, because staff members take cues from leaders about the importance of specific policies; if they sense that leaders only pay them lip service, they will be less likely to invest themselves in their implementation. Or leaders might use a style that impedes implementation, such as an excessively authoritarian approach.

Logistical factors often intrude, such as having adequate information systems, coordinating the activities of persons and organizations, and having adequate resources and supplies. We have noted, for example, that mental health centers established to help persons released from mental hospitals often found their work frustrated because no referral or tracking mechanisms allowed the community-based centers to contact the released patients.

Programs and agencies need to possess internal mechanisms of *communication* so that problems and issues can be aired and addressed. Staff members are often not fully aware of specific policies and are not encouraged to discuss issues that arise when they try to implement them.

Patterns of governance may be dysfunctional, as reflected by inadequate staff representation in agency decisionmaking; inadequate representation of persons with a range of perspectives on agencies' governing boards, which skews their decisions in certain directions; and governing boards' excessive interference in or excessive detachment from agency operations. This detachment can cause important policy issues to be overlooked.

An agency's *organizational structure* should match the nature of its functions. Agencies that emphasize innovation and staff discretion do well with relatively fluid, decentralized, and nonhierarchical patterns of administration, rather than traditional and hierarchical patterns. Traditional structures work better with programs that have standardized outputs, such as providing food stamps.

Staff members should learn necessary skills through *in-service educational programs*, which may not be provided.

We have discussed how agencies need an overarching *mission* to provide a focus for their work. They must also develop *goals* to guide their work during specific times, such as at the outset of a year. Agency staff members might decide to increase the representation of a certain population in an agency's clientele, such as Latinos, during a coming year. Staff members may even decide to make the goal more specific, such as to increase their representation by 15%.

Staff recruitment should bring in people committed to the program or agency. They should possess values and orientations congruent with its major directions. The staff should be sufficiently diverse in its ethnic, cultural, racial, sexual-orientation, and gender composition that it can adequately address the needs of clients.

Agencies need *outreach and community liaison* to make them aware of community residents' needs and to publicize their services to those persons who do not know about or use them.

Agencies' *budgets* must allocate resources in a way that allows major participants to implement their work and that directs resources toward the agency's key priorities.

Agency personnel must plan the agency's *interorganizational relations* so as to facilitate exchanges, referrals, and collaborations that are necessary to the program or agency.

Agency supervisors must pay attention to the *nature of job assignments and tasks* staff members receive. Should staff specialize in specific tasks, for example, or should their work be designed so that they have broader, generalist perspectives? Should staff be encouraged to rotate between different job assignments to make their work more interesting?

When programs use *volunteers*, agency members must examine methods of linking their work with the work of paid staff.

To the extent that conflict develops within a program, staff members and officials need to explore *strategies for conflict management*. In extreme cases, this may mean hiring an external consultant to help the staff members analyze areas of disagreement.

In relatively simple programs, such as ones where two or three staff collaborate on a project, policy practitioners can more easily identify implementation problems. In more complex situations, such as relatively large agencies, troubleshooters encounter greater challenges in diagnosing factors that impede implementation.

Political skills. Efforts to improve policy implementation often require political strategy.[39] When discussing the political challenges that practitioners often confront when changing the milieu of policy innovations, we must remember that they deal not with distant authorities, such as legislators, but with colleagues with whom they have and must maintain working relationships. Someone who tries "hardball tactics" against colleagues might find that they are not on speaking terms the next day.

Moreover, unlike advocates who seek policy changes from a legislature, persons who seek changes within organizations often find it difficult *not* to imply or state that a colleague is partly at fault. Assume, for example, that a new program failed to achieve some of the goals established at its inception; while a practitioner might implicate logistical factors, defective policies, or lack of funding, the persons actually implementing the program might conclude that they were partly to blame. Someone who confronted colleagues with the allegation that they were biased against certain types of clients would likely discover that they did not take kindly to intimations that they were acting in a prejudiced manner.

It is sometimes difficult to change policies within organizations, because people and units have a personal or collective stake in maintaining existing policies. Suppose you concluded that an operating program was not achieving its goals because it lacked sufficient resources; if you proposed a funding increase from the organization's central budget, people might oppose you, fearing that these added funds would be taken from their programs' budgets.

Persons who want to change existing agency programs may fear reprisals from those above them in the organizational chart, particularly if they oppose the proposed changes. These fears may not be merited, as our discussion of assertiveness in Chapter Ten suggests, but perceptions often shape our actions. "Higher-ups" sometimes *do* object to changes in the programs that they administer, even if they are meritorious.

The *style* of making changes in organizations differs from that of legislative settings. Legislators are used to external lobbyists or advocates who openly seek changes in existing policies. Moreover, they are accustomed to the extensive publicity often associated with policy-changing activities, such as stories in the mass media and mailings that they receive. They also anticipate considerable conflict; liberal politicians, for example, expect opposition from conservative politicians on many issues. In short, open advocacy, publicity, and conflict are expected characteristics of policy practice in legislative settings.

In organizations, by contrast, mechanisms for changing policies are often more subtle and indirect. A direct-service worker, worried that an existing program was defective, would not normally "lobby" the executive director, call in the press, and mobilize a supportive coalition that would "battle to the finish," even though she might use one of these strategies on specific, infrequent occasions. Instead, she might consider several subtler tactics. She might try to change the program by going through intermediaries, such as her supervisor or someone else in the organization, whom she could convince to mention the issue at a staff meeting or to someone above her in the organization's hierarchy. She could try to change policies informally by having other direct-service staff modify their procedures, even in defiance of high-level and written policies. She might seek data that indicated that the program was not achieving some of its goals. She could present this data to her supervisor or pass it on to someone higher in the organization's hierarchy. She might raise the issue in a staff meeting in hopes of drawing attention to it. Alternatively, she might seek relatively small changes if more fundamental reforms seemed impossible in light of political realities.

These program-changing activities are more subtle and indirect, but still qualify as policy practice as much as legislative advocacy. They both require the forming of strategy. The line-staff worker needs to consider issues of timing by trying to select an opportune moment to bring up an implementation issue. She needs to assess who might support or oppose a policy change. She must decide what channels to use; should she use her contacts with her supervisor, her contacts with other persons in the organization, a staff meeting, or contacts with other direct-service staff? She must use persuading skills. She may need to form a coalition within the organization to seek specific changes.

Interactional skills. Social workers often use interpersonal and group skills to troubleshoot agency service problems. Group skills help people participate in agency committees and task forces that examine policies. In some cases, social workers encourage these groups to brainstorm alternative policies and forestall their prematurely dismissing promising ideas. When these groups do not exist, social workers can form them, selecting people with a range of perspectives. Social workers may suggest that the group include persons from the community in some of its deliberations.

Persuading skills frequently assist social workers when they seek changes in an agency's internal workings. A staff member trying to change policy must present a convincing rationale to other staff, lest they believe that she wants change merely to advance her narrow interests within the organization. Because she often deals with staff who are well-versed in issues, she needs to use persuading tactics for expert audiences, as we discussed in Chapter Nine.

Agencies sometimes hire external consultants, or "facilitators," to help them solve problems, a decision that usually requires the executive director's approval. Facilitators often collect the staff's perceptions of the agency's problems. They use this feedback to plan brainstorming sessions in which staff identify the most important organizational problems and form task groups to solve them. These external consultants often help staff make substantial progress in addressing problems, but, without real changes in staff behavior and top administrators' leadership in implementing the changes, the short-term gains can be erased during ensuing months.[40]

Value-clarification skills. Values shape agency staff's and executives' preferences about the services they should provide and the agency's management style. A social worker in a not-for-profit agency, for example, might want it to emphasize nontraditional services, such as advocacy, free services, team services, and extensive use of volunteers. Moreover, the social worker might prefer an informal atmosphere, not a traditional one. Another social worker might favor a more bureaucratic model with hierarchical arrangements, greater use of rules, and a division of labor.

Values shape budgetary and program choices, as well. Should an agency faced with a funding crisis institute a sliding-fee schedule, even though this policy conflicts with the ideal of providing free or low-cost services to all clients? If fees are used, at what level should free services begin? Should an agency develop a profit-oriented subsidiary as a means of developing revenue, or would this policy cause the executive and staff to become increasingly absorbed in this new "revenue center"? When are writing and procuring grants consonant with an agency's mission, and when do grants become "the tail that wags the dog"?

Social workers sometimes encounter difficult value issues when they confront an incompetent or vindictive executive who is unwilling to consider important issues. Even when an executive is enlightened and skillful, political barriers often frustrate changes in agencies' administration. Persons who seek to change agencies often encounter others' opposition, whether because they are wedded to tradition, benefit from existing arrangements, or have different goals. Turf rivalries lead some persons to guard their programs and administrative roles jealously.

ETHICAL ISSUES:
COMPLIANCE AND WHISTLE-BLOWING

We discussed issues of discretion, compliance, and whistle-blowing in Chapter Ten when we analyzed power dilemmas and issues that direct-service staff sometimes confront. In the case of the Adoption Assistance and Child Welfare Act of 1980, staff members in local child-welfare units encountered the ethical dilemma of reconciling the policy pressures to reunite children with their natural families or place them with adoptive families with the paucity of social services offered to either the natural or adoptive families. Assume that courts have found a natural family guilty of abuse or neglect, but that policy pressures in the agency, such as from top executives, push supervisors and staff to return a child to this family, even when they have not been able to provide it with intensive services. In another example, assume that in the quest to move children quickly from foster care, a particularly handicapped child, such as one with severe mental disorders, is placed with adoptive parents who do not receive intensive help in caring for the child. In each of these cases, direct-service staff encounter the moral dilemmas we discussed in Chapter Ten; should they resist policy pressures when they believe that their clients (including children, adoptive parents, and natural families) will be harmed? Ethical social workers should advocate clients' needs, *even when* they encounter policy pressures from higher authorities. They should also try to have some higher-level officials reconsider policies that harm their clients, even if they encounter some job-related risks in doing this. Our discussion in Chapter Ten suggests that they could consider whistle-blowing if they fail to obtain this reconsideration, but only after careful thought.

POLICY ADVOCATES' ROLE

We have argued throughout this book that policy advocacy, which focuses on the needs of relatively powerless groups, is an important kind of policy practice. Policy advocates helped reform the implementation of the Adoption Assistance and Child Welfare Act by protesting its limited funding and subsequently low emphasis on preventive services, many child-welfare agencies' willingness to return abused and neglected children to their natural parents without giving these families adequate services, and agencies' insufficient effort to find adoptive parents in African-American and Latino communities. Advocates helped in bringing class-action lawsuits against public officials who failed to implement the program, lobbying legislators, and proposing amendments in existing legislation and administrative regulations. A number of groups performed heroic work to improve its implementation, including the Child Welfare League of America, the Children's Defense Fund, the National Association of Social Workers, and myriad local advocacy groups.

OUTCOMES OF THE ADOPTION ASSISTANCE AND CHILD WELFARE ACT

To examine how the official policy and the framers' intentions matched up with implemented policy, we would need to determine whether states that received federal funds under this act monitored local programs. Did they establish deadlines for devising a permanent plan for each child, implement tracking systems for each child, meet the six- and twelve-month requirements for reviewing each child's progress, implement permanency plans by the eighteen-month deadline, and markedly increase the amount and quality of services to reunify natural families?

Even if they did comply with the legislation's official policies, we would not have sufficient information to assess the policy's implementation. Recall our earlier discussion of the framers' *policy intentions*; they wanted children, not merely to leave the state of limbo of the foster care system, but to be placed in supportive families that would enhance their well-being. When any major policy is enacted, its implementors may comply with its formal requirements, but still subvert some of its framers' intentions. Many children's advocates hoped that establishing permanent arrangements would enhance children's developmental needs by diminishing the trauma of uncertainty and multiple placements in foster care.[41] What if some jurisdictions, anxious to comply with the formal requirements, return many children to abusive or neglectful natural families without providing them with intensive and long-term services?

The preceding discussion suggests that it is not easy to determine whether a policy has been implemented. To obtain accurate information about this legislation's implementation, we would need data from the tens of thousands of cases of children who have been removed from their homes after the 1980 legislation. Only then could we discover whether permanency plans were made and implemented in accordance with deadlines established by federal legislation. Moreover, we would need to obtain data about the children themselves, data that measured their developmental well-being after they (and their natural families in the case of reunification) received supportive services.

Obtaining this information would be difficult. Local child-welfare departments keep statistics and forward them to the state agencies that oversee foster care and adoptive services. However, we would need to view such statistics with some skepticism because some agencies have an incentive to report data that make them appear to comply with state law, even when they do not.[42] Few officials would falsify data, but some would likely ignore subtleties in the data of importance to researchers probing the implementation of the Adoption Assistance and Child Welfare Act.

These subtleties involve, not just formal compliance with the law's requirements, but also with the "spirit" or "direction" of implementation. A local child-welfare unit could, for example, require staff members to reunite children with their natural parents in order to produce permanent arrangements, but some of these reunions might not enhance the children's well-being. Indeed, the term *goal displacement*, which comes from organizational theory, captures some policy implementors' tendency to comply with formal edicts, even at the expense of the policy's intent.[43]

We will examine a number of ways that local and state authorities' program statistics could be misleading. First, as we just suggested, a local child-welfare unit might return many children to their natural families, even when they had not done sufficient investigations or provided enough ameliorative services to ensure that the children would receive minimal nurturance and safety. These children would be in permanent arrangements, their cases would appear *on paper* to comply with the law, and the cases would widely be recorded as "successes" in official statistics. However, the caseworkers would have fundamentally failed to meet the *intent* of the law.[44]

Second, some child-welfare units might place children with adoptive parents, when in fact the natural parents could have been rehabilitated. Concerned about the natural parents' rights, the legislation's framers wanted children to return to their natural homes if parents improved their parenting skills with certain services, job training, or employment. (Some children are neglected by parents because they lack the resources to provide basic essentials or because poverty induces stress that promotes abusive behavior.) Jurisdictions that unnecessarily place children in adoptions appear successful in official statistics, but violate the intent of the legislation.[45]

Third, some states might develop definitions of permanency that vary from the framers' intent. While the framers assumed that children would be placed with parents, whether natural or adoptive ones, some states might define permanency as long-term residency in one foster home or one institution or even the provision of a public guardian who would assume ongoing, legal responsibility for a child.[46] When defined more loosely to include these possibilities, permanency ceases to mean a fundamental change in the status of children who have been removed from their natural homes.

Fourth, some of the framers assumed that their legislation would increase the numbers of families willing to become adoptive parents, while retaining the existing corps of foster parents. Some local child-welfare units, in a desperate search for adoptive parents, might place considerable pressure on foster parents to adopt one or more of the children under their care. Though this sounds like a sensible policy, and sometimes it works, it probably reduces the number of available foster parents, who, like adoptive parents, are in short supply.[47]

Fifth, the framers of the legislation wanted states to provide services to natural parents to improve their parenting skills. Some localities might indicate that a certain percentage of their staff's time goes to various preventive activities when, in fact, it mostly goes to their ongoing and regular work, which includes responding to emergencies, completing paperwork, and testifying at juvenile courts.[48] (These statistical errors could stem from the intrinsic difficulty of computing how staff members allocate their time or from child-welfare staff members' desire to impress state authorities with their compliance.)

Because local units and states can use any of these five tactics, data about the implementation of the Adoption Assistance and Child Welfare Act could be misleading. Moreover, it would be difficult to reach sweeping conclusions in light of variations between states and local jurisdictions within specific states. One can imagine, for example, that in a particular county, the chief of child-welfare services and juvenile court judges aggressively promoted permanency planning, while in an adjoining county, the officials did not promote the policy. Moreover, one can imagine considerable variation between states with respect to the bill's implementation.[49]

As we have noted, as well, any full evaluation of the Adoption Assistance and Child Welfare Act would require us to obtain information about the well-being of the children and their families. Did the well-being of children and their natural families improve when they received services, compared with children and natural families who received few or no services? To obtain this information, we would need sophisticated research to resolve certain issues. For instance, what measures should we use to determine whether the well-being of children or their families is enhanced? How do we perform a "true-experiment" (where children that receive services are compared with children who receive no services) when most children in foster care receive some services funded by this legislation?

As the Adoption Assistance and Child Welfare Act nears its fifteenth year of implementation, some data exists that the legislation has reduced the numbers of children in foster care. Many jurisdictions dramatically decreased the number of children in the foster care system in the years after the bill's enactment, when the number of children in foster care was halved between 1977 and

1988.[50] Moreover, many states have complied with the legislation's tracking and case-review requirements. However, virtually no definitive data has been obtained, even by 1993, about the legislation's effectiveness in enhancing the well-being of children or their families.

SUMMARY

Policy implementation is a critical part of the policymaking process, because the fate of enacted policies is ultimately determined during this phase. We have provided a systems framework for implementation (see Figure 13.1). This framework analyzes a policy's political economy, the policy itself, implementing processes, interventions by policy practitioners to reform implementation, and policy outcomes.

Our discussion suggests that policy practitioners need several skills when they participate in implementation. They must understand the systems framework we have discussed, as well as policy advocates' role in reforming implementation.

Policy practitioners sometimes try to improve the implementation of relatively simple programs, such as ones that originate in a specific agency. In other cases, they try to reform government programs that extend to many sites, such as the Adoption Assistance and Child Welfare Act of 1980. They can seek amendments in the original legislation, try to change the administrative regulations that come from government agencies, seek funding increases, try to elicit high-level leadership and monitoring, seek changes in the milieu (such as a child-welfare office) that directly or indirectly shapes policy implementation, or work with external advocacy groups.

We can also see policy implementation as requiring policy practitioners to draw on the skills that are associated with the policy tasks we have discussed in this book (see Box 13.2). Just as practitioners might try to place social problems on decisionmakers' agendas, for example, practitioners can try to place *implementing* problems on their agendas. Just as practitioners might define and analyze social problems, they can analyze implementing problems. Similar to writing proposals to develop new programs, they can develop proposals to address problems in the implementing processes of a policy innovation. As with seeking to enact a new proposal, such as a piece of legislation, they might seek administrators' and staff members' support for a proposal to improve implementation.

Social workers often encounter issues of discretion, compliance, and whistle-blowing in their work. When confronted with unethical policies, or other staff's unethical behavior, they must weigh options in the context of ethics and pragmatic realities. When major programs are implemented, such as the Adoption Assistance and Child Welfare Act of 1980, advocacy groups can play an important role in monitoring their progress and seeking corrective reforms.

BOX 13.2
Policy-Implementing Skills Drawn from Other Policy Tasks

Using skills helpful in *building agendas*, policy practitioners can try to place implementation problems on decisionmakers' agendas, whether the decisionmakers are members of a work group, a supervisor, or highly placed executives. Aware of the problem, solution, and political streams in the agenda-building process, practitioners can do the following:

• Obtain data about problems in implementation, such as the lack of service to certain kinds of clients, noncompliance with certain high-level policies, or preliminary evidence that services are not effective (such as high rates of clients' dropping out from services)
• Revive interest in some change in the structure of services that had been discussed before in the organization, such as decentralization, but link it now to a current implementing issue
• Alert politically influential persons within the program to implementation problems
• Locate someone akin to "policy entrepreneurs" in legislative settings who is willing to bring up an implementation problem at an opportune moment, such as in an agency meeting

Using skills helpful in *defining problems*, policy practitioners diagnose implementation dysfunctions. They draw on factors that we have identified with problems in implementation, such as leadership, communication patterns, governance, logistical factors, organizational structure, and the design of jobs. Of course, they may also conclude, as we suggested in Chapter Six, that staff members sometimes diagnose their clients' problems erroneously or simplistically or use outdated treatment interventions.

Policy practitioners use *proposal-writing* skills when they construct remedies to problems in implementation. Perhaps they write a memo to a staff person that analyzes an implementation problem, its likely causes, and possible solutions. Perhaps they make a suggestion about possibly revising an agency's budget. Perhaps they suggest that better methods of collecting and analyzing data are needed. In all of these cases, then, they put forth proposals, whether in writing or orally, to address problems of implementation.

When they use *policy-enacting* skills, policy practitioners use power resources to obtain policy and organizational reforms. For example, they can do the following:

• Establish a coalition with others who favor a specific reform and work with it to develop strategy

continued

BOX 13.2 continued

- Make a presentation in an agency meeting or have someone else, such as a supervisor, make this point
- Use their autonomy to enact a certain policy on their unit without necessarily seeking policy changes at higher levels
- Work through intermediaries, such as higher-level staff, to obtain support for a policy
- Use timing skills to seek approval for a new policy at propitious moments, such as when a new leader is appointed, "slack resources" exist in a budget, or external funders support a policy innovation
- Use negotiating skills to compromise on internal issues when there is conflict

When they use *policy-assessing* skills, practitioners can do the following:

- Collect data to see if implementors are implementing enacted policies and administrative regulations
- Collect data, as we discuss in the next chapter, to see if implemented programs address specific criteria, such as effectiveness, cost, and social justice

Suggested Readings

THEORETICAL PERSPECTIVES ON IMPLEMENTATION
Erwin Hargrove, *The Missing Link: The Study of the Implementation of Social Policy* (Washington, DC: Urban Institute Press, 1975).
Yeheskel Hasenfeld, "Implementation of Social Policy Revisited," *Administration and Society* 22 (February 1991): 451–479.
Robert Montjoy and Laurence O'Toole, "Toward a Theory of Policy Implementation," *Public Administration Review* 39 (September-October 1979): 465–476.
Carl Van Horn and Donald Van Meter, "The Implementation of Intergovernmental Policy," in Charles Jones and Robert Thomas, eds., *Public Policy Making in the Federal System* (Beverly Hills, CA: Sage, 1976).

STRUCTURAL-POLITICAL PERSPECTIVES ON IMPLEMENTATION
Jeffrey Pressman and Aaron Wildavsky, *Implementation* (Berkeley and Los Angeles: University of California Press, 1974).

POLITICAL-ECONOMY PERSPECTIVES ON IMPLEMENTATION
Eugene Bardach, *The Implementation Game* (Cambridge, MA: MIT Press, 1977).
Mayer Zald, *Organizational Change: The Political Economy of the YMCA* (Chicago: University of Chicago Press, 1970).

MICRO OR AGENCY PERSPECTIVES ON IMPLEMENTATION
Yeheskel Hasenfeld, "The Implementation of Change in Human Service Organizations," *Social Service Review* 54 (December 1980): 508–520.

Mary Ann Scheirer, *Program Implementation: The Organizational Context* (Beverly Hills, CA: Sage, 1981).

STAFF PERSPECTIVES ON IMPLEMENTATION
Michael Lipsky, "Standing Implementation on Its Head," in Walter Burnham and Martha Wagner, eds., *American Politics and Public Policy* (Cambridge, MA: MIT Press, 1978).
Lyman Porter et al., *Behavior in Organizations* (New York: McGraw-Hill, 1975), pp. 274–367.

PUBLIC POLICY'S EFFECTS ON IMPLEMENTATION
Theodore Lowi, *The End of Liberalism* (New York: Norton, 1969).

LOGISTICAL OR PROCEDURAL PERSPECTIVES ON IMPLEMENTATION
Allen Spiegel and Herbert Hyman, *Basic Health Planning Methods* (Germantown, MD: Aspen Systems, 1978), pp. 239–287.

CASE STUDIES OF IMPLEMENTATION
Franklin Chu and Sharland Trotter, *The Madness Establishment* (New York: Grossman, 1974).

ETHICAL ISSUES IN POLICY IMPLEMENTATION
Sissela Bok, "Blowing the Whistle," in Joel Fleishman, Lance Liebman, and Mark Moore, eds., *Public Duties: The Moral Obligations of Government Officials* (Cambridge, MA: Harvard University Press, 1981), pp. 204–220.
Robert Goodin, *Reasons for Welfare: The Political Theory of the Welfare State* (Princeton, NJ: Princeton University Press, 1988), pp. 184–223.
Charles Levy, *Guide to Ethical Decisions and Actions for Social Service Administrators: A Handbook for Managerial Personnel* (New York: Haworth, 1982).
Donald Warwick, "The Ethics of Administrative Discretion," in Fleishman, Liebman, and Moore, *Public Duties*, pp. 93–127.

Notes

1. Theodore Lowi comments on the vagueness of the terms in many pieces of legislation in *The End of Liberalism* (New York: Norton, 1969).
2. Brian Hogwood and Lewis Gunn note that people's stated and real objectives are sometimes quite different. See *Policy Analysis for the Real World* (London: Oxford University Press, 1984), p. 156.
3. Dorothy Kupcha discusses the dual system in, "Medicaid: In or Out of the Mainstream," *California Journal* 10 (May 1979): 181–183.
4. Robert Montjoy and Laurence O'Toole, "Toward a Theory of Policy Implementation," *Public Administration Review* 39 (September-October 1979): 465–476.
5. Ibid.
6. Jeffrey Pressman and Aaron Wildavsky, *Implementation* (Berkeley and Los Angeles: University of California Press, 1974).
7. Yeheskel Hasenfeld, "Implementation of Social Policy Revisited," *Administration and Society* 22 (February 1991): 463.
8. Laurence O'Toole and Robert Montjoy, "Interrorganizational Policy Implementation: A Theoretical Perspective," *Public Administration Review* 44 (November-December 1984): 491–503.

9. Eugene Bardach, *The Implementation Game* (Cambridge, MA: MIT Press, 1977).
10. Ibid.
11. Congress, Senate, Committee on Finance, Subcommittee on Public Assistance, *Hearings on Proposals Related to Social and Child Welfare Services*, 96th Cong., 1st sess., 1979, testimony of Arabella Martinez.
12. See *Hearings on Proposals*, pp. 68–69.
13. Ibid., pp. 68–126.
14. For an overview of the strategy, see Congress, House, Ways and Means Committee, Subcommittee on Public Assistance, *Hearings on Amendments to Social Services, Foster Care, and Child Welfare*, 96th Cong., 1st sess., March 1979, pp. 22–157.
15. We argued that child-welfare and day-care issues conformed to the "politics of indifference" in the 1960s and 1970s. See Bruce Jansson, "The History and Politics of Selected Children's Programs and Related Legislation," Ph.D. diss., University of Chicago, 1975, p. 312.
16. For a discussion of declassification, see Burton Gummer, "Is the Social Worker in Public Welfare an Endangered Species?" *Public Welfare* 37 (Fall 1979).
17. Robert Kuttner, *Revolt of the Haves: Tax Rebellion and Hard Times* (New York: Simon and Schuster, 1980).
18. Bruce Jansson, *Reluctant Welfare State* (Belmont, CA: Wadsworth, 1988), p. 208.
19. Michael Wald, "Family Preservation: Are We Moving Too Fast?" *Public Welfare* 46 (Summer 1988): 33–38.
20. Julie Kosterlitz, "Not Just Kid Stuff," *National Journal* 20 (November 19, 1988): 2934–2939.
21. See, for example, the testimony of Ann Klein, the Commission of Human Services of New Jersey, in *Hearings on Amendments to Social Services*, pp. 149–154.
22. Children's Defense Fund, *A Vision for the Future, An Agenda for the 1990s: A Children's Defense Budget* (Washington, DC: Children's Defense Fund, 1989).
23. Leroy Pelton, *For Reasons of Poverty* (New York: Praeger, 1989), pp. 96–98.
24. Nora Gustavsson, "Implementation of Permanency Planning Legislation," Doctoral Dissertation, School of Social Work, University of Southern California, 1986.
25. Ibid.
26. Ibid.
27. White children are still far more likely to be adopted than minority children; see Richard Barth, "Disruption in Older Child Adoptions," *Public Welfare* 46 (Winter 1988): 23–39.
28. Wald, "Family Preservation."
29. Ibid., pp. 34–35.
30. Ibid., p. 35.
31. Gustavsson, "Implementation of Permanency Planning Legislation," pp. 106–110.
32. Ibid., pp. 106–110, 119–121.
33. Wald discusses the lack of follow-up services in, "Family Preservation," as does Barth, in "Disruption in Older Child Adoptions."
34. The writings of Besharov, Brown, and Wald suggest this need to rethink some of the assumptions of the Adoption Assistance and Child Welfare Act. See Douglas Besharov, "Rights versus Rights: The Dilemma of Child Protection," *Public Welfare* 43 (Spring 1985): 19–27; Besharov, "The Future of Child Protective Agencies," *Public Welfare* 45 (Spring 1987): 7–11; Larry Brown, "The Future of Child Protective Services: Seeking a National Consensus," *Public Welfare* 45 (Spring 1987): 12–17; and Wald, "Family Preservation."

35. See, for example, Leila Whiting, "A Different Perspective," *Public Welfare* 46 (Fall 1978): 22–25; Candace Beavers, "A Cross-Cultural Look at Child Abuse," *Public Welfare* 44 (Fall 1986): 18–22; and Paula Dail, "Unemployment and Family Stress," *Public Welfare* 46 (Winter 1988): 30–34.
36. For technical discussion of the drafting of administrative regulations, see U.S., Office of the Federal Register, *Document Drafting Handbook* (Washington, DC: U.S. Government Printing Office, 1981).
37. For a discussion of the federal budget process, see Aaron Wildavsky, *The New Politics of the Budgetary Process* (Glenview, IL: Scott, Foresman, 1988).
38. Bruce Jansson, "The Political Economy of Monitoring: A Contingency Perspective," in Harold Demone and Margaret Gibelman, *Services for Sale* (New Brunswick, NJ: Rutgers University Press, 1989), pp. 343–359.
39. Burton Gummer, *The Politics of Social Administration* (Englewood Cliffs, NJ: Prentice-Hall, 1990), pp. 92–114.
40. For discussion of organizational development, see Fred Massarik, ed., *Advances in Organizational Development* (Norwood, NJ: Ablex, 1990).
41. For a discussion of the prevailing assumption that reunification was in the child's best interest, see Wald, "Family Preservation," 33–38.
42. The absence of good data from local jurisdictions regarding children served by the Adoption Assistance and Child Welfare Act is discussed in testimony of Marylee Allen in Congress, Senate, Committee on Finance, Subcommittee on Social Security and Income Maintenance Programs, *Hearings*, 99th Cong., 1st sess., June 24, 1985.
43. See Amitai Etzioni, *Modern Organizations* (Englewood Cliffs, NJ: Prentice-Hall, 1964), pp. 10, 84–85.
44. Wald discusses this possibility in, "Family Preservation."
45. Mark Hardin discusses this possibility in, Congress, Subcommittee on Social Security and Income Maintenance Programs, 99th Cong., 1st sess., June 24, 1985.
46. See Gustavsson, "Implementation of Permanency Planning Legislation," pp. 31–32, 86.
47. Ibid., pp. 31–32, 86–88.
48. Similarly, considerable overreporting occurred in the aftermath of the 1962 welfare amendments to the Social Security Act, which required local departments to report how much time their staff members spent providing services; see Martha Derthick, *The Influence of Federal Grants: Public Assistance in Massachusetts* (Cambridge, MA: Harvard University Press, 1970), pp. 138–157.
49. See Krishna Samantrai, "Prevention in Child Welfare: States' Response to Federal Mandate," Ph.D. diss., University of Southern California, School of Social Work, 1988. Also see Jeffrey Koshel and Madeleine Kimmich, *Summary Report on the Implementation of PL 96-272* (Washington, DC: Urban Institute Press, 1983) and Madeleine Kimmich, *State Child Welfare Program Plans: Service Budgets Report* (Washington, DC: Urban Institute Press, 1983).
50. Wald, "Family Preservation."

Chapter 14
Assessing Policy

In a sense, the policy-assessing task represents both the ending and beginning of social policy practice. People often regard policy assessment as the final step in the policymaking process; having had a policy proposal enacted, they wish to determine whether it has, in fact, been a success. However, assessment is also the beginning of policy practice; when our assessments of existing policies suggest that they are flawed, we often become motivated to develop, enact, and implement policies to change them.

The technical aspects of assessment often mask its critical similarities to other topics that we have discussed, such as policy debates and analysis. To demystify assessment, we will not discuss it in highly technical terms (although we will identify some technical issues), but will analyze its fundamental logic and its similarities to policy debates and analysis. We discuss traditional, quantitative approaches to evaluation, as well as qualitative methods. Moreover, we will argue that assessment, like defense, is an enterprise that all of us can join, even if we lack the technical skills to assess a specific policy formally.

THE FUNDAMENTAL LOGIC OF POLICY ASSESSMENT

To illustrate our discussion of assessment, we will consider an example: A jurisdiction devised and implemented policies to help natural parents of children whom the courts have removed because of abuse or neglect, hoping that these enhanced services would allow more children to be reunified, decrease the costs by abbreviating foster care, and enhance the children's well-being.

Policy practitioners often want to know whether an existing policy is flawed or meritorious, not just as a matter of idle curiosity, but because the answers have important implications for several people and institutions. A policy that harms (or at least fails to help) its intended beneficiaries, such as a program's consumers, would widely be regarded as dispensable. A policy that helps consumers but absorbs "unacceptable" amounts of resources will likely receive criticism from people who wish to use resources more efficiently. A policy that

408   PART FOUR   After Enacting Policy

helps some people but discriminates against others, such as helping the male victims of a social problem while providing little help to its female victims, would be widely regarded as an unfair or inequitable policy that needed revising.

Policy assessment, then, requires examining *relationships* between implemented policies and their effects. Assessment forces us to ask how, if at all, the external world is different because a specific policy exists, and what, if any, difference it would make if we removed, deleted, or modified the policy.

When examined in this fashion, policy assessment is not that different from any kind of assessment. Direct-service practitioners who examine their work in a critical fashion often wonder whether an intervention will improve the well-being of specific clients or be counterproductive. Alternatively, has the sum of our interventions over a specific period improved their well-being?

SIMILARITIES BETWEEN ASSESSING AND ANALYZING POLICY

Readers who remember Chapter Eight, where we examined the fundamental logic of analytic reasoning, have a head start in understanding policy assessment, because assessment and analysis are strikingly similar. The decision-making matrix that we discussed in Chapter Eight (see Table 8.1) is similar to a policy-assessment matrix (see Table 14.1). To illustrate this matrix, we will consider the previous example of a jurisdiction that provides special services to the natural parents of children whom courts have removed. We will imagine an employee of the jurisdiction's bureau of child welfare who has been hired to assess the new program. She is "thinking through" how she will approach this evaluation.[1]

The policy-assessment matrix (Table 14.1) describes the policy innovation (in this case, special services for the natural parents) and one or more policy

TABLE 14.1
Policy Assessment Matrix

	Evaluative Criteria		
Policy alternatives	*Rates of reunification*	*Cost per case during the first 18 months*	*Children's developmental well-being*
1. Special services to natural parents			
2. The existing situation: the provision of relatively few services			

alternatives (in this case, the typical services provided to natural parents under these circumstances). People who assess policies usually want to compare an enacted policy with something else, because it gives them some standard for evaluation. If our policy assessor could not make comparisons, she might wonder on balance whether providing special services to the natural parents "made a difference" over receiving relatively few services.

As she wrestles with evaluating the new policy, the practitioner asks, "With respect to what criteria (outcomes) do I wish to compare the two policy alternatives?" At first glance, this would seem to be a relatively simple decision, but she soon realizes that she must choose between an extraordinary array of possible measures of outcomes. She could look at the costs of the new policy, the effects on the parents and families, the effects on the children, the implications for staff and juvenile courts, and the effects on the foster parents. Of course, as she adds more criteria or outcomes, she makes her work more difficult, because each new criterion requires her to obtain more data. After discussing this problem with many people, she finally selects three criteria: the effects of increased services to natural parents on: (1) the rates of reunifying children with their natural parents; (2) the average cost of each case during the first eighteen months, which includes the taxpayers' costs for providing services, paying foster parents, and paying for litigation in juvenile courts; and (3) the children's "developmental status" at the end of eighteen months.

Why did the policy practitioner select three measures of outcomes, rather than only one? She knew, of course, that many legislators and government officials were particularly concerned about the relative costs of the new policy experiment. Would the additional costs of providing special services, they wondered, be partially or completely offset by the savings that could accrue to government by reducing the numbers of children in foster care placements or eventually in subsidized adoptions? Indeed, some of these legislators had resisted the policy in the first place, because they doubted that it would, on balance, save funds. (One conservative legislator called it "another scheme by do-gooder social workers to get more money to fund their pet projects.")

She also wanted to check the rates of reunification of children who received and did not receive the special services. Many people wanted families to be reunified because they speculated that long-term or permanent removal of children from their natural families would detract from children's well-being. Surely, she reasoned, we should obtain information about whether special services increase the likelihood of family reunification.

She realized, however, that analysis of costs, as well as rates of reunification, could yield an incomplete, and even misleading, evaluation of the new policy. Recall our discussion of goal displacement in the preceding chapter, a phenomenon whereby implementors mistake certain secondary goals or objectives for the *basic* or most important ones. Unlike some legislators, many social workers are concerned about the ultimate effects of policies on their clients' well-being; if public authorities used the services to save the costs of providing foster care, they could easily forget that some parents do not provide a healthy environment, *even after* or while they receive intensive services. In other words, a potential exists for harming some children in order to save money. Moreover, praiseworthy as reunification may often be, she discovered when searching existing literature that no research had definitively shown that reunification is necessarily in the child's best interest.[2] Some children may thrive in foster care if it provides emotional supports that the natural home lacks.

The researcher chooses three measures of outcomes, then, to obtain a clearer picture of the new policy. She realizes, of course, that she may discover mixed outcomes; the new policy might save the taxpayers monies, for example, but not have advantages over the existing policy in promoting children's developmental needs.

SIMILARITIES BETWEEN POLICY ASSESSMENT AND POLICY DEBATES

Let us leap ahead three years after the policy practitioner has obtained her data. Assume for the moment that her evaluations suggest that the special services have indeed reduced child-welfare costs by a small but significant amount; while the jurisdiction spent an average of $7,000 on each child in the special services program, it spent an average of $9,500 on each child in the regular program, when the costs of foster care and services were aggregated.[3] Moreover, some increases in reunification occurred; while 27% of children were reunified with their parents in the special services program, only 19% of children were reunified with parents in the regular program.[4] To the practitioner's surprise, however, the children in the special services program did not on average achieve higher scores on several measures of child development than children in the regular program.

We have invented these findings, but they nicely illustrate some dilemmas that program evaluators often encounter. When subjected to rigorous, quantitative evaluations, many policies reflect relatively modest gains—they either appear not significantly different from other programs or show relatively modest changes.[5] Of course, the relatively modest changes can sometimes occur in a negative direction; in this case, for example, the children in the special services program *could* have obtained somewhat lower scores than other children on measures of their development. New policies may reveal striking findings, but, alas, evaluative research often provides less dramatic findings.

We can conjecture why many policies do not markedly transform the external world as their framers intended. Because *many* factors shape people's behaviors and development, such as their prior experiences, their economic condition, and the persons with whom they associate on a daily basis, programs in the human services system cannot be expected to transform the lives of clients, patients, and consumers dramatically and quickly.[6] The instruments that researchers use may fail to capture some important dimensions of human behavior, as well.

Whatever the reasons, policy assessments often fail to provide definitive evidence about the policy's merits. Indeed, assessments sometimes meet with considerable controversy, because the evaluator is placed in the position of arguing about "the meaning" of the findings with others. Indeed, a noted researcher, Donald Campbell, provocatively suggests that program evaluation should be regarded as a form of "argument." This position suggests that the program evaluator should make a good case that others may contest.[7] In this context, policy evaluators become like debaters, who must defend their arguments to other persons.

We can illustrate the similarities between assessment and policy debates by returning to our policy practitioner who obtained "mixed findings" when evaluating the child-welfare programs. Let us assume that she concluded her work by saying, "On balance, my findings suggest that the special services program should be enlarged so that it covers all children who are removed by the courts from their natural homes because of abusive or neglectful behavior by their parents." Let us also assume that some conservative legislators strongly contest this proposal, doubting that "hiring a lot more social workers to provide intensive services to the natural parents will really cut our costs."

The debate between the policy evaluator and conservative politicians could easily involve five dimensions, or axes.[8] First, the evaluator and conservative politicians could debate whether the glass is half full or half empty. Are the cost reductions and increased rates of reunification *sufficiently large* to continue and enlarge the special services program? No scientific method exists for resolving this dispute, because people's positions derive from their values. Conservatives who opposed the special services program at the outset and who are suspicious of social workers are likely to insist on a higher standard or threshold of evidence than are persons who favored the program at the outset. Indeed, we have already noted that many policies make, at best, marginal improvements over existing ones; thus, evaluators often encounter this magnitude-of-change argument.

Conservatives might also question the time frame of the research by asking whether the eighteen-month period is sufficiently long to discover whether the special services program is truly effective. "How do we know," one of them asks, "whether some of the children who have been reunified with their parents will not have to be placed in foster homes at some point in the near future?" (Recall that the researcher followed the cases of the children only during an eighteen-month interval.) The evaluator responds that "eighteen months is a long enough interval to make reasonable inferences." However, like the threshold argument, this one cannot be easily resolved, because values often shape one's position; someone who is skeptical about a policy is likely to want a stricter standard of proof, such as a study that follows a policy's beneficiaries for an extended period.

People could make other criticisms of the special services program, as well. They could question the practitioner's weighting of the criteria used in evaluating the program. Someone might say, for example, "It is all well and good that the special services program saves some funds and that it somewhat increases the rate of reunification, but I think that the children's well-being ought to be the *prime* consideration. On this objective, the data do not seem to demonstrate an improvement over the regular program!" Such a person develops a fundamental criticism of the special services program, *not* by questioning its superiority over the regular program in some respects, but by suggesting that it is not superior with respect to a specific objective. Here, too, individuals' values and perspectives influence their responses to evaluative information. Someone who favors the program from the outset, for example, might be willing to de-emphasize a negative finding and emphasize more positive ones. A cost conscious conservative who initially opposed the special services program might now support it because it appeared to reduce costs. A child-development expert, who initially supported the innovation, might now oppose it because it failed to improve children's scores on child-development tests.

As the policy practitioner presents her findings, she could easily encounter some questions about the accuracy of her data. "How do we know," someone could ask, "whether your findings are truly accurate? Maybe the children and families you chose for the special services program did not have as severe problems as other children and families." Someone else might ask, "How do we know that you did not select particularly talented and motivated social workers to staff the special services program? Maybe the program's success stemmed from their skills, rather than from the special services program itself." Someone else might ask whether the instruments used to measure the children's well-being (the child-development instruments) provided accurate information about the children's self-esteem.

TOOLS FOR COUNTERING CRITICISM

In Figure 14.1, we summarize some of the challenges that confront evaluators. They can address some of these challenges with methodological or technical tools. To counter some questions about the data's accuracy, evaluators have developed many technical tools. It is beyond the scope of this discussion to analyze these tools in detail, but we can describe some of them briefly.

Before discussing these technical tools, we will quickly review what criticisms evaluators wish to minimize or avoid after completing their studies. They fear that critics will contend that any program successes result from external factors that have nothing to do with the program itself. This kind of criticism is, to say the least, damaging to evaluators' credibility, because it undermines the veracity of their assertions, as a simple illustration suggests. Suppose that a direct-service counselor claims remarkable success rates in treating depression, but lacks systematic evidence. She develops a for-profit clinic, called the "Sure-Cure for Depression Clinic." Critics could easily question this entrepreneur's claims by asking how the counselor knows whether his clients' "miraculous recoveries" did not result from normal course of life events, rather than his intervention (many persons "mature out of" their problems). Background events, such as an improving economy or enhanced marital situations, may have caused clients' improvement. Critics might accuse him of selecting only certain types of clients whose prognosis was particularly promising, so

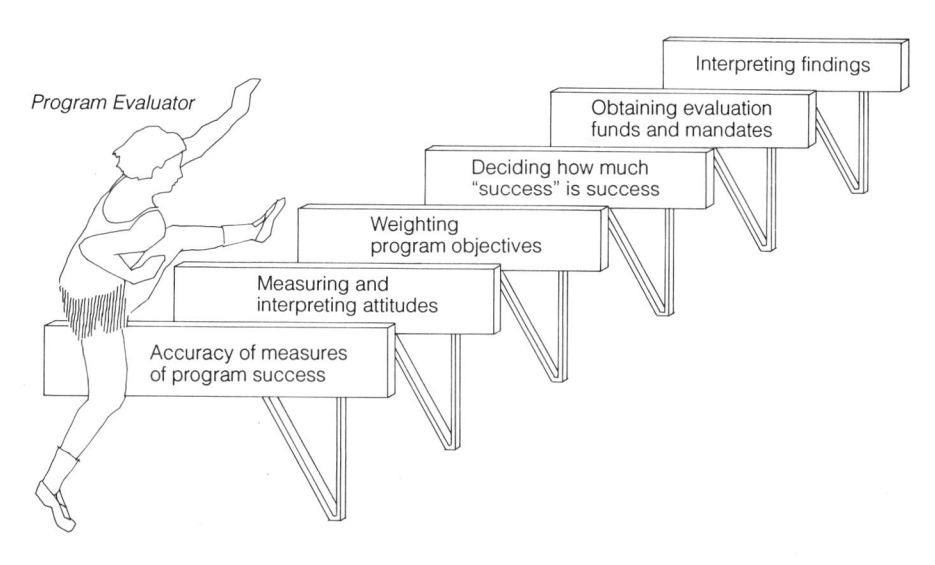

FIGURE 14.1
Evaluator's obstacle course

that his rates of improvement seemed extraordinary. They could also call his measures of clients' well-being flawed, saying that they made it falsely appear that his clients had suffered from depression in the first place or had recovered from it under his care.

Every evaluation possesses a design, a sampling and assignment strategy, instruments or measures, and statistics.[9] Design, sampling, assignment strategies, instruments, and statistics allow the evaluator to minimize these various threats to her findings. An evaluation's *design* describes the researcher's strategy in obtaining comparisons between the so-called experimental group (the beneficiaries of a specific policy or program) and the control group (persons not receiving benefits from the program). We will contrast three designs to illustrate the evaluator's options. We can place them on a continuum, extending from relatively simple (or nonrigorous) to relatively complex (and rigorous).

In a *correlational design,* the evaluator does not try to establish a new project, but seeks to analyze projects that have already been implemented. Assume, for example, that the evaluator of the special services program had found local officials unwilling to approve the program. Because of this, she could not test the effects of special services on families' reunification rates. Also assume that the child-welfare services agency had maintained excellent records of all cases in the past ten years, including detailed records of the numbers of visits that child-welfare staff had made to the natural parents of children removed by the courts from their homes. It might occur to the evaluator that she could examine the services' effects on reunification rates by studying *past* cases. Why not, she might ask, compare cases where parents received extensive services were with cases where minimal services were provided to see if people who received intensive services had higher reunification rates?

At first glance, this evaluative strategy seems brilliant, because the case materials already exist with which to construct the project. As she ponders the issue, however, the evaluator soon realizes that the criticisms that greeted the claims of the Sure-Cure for Depression Clinic could also be leveled at her findings, even if they showed a dramatic, positive relationship between the intensiveness of services and the rates of reunification. Might these higher reunification rates be caused, *not* by the intensive services, but because social workers selected primarily stable, well-functioning families for intensive services because they liked to work with that clientele? Because the cases already transpired, the evaluator would be unable to eliminate this possibility. In addition, certain events, such as an improving economy, might have influenced reunification rates *independently* of the services families received. The evaluator would encounter even more formidable research problems if she sought to examine the effects of services on the children's social and psychological functioning. Because the cases already transpired, she could not administer special tests to the children, nor would the case records be likely to yield accurate rankings of the children on social and psychological functioning.

Indeed, evaluators realize that *forward-looking research*—that is, research that analyzes current phenomena—is less subject to external criticism than correlational research, because they can limit factors that might provide alternative explanations for their findings. The researcher might begin her project by selecting a *random sample* of all children who had been subjected to child abuse during, say, a three-month period. By using a random sample, she would decrease the likelihood that the children and families in her evaluative study possessed characteristics different from those of other abused children and their families. As the children entered her sample during the three-month period, the researcher could randomly assign them either to a control group, which did not receive special services, or an experimental group, which received the services. Random assignment would decrease the likelihood that characteristics of the children and their families, rather than the effects of special services, caused differences in outcomes between the control and experimental groups.

When the evaluator controls the experiment, she can administer tests directly to participants to measure the social and psychological outcomes. She might use *instruments* whose questions have been empirically tested to increase the likelihood that they provide accurate information. Or she can observe the children in their homes or at school to assess their social functioning. Contrast this direct measurement of the children's functioning with the methods of the researcher who had to rely on information in case records.

Statistical techniques allow investigators to examine the likelihood that successful results could have occurred by chance, rather than because of the special services themselves. In studies with small numbers of subjects, it is highly possible that the investigator may have drawn successful cases merely by chance. Statistical tests allow evaluators to make definitive statements, such as, "There is only one chance in a hundred that special services could have improved reunification rates this much if chance were the explanation."

Evaluators want, therefore, to reduce the likelihood of *rival explanations* of their findings that critics can use to question their conclusions. In the case of the special services program, the evaluator hopes that she can reduce opponents' arguments about rival explanations. One can hear a conservative asking, for example, "How do we know that the special services themselves were responsible for higher reunification rates and not some other factor, such as 'creaming' by social workers who gave services to relatively stable or well-functioning families?" The evaluator is likely to feel more confident if she can respond that she has used specific design, sampling, assignment, instrumentation, and statistical procedures to decrease the likelihood that rival explanations could account for the program's positive outcomes.

We have noted that it is beyond the scope of this discussion to examine the many design, instrumentation, and sampling options in forward-looking studies. Research literature explores alternative designs, such as experimental and quasi-experimental ones, several sampling techniques, such as random sampling and stratified sampling, and a host of instrumentation or testing options, including questionnaires and observational techniques.[10]

If highly rigorous studies eliminate rival explanations, why are they not routinely used to assess programs' effectiveness? As the rigor of evaluations increases, so do their costs and the amount of time it takes to conduct them. Evaluators must be versed in the details of research and must have time—often many years—to devise and implement complex studies. Moreover, some evaluation techniques require agency members to subscribe to practices that can raise ethical problems. In the case of the special services program, for example, the evaluator might need to ask whether she could ethically *deny* special services to those families that were randomly placed in the control group.

We should not discount the role of politics when explaining many officials' failure to commission sophisticated assessments of programs, to ignore certain findings, or to bias their design or interpretations to protect their interests.[11] Advocates of new policies must often promote the likely benefits and successes in order to secure their enactment, because few politicians or officials will support policies that seem likely to fail. However, evaluations pose potential risks to the advocates of a specific program, as well as to the staff members involved in the program and its beneficiaries, because they *may* suggest that the innovations do *not* bring any, most, or some of the benefits that their advocates predicted. The special services program achieved only modest cost reductions and modest increases in reunification rates and no improvements in children's social and psychological functioning. Such mixed findings, which are typical of evaluative research, cast doubt on the innovation and make the interpretations of the findings problematic. (As we noted earlier, it is difficult to determine what magnitude of success is required to support the continuation of a program.) Moreover, evaluators are often trained to hedge even their positive findings, such as noting limitations in their methodology that *might* render their findings somewhat suspect.

Political considerations often influence interpretations of technical data. When a program receives unfavorable scores, people can question the data's validity and demand a new study or contend that the unfavorable score suggests terminating the program. They may contend that, while the program receives low scores on criteria used in the study, it might receive higher scores on criteria not used in the evaluation. Alternatively, they can maintain that the unfavorable score is not sufficiently strong to merit terminating the policy. To make matters still more complicated, someone can argue that an unfavorable score emanates not from a program's intrinsic defects, but because it has not received the funds to allow it to function properly.

The production of data, then, sometimes inaugurates a period of controversy where conflicting parties vie with one another in their interpretations of the findings. While people who favor a program are disposed to provide interpretations that support it, people who dislike it may seize upon negative findings to urge its termination.

Before we lambast officials and staff who do not routinely use rigorous policy evaluations, then, we should note that evaluations often occur in a politicized context, require significant investments of resources and time, and sometimes pose ethical dilemmas. We should also note that technical advances in evaluation methodology have not yet made findings immune to criticism. Indeed, as can be seen in Figure 14.1, which summarizes points made in the preceding discussion, evaluators encounter many obstacles during their work, each one of which can make their findings controversial, even among experts highly trained in technical procedures.

Qualitative Evaluations

Many researchers have become disenchanted with traditional, quantitative policy evaluations. They doubt that structured questionnaires capture consumers' or implementors' attitudes about the quality or nature of services they receive or provide. These researchers wonder whether evaluators, often based in consulting firms, develop simplistic criteria for assessing services without consulting consumers, clients, or providers to determine *their* perspectives. Often relying on single sources of data, such as scores on standardized instruments, evaluators often fail to gather data from several sources, including direct observations and open-ended interviews. Some researchers believe that evaluator should spend some time as participant observers in a project *before* they develop a research strategy; doing so could make them better-informed about a program.[12]

Moreover, some researchers contend that new evaluation techniques are needed for "sensitive" topics, such as evaluating programs that help people cope with or curtail stigmatized behaviors like child abuse, spousal abuse, drug use, AIDS, sexual deviance, and mental illness. People who engage in this kind of behavior are often unwilling to share their perceptions on questionnaires or even to cooperate with researchers.[13]

A feminist critique of traditional evaluations has also emerged. Though this critique lacks unity, feminist evaluators have attacked "the myth of value-free scientific inquiry." They ask researchers to acknowledge openly their biases and beliefs related to gender, race, sexual orientation, and socioeconomic class. Some evaluators want greater dialogue between researchers and their subjects rather than "interrogation" in an interview situation. Feminist researchers have developed new methods of collecting data, such as the use of visual imagery, group diaries, drama, conversation, textual analysis, associative writing, genealogy, and network tracing. Like other advocates of qualitative research, many feminist evaluators favor "triangulation," in which data are collected from three sources (such as questionnaires, in-depth interviews, and observations) and synthesized to obtain a fuller understanding of a project.[14]

Critics of traditional, quantitative evaluations want more attention to be devoted to the context of a program. We have discussed, for example, how a program's effectiveness can be shaped by many external factors, such as the blighted neighborhoods where clients often reside, the unavailability of employment, or poor schools. Or the implementing staff might be subjected to such onerous working conditions that they cannot provide services that had been planned at the inception of a program. Evaluators who failed to examine such factors might wrongly attribute the "failure" of a program to the helping techniques staff used rather than to the staff's working conditions or the blighted neighborhoods of their clients.[15]

Qualitative evaluations, then, make use of various techniques. They include multiple sources of data. In addition, qualitative evaluators often use more criteria to evaluate policies and often generate their methodology during interactions between researchers, providers, and clients.[16]

POLICY ADVOCATES' USE OF DATA

Advocates who seek policy reforms for oppressed groups and powerless populations need to evaluate policies. In some cases, they need to collect and use data, as the Children's Defense Fund and other advocacy groups do. Their data can include program statistics describing the kinds of persons who use specific programs to see if programs are reaching their intended beneficiaries. They can seek data about whether programs achieve specific goals, such as whether the Head Start Program improves children's nutritional and health needs. When program administrators lack data on vital points, advocates can pressure them to develop research projects to collect it.

Policy advocates need to participate, as well, in the politics of evaluative projects. When evaluating research reflecting that a "workfare program" for female welfare recipients effectively diminishes the welfare rolls, advocates should ask, for example, whether the program also leads to long-term improvements in the women's economic well-being, rather than merely putting them into low-wage jobs without fringe benefits. Because evaluators choose criteria that reflect their values when they assess programs, advocates should assert *their* values.[17]

WHY ALL SOCIAL WORKERS SHOULD ASSESS POLICIES

We have discussed the technical challenges of policy evaluation at considerable length, as well as the important role of technically trained evaluators. This discussion may suggest, however, that only experts can assess policies. In fact, all social workers can assess policy, even when they lack extended training in research. They can participate in arguments about research findings, cite research, use theory based on practice wisdom, and draw on moral standards.

Even when they do not produce research findings themselves, social workers can participate in critical discussions of specific evaluation projects. Social workers can critically examine evaluators' choice of criteria, methodological choices, instruments, and interpretations of findings. Indeed, in some cases, social workers should vigorously challenge evaluations that appear ill-advised, such as ones that prematurely suggest that specific policies should be abolished. Our discussion of similarities between evaluations and arguments strongly suggests that people should scrutinize evaluations, because they may wrongly propose to cast aside policies with considerable merit.

Social workers can draw on others' research as they evaluate specific programs. For example, when assessing a social program that lacks a bilingual staff, they can cite research that examines whether nonnative speakers use services when no translators exist. Social workers can adapt *suggestive findings* from other settings and programs when evaluating programs. We can infer, for example, that findings about having a bilingual staff when providing refugees with health services could also apply to other services refugees receive.

Social workers should draw on professional wisdom, as well as theory drawn from the social and human sciences, when evaluating programs. Empirical research is not available about the vast majority of decisions and policies within the human services; if we limited ourselves to empirical research, we would be silent on most issues! When they confront policies that conflict with professional wisdom or widely respected theories, social workers should draw on those sources to criticize the policies.

In the 1960s, many people thought citizens should have decisionmaking control in social agencies. Of course, citizens can make mistakes, as can any of us, but we should solicit their perspectives on specific policies. Even when citizens' opinions are not systematically surveyed, social workers can inject consumers' perspectives into debates about programs. When AIDS patients in a major city demanded special wards devoted to their problems, their preferences importantly influenced hospital officials to develop them.

Persons can support or oppose policies on purely moral grounds. We discussed in Chapter Two, for example, some moral reasons to defend social programs, even *without* specific empirical evidence about their success in rehabilitating people. For example, we can support hospice programs for terminally ill people, because they provide caring, humanistic services to those suffering from devastating trauma. An empirical finding that hospices save the government money by reducing the time people spend in hospitals would provide an *additional* justification, but we could defend the hospice program exclusively on moral grounds. Glenn Tinder argues:

> Consequences do not count, at least not decisively (when defending social programs). If someone restores a lost wallet to the owner we do not ask how the money it contained will be spent in order to determine whether this was an appropriate act. If someone helps save a friend from unemployment and poverty and the friend later dies of drink, we do not conclude that the original assistance was unwise. Indeed, a strict sense of justice is apt to be severely indifferent to consequences.[18]

Policy evaluation need not be reserved to technical experts. All of us can make important contributions and we can use many kinds of arguments to support or oppose policies. Indeed, assessing policies is the starting point for assuming leadership roles in the human services system.

Summary

We have discussed techniques for assessing policies in this chapter. When practitioners undertake this task, they should understand the following:

- Similarities between policy analysis, policy debates, and policy assessment
- Tools for countering criticism
- Obstacles that evaluators confront
- Qualitative modes of evaluation
- How policy advocates can use and interpret data

Evaluators encounter conceptual challenges similar to those that arise in policy analysis and debates. They must identify and weight criteria, such as cost and effectiveness, with which to assess policies. They have to gather data that allow them to isolate a program's effects, outcomes, or impacts on its beneficiaries. Moreover, they should obtain the data in a manner that rules out external factors as having caused the program's outcome. When they use sophisticated design and sampling strategies, they try to avoid the possibility of rival explanations, such as background economic factors, of their results. Other approaches also can be used, including qualitative methodologies. Evaluations can also use values implicit in specific programs, such as social justice and beneficence, to defend them.

Suggested Readings

GENERAL DISCUSSIONS OF POLICY EVALUATION
Scarvia Anderson and Samuel Ball, *The Profession and Practice of Program Evaluation* (San Francisco: Jossey-Bass, 1978).

Richard Berk et al., "Social Policy Experimentation: A Position Paper," *Evaluation Review* 9 (August 1985): 387–431.

Carl Patton and David Sawicki, *Basic Methods of Policy Analysis and Planning* (Englewood Cliffs, NJ: Prentice-Hall, 1986), pp. 300–328.

Peter Rossi and Howard Freeman, *Evaluation: A Systematic Approach,* 5th ed. (Newbury Park, CA: Sage, 1993).

POLICY EVALUATION IN ITS POLITICAL AND ECONOMIC CONTEXT

Richard Nathan, *Social Science in Government: Uses and Misuses* (New York: Basic Books, 1988).

Carol Weiss, "Ideology, Interests, and Information: The Basis of Policy Positions," in Daniel Callahan and Bruce Jennings, eds., *Ethics, the Social Sciences, and Policy Analysis* (New York: Plenum, 1983), pp. 213–248.

Carol Weiss, "Where Politics and Evaluation Meet," *Evaluation* 1 (1973): 37–46.

ETHICAL OR VALUE ISSUES IN POLICY EVALUATION

Bruce Jansson, "Blending Social Change and Technology in Macro-Practice: Developing Structural Dialogue in Technical Deliberations," *Administration in Social Work* 14 (1990): 13–28.

Martin Rein, "Value-Critical Policy Analysis," in Callahan and Jennings, *Ethics, the Social Sciences, and Policy Analysis,* pp. 83–111.

CASE STUDIES OF POLICY EVALUATION

Emil Posavic and Raymond Carey, *Program Evaluation: Methods and Case Studies* (Englewood Cliffs, NJ: Prentice-Hall, 1980).

Carol Weiss, ed., *Evaluation Action Programs* (Boston: Allyn & Bacon, 1972).

QUALITATIVE FORMS OF EVALUATION

Egon Guba and Yvonna Lincoln, *Fourth Generation Evaluation* (Newbury Park, CA: Sage, 1989).

Michael Patton, *Qualitative Evaluation and Research Methods* (Newbury Park, CA: Sage, 1990).

Notes

1. Michael Wald suggested this example in his article, "Family Preservation: Are We Moving Too Fast?" *Public Welfare* 46 (Summer 1988): 33–38.
2. Ibid.
3. These are hypothetical numbers.
4. These are hypothetical numbers.
5. Richard Berk and his colleagues make this point in "Social Policy Experimentation: A Position Paper," *Evaluation Review* 9 (August 1985): 387–431.
6. See Scarvia Anderson and Samuel Ball, *The Profession and Practice of Program Evaluation* (San Francisco: Jossey-Bass, 1978), pp. 6, 110–125.
7. Donald Campbell, "Experiments as Arguments," *Knowledge* 3 (1982): 327–337.
8. For a discussion of the value-laden choices that arise in program evaluations, see Martin Rein, "Value-Critical Policy Analysis," in Daniel Callahan and Bruce Jennings, eds., *Ethics, the Social Sciences, and Policy Analysis* (New York: Plenum, 1983), pp. 83–111.
9. An extended overview of program evaluation appears in Anderson and Ball, *The Profession and Practice of Program Evaluation;* and Peter Rossi and Howard Freeman, *Evalua-*

tion: A Systematic Approach, 5th ed. (Newbury Park, CA: Sage, 1993). For a brief overview, see Carl Patton and David Sawicki, *Methods of Policy Analysis and Planning* (Englewood Cliffs, NJ: Prentice-Hall, 1986), pp. 300–328.
10. Ibid.
11. See Carol Weiss, "Where Politics and Evaluation Meet," *Evaluation* 1 (1973): 37–46; Carol Weiss, "The Politicization of Evaluation Research, *Journal of Evaluation Research* 26 (1970): 57–68; and Carol Weiss, "Ideology, Interests, and Information: The Basis of Policy Positions," in Callahan and Jennings, *Ethics, the Social Sciences, and Policy Analysis,* pp. 213–248. For a discussion of how decisionmakers use social science, see Henry Aaron, *Politics and the Professors* (Washington, DC: Brookings Institution, 1981); and Richard Nathan, *Social Science in Government: Uses and Misuses* (New York: Basic Books, 1988).
12. For discussions of qualitative research, see Michael Patton, *Qualitative Evaluation and Research Methods* (Newbury Park, CA: Sage, 1990); and Egon Guba and Yvonna Lincoln, *Fourth Generation Evaluation* (Newbury Park, CA: Sage, 1989).
13. See Claire Renzetti and Raymond Lee, eds., *Researching Sensitive Topics* (Newbury Park, CA: Sage, 1993).
14. Ibid., pp. 177–180.
15. See Egon Guba and Yvonna Lincoln, *Effective Evaluation* (San Francisco: Jossey-Bass, 1981), pp. 75–76.
16. For two recent examples of qualitative research, see Rebecca Lee and J. C. M. Shute, "An Approach to Naturalistic Evaluation: A Study of the Social Implications of an International Development Project," *Evaluation Review* 15 (April 1991): 254–265; and Peter Neenan and Gary Bowan, "Multimethod Assessment of a Child-Care Demonstration Project for AFDC Recipient Families," *Evaluation Review* 15 (April 1991): 219–232.
17. Bruce Jansson, "Blending Social Change and Technology in Macro Practice: Developing Structural Dialogue in Technical Deliberations," *Administration in Social Work* 14 (1990): 13–28.
18. Glenn Tinder, "Defending the Welfare State," *New Republic* 180 (March 1979): 21–23.

PART FIVE
EPILOGUE

Policy practice is an emerging intervention within social work. We conclude this book by discussing "guiding perspectives" for policy practice. These perspectives allow us to understand tensions within policy practice, while understanding, as well, the kinds of resilience and persistence practitioners need to make policy an integral part of the professional role.

Epilogue
Perspectives for Policy Practice

We have tried to provide a framework for policy practice that can make it a major part of social workers' professional life. Having defined and discussed policy practice in agency, community, and legislative settings, we now provide some practice guidelines and orienting perspectives. Some of these guidelines and perspectives include goals and values that shape policy practice. Others involve tensions, such as ethical dilemmas, that policy practitioners encounter in policy reform.

DEVELOPING A VISION

Policy practitioners probably need a vision of a preferred state of affairs, whether in specific agencies, communities, regions, states, or in the nation. If we lack an ideal state of affairs, we are unlikely, in many cases, to find fault with existing policies. This vision derives from our values, beliefs, and ideology, as well as from a desire to help vulnerable or oppressed people who receive inferior or negligible assistance. We do not attempt to define the vision in narrowly ideological terms, because policy practice benefits from a variety of perspectives. The vision is nonetheless promoted and fueled by a sense of discontent with how existing policies and institutions measure up to an ideal.

Indeed, a vision is not only a driving force, but can enhance a practitioner's political interests and build their credibility. A person has succeeded in communicating that vision when others describe him or her as someone who "has principles," "really cares," or "is committed to changing things." We tend to be somewhat mistrustful, by contrast, of people we feel are "only in it for themselves" or who "bend with the wind." Of course, inflexibility and dogmatism can detract from policy practice, so people have to compromise between pragmatism and beliefs or values that constitute their vision.

Social workers can create a vision by developing an overview of how policies evolved in specific agencies and communities. They should also understand the policy implications of broad theoretical frameworks, such as an environmental approach. The vision could derive from identifying with the needs and aspirations of powerless groups or oppressed populations. Assuming that we have some empathy for the downtrodden, historical perspectives sensitize us to patterns of discrimination, racism, inequality, and suffering that have prompted various policy reforms. We have inherited the missions of the reformers before us, including some of the profession's founders, such as Jane Addams, who devoted remarkable energy to policy practice in a society that lacked the policies that we now take for granted. In a compelling argument, Jerome Wakefield contends that "distributional justice" provides a central mission for the social work profession, distinguishing it from other professions and traditional psychotherapy.[1]

An environmental perspective contributes to a vision by sensitizing us to factors that cause problems, such as homelessness, poverty, and inequality. This framework also alerts us to the way outmoded or dysfunctional aspects of the human services system exacerbate clients' problems.[2]

SEEKING OPPORTUNITIES FOR POLICY PRACTICE

Social workers of all stripes can assertively seek opportunities for policy practice, whether as part of their employment or outside their work. We can try to change policies in the community or in their agencies, for instance on task forces or committees. Within our agencies, as part of their employment, we can modify policies that they view as deficient or develop new programs.

Social workers can engage in policy practice outside of their working hours by helping advocacy groups, working with their professional association, or participating in campaigns.

TAKING SENSIBLE RISKS

Policy practitioners have to be sensible risk takers. Each of us possesses a finite amount of time, energy, and political resources. It is unwise to squander them on trivial or hopeless issues, even though ethical considerations sometimes prompt us to participate in difficult battles. However, we also need to be willing to take risks. Recall our discussion of assertiveness in Chapter Ten, when we noted that some policy practitioners refrain from seeking policy changes because they excessively discount their own power (or that of their allies) or exaggerate that of their opponents. Such loss of nerve—one that all of us experience several times in our careers—underscores that in policy practice, failures of omission are as important as errors of commission. In some cases, it is better to commit errors in trying to correct flawed policies than to avoid participating at all.

BALANCING FLEXIBILITY WITH PLANNING

Policy practitioners must develop plans to guide their work, but be able to improvise during unexpected events. Planning helps organize our work into a purposeful, coherent pattern and clarifies which tasks to accomplish. Improvising allows us to seize unexpected opportunities, counter opponents' arguments, and adopt new strategies that they did not anticipate in an earlier game plan. A policy practitioner makes plans by asking, "In light of the time and risk that I wish to take, what actions and arguments will help me obtain my objectives?" The practitioner considers various options, such as simple or more complex strategies. The resultant plan represents, then, a decision that specific actions and arguments, rather than other ones, will yield an acceptable outcome. In light of the uncertainties of many situations, however, these hypotheses must often be guarded and subject to modification when circumstances dictate. Policy-practice plans are made to be broken, because they reflect best initial guesses.

Policy practitioners need to be sufficiently flexible that they can alter their style or approach situationally; as with administrators, community workers, and direct-service practitioners, they need to improvise strategies in light of unfolding events.

Developing Multiple Skills

People who believe they can reduce policy practice to a simple set of recommended rules or a single style are likely to be disappointed when they discover that those rules or style are not useful in some situations. Policy practitioners need an array of analytic, political, interactional, and value-clarification skills that they use, singly or in tandem, in specific situations and during extended policy deliberations. A unidimensional policy practitioner is likely to be frustrated, because external realities require a combination of skills.

Policy practitioners need several skills, just as direct-service, community, and administrative practitioners do. Some of the skills are analytic; we need good ideas about the reforms we want, in order to be effective advocates. Other skills are process- and people-oriented ones, as our discussion of political and interactional skills throughout this book suggests. Still other skills involve ethical reasoning, particularly when we confront moral dilemmas. To develop these skills into competencies, we need to work at them in the same way as we hone direct-service, administrative, or community-work skills.

Being Persistent

Policy practitioners often need persistence, as the inspirational lives of social reformers such as Jane Addams and Martin Luther King, Jr., suggest. These people had an ability to persevere, even in the face of repeated defeats and formidable obstacles. Unlike some of their colleagues, who left reform causes after early battles, Addams and King maintained their devotion to social reform. Indeed, Jane Addams, who founded the pioneer social settlement Hull House in 1889, persevered not only during the Progressive Era, but also during the

1920s, to support innumerable social reforms. One can guess that had Martin Luther King, Jr., not been tragically assassinated, he would have been active in social reforms for decades more, because he had demonstrated that he was not inclined to rest on his laurels after securing many victories in the South.

Of course, few of us possess the persistence or the energy of these heroic figures. However, every community possesses particularly dedicated social workers who participate in many policy frays within their agencies and communities, as well as in broader arenas, even while they perform heavy direct-service, administrative, or community-work functions. We do not know why some people persevere while others cannot sustain policy practice over extended periods, but we can learn from people who possess this ability and can seek, in smaller measure, to emulate them. Perhaps their persistence stems, in part, from a combination of their vision or moral purpose and an ability not to be deterred by personal attacks or policy defeats. A vision provides a rationale for policy practice, independent of the vagaries of particular moments or the defeats and recriminations that any policy practitioner experiences.

Policy practitioners need perspective to avoid pessimism and self-recrimination in the wake of defeats or partial successes. No single person or group is likely to prevail in the complex playing field of policy deliberations. Practitioners must realize that defeats are more likely when people champion the needs of stigmatized and relatively powerless groups, which lack the clout of more powerful interests.

TOLERATING UNCERTAINTY

Policy practitioners must be able to tolerate uncertainty because policy practice often lacks structure and boundaries. While relatively few people participate in direct-service transactions, an "open field" often exists in policy practice, drawing new people into issues. Policy practitioners often do not know what to expect when they initiate a proposal. Will it be associated with conflict, consensus, or apathy? When they initiate a proposal, they often cannot predict how much time and energy will be required.

BECOMING A POLICY ADVOCATE

Policy practice can serve many purposes. In some cases, we want to advance our own interests or those of the profession, whether by seeking better reimbursement from insurances or licensing laws. Using policy practice to advance personal or professional interests is not unethical if our personal or professional activities have ethical merit. If professional social workers give counseling to persons that elevates their well-being, then policy practice that seeks licensing and reimbursement for professional social workers is ethically sound.

At the same time, social workers should include advocacy in their policy practice, which means helping relatively powerless and oppressed populations

Ethical principles, such as social justice, fairness, and beneficence, which we discussed in Chapter Two, dictate that practitioners should engage in this work, even if it brings no tangible return to them or to the profession.

When evaluating individuals' policy practice, we should take into account the degree of difficulty that they encountered. People who undertake difficult tasks or encounter formidable opposition will "lose" relatively frequently, no matter how skilled they are. Conversely, people who only contest simple issues will probably emerge victorious on numerous occasions. If we were to evaluate policy practitioners solely on the basis of their policy victories, we would risk giving high marks to excessively cautious people.

Indeed, "defeats" do not necessarily suggest that policy practitioners have been unsuccessful. When people take the initiative to propose policies, for example, they sensitize or educate other people, who may not have been aware of specific issues. While this brings no immediate successes, the defeated policy practitioner can reintroduce another proposal at a more propitious moment and hope that people, now aware of the issue, will change their positions.

Combining Pragmatism and Principles

Policy practitioners often must compromise for political reasons. With respect to controversial issues in organizational, community, and legislative settings, people rarely realize all of their goals. Yet there is a danger of making premature or excessive compromises that unnecessarily dilute a policy practitioner's goals. There is no simple way to resolve the tension between a pragmatic desire to achieve policy gains and a desire to retain provisions that a policy practitioner values. Indeed, practitioners often encounter ethical dilemmas that they can resolve only by considering the merits of alternative courses of action and making difficult choices between them.

Summary

Unique among the human-service professions, social work has emphasized incorporating a social-reform dimension into the professional role. We have named this dimension *policy practice* and have sought to identify the tasks and skills needed to implement it.

We discuss personal attributes that social workers need in order to make policy practice integral to their work in agencies, communities, and legislatures. Most fundamentally, social workers need a "vision" of a preferred state of affairs, regardless of whether that vision is derived from personal values, ideology, the examples of good leaders, or an ecological framework. Rather than believing that policy practice is limited to legislative reform, social workers should also seek opportunities for policy practice in agency and community settings.

Effective policy practitioners are sensible risk takers who select issues carefully. Possessing only scarce resources in time and political capital, they focus on issues in which they can make a difference while avoiding the danger of excessive caution. They want to plan their strategies carefully while remaining flexible so that they can alter their style or approach according to the situation. Realizing that they need multiple skills, they develop analytic, value-clarifying, political, and interactional skills.

Following the examples of such legendary leaders as Jane Addams, policy practitioners must be persistent because often they are unsuccessful in obtaining specific social reforms. They must be able to tolerate uncertainty because outcomes are unpredictable when many people participate in policy deliberations.

Policy practitioners must retain their moral principles, such as concern for social justice, while remaining pragmatic in light of the political barriers they confront. They must include policy advocacy in their policy practice by remaining attentive to the needs of oppressed populations.

The social problems of the United States in the 1990s, such as homelessness, child abuse, poverty, racism, and AIDS, suggest that the nation needs a corps of human-service professionals who not only help individuals with these problems, but also try to create more humane policies. By defining a framework, this book seeks to provide a conceptual foundation for policy practice. Each of us has to work, as well, to develop the personal attributes that motivate us to want to improve society in the first instance. In this personal arena, we each engage in a personal quest for self-definition that links us to broader issues and that expands our horizons to include advocacy for disempowered groups.

Notes

1. Jerome Wakefield, "Psychotherapy, Distributive Justice, and Social Work, Parts 1 and 2," *Social Service Review* 62 (June and September 1988): 187–210, 353–384.
2. See Carel Germain and Alex Gitterman, *The Life Model of Social Work Practice* (New York: Columbia University Press, 1980).

Name Index

Aaron, Henry, 32 n.57, 421 n.11
Abad, Vicente, 187 n.39
Abney, Glenn, 130 n.13
Abramson, Alan, 31 n.40, 159 n.32, 209
Adams, Kathleen, 296, 328 n.28
Addams, Jane, 10, 11, 427, 430
Adebimpe, Victor, 31 n.44, 185 n.8
Alexander, Chauncy, 28, 32 n.75, 296
Alinsky, Saul, 328 n.39
Amidei, Nancy, 130 n.30, 368 n.31
Anderson, James, 29
Anderson, Martin, 186 n.28
Anderson, Scarvia, 419, 420 nn. 6, 9
Arnold, R. Douglas, 129
Austin, David, 34 n.101
Austin, Nancy, 328 n.16

Bacharach, Samuel, 328 n.41, 329 n.43, 368 n.17
Bachrach, Peter, 70, 95 n.2, 276, 280, 295, 296 nn. 6, 8, 9; 297 n.16
Bagwell, Marilyn, 129, 130 nn. 8-10; 329 n.57, 369 nn. 41, 44-46, 50, 51, 53
Baker, John, 66, 66 n.22, 237 nn. 13, 14
Bales, Robert, 321, 328 n.42, 329 n.51
Ball, Samuel, 419, 420 nn. 6, 9
Banfield, Edward, 33 n.82, 82, 95 n.1, 96 n.16, 297 n.10
Baratz, Morton, 70, 95 n.2, 276, 280, 295, 296 nn. 6, 8, 9; 297n.16
Bardach, Eugene, 33 n.90, 94, 297 n.25, 327 n.9, 329 n.43, 367, 368 nn. 21, 28, 29; 380, 403, 405 nn. 9, 10
Barth, Richard, 405 n.27
Baumgartner, Frank, 157, 158 nn. 2, 3; 159 n.27
Beavers, Candace, 406 n.35
Bell, Budd, 130 n.34
Bell, William, 130 n.34

Bellah, Robert, 66 n.18
Bellamy, G. Thomas, 265 n.12
Bentham, Jeremy, 65
Berger, Peter, 31 n.53
Berk, Richard, 420, 420 n.5
Besharov, Douglas, 405 n.34
Best, Joel, 185, 186 n.23
Billingsley, Andrew, 31 n.45
Birnbaum, Jeffrey, 130 n.17, 367
Bischeff, Maurice, 61
Bisno, Herb, 8, 29 n.10, 265, 266 nn. 42, 44
Blau, Joel, 187 n.44
Bloom, Martin, 185 n.10, 210, 212 n.26
Bobo, Kim, 66 n.11, 367, 368 nn. 35, 38; 369 n.60
Boehm, Werner, 30 n.20, 32 n.71, 34 n.100
Bok, Sissela, 298 nn. 43, 44; 404
Bosk, Charles, 157
Bowan, Gary, 421 n.16
Bradshaw, Jonathan, 166, 185, 185 n.11
Brager, George, 265 nn. 15, 16; 266 nn. 32, 38; 296, 327 n.1, 328 n.41, 329 n.43, 366, 367 nn. 2, 8, 10; 368 nn. 22, 27
Briar, Katherine, 237 n.10
Briar, Scott, 237 n.10
Brieland, Donald, 31 n.39
Brilliant, Eleanor, 96 nn. 17, 19, 21; 131 n.49, 211 n.7
Brown, Jerry, 342
Brown, Larry, 405 n.34
Brown, Peter, 236
Brown, R. Douglas, 130 nn. 22, 24, 25, 29; 159 n.36
Burghardt, Steve, 115, 129, 131 nn. 38, 39; 367, 369 n.61
Burke, Vee, 297 n.21
Burke, Vincent, 158 n.9, 297 n.21
Burns, Eviline, 22, 32 n.78

431

NAME INDEX

Burns, Tom, 296 n.5
Burtle, Vasanti, 186 n.38
Bush, George, 19, 49, 103, 255–258, 338, 388

Califano, Joseph, 95 n.4, 297 n.19
Campbell, Donald, 411, 420 n.7
Campbell, Karlyn, 265 nn. 7, 8, 10
Caplan, Gerald, 32 n.62
Carey, Raymond, 420
Carroll, Harry, 209
Carter, Jimmy, 19, 147
Caulum, Sharon, 28, 32 n.68
Cegala, Donald, 265 nn. 3, 5, 11, 29, 31
Chamot, Dennis, 31 n.49, 328 n.38
Chen, Edwin, 158 n.17, 159 n.30
Cheney, Lynne, 130 n.9
Cheney, Richard, 130 n.9
Chess, Nancy, 212 n.36
Chu, Franklin, 32 n.76, 131 n.51, 288, 298 n.42, 404
Clements, Sallee, 329 n.57, 369 nn. 41, 44–46, 50, 53
Clinton, Bill, 19, 63, 99, 140, 143, 152, 153, 154, 159 n.44, 253–258, 269, 342
Cloward, Richard, 23, 30 n.26, 33 n.84, 67 n.38, 328 n.24
Cohen, Michael, 158 n.10
Conant, Ralph, 209
Conte, Jon, 186 n.26
Coons, John, 211 n.15
Coplin, William, 296 n.4, 333, 366, 367 nn. 4, 6
Cranston, Alan, 382
Craven, Bertram, 295, 297 n.11
Cunningham, James, 132 n.60
Cuomo, Mario, 253–258

Dahl, Robert, 32 n.74, 132 n.58, 293, 298 n.53
Dail, Paula, 406 n.35
Daley, Richard J., 83
Davis, Liane, 158 n.26, 210 n.1
Dear, Ron, 23, 29, 33 nn. 85, 87; 78, 96 n.15, 130 n.33, 297 n.36, 367, 367 n.1, 369 nn. 42, 43
Demone, Harold, 209, 210, 211 nn. 10, 14; 265, 266 n.42
Derthick, Martha, 406 n.48
Deutsch, Morton, 265 n.13, 297 nn. 29, 31, 32; 366
Devore, Wynetta, 32 n.58, 159 n.34, 187 n.40
Dexter, Lewis, 252, 266 n.35, 368 n.37
DiNitto, Diane, 23, 33 n.86
Dluhy, Milan, 132 nn. 62, 322, 327, 329 n.53, 54, 55, 56
Doblestein, Andrew, 23, 33 n.86

Dodd, Thomas, 111
Dole, Robert, 305
Dolgoff, Ralph, 65, 67 n.30
Doolittle, Fred, 209, 211 n.16
Dror, Yeheskel, 33 n.81, 185 n.1, 236 n.1
Dryzek, John, 236
Dukakis, Michael, 338
Duncan, Robert, 297 n.20
Dunn, William, 236
Dye, Thomas, 23, 33 n.86

Easton, Thomas, 209
Edsall, Thomas, 32 n.70, 130 n.19
Ellwood, David, 169, 170, 184, 185 n.6, 186 nn. 19–21
Emerson, Richard, 159 n.33, 326, 327 n.4
Ephross, Paul, 266 n.33, 327, 328 nn. 33, 36; 329 nn. 48, 52, 58, 62
Epstein, Irwin, 30 n.26, 236 n.3
Etzioni, Amitai, 406 n.43
Eyestone, Robert, 95 n.7, 157, 158 nn. 2, 3, 15

Fabricant, Michael, 115, 129, 131 nn. 38, 39
Fellin, Phillip, 236 n.3
Fenno, Richard, 211 n.13, 298 n.50, 368 n.19
Ferullo, Donna, 187 n.40
Figueira-McDonough, Josephina, 24, 29 n.7, 33 n.99
Finch, Wilbur, 29 n.10
Fingarette, Herbert, 184
Fleishman, Joel, 296, 327 n.8
Flynn, John, 24, 33 n.94
Folberg, Jay, 265, 266 n.45, 329 n.61
Ford, Gerald, 19
Francoeur, Robert, 237 nn. 4–6
Frank, Richard, 210, 212 n.28
Frantzich, Stephen, 367 n.5
Freeley, Austin, 264
Freeman, Howard, 420, 420 n.9
French, John, 295, 297 n.11
Fretz, Bruce, 210, 211 n.20
Froman, Lewis, 29 n.12, 129 n.7, 130 n.12, 295, 297 n.24
Fuchs, Victor, 186 n.24
Fulton, Robert, 209–210 n.3

Galbraith, John Kenneth, 67 n.26
Gates, Bill, 46
Gelman, Sheldon, 131 n.57
Germain, Carel, 18, 32 n.65, 96 n.22, 430 n.2
Gerth, Hans, 131 n.54
Gibelman, Margaret, 209, 210, 211 nn. 10, 14; 265, 266 n.42
Gil, David, 23, 33 n.83

Gilbert, Neil, 22, 32 n.64, 33 n.79, 210, 212 nn. 27, 29
Gilder, George, 66 n.23
Ginzburg, Eli, 212 n.35
Giovannoni, Jeanne, 31 n.45, 186 n.25
Gitterman, Alex, 32 n.65, 430 n.2
Glazer, Nathan, 32 n.59
Goodin, Robert, 28, 29 n.11, 66, 131 nn. 45, 53; 210, 212 n.30, 298 n.41, 404
Gorman, Paul, 209, 210 n.3
Gottlieb, Benjamin, 32 n.63
Graham, Allison, 94
Green, Arnold, 94, 185, 186 nn. 22, 27, 36
Greenwood, Ernest, 94, 185 nn. 1, 3; 236 n.1
Gruber, Murray, 131 n.50
Guba, Egon, 185, 420, 421 nn. 12, 15
Gummer, Burton, 129, 131 nn. 48, 52, 55; 263, 266 nn. 42, 43; 295, 360–361, 367, 369 n.57, 405 n.16, 406 n.39
Gunn, Lewis, 28, 94, 236, 236 n.1, 404 n.2
Gustavsson, Nora, 387, 392, 405 nn. 24–26, 31, 32; 406 nn. 46, 47

Hagan, Jan, 158 n.26, 210 n.1
Hall, Mary, 236, 237 n.22
Halleck, Seymour, 28
Hamovitch, Maurice, 67 n.39
Handler, Joel, 30 n.32
Hanft, Ruth, 236
Hanks, John, 29, 33 nn. 86, 88
Hardcastle, David, 31 n.38, 210, 212 nn. 21–23
Hargrove, Erwin, 33 n.90, 403
Hardin, Mark, 406 n.45
Harkin, Tom, 341
Hart, Aileen, 96 n.21
Hart, Philip, 307
Hartman, Ann, 30 n.21
Hasenfeld, Yeheskel, 28, 30 n.23, 31 n.48, 32 n.66, 91, 95, 96 n.20, 129, 131 nn.35, 40, 47, 56; 132 n.59, 291, 298 n.47, 368 n.15, 403, 404 n.7
Hatch, Orrin, 111
Hawkins, Augustus, 280
Haynes, Karen, 23, 29, 33 n.86, 296, 367, 369 nn. 47, 48, 52, 54–56
Hearn, Gordon, 30 n.21
Heffernan, Joseph, 212 n.31
Hickson, D. J., 327 n.4, 369 n.58
Hilgartner, Stephen, 157
Hogwood, Brian, 28, 94, 236, 236 n.1, 404 n.2
Holcombe, Marya, 237 n.24, 265 nn. 17–21
Hollingshead, August, 32 n.61
Holloway, Stephen, 265 n.15, 366, 367 nn. 2, 8, 10; 368 nn. 22, 27

Holtzman, Abraham, 129 n.3
Humphrey, Hubert, 280, 307
Humphreys, Nancy, 34 n.103, 66 n.8, 96 n.24, 296
Hyman, Herbert, 404

Imersheim, Allen, 211 n.3

Jackson, Jesse, 341
Janis, Irving, 321, 327, 329 nn. 49, 50
Jansson, Bruce, 24, 29, 30 n.18, 32 nn. 69, 77; 33 nn. 96–98; 66 n.21, 67 nn. 27, 36; 96 n.12, 131 nn. 43, 44; 158 n.23, 187 n.46, 210 n.2, 211 n. 4, 212 nn. 34, 36; 236 n.2, 237 nn. 8, 15; 295, 297 nn. 14, 18, 26, 28; 326, 327, 327 nn. 5–7, 10; 328 n.29, 368 nn. 14, 25; 405 nn. 15, 18; 406 n.38, 420, 421 n.17
Johnson, Harold, 327, 328 nn. 32, 34, 35, 37; 329 nn. 44–47, 59
Johnson, Lyndon, 19, 269, 278, 309, 342
Jones, Bryan, 157, 158 nn. 2, 3; 159 n.27
Jones, Charles, 95

Kahn, Alfred, 22, 23, 33 nn. 80, 91; 131 n.37, 185 n.1, 209, 211 n.5, 236 n.1
Kahn, Si, 367
Kamerman, Sheila, 23, 33 n.91, 131 n.37, 209
Kanter, Rosabeth, 90, 96 n.18, 293, 296, 298 n.51, 310, 311, 327, 328 nn. 19, 25, 26, 27; 369 n.59
Kaplan, John, 184
Kearns, Doris, 95 n.1, 297 n.12
Keefe, Thomas, 31 n.54
Kendall, Jackie, 66 n.11, 367, 368 nn. 35, 38; 369 n.60
Kennedy, John, 19
Keynes, John Maynard, 176
Khinduka, S. K., 212 n.25
Kimmich, Madeleine, 406 n.49
King, Martin Luther, Jr., 64, 427
Kingdon, John, 10, 30 n.13, 76, 94, 95 nn. 7–9; 139, 140, 142, 143, 144, 145, 146, 151, 157–158 n. 1, 5–8, 11–14, 16, 18–20, 24; 159 nn. 28, 29, 38–42, 45; 184, 186 n.12, 297 n.30, 368 n.12
Kitsuse, John, 185, 186 n.23
Klein, Ann, 405 n.21
Koenig, Louis, 184
Koshel, Jeffrey, 406 n.49
Kosterlitz, Julie, 66 n.5, 67 n.35, 158 nn. 21, 25; 184, 367 n.9, 368 n.11, 405 n.20
Kotler, Phillip, 186 n.15, 187 n.42, 265 n.14
Kozol, Jonathan, 41, 66 n.9
Kramer, Ralph, 211 nn. 4, 6, 8

Kupcha, Dorothy, 404 n.3
Kuttner, Robert, 405 n.17

Lauffer, Armand, 236, 237 nn. 19–21
Lauth, Thomas, 130 n.13
Lawler, Edward, 328 n.41, 329 n.43, 368 n.17
Lee, Raymond, 421 n.13
Lee, Rebecca, 421 n.16
Lemann, Nicholas, 67 n.24
Lemmon, John, 31 n.39
Leonard, Herman, 210, 211 nn. 18, 19
Levy, Charles, 237 n.16, 404
Lewin, Kurt, 333, 367 n.3
Lincoln, Yvonna, 420, 421 nn. 12, 15
Lindblom, Charles, 94
Lipsky, Michael, 296, 297 nn. 37–39; 328 n.31, 404
Loewenberg, Frank, 65, 67 n.30
Lowi, Theodore, 297 n.33, 368 n.26, 404, 404 n.1
Lynn, Laurence, 31 n.35, 129, 130 nn. 14, 23

Mackie, J. L., 7, 29 n.9, 65, 66 nn. 2, 20; 67 nn. 29, 34
MacNeilage, Linda, 296, 328 n.28
Mahaffey, Maryann, 23, 29, 33 nn. 86, 88
March, James, 158 n.10
Maslow, Abraham, 16, 31 n.51
Massarik, Fred, 406 n.40
Matthews, Christopher, 281, 295, 297 nn. 13, 23, 35; 309, 310, 327, 327 nn. 2, 11, 12; 328 nn. 14, 17, 18; 355, 369 n.49
Max, Steve, 66 n.11, 367, 368 nn. 35, 38; 369 n.60
Mayer, Robert, 94, 185 nn. 1, 3; 236 n.1
Mazade, Noel, 31 n.47
McClure, Jesse, 95 n.5, 96 n.14
McGowan, Brenda, 31 n.42, 32 nn. 67, 68
McGregor Burns, James, 129 n.1
Mechanic, David, 31 n.46, 185 n.9, 296, 328 n.30
Meredith, Judith, 130 n.11
Meyer, Carol, 18, 32 n.65
Meyer, Karl, 82–87
Mikelson, James, 29, 33 n.86, 296, 367, 369 nn. 47, 48, 52, 54–56
Milgram, Stanley, 296, 296 n.7, 298 n.49
Miller, Warren, 368 n.13
Miller, William, 186 n.37
Mills, C. Wright, 131 n.54, 293, 298 n.52
Mills, David, 210, 211 n.20
Mirin, Steven, 186 nn. 16, 34
Montjoy, Robert, 95, 95 n.6, 403, 404 nn. 4, 5, 8
Moore, Mark, 162, 164

Moroney, Robert, 94
Moynihan, Daniel, 32 n.59, 144, 281
Murphy, Michael, 210
Murray, Alan, 130 n.17, 367
Murray, Robin, 186 n.33

Nadelman, Ethan, 184
Nathan, Richard, 95, 209, 211 n.16, 420, 420 n.11
Neenan, Peter, 421 n.16
Nelkin, Dorothy, 186 n.32
Nichols-Casebolt, Ann, 95, 96 n.14
Nixon, Richard, 19, 140, 147, 308, 336

O'Leary, Michael, 296 n.4, 333, 366, 367 nn. 4, 6
Olsen, Johan, 158 n.10
O'Toole, Laurence, 95, 95 n.6, 403, 404 nn. 4, 5, 8

Paine, Stan, 265 n.12
Patti, Rino, 23, 24, 29, 32 n.75, 33 nn. 85, 87, 95; 78, 96 n.15, 130 n.33, 297 n.36, 367, 367 n.1, 368 n.24, 369 nn. 42, 43
Patton, Carl, 94, 95, 236, 420, 421 nn. 9, 10
Patton, Michael, 421 n.12
Pear, Robert, 159 n.43
Pelton, Leroy, 405 n.23
Pepper, Claude, 307
Perot, Ross, 342
Peters, Tom, 328 n.16
Pierce, Dean, 24, 33 n.94
Piven, Frances, 23, 33 n.84, 67 n.38, 328 n.24
Popple, Phillip, 93, 96 n.23
Porter, Lyman, 404
Portney, Kent, 236
Posavic, Emil, 420
Potuchek, Jean, 131 n.42, 187 n.43
Pressman, Jeffrey, 23, 29 n.5, 33 n.89, 403, 404 n.6

Quade, Edward, 33 n.81, 185 n.1, 236 n.1

Ramirez, David, 212 n.33
Rawls, John, 44, 66, 66 nn. 13–15
Reagan, Ronald, 19, 49, 73, 99, 103, 191, 195, 282, 384, 386, 388
Reamer, Frederic, 65, 66, 66 n.1, 67 nn. 30, 32
Redlich, Shirley, 32 n.61
Redman, Eric, 95, 95 n.1, 349, 367, 368 nn. 33, 34
Reich, Robert, 66 nn. 16, 17; 67 n.25, 158 n.22
Reid, Hester, 186 n.37
Reid, Robert, 265 n.24
Rein, Martin, 28, 29 nn. 1–3, 6; 94, 236, 237 n.9, 296 n.3, 420, 420 n.8

NAME INDEX

Reisch, Michael, 10, 30 nn. 14–16, 28; 67 n.40
Renzetti, Claire, 421 n.13
Resnick, Herman, 24, 29, 32 n.75, 33 n.95, 295, 368 nn. 24, 30
Rhodes, Margaret, 65, 67 n.30
Richan, Willard, 24, 33 n.92, 130 n.32, 264, 265 n.1, 351, 367, 368 nn. 36, 39; 369 n.40
Richardson, Elliot, 130 n.31
Richmond, Mary, 10, 11, 20
Ripley, Brian, 236
Ripley, Randall, 95
Roosevelt, Franklin, 99, 269, 342
Rosenthal, Elizabeth, 66 nn. 4, 5
Ross, Murray, 12, 30 n.22
Rossi, Peter, 420, 420 n.9
Rovner, Julie, 297 n.15
Rubington, Earl, 186 n.23
Russo, Nancy, 32 n.60
Ryan, Dan, 82–87

Salamon, Lester, 31 n.40, 159 n.32, 185, 209
Salcido, Ramon, 29, 64, 67 nn. 42, 43
Samantrai, Krishna, 406 n.49
Savage, Andrea, 28
Savas, Emanuel, 211 n.9
Sawicki, David, 94, 95, 236, 420, 421 nn. 9, 10
Schattschneider, Eric, 295, 297 n.27, 367 n.7
Scheirer, Mary Ann, 404
Schelling, Thomas, 368 nn. 18, 20
Schlesinger, Elfriede, 32 n.58, 159 n.34, 187 n.40
Schorr, Alvin, 7, 28, 29 n.8, 34 n.102
Scott, Ray, 209–210 n.3
Scott, Robert, 30 n.31
Seck, Essie, 29, 64, 67 nn. 42, 43
Sepulveda-Hassell, Sharon, 212 n.33
Sharwell, George, 266 n.34, 298 nn. 45, 46
Shilts, Randy, 187 n.45
Shute, J. C. M., 421 n.16
Simmons, June, 96 n.12, 131 nn. 43, 44; 295, 326, 327, 327 nn. 5–7, 10; 328 n.29
Simons, Herbert, 264, 265 nn. 2, 4, 6, 9, 14, 22, 23, 25–28, 30; 266 nn. 36, 37, 39–41; 327 n.1, 328 n.40
Sink, David, 328 n.42
Skjei, Eric, 237 nn. 17, 18, 23
Skodol, Andrew, 31 n.43, 185 n.5
Smith, Craig, 237 nn. 17, 18, 23
Smith, Hedrick, 94, 95 nn. 3, 10; 100, 129, 129 nn. 4, 6, 7; 130 nn. 15, 26, 27, 28; 157, 158 n.4, 159 nn. 27, 31; 285, 292, 295, 297 n.34, 298 n.48
Smith, James, 130 n.20, 159 n.37
Smith, Perry, 368 n.16
Smith, Stan, 209
Solomon, Barbara, 31 n.56; 32 n.66; 66 n.7, 187 n.41
Sosin, Michael, 28, 32 n.68
Specht, Harry, 22, 32 n.72, 33 n.79, 210, 212 n.29, 266 nn. 32, 38; 296, 327 n.1, 328 n.41, 329 n.43
Spector, Malcolm, 185, 186 n.23
Spiegel, Allen, 404
Spitzer, Robert, 31 n.43, 185 n.5
Stabenau, James, 186 n.33
Stanford, Rochelle, 327 n.3
Starr, Paul, 66 n.10
Stein, Judith, 265 nn. 17–21
Steiner, Gilbert, 30 n.29, 31 n.50
Stiglitz, Joseph, 186 n.35
Stogdill, Ralph, 329 n.44
Stokes, Donald, 368 n.13
Stone, Deborah, 209
Strodtbeck, Fred, 328 n.42, 329 n.51
Sugarman, Stephen, 211 n.15
Szasz, Thomas, 31 n.43, 185 n.7

Taylor, Alison, 265, 266 n.45, 329 n.61
Taylor, Robert, 30 nn. 27, 33
Teare, Robert, 212 n.24
Terrel, Paul, 210, 211 nn. 11, 12
Thayer, Frederick, 211 nn. 15, 17
Thompson, Frank, 186 n.29
Thurow, Lester, 66 nn. 12, 19
Tichy, Noel, 212 n.32, 237 n.7, 327, 328 n.15
Tinder, Glenn, 419, 421 n.18
Titmuss, Richard, 4, 28, 29 n.4, 191, 210, 211 n.5
Torczyner, James, 266 nn. 32, 38; 296, 327 n.1, 328 n.41, 329 n.43
Tripodi, Tony, 236 n.3
Tropman, Elmer, 30 n.25, 327, 328 nn. 32, 34, 35, 37; 329 nn. 44–47, 59
Tropman, John, 24, 29, 30 n.25, 33 nn.93, 94; 327, 328 nn. 32, 34, 35, 37; 329 nn. 44–47, 59
Trotter, Sharland, 32 n.76, 131 n.51, 288, 298 n.42, 404
Tsongas, Paul, 341

U.S. Department of Health and Human Services, 186 n.17
U.S. Joint Commission on Mental Illness and Public Health, 30 n.30
U.S. National Institute of Mental Health, 185, 186 nn. 13, 14
U.S. President's Commission on Mental Health, 31 nn. 36, 41

Van Horn, Carl, 403
Van Meter, Donald, 403
Vassil, Thomas, 266 n.33, 327, 328 nn. 33, 36; 329 nn. 48, 52, 58, 62
Veatch, Robert, 65, 66 n.3, 67 nn. 28, 33

Wakefield, Jerome, 62, 67 n.41, 426, 430 n.1
Wald, Michael, 405 nn. 19, 28–30, 33, 34; 406 nn. 41, 44, 50; 420 nn. 1, 2
Warren, Roland, 132 n.61
Warwick, Donald, 404
Wasserman, Harry, 21, 30 n.17, 32 n.73
Watkins, Ted, 30 n.34
Weatherford, J. McIver, 129, 130 nn. 16, 21; 310, 327, 328 nn. 13, 16, 20–22
Weber, Max, 124, 288
Webster, Stephen, 31 n.37, 131 n.36, 185
Wedel, Kenneth, 212 n.36
Weick, Kenneth, 298 n.40
Weinberg, Martin, 186 n.23
Weiss, Carol, 368 n.32, 420, 421 n.11
Weissman, Harold, 28
Weissman, Irving, 30 nn. 19, 24
Wenocur, Stanley, 10, 30 nn. 14–16, 28; 67 n.40, 131 n.49

West, Guida, 159 n.35
Whitaker, William, 296, 328 n.23
White, Robert, 16, 31 n.52
Whiting, Leila, 406 n. 35
Wilcox, Barbara, 265 n.12
Wildavsky, Aaron, 23, 29 n.5, 33 n.89, 129 nn. 2, 5; 211 n.13, 403, 404 n.6, 406 n.37
Williams, Janet, 31 n.43, 185 n.5
Williams, Walter, 33 n.90
Williamson, Richard, 211 n.16
Wilson, Michele H., 55
Wilson, William, 31 n.55, 185
Wineman, Steven, 185, 186 n.31
Wing, J. K., 185 n.4
Wofford, Harrison, 147
Wolf, Charles, 236, 236 n.8, 237 nn. 11, 12
Wood, Shelley, 186 n.18
Wyers, Norman, 7, 24, 29, 29 n.8, 33 n.99
Wylie, Mary, 31 n.37, 131 n.36

Yates, Douglas, 67 nn. 31, 37

Zald, Mayer, 14, 30 n.31, 131 n.41, 403
Zaltman, Gerald, 297 n.20
Zigler, Edward, 130 n.31

Subject Index

Abortion, 281
Absolute standard, 164
Access, 4, 201, 202
Accountability, 8
Accreditation, 87, 114, 117, 152, 198
Act-Up, 156
Administration, 12, 25
Administrative oversight, 100
Administrative regulations, 117, 148, 390, 391
Adoption Assistance and Child Welfare Act, 381-401
Advertisements, 358
Advisory boards, 125
Advocacy, 190, 197. *See also* Policy advocacy
   case, 18
   case-based, 36-40, 62
   class, 18
Advocacy groups, 42, 48, 77, 127, 149, 156, 315, 316, 359, 365, 392
Affiliations, 308
Affirmative action, 48, 201, 221
African Americans, 15, 17, 26, 43, 46, 47, 49, 101, 155, 165, 179, 387
Agencies. *See also* Social agencies
   policies of, 6, 21, 88
   agency politics, 359-364
   agenda-building task, 9-10
   defined, 71
   illustrated, 75, 76, 83, 84
   importance of, 135-139
   phases of, 141, 142
   policy advocacy in, 155, 156
   policy entrepreneurs in, 153, 154
   policy windows in, 151-153
   political stream of, 148-151
   problem stream of, 142-146
   solution stream of, 146-148
Agenda funnel, 141

Aides, 351
AIDS, 26, 41, 153, 178, 220, 221, 232-235, 250-253, 259-262, 299-304, 418
Aid to Families with Dependent Children (AFDC), 73, 77, 165, 168-172, 173, 179, 201
Alcoholics, 177
Alcoholics Anonymous, 177
Alcoholism, 75, 163, 164, 168, 175-178
Altruism, 26, 198
Alzheimer's disease, 76, 110, 315
Amending role, 331
Amendments, 78, 104, 284
American Association of Automobile Dealers, 72
American Association of Retired Persons (AARP), 72, 109, 150, 292, 357
American Civil Liberties Union, 300
American Hospital Association, 147
American Medical Association, 41, 72, 107, 147, 342
American Psychiatric Association (APA), 15, 164
Americans with Disabilities Act of 1990, 117
Analogies, 260
Analytic assumptions, 260
Analytic skills, 9, 20
   defined, 73, 74
   illustrated, 75-81, 85-87
   in agenda-building task, 139, 140, 143, 145-147, 154, 155
   in policy-assessing task, 408-410, 412-417
   in policy-enacting task, 331-347
   in policy-implementing task, 373, 374, 389, 390, 393, 394
   in policy persuasion, 244-247, 259-262
   in problem-defining task, 160-172

437

Analytic skills (*continued*)
  in proposal-constructing task, 188–208, 213–225
  theoretical development of, 22
Analytic style, 20, 74, 161, 162
Anarchy, 8, 315
Appropriations, 100, 193, 391
Appropriations committee, 391
Area Agencies for the Aging (AAAs), 203
Argumentation, 249, 259–262. *See also* Debates
Asian Americans, 17, 47
Assertiveness, 39, 40, 91, 92, 312–314, 395, 426
Assessment. *See* Policy-assessing task
Attorneys, 35–37, 41
Audiences
  apathetic, 247, 248
  diagnosing, 240–242
  expert, 247, 248, 252
  heterogeneous, 241, 251, 252
  homogeneous, 241
  hostile, 240–242, 247, 248, 250, 251
  motivation of, 241
  varieties of, 247, 248
  zone of tolerance, 241
Authoritativeness, 307
Authority, 278, 279, 292
Authorizations, 100, 193, 391
Autonomy, 14, 16, 50, 286–289, 315, 321

Battered women. *See* Spousal abuse
Behavioral frameworks, 175
Behavioral therapy, 20
Behavior modification, 15
Beneficence, 36–41, 43, 60, 63, 221, 222, 289
Benefit-cost ratio, 168–175
Bilingual staff, 228
Block grants, 195
Blocking roles, 351
Blue-ribbon committees, 284
Boards, 125, 192, 203
Boundary spanners, 126, 362
Bribes, 278
Brokerage, 36–40, 62
B.S.W.s, 14, 198
Buck-passing, 308
Budget cuts, 115
Budgets, 7, 99, 100, 121, 126, 152, 228, 234, 235, 291–293, 362, 367, 394
Bully pulpit, 99
Bureaucrats, 105
Burnout, 313
Bystander role, 331

California Children's Lobby, 301
Campaigns, 60. *See also* Political campaigns
Capitalism, 49
Case management, 197
Case records, 51–55
Categorical programs, 195
Caucus, 356
Census, 167
Center for Budget and Policy Priorities, 107
Charisma, 278, 279
Chicago School of Civics and Philanthropy, 11
Child abuse, 384
Child Care and Development Block Grant, 337
Child development legislation, 73
Child neglect, 384
Children, 43, 47
Children's Defense Fund, 107, 155, 156, 398, 417
Child welfare, 381–393
Child Welfare League of America, 382, 383, 398
Christmas-tree legislation, 281
Citizen participation, 192, 202, 203
City councils, 104
Civil rights, 140
Civil rights movement, 13
Civil servants, 150, 192, 351
  duties of, 106
  exams of, 106
  hierarchy of, 106, 114
  links with legislators, 106, 108
  links with lobbyists, 108
  mind-sets of, 113, 114
Civil service, 60, 223–226
Class-action lawsuits, 398
Classification of positions, 63, 198, 199
Clinical social workers, 62
Coalitions, 40, 60, 79, 107, 285, 314, 322, 323, 335, 337, 340, 346, 352, 354, 359, 365
Cocaine, 174, 216
Cocaine-addicted babies, 388
Codes of ethics, 36, 51
Coercion, 276, 278, 314
Coercive messages, 262–263
Cognitive therapy, 15, 20
Collaboration, 263, 264
Collective rights, 50
Combative persuasion, 259–264
Committees, 79, 310, 315–322, 338, 339. *See also* Task groups
Common Cause, 300
Communication, 393

Communities
  horizontal dimensions, 127
  vertical dimensions, 127
Community care services, 223–226
Community Emergency Service (CES) program, 205–208
Community liaison, 394
Community Mental Health Centers Act of 1963, 224
Community organization, 12, 20, 24, 25
Community-support systems, 202
Compliance, 289, 290, 380, 397
Compromises, 286, 343
Computers, 351
Conference committees, 104
Confidentiality, 50, 51–55
Conflict, 69, 283, 284, 336, 342, 343, 345, 347, 359, 360, 365
Conflict-management skills, 37, 394
Confrontation, 259, 262, 263
Consensus, 264, 342, 343
Consequentialists, 58. *See also* Utilitarians
Conservative backlash, 19
Conservatives, 46, 48–50, 173, 240, 242, 250, 251, 332, 339, 411, 412
Conservativism, 61
Constitution, 215
Consumer payments, 193
Consumers, 192–195
Consumers Union, 300
Consultants, 396
Consultation, 350, 351
Context, 239, 285, 286, 304, 305, 336–340, 384–386
Contracts, 115, 194
Cook County Hospital, 82–87
Cooptation, 279
Correlational design, 413
Cost-benefit ratio, 168–175
Cost effectiveness, 216, 380
Council on Social Work Education (CSWE), 12, 20, 24, 198
Counterproposals, 262
County boards of supervisors, 104
Court rulings, 117, 120, 149
Courts, 15
"Creaming," 4
Credibility, 305–312, 314, 355
Criminalization, 176
Crisis intervention, 197
Criteria, 213–222, 409–412
Culturally sensitive practice, 177
Cultural sensitivity, 6

Culture, 172, 173, 177, 199
Curative services, 197, 199, 200, 220

Day-care centers, 192
Day-care legislation, 73, 336, 337
Debates, 259–262, 410–412
Decentralization, 220
Decision agendas, 141
Decisionless decision, 70
Decision-making matrix, 213, 216–219, 408
Decision-making power. *See* Power
Declassification, 386
Decriminalization, 216
Defense Department, 192
Deinstitutionalization, 223–226
Delivery style, 247
Demand-side economists, 176
Democratic Party, 103, 356
Democrats, 253–258, 280, 282, 338, 342
Demography, 167
Deontology, 51
Department of Housing and Urban Development, 189, 190
Depression, 174
Design, 413
Deterrent strategies, 175
Diagnostic criteria, 200
Dictatorships, 270
Directive communication, 252
Direct-service staff, 24, 25, 387
  in agenda-building, 154, 155
  in defining problems, 179–182
  in the policy-enacting task, 271–276, 286–293, 314, 315
  in policy implementation, 402–404
  in the policy-assessing task, 418, 419
Direct-service workers, 88, 287–289, 314, 315
Disabled persons, 47, 140
Disabilities, 26, 38, 62, 169–172
Discontinuity, 4
Discretion, 21, 49, 287–289, 379, 395, 397, 398
Discrimination, 4, 62, 173, 201, 426
Dishonesty, 293, 294
Dissonance, 249
Division of labor, 346, 361, 362, 379
Donors, 114, 193
Drug addiction, 162–165, 173–176
DSM-III, 164, 178
Due process, 50
Duplication, 173

Ecological frameworks, 220. *See also* Environmental frameworks

Ecological perspectives, 173-174
Economists, 175, 176
Effectiveness, 189, 215, 201, 380
Efficiency, 189, 215, 221
Ego psychology, 11
Elderly people, 19, 47
Elected officials. *See also* Heads of government; Legislators
  campaigns of, 109
  choice-making by, 111-112
  environment of, 109, 110
  mind-sets of, 109-110
  short cuts of, 110
  varieties of, 99-105
Electoral politics, 60
Eligibility criteria, 200, 201
Empire-building, 308
Empowerment, 18, 39, 40, 42, 178
Entitlements, 201
Environmental frameworks, 16-18, 20, 92, 93, 176
Equality, 50, 179, 215, 221, 222. *See also* Social justice
Equity, 189, 201, 215
Ethical dilemmas, 35
  definition, 55
  when ethical principles conflict, 56-59
  when ethics conflict with pragmatism, 57-59
Ethical issues. *See also* Value-clarification skills
  definition, 35
  when devising policy proposals, 9
Ethical principles, 50
Ethical reasoning, 9. *See also* Value-clarification skills
  nature of, 35, 36
  need for, 59
Ethnicity, 18
Euthanasia, 57
Existentialism, 15
Existential therapy, 20
Experimental designs, 415
Expertise, 278
Externalities, 216
Evaluation, 229. *See also* Policy-assessing task
Evaluators. *See* Policy-assessing task

Facilitators, 396
Fairness, 46-48, 58, 59, 380. *See also* Equity
Fair Political Practices Commission, 300
Families, 169-172
Family Assistance Plan, 140
Family counselors, 199
Family Support Act of 1986, 375-377

Fatalism, 312, 313, 345
Feasibility, 189, 216, 221, 260
Federal government, 192-195
Federal Register, 391
Federal Shelter program, 188-204
Federated fundraising, 15
Federated Jewish Appeal, 13
Fees, 192, 200, 202
Feminists, 263, 416-417
Filibusters, 69, 104
Financing of services, 14-16
Fixers, 380
Flawed strategies, 375
Flow charts, 229
Food Stamps Program, 112, 214, 305
Force, 276
Force-field analysis, 333-336, 341, 342, 361-364
Formal policies, 7
Formats, 243-246
Forward-looking research, 414
Foster care, 384-389
Foster homes, 382-309
Foundations, 229
Fragmentation, 4, 18
Fraud, 173
Freedom, 50
Freudian theory, 11
Friendly persuasion, 238-259
Funding, 391-392. *See also* Appropriations; Authorizations
  channels of, 194, 195
  levels of, 193, 194
  sources of, 192, 193
Fundraising, 178, 192, 358

Game plan, 345
Game theory, 339
Garbage can theory, 140
Gays, 19, 26, 47, 155. *See also* Homosexuals
Gender, 18
General agendas, 141
Generalist, 25
General revenues, 192
Generic services, 220
Genetic factors, 174, 175, 199
Genetics, 15
Gestalt therapy, 15, 20
Goal displacement, 399, 409
Goals, 228, 233. *See also* Objectives
Golden Rule, 45
Governance, 202, 393
Government intervention, 48
Grant proposals, 116, 230-235
Grants, 194, 231-235

Great Society, 20
Group process, 315–325. *See also* Task groups
Groups. *See* Coalitions; Task groups
Group skills, 396
Guest editorials, 355

Hardball tactics, 263, 395. *See also* Machiavellian tactics
Heads of government, 352
　budget roles of, 99
　ideology of, 99
　powers of, 99
Head Start Program, 48, 140, 190, 378
Heroin, 162–165
Hierarchy, 361, 362, 379
Hispanics. *See* Latinos
Homelessness, 81, 178
Homosexuals, 259–262, 299–304
Honesty, 50, 56, 57
Hospitals, 119
Host organizations, 118, 119
House of Representatives, 101, 103
Humor, 248, 324, 325
Huntington's disease, 175

Ideologues, 342
Ideology, 48–50, 99, 342, 359
Implementation, 228. *See also* Policy implementation; Policy-implementing task
Improvisation, 341
Incidence, 165
Incrementalism, 332
Incrementalists, 139, 140
Indirect power. *See* Power
Inequality, 43, 179, 426
　ethics of, 44–46
　in opportunities, 43
　of status, 43
　thresholds of, 44
　varieties of, 43
Informal policies, 7, 360
Informal relationships, 363
Initiators, 351
Innovations. *See* Policy innovations
In-service training, 394
Instruments, 414
Integrity, 307
Interactional skills, 9, 20
　in agenda-building tasks, 139, 140, 145, 146, 154, 155
　defined, 74
　illustrated, 75–81, 85–87
　in policy-enacting task, 299–326
　in policy-implementing task, 396

Interactional skills (*continued*)
　in problem-defining task, 183
　in proposal-making task, 208, 242, 243, 247
Interest groups, 23, 72, 106, 108, 140, 292
Intermediaries, 277, 278–363, 395
Internal contradictions, 375
Internal Revenue Service, 191
Interorganizational relations, 377, 394
Interventions, 172
Intimidation, 313
Intrapsychic factors, 175
Intuitionism, 51
Involuntary commitments, 15, 222
Iron triangles, 108

Jewish Americans, 47
Jewish Appeals, 115
Jewish Federated Fundraising, 122
Job Training Partnership Act, 143
Jurisdiction, 190, 191
Juvenile courts, 382, 383

Latinos, 15, 17, 26, 43, 47, 49, 101, 139, 141, 143, 153, 155, 177, 387
Leaders, 317, 318, 324, 325
Leadership, 91, 92, 319, 345, 346, 377, 392
Learning disorders, 280
Legislative bills, 352
Legislative committees
　chairs of, 101
　committees of, 101–104
　hearings of, 100
　internal structures, 104
　jurisdiction of, 103–104
　subcommittees of, 104
Legislative testimony, 354, 355
Legislators
　aides of, 110
　budget roles of, 100
　campaigns of, 110
　choice processes, 111, 112
　committee assigments of, 100
　districts of, 101
　links with civil servants, 100
　links with lobbyists, 108
　priorities of, 110
　powers of, 100, 101
　procedures of, 104–105
　short cuts of, 110
Legislatures. *See also* Budgets; Lobbying; Testifying
　agenda-building in, 150, 151
　chambers of, 101–104
　leadership of, 101–104
　structures of, 101–104

SUBJECT INDEX

Lesbians, 19, 26, 47, 155. *See also* Homosexuals.
Letter-writing campaigns, 356
Liaison, 36–40
Liaison assistance, 62
Liberalism, 49, 50, 61
Liberals, 240, 242, 338, 339
Library searches, 351
Licensed Clinical Social Worker (LCSW), 198
Licensing, 63, 87, 194, 197–199
Lobbying, 40, 353, 354
Lobbyists, 147, 250–253, 292, 299–304
  links with civil servants, 108
  links with legislators, 108
  personal qualities of, 107
  power of, 106, 107
  tactics of, 116, 107
Local government, 192–195
Logistical factors, 393
Loopholes, 202
Los Angeles uprising, 45
Lying, 35, 36, 55–57. *See also* Honesty

Machiavellian tactics, 36, 305, 308, 309
Macroeconomics, 176
Majority leader, 101
Majority whip, 101
"Management by Walking Around," 309
Manifestations, 162
Manipulation, 293, 294
Marketing, 149, 178, 181, 192, 358, 379
Marriage counselors, 199
Mass media, 69, 146, 147, 150, 156, 262, 285, 287, 290, 291, 355, 356
Mayors, 104, 195
Means-testing, 200, 201
Mediation, 37, 264, 325
Mediators, 264, 325, 342
Medicaid, 173, 195, 224
Medical models, 174
Medicare, 119, 193, 201, 224
Members, 317, 318, 324, 325
Memos, 222
Mental Health Centers Act of 1963, 224
Mental illness, 26, 62–63, 173, 178, 179, 223–226
Mentors, 310, 311
Methadone, 174
Mind-sets, 376
Minority leader, 103
Mission, 152, 189, 190, 362
Mission enhancers, 126
Mission statements, 120
Momentum, 285, 320
Monetarists, 176

Monitoring, 202, 203, 392
Monopolies, 198
Morale, 319, 361
Moral reasoning. *See* Ethical reasoning
Motivation, 260, 345
M.S.W.s, 14, 115, 199, 200, 390
Multiculturalism, 17
Multidiversity, 177
Multiprofessional teams, 220
Myths impeding policy practice, 21, 22

Naiveté, 346
National Association for the Advancement of Colored People (NAACP), 128
National Association of Social Workers (NASW), 16, 19, 27, 42, 48, 60, 87, 108, 114, 156, 290, 311, 315, 357, 398
National Health Service Corps, 349
National Institute of Mental Health, 167, 190
National Organization for Women (NOW), 75, 128, 317, 340
National Rifle Association, 72, 285
National Welfare Rights Organization, 149–150, 291
Native Americans, 15, 26, 44, 47, 155
Needs assessment
  comparative need, 166
  expert need, 166
  expressed need, 166
  felt need, 166
Negotiation, 263, 264
Networking, 107, 309–311, 314
Networks, 301, 309, 323
New Deal, 19
New York School of Philanthropy, 11
Nonelected officials. *See also* Political appointees; Civil servants
  mind-sets of, 112–114
  varieties of, 105, 106
Nonpartisan elections, 104
Not-for-profit agencies, 15, 114–118, 148, 149, 191, 192. *See also* Social agencies
Nursing homes, 192

Objectives, 7, 233, 239, 240, 331, 332, 345
Office of Economic Opportunity (OEO), 190
Office of Education, 190
Office of Management and Budget (OMB), 292, 391
Old-boy networks, 43, 310, 311
Open-ended funding, 193, 201
Oppressed groups, 365, 417
Oppressed populations, 144, 155–157, 178, 179
Options. *See* Policy options
Organizational structure, 394

Organizational theory, 16
Organizational units, 118, 119
Organization charts, 123–126
Organizations. *See also* Social agencies
Outcomes, 380, 381, 398–401
Outgroups, 311, 312
   definition, 47
   dependent, 47
   deviant, 47
   model, 47
   radical, 47
   sociological, 47
Outlines, 243–246
Outreach, 6, 394
Outreach services, 228

Paradigms, 173, 197, 220, 221
Parental rights, 399
Parent participation, 190
Parliamentary assistance, 353
Parliamentary strategy, 104, 282
Partnerships, 379
Patient rights, 15, 50–55
Payroll taxes, 193
Permanency planning, 382–393
Persistence, 286, 427
Personnel policies, 119
Person-to-person power. *See* Power
Persuasion. *See* Policy persuasion
Physicians, 35–37, 41
Placement of facilities, 202
Polarization, 70, 336, 342
Policies. *See* Social policies
Policy advocacy, 26, 428, 429
   in agenda-building task, 155–157, 178–179
   in policy-assessing task, 417, 418
   in policy-enacting task, 299–304, 322, 323, 350–359, 365, 366
   in policy-implementation task, 389–398
   in policy practice, 428, 429
   in problem-defining task, 178, 179, 220–222, 259–263
Policy alternatives. *See* Policy options
Policy analysis, 20. *See also* Analytic skills
Policy-assessing task, 9–10
   defining, 71
   fundamental logic of, 407, 408
   illustrated, 80, 83, 84
   interpreting data, 410–412, 415, 416
   qualitative approaches, 416, 417
   quantitative approaches, 408–410, 412–416
   similarity to policy analysis, 408–410
   similarity to policy debates, 410–412
   technical tools for, 412–417

Policy-assessment matrix, 408–410
Policy brief, 351, 352
Policy bystanders, 69
Policy context. *See* Context
Policy criteria. *See* Criteria
Policy-enacting task, 9–10
   defining, 71
   illustrated, 79, 83, 84
   strategizing in, 331–366
   task groups in, 315–325
   use of power in, 276–286
Policy entrepreneurs, 153, 154
Policy goals. *See* Objectives
Policy implementation, 23, 203, 204. *See also* Policy-implementing task
Policy-implementing task, 9–10
   defining, 71
   determining outcomes, 398–401
   developing diagnoses, 393, 394
   developing remedies, 389, 390
   framework for, 373, 374
   illustrated, 80, 83–84
   political economy of, 376–378, 384–385
   processes of implementation, 378–379
   stages of, 386–389
   using agenda-building skills in, 402
   using policy-assessing skills in, 403
   using policy-enacting skills in, 402, 403
   using problem-defining skills in, 402
   using proposal-writing skills in, 402
Policy initiators, 68
Policy innovations, 374–376, 381–383
Policy intentions, 375, 398
Policy issues, 188–204
Policy leadership, 91, 92
Policy opposers, 69
Policy options, 22, 188–212, 213, 214, 216–226, 231
Policy orientations, 7
Policy oversight, 203
Policy persuasion, 40
   collaborative techniques, 263, 264
   combative persuasion, 259–263
   delivery style, 247
   devising strategies in, 242–253
   diagnosing audiences, 240–242
   fine-tuning of, 246, 247
   formats for, 243–246
   friendly communication, 238–262
   oral, 242
   setting objectives in, 239, 240
   written, 243

SUBJECT INDEX

Policy practice. *See also* Agenda-building task; Policy-assessing task; Policy-enacting task; Policy-implementing task; Policy practitioners; Policy skills; Problem-defining task; Proposal-making task
  agency-based, 88
  assessing, 81–83
  by social workers, 61–63, 93
  context of, 68, 69, 72, 73
  definition, 8–9
  demystifying, 21–22
  ethical rationale for, 40–50
  evaluations of theory, 22–24
  framework for, 68–70
  generic approach to, 88, 89
  issues in conceptualizing, 24–26
  in environmental frameworks, 92, 93
  in legislative settings, 88
  lack of emphasis on, 20–21
  multiple skills in, 74
  origin of the term, 24
  outside of employment, 90
  part of professional work, 89, 90
  securing mandates for, 89, 90
Policy practitioners, 25, 26. *See also* Policy practice
Policy proposals, 188–209, 213–235
Policy-related practice, 36–40
Policy responders, 69
Policy sectors, 190
Policy-sensitive practice, 36–40
Policy skills, 9. *See also* Analytic skills; Interactional skills; Political skills; Value-clarification skills
Policy tasks. *See* Agenda-building task; Policy-assessing task; Policy-enacting task; Policy-implementing task; Problem-defining task; Proposal-making task
Political Action Committee of NASW (PACE), 19, 60, 114, 156, 357
Political action committees (PAC), 356, 357
Political appointees
  appointments of, 106
  mind-sets of, 112, 113
Political campaigns, 40, 356–359
Political clubs, 356, 357
Political economy, 361
  of organizations, 114–118
  of programs, 118, 119
  of social-work units, 118, 119
Political parties, 356, 357
Political skills, 20
  centrality of, 90, 91
  defined, 74
  illustrated, 75–81, 85–87

Political skills (*continued*)
  in agenda-building task, 139, 140, 143, 145–157
  in policy-assessing task, 410–412
  in policy-enacting task, 299
  in policy-implementing task, 380, 389–393, 395, 396
  in problem-defining task, 172–179, 183
  in proposal-making task, 208, 220–222
Political social work, 25
Political strategy
  addressing six issues, 344–347
  analyzing context, 336–340
  building scenarios, 340, 341
  establishing time frame, 332
  force-field analysis, 332–336
  illustrations of, 348–350
  in community settings, 364–365, 366
  in governmental settings, 350–359
  in organizational settings, 355–364
  objectives in, 331, 332
  selecting a strategy, 341–344
Political stream. *See* Agenda-building task
Politicization of services, 13–16
Politics, 23, 60
  contrasted with analytic approach, 270
  definition, 269
  in community settings, 365, 366
  legislative politics, 359–361
  organizational, 148, 149, 272–275, 359–364
  political model of policy practice, 270, 271
  positions, 333–336
  positive functions, 269, 270
Poverty, 17, 73, 169, 169–173, 199
Power, 90. *See also* Assertiveness
  as a professional resource, 92
  autonomy, 286–289
  context-shaping power, 285, 286
  decisionmaking power, 282, 283
  definition of, 276, 277
  demystifying of, 92
  differentials in, 291–293
  discomfort with, 90, 91
  ethics of, 91, 92
  indirect power, 281–286
  measuring, 334
  methods of developing, 304–315
  person-to-person, 278, 279
  procedural, 282
  process power, 283–285
  power relationships, 276–278
  resources, 345
  in political strategy, 345, 346

Power (*continued*)
  substantive, 280, 281
  use in groups, 324, 325
Power dependence, 306, 307
Power differentials. *See* Power
Powerlessness, 92
Pragmatism, 57, 58, 305, 306, 341
Preambles of legislation, 189
Preservation of life, 50
Presiding officers, 101–104
Press conferences, 355
Prevalence, 165, 166. *See also* Analytic skills
Prevention, 145, 168, 197, 199, 200, 220, 228, 233–235
Primary prevention, 199, 200
Priorities, 376
Privacy, 215
Private philanthropy, 15, 193
Problem-defining task, 9–10
  analyzing causes of problems in, 168–176
  classifying problems in, 162–165
  defining, 71
  illustrated, 76–78, 83, 84
  locating problems in, 167
  measuring prevalence of problems in, 165–167
Problems. *See* Social problems
Problem stream. *See* Agenda-building task
Procedural power. *See* Power
Procedures, 320
Process power. *See* Power
Professional associations, 292
Professions, 198
Profit-oriented agencies, 148, 149, 191, 192. *See also* Social agencies
Program evaluation, 214. *See also* Policy-assessing task
Program titles, 202
Proposal-making task, 9, 10
  defined, 71
  developing proposals, 227–235
  identifying recurring policy options, 188–209
  illustrated, 78, 79, 83, 84
  policy persuasion, 238
  selecting options in, 213–226
Proposition 13, 384
Protocols, 250
Psychiatric evaluation teams (PET), 222
Psychodynamic therapy, 15
Psychologists, 199
Psychotherapy, 63, 426
Public agencies, 15, 115, 116, 148, 149, 191, 192. *See also* Social agencies
Public guardians, 400

Public health perspectives, 173
Public opinion, 108, 109
Public opinion polls, 108, 109
Purchase of services (POS), 223–226

Qualitative approaches
  in selecting options, 219–222
  qualitative evaluations, 416, 417
  qualitative research, 169, 171
Quantitative approaches
  in selecting criteria, 221
  in selecting options, 213–219
  quantitative research, 169–172
  quasi-experimental designs, 415
Quotas, 201

Racism, 47, 426
Radicalism, 62
Radical perspectives, 23, 174
Radicals, 174, 179, 305
Rainbow Coalition, 127
Random sample, 414
Rates, 165
Rationalists, 74, 139, 140
Rationality, 162
Rationing, 58, 200–202
Reapportionment, 101
Redistribution, 44–46, 63
Red tape, 173
Referral patterns, 229
Referral services, 197
Referral sources, 116
Regional government, 192–195, 203
Regulations, 7, 21, 203, 315. *See also* Administrative regulations
Relative standard, 163
Republican Party, 103
Republicans, 253–258, 280, 282
Research instruments, 414
Resource allocation, 376
Resource path. *See* Funding, channels of
Reverse discrimination, 221
Rewards, 239, 262, 278, 279, 314
Risk taking, 426
Rivalries, 338
Rules, 7
Russell Sage Foundation, 11

Salience, 333–336
Sampling, 413
Sandbagging, 308
Scapegoating, 221
Scenarios, 229, 340–344
Schizophrenia, 174
School boards, 104, 365

Secondary analysis, 170
Secondary prevention, 199
Self-determination, 51–55, 57, 215, 222
Self-help groups, 203
Self-interest, 26, 198
Senate, 101
Settlement House Movement, 11
Sexism, 199
Shelters, 189–204
Shoestring lobbyists, 107
Sickle-cell anemia, 167
Situational realities, 338, 339
Skills. *See* Policy skills
Sliding fees, 193, 202
Social agencies
  budgets of, 121, 126
  budget cuts of, 114–118
  conflict within, 123, 124
  division of labor in, 124–126
  funding of, 114–118, 120, 148, 149
  hierachy of, 124–126
  informal relations within, 126, 127
  policies of, 119–124
  politics of, 148, 149
  political economy of, 114–118
  sources of clients, 116
Social class, 18
Socialism, 49, 50–59, 62
Social justice, 43, 60, 62–63, 215, 221, 380
Social movements, 60, 127, 292
Social policies
  definition of, 3–8
  diversity of, 87–89
  malleability of, 88
  varieties of, 3–8
Social problems, 4–5
  analyzing causes of, 168–176
  defining, 163, 164
  developing interventions, 172
  establishing typologies, 162–165
  locating spatially, 167
  measuring impacts of, 168
  measuring prevalence of, 165–167
  nonrational factors, 172–178
  stages of development of, 162
  threshold of, 163, 164
  variations in, 177, 178
Social psychologists, 17
Social psychology, 249
Social Security, 140, 193, 201
Social Services Block Grant, 386
Social support, 17
Social workers
  assertiveness of, 91, 92
  developing leadership skills, 91, 92

Social workers (*continued*)
  discomfort with power, 90–92
  policy practice of, 41–63
  policy-related practice by, 37–40
  policy-sensitive practice by, 37–40
Social work profession. *See* Council on Social Work Education; Licensing; National Association of Social Workers; Social workers; Staff
Sociologists, 17
Solution stream. *See* Agenda-building task
Special taxes, 193
Sponsors, 352, 353
Sponsorship, 352, 353
Spousal abuse, 189, 196, 197, 199, 202, 203
Staff, 14–15, 317, 318, 321, 324, 325
Standardized instruments, 416
Standard operating procedures, 376
State government, 192–195
Statistics, 413–415
Strategy. *See* Political strategy
Style of services, 197, 202, 203
Subcommittees, 104, 320, 325, 391
Substance abuse, 199
Substantive power. *See* Power
Suburbs, 116
Supplementary Security Income (SSI) Program, 170, 224, 281
Supply-side economists, 176
Supply-side economics, 254, 255
Supreme Court, (U.S.) 19
Survival skills, 39–40
Systems frameworks. *See* Environmental frameworks

Task forces, 88, 310
Task groups
  context, 321
  definition, 316
  deliberative processes, 320
  developmental needs, 319, 320
  dysfunctional processes, 324
  functions, 317
  kinds, 316
  leadership, 319
  missions, 318, 319
  procedures, 320
  roles within, 316, 317
  staff and resources, 321
  structure, 326
Tax credits, 170, 195
Tax deductions, 195
Taxes, 49
Tax exemptions, 196
Taxpayer revolts, 192

Tax revolts, 115, 384
Tay-Sachs disease, 167
Teachers, 35–37, 41
Team players, 306, 307
Telephone campaigns, 353
Terminal illness, 35, 56
Testifying, 354, 355
Think tanks, 107, 150
Threats, 239, 262, 278
Thresholds, 411
Time frame, 332, 345
Time lines, 229
Title XX, 224
Track records, 308
Trade-offs, 213–226, 261
Traditions, 336, 337
Transactional relationships, 276, 277
Transactional therapy, 15, 20
Trend data, 228
Triangulation, 417
Typologies, 162–165

Unanticipated consequences, 260
Underclass, 144, 179
Unemployment, 169, 170
Unilateral relationships, 276, 277
Unions, 16, 192, 223–226, 214, 314, 362, 379, 385
United Way, 13, 115, 122, 193
Units. *See* Organizational units
U.S. Chamber of Commerce, 322
U.S. Congress, 103
Universal eligibility, 220
Utilitarianism, 51
Utilitarians, 58
Vagueness, 261, 280
Value-clarification skills, 9, 20. *See also* Ethical issues; Ethical reasoning
   defined, 74
   illustrated, 75–81, 85–87
   in agenda-building task, 143, 145, 146, 155–157
   in policy-assessing task, 417–419

Value-clarification skills (*continued*)
   in policy-enacting task, 282, 293, 294, 307–309
   in policy-implementing task, 396–398
   in problem defining task, 173–176, 178, 179, 183
   in proposal-constructing task, 208, 220–222
Values, 173, 259–260. *See also* Ideology
Veil of ignorance, 44–46
Vendor payments, 195
Venereal disease, 260
Vested interests, 337
Vetoes, 100, 104, 113
Victim mentality, 312–314
Vietnam War, 19
Visibility, 314
Vision, 425, 426
Volunteers, 192, 199, 394
Voter registration, 60, 356
Vouchers, 115, 194, 195

Waiting lists, 59, 199, 200
War on Poverty, 375. *See also* Office of Economic Opportunity
Wastage, 4
Waste, 173
Watergate, 100
Ways and Means Committee, 103
Welfare Council of Chicago, 82–87
Welfare reform, 76–80
Whistle-blowing, 64, 290, 291, 397, 398
Windows of opportunity, 76, 151–154
Win-lose politics, 263–284
Win-win politics, 263, 284, 365
Women, 19, 43, 46, 47, 90, 155
Written policies, 375

Young Men's Christian Association (YMCA), 14, 117, 127
Young Women's Christian Association (YWCA), 117, 127

Zones of discretion. *See* Discretion
Zoning boards, 365

TO THE OWNER OF THIS BOOK:

I hope that you have found *Social Policy: From Theory to Policy Practice*, Second Edition, useful. So that this book can be improved in a future edition, would you take the time to complete this sheet and return it? Thank you.

School and address: _____

Department: _____

Instructor's name: _____

1. What I like most about this book is: _____

_____

2. What I like least about this book is: _____

_____

3. My general reaction to this book is: _____

_____

4. The name of the course in which I used this book is: _____

_____

5. Were all of the chapters of the book assigned for you to read? _____

   If not, which ones weren't? _____

_____

6. In the space below, or on a separate sheet of paper, please write specific suggestions for improving this book and anything else you'd care to share about your experience in using the book.

_____

_____

_____

_____

_____

_____